THE NEW TERRAIN OF INTERNATIONAL LAW

THE NEW TERRAIN OF INTERNATIONAL LAW

Courts, Politics, Rights

Karen J. Alter

PRINCETON UNIVERSITY PRESS
Princeton and Oxford

Published by Princeton University Press, 41 William Street, Princeton, New Jersey 08540
In the United Kingdom: Princeton University Press, 6 Oxford Street, Woodstock, Oxfordshire OX20 1TW

press.princeton.edu

Portions of the text and figures 2.1, 3.4, and 3.13 have appeared in *Interdisciplinary Perspectives on International Law and International Relations: The State of the Art*, edited by Jeffrey L. Dunoff and Mark A. Pollack. New York: Cambridge University Press. Reprinted with permission

Library of Congress Cataloging-in-Publication Data

Alter, Karen J.
The new terrain of international law : courts, politics, rights / Karen Alter.
pages cm.
Includes bibliographical references and index.
Summary: "In 1989, when the Cold War ended, there were six permanent international courts. Today there are more than two dozen that have collectively issued over thirty-seven thousand binding legal rulings. The New Terrain of International Law charts the developments and trends in the creation and role of international courts, and explains how the delegation of authority to international judicial institutions influences global and domestic politics. The New Terrain of International Law presents an in-depth look at the scope and powers of international courts operating around the world. Focusing on dispute resolution, enforcement, administrative review, and constitutional review, Karen Alter argues that international courts alter politics by providing legal, symbolic, and leverage resources that shift the political balance in favor of domestic and international actors who prefer policies more consistent with international law objectives. International courts name violations of the law and perhaps specify remedies. Alter explains how this limited power—the power to speak the law—translates into political influence, and she considers eighteen case studies, showing how international courts change state behavior. The case studies, spanning issue areas and regions of the world, collectively elucidate the political factors that often intervene to limit whether or not international courts are invoked and whether international judges dare to demand significant changes in state practices"— Provided by publisher.
Includes bibliographical references and index.
ISBN 978-0-691-15474-9 (hardback) — ISBN 978-0-691-15475-6 (paperback) 1. International law. 2. International courts. 3. Human rights. I. Title.
KZ3410.A44 2013
341—dc23
2013022405

British Library Cataloging-in-Publication Data is available

This book has been composed in Sabon LT Std

Printed on acid-free paper. ∞

Printed in the United States of America

10 9 8 7 6 5 4 3 2 1

For Abby and Elliot

Contents

Illustrations

Case Study Index

DISPUTE SETTLEMENT

5.1 ICJ—"Bahrain v. Qatar territorial dispute"—International Court of Justice resolves a territorial dispute, which facilitates regional economic development

5.2 ITLOS—"Japan v. Russia—seizing of vessels"—International Tribunal for the Law of the Sea assures fair treatment of Japanese vessels seized for illegal actions in Russian waters (*Tomimaru* and *Hoshinmaru* cases)

5.3 "Iran-US mass claims tribunal"—Adjudicating disputes arising from the Iranian revolution

5.4 "OHADA business law"—The Organization for the Harmonization of Business Law in Africa as an appellate body for cases involving OHADA "Uniform Acts"

ADMINISTRATIVE REVIEW

6.1 ECJ—"Microsoft" and "GE/Honeywell merger" cases—Oversight of Commission administrative decisions

6.2 ATJ—"Belmont case"—The Andean Tribunal fills lacunae and coordinates transnational administrative decision making

6.3 NAFTA and WTO—"Softwood lumber"—NAFTA binational and WTO review of national determinations of dumping and countervailing duties

6.4 ICSID— "Metalclad" ICSID investor dispute settlement systems to compensate for administrative "takings"

Administrative Cases in Other Chapters

ITLOS—Japan v. Russia—seizing of vessels (5.2), "Second use patent case"—ATJ annulment of Peruvian second use patent decree (7.2), "Seizing private assets"—(Kadi) case (8.2)

LAW ENFORCEMENT

Enforcement Cases in Other Chapters

CONSTITUTIONAL REVIEW

CASE STUDIES BY SUBJECT MATTER AND COUNTRY

Economic Law

Human Rights Law

War Crimes

Other

Preface

This book is motivated by the changing world around us. The growing role of judges, both domestic and international, is self-evident. In the United States and Europe courts review most major policy initiatives, and judicial rulings are front-page news. In many other parts of the world judges are also becoming increasingly emboldened, willing to challenge powerful individuals and governments. International courts are part of this global trend and a powerful symbol that law and legalism have become part of foreign affairs and international politics. What draws the attention of international relations scholars is the fact that international courts increasingly speak to issues that used to fall exclusively within the national domain. There are literally thousands of international judicial rulings reviewing the human rights and economic practices of governments. International adjudication has even entered the might-equals-right world of security relations. These developments are further evidence of evolving norms of state sovereignty.

Despite clear changes in the world around us, much of the academy remains trapped in old ways of thinking. The new international courts are quite different from the archetype in most scholars' heads—the International Court of Justice—and the substance of international law has also changed, becoming more detailed and far reaching in its scope. International relations and international law scholarship is yet to catch up. Most international relations scholars still assume that international courts exist primarily to resolve disputes between states, that the desires governments express unquestionably reflect "the national interest," and that the wishes of powerful governments invariably do or should prevail. Of course governments remain key actors in international politics. World leaders dominate the global bully pulpit, and usually governments are the only voting participants within international institutions. Moreover, it is increasingly clear that the only thing worse than a state with a predatory leader is the chaos of a country lacking a government. Governments are and will remain essential actors in domestic and international politics.

But government's defended perch on the mountaintop of power politics is increasingly questioned and challenged from below. Governments may still prefer the polite rules of diplomacy, including respect for national sovereignty. And lawyers, whose background and work makes them closely attached to state power, may still regularly question the notion that international agreements are or should be domestically binding. But this view from inside of office buildings and ivory towers overlooks something vital: that most people accept at face value that governments should play by the legal rules of the game. International courts traffic in the currency of rule of law expectations, and most people believe in international law's good faith ideal of *pacta sunt servanda*. These developments reflect a changed social understanding that international law generates rights.

Some governments are used to ruling by executive fiat or decree, and some governments respond to binding adverse legal rulings by taking out their pens to write a new legal decree. But most people expect signing and ratifying a treaty to give rise to a binding obligation. There is also a largely unquestioned presumption that legal obligations should be meaningful, that they should give rise to rights, that the legal bodies tasked with interpreting and applying applicable laws should be prioritizing the law over the wishes of governments, and that legitimate governments should display a fundamental respect for the rule of law, including international law. Perhaps these presumptions should be questioned, but in any event most people make the domestic analogy. Why should an international agreement, negotiated and duly ratified, be any different from a national law? Why should rulings by international courts be any less binding than rulings by domestic courts? Lawyers can explain the complicated reasons why international law is somehow different—international law is not self-executing, international law operates in a separate legal order, international legal rulings do not generate domestic effects—but for most people these reasons seem convoluted.

There may be a cynicism about how the rule of law operates in practice, and the gap between expectations and the international legal situation remains profound. But this does not change the reality that people want, hope, and expect that in a well-functioning polity legality matters. This expectation transfers into the political realm, carried forward by advocates of international law and the tacit backing of commonsense assumptions of most people. The reality that legitimate governance is increasingly equated with rule of law governance is why governments bend over backward not to be seen as violating the law. One must only look at the tortured "torture memos" to recognize the lengths governments will go to be seen as rule of law actors. Pinochet's Chile and even

Communist China have been equally committed to keeping up a rule of law appearance.

I have just used a lot "shoulds" in noting that people think governments should follow the law. My invocation of norms and values perhaps suggests that this book is a normative enterprise. It is not. This book is a positive political science enterprise that sees law and the preferences of people as important political forces. *The New Terrain of International Law* represents an international relations and comparative politics analysis of the politics of law, taking very seriously that the law and the legal rules of the game matter to lawyers, judges, and people.

Litigation is a tool of the weak. Chapter 2 explains how governments use law to regulate the behavior of citizens. Powerful actors that are able to influence government policy making can rule by law, using the legislative process and government support to promote their priorities. For individuals and groups who do not find government doors wide open, litigation can be a political means to overturn the decisions of governments. Individuals living in authoritarian countries and in countries with weak rule of law institutions generally invoke international law to circumvent blockages created by domestic institutions that are captured by governments. International law is also a resource vis-à-vis powerful states because the United States and Europe are rule of law countries, where legitimate action must also be legal action. International law is an attractive political resource because governments do not control it. No one government can change international law. And while international courts are surely political actors, they are legal institutions comprised of judges from multiple countries with a formal mandate to apply the law. Governments can personally threaten judges, but really the best way to influence legal bodies is to use legal and public policy arguments. And even then, judges get to decide.

This book is about how litigant pressures interact with domestic and international forces to propel change in the direction the law indicates. The power of courts will always be limited. To take on power with law is perhaps akin to the battle between David and Goliath. Goliaths also sometimes use law. American and European actors understand law's power, and they are often participants in foreign litigation as consultants, lawyers for hire, or pro bono nongovernmental advocates showing others how to play the litigation game to influence policy.

Since we live in a world with expensive international judicial institutions that have the ability to be effective, ineffective, or to act in ways that are counterproductive, I think it is important to investigate how international courts affect political outcomes. Rather than studying the hundreds of ways that institutions can fail, I prefer to study what helps public bodies succeed in some cases yet then fail in others. If it seems like I find much success in international legal institutions, it is probably because my expectations are so low. In the Bible, David always wins. In the real world, the odds remain in Goliath's favor. But increasingly international law—words on paper imbued with legal authority—provides a legal and political resource that makes a political difference. The ability of international courts to speak law to power and thereby influence governments to alter their behavior is in my mind somewhat akin to David's miracle victory over Goliath.

This book has four main audiences. For international relations scholars, *The New Terrain of International Law* explains why today's international courts are more politically prominent than international courts of the past. I document a new style of international courts and explain how this new style combines with the growing practice of embedding international law into domestic legal orders and empowering national judges to apply this law. I also focus on how law is a different sort of political resource, operating by its own rules of the game, able to mobilize a transnational constituency of lawyers and judges and to tap into diffuse support for the rule of law. Legal politics *are* different from electoral politics and diplomacy, and this is precisely law's attraction.

For specialists of law and courts, this book conceptualizes and studies international courts using categories and tools that have been developed for studying comparative courts. I examine international courts as tools of social control that powerful state actors use to lock in their policy preferences. By delegating legal interpretation to courts, the authors of the law gain a slow time-release mechanism that litigants can activate to push in the direction the law indicates. International courts are designed to promote the objectives of economic and political liberalism written into the DNA of international law, enforcing the legal rules that governments agreed to perhaps expecting that they would never truly be held to these legal commitments.

For specialists of international law and institutions, this book helps to move beyond the "usual suspects" scholars tend to focus on. The book considers twenty-four international courts based around the world. I include courts and legalized dispute adjudication systems that Americans and Europeans care about. Still, United States actors are litigants in only six and European actors are litigants in four of my eighteen case studies. I compare ICs constraining very powerful countries to contexts where governments are not known to be supporters of international law, international legal institutions, or even the rule of law. My goal is to broaden the focus of scholars, to show that international law can constrain the powerful but it is also an important resource to promote rule of law objectives outside of Organisation for Economic Co-Operation and Development (OECD) countries.

Finally, this book is a theory-generating enterprise that brings comparative politics tools and the best of what qualitative methods uniquely provide—a careful attention to the causal pathways of political change, taking seriously the importance of local context and priorities, world history, and the complexities of the real world. By identifying like cases, institutions, and categories that others might compare in their own work—quantitative or qualitative—I hope this book makes the study of comparative international judicial systems less daunting. The case studies are designed to bring theories and institutions into the nitty-gritty of actual cases, revealing the complexity that is often lost when political scientists engage in deductive theorizing and macro analysis. Scholars can mine the case studies and the role-based chapters to identify factors to explore more systematically. I also hope the case studies make this book more teachable, and the new terrain of international law less abstract.

When I first began presenting this research a number of years ago, especially older members of the audience would sometimes become very upset. I understood the source of their consternation, although I thought that venting on me was fundamentally misdirected. I did not create the ICs I study. Nor did I have any say over how international courts were invoked or how legal rulings affected political outcomes. Quite honestly, if I had been asked, I might have recommended that some of the ICs in this study not be created and some of the cases not litigated. I try to adopt a value-neutral approach when it comes to studying international courts. Still, this work is upsetting to some because it upends taken-for-granted assumptions.

If you are over forty-five years old, chances are you studied international law during the Cold War when power politics mattered more than law, and when most international legal institutions were virtual entities that barely met and rarely said anything of political or legal consequence. For lawyers who have not updated their knowledge and for litigators who have little direct contact with international law and international courts, this book's conversation may seem esoteric and even fantastical. Numerically speaking, most lawyers probably fit into this category, which means by definition that this book presents what is probably a minority view of how international law operates in the real world. Mine may be a minority view, but it is also a far more informed view than that of most practicing lawyers. Today's judges and lawyers have specialized, so that their job likely does not bring them into contact with a broad range of international law and international courts. Also, just as most of the national economy remains domestic in nature—for example, most of a family's income is spent on locally produced goods and services and most citizens never venture beyond their borders—most of the daily life and practice of lawyers remains untouched by international law. Add in our preference to focus on what is close to home and familiar, and to avert our gaze from any international or external origins of decisions we make, and it is not hard to see why the changes in the international judicial world remain peripheral for most law faculties and lawyers. But just because international law feels distant and everything we call law seems homegrown does not mean that politics, law, and legal practice today is not colored by international legal precepts. Nor do traditional views mean that the international legal world is unchanging.

Clearly and undeniably international courts are growing in political importance. Newspaper coverage reflects this reality, and scholarship follows the front pages. International law is a burgeoning area of academic writing. This book is motivated by the changing world around us. What *The New Terrain of International Law* identifies, names, and explains is but the tip of the iceberg of how legalization already is and will continue changing our world.

This book has been incredibly challenging to write, and I have had much help along the way. With twenty-four courts, very diverse legal subject matters, four judicial roles, eighteen case studies involving institutions and countries from around the world, it has been hard to keep the many pieces organized and accurate while staying focused on the larger argument. I have worked hard to get beyond an alphabet soup of institutions, so as to make the international judicial architecture more tractable. Yet collecting and managing information about international courts is at times bewildering. Something as straightforward as when a court was established can actually be quite hard to pin down, and the design, legal jurisdiction, the way rulings get reported, and the membership that falls under a court's jurisdiction are constantly moving targets. To give but one example, the European Court of Justice was created in 1952, but only became the Court of today starting with the launching of the European Economic Community. This Court has been redesigned at least four times, because the European project has grown, the number of judges sitting on the court has increased from six to twenty-seven, and member states added a Tribunal of First Instance. The European Court's jurisdiction continues to grow every time European states decide to regulate a new area of the economy, and both the European Court of Justice and the Tribunal of First Instance have changed their names so it is hard to know what to call the European Court of the 1980s. I have intentionally eschewed the details that lawyers often hold dear, trying instead to create heuristics that allow readers to follow the analysis without needing to stay on top of moving targets. I imagine and expect specialists on each of these cases, institutions, and legal topics will object to or find small errors in what I have written. As I say in the book's conclusion, this book is a "lumping" exercise, which means that it glances over important details and nuances that are of meaningful legal importance for the purpose of comparison. I have done my best to accurately discuss diverse laws and institutions, and to get the dates, actors, and details right. I apologize in advance for the errors that surely exist.

If this book is relatively clearheaded, comprehensible, accurate in its details, and readable, it is because of the feedback I have had along the way. Larry Helfer has been a partner in studying and writing about Latin American and African courts. Not only is he willing to travel to remote places, he has also with amazing cheer read many drafts, encouraged me, and provided incisive comments at many stages during the writing of this book. It is a rare gift to find a fellow traveler who is also curious and open to wherever the data takes us. As a bonus, David Boyd comes as part of the Larry package, making travel delicious and enjoyable, and ensuring that we also talk about something other than international law. Cesare Romano has been a resource from the time I barely knew anything about courts outside of Europe. He has read many drafts of this book and articles, and has always been encouraging, helpful, and a supportive friend despite my very many blunders. Erik Voeten and Jonas Tallberg have also read multiple drafts multiple times, giving me extremely helpful feedback, even on the fifth version they read! Thanks for all of your patience and help.

Many others have looked at pieces of this project, come to workshops, or created opportunities to get feedback. Thanks to Samantha Besson, Tanja Börzel, Damian Chalmers, Tom Ginsburg, Larry Helfer, Ian Hurd, Mattias Kumm, Peter Lindseth, Franz Mayer, Steve Nelson, Jide Nzelibe, Joost Pauwleyn, Henrik Palmer Olsen, Chris Reus-Smit, Thomas Risse, Cesare Romano, Hendrik Spruyt, Jonas Tallberg, Stephen Toope, Leslie Vinjamuri, Erik Voeten, and Michael Zürn for coming to workshops where we could talk about the book in depth. Thanks to Francesca Bignami, Rachel Cichowski, John Crook, Paul Diehl, Jeff Dunnoff, Andreas Follesdahl, Michael Geyer, Brian Hanson, Nick Hatzis, Darren Hawkins, Alexandra Huneeus, Beth Hurd, Ian Hurd, Vicki Jackson, Wade Jacoby, Peter Katzenstein, Judith Kelley, Bob Keohane, Michael Rask Madsen, Sally Merry, Alexander Panayotov, Mark Pollack, Tonya Putnam, Morton Rasmussen, Duncan Snidal, Richard Stewart, Bernhardt Zangl, and others who read and commented on pieces of this book and its arguments. Thanks to Ji Li, Stephen Bychowski, Alexander Panayotov, and Aleksandr Sverdlik for invaluable research assistance (the diagrams of regional regime complexes were Aleksandr's creation). Thanks to Sophie

Meunier, Wade Jacoby, and Judith Kelly, colleagues who have also become important friends. I feel like I have been working on this book for years, and I know I have forgotten to mention some people—so a blanket thanks to the many people who have answered my e-mails and offered their feedback along the way.

I have developed the pieces of this argument over the years, mostly through articles presented at various workshops and published in various forums. These articles probed ideas, for example, the category of new-style courts, the idea that delegation to courts is both self- and other-binding, that ICs are trustees, that ICs play multiple judicial roles, and that international regime complexity matters, have all appeared in articles published from 2006 on. This book updates all of these ideas, qualifying my earlier claims while creating a simplified snapshot of the international judiciary as of 2011.

I would not have started this book without Joseph Weiler inviting me to spend a year at Harvard Law School where he guided me to audit courses on property law, constitutional law, and administrative law. I would not have pursued my intuition about the four judicial roles without Mike Tierney, Darren Hawkins, and Dan Neilson pushing me to write memos that explained my ideas. And I would not have finally finished this book were it not for the John Simon Guggenheim Foundation and the American Academy of Berlin, which provided a wonderful respite for me to push through the bulk of the writing and revisions. This project has also had support from Northwestern University, the Howard Foundation, and research support from Northwestern and Vanderbilt University has been critical for field research in Latin America, Europe, and Africa and for research assistance. Residential stays at the American Bar Foundation and Northwestern Law School also pushed my thinking on this project. Mostly, this book is reflective of the rich intellectual and interdisciplinary pluralism that flourishes at Northwestern University. The Department of Political Science's commitment to multiple methods and strength in all social science and theoretical perspectives, and the Buffett Center for International and Comparative Studies' relentless efforts to get scholars from different disciplines to work together have had a formidable influence on my thinking.

The only people who have given as much to this book as I have are my family who endured me through what has been a very consuming project. Brian is my better half who makes everything I do both possible and meaningful. My father, mother, sisters, and in-laws are always great cheerleaders and listeners. My daughter wanted me to include our dog in the book's dedication. I call Quinn "happiness" for his unabated enthusiasm whenever I walk through the door, and his company as he follows me from room to room. But I dedicate this book to Abigail and Elliot, who shared their mother even when they really did not want to. In some ways, I have been working on this book your whole lives. You came with me to Berlin and joined in life's adventure of living abroad. Especially in the last year and a half there has been more work than play because of this book. I hope you are proud of this book, as it reflects our collective achievement. That said, please do hold me to my promise not to work as much or be as distracted now that this book is out the door.

Abbreviations

ACtHPR	African Court on Human and Peoples' Rights
ADIFAN	Association of Pharmaceutical Industries of National Origin
ASEAN	Association of Southeast Asian Nations
ATJ	Andean Tribunal of Justice
BENELUX	Belgium Netherlands Luxembourg cooperation system
BIT	Bilateral Investment Treaty
CACJ	Central American Court of Justice
CCJ	Caribbean Court of Justice
CEMAC	Central African Monetary Community
COMESA	Common Market of Eastern and Southern Africa
DISC	Domestic International Sales Corporation
EACJ	East African Court of Justice
ECCIS	Economic Court of the Commonwealth of Independent States
ECCJ	Economic Community of West African States Court of Justice
ECJ	European Court of Justice (a.k.a. Court of Justice of the European Union)
ECOWAS	Economic Community of West African States
ECtHR	European Court of Human Rights
EFTAC	European Free Trade Area Court
EU	European Union (a.k.a. EC—European Community)
FSC	Foreign Sales Corporation
GATT	General Agreement on Tariffs and Trade
IACtHR	Inter-American Court of Human Rights
IC	International court
ICC	International Criminal Court
ICJ	International Court of Justice
ICSID	International Centre for the Settlement of Investment Disputes

ICTY	International Criminal Tribunal for Former Yugoslavia
INDECOPI	National Institute for the Defense of Competition and the Protection of Intellectual Property
INTAL	Institute for the Integration of Latin America and the Caribbean
ITLOS	International Tribunal for the Law of the Sea
LAFTA	Latin American Free Trade Area (a.k.a. Aladi)
MERCOSUR	Southern Common Market
NAFTA	North American Free Trade Agreement
OAPEC	Organization of Arab Petroleum Exporting Countries
OAS	Organization of American States
OAU	Organization for African Unity
OHADA	Organization for the Harmonization of Business Law in Africa
SADC	Southern African Development Community
UN	United Nations
UNCLOS	United Nations Conference for the Law of the Sea
UNIDA	l'Association pour l'Unification du Droit en Afrique (Association for the Unification of African Law)
WAEMU	West African Economic and Monetary Union
WTO	World Trade Organization

Part I: Delegating Authority to International Courts: A Global View

CHAPTER 1

The New Terrain of International Law

Courts, Politics, Rights

International relations have long been considered outside of the domain of law. Most people presume that law is only meaningful when backed by a central enforcer. By this logic, absent a world state international law cannot meaningfully exist. But since the end of the Cold War, the rulings of international judges have led Latin American governments to secure indigenous peoples' land rights; the United States Congress to eliminate a tax benefit for American corporations; Germany to grant women a wider role in the military; Niger to compensate a former slave for her entrapment in Niger's family law justice system; and Congolese warlord Thomas Lubanga Dyilo, Liberian president Charles Taylor, Jean Paul Akayesu, and others to be convicted for conscripting child soldiers, abetting insurgents in neighboring countries, and tolerating rape. How have international courts around the world come to be ruling on issues such as these, which once fell under the exclusive domain of sovereign states? There still is no central enforcer for international law, so how do international courts get governments to follow their legal rulings? How is the possibility of an international judicial remedy changing the influence of international law in domestic and international politics? This book is inspired by these questions.

The goal of this book is threefold. First, it reveals a paradigm change in creating and using international courts. The first standing international courts were voluntary interstate dispute settlement bodies that could be invoked in the rare event that governments wanted a legal resolution of a transborder disagreement. This book documents the new international judicial architecture, which is more far-reaching than most people realize. ICs today review the validity of administrative decisions, assess state compliance with international law, and speak to constitutional issues affecting both international and domestic politics. There are now at least twenty-four permanent international courts. Eighty percent of operational ICs have a broad compulsory jurisdiction, and 84 percent authorize nonstate actors—supranational commissions, prosecutors, and/or private actors—to initiate litigation. These ICs have collectively issued over 37,000 binding rulings in individual contentious cases, 91 percent of which were issued since the fall of the Berlin Wall. Since few of these ICs and cases are about interstate dispute adjudication, we need to update our understandings about international courts.

Second, this book conceptualizes how new-style international courts affect domestic and international politics across countries, courts, cases, and issues. An international court's political influence comes from its authority to say what the law means for the case at hand, its jurisdiction to name violations of international law, and its ability to specify remedies that follow from international legal violations. This book explains how speaking the law translates into meaningful political influence over international and domestic politics. And it theorizes why IC influence varies across countries, issues, and cases.

Third, this book aims to create nonutopian and thus more realistic expectations for international courts. This inquiry builds on theories developed in the study of domestic courts and uses the presence of similarly designed international courts, of cross-time design changes, and variations in the influence of the same ICs across countries and issues to inductively elucidate factors that contribute to the ability of international judges to influence state behavior. This approach inherently stresses the courts rather than the international aspects of what I am studying. International judges, like their domestic counterparts, wield neither the sword nor the purse; they only have the power to speak the law. To subordinate powerful actors to the rule of law, international judges must draw on diffuse support for the rule of law and the power and preferences of domestic and international interlocutors. As in the case of the domestic rule of law, critical zones of social interaction occur in contravention of legal rules, with most disagreements settled out of court sometimes without full compliance with the law. But even when law is not 100 percent followed, law still serves a regulative role of creating guidelines and setting expectations, and the judicial system helps to clarify the meaning of the law and create some remedy for law violations, as imperfect as they may be.

The implications of these developments for national sovereignty and international relations are profound. ICs are new political actors on the domestic and international stage. Their *international* nature allows ICs to circumvent domestic legal and political barriers and to create legal change across borders. Their *legal* nature allows ICs to provoke political change through legal reinterpretation and to tap into diffuse support for the rule of law and pressure governments. Their *legal* and *international* nature allows litigants to harness multilateral resources and to knit together broader constituencies of support, linking communities that care about the larger policy domain (for example, free trade, human rights, and such), with supporters of the rule of law, with advocates for the particular legal regime (for example, regional integration or the World Trade Organization), with self-interested litigants pursuing personal agendas and with the legal community of lawyers, judges, and scholars. The result is a judicialization of international relations and diminishing government control over how international legal agreements are understood domestically and internationally.

The rest of this introduction summarizes the main pieces of this argument. Section I describes the courts part of this story. I explain what has actually been delegated to international courts, how the new-style features of international courts change their political influence, and how the new-style features are an artifact of the desire of states that ICs assume a broader range of judicial roles. This section also defines the four judicial roles states have delegated to ICs, which serve as a framing device for exploring where and how ICs are influencing international and domestic politics. Section II explains the politics part of the story. ICs alter politics through alliances with compliance constituencies—ever-changing sets of actors that for a variety of reasons want to see law respected. Law is the source of the ICs' power, and it is what broadens and unites compliance constituencies. Section III explains the rights part of the story, how delegation to ICs helps generate rights by allowing rights holders or defenders to ask judges for a legal remedy. Section IV provides a roadmap for the book.

I. THE RISE OF NEW-STYLE ICS: THE COURTS PART OF THE STORY

The courts part of the story begins with a fundamental change in international court design, which transforms the political importance associated with delegating authority to international courts. Old-style international courts lack compulsory jurisdiction so that cases can only proceed with the consent of the defendant-state. New-style ICs have compulsory jurisdiction, and they allow nonstate actors—international commissions, prosecutors, institutional actors, and private litigants—to initiate litigation. New-style ICs reflect the reality that states have tasked ICs with helping to enforce international law, and with reviewing the application of international law by state and international administrative and legislative actors.

The importance of these design features is sometimes overlooked because scholars focus on whether there is delegation to third-party adjudicators rather than the form delegation takes and because the formal power of courts is the same regardless. But this shift from "old" to "new" style combines with the broader range of roles states have delegated to ICs to generate a paradigmatic shift from a contract-based to a rule of law conceptualization of the meaning of international law. The interstate arbiter approach to international adjudication envisions international law as a contract among signatory states where the role of courts is limited to specifying the terms of the contract. Legal agreements in this view mostly affect signatory parties with law being reciprocally binding, generating no obligation to others besides honoring the terms of the contract with respect to other signatory-states. By contrast, a rule of law perspective assumes that law brings obligations regardless of what other states do and that governments are not above the law.

The Political Importance of ICs' New-Style Design Features

The old paradigm of international law circumscribes international courts to a voluntary interstate dispute settlement role. Eric Posner and John Yoo build their theory of international adjudication around the dispute settlement role beginning with an observation about the design of international courts. ICs that lack compulsory jurisdiction, they argue, are more dependent on states wanting to use them. This dependence, they argue, leads ICs to work harder to please governments and especially the governments of powerful states, which according to Posner and Yoo makes the courts more effective.[1] While much of Posner and Yoo's analysis is controversial,[2] most agree that ICs with judges appointed to fixed

1 Posner and Yoo's goal is to show that judicial independence is not linked to judicial effectiveness. They argue that judicial "independence exists when judges have fixed terms and are not appointed by the parties of a dispute; when the judges are not, or are not necessarily, the nationals of a state party to the dispute; when the judges observe regular, predetermined rules of procedure; and when stare decisis and other legal conventions are observed. In addition, jurisdiction must be compulsory, or states will simply deny jurisdiction of a court when they believe they are likely to lose." (Posner and Yoo 2005, quote at 12).

2 The main controversy surrounds Yoo and Posner's conflation of compliance with effectiveness. Dependent ICs may only be invoked when states intend to comply with a ruling, which will increase compliance with IC rulings. But effectiveness is different than compliance. Effectiveness entails inducing a change from the status quo in the desired direction, even if the result is less than full compliance. For a more far reaching critique of Posner and Yoo's analysis, see Helfer and Slaughter (2005). Central features of this argument get repeated in (Goldsmith and Posner, 2005), which has generated even more critique.

terms and with compulsory jurisdiction are in fact more independent, for the reasons the authors suggest. When ICs lack compulsory jurisdiction, legal disputes reach a court only where the respondent state also prefers a legal resolution. Also, a lack of compulsory jurisdiction leads international judges to work harder to please governments, so as to encourage the bringing of more cases and to build support among governments for signing on to compulsory jurisdiction protocols. This dependence on states limits the ability and the opportunity for ICs to build law or their relationship with broader compliance constituencies. By contrast, when ICs have compulsory jurisdiction, cases will proceed despite the reluctance of the defendant state, and ICs will have more opportunities to shift the meaning of the law in ways the defendant government may dislike but that individuals, groups, and other governments may actually prefer.

Access for nonstate actors further enhances an IC's independence from governments, and it makes litigation more likely. Governments tend to be reluctant to initiate international litigation against other states, concerned that litigation will antagonize other governments and undermine the achievement of other goals. Governments may also worry that raising a legal suit will provoke actors in other countries to scrutinize their own compliance record and to raise a retaliatory legal suit.

Supranational prosecutors and international commissions, compared to state litigants, tend to be more willing to raise cases, both because they have a mandate to help enforce the law and because unlike state-plaintiffs, they do not have as many cross-cutting relations and objectives that compete for attention and are perhaps a higher priority.[3] Also, whereas states will use ICs to promote national interests, supranational prosecutorial actors will also pursue noncompliance cases of concern to individuals and groups but perhaps not other states. But international prosecutorial actors are also subject to political pressure. There are many cases that prosecutors choose not to pursue, preferring instead to rely on political means to address the issue.

Allowing private litigants to initiate litigation further changes international legal dynamics. Private litigants are more numerous, and they often bear the concentrated costs of state noncompliance and errant administrative decision making. Private litigants may be less easily dissuaded from pursing a legal suit compared to international prosecutorial actors, and they may pursue cases that promote their own objectives regardless of the preferences of others. When litigants and advocacy groups use litigation as a political strategy to promote their objectives, ICs are likely to have ready-made compliance constituencies who will work to see the IC

3 For more, see McCall Smith and Tallberg (2012).

ruling implemented.[4] Thus private access may enhance the likelihood that ICs find domestic interlocutors, leading to a stream of cases that enable IC law making and generating constituencies that pressure for compliance with international law.[5]

I focus on these design features in part because they allow us to readily see the difference in ICs today. Before the Cold War ended, it perhaps made sense to see ICs as voluntary dispute settlement bodies, and Europe's Court of Justice as a sui generis case of one. But today, new-style ICs are more typical, and cases raised by nonstate actors generate the lion's share of all international legal rulings.

The Power of International Judges

The design of ICs has changed, but their formal power has not. My perspective regarding the power of international judges differs from a traditional conception wherein law and adjudication are politically meaningful because they enjoy the backing of the state's coercive power. This Austinian view stands behind the presumption that absent a world state, international law is wholly dependent on state consent and therefore quite limited in its ability to influence state behavior or international relations.[6] International judges clearly do face political limitations, but the biggest constraint is neither the lack of a world state, nor the lack of strong coercive tools. Indeed, it really is not clear that adding either of these features would change the reality that international judges, like all judges, are legally and politically constrained.

International law is different from municipal law. Later I will argue that the key difference is that international law must compete with domestic rule of law conceptions. For now, what interests me is the power of international judges that comes by virtue of their legal mandate. ICs have the power to issue binding rulings in the cases that are raised. Like their domestic counterparts, international judges issue rulings pertaining to the authority and legality of government actions even though they have no way to force governments to comply with their rulings.[7] So how do

4 (Harlow and Rawlings 1992, especially chapter 4).

5 (Helfer and Slaughter 1997; Keohane, Moravcsik, and Slaughter 2000, 482; Stone Sweet 1999, 314–18).

6 John Austin argued that law reflects the commands of a sovereign and has influence because it is backed by that sovereign's coercive power (Austin 1832). The Austinian perspective still holds sway in international relations, although it has been much critiqued by jurists and philosophers. For an excellent discussion of Austin's approach alongside other perspectives, see O'Connell (2008, 19–55).

7 Goldsmith and Levinson consider the similarities between ICs and domestic courts in their public law roles. See Goldsmith and Levinson (2009).

international judges promote greater government respect for the rule of law?

Delegating interpretive authority to ICs is politically significant because it introduces an independent outside actor with the legal authority to say what international law means. ICs become the trustees of the legal agreement, and their legal interpretations are presumed to be more independent and disinterested compared to self-serving arguments litigating states put forward. To understand this claim, we must think about what exists when there is no delegation to ICs. Where there are no authoritative international adjudicators, each party can proffer their own interpretation to support their cause. Although domestic judges may be called upon to interpret international rules, national judges often defer to governments because the executive branch enjoys foreign affairs power, because governments have more insight into what an international agreement was supposed to mean, and because diplomats often have a better sense of how different legal interpretations might impact foreign relations. But delegation to ICs creates a legal actor that resides outside of the control of litigating states with the authority to say what international law means, to apply the law to concrete cases, and thus to indicate what compliance with international law entails. Delegating interpretive authority to ICs does not supplant the role of domestic actors, and in most cases ICs will be working with domestic supporters of the rule of law. But it does remove from governments and domestic judges the monopoly power to define what international law requires at home.

Being a trustee does not mean that international judges are entirely neutral or fully independent actors. The term comes from the common law concept of a trust, where the trust's creators specify the terms of the agreement and transfer oversight to a third party "trustee," who implements the agreement on behalf of the trust's beneficiaries.[8] The creator of the trust writes the trust agreement and selects the trustee to supervise the agreement, and in this respect, trustees are the agents of those who created the trust. The key conceptual point is that judges exercise their power on behalf of the trust's beneficiaries. A single state cannot change the trust agreement (international law), nor can they remove an international judge from office. This is why simply creating an IC involves a sovereignty risk. Governments can appoint a political ally to an IC, and they can choose to disregard an IC ruling. But there will remain a concrete risk that international judicial rulings will shift the meaning of law in ways that are unexpected and politically irreversible, putting governments on the

8 I have developed this idea further in Alter (2008). Chapter 2 qualifies this earlier work, arguing that the interests of states and ICs align when ICs are binding others to follow the law, and that ICs are most like trustees in self-binding judicial roles.

defensive. This risk is not just hypothetical. Constitutional review involves nullifying laws passed by legislative bodies, while administrative review involves rejecting decisions made by public actors. Thus if judicial actors play their intended roles, judges will at times disagree with, rule against, or render interpretations that run counter to what the makers and the enforcers of the law might have wanted.

In chapter 4 I take up the question of why states became increasingly willing to submit to international judicial oversight, and chapters 5, 6, 7, and 8 further consider why states might delegate a specific jurisdictional role to specific international courts. These arguments help make sense of the trends this book documents, but for me the reasons are secondary. What matters is that states have consented to IC authority, binding ever-changing governments to international judicial oversight of their adherence to international legal agreements and also empowering ICs to review the creation and application of law by international and national legislative and administrative actors. Once ICs exist, they become opportunity structures that litigants can activate to promote greater respect for international law. International judges may not be able to call upon centralized tools of coercion to enforce their rulings, but they can often call upon legal and political actors around the world to pressure governments to respect international law as defined by IC rulings.

Four Judicial Roles: Dispute Settlement, Administrative Review, Enforcement, and Constitutional Review

I assess the influence of ICs in action by looking at four different roles international courts play in the international political system: dispute settlement, administrative review, enforcement, and constitutional review. Old-style ICs were primarily interstate dispute settlement bodies with jurisdiction to adjudicate disputes and access rules that allowed only states to initiate binding litigation. New-style ICs have more extensive mandates that can include jurisdiction to rule on state compliance with international law and jurisdiction to review the legal validity of state and international legislative and administrative acts. Chapter 2 explains how dispute settlement and administrative review tend to be other-binding judicial roles that extend the central state's power, while enforcement and constitutional review tend to be self-binding judicial roles that check the state's exercise of power. Although each role can have both self- and other-binding dimensions, quite often delegation to ICs remains other-binding, which is to say a tool powerful state actors use to bind others to follow the law. This reality helps us understand why states so readily extended compulsory jurisdiction and access to nonstate actors and why most dispute settlement and administrative review IC rulings are not politically controversial. In short, states and ICs share the objectives of seeing the legal agreements implemented and the law respected.

The book has four chapters that correspond to these different roles. My coding of IC legal instruments reveals that governments made decisions to delegate certain roles to certain courts. These decisions are reflected in the initial grant of jurisdiction and in variation in access rules and remedies associated with different IC roles. I begin each empirical chapter by charting the universe of permanent ICs delegated a specific role, and in doing so I document a baseline of state consent while implicitly arguing that it makes the most sense to compare ICs within a given role, rather than to mix, match, and compare ICs playing fundamentally different roles. I document design variation within the role and include a number of case studies, using the case studies to identify how ICs are influencing international relations and state behavior in the particular role. The case studies also allow me to relax the categories somewhat, to consider international adjudication by nonpermanent courts, the influence of ICs in assumed rather than explicitly delegated roles, and to explore cases that combine roles. The rest of this section summarizes the four roles and reports broad trends the coding of IC legal instruments reveals.

Before proceeding, it is worth mentioning that these role categories are somewhat controversial. The idea that judicial roles can be separated by function—dispute settlement, administrative review, enforcement, and constitutional review—tends to be more recognizable and accepted by lawyers educated in the civil law tradition where branches of the judiciary are often divided by role. Lawyers most familiar with common law legal systems, by contrast, tend to see the judicial roles as overlapping, and they are more likely to expect that judges will fluidly migrate across roles. ICs are a melding of civil and common law traditions.[9] Since ICs are expensive to create and maintain, states often follow the common law tradition of giving multiple roles to single international legal institutions. Also, ICs tend to use the common law practice of citing precedent. But the legal instruments specifying IC jurisdiction intentionally vary IC design for different types of legal jurisdiction, extending access for certain roles so that ICs can perform additional legal functions. And my sense is that

9 Civil law systems (especially those that copy the French and German models) have separate private law dispute settlement, criminal enforcement, and public law administrative courts. When civil law systems added constitutional courts, they created separate institutions so as to underscore that ordinary courts still lacked judicial review authority. Common law countries, by contrast, tend to have unified legal systems where a single court may hear cases across categories, where lawyers might raise constitutional questions in the context of any type of dispute, and where judges regularly conduct judicial review and engage in lawmaking. The two traditions are increasingly merging. See Merryman and Pérez-Perdomo (2007, 86–90).

consistent with the civil law tradition, ICs are likely to stay within a given role. This is especially so because the authority of ICs is often contested by national judges who expect ICs to stick to their designated jurisdictional mandate.

What matters for me is that delegating specific roles to ICs tends to create a self-fulfilling prophecy. I do not expect that delegating an IC a given role means the court actually plays this role in practice. ICs influence law and politics when potential litigants invoke them. But the jurisdictional mandates define where ICs are more likely to be invoked, where ICs are more likely to rule against state defendants, and where international judges are more likely to be defended and politically protected because they are doing exactly what they were tasked to do. In any event, I am less concerned with creating hermetic distinctions than I am in understanding how and when ICs make contributions in the four roles.

Dispute settlement

In their dispute settlement role ICs adjudicate legal disagreements between contracting parties, helping the two sides resolve disagreements that turn on definitions of law. Most international treaties include provisions requiring the peaceful settlement of disputes, and many agreements designate ICs as the final legal venue for the settlement of disputes related to the treaty. Perhaps for this reason dispute settlement remains the role scholars most commonly associate with international courts, even though it is not the role most often delegated to ICs, nor the function ICs most often perform. The majority of ICs (seventeen of twenty-four) have dispute settlement jurisdiction. States do not have to use ICs to resolve disputes; the only legal obligation is that the dispute be resolved peacefully. Litigating parties can settle out of court or mutually agree to any venue for dispute resolution, including legalized and nonlegalized dispute settlement (for example, arbitration, mediation, good offices). The upshot is that ICs' dispute settlement jurisdiction is usually general, abstract, neither exclusive nor mandatory, and often never invoked.

It is nonetheless helpful to consider ICs involved in dispute settlement, since sometimes ICs do help contracting parties resolve disagreements. Chapter 5 identifies the seventeen ICs with the formal jurisdiction to adjudicate disputes pertaining to a broad range of issues. Fourteen of these ICs have jurisdiction to adjudicate disputes between state parties; thirteen have jurisdiction regarding disputes involving nonstate actors (international institutional actors or private litigants). Quite often the dispute settlement role primarily binds others to follow the terms of the legal agreement, and quite often the IC has also been delegated other roles. Indeed all but three of the ICs with a formal dispute settlement jurisdiction also have been delegated either enforcement, administrative, or constitutional review roles. These facts may help explain why more often than not IC's have compulsory jurisdiction for their dispute settlement role. After all, if ICs are primarily binding others to follow the terms of legal agreements, and if ICs also have compulsory jurisdiction for their enforcement role, why not extend compulsory jurisdiction to the dispute settlement role?

The goal of judging in this judicial role is to apply the law, but also to facilitate the settlement of disputes in the shadow of the law. ICs' key compliance partners in this role are the litigants themselves. ICs specify what the law requires, issuing a ruling that more often than not is a legal compromise designed to facilitate voluntary compliance. The legal solution is embraced because the parties brought the issue to the IC so that they could have a legal solution, the parties prefer legal certainty and want to move on, and perhaps because it is convenient for governments to blame the IC for disappointing domestic actors.

Case studies in chapter 5 examine how the International Court of Justice (ICJ) helped resolve a territorial disagreement between Qatar and Bahrain; how the International Tribunal for the Law of the Sea could help resolve disputes involving Russian authorities seizing Japanese vessels despite the fact that the two countries still contest the underlying boundaries where the vessels were fishing; and how the US-Iran Claims Tribunal and the Organization for the Harmonization of Business Law in Africa are able to resolve complex legal disagreements involving public and private litigants.

Administrative review

In their administrative review role, ICs review the legal validity of contested administrative decisions, creating a legal remedy for the subjects of those decisions. Depending on the standard of review, the judge will be checking to make sure that the administrator was faithful to the law, followed prescribed procedures, had legally defensible reasons for the decision, and that the decision was not discriminatory. Chapter 6 identifies thirteen ICs with administrative review jurisdiction and explains how delegation of administrative review authority is associated with systems where international and/or domestic administrative actors apply international regulatory rules. Whereas international dispute settlement involves a broad range of issues, administrative review tends to be concerned with economic aspects of international agreements. Eleven ICs have jurisdiction to review administrative acts of supranational administrators; eight have jurisdiction to review national implementation of international administrative rules.

All ICs with designated administrative review roles have compulsory jurisdiction associated with this role and allow private actors to initiate litigation so that the subjects of administrative decision making can pursue a legal remedy. Twelve ICs also allow national judges to refer to the IC cases where community rules are at issue. ICs' key compliance partners in this role are administrators who seek help in interpreting legal lacunae and in coordinating interpretation across actors and borders, and who deflect criticism and benefit from judicial validation of their rulings via administrative review.

Governments delegate administrative review to ICs because such review primarily binds others, providing a fire-alarm system of oversight for administrative actors who rely on delegated authority.[10] Governments learn about errant administrative decisions, which they can then repudiate, and judges can help administrators to resolve thorny interpretive questions. Where governments do not like how their regulatory rules are being interpreted, they can issue a clarifying declaration (as occurred in the Belmont and Metalclad cases discussed in chapter 6) or change the regulation. When ICs review international administrative decisions, they provide a legal redress that would otherwise not be available through domestic legal systems. When ICs review state administrative acts, they serve as a backup to domestic procedures, helping to generate a uniform interpretation of supranational administrative rules and providing an international redress that can be assuring to foreign litigants. Compared to domestic administrative review, international administrative review is more likely to leave fact finding to administrators so that in practice international administrative review provides a legal redress that fails as often if not more than it succeeds, thereby helping domestic and international administrators defend their actions against firm claims of illegalities. Where international adjudicatory bodies do scrutinize fact finding, administrative review is more likely to be contested by local administrators and to turn into a de facto enforcement role.

Case studies in chapter 6 include the European Commission's regulation of Microsoft and GE/Honeywell's decision to merge; the Andean Belmont litigation, which involved multiple countries disagreeing about which firm owned rights to the Belmont trademark; the softwood lumber case study involving binational panels under the North American Free Trade Agreement (NAFTA) and the WTO's dispute settlement system; the International Centre for the Settlement of Investment Disputes (ICSID)

10 On administrative review as oversight for administrative actors see McCubbins, Noll, and Weingast (1989). The general idea is that fire departments wait for a private actor to trigger a fire alarm before deploying fire trucks. By contrast, policemen are out on the streets monitoring citizens so as to discourage crime. Fire alarm oversight systems are especially attractive for international institutions with limited central resources, and where there is an effort to respect the autonomy of national regulators. See Kelemen (2011); Raustiala (2004).

dealing with Mexican decisions affecting the American firm Metalclad. Other chapters also include cases that involve administrative issues. The second-use patent case in chapter 7 involves a supranational commission challenging an illegal national regulation of an administrative nature. The Kadi case in chapter 8 involves a private litigant raising a constitutional challenge to a supranational regulation.

Enforcement

ICs in their enforcement role assess state compliance with an international agreement, naming violations of the law and thereby increasing the costs of noncompliance. Nineteen ICs have enforcement jurisdiction, meaning jurisdiction to adjudicate state compliance with international legal rules. IC enforcement cases nearly always involve state defendants (or individuals acting in a public/leadership capacity), and nearly all ICs with explicitly delegated enforcement roles (seventeen of the nineteen) have compulsory jurisdiction associated with this role. Fourteen of these systems allow states to initiate noncompliance suits; thirteen allow supranational commissions and eleven private litigants to initiate a review of state compliance with international law. Today one finds international courts with compulsory enforcement jurisdiction in the substantive areas where ICs operate: economic agreements, human rights treaties, and international criminal law. ICs primarily name a state practice as legal or illegal and secondarily authorize remedies designed to compensate victims and create costs associated with illegal behavior. The types of remedies ICs are able to specify vary by court, and ICs' compliance partners vary by issue area and case depending on what compliance with the law actually entails, which in turn determines which actors have the power to choose compliance.

Chapter 7 presents four case studies covering all of the substantive domains in which international courts operate. The case studies show WTO litigation pressuring the US Congress to change a tax policy that promoted US exports; the Andean Tribunal facilitating a retreat on the issuing of "second use patents"; and the Community Court of the Economic Community of West African States (ECOWAS) leading Niger to compensate Hadijatou Mani for enslavement in the customary family law system and the indictment and arrest of Charles Taylor, a sitting head of state, for crimes committed in a neighboring country. Chapter 8 includes four additional case studies of ICs reviewing state practices (previewed in my discussion of the constitutional review role). In all of these case studies, the ability of ICs to offer a remedy mobilized litigants, and ICs' rulings constructed focal remedies that compliance supporters could demand. IC rulings also provided legal, symbolic, and political resources that those actors who preferred law compliance could use as levers for their cause.

Political mobilization and the legal, symbolic, and political resources supplied to compliance constituencies generated costs for violating international law.

Constitutional review

In their constitutional review role, ICs hold international and state actors accountable to constitutional procedural and rule of law expectations, invalidating legislative acts that conflict with higher order legal requirements. Constitutional review is perhaps the most controversial IC role in that it involves ICs confronting highly legitimated actors and rejecting policies that may have been legally enacted.[11] Ten ICs have this self-binding jurisdiction to assess the legal validity of public acts, with the remedy being the nullification of illegal acts. Nine of these ICs have jurisdiction to review the validity of supranational laws and acts; four have explicit jurisdiction to review the validity of national acts.

Whereas ICs' enforcement role creates costs associated with state noncompliance, ICs' constitutional review in theory nullifies and vacates illegal acts. The discussion of constitutional review authority in action explores how local cultures of constitutional obedience condition whether IC constitutional rulings are seen as rendering unconstitutional acts null and void. If governments or judges see IC rulings as authoritative, and the applicable international law as legally supreme, then ICs may be able to foster a culture of constitutional obedience to international law where acts condemned by ICs are seen as ipso facto invalid. Like their domestic counterparts, ICs cannot really force governments to comply with their ruling. Where national cultures of international law adherence emerge, however, national legislators and judges will usual voluntarily vacate policies that run afoul of higher order international laws.

I suggest that building a culture of constitutional obedience to international law may be easier with respect to the review of international acts, because the political legitimacy of international legislative acts is already considered suspect. Chapter 8 includes two case studies of ICs invalidating contested supranational legislation.

The chapter then examines four cases where ICs are arguably engaged in constitutional review of domestic acts. These cases are even more difficult in that domestic actors need to see international law as supreme to national law. In the women in combat support roles and indigenous land rights cases, IC rulings were widely seen as requiring governments to create a positive remedy for the constitutional breach, and this remedy was not required by domestic law. These case studies are contrasted with the

11 For more on the debate about constitutional review by international courts, see Dunoff and Tractman (2009).

alcohol-related practices case study where the Andean Tribunal of Justice (ATJ) condemned Colombia's alcohol policies but the Colombian Supreme Court hindered the supreme application of Andean community rules. I also contrast the positive obligation to make land rights meaningful in the "indigenous land rights case" to the politically easier requirement of a compensatory award in the modern-day slavery case study discussed in chapter 4. Finally, the chapter discusses the rape as a war crime case study where the International Criminal Tribunal for Rwanda (ICTR) constructed a new definition of criminal responsibility with constitutional import.

The Four Judicial Roles Together

I am interested in the multiple roles ICs play because they allow us to appreciate the many different contributions ICs make to international politics. ICs engage in interstate dispute settlement, and they adjudicate state compliance with international agreements. But this is not all they do. Wherever there are common regulatory rules that are to be applied transnationally, policy makers worry about rules being interpreted and applied differentially across borders. Wherever there are supranational administrators making binding decisions, lawyers and policy makers worry about how to monitor the international actors to ensure basic competence and as a check against institutional capture. International systems of administrative review are designed to address these concerns. National legislatures and states in federal systems worry that their sovereign rights may be usurped when the executive operates through international institutions. Human rights advocates and national judges worry about unchecked international authority. International constitutional review helps to address these concerns. Even the dispute settlement role is broader than interstate dispute settlement. It does more than resolve legal ambiguities; it transfers private litigant complaints about broken promises to a venue where disinterested actors can investigate the charges and hopefully create some legal finality that helps stakeholders move on.

My larger argument is that state-IC politics vary by judicial role. Some judicial roles—in particular the dispute settlement and administrative review roles—are primarily other-binding roles, where the power of central governments is more likely to be reinforced by independent judicial review than it is to be undermined. Other judicial roles—particularly the enforcement and constitutional review roles—self-bind governmental and legislative actors and by design check the exercise of sovereign power. Also, the ICs' key interlocutors—those who help give IC rulings a political effect—vary by role. In the dispute settlement role, ICs' key interlocutors tend to be the litigants who choose to embrace the IC ruling and end their disagreement. In the administrative review role, ICs' key interlocutors tend to be administrators who assent to interpret and apply regulatory rules in the ways defined by the IC. In the constitutional review role, ICs' key interlocutors are national supreme court judges whose support for the notion that international law imposes higher order legal obligations makes it harder for governments to simultaneously violate international rules and maintain their claim to be rule of law actors. For the enforcement role, ICs' compliance partners will vary because what compliance with the law entails will vary, and ICs may need to draw on the support of broader compliance constituencies who leverage IC rulings to pressure for political change.

New-Style ICs and the New Terrain of International Law

In certain respects, basic elements of ICs have not changed. States still create ICs; governments still appoint international judges; ICs still have the same formal power to render binding rulings in the cases that are adjudicated. But expectations have changed. Under the contract-based approach, when one side breaks a contract, the other side is released from their legal obligations under the contract. This contractual approach still operates to some extent in the ICJ and for some economic systems, but the shift to new-style ICs reflects a changed notion of legal obligation.[12] For human rights, mass atrocities law, and much international economic law, we don't expect one country's violation to dissolve the obligation of other states. We will see in the book's case studies that the practice of many ICs today reflects this shift toward rule of law expectations of compliance with the rules regardless of what other states might be doing.

Politically speaking the new-style design of ICs is important because compulsory jurisdiction and access for nonstate actors makes it harder for governments to block inconvenient cases. Because the content of international law has expanded and the opportunities to legally challenge state practices increased, international courts are adjudicating legal issues that used to fall within the exclusive prerogative of states.

This change in IC design combines with the embedding of international law into domestic legal orders to bring with it a loss in government control over both the litigation process and legal understandings. But it is also true that the reach and scope of international law into the domestic realm varies. The starting point for ICs remains state consent.

12 Article 36 (3) of the ICJ's statute recognizes that some legal obligations depend on reciprocity, but it also allows that countries can create agreements that do not depend on reciprocity.

Governments must craft international agreements, incorporate international law into national systems, and create international legal mechanisms that are actually useful for those actors that want to see law respected. Litigants must be able to invoke ICs, and ICs must be able to connect with compliance supporters in order for delegation to ICs to increase the shadow of international law in domestic and international politics. Chapter 3 identifies significant variation in where states have consented to compulsory international judicial oversight. The reach of ICs and international law varies, but where there is international law that litigants can invoke in court, the circle of actors involved in defining what international law means, and what it means for governments to be rule of law actors, expands. This expansion brings with it a shift in international relations, away from state control in both the domestic and international realms.

II. ALTERING POLITICS: THE POLITICS PART OF THE STORY

The larger question of this book is when and how delegation to ICs influences international and domestic politics. Although an IC's influence varies by judicial role, I have one general argument about how ICs influence political outcomes. The existence of an international legal remedy empowers those actors who have international law on their side, increasing their out of court political leverage. ICs then alter political outcomes by giving symbolic, legal, and political resources to compliance constituencies, ever-changing groups of actors that for a variety of reasons may prefer policies that cohere with international law. The general dynamic is present across roles and cases, but variations in the law, what compliance entails, and the mobilization, political power, and leverage of compliance constituencies creates important variation in when delegation to ICs ends up altering domestic and international outcomes.

This argument is challenging for those who expect ICs to be beholden to the interests and preferences of governments. International relations scholarship generally conceives of international courts as a cipher of state interests. This is partly true, although not in the way that many international relations scholars posit. Scholars who expect ICs to be guided by the preferences of litigating governments generally build their theories from the insight that ICs have no way to compel compliance with their rulings. They then make the following corollary: if ICs can neither compel compliance nor enact strong sanctions for violating the law, the only choice left to an international judge who wants to be useful and relevant is to make rulings that appeal to a litigating state's national interest. Thus all ICs can really do is serve as coordination devices for states.[13]

No one disputes that ICs can be interstate arbiters, helping governments identify areas of common interests. The real question is whether ICs are only able to serve as coordination devices. Conservative and law and economics scholars make this leap.[14] But the corollary—a lack of coercive power limits ICs to the role of ascertaining median preferences of the litigating governments—has within it a flawed logic.

All courts lack coercive power; it is states not judges that have the monopoly on the legitimate use of force. Nor is the main constraint of ICs their lack of overt sanctioning tools. Indeed, ICs are no different from domestic constitutional courts in facing these constraints. Rather, ICs, like their domestic constitutional counterparts, must create indirect costs for political actors inclined to ignore them.

The problem for ICs is that governments can choose not to comply, defending noncompliance as consistent with the domestic rule of law.[15] Moreover, domestic populations may actually prefer noncompliance with international agreements. But where domestic actors are unhappy about government violations of international agreements, and even where populations are mostly indifferent, ICs can work with domestic and transnational interlocutors to either orchestrate compliance or construct counterpressures that alter the political balance in favor of policies that better cohere with international legal obligations.

ICs help alter state policy by using their institutional position to aid actors inside and outside of states that share the objectives inscribed into the law. Chapter 2 distinguishes between compliance partners and compliance supporters. *Compliance partners* are actors that have the power to generate compliance with an IC ruling on their own. In other words, compliance partners can embrace an IC ruling and thereby create compliance without any decision, mobilization, or action by governments or legislatures. For the dispute settlement role, the litigating parties are the IC's compliance partners. In the administrative review role, administrators are the IC's compliance partners. In the constitutional review role national supreme court judges are compliance partners. *Compliance supporters* are broader coalitions of actors whose tacit or mobilized support is needed to protect compliance partners

13 (Garrett and Weingast 1993; Goldsmith and Posner 2005; Posner and Yoo 2005).

14 For more, see the discussion of the interstate arbiter model in chapter 2.

15 Not all constitutions grant supremacy to international law, so that conflicts between international and domestic laws are not necessarily resolved in favor of international law. Even where international law is seen as formally supreme, domestic courts adjudicate the internal effects of international law.

from political retaliation or to induce reluctant governmental actors to embrace an IC ruling. The two together—partners and supporters—are the IC's compliance constituency.

The path to mobilize these compliance constituencies can take a few different routes. The existence of these alternative routes means that ICs do not need to pander to the interests of governments in power. Perhaps the easiest route politically is for ICs to co-opt the support of compliance partners, since they already have the power to choose compliance. ICs can co-opt governments, providing legal rulings that governments can use to deflect blame and overrule the arguments of domestic opponents. ICs can also circumvent governments. If ICs induce administrative agencies and national judges to reinterpret existing domestic laws, ICs can produce policy changes regardless of or even despite of the preferences of ruling governments. Using reinterpretation as a mode of political change is relatively easier because it does not require mobilizing governments or legislatures to act. Domestic compliance partners can be fairly easily co-opted where they believe that ambiguity in the rules themselves, unintended errors, incompetence, indifference, or corruption has generated noncompliance, or where they think that the government is pursuing an agenda that runs counter to domestic legal and constitutional requirements.

Where compliance partners are either unwilling or unable to deliver full compliance with an IC ruling, ICs must instead rely on others to exert political pressure on those actors that do have the power to choose compliance. ICs can appeal to actors in other states, invoking multilateral politics as a tool to influence a recalcitrant government. For example, the World Trade Organization (WTO) allows other states to retaliate for violations of WTO rules by raising tariffs against politically sensitive industries and regions. The Foreign Sales Corporation case discussed in chapter 7 shows how the legally authorized retaliation of the European Union shifted US firm preferences, so that firms now wanted the US Congress to eliminate a special tax break for exporters. The Charles Taylor case shows governments and advocates invoking the Special Court for Sierra Leone's indictment of Charles Taylor to justify creating sanctions and repealing Taylor's grant of asylum in Nigeria. The key point is that sanctions occur as a consequence of IC involvement. In other words, in the new terrain of international law nonstate actors can initiate international litigation, provoke an IC condemnation, and then harness multilateral and interstate politics to support their objectives.

ICs can also try to inspire the "spiral strategy" where national and transnational activists use an international legal ruling as evidence that political leaders are deviating from their promises of respecting the rule of law, or from adhering to the goals and standards inscribed into national and international law.[16] In this transnational politics strategy, ICs work with grassroots organizations to influence government policy. For example, the indigenous land rights case discussed in chapter 8 shows how supporters of indigenous rights used the Inter-American Court of Human Rights (IACtHR) judicial system to pressure Nicaragua's government to adopt new policies demarcating the land ownership of indigenous peoples.

ICs' institutional position allows them to contribute meaningful leverage to compliance supporters, which is why raising cases in front of an IC can be attractive. IC rulings provide legal justifications for actors within states—the police, governments, national administrators, and national judges—who might otherwise be reluctant to push back against the preferences of a powerful domestic actor. The presumed authority of IC rulings also provides compliance advocates with a tool to delegitimize the interpretations of the law that opponents are using to defend the validity of their actions. IC rulings can mobilize lawyers, law professors, and public interest law groups to find similar cases and to use domestic legal channels to increase the political pressure. IC rulings can also mobilize actors who benefit from the international legal system overall. For example, business groups might support certain interpretations of WTO law because they see compliance as furthering their international economic interests. Even if these groups do not mobilize, their tacit support provides cover for actors who are facing counterpressures. The public nature of IC rebukes also creates potential costs. Flaunting an IC ruling can make it harder for a government to pressure other states to follow rules of the international regime. For example, if the United States violates the consular affair rights of foreigners within its prison system, American citizens arrested abroad may find that their legal pleas carry less weight. And for this reason the State Department may become an advocate of following international law. In these ways ICs are able to knit together broader constituencies of political support to push in the direction of law compliance. IC involvement can also lead to changes that span borders. The indigenous land rights ruling led to legal claims in other Latin American countries. Erik Voeten and Laurence Helfer further show how European Court of Human Rights jurisprudence regarding the rights of gay, lesbian, and transsexual individuals and their partners contributed to broader change in practices across members of the Council of Europe.[17]

The ability of ICs to alter internal and external politics means that simply creating an international court is a politically significant act. What

16 (Risse, Ropp, and Sikkink 1999; Thomas 2001).
17 (Helfer and Voeten 2013).

delegation to ICs does most often is entrench politics across time. States delegate authority to an IC so as to ensure that subsequent governments do not walk away from the set of policies inscribed in the law. Thus quite often ICs help alter the balance in the direction the law's authors inscribed into the DNA of the law. ICs enforcing international economic rules will tend to promote market openness. ICs enforcing human rights rules will tend to promote a human rights agenda. International war crimes tribunals will tend to condemn state practices that harm noncombatants. This means that to the extent that international agreements codify the goals and objectives associated with economic liberalism, or liberal democracy, ICs will more likely than not be contributing forces for these goals. The role of ICs in reinforcing the current order may not be visible because states may avoid violations that are likely to be challenged, or governments may settle out of court, granting concessions but perhaps not complying in full. But delegating authority to ICs will nonetheless have the effect of increasing the negotiating leverage of the party that favors what the law requires.

The argument itself implies no specific trajectory for how law gets interpreted. The argument does, however, mean that ICs actually contribute to constituting understandings of international law, and thereby the preferences of actors that care about the legality of their behavior. The role of ICs in constructing interests is easier to observe when ICs are seized and when their rulings lead to changes in domestic policy, but ICs' very presence can discourage actions that would expose legal vulnerabilities and thereby hinder change that may otherwise have occurred. In either case, in order to reconstitute politics ICs must have domestic- and international-level interlocutors that support their interpretations of the law.

This argument takes legal obligation and the autonomy of law seriously and suggests that international judges are equal parts legal and political actors. The legal part of the analysis is the claim that international judging is deeply shaped by the jurisdiction delegated to ICs, which defines the judicial roles ICs may be asked to play and are likely to embrace, and by the "legal facts" by which I mean what a plain reading of the law requires. The political part—captured by the altered politics framework—focuses on how variation in what compliance entails and variation in the mobilization and political power of judges' compliance constituents influences litigant strategies, IC decision making, and whether state behavior changes.

The altered politics argument suggests that the greatest limitation on ICs is not the lack of a world government but rather the reality that where ICs lack domestic support constituencies, governments can defend noncompliance with international rules as consistent with the domestic rule of law. But where there are governmental and nongovernmental actors who *do* prefer to follow international law, ICs can help construct coalitions of counterpressures that alter the political balance in favor of policies that better cohere with international legal obligations.

This analysis suggests that ICs become politically weak not because governments oppose them—indeed, opposition to existing government policies is probably the reason why ICs are invoked in the first place. Rather, ICs become politically weak when legal and policy defenders will not organize to demand that governments adhere to the particular legal covenants or to the particular interpretations of the law the IC is promoting.

Explaining Variation in IC Influence: A Brief Theory and Methods Discussion

Overall this book is a theory-generating exercise with the goal of theorizing ICs' varied influence in domestic and international politics. My claim is not that IC design necessarily translates to IC effectiveness. On the contrary, I argue that by comparing like institutions operating in different contexts, we can gain insight into when and how ICs become politically effective, meaning helpful for engendering greater respect for the law.

My method of investigation is inductive. I start by understanding the world as it exists, with twenty-four ICs that states have differentially empowered to adjudicate a variety of types of legal cases. A key question for me is how the existence of the IC affects political strategies both inside and outside of court, and whether invoking international law contributes to changing government behavior in the direction of greater respect for the law. Since this is my question, I need to explore the political dynamics that lead cases to get to court, ICs to be willing to challenge powerful political actors, and governments to change their behavior. Case studies are the best way to do this. The chapter case studies combine to elucidate variation within a given judicial role. I looked for cases that represent a variety of legal and structural situations, varying the actors that initiate litigation, what compliance entails, and the pathways toward compliance. I generally pick hard cases, situations where important interests are at stake, where the policies leading to law violations are politically entrenched, and where law operates in places and ways that are counter to the expectations of international relations scholars and domestically focused lawyers. Since we would expect IC influence to be less in these cases, a focus on hard cases is a good qualitative tool to "test" how meaningful IC influence actually is. The case study method allows me to compare single institutions across time, and I explore political dead ends alongside success stories so as to elucidate how invoking ICs does and does not influence state behavior across cases.

If I were testing as opposed to inductively building theory, I would carefully select case studies to fit theoretical arguments. Instead, I put side by side a variety of ICs and other international legal bodies as they adjudicate disputes that occur in diverse contexts and that involve economic issues, human rights, mass atrocities, and other issues so as to underscore the similar altered-politics dynamics at play. My selection bias is that I focus on cases that are litigated and where the defendant government lost because it is easier to see the influence of ICs in such cases. The qualitative method of investigation also allows me to examine how change occurs over time, to move beyond binary views of law compliance, to evaluate varying causal factors influencing state behavior, and to better see the broader (for example, non-case-specific) influence of ICs on international and domestic politics.

Case studies allow me to relax the focus on permanent international courts and state consent that dominate in part I of the book, so as to show how these are not essential criteria for domestic and international politics to become judicialized. Although there are *many* European cases one could examine, only three of the eighteen case studies in this book focus on European legal institutions because I want to show that the new terrain of international law exists beyond Europe. Because I prefer less likely cases, I focus on human rights courts from Latin America and Africa, and cases where ICs with economic subject matter jurisdiction end up speaking to human rights issues, rather than a case study involving the European Court of Human Rights. I also use case studies to make the theory less abstract. Through the case studies we see how international legal politics works in the real world, warts and all. We can also identify how the introduction of compulsory international adjudication and access for nonstate actors has affected domestic and international politics.

Throughout the book I generate hypotheses that one could systematically test. Chapter 2 develops the altered politics framework, a process-based approach to studying the influence of ICs across issues and cases where I break down the stages of the litigation process. Each time frame is a threshold where different actors play a decisive role. In Time 1—bargaining in the shadow of the court—the key decision makers are potential litigants, legal factors shape the credibility of the legal threat, and the political reality of what compliance with the law requires shapes bargaining politics. In Time 2—litigation politics—the key decision makers are international prosecutorial actors and judges, legal factors and compliance concerns shape IC decision making, and rhetorical politics dominate. In Time 3—leverage politics—the willingness of compliance constituencies to remain mobilized, and to leverage rulings into costs for noncompliant governments, shapes politics and outcomes. I explain how variation in each of these steps of the litigation process and interactive effects across steps can lead to variation in the influence of ICs. Role-based chapters further hypothesize about sources for ICs' varied activation and influence in a given role.

Rather than constructing stylized cases to fit theories, my case studies are brief narratives, compelling stories that acknowledge the complexity of the issues at stake. By revealing the contemporary international judiciary, and comparing disparate cases with their inherent complexity, I implicitly suggest the way to understand the growing and varied influence of ICs today and to test theories is through comparative analysis—comparing ICs, comparing issues, comparing pathways toward greater respect for the law. I hope that presenting a broader array of courts and cases will push others to move beyond the "usual suspects," as there are important issues we can explore by looking at how international law works in varied contexts.

III. MAKING LEGAL RIGHTS MEANINGFUL: THE RIGHTS PART OF THE STORY

This book explains how legal norms and politics are imposing rule of law expectations on international deal making and bringing international law into domestic politics. Rule of law politics are often closely related to rights politics. A key legal notion is that rights can only meaningfully exist when there are remedies. International law has long lacked remedies, and in truth there may be no remedy for certain international law violations. War that is illegally instigated, human rights violations that affect hundreds and thousands of individuals, and even the death or rape of a single person can never be rectified. It is also questionable whether remedies in the form of restitution should be a goal for international politics. Seeking restitution keeps people focused on the past, and it may be less practicable and useful than stopping new violations from occurring or simply helping parties move on.

Delegation to ICs is part of a forward-looking project of building respect for international law. To create an IC is to introduce the possibility of a legal remedy. Not only does the existence of this remedy instantiate the legal right, making it meaningful, the prospect of the remedy also mobilizes stakeholders to claim their rights. Formally speaking, the IC's contribution is to offer a legal interpretation that validates the existence of the legal right, to put a scarlet letter on a violation, and perhaps to specify what compliance with the law and respect for the right requires. The modern-day slavery, softwood lumber, and Metalclad case studies led to compensation for harms illegal acts generated. The indigenous land rights, women in combat support roles, Belmont, seizing private assets

(Kadi), and rape as a war crime case studies led to the creation of obligations and rights that extend into the future.

Politically speaking, the IC's contribution is to become a catalyst for rights holders to assert their rights and governments to recognize these rights. Litigants claim their rights, and this claiming instigates bargaining in the shadow of the law. Rights holders may well settle for far less than the full realization of their right, and the settlement may reflect power more than law. But in offering to settle, or in letting the case proceed to litigation, the existence of the right gets recognized. Rights claimers of the future can draw inspiration, future litigants can invoke legal precedent, expectations can shift, and in the next iteration litigants, advocates, and judges can ask for more.

My approach to rights creation is dynamic, showing how the common international relations baseline—that governments pursue their own and the nation's interests—shifts over time. International treaties and secondary legislation get created at one point, for specific reasons. Governments might ratify an international treaty without considering what compliance involves, or political leaders might think that they will control how international law is applied by writing protections for cherished national policies into international treaties and secondary legislation. Delegation to ICs may come at the same time the law is made, or much later. And states may begin by significantly limiting access to the IC, by making the IC ruling purely declaratory, and by filling ICs with their allies. Over time, however, governments and politics change. New leaders emerge, and they may want to signal their new politics by strengthening existing international legal systems or by complying with a ruling a previous government flaunted. A new government's embrace of democratic values or the growing power of judges in general may itself spur litigants, and ICs may find they have new constituencies of support to draw on. ICs may then interpret existing laws in unexpected ways. Delegation to ICs in this way becomes a slow time-release mechanism that promotes political change in the direction indicated by the law. International judicial review can be a mode of institutional change, of changing understandings of law, of circumventing national legal and political barriers, and of incrementally shifting expectations about what compliance with the law entails.

The book's case studies allow us to see ICs' varied contribution to generating rights. In terms of the legal finding, international judges' room for interpretive maneuver may be limited by the law and by shared legal understandings of compliance partners. Variation may mostly come in the form of the remedies demanded. The cases present a sliding scale of legal remedies and show how ICs and litigants vary remedies to make it easier for compliance partners—administrators, judges, or government officials—to circumvent political opposition. When the political moment is right—when new coalitions of support arise and mobilize, when opponents of policy change are no longer upset, mobilized, or powerful; when support for certain norms becomes broader or captures the attention of political leaders; or when political leaders change—international judges can ask for a fuller remedy. In the meantime, the ability to offer a scaling and adjustable remedy provides an incentive for advocates to invoke courts, judges to declare rights, and a starting point for ideas and understandings to shift.

This long-term view is admittedly optimistic. Legal strategies can of course lead to new impediments for rights claimers, which may then inhibit future litigation. It is also possible that IC involvement can provoke a political backlash, even where ICs are doing exactly what they have been asked to do. In the short run, the inadequacies of international legal remedies raise serious normative questions. Opponents will ask: who consented to let ICs adjudicate compliance with international law? On whose behalf do ICs monitor compliance and help enforce the law? What if governments and citizens do not like how ICs apply the law? What if state and substate actors want to change their mind about consenting to an international law or to IC adjudication? Even sympathetic supporters will wonder: How can huge atrocities generate such short and relatively cushy prison terms? Why are my country's fairly minor violations pursued while major violations in country *x* escape adjudication? These normative questions are important, and vigorously debating them may well end up shaping what international legal rights become. The fact that we bother to raise these questions is itself testament to the growing power and influence of ICs, and our rising expectations for international law.

Overall, this book shows that ICs are increasingly part of legal contestation about the meaning of international law and what government respect for the rule of law entails. ICs' contribution to these politics is to increase the credibility of legal threats, and then to state what the law means in the cases that are adjudicated, sometimes naming violations of the law, sometimes specifying remedies. ICs effectuate change by working with compliance constituencies to facilitate greater respect for international law. Because governments can no longer block litigation or control which cases get adjudicated, because ICs are legal actors that traffic in the currency of rule of law expectations, because international law is increasingly embedded into domestic legal orders, the prospect of an IC remedy and IC legal edicts are politically meaningful. But international judicial dependence on state and substate interlocutors is both empowering and constraining. Ultimately, rights are intersubjective; they exist when both the rights holder and those actors who have legal duties recognize the right. Delegation to ICs ratchets up the pressure to recognize rights, and this in itself contributes to generating such rights.

CONCLUSION: A ROADMAP FOR THIS BOOK

In the new terrain of international law, international law governs issues and policy arenas that were once the exclusive domain of national governments. Litigation can be a tool to reinforce the regulative role of international law and a way to help the individuals charged with applying international rules better understand *how* they are supposed to implement international laws. This regulative role of international law and IC adjudication is important to recognize, and it is the main focus when I examine the other-binding dispute settlement and administrative review roles of ICs. But I am especially interested in when ICs serve as change agents, reinterpreting law on the books, applying existing rules to new domains, and helping to generate rights that have value and meaning. Because ICs can be change agents, delegation to ICs introduces a dynamic element into international politics. ICs are rival authorities, able to contest interpretations of the law powerful domestic and international actors use to defend the legality of their actions. ICs are also able to introduce a finality to disagreements about what the law means, clarifying the meaning of the law for the case at hand in a way that creates a new status quo that all political actors must respond to.

Part I of this book considers the international judiciary as a whole. Chapter 2 develops the altered politics framework in theoretical terms. Chapter 3 maps the international judicial landscape today by presenting a bird's-eye overview of the contemporary international judiciary, revealing temporal, substantive, and regional trends in delegating authority to ICs. The bird's-eye perspective helps us grasp what delegation to international courts looks like today. But the perspective is largely static, a snapshot in time that obscures how legal practice, international law, and international legal institutions evolve. Chapter 4 explains why governments have become increasingly willing to consent to compulsory international judicial oversight, highlighting how legal practice has changed and how international law has increasingly become embedded into domestic law and institutions.

Part II of the book examines the politics of ICs in action. Chapters 5 through 8 consider the four judicial roles—dispute settlement, administrative review, enforcement, and constitutional review—independently. I document which ICs have explicitly been delegated the role, provide more fine-grained distinctions about design variations across ICs with respect to the role, and speculate about why the identified set of courts (and not others) were delegated the role in question. Appendixes to each chapter provide more detail regarding access rules and jurisdiction for a given role. Case studies then examine the politics of ICs within each role, suggesting both similarity and divergence in how different ICs play a given role. This book presents a total of eighteen case studies of ICs in action. The cases get increasingly contested as the chapters proceed because the discussions move from ICs in other-binding roles, where international judges are reinforcing and extending the power of the central state, to ICs self-binding governments and invoking higher order legal norms as they challenge state prerogatives and entrenched behaviors.

The conclusion recaps and starts to build on the main findings in the book through a focus on the normative question of how to reconcile international law with democratic politics. The most obvious way to build on this book is to engage in deeper comparative theorizing about how and when delegation to ICs alters international and domestic politics. By identifying how different factors matter at each stage of the litigation process, and how litigation efforts can succeed or fail at each step of the process, the altered politics framework provides a natural starting point for developing scope conditions and testable hypotheses. The role-based chapters identifying similarity and difference in ICs' formal mandate and access provisions, the varying data, and the juxtaposition of case studies highlight the many different pathways toward compliance as well as challenges ICs face, providing detail from which scholars can develop their own hypotheses to test. A second way to build is to begin a policy discussion about how we want to use international legal mechanisms as a tool to enhance the influence of international law in domestic and international politics.

The fuller picture of how a broad range of ICs are influencing politics requires us to throw away our stereotypes about courts, which are usually utopian ideals that do not even exist in the best national rule of law system. The fuller picture also requires us to recognize international law not as a luxury good, but as a basic necessity for countries and individuals where the domestic rule of law and the best efforts of their supporters nonetheless fall short. Elites may chafe when international judges rule against countries on issues that used to fall within the prerogative of domestic governments, but this is a new reality that states created for themselves when they combined a commitment to international laws with international judicial oversight. More importantly, this is an evolution in legal practice that is unlikely to change.

Going back in time to the world after World War II, where governments could choose whether or not to submit to judicial oversight, is not a realistic or viable political option. Rather than lament the new reality, we should learn to harness delegation to legal bodies as a means to promote shared political objectives. Most ICs do exactly what governments asked them to do. ICs adjudicate disputes, fill in legal lacunae, review administrative decision making, and assess state compliance with international law. Most IC rulings are not controversial, and those that raise objections are controversial mostly for those whose argument lost in court. The involvement of courts and judges in adjudicating state compliance with international law is an interesting and important evolution in contemporary politics, one that is growing and unlikely to be reversed any time soon.

CHAPTER 2

International Courts Altering Politics

International courts have the power to issue binding rulings in cases that are adjudicated. How does creating an international court with such limited powers change international politics? This chapter answers this question by considering the power of courts in general. Although we often talk about courts enforcing the law, the truth of the matter is that no courts enforce the law. States, with their monopoly on the legitimate use of force, enforce the law. But at the national level court rulings are arguably backed by state power. Many people consider international courts to be particularly handicapped because there is no world state to back their rulings. On the one hand, ICs are no different from national constitutional courts in this respect; they can issue binding and authoritative rulings, but international judges cannot force governments to respect their rulings.[1] On the other hand, supporters of international courts will agree with critics that international judges do not have a sufficient inherent authority on their own to compel governments to abandon valued policies. While international courts are different from their domestic counterparts, it is nonetheless true that for all courts legal rulings must combine with other factors to influence political outcomes.[2]

For political science realist scholars, IC rulings must combine with preexisting national interests. Others see government preferences as changeable and IC rulings as part of a process that leads to change. Adjudicating between these two very different perspectives may be impossible. If ICs are anticipating state reactions, we may never know if governments follow an IC ruling because they were persuaded to do so or

1 (Goldsmith and Levinson 2009; Hathaway and Shapiro 2011).

2 Law and society scholarship commonly presumes that societal factors are perhaps even more important than legal rulings in shaping political outcomes. See Epps (1998); Rosenberg (1993).

because the IC correctly deduced the state's national interest.[3] Scholars have sought to disentangle this conundrum by employing increasingly sophisticated qualitative and quantitative methods to investigate how political factors shape IC decision making. If critics can demonstrate that ICs tailor their rulings to the interests of powerful governments, they can undermine any claim that ICs are independent or capable of influencing powerful states. Tests of varying hypotheses have met with contested results. The evidence that international judges cater to the interests of certain states is weak at best, as is the evidence that judges are primarily influenced by a fear of being legislatively reversed or passed over for reappointment. The only point of some agreement is that compliance concerns probably shape the decisions of international judges to some extent.[4] Since the debate pivots around the issue of what shapes government compliance with international law, this chapter begins by considering when compliance with IC rulings is puzzling.

Section I builds on Martin Shapiro's argument that delegation to courts extends the power of the central state. If much of what international courts do is bind other actors—private litigants, administrative actors, international institutions, or weaker states—to follow the law powerful states wrote, then compliance is not a puzzle nor is it surprising that states would consent to compulsory jurisdiction and private access provisions to ICs. In other-binding contexts, international judges should not have to be focused on eliciting compliance; high levels of compliance should be the norm; and the factors shaping IC decision making are more likely to be legal and/or related to the professional background and appointment politics of judges.

The rest of the chapter focuses on the more narrow category of self-binding, where the rule of law objectives of ICs and the priorities of

3 On how the endogeniety of international agreements makes it hard to know why states comply with international agreements, see Downs, Rocke, and Barsoom (1996). An equally great challenge is how do we know a state's national interest? On the fungibility of national interests and the problem of relying on post hoc "revealed" state preferences, see Alter (2008, 36–38); Finnemore (1996).

4 A partial list of studies include Carrubba, Gabel, and Hankla (2008); Garrett, Kelemen, and Schulz (1998); Ginsburg (2005); Pollack (2003); Posner and De Figueiredo (2005); Posner and Yoo (2005); Steinberg (2004); Stone Sweet (2004; 2010). Most of these studies try to explain variation based on what are often fairly crude proxies scholars use to operationalize their hypotheses. Since it can be hard to measure how legal concerns or the merits of the case are affecting IC decision making, most of these studies only consider how political factors shape IC decision making. The strongest finding of state influence comes from Carrubba, Gabel, and Hankla (2008). Their finding has been persuasively contradicted by Stone Sweet and Brunell (2012). Erik Voeten (2008) has found creative ways to overcome the limitations of these studies. Meanwhile, a host of systematic qualitative studies have called into question the claim that ICs tailor their rulings to reflect the preferences of powerful governments (Cichowski 2007; Conant 2002; Pollack 2003; Tallberg 2003).

powerful states may not be aligned. Section II defines three models of how ICs might influence state behavior in a self-binding context. Since ICs can influence politics via the mechanisms in each model, it is somewhat pointless to argue that one model is better than the others. Instead I identify the domains that each model applies, and argue that single model conversations cannot ascertain the limits of international law or international courts. Section III brings the three models together into a unified altered politics framework that explains how delegation to courts increases the credibility of legal threats, mobilizes potential litigants to claim their legal rights, and builds connections to and pressure on domestic compliance partners, thereby pushing international law deeper into the domestic realm. Section IV builds on this framework by theorizing how legal and political factors generate variation in IC influence across contexts. ICs alter politics by merging domestic and international understandings of legality, so that compliance with international law is seen as consistent with and perhaps even required for the domestic rule of law. The conclusion considers how such a change occurs.

I. WHEN IS COMPLIANCE A CONCERN FOR ICS?

This book explains how rule of law values are infiltrating the anything-goes world of international politics and how international law is entering into domestic rule of law debates. We might think that governments prefer not to be constrained by law. This section, however, reminds us that governments have a huge stake in promoting the rule of law, because the first accomplishment of the rule of law is to extend the power of the central state.

In his book *Courts: A Comparative Political Analysis*, Martin Shapiro creates a seminal theory of judicial politics. Shapiro starts with the prototype of judging, what he calls "triadic dispute resolution." Two parties bring a dispute to a third party judge, because the judge is considered a neutral arbiter. In this archetype, the judge picks a side in the controversy, which invariably calls into question the judge's neutrality. Shapiro explains that this entire triadic structure is an unstable myth. Judges do not create binary resolutions, and since judges work for the state, they are not in fact neutral arbiters. Rather, "by applying pre-existing rules not shaped by the parties themselves, the judge acts not independently but as a servant of the regime [that wrote the rules], imposing its interest on the parties to the litigation."[5] The triadic dispute resolution logic of judging, however, requires that judges maintain the fiction of their neutrality.

5 (Shapiro 1981, chapter 1, quote at 26).

Judges, in Shapiro's view, essentially mediate disputes by constructing compromise outcomes. When no compromise is possible, judges rely on legal techniques to "substitute office for consent." Judges ensconce themselves in symbols of legal authority and suggest that they are using objective legal techniques, neutrally applying preexisting rules. The noble lie of judicial neutrality extends both the power of judges and the central state. Indeed, according to Shapiro, political bodies tolerate independent judging only so far as judicial action promotes the objectives of the central state.[6]

Shapiro's primary goal was to identify fundamental legal-political logics that apply across diverse legal systems. My goal is different. This study seeks to understand judging across public and private law roles, since governments are often defendants in international litigation. Shapiro's argument also needs to be updated. In 1981, few countries had constitutional courts that were powerful enough to meaningfully constrain governments. Today, one can find numerous examples of judicial power operating independently of the will of national governments. Thus I recover the categories of judging that Shapiro intentionally suppressed.[7]

Whenever ICs are primarily engaged in binding others, including public administrators and officials, delegation to ICs reflects Shapiro's understanding of delegation to courts as extending the power of the central state. The rest of this section argues that very often, although not always, ICs are binding others, and government and IC interests align, which should mean that power, although not necessarily tools of coercion, implicitly backs an IC ruling. We will need a different sort of explanation, however, for self-binding delegation when courts are creating limits on the exercise of sovereign authority.

Other-Binding vs. Self-Binding Delegation to Courts

It is easiest to introduce the distinction between self-binding and other-binding delegation to courts by beginning with a stylized historical narrative.[8] In earlier times and in smaller societies there was no delegation to judges; chiefs and kings made law and served as interpreters of the law. As territories grew, delegation of interpretive authority became unavoidable. Sovereign actors—those with the authority to make law—primarily

6 Ibid., 34.

7 Shapiro wanted to avoid "artificial compartmentalization of judicial roles" that could obscure the extent to which all judges mediate and engage in social control. While agreeing that different judicial roles can be located on a continuum of consent and social control, Shapiro emphasized that all judicial roles involve seeking consent and participating in social control on behalf of the central state (ibid., especially 17–24).

8 An earlier version of this discussion appeared in Alter (2008b; 2012b).

delegated dispute settlement authority to judges, meaning the power to make a decision about a controversy or a dispute. While sovereign actors were ceding interpretation of the law, they were not themselves subject to the interpretations of their judges mainly because no judge would presume to know better than the sovereign what the law meant. This delegation was other-binding—sovereigns were subjecting others to judicial interpretations of the law. As the state apparatus grew, the role of judges grew. Cases still appeared as controversies judges were asked to resolve, but when the subject of cases became state actors, judges ended up in a monitoring and enforcing role with judges reviewing whether the central state's other agents (for example, tax collectors, local rulers, state administrators) were faithfully following the government's laws. Neither type of delegation—dispute settlement or monitoring and enforcing—bound the central state so long as executive and legislative actors were never subjected to the authority of the court.

As Shapiro showed, other-binding delegation extends state authority in a few ways. Delegating the role of judging provides efficiency gains, harnessing citizens as monitors of state's agents and saving the king from having to hear endless disputes. Law is also a tool of state social control. Since judges apply the state's law, courts extend the central state's authority into the economy, the family, and throughout the land.[9]

Thus far I have only considered delegation in an authoritarian context, where the supreme leader both makes and enforces the law. Constitutional democracy differs in that it is premised on the notion of a social contract between leaders and their people. Government acts legitimately only when citizens can select their rulers and when governments respect the rule of law.[10] Developments in constitutional democracy led to self-binding delegation wherein branches of government agreed to limit their powers by binding themselves to the authority of others, including to the authority of courts. When the central state uses delegation to courts to monitor private litigants and its agents, delegation to courts remains primarily other-binding. When the central state uses courts to check its exercise of power, delegation to courts is primarily self-binding.[11] Especially in self-binding contexts, judges will need to substitute the authority of their office for the consent of the litigants. Judges today can draw on wells

9 (Shapiro 1981, 22–28).

10 Scholars of the rule of law in authoritarian contexts distinguish between rule *of* law and rule *by* law. In a rule of law system, courts can hold governments accountable to the law. In a rule by law system, governments use law and courts to control the polity. For more, see Ginsburg and Moustafa (2008).

11 Of course this binding is somewhat fictitious, since the self-binding could be undone through a new constitutional act. Jon Elster (2000) uses the metaphor of Ulysses, who asked his crew to bind him to the mast of a ship so he could resist the temptation of the Sirens.

of judicial power, such as relative trust in the judiciary in comparison to the political branches, diffuse support for the rule of law, and the power and prestige associated with judges themselves.[12]

At the domestic level, it is easy to see how delegating different judicial roles binds the central state in different ways. Courts playing a *dispute settlement* role, hearing private litigant cases, mostly bind others by bringing state law into the resolution of private disputes. In *administrative review*, a judge checks the legal validity of the decisions, actions, and nonactions of public administrative actors, who rely on delegated authority. Administrative actors may find themselves constrained, but that is the point of subjecting administrative authority to judicial oversight. Indeed, Shapiro's argument suggests that even authoritarian leaders have good reasons to delegate meaningful administrative review and dispute settlement jurisdiction to fairly independent judges.

Self-binding occurs in the enforcement and constitutional review roles. In the *enforcement* role, a judge monitors police and prosecutors as they use the state's coercive power. Force can only be legitimately used against citizens when it is lawful. *Constitutional review* checks whether the law created by legislatures or interpreted and applied by governments, or both, cohere with the constitution. Although delegating enforcement and constitutional review roles is sovereignty compromising, submitting to judicial review reinforces the legitimacy of the central state's actions. Judicial review will only reinforce the government's rule of law legitimacy, however, when the subjects of the law can truly believe that judges are independent adjudicators of state action.[13]

The international level is different from the domestic level in that ICs are often ruling on the actions of governments and their agents, and the international realm introduces cross-state power dimensions. Thus we must amend the above discussion of how judicial roles implicate state autonomy. It is still the case that dispute settlement and administrative review are primarily other-binding while enforcement and constitutional review jurisdiction are primarily self-binding judicial roles. But circumstances can arise in each role that will lead ICs to be issuing interpretations that impinge on national autonomy.

When ICs are helping to resolve private actor disputes, the *international dispute settlement* role remains analogous to the king's representative resolving disputes. For example, chapter 5 will discuss the Iran–United

12 On growing judicial power, see Cappelletti (1989); Hirschl (2004); Lindseth (2010); Stone Sweet (2000). On judges drawing on trust and diffuse support for the rule of law, see Gibson and Caldeira (1995); Gibson and Caldeira (1993); Gibson, Caldeira, and Baird (1998).

13 (Majone 2001, especially 110). I further develop the difference between efficiency-enhancing and legitimacy-enhancing delegation to judges in Alter (2008).

States Claims Tribunal, created to deal with private actor disputes arising from the Iranian revolution and the United States' decision to freeze Iranian assets.[14] Since decisions of the Claims Tribunal were binding on US banks, the US government, and Iranian actors, this delegation was in some ways a self-binding delegation of authority. But since Iran and the United States collectively defined the terms the Claims Tribunal would use to resolve disputes, they were able to decisively shape how judges applied the law as they resolved private litigant claims.

International dispute settlement can become self-binding when the subject of concern is a government's policy. The interstate arbiter model, discussed in the next section, is designed for situations where governments self-bind because they want to cede responsibility for a decision. So long as an IC's jurisdiction is noncompulsory, governments are able to select on a case-by-case basis whether to cede resolution of the dispute to an international judicial body. Delegation to ICs is still, thus, subject to state control. Once ICs gain compulsory jurisdiction, and especially if nonstate actors are empowered to initiate litigation, governments lose their tight control over international dispute settlement. At this point, dispute settlement can morph into law enforcement with judges attempting to substitute the authority of their office for the consent of the litigants.

International *administrative review* remains mostly an other-binding grant of jurisdiction. When ICs are reviewing administrative decisions of international actors, and as long as administrative review focuses on questions of procedure or clarifying unclear rules, international administrative review will mostly reinforce the central state's authority. For example, where ICs affirm state administrative decisions contested by foreign investors, delegation to ICs bolsters the central state's claim to be applying national regulatory rules consistent with the rule of law. ICs can also facilitate the uniform application of international rules across borders, keeping firms from playing jurisdictions off against each other. Chapter 6 will discuss a multicountry fight over use of the Belmont trademark where the Andean Tribunal of Justice helped fill in legal lacunae without compromising national autonomy. Chapter 6 also discusses cases where international administrative bodies questioned the fact finding of national administrators, using administrative review as a tool of law enforcement. The administrative review systems where this occurred—NAFTA binational review panels, and ICSID arbitration—were intended to help enforce international agreements, thus it is less surprising that administrative review morphed into a self-binding tool of law enforcement in these two legal domains.

14 See the discussion of the US-Iran Claims Tribunal case in chapter 5 for more.

Enforcement jurisdiction remains a primarily self-binding delegation of jurisdiction to an IC. In delegating to ICs a compulsory enforcement role, states accept that their actions might become the subject of international judicial review. We should not assume, however, that the central state would rather not be bound. For example, the Chinese Communist Party may have little to gain from the rampant piracy of intellectual property. It may welcome WTO pressure so far as such pressure helps convince domestic producers that cheating on Chinese intellectual property and regulatory rules may undermine access to world markets. Newly democratic governments may also want to bind future governments to supranational review.[15]

International law enforcement can sometimes be an other-binding tool. The International Criminal Court (ICC) binds states that have ratified the ICC's Rome Statute, but it also allows the Security Council to refer cases to the International Prosecutor. The ICC is thus self-binding for signatory states and other-binding vis-à-vis nonsignatory states and especially states that lack a Security Council veto. The ICC is also other-binding vis-à-vis substate rebels. Governments can invoke international criminal tribunals to undermine international support of rebel factions, or to challenge the actions of neighboring governments as occurred in the Charles Taylor case (discussed in chapter 7).

The delegation of *constitutional review* jurisdiction is primarily self-binding. When states authorize ICs to nullify illegal international acts, they are limiting their ability to use international institutions to achieve objectives other than what has been explicitly allowed in the original treaty (the constitution of the international institution). But as the constitutional review chapter explains, international judicial checks can be useful for central governments, helping to reassure national parliaments that they are not giving the executive a blank check for actions undertaken at the international level. International constitutional review can also reassure national judges that legal means of redress exist at the international level. Chapter 8 discusses how constitutional review depends on cultures of constitutional obedience, and how national high courts insert themselves into conversations about higher order international law as a check to ensure that international law does not compromise cherished values associated with national constitutions.

The point is not that delegation to ICs is either self-binding or other-binding. Rather, the main insight is that wherever ICs are binding others to follow the law, the role of compliance concerns in shaping IC decision making should recede. Moreover, even in self-binding contexts, states may share with an IC an interest in having international rules correctly applied

15 (Moravcsik 1995).

FIGURE 2.1: Other-binding and self-binding logics in delegation to ICs

	Other-binding situations	Self-binding situations
Dispute Settlement Helping litigating parties resolve disagreements that turn on definitions of law.	Compulsory dispute settlement between private litigants (e.g., US-Iran Claims Tribunal, OHADA cases). Compulsory dispute settlement between IOs and private contractors (found in many IOs).	Interstate dispute settlement. *When noncompulsory, states control which cases reach the IC. Compulsory dispute settlement easily morphs into the enforcement role.*
Administrative Review Reviewing the legal validity of contested administrative decisions.	Review of administrative decisions of IO actors (ITLOS, ECJ, ATJ, and others). IC review of national application of international rules (BCJ, ECJ, ATJ, and others) so long as IC review is gap filling and procedural, leaving fact finding to national actors.	*Administrative review that questions administrative fact finding morphs into enforcement.*
Enforcement Naming violations of the law and sometimes defining remedies.	Criminal prosecutions initiated by the Security Council (e.g., ICTY and ICTR, and referrals to international prosecutor). Central states binding rebel actors to international criminal law.	Most international enforcement contexts (trade, human rights, war crimes).
Constitutional Review Holding international and state actors accountable to higher order norms.		Review of the legality of IO actions (ECJ, ATJ, and others). *When international law is seen as domestically supreme, the enforcement role may morph into constitutional review.*

and respected. Figure 2.1 summarizes this discussion of how delegation of different roles to ICs is self- and/or other-binding. Italics indicate the morphing of judicial roles into a self-binding category.

Because most of the boxes on the table above are filled, it may look like ICs are binding states as much as they are binding others. But this would only be true if the number of cases in each box were equal and thus if ICs spend as much time reviewing state compliance with international rules as they do fulfilling the many other-binding tasks they have been delegated. Chapter 7 suggests that most of the caseloads of the busiest ICs involve other-binding administrative review. Even if ICs spent equal time across self-binding and other-binding roles, this discussion still provides an important corrective for much of the debate about delegation of authority to ICs. Critics of ICs suggest that ICs primarily are about questioning and compromising state authority. But in ways that are quite analogous to the domestic context, delegation to ICs often extends central state power.

ICs also contribute in ways that domestic judges cannot. A certification of good standing by ICs can reassure foreign actors, who may otherwise believe that national judges are influenced by their government or favor national producers. ICs can also help coordinate interpretations across borders in ways that are difficult for domestic judges. ICs can create legal checks on international action, reassuring domestic actors that international governance is subject to the same sorts of legal checks as domestic governance. And ICs can challenge interpretations of powerful interests, providing legal cover for actors within states that also disagree with the contested interpretation.

A number of puzzles become solvable when one considers that delegation to courts can reflect a self-binding and/or other-binding logic. For example, it is perhaps less surprising that states consent to ICs with compulsory jurisdiction and private access when we consider that these ICs might be mostly binding others to follow law. To think of the ICC as both self- and other-binding helps us understand why many people see in the ICC a good limit on rights-violating governments and a tool of the North to intervene in the South. One might also hypothesize that compliance with IC rulings will be highest with respect to international judicial decisions made in other-binding judicial roles.

But internationally and domestically, this argument about the rationality and logic of other-binding delegation to courts starts to run out once judges become powerful enough to substitute the authority of the law and the office of the judge for the consent of governments. International law and ICs have clearly reached this point. We move furthest from states using international law to bind others in the enforcement and constitutional review roles, which is why the case studies in chapters 7 and 8 are more contentious. The rest of this chapter focuses on why states might comply with adverse IC rulings in self-binding contexts, when international judicial review compromises government autonomy.

II. THREE CONCEPTUAL MODELS OF HOW ICS INFLUENCE STATE BEHAVIOR

Political scientists like models because they help isolate causal mechanisms and clarify the assumptions underpinning different types of arguments. The three models discussed in this section map onto different theoretical traditions, and this chapter uses the models as a substitute for a literature review. International relations realists and law and economics scholars will find affinity with the interstate arbiter model because it assumes that states have predefined national interests, and compliance with international law is a voluntary decision made on a case-by-case basis. Scholars and practitioners who believe that principled decision making and international cooperation furthers national interests find affinity with the multilateral politics model. Comparative politics scholars, who find the notion of a single discrete "national interest" to be somewhat implausible are more likely to embrace transnational politics model.

Before I begin, however, I need address a question that often arises at this juncture. All three models presuppose that ICs are independent actors. If international judges were dependent on governments, judicial decision making would itself be endogenous to the preferences of governments. In 1993, Geoffrey Garrett and Barry Weingast borrowed from the American politics literature to make the following claim:

> Embedding a legal system in a broader political structure places direct constraints on the discretion of a court, even one with as much constitutional independence as the United States Supreme Court. This conclusion holds even if the constitution makes no explicit provisions for altering a court's role. The reason is that political actors have a range of avenues through which they may alter or limit the role of courts. Sometimes such changes require amendment of the constitution, but usually the appropriate alterations may be accomplished more directly through statue, as by alteration of the court's jurisdiction in a way that makes it clear that continued undesired behavior will result in more radical changes . . . the possibility of such a reaction drives a court that wishes to preserve its independence and legitimacy to remain in the area of acceptable latitude.[16]

Garrett and Weingast used this argument to argue that the European Court of Justice was actually more constrained than the United States Supreme Court.

I will be short and perhaps somewhat curt, as I have explored this argument at length elsewhere and I will return to its more viable parts in the

16 (Garrett and Weingast 1993, 200–201).

book's conclusion. The assertion that the European Court of Justice (ECJ) "rationally expects" and therefore avoids displeasing states is a methodologically problematic argument that Garrett and Weingast supported with tautological and post hoc reasoning.[17] The tenacity of their argument is surprising given the significant evidence of the ECJ making decisions that governments neither advocated nor wanted.[18] In chapter 9 I will explain why this "executive control" thesis does not work as a general theory of IC behavior. My main objection at this point is with any attempt to derail analysis by shifting the burden of proof, by positing that IC rulings *are* endogenous of state preferences so as to demand that others first prove that court rulings are *not* endogenous to government preferences. For reasons I will explain in the book's conclusion, this is an impossible challenge that sets up an irrational search for a systematic divergence between government preferences and IC rulings.

Given how often I hear this argument, I want to reiterate that my claim is not that ICs are wholly independent. Chapter 1 noted that trustees implement a trust agreement and the creators of the trust handpick the trustees. The next section argues that ICs are deeply dependent on maintaining the support of compliance partners, who are generally public actors, and with maintaining the support of a larger compliance constituency. My claim is also not that government preferences are irrelevant. Governments are sometimes ICs' compliance partners. Mainly I disagree with the implicit assumption that since governments have tools to politically sanction judges, government preferences should be the most important factor judges consider. Rather than embark on a hunt for this red herring of judicial rational expectations, it is more plausible that we accept the possibility that ICs can rule against the preferences of governments and then ask how ICs get governments to then change their behavior.

The Interstate Arbitration Model: ICs Construct Focal Points

In the *interstate arbiter* model ICs influence international politics by constructing a focal point legal understanding that represents an equilibrium

17 (Alter 1998; 2008a). This debate renewed again when Clifford Carrubba, Mathew Gabel, and Charles Hankla suggested that their new statistical analysis proved that the ECJ responded to member state interventions in court because of a concern of judicial override (Carrubba, Gabel, and Hankla 2008). Alec Stone Sweet and Thomas Brunell dismantled their argument using the same data, arguing that ECJ decision making aligns more closely with Commission interventions rather than member state interventions. Stone Sweet suggests that the Commission represents the majoritarian preferences of member states, and that in practice override threats are not credible (Stone Sweet and Brunell 2012).

18 (Cichowski 2007; Rasmussen 1986; Stein 1981; Stone Sweet 2004; Stone Sweet and Brunell 2012; Weiler 1981).

position acceptable to state litigants. This minimalist model, favored by rational choice and law and economic scholars, assumes that state interests are largely fixed and that international litigation mainly influences international politics by providing new information to guide state decision making. ICs may in fact influence state behavior by helping to coordinate governments, but the model generally precludes the notion that ICs can fundamentally change domestic politics or international relations.

There are many reasons why governments might want an IC to "impose" a legal solution on them. Governments might want ICs to resolve legal ambiguities and specify details of vague rules. Sometimes it is helpful to have a judicial actor to blame for a controversial decision. IC rulings can also create legal certainty, allowing firms and individuals to make important decisions. And an IC endorsement can elevate the legal authority of an interpretation that the government also supports.[19] Sometimes the IC's legal solution will differ from what governments might have chosen on their own, but in all of these scenarios the IC coordinates states, helping governments to find a shared understanding of the law that reflects preexisting national interests.

Figure 2.2 captures the task of the international judging in this model. This figure imagines ICs operating in the space defined by the interests of the litigant states (represented by the x and y axes), bounded by what legal rules allow (represented by the curved line). ICs essentially pick the spot that is both on the line defined by the law and on the indifference curve of the *litigants*. So long as the IC ruling is somewhere on each state's indifference curve, the IC ruling will represent a Pareto improvement. The ruling is politically meaningful. It provides legal certainty that did not exist before, creates a shared understanding of how the law applies to the case, and helps governments move on by ending the dispute. The IC ruling may induce a change in state behavior by elevating the expressive value of the court-endorsed legal interpretation. But IC-induced change is only possible because governments are precommitted to accepting any point on the curve. Rather than a change in a state's underlying preference, the change in behavior either reflects an updating of the government's articulated position based on new information or a confirmation of a government's underlying preference with the government using the IC to absorb domestic blame.

These are important but fairly limited contributions of international adjudication. Rational choice scholars admit the possibility that international

19 Garrett and Weingast saw delegation to ICs as an efficient way to fill in incomplete contracts, with the ECJ ascertaining the preferences of litigating and powerful states. Others stress both incomplete contracting and blame-shifting dynamic (Goldsmith and Posner 2005; Guzman 2008; Simmons 2002). Richard McAdams (2004) develops the idea of law's expressive contribution.

FIGURE 2.2: ICs as interstate arbiters constructing focal points

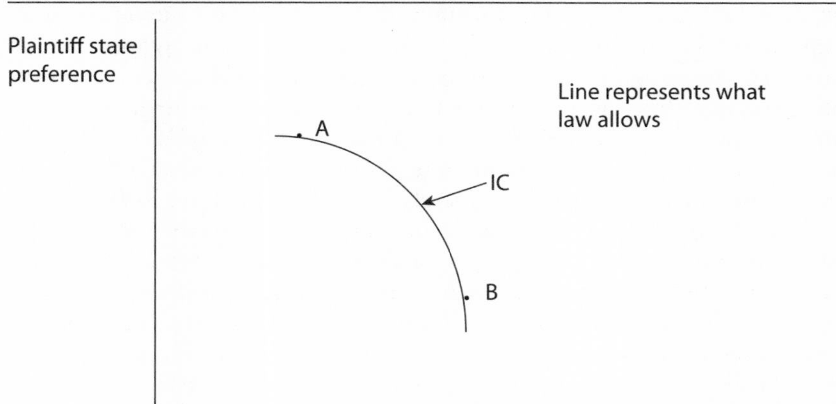

law can change state interests. Nonetheless the advocates of law and economics approaches posit that disputes over law provide information rather than redefine national interests.[20] One can add more nuances to this model.[21] Still, the core model contains limiting assumptions captured by figure 2.2. The only relevant actors in this model are the litigating states, which are assumed to have predefined fixed national interests. ICs could, of course, create focal points that nonstate actors coalesce around. But international law scholars employing law and economic theories tend also to posit that compliance with IC rulings is a voluntary decision that governments make.[22] Posner and Yoo suggest that ICs can only be effective if they are willing to choose from the set of interpretations acceptable

20 Posner and Yoo conceptualize ICs as simple problem-solving devices that do not transform interests (2005, 6). Goldstein and Posner note that they cannot rebut the constructivist challenge that international law can reconstitute state preferences, but they "doubt it is true in any important degree" and note that "constructivists have not shown that international law transforms individual and state interests" (2005, at 9). Andrew Guzman assumes away the constructivist notion that interests can be transformed, defending the choice by noting that "developing a theory of international law requires us to make certain initial assumptions and to stick with them as much as possible" (2008, 215).

21 Guzman (2008), Tom Ginbsurg (2005), and McAdams (2004 and 2005) have added quite a number of nuances to law and economics approaches, providing a bridge to the next model.

22 See Goldsmith and Posner (2005). The point is even clearer in Posner and Yoo (2005, 6).

to litigant governments; Posner and Alan Sykes argue that the best (that is, most "efficient") outcome for international law *is* the outcome reflecting the equilibrium preference of governments.[23] In other words, proponents of this model accept Shapiro's argument that judges seek compromise solutions but reject the notion that judges can substitute the authority of law and office for the consent of state parties. As Sykes and Posner baldly say: "It is neither rational nor desirable for states to behave as if bound by international law . . . merely because of its status as law."[24]

The model of ICs as interstate arbiters is most applicable where interstate dispute settlement is not compulsory. In such contexts, countries are likely to refuse to submit international adjudication *unless* they prefer legal resolution of the dispute and are fairly indifferent to where on the curve the outcome resides. This model may also apply to compulsory adjudication in coordination contexts where states primarily seek a common standard.[25] The dispute settlement chapter will illustrate this argument through an example of ICs facilitating cooperation in the Qatar v. Bahrain territorial dispute. Chapter 5 also includes the seizing private vessels case, a coordination case where the International Tribunal for the Law of the Sea helps define the terms for seizing vessels engaged in arguably illegal activities. The Microsoft and GE/Honeywell merger cases, Iran-US mass claims tribunal, Belmont trademark, Charles Taylor, and women in combat support roles case studies did not necessarily involve ICs ascertaining the preferences of governments, but they are cases where ICs made legal determinations that governments favored.

The more legal rules are subject to interpretative latitude, the more state interests are mutable, the more authority international law has, and the more compliance constituencies are mobilized to press states to respect international law, the less helpful this model becomes. Said differently, the more ICs can reshape the law and draw on law's authority, the less likely that the IC will be looking primarily to government or litigant interests to decide cases.

23 (Posner and Yoo 2005, 17–18; Posner and Sykes 2011). Posner and Yoo's claim about effectiveness is controversial because they conflate compliance with IC rulings with effectiveness, presuming that ICs are *only* effective if states will immediately comply with their ruling. For a critique of their analysis, see Guzman (2008, 53); Helfer and Slaughter (2005).

24 Sykes and Posner also suggest that "efficiency" should be a "political efficiency" defined based on the willingness of states to retaliate or deviate from the law rather than a welfare-maximizing efficiency (2011, 294).

25 On the difference between coordination and cooperation contexts, see Raustiala (2000); Stein (1983).

Multilateral Adjudication Model: ICs Reshape the Strategic Space of International and Domestic Politics

In the *multilateral politics* model we move from a world defined by the interests of the state parties to a world where law renders certain policies more or less legal, and legal legitimacy is politically important. This world of law encapsulates a multidimensional policy space where there are many different state interests, some of which are compatible with the law and some of which are not. Multilateral politics leads to the creation of legal rules within this policy space, rules intended to balance the differing interests of states. The square in figure 2.3 represents a simplified two-dimensional policy space that defines the realm of potential outcomes for a policy issue. Figure 2.2 showed ICs constructing a focal understanding, a single legal interpretation that parties coalesced around. This idea was represented by a point that reflected a median position of litigating states. By contrast, figure 2.3 uses a circle within the policy space to represent the discursive space created by international law. The discursive space is a circle rather than a point because legal rules often have ambiguity and flexibility built in. Depending on how precise the legal rule is, the size of the circle—and thus the extent of state discretion within this legal discursive space—will vary. The interests of the many state actors affected by the law are scattered all over the policy space. Some states will prefer outcomes that are hard to locate within the discursive space of legal interpretation. For these actors, law will constrain the choices they make to the extent that violating the law creates costs. The most powerful actors will find themselves within the legal discursive space because they will have written the law to suit their interests. Time and elections, however, can lead to changing preferences so that powerful and weak states can all find themselves wanting to adopt or maintain a policy that arguably lies outside of the discursive space defined by extant international law.

Litigants bring a case to an IC in the hope that the IC will validate their interpretation of the law. I illustrated this case in figure 2.3 by mapping the WTO's shrimp-turtle decision where developing countries challenged a US policy that blocked market access for their shrimp. The US justified its trade restrictions by giving environmental reasons. The WTO allows countries to apply domestic regulations designed to protect the environment to foreign imports. In this example, the developing country (litigant L) lacked the power to change WTO law, but it could gain market access if the interpretation of permissible environmental barriers shifted. Seeking to create this legal change, litigant L asks the IC for a legal interpretation. The WTO's appellate body required the US government to apply the least

FIGURE 2.3: Multilateral adjudication politics shifting the costs of noncompliance

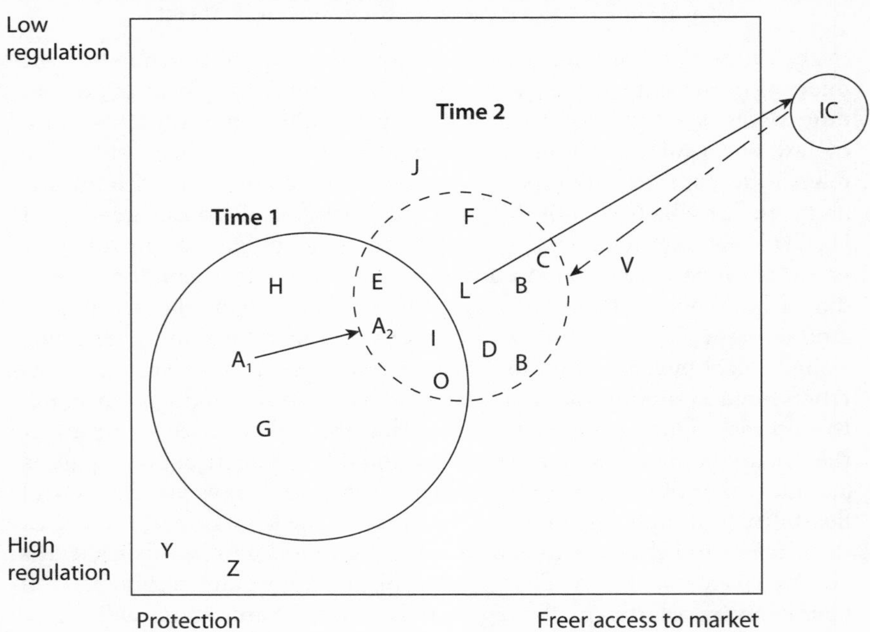

restrictive means to pursue its environmental objective, which meant that the United States (government A) had to accept the validity of litigant L's argument. Figure 2.3 depicts the IC shift in Time 2, which redraws and shrinks the discursive space of legality. Policy A_1 no longer falls in the zone of legality, and the new legal interpretation encapsulates the preferences of more states.[26]

Why would state A ever shift their position to point A_2 if it involved moving away from their preferred policy? In the minimalist interstate adjudication model, states moved from point A_1 to the point defined by the IC because litigation revealed new information—the focal point solution—that reflected preexisting government interests. By contrast the multilateral politics model assumes that ICs can alter the cost-benefit analysis of governments. It also allows that even powerful actors can be constrained by international perceptions regarding the rule of law. Governments in this model are persuaded to change their policy because of tactical considerations. Perhaps the government realized that fighting this

26 This case is discussed in Shaffer (2000).

issue is not worth it—that the particular fight is far less important than the larger set of benefits the international institution confers. Perhaps the government has reputational concerns. Or perhaps there is a concern about sanctions that might follow from state noncompliance. There are clear winners and losers in this redrawing of the law. H, G, and A_1 are no longer within the circle of the law, but now a larger set of actors finds the law pleasing to them and thus state A is unlikely to be able to sanction the IC or shift the meaning of the law back to where it arguably was in Time 1.

The multilateral politics model works where ICs have compulsory jurisdiction, and thus where state A cannot block the case from proceeding. The model may also require majoritarian or unanimity decision-making rules that keep losing states from unilaterally changing international rules or sanctioning judges. Whereas in the interstate arbiter model compliance concerns forced ICs to pick an equilibrium point between the interests of litigating states, in this model IC judges pick from among the legally valid interpretations an outcome that garners support among a majority of state actors, including states that did not participate in the legal proceedings.[27]

This model also suggests that decisions about state compliance will be shaped by the costs the multilateral system can generate, be they reputation or sanction-based. Chapters 6 and 7 illustrate the sanctions-based mode of inducing compliance through the discussion of the softwood lumber dispute and Foreign Sales Corporation case studies. The modern-day slavery case study illustrates a reputation-based reason to comply.

This multilateral politics model is better able to capture how time and larger international politics can change government preferences. But this model still has international law being a contract among states. In representing state interests as a single point, and thus as monolithic, the multilateral politics model still does not capture the reality that international law can penetrate states, and that international courts can be activated by private litigants as part of domestic political strategies. Also like the interstate arbiter model, the multilateral politics model assumes that governments control decisions about compliance. The final transformation of international politics, discussed below, provides another explanation for why state A could move from A_1 to A_2—perhaps the international level politics scrambles domestic politics, advantaging and empowering domestic actors who prefer that domestic policy coheres with international law.

27 Stone Sweet's concept of international judicial trusteeship posits this logic (Stone Sweet and Brunell 2012).

Transnational Politics Model: ICs Reshape Domestic and Transnational Legal Politics

The *transnational politics* model involves perhaps the most radical transformation of international politics with ICs connecting with actors within states to help redefine government policy. Delegation to ICs brings international law into domestic debates leading governments to choose compliance with an IC ruling for reasons that are domestically rather than multilaterally defined. In this third model, states are no longer monolithic actors captured by a single point in the policy space. Rather, each state is a collection of quasi-independent actors—judges, administrators, criminal prosecutors, political parties and interest groups, and such. Figure 2.4 captures this idea by suggesting that domestic actors within a state disagree about whether certain coercive interrogation techniques constitute torture (*y*-axis), and about the habeas corpus right of plaintiffs to have their claim heard in either domestic or foreign courts (*x*-axis).[28] In this model, either actors within the state reach outside, or transnational actors (nongovernmental organizations [NGOs], other states, international prosecutors, and such) bring the case with the tacit support of domestic actors. As in the multilateral politics model, ICs' interpretation shifts understandings of what the law means.

This model allows for IC legal precedent to be used by domestic judges to scrutinize the policies and actions of the government, even if the IC affirms the government's policy in the case at hand. In the notional case below, the box drawn by the IC is fairly large, suggesting that national judges will be left to decide the contours of what constitutes torture as well as the legal rights of private actors. But the political debate will be shifted because national judges will now have a clear legal reason to more vigorously review governmental assertions regarding coercive measures. Thus compared to the other two models, the transnational politics model opens the possibility that IC review can lead to deeper structural changes in how legality and national interests get defined.

Compulsory jurisdiction is arguably necessary for this model to work; otherwise, the defendant state would block litigation. But the key to ICs having influence in this model is the existence of substate compliance

28 While this case is fictional, the first interstate case heard by the European Court of Human Rights concerned the issue of whether certain police tactics constitute cruel and unusual punishment. (See Ireland v. United Kingdom, 1976 Y.B. Eur. Conv. on Hum. Rts. 512, 748, 788–94 [Eur. Comm'n of Hum. Rts.].) The ECtHR has gone on to rule on many cases regarding government interrogation tactics; indeed, there is an entire guidebook of European Human Rights law concerning what does and does not constitute torture. The handbook is replete with references to European Court of Human Rights rulings (see Reidy 2002).

FIGURE 2.4: Transnational judicial politics model co-opting domestic compliance constituencies

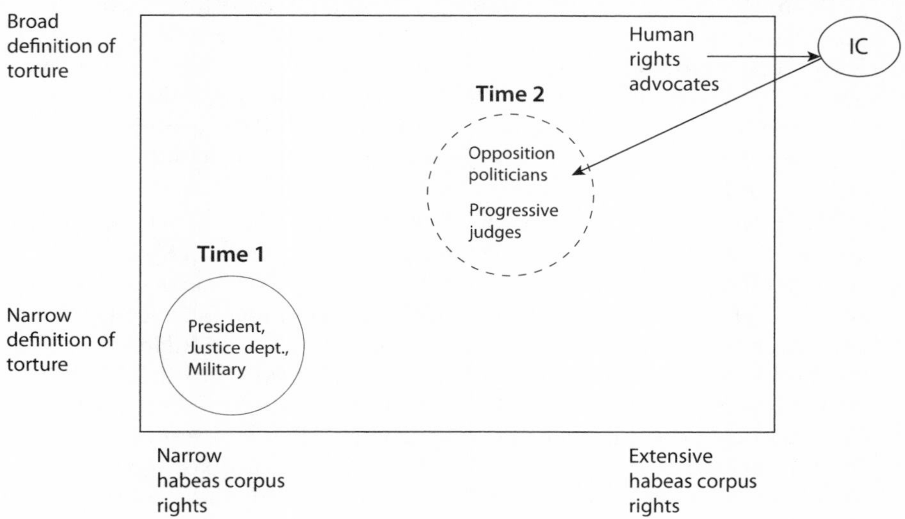

partners that favor an outcome closer to what international law requires. An example of this model is the second use patent case study where the ATJ drew on its established close working relationship with national intellectual property agencies and national administrators who preferred Andean law. These actors disallowed second use patents even though Peru's government never removed the offending law from the books. The model does not explain why domestic actors might coalesce around an IC interpretation. One could use either rational institutionalist or constructivist arguments to explain such a change. The constitutional review chapter discusses how cultures of constitutional obedience facilitate compliance with IC constitutional rulings. The indigenous land rights, rape as a war crime, and modern-day slavery case studies all show the importance of substate or transnational actors creating political pressure to facilitate implementation of international law, as interpreted by the IC.

Moving beyond a Single Model

Most scholars develop hypotheses from within a single model, focusing on factors that are important only so long as the assumptions and conditions for the model hold. Considered in isolation, each model suggests absolute limits to the possibilities for international law and IC influence. The interstate arbiter model suggests that international law cannot work when there is no indifference curve uniting the position of litigating states.

The multilateral politics model suggests that international law cannot work absent sanctioning and multilateral reputation costs for noncompliance. The transnational politics model suggests that absent domestic interlocutors, international law cannot exert any independent influence on state behavior. Moving across models, however, calls each of these claims into question. If ICs can influence state behavior via all three models, then one cannot determine the limits of international law or IC influence by staying within a single model.

The point of keeping the models separate is to identify assumptions underpinning each approach. The interstate arbiter model assumes little meaningful pressure on states to comply with international law. This model may help us understand ICs engaged in voluntary interstate dispute settlement, and it works best for cases in chapter 5. The multilateral politics model can consider politics in ICs with compulsory jurisdiction, but the multilateral model only really speaks to the coordinated interests of governments and the types of pressure that multilateral institutions can exert. This model does not capture issues that interest peoples and private actors more than governments, and it works less well when private and nonstate actors pursue cases that are of individual but perhaps not interstate concern, such as human rights cases and many economic cases. And neither the interstate arbiter or multilateral politics models can help us think about how it may matter that international law is increasingly embedded within national legal systems, allowing international actors to coordinate legal interpretation with domestic actors.

The models are, of course, artificial in many ways. To see states as unified actors with distinct and stable national interests is a simplifying assumption; few people believe that states are actually unified actors or that government preferences are structurally given or immutable. The models present decisions about compliance as largely binary, truncated in time and independent from all other issues and events at play. All three models are instrumentalist and have a hard time capturing normative forces, world historical forces, or dynamics introduced by the autonomy of law. Anyone who studies judicial politics over time knows that that these assumptions are false. The next section considers how one might bring the models together into a single framework so as to better understand international judicial politics in a world where new-style ICs operate in highly diverse contexts, and where time is a factor that shifts state preferences. The conclusion will suggest that bringing the models together is also a way to free up our thinking about how to reconcile democracy and international law.

III. THE ALTERING POLITICS FRAMEWORK

In social scientific terms, I seek to explain IC-induced change in state behavior in the direction of greater respect for international law. I refer to this as pressure toward greater compliance, slipping into the language of compliance because compliance is the way participants gauge whether or not governments are adhering to the rule of law. But my goal is not to explain compliance with international law or IC rulings per se. My actual metric is whether the presence and/or actions of an IC induces policy change in the direction indicated by the law, and thus legal effectiveness.[29]

My main argument is that ICs influence governments through alliances with compliance constituencies, ever-changing groups of domestic and international actors that actively or tacitly support compliance with international law and IC rulings. Compliance constituencies encompass diverse actors with diverse motivations. I give the name *compliance partners* to actors within states—judges, government officials, members of administrative agencies or militaries—that already have the power to choose compliance. These actors often do not have a dog in the fight, and they are usually predisposed to embrace legal solutions because they see themselves as rule of law actors, and because following a court-mandated legal interpretation is often the politically safest strategy where two parties or where groups of organized interests vehemently disagree.

Compliance supporters represent a broader group of actors who for a variety of reasons support adherence to a specific international law. Some compliance supporters will be motivated by the substantive goals embedded in the law, such as the promotion of human rights and free trade. Some supporters will be self-interested, seeking rulings that benefit themselves and their clients or that help counter an interpretation proffered by political opponents. And some compliance supporters are primarily motivated by their normative commitment to the rule of law and a belief that the IC ruling correctly applies the law.

Compliance constituencies encompass partners with the power to choose compliance and supporters whose tacit or active support helps to protect those who implement politically contentious decisions mandated or inspired by international law. Although politics may at times eclipse law in the resolution of a contentious case, law remains the bedrock of IC power in this argument. Litigants bring cases to the court expecting that clear violations of international law will lead ICs to rule against powerful governments, even when international judges can clearly anticipate defiance rather than compliance (as in the Colombia and Ecuador alcohol-related practices and softwood lumber case studies). Support for the rule of law broadens and unites the compliance constituency, bringing civil society groups and countries that are substantively self-interested together with individuals, groups, and foreign governments that care about correct legal interpretation and the rule of law more generally. Since ICs are

29 Scholars who study international cooperation know that compliance is a problematic metric. For more see Helfer (2013); Martin (2012); Raustiala (2000); Huneeus (2013).

dependent on the continued support of compliance constituencies, ICs must rule against powerful governments where violations are clear. In other words, the external, independent, and legal nature of international courts is their chief attraction, their main source of power, and a constraint on IC decision making.

Governments from targeted states may be compliance partners or part of an IC's broader compliance constituency. Government support is always helpful, and sometimes a government's endorsement is all that is needed to trigger compliance with an IC ruling. For example, in the Qatar v. Bahrain territorial dispute, women in combat support roles, and modern-day slavery case studies, executive endorsement led to rapid compliance with the IC ruling. But the case study discussions also reveal a broader domestic and international base of support for the IC rulings, which may be why targeted governments so readily endorsed the IC's legal solution. Other case studies have governments as either reluctant participants or largely uninvolved with decisions about compliance. This pattern leads me to conclude that government support is not a necessary condition for compliance to occur. Where governments lack the legal power to orchestrate compliance, government support may not even be a sufficient condition for compliance to occur.[30] This book discusses the WTO's Foreign Sales Corporation case and the Colombia and Ecuador alcohol-related practices case studies where executive support alone proved insufficient to generate compliance with the IC ruling.

A key analytical move is to introduce time into my argument (figure 2.5). I break the litigation process into three time periods, indicated by the boxes at the bottom, which allows me to capture IC influence before and after the issuing of a ruling. Time 0, not indicated, is when the state violates an international law either by intention or accident. Litigants can comply or settle during any of the three time periods, ending the litigation process before it runs its full course. Thus the time periods should be seen as thresholds that occur sequentially but somewhat independent of the steps that precede and follow because the key decision makers vary in each time period. In Time 1 (T1), the plaintiff will identify which actors have the power to choose compliance and speculate about the factors that motivate these actors. The shaded columns, which repeat in T1 and T3, identify the set of substate actors with the power to choose compliance.

30 For example, President George W. Bush actually tried to orchestrate compliance with the International Court of Justice's (ICJ) *Avena* decision by instructing his attorney general and state courts to conduct the legal review the ICJ demanded. The United States Supreme Court, however, found the ICJ's ruling generated no domestic effects and the president's order unconstitutional. Only a congressional act could require states to conduct the legal review the ICJ had required. (The US Supreme Court ruling is *Medellín v. Texas* 552 U.S. 491 [2008].)

FIGURE 2.5 ICs altering politics by issue area

	National system		International system				
	Domestic enforcement strategy	Compliance partners	International legal strategy	IC ruling	Legal remedy	Post-ruling political strategy	Compliance partner policy change
Economic issues	National court ruling or request preliminary reference to IC	Legislature **Executive branch** Administrative actor	Pre-litigation negotiations with other parties or supranational monitors		National judge applies IC ruling Government pays compensation	Retaliatory sanctions (withholding market access)	Legislature **Executive branch** Administrative actor
Human rights issues	National legal appeals (required to exhaust local remedies)	National judge	Commission investigation/ Report/ Advisory opinion	IC ruling condemns state and requires specific remedies	Government undertakes prescribed political remedy	Diplomatic pressure Publicity	National judge
Mass atrocities	National prosecution of war crimes	Security apparatus **President/Prime Minister** Military leaders	International Prosecutor inquiry		Incarceration of convicted criminals	Withholding existing inducements Economic, political & military sanctions	Security apparatus **President/Prime Minister** Military leaders
	T1: Bargaining in the shadow of an IC			T2: Litigation politics		T3: Leverage strategies	

In bold are executive actors, which are a proxy for the idea that governments choose compliance. The unbolded compliance partners—administrative actors, judges, the security apparatus, and military leaders—can make choices independently from what the executive branch may want, and their decisions may themselves lead to greater state respect for the law. Issue areas are indicated on the left, and we can see that IC compliance partners likely vary by issue area. Arrows indicate direction of political pressure. Bargaining in the shadow of the law (T1) targets those actors with the power to choose compliance. During litigation politics (T2), advocates focus on swaying IC decision making. Post-ruling politics (T3) seek to maximize political pressure to comply with an IC ruling. The arrows indicate pressure and suggest that certain types of pressure work better with certain types of actors.

International politics becomes judicialized during T1, when legal advocates invoke international law and IC authority to pressure those actors with the power to choose compliance. The IC may be doing little more than simply existing at this stage, with the law, established legal doctrine, and the prospect of a court-ordered remedy doing the work of altering politics. IC's influence is nonetheless channeled through the actions of potential litigants who first suggest litigation, then file formal complaints, leading perhaps to formal investigations and reasoned opinions, each step of which ratchets up the pressure to settle in the shadow of the law. Many cases will settle during this bargaining stage. Most of the politics in the Microsoft case, and all in GE/Honeywell merger case discussed in chapter 6 occurred in the shadow of IC review because the litigants could easily anticipate that the European Court of Justice would back the Commission's actions. For international criminal law especially, litigation only proceeds when the indicted individual is in custody, at which point conviction (T2) followed by a prison sentence (at T3) are highly likely. For this reason, T1—when indictments were fashioned and arrest warrants executed—is especially important. My discussion of the Charles Taylor case focuses mostly on the prelitigation stage for this reason.

T2 is when adjudication occurs: litigating parties muster an interpretation of the law that favors their side and attempts to influence international judicial decision making. As an IC deals with procedural issues, litigants can get a sense for the likely legal outcome and perhaps choose to settle so as to avoid a legally binding ruling. If the case does not settle, ICs will issue a ruling that defines the law, identifies an action as legal or illegal, and perhaps specifies a remedy. Sometimes compliance occurs at this stage. The rape as a war crimes case shows how litigation politics can be important in developing the law, which will then shape the legal remedy and future out-of-court bargaining. In the Qatar v. Bahrain territorial

dispute, seizing private vessels, Iran-US claims tribunal, Belmont, Metalclad investor dispute, modern-day slavery, second use patent, and women in combat support roles cases, the relevant actors immediately complied with the IC legal ruling.

Where the legal ruling and the remedies awarded are themselves insufficient to induce meaningful change in state behavior, compliance constituencies turn to leverage strategies (T3) to ratchet up the costs of noncompliance. The case studies identify a number of leverage strategies that occur leading up to and following IC rulings. In the Foreign Sales Corporation case study, the European Union started levying escalating tariffs on US products. In the softwood lumber, seizing private assets (Kadi), and indigenous land rights case studies, litigants raised a number of subsequent legal suits to force implementation of international legal rulings. If litigation provides tools of political and legal leverage, and if the result is change in the direction of greater respect for international law, we can see the existence of ICs as altering politics, and we can then assess the extent of IC influence and effectiveness.

This argument essentially inserts ICs into the sort of mobilization strategies long discussed by others. In this respect we might see a consensus view emerging that domestic actors influence state behavior by invoking international commitments and a government's public claims to be a rule of law actor so as to pressure governments to live up to their international legal commitments.[31] The argument also fits with the view that external factors and rules can mobilize and organize domestic supporters.[32] The dispute settlement, administrative review, and enforcement roles chapters stay in the familiar political science instrumentalist perspective of showing how legal invocations and state compliance help serve the objectives of certain actors. The constitutional review chapter, however, introduces the idea of a culture of constitutional obedience. In combination, part II of the book suggests that international law can be a tool of instrumental politics but at a certain point a culture of law can emerge. When international law becomes part of the fabric of domestic legal culture, compliance with international law becomes an inherent part of exercising legitimate authority.

The IC's contribution to compliance politics across all three stages is to offer a prospect of a legal remedy, to offer authoritative legal interpretations, and perhaps to name violations and specify remedies, thereby creating a legal claim for compliance supporters to coalesce around. The existence of an international legal remedy helps instantiate internationally defined legal rights, and commitment to legal rights widens the number

31 (Risse, Ropp, and Sikkink 1999; Sikkink 2011).

32 (Dai 2007; Shaffer 2003; Simmons 2009).

of actors that become involved in compliance politics. Potential litigants gain a new tool of negotiating leverage, and the IC ruling can provide a reason for domestic administrators and judges to use their discretion to promote respect for international rules. Sometimes international legal violations will also trigger domestic and international actions. For example, the United States prohibits certain types of foreign aid and market access for governments that violate human rights. Advocates can use an IC finding of a human rights violation to lobby American foreign policy and congressional actors to enact or apply US legislation so as to punish recalcitrant governments. The second use patent, modern-day slavery, Charles Taylor prosecution, and indigenous land rights case studies show how a number of private and nongovernmental actors worked in tandem with international law and IC review to promote their causes.

My metric of IC effectiveness is whether IC-induced politics lead to changes in state behavior in the direction indicated by the law and the IC. But other sorts of changes are also possible. For example, the Metalclad case study shows a Canadian judge overturning an arbitral ruling, and representatives of Canada, the United States, and Mexico issuing a clarifying interpretation that endorsed the Canadian appellate judge's position over that of the arbitral panel. The Belmont case study discusses how Colombia responded to an ATJ ruling by clarifying how local administrators should use their discretion allowed by Andean law. These clarifications did not actually reverse IC rulings; rather, they brought administrative and judicial interpretations closer to the government's intent when they wrote the law. An IC ruling may also trigger a political backlash that changes existing law to protect national sovereignty. While finishing this book, Southern African leaders responded to Southern African Development Community (SADC) legal rulings regarding land rights of Zimbabwean farmers by qualifying the grant of private access to the SADC. For advocates of the court, this political intervention "stripped" the court of its human rights jurisdiction, delivering a "fatal blow" that will perhaps "destroy" the court. The August 2012 intergovernmental decision is the first example of an IC actually having its jurisdiction curtailed as a result of its judicial rulings.[33] Other backlashes in Africa have led to creating an appellate system for the East African Community and a judicial council for ECOWAS, both of which arguably shore up the independence and authority of the respective legal bodies.[34]

33 On the rulings and political responses precipitating the change in SADC, see Ebobrah (2010, 261–63). de Wet (2013).

34 We discuss the ECOWAS controversy in Alter, Helfer, and McAllister (2013).

IV. Theorizing Variation in IC Influence: Law and Politics

We have long known that the design of ICs contributes to their varying effectiveness because the credibility of a legal threat depends on whether the plaintiff has standing to pursue the issue.[35] The Foreign Sales Corporation, second use patent, and softwood lumber cases reveal how the addition of compulsory jurisdiction and access for nonstate actors contributed to the outcome of greater compliance with the law by making the legal threat credible and litigation unavoidable. But not all ICs with compulsory jurisdiction are active, so clearly design is not a sufficient explanation of ICs' varied influence. Any explanation of IC influence must be able to account for variation in the activation and influence of similarly designed international legal institutions, and for similarity in the influence of diversely designed international legal institutions. This section begins to theorize from the altered politics framework, identifying a number of forces for variation in IC activation and influence.

As mentioned, the three time periods—bargaining in the shadow of the law, litigation politics, and leverage politics—represent sequential thresholds for litigants to surmount. If out of court bargaining is insufficient, litigants will have to bring their case to court. If litigants win in court, yet the ruling itself does not engender compliance, advocates will need to pursue leverage strategies. The venues at each stage differ, the key actors involved vary, the tools of influence vary, and the modes of politics vary. In T1, potential litigants are the key actors that matter. Bargaining in the shadow of the law tends to be more akin to diplomacy, occurring outside of the spotlight and open to all sorts of political compromises. In T2, international judges shape legal outcomes. Litigation politics occurs through written exchanges and courtroom interactions. International judges are most likely to be swayed by legal arguments, thus lawyers will use the language of law to advance their case. Litigation generates a paper trail that might one day become public, and legal rulings must be defended in legal terms if ICs are to draw on law for their political power. Leverage politics (T3) generally involve a wider group of actors, and publicity may be a key element in encouraging recalcitrant actors to follow the IC's ruling. Since the actors and politics vary at each stage of the litigation process it is hard to make blanket arguments about what will matter for each case. Cases that settle at T1 might involve very little publicity about legal violations and legal solutions. For cases that proceed to T3 publicity may become very important in pressuring governments.

35 (Helfer and Slaughter 1997; Keohane, Moravcsik, and Slaughter 2000).

Interacting with these varied actors and modes of decision making are legal and political factors that are largely exogenous to the court and the specific contentious case. Variations in the content of the law, and in which actors have standing to access the court, will generate varied IC activation and influence. Litigants must figure out which actors within states have the power to choose compliance, and whether litigation might influence these actors. Sometimes compliance with the law requires mobilizing the executive and legislative branches, and other times compliance will involve influencing a single person or office. All of this—the varied legal and political facts, the varied actors involved, and the varied incentives of these actors—generate variation in the influence of ICs across issues and cases. Figure 2.6 captures sources for variation and interactive effects, separating how legal and political factors matter at each stage of the litigation process.

Most political scientists focus on how political factors shape legal outcomes, suggesting that legal factors are either epiphenomenal or constant across cases. Law matters, however, because judges are legal actors and because the IC's compliance constituency includes actors committed to the rule of law as an end in itself. But within the constraints of law, flexibility exists in the form of varying interpretative traditions,[36] and especially with respect to remedies the court orders. Indeed, the issue of remedies may be where we are mostly likely to see ICs adjusting to the realities of their environment. ICs can require no remedies, in which case compliance becomes much easier to arrange. For example, in the Peru exceptions case the ATJ followed the well-known judicial strategy of finding that the legal breach had already been rectified. Other case studies show ICs framing remedies to be more politically achievable. For example, the modern-day slavery case raises a fundamental question about whether family law practices trap women in slave relations. By refusing to review the validity of national laws and practices, and instead requiring compensation for a found violation, the ECOWAS court made compliance with its ruling relatively easy to orchestrate. Chapter 8 contrasts this outcome to the Inter-American Court of Human Right's indigenous land rights ruling, where the Court required restorative remedies. The conclusion will further hypothesize about how environmental factors lead to variation in IC behavior and influence.

Figure 2.6 suggests that *many* factors can matter, which can present a dilemma for political scientists who value parsimony. My goal is to present an analytical framework from which one can generate more specified yet accurate hypotheses about the factors that contribute to or undermine

36 For how interpretative traditions influence IC decision making, see Pauwelyn and Elsig (2012).

FIGURE 2.6: Legal and political factors shaping the influence of ICs

Time 1: Bargaining in Shadow of IC	Time 2: Litigation Politics	Time 3: Leverage Politics
Key actors: Potential litigants and potential compliance partners	*Key actors:* International prosecutorial actors and judges	*Key actors*: Transnational actors, foreign governments
International legal factors: Variations in international legal standing and IC jurisdiction will shape the credibility of litigation threats. **Domestic legal factors:** Where private litigants gain access to ICs via domestic courts, factors shaping whether national judges refer cases and follow IC rulings may influence the credibility of legal threats. **Political factors:** Differing mobilization capabilities and incentives (e.g., varied legal resources and skill) shape whether potential litigants invoke the IC. Variation in political incentives to litigate (e.g., variation in whether pressure through law is considered a politically legitimate advocacy strategy, variation in how interests are organized as it affects the definition of goals and objectives).	**International legal factors:** The clarity of the legal violation and the IC's jurisdiction may affect IC willingness to rule against a state. Fact finding constraints and differing burden of proof may also shape litigation politics. **Political factors:** Concerns about co-opting compliance partners, about the political impracticality of certain legal outcomes, about harming rather than helping the cause of compliance supporters or about fomenting backlash may shape IC decision making.	**Transnational legal factors:** Variation based on the legal levers of pressure (e.g., statutory links between foreign aid and the behavior of aid recipients, legal rules regarding bilateral or multilateral sanctions). **Domestic legal factors:** Factors affecting the domestic legal effect of international legal rulings. **Political factors:** Variation based on the preferences of governments with political levers of influence. Variation based on the existence and resources of transnational advocates.
Interactive effects		
Relevant questions: How might an IC rule in the case (T2)? Who has the power to choose compliance? What motivates these actors? What sorts of leverage exist to influence these actors (T3)?	*Relevant questions:* What sort of specified remedies would most help compliance supporters (T3) and future litigants (T1) induce policy change in the direction of respect for international law?	*Relevant questions:* What does compliance with the IC ruling entail (T2)? Will there be follow-up litigation (e.g., copy-cat cases) (T1)?

IC effectiveness. The altered politics argument suggests four necessary conditions for ICs to alter domestic and international politics: (1) litigants must be able to seize the court; (2) actors within states must care about legality; (3) entrepreneurs must invoke a court and help build a compliance constituency; (4) international rules must enjoy the political support of constituencies that have power. The first condition is met by new-style ICs but shaped by legal standing requirements and the substance of the law. Conditions two through four are determined by political factors, and variation in these factors will generate variation in the influence of ICs across institution, issue area, and case. One can generate hypotheses based on each of these four variables, hypothesizing for example about the conditions and issues that make actors care more or less about legality. One can investigate when potential litigants will be more or less likely to seize an international court. One can hypothesize about when key compliance partners are more or less likely to coalesce in support of international legal rulings. I make a number of such conjectures in the chapters that follow and elsewhere, returning to this question in the book's conclusion.[37] For now, I rest with the claim that politics varies across time periods, and legal and political factors will matter in different ways within each time period.

How the Altered Politics Framework Differs from Alternative Explanations

Since the altered politics framework can incorporate the causal forces of all three models, it may seem like everything matters for my argument. But the framework suggests that certain arguments one reads about may matter less than is often implied. That there are three alternative pathways toward compliance—pleasing litigants, creating tools of international leverage, or co-opting domestic compliance partners—means that international judges do not need to cater exclusively to the interests of litigating governments or politically powerful states. In this respect I disagree with Eric Posner and Jack Goldsmith who see international law as little more than a "coordination device of governments."[38]

My emphasis on *preferences*, *priorities*, and *choices* implicitly suggests that structural domestic legal factors are less of a barrier than is sometimes claimed. My claim is not that national legal attributes are irrelevant. ICs may well draw on national legal traditions to build support for their rulings within national judiciaries. But national legal attributes do not themselves create insurmountable barriers. This is why I stress the opportunities

37 (Alter 2009, 22–25, 204–14).
38 (Goldsmith and Posner 2005).

created by embedded international law, rather than whether or not a national legal system is monist or dualist, civil law or common law. Where states and judges do not want to draw on international law, they invoke national legal barriers to explain their actions. Where states and judges *do* want to follow international law, they find ways to do so (this argument is further developed in chapter 8, where I explain my focus on constitutional cultures instead of domestic legal attributes).

Real implications follow. If ICs were dependent on pleasing governments, then international law would be nothing more than a cipher for the interests and purposes of hegemonic power. Critical theory scholars may believe such arguments, but it means that international law can never be a tool to meaningfully subordinate power to law. This book shows otherwise. If certain international legal design features—like private access rules or the existence of strong sanctioning tools—were the key to IC effectiveness, then we would either need to increase the sanctioning power of ICs or conclude that certain international courts can never meaningfully influence international relations. We would also become lackadaisical whenever there were superficial resemblances between international legal systems and ideal type models, putting false faith in the power of strong sanctions and expecting too much from ICs that mimic design models associated with effective international courts.

If national legal structures generated fundamental barriers to international law's influence, then the lesson would be that to generate greater respect for international law we should work to change structural elements of national legal systems. My argument suggests that such structural change is not necessary. In rejecting these alternatives, the altered politics argument suggests a specific path forward.

Overall, the altered politics argument suggests that ICs are politically influential when there are clear legal rules to enforce, when litigants are mobilized to seize ICs and demand compliance with the law, and when ICs have politically strong compliance constituents. ICs become weak when the legal rules they oversee have critical loopholes and when courts lack mobilized litigants or have weak compliance allies. What is not on this list is also of interest. Government opposition and the lack of sanctioning systems do not per se make ICs politically weak. Indeed, legal violations by governments are more likely to activate than they are to undermine IC influence. The altered politics framework suggests that the way to encourage state respect of international law is to create clear law and then work to shift the attitudes of key compliance supporters—potential litigants, lawyers, judges, and those actors that can create helpful tools of political leverage. In other words, to have political influence ICs need to co-opt domestic legal actors, to convince them that it is illegal to violate international law, ignore the IC ruling, or maintain a government practice that has been internationally condemned. ICs can appeal to the instrumental incentives of compliance partners, so that rationalist interests may explain changes in government policy. But ICs intervene in politics using the language of legality, thus normative forces will also matter. At the end of the day, IC legal interpretations must hold sway, which is to say that the remedies international courts articulate must be seen as the legal way forward, both domestically and internationally.

CONCLUSION: BREACHING THE SOVEREIGNTY OF DOMESTIC LAW

The judicialization of politics occurs when politicians conceive of their policy and legislative options as bounded by what is legally allowed and when courts gain authority to define what the law means. At the domestic level, we might expect politics to be judicialized wherever independent judges and courts exist. But applying this same expectation to the international level presents problems. Even if international judges are independent actors, ICs must worry about whether governments will comply with their rulings.

Many practitioners and scholars expect ICs to be so concerned about eliciting compliance that international judges perforce look to the preferences of powerful governments as they adjudicate cases. This chapter offered a number of reasons to question such claims. First, I explained that in many instances states and ICs will share a general interest in seeing the relevant laws followed. In other-binding roles, such as when ICs serve as dispute settlement bodies for private actor cases and when ICs are administrative review bodies for international administrators, ICs will be acting as agents of states helping to monitor the extent to which other actors are following the law. In coordination contexts—situations where states want common rules given a common interpretation—governments will also happily let ICs facilitate the uniform interpretation of international rules. These situations are not apolitical; real interests are at stake, and the subjects of the law care greatly about legal interpretation and judicial decision making. But governments delegated decision making to ICs so that judges can fill in the law and resolve these types of disputes. Delegation to ICs in such contexts mostly extends or at least does not unduly impinge on the sovereignty of nations and the power of governments.

The chapter then focused on situations where states have bound themselves to international judicial oversight. Self-binding limits state autonomy, but it also brings benefits. States self-bind to increase the credibility of their commitment in the eyes of other actors. Where governments want to encourage foreign investment and where governments want to bolster a promise to their own population or to other states, they may happily submit to international judicial oversight and readily respect IC rulings to provide proof of the government's commitment to the rules in question. Or, governments may actually want external pressure to adopt a domestically controversial policy. In all of these contexts, international law can rationally coexist with national legal sovereignty. The interstate arbiter model speaks to these situations, reconciling international adjudication and national sovereignty by making ICs wholly dependent on governments choosing to comply with their rulings. Such a view fits nicely with a realist perspective of international relations. It allows international law to matter when diverse national interests converge, but not to constrain by creating obligations or serious reputational costs.

The altered politics framework is different because it allows for law to exist independent of the will of governments, for ICs to be able to rule against powerful governments, for a grassroots political preference for legality to foreclose certain government options, and for a culture of constitutional obedience to internationally defined law to emerge. This argument dovetails with the work of Beth Simmons, Kathryn Sikkink, Thomas Risse, Xinyuan Dai, Charles Epps, and others. The primary difference is to stress that international adjudication involves *international law*. The legal and international nature of ICs is crucially important. International adjudication mobilizes not just advocacy communities who share a particular agenda or worldview, it mobilizes the legal community—lawyers who can earn money by developing legal expertise, judges who are asked by litigants to adjudicate cases involving international rules, scholars and practitioners who are attracted to legal conundrums, and populations who believe they have a stake in governments respecting the rule of law regardless of the substantive issue at hand. The international nature of the laws ICs apply helps to circumvent domestic barriers, and it frees legal review from the grip of a national government.

Governments have long considered international law in their foreign policy decision making, thus it is not new for international law to shape international relations.[39] Governments have also long used legal arguments to justify policies, and then come to find themselves constrained by their legal invocations. Thus it is also not new for international law to be domestically constraining.[40] What is new, however, is the ability of state and nonstate actors to seek an international legal remedy, and thereby circumvent domestic legal and political barriers. Also new is the possibility that ICs can draw on law's autonomy and construct compliance constituencies within and across states.

39 (Chayes 1974).

40 (Hurd 2005; Risse, Ropp, and Sikkink 1999).

The altered politics framework is about *how* ICs transform politics. ICs influence politics by drawing on the autonomy of law, specifying what law requires, creating legal remedies, and building legal and political constituencies that co-opt the ICs' definition of legality. New-style ICs—meaning ICs with compulsory jurisdiction and access for nonstate actors to initiate litigation—make it increasingly possible for ICs to broaden the constituency of actors within and across states who support the goals and objectives associated with international legal regimes. The fact that much international law today is embedded into national legal systems provides a way to reconcile international and domestic legality, and to breach the domestic sovereign legal barrier. Realizing this reconciliation—which is to say convincing domestic actors that international law violations are also domestic rule of law violations—may require shifting legal understandings about the domestic standing of international law, or shifting interpretations of domestic law so that domestic practice no longer conflicts with international law. This may be a long-term project, and it may require that a generation of judges and law faculty steeped in national legal approaches first retire. But it is possible to promote legal change through small intermediary steps, each of which leads to change from the status quo ante in the direction implicated by the law.

I focus in this book on ICs working with compliance supporters who bring international law into domestic debates and foreign relations. Of course the democratic legitimacy of international law surely depends on building public support for international law domestically and globally. An American, however, cannot help but observe that public opinion is not enough. Legality is the currency of international courts, and domestic lawyers, law professors, and judges are the gatekeepers of domestic legality. The future of international law resides in the choices of these actors, because the IC's key compliance partners are motivated at least in part by a desire to be respecting the rule of law.

The analysis in this chapter is admittedly legal realist and instrumentalist in nature. I am arguing that international judges should, and probably do, consider whether or not there is legal and political support for the interpretations they advocate. I agree with those who argue that law greatly shapes and constrains the discursive space where conversations about legality and compliance occur. Moreover, because ICs are legal actors, and because many IC compliance partners will be motivated primarily, if not exclusively, by conceptions of what the law requires, international judges *should* be faithful to the law. But especially international judges should take into account how international law interacts with societal preferences, and how different international legal rulings might be helpful or harmful to those actors that support the goals of international law. Such an argument is an anathema to legal positivists and strict constructionists who believe that judges should *only* consider factors inherent to the law itself.

By now it should be clear how my argument raises serious normative questions. The altered politics framework allows for circumventing elected political bodies and domestic judges and by substituting international legality for domestic legality. When the conversation is about whether war criminals should escape prosecution, or whether extraconstitutional actions violate human rights, we may believe that circumventing domestic bodies is acceptable and even desirable. Circumventing the power and authority of highly legitimated domestic actors, however, is another matter entirely.

On the one hand, the whole point of self-binding to international law and trusting interpretation of international law to ICs is so that new governments feel pressure to respect past agreements. And the whole point of human rights and mass atrocities law is to protect minorities from a tyranny of the majority. On the other hand, it is sometimes normatively problematic to insist that today's domestic choices be subservient to past international promises. I return to the normative desirability of further opening domestic spheres to international forces in the book's conclusion where I consider the implications of delegating authority for ICs for democratic politics.

CHAPTER 3

The New International Courts

When the Cold War ended in 1989, there were six permanent international courts plus the noncompulsory dispute settlement system of the General Agreement on Tariffs and Trade (GATT). The European Court of Justice (ECJ) offered the model of an active and effective new-style international court. The other six international adjudicatory mechanisms had collectively issued only 373 binding judgments between 1945 and 1989. Today, there are at least twenty-four permanent international courts that have collectively issued over 37,000 binding legal judgments. The greater influence of ICs today is not simply a matter of numbers. Today's ICs are fundamentally different from their historical predecessors. Before the Cold War ended, scholars and practitioners conceived of ICs as voluntary dispute settlement bodies, institutions litigants could use if they wanted a legal resolution to a disagreement. Europe's Court of Justice was clearly different, but it was seen as a sui generis case of one. Meanwhile, the existing human rights institutions seemed either mostly irrelevant or ineffective. Today's ICs, what I call "new-style ICs," have compulsory jurisdiction, and they allow nonstate actors to initiate litigation. Today, the lion's share of all international legal rulings are issued in cases instigated by supranational commissions and prosecutors or private litigants with the plaintiff seeking to have state or international actions reviewed and international legal rules enforced.

This chapter and the next provide a global view of the transformation of the international judiciary since 1945. A key objective of this book's global perspective is to identify connections across international judicial developments and variation that can be used to research when and how international courts become politically influential.

Section I identifies important temporal variation in creating international courts. Rationalist explanations provide compelling arguments about the political benefit of delegating authority to ICs. Such explanations should, however, be valid across time and space. This section documents a first trend, a proliferation of international courts since the end of the Cold War. It also explains important definitional and methodological choices and defines the universe of operational permanent international courts analyzed in this book.

Section II documents the second trend, a shift from "old-style" voluntary dispute adjudication to "new-style" ICs with compulsory jurisdiction and access for nonstate actors to initiate litigation. "Old-style" international courts, like the International Court of Justice, can facilitate the peaceful settlement of interstate disputes, but they are limited in their ability to enforce or develop international law. I show that most ICs today are "new-style" bodies, and that Cold War–era international legal bodies also changed in the post–Cold War era. Thus this section also documents a tendency to augment rather than scale back the jurisdiction and design of ICs over time.

Section III identifies subject matter and regional clumping in creating ICs and an increase in international litigation since the end of the Cold War. Most ICs today have jurisdiction over economic, human rights, or crimes associated with mass violence. ICs with similar subject-matter jurisdictions share certain basic design traits. Delegation to ICs is also regionally clustered. European and African countries are most likely to submit to compulsory international judicial oversight, followed by Latin American countries. Delegation to ICs is not wholly absent in Asia and the Middle East, but certain countries display a significant aversion to submitting to the compulsory jurisdiction of international courts.

Overall, this chapter presents rich regional, subject-matter, and temporal variation in creating ICs. The existence of new-style ICs is the critical starting place that allows ICs to alter domestic and international politics. Inquiring minds, however, will want to know why the changes identified in this chapter occurred. The fundamental logic underlying delegation of compulsory jurisdiction to ICs is a distrust of national governments. Rationalist explanations suggest reasons why governments might want to self-bind to international judicial oversight, but the dearth of new-style international courts before the end of the Cold War is testament to the reluctance of governments to submit to compulsory international judicial oversight. What then changed to make governments more willing to create new-style international courts? I leave this question to the next chapter. For now I want to underscore how chapter 4 is an important complement to this chapter. This chapter dates and locates governmental decisions to create or change the design of international courts, which suggests that government choices are perhaps more important than legal practice. Chapter 4 corrects such a misperception by identifying how world historical forces and legal practices have changed the choice-set governments face.

I. INTERNATIONAL COURTS: SOME IMPORTANT DEFINITIONAL ISSUES

This book focuses on permanent international courts and uses the number of binding rulings as an indicator of the court's growing political and legal relevance. These choices lead me to understate the trend of creating and using ICs. I prefer to understate trends since this study already paints a picture of the international judiciary that is larger and more active than most people expect. I include as case studies international legal bodies that do not meet the definitional criteria used to create a universe of ICs, so as to highlight how functional equivalents of the permanent ICs can also alter domestic and international politics. Here I specify my methods and choices.

The Twenty-Four Permanent International Courts in This Study

This study adopts the definition of an international court developed by the Project on International Courts and Tribunals (PICT). The virtue of PICT's definition is that it creates a coherent category of international adjudicatory bodies that bear a meaningful resemblance to domestic courts. PICT's definition requires that international court be (1) a permanent institution, (2) composed of independent judges (3) that adjudicates disputes between two or more entities, one of which can be a state or international organization. They (4) work on the basis of predetermined rules of procedure and (5) render decisions that are legally binding.[1] PICT's definition generates a large but nonetheless tractable universe of twenty-eight permanent ICs; my focus on operational ICs creates a slightly circumscribed universe of twenty-four ICs.

By relying on PICT's definition, I can include the courts that most interest politicians and scholars—namely, ICs that adjudicate cases involving states. I can also create a basic uniformity across judicial institutions. ICs meeting PICT's definition can issue legally binding rulings, which also means that the law these courts apply is legally binding. We know that all ICs meeting PICT's definition have a predefined pool of judges so that litigants cannot choose who will hear the case on final appeal.[2] These judges

1 Cesare Romano created this definition in 1999, documenting ICs that met this definition and quasi-legal bodies that did not (Romano 1999, 711–23). See http://www.pict-pcti.org/matrix/matrixhome.html. This definition is explained and the information updated in Romano (2011); Romano, Alter, and Shany (2014, chapter 1). Some IC rulings are only advisory, but this book is focused on IC rulings that are defined by treaties as being binding in the legal sense.

2 The ICJ's system of allowing countries without a judge on the IC to appoint an ad hoc judge is a partial exception.

are independent in that they have taken an oath not to be government representatives but rather to uphold the law. ICs are also independent because they have rules that ensure that judges cannot be removed except for malfeasance, and that the working conditions for judges cannot be altered because states are unhappy with legal rulings. Like all judges, the men and women who staff international courts bring their own worldviews and experiences to the task of judging, and they are influenced by their larger political context.[3] But since ICs are composed of judges from multiple countries, and because each country gets to nominate its candidates of choice, international courts are also independent in that they are virtually impossible to stack. The political environment in which they work may be politically fraught, but the ability of governments to inflict personal retribution is far more limited than most suspect, and arguably much less of a factor in international judicial politics than in domestic judicial politics.[4]

Figure 3.1 provides basic information about the operational ICs that meet PICT's definition, organized chronologically to highlight how the creation of ICs accelerated after the end of the Cold War. The table presents the number of states falling under the legal body's jurisdiction and the number of binding rulings each court has issued by December 31, 2011, revealing variation in litigation rates that cannot be explained based on years of operation or the size of membership per se. The rest of this chapter extrapolates from this table. Excluded from this book's universe of ICs is one old-style court, the dispute settlement court for the Organization of Arab Petroleum Exporting Countries, created in 1980 but by all appearances now defunct. Also excluded are a handful of post–Cold War new-style ICs that exist only on paper[5] and the compulsory ad hoc adjudication system of the International Centre for the Settlement of Disputes, which allow nonstate actors to initiate litigation. The book's online appendix includes a brief description of the twenty-eight ICs

3 For more on who international judges are, see Terris, Romano, and Swigart (2008).

4 Countries can nominate whomever they want, so long as the nominee meets the defined professional criteria. The politics of selecting among nominees can be politicized, but the decentralized nomination process significantly limits the ability of any one country or subgroup of countries to shape the overall composition of an IC. This decentralized appointment system is intentional, designed to provide geographic representation and thereby reassure less powerful countries by limiting the ability of the most powerful countries to stack or control an international court. For more, see Alter (2006). See also Staton and Moore (2011). For empirical studies of IC appointment politics see Voeten (2007; 2008).

5 Cesare Romano (2014) identifies twenty stillborn bodies meeting PICT's definition of an IC. The online appendix includes a few ICs with binding Court Treaties but no judges appointed, including ASEAN which had a ratified statute but as of yet no appointed judges. Also included is an Arab Investment Court, where available information is extremely limited and in Arabic. See the online appendix for more.

FIGURE 3.1: International courts in this study (ordered by date IC became operational)

International Courts	Geographic Reach	Subject Matter Jurisdiction
ICs created following WWII		
International Court of Justice (ICJ) *Previously the Permanent Court of Justice, created in 1919.*	All regions	Any interstate issue + authority regarding the UN Charter + other international treaties where ICJ is designated as the final interpreter
European Union's Court of Justice (ECJ) and the first instance General Court (GC)	Europe	Trade and other issues governed by European Union law
European Court of Human Rights (ECtHR)	Europe	Human rights
ICs created during the Cold War		
BENELUX Court (BCJ)	Europe	Economic issues plus some civil and criminal affairs
Inter-American Court of Human Rights (IACtHR)	Latin America	Human rights
Andean Tribunal Of Justice (ATJ)	Latin America	Trade
ICs created following the end of the Cold War		
European Free Trade Area Court (EFTAC)	Europe	Economic issues
Central American Court of Justice (CACJ)	Central America	Any interstate issue
International Criminal Tribunal for the Former Yugoslavia (ICTY)	Europe	Mass atrocities
Economic Court of the Commonwealth of Independent States (ECCIS)	Commonwealth of Independent States	Primarily economic issues
International Criminal Tribunal for Rwanda (ICTR)	Africa	Mass atrocities
World Trade Organization Appellate Body (WTO) *General Agreement on Tariffs and Trade (GATT)*	All regions	Economic issues (international trade)
West African Economic and Monetary Union Court of Justice (including its Court of Auditors) (WAEMU/UEMOA)	Africa	Economic issues Members are also part of ECOWAS system.

Date Created	First Ruling	Member States	Binding Rulings (Founding–2011)
1945	1947	193 69 countries accept optional compulsory jurisdiction	152 cases filed, 77 binding rulings, 26 advisory opinions. *29 judgments (1929–44)*
1952 (GC–1988)	1953	27	18,511 binding rulings
1958	1960	47	14,940 binding rulings
1974	1975	3	146 binding rulings
1979	1987	21	239 binding rulings and 20 advisory opinions
1984	1985	4	2,197 binding rulings
1992	1994	3	126 binding rulings
1992	1994	4	65 rulings in contentious cases, 12 preliminary rulings, 43 advisory opinions
1993	1994	7	93 completed cases
1993	1994	9	67 binding rulings, 30 advisory rulings
1994	1998	1	72 completed cases with binding outcomes
1994 *1948–94*	1994 *1948*	153	402 disputes initiated, 176 panel decisions adopted + 108 appellate rulings adopted *117 panel reports adopted*
1995	1995	9	44 binding rulings (data through 2009)

FIGURE 3.1: (*Continued*)

International Courts	Geographic Reach	Subject Matter Jurisdiction
International Tribunal for the Law of the Sea (ITLOS)	All regions	Law of the Sea Convention (UNCLOS III), plus oversight of the Seabed Authority created by UNCLOS III.
Organization for the Harmonization of Corporate Law in Africa Common Court of Justice and Arbitration (OHADA CCJA)	Africa	Economic issues (business law)
Southern Common Market (MERCOSUR)	Latin America	Economic issues
Eastern and Southern Africa Common Market Court of Justice (COMESA)	Africa	Economic issues
Central African Economic and Monetary Community Court of Justice (CEMAC)	Africa	Economic issues
East African Community Court of Justice (EACJ)	Africa	Economic issues Good governance
Caribbean Court of Justice (CCJ)	Latin America/ Caribbean	All issues, plus appeals of domestic civil & criminal law cases
Economic Community of West African States Court of Justice (ECOWAS CJ)	Africa	Economic issues Good governance Human rights
International Criminal Court (ICC)	All regions	Mass atrocities
Southern African Development Community (SADC)	Africa	Economic issues Good governance
African Court on Human and Peoples' Rights (ACtHPR)	Africa	Human rights
Totals each category (N = 24)		

Date Created	First Ruling	Member States	Binding Rulings (Founding–2011)
1996	1997	162 33 countries accept optional compulsory jurisdiction	17 binding rulings and 1 advisory ruling
1997	1999	15	569 binding rulings
1999	1999	4	12 panel reports, 5 appellate body reports, 3 preliminary ruling consultations
1998	Not available	19	7 rulings (data incomplete)
2000	Not available	6	Not available
2001	2006	5	26 binding rulings
2001	2005	13	9 original jurisdiction, 51 appeals of national court decisions
2001	2004	15	51 binding rulings
2002	2012	121	1 conviction in 2012, cases involving 24 indicted individuals underway.
2005	2007	15	24 binding rulings (no new cases allowed after 2010)
2006	2009	26	8 binding rulings
			37,236 binding rulings in contentious cases

meeting PICT's definition, provides references to the legal instruments that define an IC's jurisdiction, and provides sources for the litigation data.

PICT's definition is not perfect. Perhaps the most arbitrary part of the definition is the requirement that a legal body be permanent. Cesare Romano justified the focus on permanent courts because their existence is "independent of the vicissitudes of a given case."[6] Because international judges are part of ongoing institutional and legal structures, they are more likely to act with an eye toward the future, resolving cases in ways that generate precedent and defending the court's institutional authority when it is challenged. After some definitional consideration, the PICT project included the International Criminal Tribunals for Rwanda and Yugoslavia in its count of international judicial bodies, perhaps because their legal jurisdiction is permanent.[7] But the requirement of permanence ends up excluding legal bodies that are similar if not identical to permanent courts in their operation and political influence. For example, the US-Iran Claims Tribunal, discussed in chapter 5, was a special international body given a finite mandate of dealing with disputes arising from the Iranian revolution and the United States' decision to freeze Iranian assets. This body was composed of independent judges, issued binding rulings using legal decision making, and contributed significantly to the development of international law regarding the rights of private claimants in complex political contexts.[8] Yet it was not a permanent court and is for this reason excluded from PICT's count. Also, the dispute settlement systems of the World Trade Organization (WTO) and Southern Common Market system (MERCOSUR) meet the definition because they have permanent appellate bodies, while the nearly identical dispute settlement system of the North American Free Trade Agreement (NAFTA) does not count even though NAFTA adds a system of binational panels, discussed in chapter 6, which are functional equivalents of ICs conducting administrative review, and its enforcement politics are not all that different MERCOSUR's enforcement politics. The Special Tribunal for Sierra Leone discussed in chapter 8 also falls outside of the definition of an IC, even though this court and the other hybrid international criminal tribunals function very similarly to their more permanent brethren.

PICT's definition allows me to compare an entire category of like institutions—operational permanent international courts—and at the end of

6 (Romano 1999, 713).

7 See PICT's synoptic chart, reference at note 1. *The Oxford Handbook on International Adjudication* (2014) will have updated charts.

8 See the case study discussion in chapter 5 for citations and more about the US-Iran Claims Tribunal.

the day nothing significant hangs on the decision to focus on permanent ICs. It is better to use objective definitional criteria, and it is preferable to include ICs that are operational but inactive because inactive ICs present an opportunity to investigate why similarly designed ICs do not end up playing the roles that have been delegated to them. Moreover, once one opens the door to include ad hoc and quasi-judicial bodies, it becomes difficult to identify a universe of like bodies to compare, and the legal institutions included can end up quite different in nature. For example, arbitration is fundamentally different from adjudication by permanent courts in that litigants select their judges and the panel disbands after adjudicating a case. Political human rights treaty bodies are also different in that member affiliations to governments politicize them, and their decisions are not legally binding. But if one added international court-like institutions that American or European lawyers see as important, adding for example NAFTA and International Centre for the Settlement of Investment Disputes (ICSID), and excluding the Rwandan and Yugoslav Criminal Tribunals or international courts that have issued less than ten rulings, the trends would be the same, and the argument about how these bodies influence international relations would be the same. All that would change is that the number of legal rulings issued and the phenomenon I am studying would look even larger.

Litigation Data as Indicators of Legal Demand and Rights Claiming

While I do not equate litigation with political salience or legal effectiveness, litigation indicates a faith that ICs will act as independent legal interpreters, that a legal ruling in one's favor will have a legal and political resonance, and that the legal rights established by international law are seen as valuable. Governments may consent to international judicial oversight to send a signal to powerful foreign governments, international agencies, and potential investors. Especially when few cases end up being adjudicated, this signal may be relatively costless. Litigation, by contrast, is never costless. At a minimum, litigation involves nontrivial legal expenses. Losing a case may also generate costs in the form of legal fees where the loser pays the winner's expenses, restorative remedies, punitive sanctions, and reputational costs since most IC rulings are public. It is safe to assume that litigants are only willing to pay the costs when they expect that doing so may be useful.

I collected data from ICs that post reports or rulings on the Internet, or that responded to my queries (twenty-three in all), counting the number of final and binding rulings in contentious cases issued in any given year.[9] Unless otherwise noted, the over 37,000 binding international judgments documented in this chapter are rulings on the merits issued in individual contentious cases. (Figure 3.1 lists IC advisory opinions, which can also have political resonance, but the rest of this chapter excludes advisory rulings so as to underscore the binding nature of the legal rulings of ICs.) To avoid double counting individual contentious cases, I exclude interim rulings and appeals. I also exclude rulings regarding the staff of international organizations, since these cases will not have a meaningful effect on domestic or international politics.[10] Repeat player cases, meaning cases with the same plaintiff and similar fact patterns, get counted separately when legal rulings are issued separately. Where the same public source, for example IC reports, changed the data reported for a given year I took the lower figure so as not to double count cases.

This conservative counting method significantly understates the activity of ICs; readers should thus keep in mind that international judges are quite a bit busier than my numbers suggest. For example, the more than eighty cases filed before the ECOWAS court through 2011, which includes rulings on procedural and jurisdictional questions and staff cases, ends up counting as fifty-one binding rulings. Over 150 cases have entered the ICJ's general list from its founding to today. After eliminating cases withdrawn and cases where a final ruling on the merits is still pending, my count of ICJ rulings end up with seventy-seven binding rulings in contentious cases.[11] The WTO lists 427 cases formally filed in its dispute settlement system between 1994 and 2011.[12] I count panel decisions, since these are first-instance binding rulings even if the bodies that issue them are not permanent. I exclude cases settled without the formal adop-

9 See the appendix for data sources. Where possible, I draw on the data of scholars who have systematically analyzed the legal outputs of specific systems. For analysis of ECJ outputs see Stone Sweet (2004); Stone Sweet and Brunell (2012). For analysis of ATJ outputs see Alter and Helfer (2010); Helfer and Alter (2009); Helfer, Alter, and Guerzovich (2009) (we are also currently analyzing the ECOWAS court's rulings). Robert Hudec analyzed legal outputs of the disputes settlement system of the General Agreement on Tariffs and Trade (Hudec 1993). Eric Reinhardt and Marc Busch updated this data (Busch and Reinhardt 2000). Henrik Horn, Louise Johannesson, and Petros Mavroides analyze WTO dispute settlement outputs (Horn, Johannesson, and Mavroides 2011). James Meernik has coded rulings of the Yugoslavian and Rwandan Criminal Courts. There are also systematic analyses of IACtHR legal outputs (Hawkins and Jacoby 2010; Huneeus 2013).

10 Where ICs report staff cases separately, and where I manually coded IC data, I was able to exclude staff cases. The data sources are listed in the Court Treaty bibliography.

11 My count excludes the ICJ advisory opinions (twenty-four), cases that are settled or dropped before the ICJ issues a ruling related to the merits of the case (thirty-one), and cases where a party asks the ICJ to reconsider or clarify aspects of previous rulings. I do, however, include twenty-six ICJ rulings where the cases ended with the Court declaring the case inadmissible or that it lacked jurisdiction to proceed.

12 http://www.wto.org/english/tratop_e/dispu_e/dispu_status_e.htm.

tion of a panel report, interim and implementation rulings, and appellate body rulings, thus my data include only 176 binding panel rulings from the WTO period. I also do not capture rulings by ad hoc bodies (like the International Centre for the Settlement of Investment Disputes) or domestic rulings involving international law, which by all counts are significantly more numerous.[13]

A final caveat is that my data lag in time. Most ICs report on their activity of the year, which means that IC decisions get counted in the year the decision is issued, not the year the case began. For consistency, I maintained this practice for rulings that I coded. Especially for international criminal courts, where years may pass between the intiation of a formal investigation and the issuing of a legal verdict, the lag and counting method surely understates the influence of international tribunals at any given moment. The upshot of these choices is that these data understate the extent to which international litigation is increasing and do not fully capture how ICs' existence is affecting negotiated outcomes.

Court Treaties and Coding Delegation of Judicial Roles

This book is organized around four roles ICs play in international politics: dispute settlement, administrative review, enforcement, and constitutional review. Chapter 1 overviewed the roles, and separate chapters document ICs explicitly delegated specific roles, identifying variation in the design of ICs in the given role. These discussions are based on coding ICs' legal instruments, which arguably define what governments expected ICs to be doing. IC jurisdictions are defined and amended across a number of legal documents, including the charter of the international organization and subsequent treaties, revisions, and legislative acts. I sum up the varied formal legal texts, provisions, and revisions agreed to by member states through a generic construct of a "Court Treaty," which encapsulates the jurisdiction governments have formally endorsed across diverse legal texts.

This coding is meant to simplify legal reality for the purposes of comparison. I looked for wording in Court Treaties that grants jurisdiction to the IC (see the chapter's appendix for examples). Usually, jurisdictional powers are delegated to ICs in different articles of the agreements, thereby allowing negotiators to pick specific design features for specific judicial

13 Kathryn Sikkink tries to get a handle on this difference by comparing domestic, foreign (e.g., extraterritorial domestic), and international human rights prosecutions. The lion's share of prosecutions are domestic; foreign and international prosecutions are roughly the same in number, although international prosecutions may be eclipsing foreign prosecutions (Sikkink 2011, 21).

roles. More than one role can be delegated to a single court, and design features, such as whether the IC's jurisdiction is compulsory, which actors can raise a suit, and such, can vary by role. For the most part, the coding is straightforward. ICs either have been given constitutional, administrative, or enforcement powers, or they have not. And it is usually quite clear which actors are allowed to initiate litigation for each role. For example, the coding reveals that the International Tribunal for the Law of the Sea (ITLOS) has a dispute settlement system that governments can activate. There is also a special Seabed Disputes Chamber that allows private actors to challenge administrative decisions of the supranational Enterprise, which oversees mining of the deep seas. Thus the ITLOS court's dispute settlement jurisdiction is mostly noncompulsory and accessible only for states. The ITLOS administrative review jurisdiction is compulsory, and private actors can initiate litigation. The coding does not capture how judges qualify access rules through their rulings on legal standing, and there can be nuances not captured by the coding. For example, lawyers consider ITLOS to have compulsory jurisdiction for cases involving the seizing of vessels, and, at least in theory, ITLOS allows governments to consent to let the owners of vessels pursue a case on their own. Each role chapter has an appendix that paraphrases and references the relevant treaty articles for each court delegated the role, thereby indicating the provisions that generated the coding. Relevant exceptions can be found in footnotes, but interested scholars should consult expert analysis for a more precise clarification of the court's standing and jurisdiction rules.

I recognize that judicial roles can morph so that ICs assume roles not explicitly delegated. Still, this basic coding provides a helpful baseline that reveals that sometimes governments only want ICs to be available should parties seek a legal resolution to their disagreements; other times governments want ICs to monitor compliance with the agreement. We can also observe governments limiting access to ICs for specific judicial roles. The formal grants of jurisdiction are important because they send powerful signals. Potential litigants examine the court's jurisdiction as they consider the types of cases a court will welcome, and international judges reference the founding legal instruments, so that the formal jurisdiction shapes legal practice. Also, because states have so clearly endorsed ICs playing certain roles, the formal mandate creates a zone of relative safety for international judges. Litigants that are unhappy with judicial outcomes often want to shoot the messenger—to claim that the court was political or somehow going beyond its mandate. Such claims are less likely to stick when ICs are hewing closely to their founding charters and the law they are applying, because supporters are more likely to rally behind a judicial institution that is being critiqued for doing exactly what it has been asked to do. In other words, an IC explicitly authorized to oversee state compliance with the law is likely to receive cases involving states' compliance, and an IC and its supporters are usually more willing to defend an exercise of clearly delegated jurisdiction. In this way, the delegation mandate contributes to generating a self-fulfilling prophecy.

The analytical construct of a Court Treaty identifies a moment in time when states defined the IC's jurisdiction. Given that not all ICs are very active, my coding of the formal grants of jurisdiction to ICs overstates what ICs do in practice. A disjuncture between the founding treaty and IC practice calls for some sort of explanation. Role-based chapters will explore under what condition ICs come to actually inhabit a judicial role. We can only explore such developments, however, after we know what governments have consented to.

A Trend toward New-Style International Courts

Not only are there more ICs today, these ICs are fundamentally different from international courts of the past. International legal bodies adjudicating cases involving governments have long existed. The 1794 Jay Treaty created an early form of transnational mass claims arbitration to adjudicate private and governmental claims that arose when the United States and Britain renegotiated the US-Canadian boundary.[14] International war crimes prosecutions arguably began with Napoleon's banishment to St. Helena in 1815.[15] The first generation of permanent ICs—standing bodies that preexisted the particular dispute with judges who were not chosen by the litigants—began with the Hague Peace Conference in 1899. Today's ICs are different from these bodies as well. Perhaps the most important trend in delegation to ICs is that international legal bodies today are more likely to have a far-reaching compulsory jurisdiction and allow non-state actors to initiate international legal review.[16]

I give the name "old-style" to international courts that lack compulsory jurisdiction and that only allow state parties to initiate litigation. Chapter 4 explains that "old style" ICs are representative of the Hague Peace Conference vision of politically feasible international courts. Writing in 1976, Werner Levi argued that "old-style" international adjudication was the defining feature of *Law and Politics in International Society*:

> The reluctance of states to have their disputes adjudicated finds expression, first, in limiting their obligation of submitting to judicial procedures, and second, in limiting the jurisdiction of the Court when they do submit to judicial

14 (Hudson 1944, 3).

15 (Bass 2000).

16 This section develops arguments previously published in Alter (2006, 50–64).

> procedures. States have consistently rejected the notion of a general and universal obligation of submitting all their disputes to an international court. They have almost as adamantly opposed agreements to submit their disputes to judicial decisions by international courts (the so-called "compulsory jurisdiction"). This was true, for example, in the case of arbitration in general of the international courts, of the Law of the Sea Conference (1958), the Conference on Diplomatic Intercourse and Immunities (1961), the Conference on Consular Relations (1963), the Conference on the Law of the Treaties (1968–1969), the Third Law of the Sea Conference (1975). Whenever "compulsory" jurisdiction was proposed it was rejected in favor of "optional procedures" by which states had the option of choosing which method for peaceful settlement of disputes they wanted to apply. The nearest to an obligation for judicial settlement is the "optional clause" in Article 36 of the Statute of the International Court of Justice and certain commitments of Western European States to the use of the European Court of Justice.[17]

The optional provisions Levi references let governments enjoy the benefits of being a member of the larger institution while being able to opt out of judicial oversight should such oversight become inconvenient. As Eric Posner and John Yoo explain, the opt-out possibility keeps international judges dependent on pleasing litigating governments so as to encourage litigation and avoid states opting out of their jurisdiction.[18] The European Court of Justice was in 1976 the only new-style IC, a clear exception to the general aversion governments displayed vis-à-vis international adjudication. Old-style ICs still exist; indeed, chapter 5 will discuss litigation in old-style international dispute settlement bodies. But such bodies today are the exception more than the rule.

What I am calling "new-style" ICs are international courts with a far-reaching compulsory jurisdiction and access for nonstate actors—private litigants and/or supranational prosecutorial bodies—to initiate litigation. The extension of compulsory jurisdiction is arguably the most prevalent and important IC design change since the end of the Cold War. Granting an IC a broad compulsory jurisdiction, and associating this jurisdiction with community membership, means that the only way to "opt out" is to withdraw entirely from the multilateral institution. As chapter 1 explained, empowering supranational prosecutors to raise noncompliance cases further undermines a target state's ability to block inconvenient litigation, because commissions may see enforcement as part of their job description, and because retaliation in the form of a reciprocal legal suits

17 (Levi 1976, 70–71).

18 (Posner and Yoo 2005). See chapter 1's discussion of dependent versus independent courts for more.

is less likely when a commission raises a case. Private access increases the number of potential litigants, making it more likely that state noncompliance cases will be challenged. The combination of these new-style features undermines a government's ability to block inconvenient legal suits from proceeding.

Figure 3.2 captures the trend toward new-style ICs. Old-Style ICs are listed in white boxes, ICs with hybrid designs are in light gray boxes, and new-style ICs are in dark gray boxes. The ICJ and perhaps the International Tribunal for the Law of the Sea still fit the description of "old-style" ICs. Both courts allow for some compulsory jurisdiction and limited access for nonstate actors to initiate litigation, but these features are circumscribed in their reach.[19] ICs with compulsory jurisdiction tend to be part of member organizations where all members are equally accountable to binding rules. The Organization of American States and the African Union allow countries to opt in to the court's jurisdiction, but regional integration, trade systems, and the Council of Europe require members to submit to the regional court's compulsory jurisdiction. Overall, twenty-one ICs have mandatory compulsory jurisdiction for certain roles (88 percent), sixteen allow international actors, and a different set of sixteen allow private litigants to initiate binding litigation (67 percent). In italics I list a few important exceptions to the old-style or hybrid classification of an IC. Role-based chapters and case studies provide finer-grained descriptions of IC designs, which sometimes include caveats on these design features. Appendixes to the role chapters document the provisions upon which this categorization is based.

Designers of ICs are clearly aware of how new-style design features matter, as evidenced by the decision to vary IC design by judicial role. For administrative review, for example, Court Treaty negotiators tend to allow broad access so that private litigants can monitor the behavior of supranational and national administrators. For enforcement, however, Court Treaties often limit access to protect national sovereignty. I label these sovereignty-protecting limitations "design hobbles" since the intent is to hinder unwanted adjudication.[20] When governments want a legal system to be more effective, they often release the hobbles, removing

19 Specific treaties can confer compulsory jurisdiction on the ICJ, but such jurisdiction is subject to revision by signatory states. The United Nations General Assembly can seek an advisory opinion from the ICJ, but such opinions are not binding. ITLOS jurisdiction is compulsory with respect to cases involving the seizing of vessels, and signatory states have also declared themselves bound to compulsory adjudication of such cases, which means they can in theory later declare themselves unbound. Private access and compulsory jurisdiction does, however, exist with respect to the Seabed Chamber.

20 Hobbles strap together the legs of a horse or other large animal to keep them from straying. A hobbled horse cannot run, and even walking becomes difficult and awkward.

FIGURE 3.2: Trend toward ICs with new-style design features

	Optional Provisions	Compulsory Jurisdiction
State initiation rights only (N = 4)	International Court of Justice (binding rulings) International Tribunal for the Law of the Sea (ITLOS) →	Economic Court of the Commonwealth of Independent States World Trade Organization *ITLOS seizing of vessels cases*
Supranational Commission or Prosecutor initiation rights (Total ICs with supranational actor initiation rights = 13 + ICJ advisory opinions)	*ICJ advisory opinions (opinions not binding)* African Court on Human and Peoples' Rights (ACtHPR) → Inter-American Court of Human Rights (IACtHR) → International Criminal Court (ICC) →	International Criminal Tribunal for Former Yugoslavia International Criminal Tribunal for Rwanda Common Market of Eastern and Southern Africa Court of Justice *(requires Council assent for case to proceed)* *ACtHPR—26 of 54 member countries accept compulsory jurisdiction* *IACtHR—22 of 35 member countries accept charter and compulsory jurisdiction* *ICC jurisdiction compulsory for 120 signatory states and when Security Council refers case*
Supranational actor *and* private initiation rights D = Direct PR = via national courts (preliminary ruling references)		Andean Tribunal of Justice (D + PR) Central African Economic and Monetary Union (D + PR) East African Community Court of Justice (D + PR) Economic Community of West African States Court of Justice (D + PR) European Union Court of Justice (D + PR) European Free Trade Area Court (PR *advisory only*) West African Economic and Monetary Union Court of Justice (PR)
Private litigant initiation rights (Total ICs with private initiation rights = 16)		BENELUX Court (PR) Caribbean Court of Justice (D) Central American Court of Justice (D) Common Market of Eastern and Southern Africa (PR) European Court of Human Rights (D) Organization for the Harmonization of Business Law in Africa (D) ITLOS Seabed Chamber (D) Southern African Development Community (D + PR)* Southern Common Market (PR *advisory only*)

*Direct access is likely to be removed. PR access will likely remain.

limitations on access, jurisdiction, and the checks required before a case proceeds to court. For example, the Andean Tribunal copied most of the design features of the European Court of Justice, except its designers refused to allow the General Secretariat to consider private litigant noncompliance complaints. When governments wanted to increase the effectiveness of the Andean legal system, they authorized private actors to complain to the Secretariat, and to bring noncompliance suits to the ATJ directly.[21] Figure 3.3 identifies the significant changes in the design of six existing international legal systems over time. These changes are all in the direction of enhancing the new-style design features of ICs.

All of the design changes indicated above were agreed to by governments. The reasons for these changes will be explained in chapter 4. There are also important changes created by participants in the system. For example, the ECJ declared the direct effect of community law in 1962, creating legal standing for private litigants to invoke the ECJ in front of national courts. In the 1980s the European Commission on Human Rights decided on its own to refer more cases to the ECtHR, a move followed by the Inter-American Commission in 2001. The IACtHR and the ECOWAS court have also decided to allow nongovernmental actors to have legal standing before the court, and the WTO appellate bodies has allowed nongovernmental actors to file amicus briefs.

Together with figure 3.2, figure 3.3 suggests a tendency to augment rather than scale back the jurisdiction and design of ICs over time. The increased willingness to accept compulsory oversight and private initiation of litigation is also present with respect to nonpermanent adjudicatory bodies. We can thus see a general trend toward governments choosing IC designs that will increase the likelihood of international litigation. Indeed, the only example of a scaling back of an IC's subject-matter jurisdiction or design is a recent decision to remove private litigant access to the court of the Southern African Development Community. This decision came in response to rulings supporting the land rights of white farmers.[22]

II. SUBJECT MATTER, REGIONAL AND COUNTRY VARIATION IN DELEGATION TO ICS

Delegation to ICs generally clusters around three issues—economic issues (for example, trade, foreign investment regulation, contract disputes, intellectual property rights, business law), human rights, and mass atrocities

21 (Alter, Helfer, and Saldias 2012, 727–32).

22 At the time of writing, the details of the August 2012 revisions are not clear. For a discussion of the controversy giving rise to this action, see Ebobrah (2011); de Wet (2013).

FIGURE 3.3: ICs with significant design changes over time

Court	System First Established	Year of Reform	Most Significant Design Changes
European Union Court of Justice (ECJ)	1952	1988, 1993, 1994, 2004, 2009	A new Tribunal of First Instance, created in 1988, added judicial capacity. In 1993 member states added a system for financial sanctions for noncompliance with ECJ rulings. Member states extended the Court's subject matter jurisdiction in 1993, 1994, 2004, and 2009. The 2009 extension included a formal endorsement of the ECJ's assertion of jurisdiction to assess the validity of European law vis-à-vis the European Convention on Human Rights and national constitutional provisions. In 2009 the Tribunal of First Instance was renamed the General Court and the ECJ the Court of Justice of the European Union.
World Trade Organization (WTO)	GATT 1948	1994	Reforms passed as part of the single undertaking to create the WTO made the formation of dispute settlement panels automatic and states could no longer veto the adoption of a panel report. In other words, the WTO system has compulsory jurisdiction where the GATT system did not. The WTO also added a permanent appellate body, which has arguably contributed to legalizing dispute adjudication.
Andean Tribunal of Justice (ATJ)	1984	1996	Private actors gained the right to complain about state noncompliance to the Andean General Secretariat, and to raise a suit directly in front of the ATJ.
European Court of Human Rights (ECtHR)	1958	1998	ECtHR's jurisdiction became compulsory for all Council of Europe members. Private actors gained direct access to the Court.
Southern Common Market (MERCOSUR)	1991	2002	Reforms of the Asunción system allow states to appeal decisions of the Common Market Council to a Permanent Review Court. National supreme courts were later authorized to refer cases to the Permanent Review Court, so now private actors cases may reach the MERCOSUR Permanent Review Court although its decisions in these cases are advisory rather than binding.
Economic Community of West African States Court of Justice (ECOWAS CJ)	2001	2005	The ECOWAS court gained a human rights jurisdiction, private litigants gained direct access to pursue human rights violations, and national courts were authorized to send preliminary ruling questions to the Community Court.
Southern African Development Community (SADC)	2005	2012	Unclear at the time of writing what changes occurred, but member states clearly intend to limit private access to challenge national policies, except for where subsidiary protocols explicitly authorize such access.

crimes. There is significant regional variation in the willingness to submit to compulsory international judicial authority. For figure 3.4 and what follows, I am primarily interested in jurisdiction to review state policies, thus the enforcement role. A court can be listed more than once if its subject-matter jurisdiction extends beyond a single category. I indicate a second listing by using the acronym only. General jurisdiction refers to the right of the court to hear pretty much any interstate dispute involving member states.[23] Within each cell, the information is presented in the order the court was created, revealing that Europe's ICs are the oldest, followed by Latin American courts and the much newer African courts. Asia, the Middle East, and Oceana do not appear because these regions lack regional ICs.[24] Europe and Africa have ICs with economic, human rights, and criminal jurisdictions. The Americas lack regional criminal tribunals, but all countries accepting the IACtHR's compulsory jurisdiction are signatories of the Rome Statute.[25]

The number of ICs is at best a crude indicator of international legalization trends. The standard definition of legalization considers the extent and precision of binding legal rules, and it considers functional equivalents of ICs that monitor compliance and interpret legal agreements.[26] The different human rights and criminal courts apply similar bodies of law, thus the extent to which countries submit to the jurisdiction of these courts is a reasonable indicator of legalization. But many African and Latin American common market systems lack detailed secondary legislation, so while the formal power of ICs may appear extensive the amount of binding and enforceable law may be still be minimal. Scholars are coming up with ways to assess the extent and precision of rules associated with regional governance structures, and to thus better capture varied legalization trends across regional integration systems.[27]

IC Design Templates

We might consider it plagiarism or a violation of intellectual property if individuals assiduously copied the ideas of others, but in the legal realm the name for the phenomenon is "legal transplants." As lawyers well

23 Regional ICs' general jurisdiction usually applies to agreements within the larger regional institution, although some regional ICs can hear any dispute among member states, and many Court Treaties allow states to adopt additional provisions that extend the IC's jurisdiction for specific agreements.

24 The Arab Investment Court, discussed in the online appendix and identified in figure 3.9, is a recently discovered exception to this statement.

25 Guatemala, the last holdout, became a signatory state in April 2012.

26 (Abbott et al. 2000).

27 See, for example, Hooghe, Marks, and Schakel (2010).

FIGURE 3.4: Regional distribution of ICs (year IC became operational)

	Europe	Latin America	Africa	Panregional
International Economic Courts 16 ICs	European Court of Justice (1952) BENELUX court (1974) Economic Court of the Commonwealth of Independent States (ECCIS) (1993) European Free Trade Area Court (1992)	Andean Tribunal of Justice (ATJ) (1984) Central American Court of Justice (CACJ) (1992) Caribbean Court of Justice (CCJ) (2001) Southern Common Market (MERCOSUR) (2004)	West African Economic and Monetary Union (WAEMU) (1995) Common Court of Justice and Arbitration for the Organization for the Harmonization of Corporate Law in Africa (OHADA) (1997) Court of Justice for the Common Market of Eastern and Southern Africa (COMESA) (1998) Central African Monetary Community (CEMAC) (2000) Court of Justice of the East African Community (EACJ) (2001) Economic Community of West African States Court of Justice (ECOWAS CJ) (2002) Southern African Development Community (SADC) (2005)	World Trade Organization Appellate Body (1994)
International Human Rights Courts 5 ICs[1]	European Court of Human Rights (1958)	Inter-American Court of Human Rights (1979) CCJ[2]	African Court on Human and Peoples' Rights (ACtHPR) (2006) ECOWAS CJ (2005) [The EACJ envisions adding a human rights jurisdiction]	

International Criminal Tribunals 3 ICs	International Criminal Tribunal for Former Yugoslavia (ICTY) (1993)		International Criminal Tribunal for Rwanda (ICTR) (1994) [Special Court for Sierra Leone is a hybrid international criminal tribunal]	International Criminal Court (2002)
General Jurisdiction 8 ICs	BCJ	CACJ CCJ	WAEMU, CEMAC, EACJ, SADC	International Court of Justice (ICJ) (1945)
Specialized Jurisdiction 1 IC				International Tribunal for the Law of the Sea (ITLOS) (1996)
Total courts by region N = 24	6	5	9	4 Panregional ICs

[1] I do not list the ECJ as a human rights court, since its human rights jurisdiction extends only to the review of European legislation.

[2] CCJ's de facto human rights jurisdiction applies to countries that allow the CCJ to replace the Privy Council as the highest court of appeals.

know, there are tremendous similarities in national constitutions and bodies of law, and in fact most national legal systems are based on European models, known as "legal families."[28] It should thus come as no surprise that the multiplication of ICs involves copying preexisting models. What is perhaps surprising, however, is the extent to which international courts follow European models, because Europe's ICs are known for being activist and sovereignty compromising.

International economic courts tend to follow one of two basic models. The GATT/WTO model has compulsory jurisdiction, and only states can initiate noncompliance suits. This design ensures that only the disputes governments care about are adjudicated. Regional systems that adopt the WTO model often also adopt its panel system of dispute settlement, which allows governments to first try consultation followed by a more arbitration style of dispute adjudication before any appeal to a more legalized appellate body.[29] The other basic template is the ECJ model, which has a supranational commission that monitors state compliance and brings noncompliance cases to the supranational court; a preliminary ruling mechanism that allows private litigants to raise cases in national courts, which can then be referred to the supranational court; and systems of administrative and constitutional review that allow states, community institutions, and private litigants to challenge community acts in front of the supranational court.[30] Figure 3.5 identifies the basic design similarities of economic ICs, dividing according to the two basic models. What I am calling the basic model is listed first and shaded. Chapters 6 and 8 further discuss the borrowing of the European model for designing administrative and constitutional review mechanisms for ICs. Elsewhere I explore meaningful variations in these basic designs.[31]

Figure 3.6 highlights the basic design templates of human rights and international criminal tribunals. ICs with human rights jurisdictions follow one of two models, both of which are associated with the European Court of Human Rights (ECtHR). The original ECtHR model relied on states to consent to the Court's compulsory jurisdiction. States could consent for short periods of time and withdraw their consent if they were unhappy with Court rulings. The original ECtHR also had a supranational commission that vetted human rights complaints and served as a gatekeeper to the Court. This is the model copied by the African Court on

28 (Berkowitz, Pistor, and Richard 2003; Ginsburg 2012; Watson 1993).

29 Disputes start as consultations among states, proceeding to the ad hoc panel stage where litigants can help choose the adjudicators. Panel rulings are generally binding, and matters of law can be appealed to a permanent appellate body.

30 States can also bring disputes against other states, although they seldom do, preferring to let supranational Commissions pursue violations instead.

31 See Alter (2012a); Alter et al. (2014).

Human and Peoples' Rights (ACtHPR), and it has contributed to the dearth of cases reaching that court. It is also the model copied by the Inter-American Court of Human Rights, but the Inter-American Court has made it hard(er) for states to withdraw consent once given, and the Inter-American Commission has been increasingly willing to refer cases to the Inter-American Court.[32] The post–Protocol 11 ECtHR has compulsory jurisdiction and direct private access. This is the model copied by the ECOWAS Community Court. Figures 3.12 and 3.14 will offer an evolutionary perspective on human rights litigation where design differences contribute to different amounts of litigation.

International criminal tribunals (ICTs) build on the basic design of the Nuremberg trials. Criminal tribunals have compulsory jurisdiction, and an international prosecutor selects which cases to pursue. Modern international criminal tribunals improve on the Nuremberg model in that all parties to the conflict can be prosecuted, the international prosecutorial office and tribunals includes a broader representation of states, and there is an appeals mechanism.

The fact that many newer ICs are based on general templates provides a partial explanation of the trend toward new-style ICs. Economic ICs and human rights ICs tend to have at least some new-style features. ECJ emulators and human rights courts copying the current design of the ECtHR are all new-style ICs. All criminal tribunals are new-style ICs. The prevalence of IC design copying also suggests that emulation is a factor in the proliferation of ICs.

Country Level Variation and Overlapping IC Membership

This section maps regional judicial complexes. A "regime complex" refers to the set of overlapping nonhierarchal institutions governing an issue or geographic area. The leaders of international organizations try to avoid conflicts across regimes by taking into account state obligations in parallel institutions and by trying to close off forum shopping opportunities for litigants. But the existence of parallel institutions nonetheless shapes politics within any individual regime because of differences in international organization membership and the desire of some governments to create legal openings that might protect cherished policies.[33] Figures 3.7–

32 A meaningful difference for the IACtHR is that the Inter-American Commission has always allowed private litigants complaints, whereas states in Europe and Africa must opt in to before the commissions can investigate private litigant complaints. Also, the IACtHR has through its jurisprudence created some limits on the right of states to withdraw from its jurisdiction.

33 For more on regime complexes and the politics they generate, see Alter and Meunier (2009); Keohane and Victor (2011); Raustiala and Victor (2004).

FIGURE 3.5: Economic ICs following the WTO and ECJ models (year IC created, organized chronologically)

International Court	Interstate dispute settlement	Supranational Commission can raise noncompliance suits	Preliminary ruling system of national court referrals	Explicit administrative review jurisdiction	Explicit constitutional review jurisdiction
WTO Model					
World Trade Organization (WTO) (1994)	X				
Economic Court of the Commonwealth of Independent States (ECCIS) (1993)	X				
Southern Common Market (MERCOSUR) (2004)	X		X		
ECJ Model					
European Court of Justice (ECJ) (1952)	X	X	X	X	X
BENELUX court (BCJ) (1974)	X		X	X	Consultative jurisdiction
Andean Tribunal of Justice (ATJ) (1984)	X	X	X	X	X
Central American Court of Justice (CACJ) (1992)	X		X	X	X
European Free Trade Area Court (EFTAC) (1994)	X	X	Advisory opinions only	X	

West African Economic and Monetary Union (WAEMU) (1995)	X	X	X	X	X
Organization for the Harmonization of Business Law (OHADA) (1997)	Advisory opinions		X (Plus appellate jurisdiction for national rulings)		Consultative jurisdiction
Common Market for East African States (COMESA) (1998)	X	X	X	X	X
Central African Monetary Community (CEMAC)(1999)	X	X	X	X	X
East African Community Court (EACJ) (2001)	X	X	X	X	X
Caribbean Court of Justice (CCJ) (2004)	X	Currently under discussion	X	X	X
Economic Community of West African States Court of Justice (ECOWAS CJ) (2002)	X	X		X	X
Southern African Development Community* (SADC) (2007)	X	X	X	X	X
Total ICs with this feature	16	9	12	12	10

* SADC private access provisions revised in 2012. Changes are not reflected in this table.

FIGURE 3.6: Design templates of human rights and criminal tribunals (year IC operational)

International Court	Compulsory or optional jurisdiction	International actor initiate litigation	Private litigant initiate litigation
Human rights courts templates (ECtHR model)			
European Court of Human Rights (1958)	Optional (1958–97) Compulsory (1998)	Commission (1958–97)	X (1998)
Inter-American Court of Human Rights (1979)	Optional	Commission	
Caribbean Court of Justice (2004)	Optional		Appellate review for certain countries
Economic Community of West African States Court of Justice (2005 for human rights jurisdiction)	Compulsory		X (2005)
African Court on Human and Peoples' Rights (2006)	Optional	Commission	
Criminal tribunal templates (building on Nuremberg model)			
International Criminal Tribunal for the Former Yugoslavia (1993)		Prosecutor	
International Criminal Tribunal for Rwanda (1994)		Prosecutor	
International Criminal Court (2002)	Optional (except for Security Council references)	Prosecutor	

3.10 map regional judicial complexes, helping to understand how IC jurisdictions complement each other and allowing us to envision how regional dynamics may affect the creation, use, and influence of individual ICs. Unless indicated, the courts listed have compulsory jurisdiction for the set of rules they oversee, thus we can view these tables as identifying which countries fall under which court's compulsory jurisdiction. Next to each complex is a list of countries in the region that do not fall under the jurisdiction of regional ICs. The list further specifies regional trends.

Figure 3.7 and 3.8 capture delegation trends in Europe and the Americas, showing that membership overlap mainly reflects subregional

FIGURE 3.7: Europe's overlapping international courts (2012)

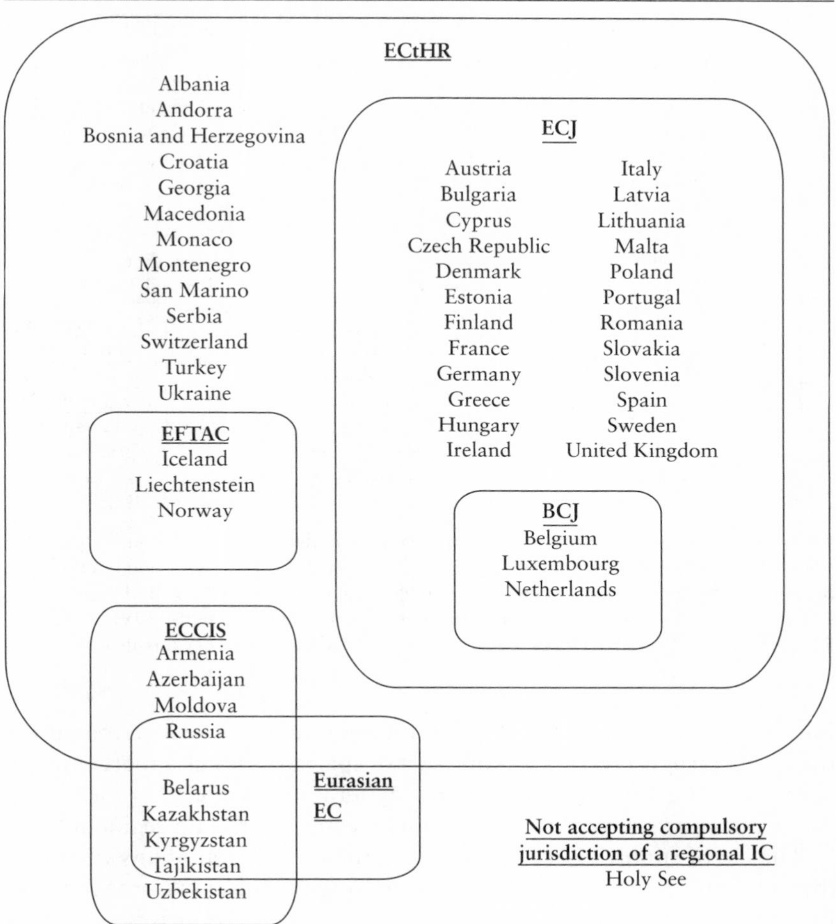

specialization. There is membership and some jurisdictional overlap in the human rights jurisdictions of the ECJ and the ECtHR, although the jurisdictional overlap is limited because the ECJ will only be reviewing the compatibility of European Union law with European human rights law. For the other European ICs, each court has a singular substantive jurisdiction. The BENELUX court deals with regional law that is not EU law; the European Free Trade Area Court (EFTAC) oversees the enforcement of regional trade rules in countries that are not members of the EU; and the ECCIS handles disputes involving agreements concerning members of the Commonwealth of Independent States. (Included is the brand new

FIGURE 3.8: American and Caribbean overlapping international courts (2012)

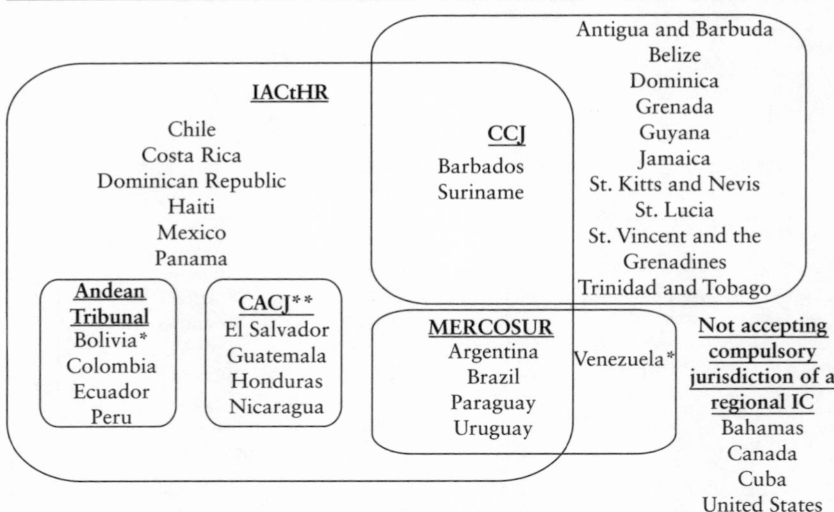

*Venezuela was subject to the Andean Tribunal's compulsory jurisdiction until Hugo Chavez left the Andean Community in 2006. Venezuela and Bolivia will soon fall under the compulsory jurisdiction of the MERCOSUR Permanent Review Body and Chavez withdrew from the Inter-American human rights system (effective August 2013). **Costa Rica, Belize and Panama have not consented to the CACJ's compulsory jurisdiction.

Eurasian court. Not pictured is the International Criminal Tribunal for the Former Yugoslavia.) The same sort of specialization is apparent in the Americas. The IACtHR is a human rights body, while the other Latin American courts have their own unique memberships and regional laws.

The list of countries not falling under the jurisdiction of any IC shows that in Europe, membership in regional organizations is broad. Every European country except the Holy See falls under the jurisdiction of at least one IC with compulsory jurisdiction; most European countries fall under the compulsory authority of more than one IC because there are separate economic and human rights systems. By contrast, for the Americas, delegation to regional ICs generally stops at the US border.

We can also see that all European countries, except the Holy See, fall under the jurisdiction of the ECtHR, and most Latin American countries fall under the jurisdiction of the IACtHR. This fact may explain why the economic courts in these regions are not very involved in human rights adjudication.[34] Figure 3.8 notes that many Caribbean island states have

34 The ECJ created for itself a jurisdiction to review human rights complaints regarding European Union rules, and this jurisdiction was later codified in a treaty reform. Notwithstanding the ECJ's well-known penchant for interpreting its own authority broadly, the ECJ

FIGURE 3.9: Asia and the Middle East's negotiated international courts

ASEAN
Brunei
Cambodia
Indonesia
Laos
Malaysia
Myanmar
Philippines
Singapore
Thailand
Vietnam

OAPEC*
Algeria

Arab Investment Court**
Bahrain
Egypt
Iraq
Kuwait
Libya
Qatar
Saudi Arabia
Syria
United Arab Emirates
Djibouti
Jordan
Lebanon
Mauritania
Oman
Palestine
Somalia
Sudan Tunisia
Yemen

Not accepting compulsory jurisdiction of a regional IC

Asia and Pacific
Australia
Afghanistan
Bangladesh
Bhutan
China
India
Japan
South Korea
North Korea
Maldives
Mongolia
Nepal
New Zealand
Pakistan
Palau
Sri Lanka
Timor-Leste
Many island states

Middle East
Iran
Israel
Comoros

*Note: The Arab League includes countries from both the Middle East and Africa. The Organization of Arab Petroleum Exporting Countries, which is mostly defunct, has compulsory jurisdiction, but it allows states to exclude cases involving sensitive issues.
**The statute for the Arab Investment Court came into force in 1988, but only in 2003 did the Arab League decide to activate the body. Comoros and Algeria had not yet signed on. The Investment Court has adjudicated a few investment disputes, and has regularly appointed judges. See the book's online appendix for more.

opted out of the Inter-American Court of Human Rights system. These countries generally rely on regional courts to conduct human rights review, either the Caribbean Court of Justice (noted in figure 3.8) or the East Caribbean Supreme Court, which serves as an appellate body for nine Caribbean island states.[35] Also not indicated is that Costa Rica, Belize, and Panama are part of the Central American Integration System, but they have opted out of the Central American Court of Justice's (CACJ) compulsory jurisdiction.

Figure 3.9 examines the countries falling under the jurisdiction of regional ICs in Asia, the Middle East, and Pacifica. This figure is mainly

has limited its human rights review of national actions, a legal domain that is covered by the ECtHR (De Burca 2011). In Latin America, with the exception of the CCJ, most regional economic courts also do not hear human rights cases. The CCJ has heard a number of death penalty cases in part because some countries have chosen to designate the CCJ as a replacement for the Privy Council. It is also true that Trinidad and Tobago withdrew from the Inter-American system because of unhappiness with the IACtHR's death penalty rulings (Helfer 2002). The CCJ may thus be more willing to move into a human rights domain compared to the other regional courts in Latin America, providing a human rights review tailored for the customs of the states falling under its jurisdiction.

35 The East Caribbean Supreme Court is the appellate review body for Anguilla, Antigua and Barbuda, Commonwealth of Dominica, Grenada, Montserrat, Saint Kitts and Nevis, Saint Vincent and the Grenadines, Saint Lucia, and Territory of the Virgin Islands. See the book's online appendix for more.

interesting in comparison to the other regional charts. I included the non-functioning dispute settlement systems of ASEAN and the Organization of Arab Petroleum Exporting Countries (OAPEC), and the Arab Investment Court which has adjudicated a handful of cases (all of these bodies are described further in chapter 4 and in the book's online appendix). The formal commitment to these bodies is at this point rather thin, and in conjunction with the list of countries not falling under the jurisdiction of any regional IC this figure is testament to the lack of judicialization in Asia, the Middle East, and Pacifica. Perhaps the dearth of near neighbors submitting to robust regional or global judicial oversight dissipates pressure on any one country to submit to international judicial oversight.

The international judicial complex in Africa is by comparison quite different. Figure 3.10 includes eight African ICs in this study (the International Criminal Tribunal for Rwanda is not listed) and the African Maghreb community (Arab Maghreb Union), which is not yet operational. As in Europe, nearly every African country is part of at least one regional judicial system. But African countries are also more likely to be part of multiple regional legal systems.[36]

Many of these African ICs are fairly new and as of yet of marginal political import. It can be hard to separate the wheat from the chaff. But considering these overlaps in memberships and jurisdictions allows for some speculative observations. The first observation concerns the African Court on Human and Peoples' Rights. Unlike the European and Inter-American human rights systems, the majority of African countries have not accepted this Court's jurisdiction, which likely contributes to the reluctance of the African Commission to refer polemical cases to the Court. The political limitations of the African Union's human rights system have arguably facilitated the expansion of African regional courts into human rights issues. Most of Africa's regional systems work to address problems related to poverty, poor governance, and development. As figure 3.3 indicates, the ECOWAS court gained a human rights jurisdiction in 2005, in large part because human rights advocates were frustrated by the limitations of the African Union system.[37] The East African Court of Justice (EACJ) has a provision that allows member states to add a human rights jurisdiction to the Court.[38] And in fact most litigation in the EACJ, SADC, and ECOWAS systems has focused not on economic claims but rather on good governance and what can be classified as human rights-related claims.

36 (Gathii 2011, 65–75).

37 (Alter, Helfer, and McAllister 2013).

38 Article 27 (2) of the Treaty for the Establishment of the East African Community (chapter 8) available in Ebobrah and Tanoh (2010, 43).

FIGURE 3.10: Africa's overlapping international courts (2012)

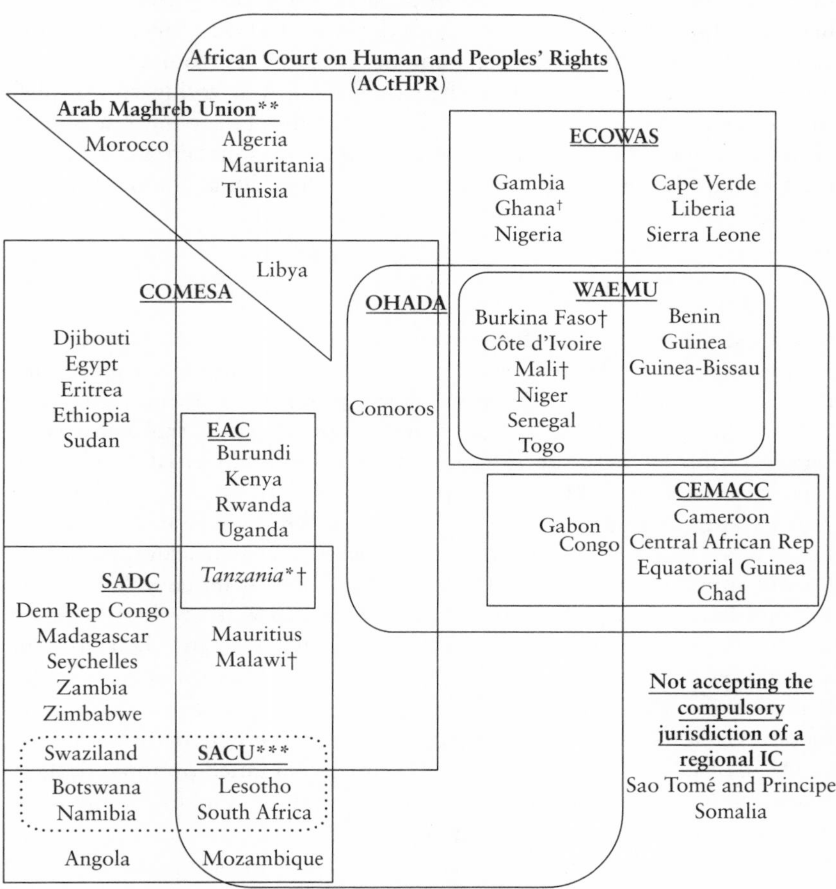

*Note: Tanzania is a member of ACtHPR, EACJ, and SADC but not COMESA
**Court not yet in operation. See the book's online appendix for more on the African Maghreb court.
***Southern African Custom's Union (SACU) lacks a court, but it sets the customs rules and rates for trade between its members
†Countries also accepting right for the ACtHPR to receive cases raised by private actors. Rwanda and Ivory Coast joined this list in 2013.

From what I can tell, the Arab Maghreb Union and the Common Market of Eastern and Southern Africa (COMESA) systems do not yet function as politically meaningful entities. The overlap in membership is part of the problem. South Africa has a customs union with its key trading partners in SADC, and other SADC members are in COMESA. This overlap saps commitment to SADC.

Given that Africa's ICs are very new, it is hard to know what they will become. Figures 3.14 and 3.15 will present evolutionary charts that can help us think about how building legal authority takes time. When one controls for years in existence, some of Africa's very young ICs appear more similar to Europe's ICs when they were first trying to establish themselves. In any event, we should be careful about drawing assessments about very new African ICs, or dismissing these regional entities based on the fact that they are located within fairly dysfunctional common market regimes.[39]

Global ICs

Of course the larger international judicial complex also includes ICs with a global reach, of which there are four. Figure 3.11 considers which countries have consented to the compulsory authority of the International Court of Justice (ICJ), the dispute adjudication system of the World Trade Organization (WTO), the International Criminal Court (ICC), and the International Tribunal for the Law of the Sea (ITLOS).[40] The ICC's compulsory authority applies to all signatories of the Rome Statute, 121 as of December 2012.[41] The WTO dispute settlement system's compulsory authority applies to all members of the WTO, 153 as of January 2012.[42] The ICJ and ITLOS courts have optional declarations whereby states can assent to the court's compulsory authority, later withdraw their consent, and file reservations that limit the court's jurisdiction for specific issues. Signatories to the optional declarations accept the IC's compulsory jurisdiction vis-à-vis one another, except for issues where formal reservations exist. As of January 2012, sixty-nine countries had filed optional declarations accepting the ICJ's reciprocal compulsory jurisdiction.[43] Far fewer have accepted the compulsory authority of the ITLOS court (thirty-three states), which may only mean that member states would prefer to let the

39 (Gathii 2010).

40 This figure includes 186 countries, whereas the UN lists 193 countries. Excluded are a number of island states, the Holy See, and states that are so new they have not had time to join ICs.

41 http://www.icc-cpi.int/en_menus/asp/states%20parties/Pages/the%20states%20parties%20to%20the%20rome%20statute.aspx, last visited December 20, 2012. This includes thirty-three African states, eighteen Asian-Pacific states, eighteen East European states, twenty-seven Latin American and Caribbean states, and twenty-five West European and other states.

42 http://www.wto.org/english/thewto_e/whatis_e/tif_e/org6_e.htm, last visited January 24, 2011.

43 See http://www.icj-cij.org/jurisdiction/index.php?p1=5&p2=1&p3=3, last visited December 18, 2012.

FIGURE 3.11: Countries consenting to compulsory jurisdiction of ICs with a global reach* (2012)

ICJ, WTO, ICC & ITLOS	3 ICs with global reach (usually WTO, ICC, and ICJ)	2 ICs with global reach (Usually ICC & WTO)	1 IC with global reach	None
Australia Austria Belgium **Canada** Estonia Finland Germany Greece Hungary Lithuania Portugal Switzerland Madagascar Mexico Uruguay Bulgaria	Argentina Barbados Belgium **Bangladesh** Botswana **Cambodia** Cape Verde Chile Costa Rica Côte d'Ivoire Croatia Cyprus Democratic Rep. of Congo Denmark Djibouti Dominica Dominican Rep. of Congo Ecuador Gambia Fiji Georgia Guinea Honduras Italy Ireland Japan Kenya Latvia Lesotho Liechtenstein Luxembourg Malawi Malta Mauritius Montenegro Netherlands Nigeria **New Zealand** Norway Panama Paraguay Peru Philippines Poland Senegal Slovenia Slovakia St. Vincent & Grenadines Suriname Spain Sweden Tanzania **Timor Leste** Trinidad & Tobago Tunisia Uganda United Kingdom	Albania Angola Antigua and Barbuda Belize Benin Bolivia Brazil Burkina Faso Burundi Cameroon Central African Republic Chad Chile Colombia Congo (Republic) Czech Republic Egypt France Gabon Ghana Grenada Guatemala Guinea-Bissau Guyana Haiti Iceland **India** **Jordan** Liberia Macedonia **Maldives** Mali Mongolia Moldova Montenegro Namibia Nicaragua Niger **Oman** **Pakistan** Romania Samoa Senegal Sierra Leone Slovenia South Africa **South Korea** St. Kitts &Nevis St. Lucia Swaziland Tajikistan Tanzania Togo Vanuatu Venezuela Zambia	***ICC only*** **Afghanistan** Andorra Bosnia and Herzegovina Comoros Cook Islands Macedonia Marshall Islands Republic of the Congo Naurau San Marino Serbia Seychelles Tajikistan ***WTO Only*** Armenia **Bahrain** **Brunei** **China** **Cuba** El Salvador **Indonesia** **Israel** Jamaica **Kuwait** Kyrgyzstan **Laos (2013)** **Macao** **Malaysia** Mauritania **Moracco** Mozambique Myanmar **Nepal** Papua New Guinea **Qatar** **Russia (2013)** Rwanda Samoa **Saudi Arabia** **Singapore** **Sri Lanka** **Solomon Islands** **Taiwan** **Thailand** Turkey Ukraine **United Arab Emirates** **United States** **Vietnam** Zimbawe ***ICJ only*** Sudan	Algeria Azerbaijan **Bahamas** Belarus **Bhutan** Equatorial Guinea Eritrea Ethiopia Holy See Monaco **Iran** **Iraq** **Kirabati** Kosovo **Laos** **Lebanon** Libya **Micronesia** **Monaco** **North Korea** **Sao Tomé & Principe** Somalia **Syria** Turkmenistan Uzbekistan **Yemen**

*Bold indicates that country has not consented to an operational regional IC with compulsory jurisdiction. ICs listed in Figure 3.9 are not considered operational. For the ICJ, only the sixty-nine countries signing optional protocol are included. For ITLOS, only the 33 countries signing the optional protocol are included. Not listed are a number of island states and very new countries.

ICJ deal with disagreements regarding the ITLOS convention and its subsidiary agreements.[44]

Mapping the global judicial complex is difficult. Instead I note the number of global ICs where the state has assented to its compulsory international judicial authority. In bold are the countries that also do not fall under the compulsory authority of regional courts, thus their categorization on this table represents their sole commitment (or lack thereof) to compulsory international judicial oversight. We can see that although Canada does not participate in regional ICs, it remains willing to accept the compulsory oversight of all of the main global judicial bodies, suggesting that its exclusion from regional courts does not indicate a general aversion to ICs. We can also see that the WTO has attracted membership from a number of countries that are otherwise not part of regional or global legal systems. These countries were perhaps enticed by the most-favored-nation trade rules of the WTO system, committing to legal oversight primarily because doing so was part of the cost of admission to the WTO system. Less apparent is the reality that a number of countries located in Africa and Europe fall under the jurisdiction of the most ICs (five or six).

Figure 3.11 reinforces the sense that island states, the Middle East, and Asia stand apart from broader trends in international legalization. For the Middle East the lack of ICs may be less surprising given the many authoritarian political systems in the region. The geographic isolation of many small island states combines with the expense and challenge of providing funds and staff to help explain their outlier status. Asia is a different sort of outlier. Scholars have long talked about Asian exceptionalism, an idea put forth by Asian leaders themselves as they contrast their so-called communitarian and cooperative approach to resolving disagreements.[45] Erik Voeten implicitly raises the question of whether this Asian exceptionalism is changing. Asian economies are very integrated into the world economy, and most Asian countries are part of the WTO system. Analyzing usage of the WTO system, Voeten finds that Asian countries do not stand out as avoiding the WTO dispute resolution system, or as avoiding international mechanisms designed to deal with territorial disputes. Looking at comparative data regarding Bilateral Investment Treaties, Voeten also found that Asian countries are not more reluctant to agree to compulsory arbitration clauses compared to other countries.[46] Asian countries are increasingly embracing compulsory international arbitration, and a number of Asian countries are promoting the rule of law at home and respect for their contracts abroad.

44 Countries can file Article 287 declarations indicating which designated dispute settlement body. States can also submit reservations to ITLOS jurisdiction via Article 298 statements.

45 (Kahler 2000).

46 (Voeten 2010).

FIGURE 3.12: ECJ (including its General Court) and ECtHR binding rulings in contentious cases (founding–2011)

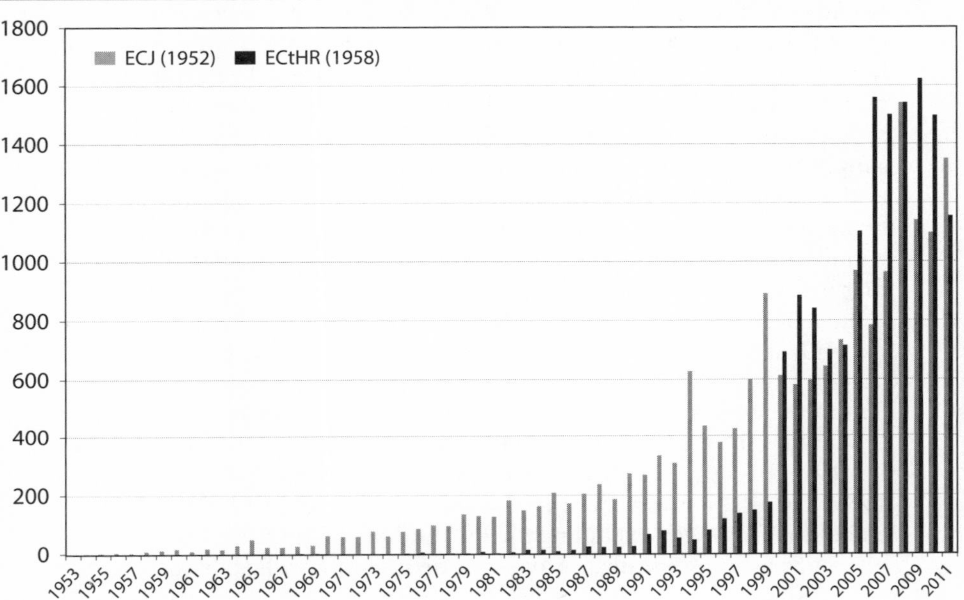

III. LITIGATION IN ICS OVER TIME: EUROPEAN EXCEPTIONALISM AND INCREASING INTERNATIONAL LITIGATION

Two of Europe's ICs stand out as being exceptionally active: the European Court of Justice (ECJ) and the European Court of Human Rights (ECtHR). While legal activity does not necessarily mean that ICs are politically influential, perusal of European newspapers, law faculties, and legal scholarship shows that these two courts are very legally and politically relevant in European politics today. Indeed, the extent of activity and influence of these two ICs can make all other ICs pale in comparison.

Figure 3.12 shows litigation rates in Europe's main supranational adjudicatory bodies over time. This figure shows that the ECJ and ECtHR took a very long time to become active. Chapter 4 will explain the rise of litigation following the ECJ's judicial revolution, the increase in secondary legislation in the European Community, and the declining threat that states might withdraw from the Council of Europe. ECtHR litigation rates increase at the end of the Cold War, and especially in 1998 when direct private access to the Court became compulsory for all Council of Europe members.

These two European ICs are exceptionally active. Demographics contribute to the business of Europe's courts. The European Union now has twenty-seven member states with a population that today encompasses more than five hundred million people;[47] the ECtHR is today the final human rights appellate body for forty-seven countries. The extent of secondary legislation in the European Union also surely matters. But without a doubt, the political context of these courts matters. The issue is not simply that Europe has many well-functioning liberal democracies. If this is all it took for ICs to be active and effective, then we should have seen higher litigation rates in Europe from each court's founding. Chapter 4 will discuss how World War II created a conjunctural moment in Europe that has contributed to the success of these two bodies.

Europe is exceptional, but all ICs have seen a growth in activity since the end of the Cold War. Figure 3.13 shows increased post–Cold War usage of the other twenty-one ICs for which I could find reliable data. Before the end of the Cold War, there were four operational permanent ICs besides the ECJ and the ECtHR, plus the ad hoc GATT system; these ICs had collectively issued 214 decisions from their founding through 1989. The first bar includes the judicial activity of existing ICs before the end of the Cold War, excluding the ECJ and the ECtHR. For the purposes of comparison over time, I have included binding rulings issued by the WTO's precursor body, the dispute settlement system of the General Agreement on Tariffs and Trade (GATT). The rest of the chart includes litigation by year. The legend notes the date the court first became operational. The width of the bands suggests the relative level of activity of different ICs. After the ECJ and the ECtHR, the next most active courts are the Andean Tribunal of Justice (ATJ) (2,178 rulings), the Organization for the Harmonization of Business Law in Africa (OHADA) court (569 rulings) and IACtHR (238 rulings), and the WTO legal system (137 GATT-era panel rulings, 161 WTO-era panel rulings; to avoid double counting the 108 appellate body rulings are not included).

It appears from this chart as if the overall litigation rate drops in recent years. International litigation peaked in 2005, and in general litigation rates tend to jump around. The bandwidth for most courts does not decline over time, instead the downward slope is an artifact of a precipitous decline in OHADA litigation due to instability following a peace agreement adopted in the Ivory Coast in 2007, the seat of the OHADA court.[48]

47 European Commission Directorate-General for Employment, Social Affairs and Inclusion, Eurostat, the Statistical Office of the European Union "Demography report" 2010, at http://epp.eurostat.ec.europa.eu/portal/page/portal/population/documents/Tab/report.pdf, last visited April 25, 2013.

48 The OHADA court is based in Ivory Coast, and lawyers must file cases in person, by relying on local law firms. Also, many OHADA cases involve the Ivory Coast. The peace

FIGURE 3.13: Growth in IC binding rulings through 2011 (ECJ & ECtHR excluded)

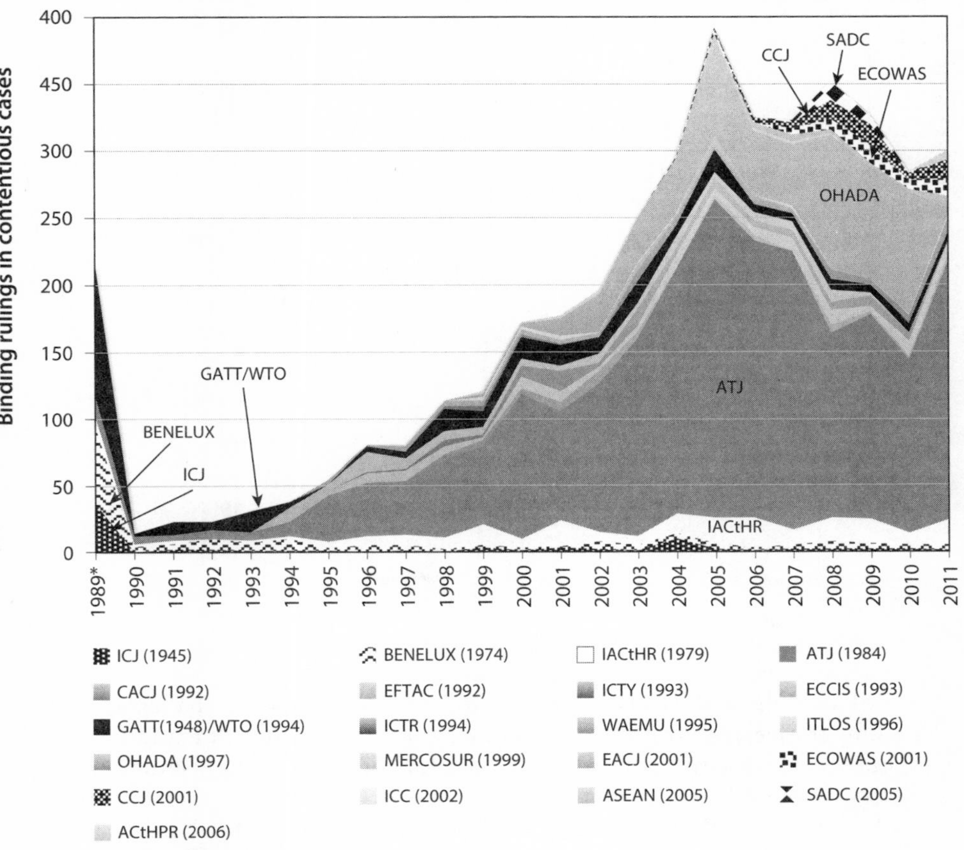

*Rulings from founding through 1989.

The SADC court also experienced a precipitous decline when a Zimbabwean backlash led to a decision not to allow the court to hear new cases or replace its judges.[49] When and if these courts rebound to previous levels, the chart is likely to even out or resume its assent.

agreement of 2007 envisioned elections, which were then postponed and later contested, leading to a civil war. Many normal business transactions came to a halt during this period, and at a certain point the OHADA court closed so as to ensure the safety of staff.

49 In August 2012 member states decided to revise the SADC court. This book discusses the SADC court during the period of study (through 2011), in part because there is no new protocol for the SADC court. But the court remains in abeyance since member states are yet to redefine the court's jurisdiction or replace outgoing judges. For more, see de Wet (2013, 3–4).

FIGURE 3.14: Evolutionary perspective on litigation in human rights courts (year operational/year first ruling)

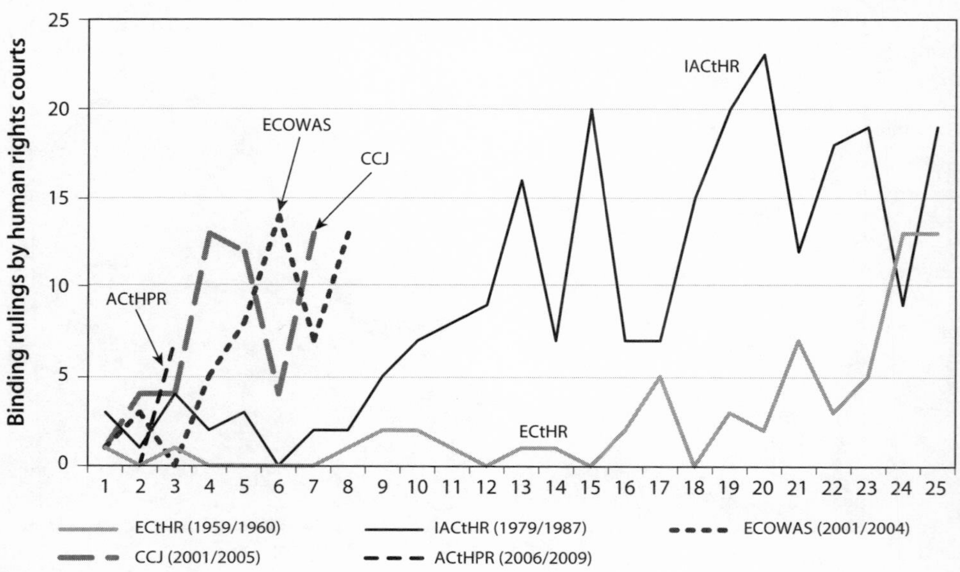

1= first year court issued a ruling.

The high level of litigation in Europe's ICs presents a challenge for comparative analysis of ICs. It becomes hard to know how it matters that Europe has a large population, highly functioning national judiciaries, very mobilized legal communities, extensive legislation that litigants care about, and ICs that have built a reputation for solid legal decision making. Time, however, can provide a clue. Europe's ICs did not always have large membership. Indeed, there was a time when the Council of Europe and the European Community worried that aggressive legalism might deter institutional expansion, which leaders of both systems desired. The figures below crudely capture what might be considered an "evolutionary perspective" on international courts. New international legal systems begin slowly, as awareness of the legal system is low, and potential litigants are uncertain as to whether or not litigation makes strategic sense. Especially during this early period, ICs will proceed with caution because they are unsure of their ability to influence political behavior. The real question is what happens over time? Figures 3.14 and 3.15 control for time by using 1 to denote the year the court issued its first binding ruling (the legend notes the year the court was created and the year it issued its first ruling). I then overlay ICs by years operational. Lines end depending on the age of the IC, and thus the number of years for which there are

FIGURE 3.15: Evolutionary perspective on litigation in economic courts

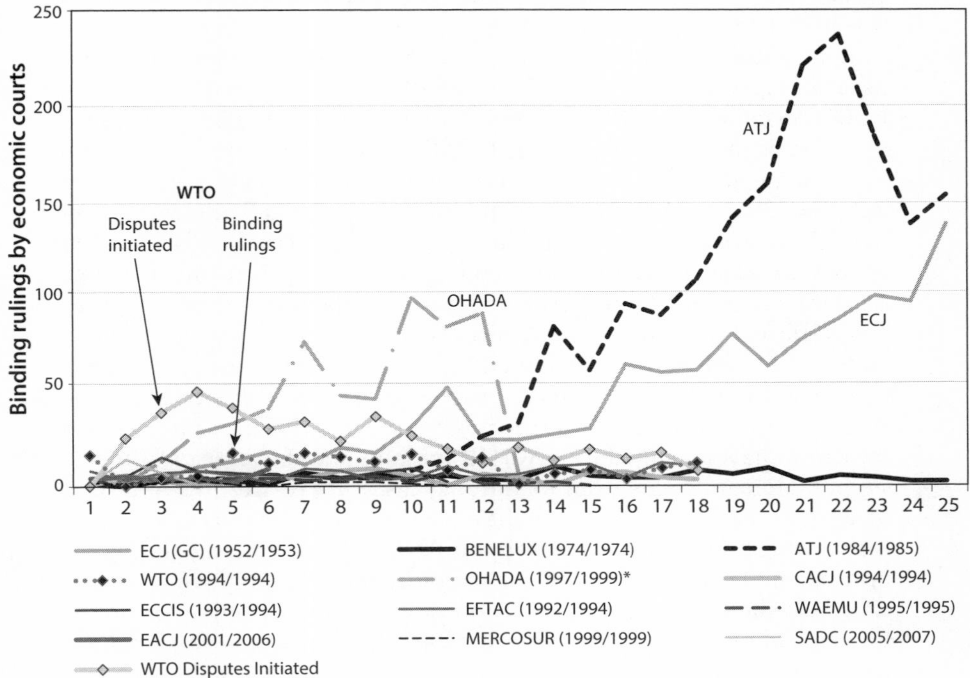

1= first year court issued a ruling. *OHADA data declines due to instability in the court's host country of Cote d'Ivoire.

data. This "evolutionary perspective," which considers that it takes time for ICs to establish their authority, provides a different way to assess litigation rates as a sign of legal demand.

Figure 3.14 focuses on litigation in human rights courts. The figure includes the ECOWAS Community Court of Justice and the Caribbean Court of Justice, since all of the ECOWAS court and much of the CCJ's binding judgments involve human rights issues.

The evolutionary perspective helps us to compare the IACtHR and the ECtHR. If one compares today's IACtHR, with twenty-two members and a commission as a gatekeeper, to the now very established European human rights court with forty-seven members and direct access for litigants, the IACtHR seems like a poor cousin. A more apt comparison is to consider the ECtHR's first thirty years, from 1960 to 1990, a period when the ECtHR also had a commission that served as a gatekeeper to the system and a time during which its membership grew to twenty members. Making this more appropriate comparison, the Inter-American Court is more active than the ECtHR was in the 1960s and 1970s, perhaps because political tolerance for legal oversight in Latin America in the 1990s was higher than it was in Europe in the 1960s.

Returning to the design templates and the maps of international judicial complexes helps to make sense of the situation in Africa. The ECOWAS court, which has compulsory jurisdiction and direct access for private litigants (like the current ECtHR), has been immediately much busier than either the Inter-American or European human rights bodies were initially, both because it operates in the post–Cold War environment and allows private litigants to initiate legal review. The CCJ is also relatively busy as an appellate review body activated by private litigants. The ACtHPR is new, and half of African Union members are yet to accept the Court's jurisdiction. In Europe, concerns about undermining government willingness to be part of the human rights legal regime led the European Commission of Human Rights to proceed with caution, limiting the substance and numbers of cases reaching the ECtHR.[50] This same concern seemed to have hindered the IACtHR initially, and the African Commission on Human Rights from forwarding cases. There are, however, signs of change. The ECOWAS court has been issuing human rights rulings, introducing human rights review to the African continent. And during the uprising in Libya, the African Commission and its Court of Human Rights called on the Libyan government to cease its military action. Since the Libyan and Ivory Coast civil wars, a trickle of cases have been allowed to reach the ACtHPR.[51] This chart captures only twenty-five years of operation, thus it ends before litigation in the ECtHR took off.

For economic courts, by contrast, the evolutionary perspective mainly helps identify large diversity in litigation levels across ICs. Figure 3.15 shows that the ECJ began as a relatively active IC; the lesser known OHADA and Andean courts seem to be following a similar trajectory. Greater activation of these courts has something to do with private access provisions and secondary legislation that affects private litigants. The WTO's caseload starts out strong because of pent-up demand and declines over time (the figure includes as separate lines cases initiated and binding rulings). Meanwhile many ICs remain clustered at the bottom of

50 As I discuss in chapter 4, European governments were concerned that struggles related to decolonization could generate human rights violations. Originally only Sweden, Ireland, Denmark, Iceland, Germany, and Belgium accepted ECtHR's compulsory jurisdiction and only Sweden, Ireland, and Denmark accepted the right of individual petition. Moreover, a number of these acceptances were provisional, made for only a few years at a time. The refusal of France and Britain to consent to the right of individual petition or to the ECtHR's authority diminished the sense that Europe as a whole was seriously committed to a robust regional human rights regime. For more, see Madsen (2010).

51 Starting in 2011, the Commission began to refer more cases to the ACtHPR.

the chart for many years. In some cases, the low level of litigation is not surprising. Compared to the ECJ, the EFTA, BENELUX, MERCOSUR, and EACJ systems have few member states, and less enforceable secondary legislation. In other cases, low levels suggest that something else is hindering courts from building their legal authority and establishing useful rights that litigants want to claim.

The point of these comparisons is not to suggest that all ICs will follow a European trajectory. As chapter 4 will explain, the historical context of the ECJ and the ECtHR clearly contributed to increasing political relevance of these two courts. Rather, my point is to underscore that it takes time for an IC to develop a reputation that encourages litigation. The images raise many interesting questions one could investigate. What counts for rising litigation or declining litigation levels in some systems? Endogenous sources of change—learning about the international judicial system and the development of international jurisprudence, the building of legal fields, and changes in regional legal orders adopted in order to improve the systems' functioning—should contribute to rising litigation levels. Exogenous sources of change may also matter. For human rights courts, for example, litigation rates may rise in tandem to human rights violations. For economic courts, litigation may track the extent of secondary legislation, which may itself affect the extent of trade among member states.[52] All of these forces suggest rising litigation rates over time, but there are also forces for declining litigation rates. When legal issues are decisively resolved, litigation rates may fall because parties are more likely to settle in the shadow of the court. Dissatisfaction with IC rulings may also lead litigants to avoid the IC. And many ICs never leave the starting gate, experiencing years of very low levels of litigation.

This evolutionary approach is less helpful for studying international criminal tribunals because it may take a long time to apprehend and prosecute war criminals, and increasingly war crimes tribunals limit prosecutions to top officials. Especially since most prosecutions should occur at the national level, litigation rates are no indication of real-time demand for international law enforcement or the political salience of international criminal tribunals.

A final limitation with this evolutionary approach is that it collapses world time. World time is more important in understanding why litigation rates grew in the Inter-American human rights system in the 1990s than is the fact that the court had celebrated its tenth anniversary. The next chapter considers how world events have affected the patterns this chapter has identified.

52 (Stone Sweet 1999, 57–63).

CONCLUSION: A TRANSFORMATION IN SEARCH OF AN EXPLANATION

Bringing these four trends together reveals the architecture of the contemporary international judiciary. The old terrain of international law had few international courts. Those that did exist allowed states to refuse or opt out of the court's compulsory jurisdiction, making old-style ICs dependent on and deferential to governments. As chapter 5 will show, old-style ICs can still facilitate the peaceful resolution of disputes, when governments want a legal solution. But old-style ICs are limited in their ability to alter international relations or domestic politics, reduced to the interstate arbiter model of political influence. In this model, ICs can help coordinate governments and construct focal legal understandings of the law, but they cannot generate leverage that might induce governments to follow rulings they oppose.

The end of the Cold War led to the reform of existing ICs, the creation of many new ICs, and increased litigation in all ICs. Today's ICs are overwhelmingly new-style ICs that copy a small repertoire of basic models. Many of these ICs are associated with club goods, where membership includes submitting to an IC's compulsory jurisdiction. Chapter 4 will explain that this new-style IC is coupled with embedded international law, which allows ICs to connect with compliance constituencies—other governments and actors within states who want to see their government respect international law.

This chapter showed how the contemporary international judiciary remains variegated and uneven in its subject matter and geographic coverage. While ICs today can hear cases that touch on security and environmental issues, there are no ICs dedicated to overseeing compliance with environmental or security agreements. Also, countries in Europe, Latin America, and Africa seem far more willing to embrace ICs compared to countries in Asia and the Middle East.

Adaptations in the design of ICs, and increased litigation in front of ICs suggest a gradual strengthening of international judicial institutions over time. Some ICs experience crises and moments of political backlash, but the larger trend over time has been in the direction of extending access, expanding subject-matter jurisdiction, adding remedies, and increasing litigation. Whether this trend will continue is yet to be seen. On the one hand, the global economic crisis, and the decline of US and European economic, military, and political influence in the world, have contributed to slowing litigation rates in some ICs. On the other hand, the more China ascends in economic dominance the more Communist leaders want to embrace the rule of law in economic matters both at home and abroad.

Institutions, once created, tend to be sticky. The evolutionary charts suggested that ICs can undergo long hibernations, waking once litigants believe that governments and publics are truly concerned about international legality, and when litigants see ICs as positively contributing to debates about international legality.

This chapter emphasized the decisions of governments to create ICs. These decisions are important, but legal practice shapes what institutions become. The next chapter shows the importance of legal practice in the evolution of the international judiciary.

CHAPTER 4

World History and the Evolving International Judiciary

My objective for this book is to understand how and when the creation of international courts affects international and domestic politics. This chapter, however, speaks to the question of why there are more international courts today than at any point in history.[1] Delegation to international courts (ICs) at its core is inspired by a distrust of governments, a belief the rule of law is enhanced when individuals, including elected officials, are not judges of their own causes and that domestic checks and balances are also insufficient to ensure that governments keep their international covenants. Citizens and investors have increasingly desired independent judicial oversight, and in some respects international judicialization reflects global trends in rights claiming.[2] But how do you get governments to agree that domestic legal oversight is insufficient and thus to consent to international judicial oversight?

This chapter provides a partial explanation of the trends discussed in chapter 3, focusing on how global forces shaped decisions about ICs. Although the same fundamental motive drives delegation to courts across time, key historical events were needed to increase bottom-up demands and make governments and legislatures open to accepting greater international judicial oversight. The sum of the argument is that at the end of World War II governments were able to reject proposals for compulsory international judicial oversight of their behavior. Changes in legal practice in the United States and Europe during and after the Cold War meant that foreign legal and quasi-legal bodies increasingly adjudicated allegations of economic and human rights violations abroad. Given the choice of European and American judicial review or international judicial review, many governments preferred international judicial review especially because international initiatives—World Bank and IMF projects, US and

1 An earlier version of this chapter appeared as Alter (2011).

2 (Reus-Smit 2011; Sassen 2006).

European foreign policies, and the Millennium Development Goals—created added incentives for governments to show progress toward democracy and human rights protection by embracing binding rules and international legal oversight. The interaction of legal and political dynamics helps us understand why Europe became the model for many new ICs, why the tendency is to enhance IC designs over time, and why American opponents of international law and international courts delayed but were ultimately unable to halt the evolution of the modern international judiciary.

Section I identifies three critical junctures in the creation of international courts and provides an overview table that puts developments in international economic, human rights, and mass atrocities law side by side. Section II focuses on the Cold War period (1945–89), explaining how legal practice changed the way the European Community's legal system worked, generating a model of an effective international legal system that became politically and legally entrenched and earned many adherents. Section III explains how the end of the Cold War unleashed political forces that contributed to the strengthening of existing international legal systems and the global spread of new-style ICs, many of which also emulated Europe's embedded model of international law enforcement. Section IV extracts from this history some general explanations of the political forces shaping the evolution of the modern international judiciary. Section V concludes by explaining how the embedded approach of international law enforcement facilitates respect for international law and shapes how international legal institutions evolve.

I. SYSTEMIC CHANGE CONTRIBUTING TO THE CREATION OF INTERNATIONAL COURTS

Scholars and practitioners have a tendency to write institutional histories as if moments of genesis are unconnected. It is understandable that the meetings where government leaders come together to negotiate and endorse Court Treaties draw our attention. But such gatherings are preceded by long discussions, and by experimentation and lesson drawing in parallel institutions. Individuals who work or otherwise participate in predecessor institutions form an interconnected network that debates the strengths and limits of existing systems while waiting for a political opportunity to put forth proposals for improvements. Disappointment with existing institutions gives rise to a thirst for change. When alternatives are exhausted, and when politicians are willing to agree that something needs to change, advocates will put forward their proposals. This larger process of institutional genesis is how systemic factors and activities in parallel institutions end up shaping the development of individual institutions.

Critical Junctures as Moments for Institutional Change

One can identify three moments where systemic, large-scale international upheaval contributed to the creation of international courts: the Hague Peace Conferences (1899–1914), the end of World War II and the onset of the Cold War (1945–52), and the end of the Cold War (1989). Advocates of international courts seized on these moments, offering packaged solutions that drew lessons from previous international judicial experiences. The three moments together encapsulate the shift from old- to new-style ICs.

The Hague Peace Conferences: A vision for international relations governed by international law and international courts

The Hague Peace Conferences were moments for legal idealists to crystallize their bold vision of subordinating power politics to an international rule of law. The first Hague conference in 1899 led to the creation of the Permanent Court of Arbitration (which is primarily a list of arbiters, and thus neither permanent nor a court). The second Hague conference in 1907 generated the ten-year experiment of a Central American Court of Justice (1908–18). World War I's destruction reinforced in the mind of Hague supporters the need for the Hague peace formula. The League of Nations, created as part of the peace settlement from World War I, was the first worldwide intergovernmental organization dedicated to maintaining peace. The league created the Permanent Court of International Justice, which held its inaugural sitting in 1922.

The Hague vision is most accurately associated with old-style ICs. The first international courts existed for the use of signatory states; their primary purpose was to facilitate the peaceful resolution of interstate disputes. Supporters drafted proposals to create a number of ICs, but the ICs created at the beginning of the twentieth century operated entirely within the voluntary interstate dispute settlement paradigm because the political context of the times made the Hague approach to ICs highly deferential to governments. According to Jean-Michel Guieu, already in the 1920s and 1930s international legal experts were beginning to wonder whether regional approaches made more sense than a "universalist" strategy. This thought arose because United States opposition limited the prospects of universalist strategies, and because it was increasingly clear that weak League of Nations strategies were insufficient in the face of the fascism and war in Europe.[3]

For many lawyers and politicians the outbreak of World War II was a death knell for the larger Hague Peace Conference vision, since it seemed to show the futility of the League of Nations project. Self-described

3 (Guieu 2012).

"political realists" denounced the "idealist" notion that systems of rules and reasoned interaction could ever replace war and balance-of-power politics as the primary tools of international relations.[4] Manley Hudson's treatise on international tribunals, published in 1944, made a last plea for the Hague peace approach to international courts. Hudson repeatedly stressed the many useful roles that ICs could play. But Hudson also noted the serious political limits regarding what governments would consent to with respect to international judicial oversight.[5] The onset of the Cold War essentially killed any chance to advance the Hague agenda, even Hudson's limited highly deferential version.

The Hague Peace Conference juncture continued to matter, however, because its ideals and lessons lived on in the minds of advocates. The success of the Hague Peace Conferences raised the hope that governments might once again sign on to bold multilateral political and legal ventures. Post–World War II, Hague idealists flocked to the world federalist association and the Mouvement Européen, and became jurisconsult representatives during conferences that ended up defining many international legal initiatives. The commitment of jurist advocacy movements to having law replace power politics and war directly influenced the European and Latin American economic and human rights projects, and later developments in international criminal law.[6]

Although the Hague Peace Conferences did not accomplish their goals, Christian Reus-Smit sees the Hague conferences as the foundational cornerstone of the modern international system.[7] The United Nations (UN) is not the League of Nations, but it is a league of nation-states, and today multilateral institutions are key venues for discussing collective responses designed to maintain peace and security. Even the Hague conference's legal agenda has been largely realized. International relations is increasingly legalized, with treaties and institutions overseeing international laws that cover many of the legal issues discussed during the Hague conferences.

The end of World War II and the onset of the Cold War

The major international judicial systems of today—the ICJ, ECJ, ECtHR, IACtHR, the WTO, and even the ICC—can trace their origins to the con-

4 (O'Connell and VanderZee 2014).

5 Plans included creating an International Criminal Court, an International Prize Court, and an International Loans Tribunal. Manley Hudson's book discusses the state of play for each proposed international judicial body (Hudson 1944). Cesare Romano (2014) discusses what became of these proposals.

6 Historians are investigating legal networks as they promoted change from 1920 to 1960. See Rasmussen (2013).

7 (Reus-Smit 1999).

junctural moment that was the end of World War II. The end of World War II brought both a closing and an opening. The political door to The Hague peace vision of subordinating power politics to law closed. The Soviet Union emerged from World War II committed to securing the Soviet empire, and to deepening and extending the Communist revolution around the world. China was also committed to this Communist vision, albeit in a more inward looking way. By contrast, the United States and Western Europe sought to build a liberal order based in multilateral institutions, human rights, and democracy. This liberal vision mainly applied within Europe; colonial powers did not want to extend human rights and democracy to their colonies, nor did they want to be held accountable for their actions in suppressing independence movements. Many Americans also remained committed to this liberal vision, but in the United States a Brickerite coalition made ratifying global treaties, especially human rights treaties, difficult if not impossible (see section IV for more). The different priorities and visions limited what was politically possible within the UN framework.

The closing of political space within UN bodies opened room for European and Latin American leaders to develop their own international legal institutions. Section II will explain how European legal initiatives began and developed during the Cold War, and how the seeds were planted for the World Trade Organization and Latin American legal systems to develop.

The end of the Cold War: The global spread of new-style ICs

The end of the Cold War signaled the demise of the Communist alternative to the West's capitalist liberal democratic order. Section III will explain how the fall of the Berlin Wall gave new energy to Europe's integration and human rights projects, and how the post–World War II Bretton Woods institutions (the International Monetary Fund and World Bank, plus the General Agreement on Tariffs and Trade) became conveyers of economic and political liberalism in developing countries. These trends are reflected in the reform of existing international judicial systems and the rise of many new-style ICs following European models. Many of these ICs took years to become operational, because it took time for treaties to be negotiated and ratified by a sufficient number of states and thus to enter force. But the initiatives to reinvigorate regional integration projects and to create new ICs can be linked directly to the end of the Cold War.

Each successive moment built on the past lessons learned. The end of World War II suggested to legalization proponents the need to improve on the "failed" international courts of the interwar period. Such improvements could not occur at the UN level, thus proponents turned to regional strategies. The end of the Cold War presented an opportunity to draw lessons from the Nuremberg trials, and from Europe's great postwar experiment with supranational adjudication. The path-dependent nature of institutional change meant that the form and nature of international judicial institutions did not repeat; rather, it evolved across iterations.

Legal Practice as a Means of Institutional Change

Governments create ICs by ratifying Court Treaties and agreeing to the appointment of international judges. But between international legislative moments, lawyers and judges are adjudicating cases within the legal frameworks they have, and international secretariats are working with judges, advocates, and governments to adjust existing systems so as to address known problems. The process of adjudication and adjustment leads to institutional changes that occur with less fanfare but which can cumulate into large and meaningful institutional change.[8]

During the Cold War's long hibernation, two deep structural changes occurred in domestic judicial institutions, which contributed to shifting the choices facing governments in the United States, Europe, and elsewhere. First, constitutional and administrative courts grew in political power in the United States and Europe.[9] Domestic and international legal change meant that by the 1990s European governments found themselves inextricably bound to their European law commitments. Second, extraterritorial assertions of legal jurisdiction grew in number and nature.[10] Beginning in the 1960s and accelerating over time, judges around the world began to assert more types of extraterritorial legal authority, including claiming jurisdiction over the actions of foreign leaders. For example, in 1960 the Israeli secret service kidnapped former Nazi Adolph Eichmann, and shortly thereafter, Israeli courts claimed universal jurisdiction as they prosecuted Eichmann for crimes committed in Europe before the state of Israel existed. In the 1970s the United States began limiting foreign sovereign immunity and unilaterally sanctioning "unfair" trade practices, and in 1980s US courts reinvigorated the defunct Alien Tort Statute to claim federal jurisdiction for violations of international law that occur abroad.[11] Ratification of the Convention against Torture and Other Cruel,

8 (Streeck and Thelen 2005; Thelen 2004).

9 (Cappelletti 1981; Shapiro and Stone Sweet 2002).

10 (Putnam 2014; Raustiala 2009).

11 The reform of the Foreign Sovereign Immunities Act occurred in response to Cuba's Communist revolution (Foreign Sovereign Immunities Act of 1976, Pub. L. 94-583, 90 Stat. 2891, 28 U.S.C. Sec. 1330, 1332(a), 1391(f) and 1601–1611.) Many other countries copied this act, creating broader limits on foreign sovereign immunity. Section II will explain how in 1974 the United States passed the United States Trade Act that allowed the United States Trade Representatives to investigate and sanction "unfair trade." Then, in 1980 a US circuit

Inhuman or Degrading Treatment or Punishment involved creating domestic legislation to prosecute torture regardless of where the torture occurred. Following the end of the Cold War, Belgium's Parliament passed a "law on universal jurisdiction" that allowed Belgian courts to prosecute individuals for crimes committed abroad.[12] In 1998, Britain arrested Augusto Pinochet based on a Spanish warrant for prosecution.[13] These changes meant that even though governments in Latin America and Africa may not have consented to be held accountable to international law, the notion of individual and state accountability developed through legal practice, and in fact Latin American and African leaders *were* being held accountable for their international legal violations.

The rest of this chapter will explain how these global forces reverberated across regions, institutions, and issue areas. Figure 4.1 organizes and presages key historical developments, noting the creation of permanent ICs in bold. The table helps us see how developments with respect to international economics, human rights, and war crimes are being affected by similar world historical events, reminding us of the larger context and the permissive conditions that give rise to individual agency and that shape political decision making and developments within specific institutions.

II. COLD WAR LEGAL PRACTICE AND THE EMERGENCE OF EUROPE'S EMBEDDED APPROACH TO INTERNATIONAL LAW

International judicial developments during the Cold War laid the foundation for the post–Cold War proliferation of international courts. This section explains why global international legal efforts closed, why Europe went its own way, and why other regions did not immediately follow in Europe's footsteps. The story is one of disappointment fueling legal idealists, who drew lessons and stood ready to advocate for more effective international legal institutions when the opportunity presented itself. By the 1980s, much of the core foundation for the contemporary international judiciary had been laid. As is true with most foundations, a 1980s perusal

court asserted federal jurisdiction over violations of international law occurring abroad, where both the perpetrators and the victims were foreign nationals (Filártiga v. Peña-Irala). This ruling was limited to the finding of torts, and it did not speak to the question of whether sovereigns might be immune from tort prosecution, but subsequent US cases have involved crimes committed by political leaders.

12 For a discussion of Belgium's universal jurisdiction law, see Hurwitz (2009), Roozbeh (2009). As these articles explain, Belgium's law was repealed in 2003, replaced with a more restrictive law on extraterritorial jurisdiction.

13 See the discussion in section III for more.

of rudimentary stone supports would provide few clues about as to whether a larger building would be created or what such a building might look like.

The Global Level: The Door to International Efforts Closes

Section I discussed the old-style international courts of the Hague Peace Conference era: the Central American Court of Justice (1908–18) and the Permanent Court of Justice (1922–46). To many the inability of international law and international judicial bodies to avert war in Europe suggested that disputes between states would not be resolved in court. One can find in the United Nations system remnants of the legal and political conceptions that had animated the League of Nations, and the International Court of Justice (ICJ) in many respects resurrected the Permanent Court of Justice. But expectations were lower this time.[14]

The discrediting of old international legal beliefs combined with the Cold War, however, to make a limited international legal approach newly attractive. Already in the 1920s and 1930s European and Latin American legal scholars were concluding a regional strategy might make more sense than a "universalist" strategy.[15] The atrocities of World War II generated a willingness, if not a desire, to experiment with international courts. The Allied victors of World War II did not want to repeat the mistake of World War I by pursuing collective retribution against all Germans, thereby generating anew the sorts of grievances Adolph Hitler exploited in his rise to power. They also sought to create a clear difference between the summary execution/political trial approaches of Soviet President Josef Stalin. The Nuremberg tribunals used law and legal processes to hold specific Germans accountable for specific crimes. The Tokyo trials repeated this strategy, although concerns about inflaming Japanese nationalists led to the decision not to prosecute Japan's wartime emperor. Traditionally, international law had been conceived of as a contract between states. Governments might be required to pay compensation for violations of contracts with private actors, but international legal bodies generally did not hold individuals personally accountable for international actions undertaken in a public capacity.[16] Nuremberg held individuals accountable, but only

14 The Central American Court of Justice heard ten cases before its founding treaty expired. The Permanent Court issued thirty-two binding rulings from the sixty-six contentious and advisory cases raised. For an early history of international adjudication, see Allain (2000), O'Connell and VanderZee (2014). Katzenstein (2014).

15 On the frustrations of European juris-diplomats during the Hague Peace Process period, see Guieu (2012).

16 The banishment of Napoleon Bonaparte to Saint Helena after the hundred-day war, however, is an exception. For more on the history of war crimes prosecutions see Bass (2000).

FIGURE 4.1: The creation of international courts in their historical context (**Permanent ICs in bold; ad hoc international courts in italics**)

World History	Key International Legal Developments	International Economic Legal System	Mass Atrocities and War Crimes System	International Human Rights System
1940s				
WWII ends India gains independence (1947) Decolonization begins	United Nations founded (1945)	General Agreement on Tariffs and Trade adopted as a precursor to International Trade Organization (1947)	*Nuremberg Trials (1945–46)* *Tokyo Trials (1946–48)* International Law Commission proposes International Criminal Court (1948)	UN Human Rights Commission created (1947) American Declarations on Human Rights (1948) Universal Declarations on Human Rights (1948) European Convention on Human Rights (1950)
Cold War Sets In				
1950s				
Korean War (1950–53) Decolonization gains political momentum, fueled in part by Cold War rivalries	United Nations Convention Relating to the Status of Refugees (1954) Treaties for European Political and Defense Communities rejected (1954)	**European Court of Justice** (ECJ) founded as part of Coal and Steel Community (1952) Treaty of Rome creates European Economic Community, transforming and extending the ECJ's subject matter jurisdiction (1958)		European Commission on Human Rights begins operations (1954) **European Court of Human Rights (ECtHR)** created (1958) Inter-American Commission on Human Rights established (1959)

1960s Civil rights movements Wars of independence among former colonies US gets involved in Vietnam War (1962–75)	Organization of African Unity founded (1963)	GATT's noncompulsory dispute settlement system has its first codification/reform (1966)	Eichmann trial in Jerusalem (1961-2) German trials of Treblinka and Auschwitz Guards (1960s and 1970s) American Military courts convict William Calley for crimes associated with the My Lai Massacre; his short sentence provokes outrage (1971)	Amnesty International founded (1961) Signing of UN human rights conventions: Racial Discrimination (1965); Civil and Political Rights (1966); Economic, Social and Cultural Rights (1966) UN Human Rights Commission starts investigating and reporting on human rights violations (1967) American Convention on Human Rights signed (1969). It included a protocol envisioning the creation of the IACHR
1970s East-West détente—Brandt's *Ostpolitik* (1970), Nixon goes to China (1972) Chile's and Argentina's Dirty Wars (1974–78) Cambodian Politicide (1975–79) Carter elevates human rights in US foreign policy (1977–81)	Organization for Security and Cooperation in Europe founded. Helsinki Act (1975) Convention on the Elimination of all Forms of Discrimination against Women (1979)	**BENELUX court** created (1974) United States Trade Act creates Section 301 mechanism providing for unilateral sanctions for "unfair" trade practices (1974)		Charter 77—a Czech group to monitor progress toward Helsinki human rights goals—is founded (1976) Inter-American Court of Human Rights (IACHR) created (1979)

FIGURE 4.1: (*Continued*)

World History	Key International Legal Developments	International Economic Legal System	Mass Atrocities and War Crimes System	International Human Rights System
1980s Gorbachev era reforms in Soviet Bloc (Perestroika and Glasnost) Berlin Wall falls (1989), Cold War ends	Law of Sea III signed (1982)	**Andean Tribunal of Justice (ATJ)** (1984) Uruguay Round negotiations in GATT system begin (1986)		US revival of Alien Tort Statute—Filártiga v. Peña Irala (1980) African Charter on Human Rights signed (1981) Convention against Torture and Other Cruel, Inhuman or Degrading Treatment or Punishment signed (1984)
Cold War Ends				
1990s German Reunification Washington Consensus (US, IMF, World Bank) regarding economic policy War breaks out in Yugoslavia (1991).	Maastricht Treaty and reforms of European Union and its legal system (1992). **International Tribunal for the Law of the Sea** finally created (1996)	**Economic Court of the Commonwealth of Independent States (ECCIS)** (1993) **European Free Trade Area Court** (EFTAC) (1992) **World Trade Organization's** (WTO) compulsory dispute resolution (1994)	**International Criminal Tribunal for the Former Yugoslavia (ICTY)** (1993) **International Criminal Tribunal for Rwanda (ICTR)** (1994)	Belgium Parliament passes "law of universal jurisdiction" (1993) ECtHR reformed (Protocol 11 signed 1994, implemented in 1998) European Commission abolished and ECtHR's reformed system comes into force (1998)

Failed UN intervention in Somalia (1992) Rwandan genocide (1994) EU and Council of Europe first post–Cold War enlargement (1995)	Rome Statute of International Criminal Court signed (1998)	**Central American Court of Justice** (1994) **Court of West African Economic and Monetary Union (WAEMU)** (1994) **Court of Justice for the Common Market of Eastern and Southern Africa (COMESA)** (1994) **Common Court of Justice and Arbitration for the Organization for the Harmonization of Corporate Law in Africa (OHADA)** (1997)	*Hybrid international criminal tribunals for East Timor, Kosovo and Sierra Leone* (1999-2001)	Spanish extradition request for Augusto Pinochet to prosecute human rights violations (1998) Organization of African Unity agrees to create an African Court on Human and Peoples' Rights (1998)

FIGURE 4.1: (*Continued*)

World History	Key International Legal Developments	International Economic Legal System	Mass Atrocities and War Crimes System	International Human Rights System
2000s				
Millennium Development Goals defined (2000) Attack on United States World Trade Towers (2001) EU and Council of Europe enlargements reach Soviet states (2004, 2007) Arab Spring (2012)	Protocol to establish an African Court of Justice created (2003) Merger of African Court of Justice and ACtHPR still under discussion	**Central African Economic and Monetary Union Court** (2000) **Community Court of Justice of the East African Community (EACJ)** (2001) **Caribbean Court of Justice (CCJ)** (2001) **Economic Community of West African States (ECOWAS CJ) Court** (2001) **Southern Common Market (MERCOSUR)** (2002) Association of Southeast Asian Nations (ASEAN) dispute settlement system agreed to (2004) **Southern African Development Community Court (SADC)** (2005)	**International Criminal Court** (ICC) (2002)	Inter-American Human Rights Commission decides that it will refer all unresolved cases to the IACtHR (2001) **ECOWAS Court** gains human rights jurisdiction (2005) First judges are appointed to the **African Court of Human and Peoples' Rights (ACtHPRs)** (2006) ACtHPR delivers first judgment (2009)

leaders on the losing side of the conflict. Still, this post–World War II idea of using international law to hold individuals accountable presaged a larger shift toward an international rule of law.[17]

Among Western lawyers and politicians, the Nuremberg trials were seen as a very important success in that they opened German eyes to the atrocities of World War II, convinced Germans that actual war criminals were prosecuted and dealt with relatively fairly, and helped to construct a historical memory of World War II.[18] But the trials were far from what idealistic international lawyers might aspire. Legally problematic was the notion that the defendants could be held to account for crimes that did not exist as a matter of law. Only after Nuremberg were laws established so that future trials would not violate the fundamental due process notion of "no punishment without law." Politically problematic was that only the war crimes of Germany (and at the Tokyo trials the crimes of the Japanese) were prosecuted. Moreover, prosecution was highly selective in terms of which actors and crimes were pursued, suggesting to many that the Nuremberg and Tokyo trials were yet another example of victor's justice.[19] These problems would be addressed when advocates resurrected the model of international criminal prosecution following the post–Cold war outbreak of war in Yugoslavia.

Even though the Nuremberg and Tokyo prosecutions were in many ways problematic, their perceived success contributed to the decision to give the new International Court of Justice jurisdiction to help enforce the Convention on the Prevention and Punishment of the Crime of Genocide.[20] This decision proved controversial as a number of countries ratified the genocide convention with reservations and declarations associated with their signatures. The clause generating the most reservations was the agreement to submit disputes to the International Court of Justice.[21] The UN Declaration on Human Rights was similarly controversial.

17 There were discussions during the interwar years about the need to create a "High Court of International Justice" with jurisdiction to try crimes "against international public order and the universal law of nations." See Shabas (2014, n. 14).

18 (Savelsberg and King 2007; Shklar 1964, part 2).

19 (Bass 2000, chapter 5).

20 Convention on the Prevention and Punishment of the Crime of Genocide adopted by Resolution 260 (III) A of the UN General Assembly on December 9, 1948. Article IX states, "Disputes between the Contracting Parties relating to the interpretation, application or fulfillment of the present Convention, including those relating to the responsibility of a State for genocide or for any of the other acts enumerated in article III, shall be submitted to the International Court of Justice at the request of any of the parties to the dispute."

21 There were twenty-seven reservations involving article IX: Albania, Algeria, Argentina, Bahrain, Bangladesh, Belarus, Bulgaria, China, Czech Republic, Hungary, India, Malaysia, Mongolia, Morocco, Philippines, Poland, Romania, Russian Federation, Rwanda, Singapore, Slovakia, Spain, Ukraine, United States, Venezuela, Vietnam, and Yemen. After

Many governments refused to agree to anything too concrete or legally binding, so the declaration became a soft law aspirational statement the General Assembly adopted. Even this nonbinding declaration was too much for some states; the UN Declaration on Human Rights was adopted with forty-eight votes in favor, zero votes opposed, and eight abstentions that mostly came from Soviet bloc states.[22] The UN Commission on Human Rights, from its establishment in 1947 until its reconstitution and renaming in 1967, concentrated on promoting human rights and helping states elaborate treaties, but not on investigating or condemning violators. The clear limits of the UN system spurred Europeans to go their own way.

In terms of international economics, at the end of World War II world leaders banded together to try to avoid the sort of economic collapse that had led to the Great Depression and the rise of fascist governments. At Bretton Woods in 1944, 738 delegates from forty-four Allied governments negotiated agreements. Finance ministries dominated the Bretton Woods negotiations, generating the international financial institutions (the International Monetary Fund and the International Bank for Reconstruction and Development, which is today part of the World Bank). The International Trade Organization was to be a trade-related addition to the Bretton Woods institutions, but Cold War tensions quickly interceded. Fifteen Western countries created the General Agreement on Tariffs and Trade (GATT) in 1945 and began negotiating the first set of tariff reductions at the same time as a larger coalition of states negotiated the International Trade Organization's Havana Charter. This draft charter included a mechanism for resolving disputes related to the agreement, which expected that the ICJ would adjudicate unresolved cases. Anticipating that the International Trade Organization would supersede the GATT, little thought was given to how trade conflicts might be resolved in the GATT system. When the United States Congress refused to ratify the Havana Charter, the GATT became a default trade institution that included only a small number of Western-oriented countries. At its founding, the GATT lacked any legalized dispute settlement system.[23]

---

the Cold War ended, eleven of these countries removed their reservations regarding the ICJ's authority. See http://www.preventgenocide.org/law/convention/reservations/, accessed May 20, 2011.

22 Countries abstaining included: Byelorussia, Czechoslovakia, Poland, Ukraine, USSR, Yugoslavia, South Africa, and Saudi Arabia. See http://www.un.org/rights/HRToday/declar.htm, accessed May 20, 2011.

23 (Barton et al. 2006, 27–47; Dunoff 2009, 327–33).

Changes in Europe: A Judicial Revolution Generates the Embedded Model of International Law Enforcement

Dismayed by the limited UN initiatives to protect human rights, and wanting to demarcate Western European practices from Soviet practices in the East, the Council of Europe decided to create its own human rights system in 1950.[24] Many of the architects of the European Convention on Human Rights were members of the European Movement, a group that included former antifascist resistance fighters and government officials overseeing national purges of Nazi collaborators. The European Movement envisioned a robust system of international oversight that according to Pierre-Henri Teitigen could "sound the alarm to the minds of a nation . . . to warn them of the peril and to show them that they are progressing down a long road which leads far, sometimes even to Buchenwald or Dachau."[25]

Given this history, we might expect Europe's flagship to be its human rights system. But the dreams of the ECtHR's legal architects were immediately tempered by state sovereignty concerns. Especially given the wars of independence occurring in Europe's colonies, key European governments did not want a highly independent international oversight mechanism,[26] thus the Commission's formal mandate prioritized friendly reconciliation over enforcement actions.[27] Also, states made optional the consent for the right of individuals to petition the Commission and for the Commission to be able to bring cases to the ECtHR. Henry Schermers stated the dilemma:

> Proper human rights protection requires international supervisory organs. This, however, would be a further infringement of national sovereignty. The supremacy of national courts would be degraded if an international organ would be permitted to criticize their judicial decisions. For many states, this went too far. An inter-European commitment to protect human rights was acceptable, but a European court supervising the Convention would undermine the sovereignty of the state and could not be generally accepted.[28]

Originally only Sweden, Ireland, Denmark, Iceland, Germany, and Belgium accepted ECtHR's compulsory jurisdiction, and only Sweden,

24 (Madsen 2010, 36–39).

25 Henri Teitgen, quoted in Bates (2011, 7). See also Bates (2011, 44–76); De Burca (2011, 653–64).

26 (Madsen 2010, chapter 2).

27 (Robertson and Merrills 1994, 5–12, 295–96).

28 (Schermers 1999, 822).

Ireland, and Denmark accepted the right of individual petition. Moreover, a number of these acceptances were provisional, made for only a few years at a time. The refusal of France and Britain to consent to the right of individual petition or to the ECtHR's authority diminished the sense that Europe as a whole was seriously committed to a robust regional human rights regime.[29] The politically fragile nature of Europe's human rights system led the European Human Rights Commission to proceed with great caution. In the early years, the European Human Rights Commission acted primarily as a political gatekeeper limiting the types of cases the ECtHR heard. Between 1954 and 1961, fewer than one-half of one percent of the 1,307 applications filed with the Commission were declared admissible—with the result being that in its first ten years of operation, the ECtHR ruled on only seven cases.[30]

The Commission's timid approach to human rights oversight was a disappointment to legal idealists, and arguably a sign that postwar international law approaches would not achieve much more than interwar international law had achieved. Britain agreed to the ECtHR's optional provisions in 1966, the second major European power to do so, but only because "it was thought that the Court, and the Convention more generally, would have little influence on domestic law."[31] In 1974 the European human rights system teetered on the brink of failure. To signal its displeasure, the United Kingdom shortened its acceptance of the Court's authority to two years and suggested that it would withdraw from the right of individual petition. But at around the same time domestic political efforts culminated in Italy, Switzerland, Greece, and France accepting the ECtHR's jurisdiction, and the ECtHR issued a number of important rulings that reinforced the object and purpose of human rights law in Europe. Edward Bates argues that what looked like a near collapse ended up being an awakening of Europe's human rights system, a turning point where Europe transitioned from ambivalent concern about the ECtHR to an onus to accept the ECtHR's authority to demonstrate commitment to liberal democratic ideals.[32]

European integration generated the other European approach to international law enforcement after World War II. The main impetus for

29 (Moravcsik 1995, 171; Robertson and Merrills 1994, 13–14).

30 (Schermers 1999, 825). The rate improved only slightly over time. By 1990, the Commission had received 15,457 complaints, of which 14,636 were declared inadmissible. The Court ruled on 251 cases, thus by 1990 1.6 percent of the applications filed reached the ECtHR for a ruling (Moravcsik 1995, 170–71). On the factors shaping Commission decisions to refer cases, see Greer (2006, 33–98); Robertson and Merrills (1994, 264–74, 300–301).

31 (Bates 2011, 12).

32 Ibid., 277–318.

founding the European Coal and Steel Community was a concern that the United States intended to return to Germany full sovereignty over its coal and steel industry. France, Italy, Belgium, the Netherlands, and Luxembourg feared that Germany would exploit its dominance in coal and steel, putting its neighbors at a competitive disadvantage at a time that they needed to rebuild their economies.[33] The Coal and Steel Community included domestically binding supranational legal rules, overseen and enforced by the powerful supranational High Authority. The six founding member states added a European Court of Justice (ECJ) as a check should the High Authority be dominated by the more powerful member states. The Coal and Steel Community generated a European Court of Justice that already in 1952 had compulsory jurisdiction and private access so that the individuals could challenge arguably illegal High Authority actions.

Members of the European Movement hoped that the Coal and Steel Community would be the launching point for further integration endeavors. European federalists imagined that the European human rights system would become part of a larger federal Europe united under the supreme authority of a European Constitution and a European Constitutional Court. The first steps toward both groups' visions were the drafting of charters for the European Political Community and European Defense Community. Sovereignty concerns interceded again when the French Parliament rejected the European Defense Community in 1954. In this sense, the 1958 Treaty of Rome, which created the European Economic Community (EEC), was a big disappointment.[34] The Treaty of Rome rechristened the High Authority as the Commission (not to be confused with the completely separate European Commission on Human Rights). The EEC Commission could not rule itself on state or firm compliance with European rules; rather, it was authorized to bring state violations to the European Court of Justice, which could declare that a member state had "failed to fulfill its obligations" under the Treaty of Rome. Such a declaration was largely toothless in that no remedies were associated with an ECJ finding of a violation of European law.[35]

For the activists of the European Movement, both the Treaty of Rome and the legal system of the European Convention on Human Rights were disappointments. Concerns about state sovereignty had watered down the agreements, leaving only a minimalist commitment to integration and supranationalism. Integration enthusiasts then watched in further dismay as French President de Gaulle assumed office in 1959 and led a successful

33 (Gillingham 1991).

34 (De Burca 2011, 658–67; Milward 1992, 186–223).

35 (Boerger-De Smedt 2012).

full-on assault on the supranational elements of the EEC, culminating in the arguably illegal "Luxembourg compromise" where the treaty-mandated switch to qualified majority voting was derailed by political agreement.[36] Equally disconcerting was de Gaulle's assault on the domestic rule of law so as to avoid scrutiny of the military commissions operating in Algeria.[37] De Gaulle's efforts led activists to turn to a legal strategy to promote European integration.[38] With so few countries accepting the authority of the ECtHR, the ECJ became the focus of their legal activities.

Scholars use the term "revolution" to characterize what then happened. Basically, in the 1960s the ECJ made a number of legal rulings that repudiated existing international legal doctrine and boldly asserted the supreme authority of European law within national legal orders. In 1962 the ECJ declared the direct effect of European law, finding that the EEC treaty created legal rights that private litigants could claim in domestic courts. In 1964 the ECJ declared European law supreme to conflicting national law. In 1978 the ECJ instructed national courts to use their power to ensure that national practice respects European law.[39] We now know that members of the European Movement, who had helped found associations of lawyers, judges, and scholars committed to or merely interested in the laws of European integration, spurred on these revolutionary rulings. Euro-law jurist advocacy movements located test cases that allowed the ECJ to develop European law and used their positions of legal power to suggest domestic legal support for them.[40] Legal practitioners and scholars wrote articles trumpeting ECJ rulings and worked to constitute a legal field of community law based on ECJ doctrine.[41] In the 1960s, the direct effect and supremacy of European law was mostly dicta, but the ECJ's doctrines became increasingly authoritative in the 1970s as lawyers and national courts adjusted national legal doctrine to incorporate the ECJ's radical legal innovations.[42] By the 1990s, the ECJ's understanding of the direct effect and supremacy of European law had captured the entire European legal complex. European law became a subject taught to new generations of lawyers and judges, who all learned that European law by its very nature generates direct effects and is supreme to ordinary national law. These legal and institutional changes, which are today taken-for-granted elements of the EU's legal order, were the result of

36 (Hoffmann 1966).
37 (Lagneau-Devillé 1983).
38 (Cohen 2007).
39 These changes are discussed in Stein (1981), Weiler (1991).
40 (Alter 2009, chapter 4; Rasmussen 2010; Vauchez 2010).
41 (Cohen and Madsen 2007).
42 (Alter 2001; Davies, 2012).

extraordinary efforts of lawyers, judges, and legal scholars committed to the idea of European integration under a rule of law.

Much more could be said about this revolution, but the key point is that it changed the way the European Community's enforcement system operated. For both the EEC and the European Convention on Human Rights, the main enforcers were supposed to be the more politically controllable supranational commissions—the EEC Commission and the Council of Europe's Human Rights Commission. In the 1960s, both of these commissions were understandably deferential to the concerns of national governments. But the ECJ's legal revolution harnessed private litigants as monitors of state compliance with European law and national courts as key enforcers of community legal obligations. At around the time that the ECJ was flexing its new legal muscle (1980s), the European Commission on Human Rights began to let more cases proceed to the ECtHR. Schermers explains that "over the years the Commission became more critical of the behavior of governments. In 1993 there was no longer a reasonable risk that member states would not renew the right of individual petition or that they would withdraw from the Convention. Public opinion in the member states and the Council of Europe would not easily accept such a step."[43]

The transformation of Europe's supranational legal systems introduced to the world a new form of international court and a new approach to making international law effective. Both the European Community and the European Convention on Human Rights made supranational legal rules supreme to and part of national legal systems, essentially embedding the *acquis communautaire* and the European Convention on Human Rights into the domestic legal fabric.[44] The act of embedding international law into domestic law is not new per se. Treaty ratification generally involves making the international treaty part of domestic law. What was different was that the Council of Europe and the European Community combined embedded supranational law with international judicial oversight of how this law is interpreted and applied domestically. Private litigants could trigger this oversight, pursuing cases that the EEC Commission had dropped out of political concerns and framing their challenges boldly. The likely prospect of international judicial review of national actions creates an incentive for domestic actors to coordinate their interpretation of European law with ECJ and ECtHR judges. National court enforcement ended up providing a number of benefits. There were few international costs to ignoring ECJ rulings, but ignoring national

43 (Schermers 1999, 825).

44 The *acquis communautaire* is the body of substantive secondary law and common law of the European Community.

court rulings was politically more difficult.[45] National courts could also apply the same remedies for violations of European law as existed for violations of domestic law.[46] There are, of course, significant sovereignty costs associated with Europe's international judicial model. Private litigants have turned to the ECJ to pursue social, economic, and political objectives only distantly related to facilitating trade.[47] Litigants have turned to the ECtHR as a sort of constitutional court for Europe, garnering legal precedents that occasionally go beyond what domestic law requires.

At times European governments have chafed at the ECJ and ECtHR's growing power. In the 1980s Thatcherite conservatives and even officials within Helmut Kohl's pro-Europe government began to openly question whether the ECJ's legal revolution should be revisited. But by then European leaders were also becoming concerned that economic competition from the United States and Japan would threaten the European economic system. Curbing the European legal system's perceived excesses would be a blow to European integration at the very moment that national governments were embracing European integration as the central tool to ensure that European economies remained internationally competitive.[48] The end of the Cold War introduced the prospect of enlarging both the Council of Europe and the European Community. European governments wanted to expand membership in both systems so as to secure democracy in the newly freed central European countries. With the fall of the Iron Curtain the window of time to reverse or sanction the ECJ for its earlier activism closed.

Changes In Latin America: Creating Sleeping Bears?

Most Latin American countries achieved colonial independence in the early 1800s, thus unlike Africa the decolonization wars following World War II did not directly impact Latin America. Following their initial independence, Simón Bolivar—a charismatic leader who helped liberate Venezuela, Colombia, Panama, Peru, Ecuador, and Bolivia from Spanish rule—advocated various forms of regional unification as a way to balance against European and US power. Bolivar's dream is repeatedly invoked in association with ever-changing regional unification plans, but is yet to be realized. The end of World War II generated yet another missed opportunity to resurrect regional integrationist ideas.

45 (Alter 2009, chapter 6; Burley and Mattli 1993; Weiler 1991).

46 (Helfer and Slaughter 1997).

47 (Cichowski 2007; Harlow and Rawlings 1992).

48 These changes are discussed in more detail in Alter (2009, especially chapters 4, 5, and 6).

In 1948 Latin American leaders launched the Organization of American States (OAS), an American counterpart to the Council of Europe. At the same time, founding states adopted the American Declaration of the Rights and Duties of Man. Lawyers from the region like to point out that the first international court was in Latin America (the Central American Court of Justice [1908–18]),[49] and that the American Declaration preceded the UN Declaration on Human Rights (by six months). But neither initiative went much beyond its League of Nations/UN counterpart. Like the UN Declaration, the American Declaration was a nonbinding catalog of rights. The Economic Agreement of Bogotá, negotiated at the same time as the American Declaration, never entered into force. Limiting OAS initiatives was a tradition of executive rule in Latin America, a lack of trauma during World War II that might have called this tradition into question, and a lack of US support for more binding and precise American initiatives.

What mattered, however, is that Latin America had its own human rights system; the OAS was not dependent on Soviet assent to take the next steps. In 1953 Fidel Castro led an insurgent movement that in 1959 created the first avowedly Communist government in the Americas. In 1959 the OAS finally agreed to create an Inter-American Commission on Human Rights to monitor respect for the American Declaration for the Rights of Man. This Commission could launch its own investigations of human rights abuses based on individual complaints. The Inter-American Commission was more involved in international oversight of human rights than its UN counterpart; unlike its European counterpart, however, the Commission was unable to refer cases to a court. Moreover, since the American Declaration was not yet a legally binding instrument, Inter-American Commission findings were not themselves legally binding.

In the 1960s the civil rights movement reverberated around the world, and along with decolonization contributed to a global demand for international human rights. The drafting of key international human rights conventions and the decision to allow the United Nations Human Rights Commission to investigate rights violations occurred at this time.[50] The

49 The so-called Permanent Court of Arbitration preceded the Central American Court of Justice, but this "court" is actually just a list of arbiters. It does not meet the definition of an IC discussed in chapter 3, and most international lawyers do not consider the Permanent Court of Arbitration to be an IC. For more on these early international legal bodies, see O'Connell and VanderZee (2014).

50 The International Convention on Civil and Political Rights (1966); International Covenant on Economic, Social, and Cultural Rights (1966); and Convention on the Elimination of All Forms of Racial Discrimination (1965) were negotiated and adopted at this time. In 1967 the UN changed the mandate of its Human Rights Commission to include investigating abuses.

Latin American corollary took the form of a binding American Convention on Human Rights, agreed to by OAS members in 1969, which included a provision establishing an international court to oversee respect for the agreement. Shortly thereafter, the United States supported a coup in Chile to unseat its democratically elected Marxist government.

The Cold War began to thaw in the 1970s. West German Chancellor Willy Brandt engaged in Ostpolitik, and US President Nixon went to China. The end of the Vietnam War and the departure of the Nixon/Kissinger administration led to a change in US policy toward Latin America. As part of a broader set of policies aimed at promoting human rights in Latin America, President Carter and human rights activists threw their support behind ratification of the American Convention on Human Rights.[51] Ten years later, after enough states had ratified the American Convention and accepted the Inter-American Court's authority, the first judges were appointed to the Inter-American Court of Human Rights (IACtHR). But the Inter-American Commission, which had for many years been the sole human rights body in Latin America, proved reluctant to bring cases to the Court.[52]

A number of economic initiatives proceeded outside of the OAS.[53] The two most important initiatives were the Latin American Free Trade Association (LAFTA, a.k.a. ALADI in Spanish) and the Andean Pact. In 1960, Argentina, Peru, Brazil, Uruguay, Peru, Paraguay, and Chile launched LAFTA to promote a free trade area in the Americas. Four additional countries joined in the next few years. Concerned that larger countries would dominate the LAFTA, in 1969 Peru, Ecuador, Chile, Colombia, and Bolivia agreed to pursue deeper economic integration. The Andean Pact copied the political institutions of the European Community, but its economic project was quite different. Andean countries' left-leaning political leaders envisioned harnessing captive profits from foreign investment to promote grand industrial programs.[54]

The Andean Pact did not, at the time, make Andean secondary legislation directly applicable within national legal systems, nor did Andean leaders copy the European Community's legal system. Instead, Andean leaders expected to be able to implement Andean Pact Decisions via executive decree. But legal challenges in Colombia and Chile regarding

51 (Sikkink 2004, chapter 6).

52 (Cosgrove 2000, 52–53).

53 These agreements and their legal mechanisms are discussed in David Padilla's 1979 survey of Latin American regional integration systems. Padilla saw the LAFTA system as similar to the European legal system, but it was really more similar to the GATT system. Padilla also noted that only in the Andean Pact was there any movement toward creating a true European-style IC (Padilla 1979, 80).

54 (Helfer, Alter, and Guerzovich 2009, 6–8).

executive implementation of the Andean Pact's foreign investment rules raised questions about the binding nature of Andean secondary law in national legal orders. These challenges led Andean leaders to turn to the European model as a solution. By making Andean law directly effective and supreme, Andean leaders could address the concern that domestic judges might undermine the legal validity of Andean Decisions. In 1979 Andean leaders formally endorsed creating an Andean Tribunal modeled on the ECJ.[55] Originally, member states added in design hobbles intended to protect national sovereignty. These hobbles would be removed in 1996, bringing the design of the ATJ even closer to its ECJ model.[56]

By the end of the Cold War, Latin America had two regional courts. The IACtHR followed the model of the ECtHR, as it existed at the time. The Andean Tribunal of Justice (ATJ) intentionally copied the model of the European Court of Justice, with some adjustments designed to protect national sovereignty. The models were in place, but both legal initiatives only really began to work once military governance ended, a process of democratization and economic liberalization in Latin America began, and Andean countries decided to join the WTO.

Changes in Africa: The Birth of Nationalist Movements

Africa emerged from World War II still controlled by European colonial powers. African peoples focused on liberation from European domination, believing that self-governance would provide respect for human rights and economic justice that was so lacking in colonial Africa. Cold War politics intervened, leading to a series of violent civil conflicts fueled by Communist and anti-Communist ideologies and American and Soviet political and military backing. As section III will explain, the end of the Soviet backing led to a search for new sources of political and financial support.

The first African wars of independence generally took place in the 1950s and early 1960s. In 1963, thirty-two newly independent African governments launched the Organization for African Unity, a precursor to today's African Union, with a stated goal of promoting solidarity and cooperation and helping African countries overcome the legacy of colonialism. For nearly twenty years the Organization for African Unity

55 (Alter, Helfer, and Saldias 2012, 722–26; Saldias 2010, 16–17).

56 Andean leaders only allowed the legal secretariat to investigate noncompliance complaints raised by governments, barring the investigation of private litigant complaints and any "failure to act" suits against community or state actors. In other words, the Andean system was designed to help enforce the Andean rules that governments endorsed. The decision to add design hobbles, and to then change the ATJ design are discussed in Alter, Helfer, and Saldias (2012, 727–29, 730–32, 734–39).

focused on decolonization efforts and fighting South Africa's apartheid system, two objectives the varied African governments could all endorse.

In 1979 African leaders agreed to ask a committee of experts to create an African Declaration of Human Rights similar to what existed in Europe and Latin America. The committee drafted what became the Banjul Charter, which identifies a series of rights and duties for individuals and peoples. The committee's drafters considered Africa "not ready for a supranational judicial institution at that time," thus they recommended the creation of an African Commission on Human Rights to oversee respect of the African charter. The recommendations of the Committee of Experts were approved in 1981, and the African charter came into force in 1986 after ratification by half of the Organization for African Unity members.[57] Shortly thereafter, the African Commission on Human Rights began to oversee signatory states' respect for the African charter. Proceedings of the Commission are notoriously politicized and slow, and as was the case in the Inter-American system, Commission decisions are widely regarded as nonbinding. Only after the Cold War ended did African states agree to add a court to their human rights system.

In the 1960s, 1970s, and 1980s, African countries also began a number of regional initiatives aimed at economic cooperation. These initiatives generally faltered under the weight of decolonization. Joseph Nye studied what was perhaps the most promising of Africa's early integration endeavors, the integration scheme of the East African Community. The states of the former British East Africa (Kenya, Tanzania, and Uganda) could build on the colonial ties and the infrastructure connections the British had left behind. They had shared language ties (English and Swahili), similar colonial institutions, the regional elite had been socialized through the same elite institutions, and workers in the region were used to traveling across borders to find jobs. There were also a number of existing institutions to promote functional cooperation in the region, and a new regional integration initiative that included an economic union adopted in 1963 and steps toward building a federation.[58] Nye found, however, that new African leaders were more interested in establishing nation-states, which meant dismantling existing infrastructures so as to inhibit the free movement of labor and capital.

Involvement of former colonial powers also hindered integration initiatives. Support for authoritarian leaders and the funding of proxy wars kept African governments divided. Also, most African countries traded very little with each other; economic relationships with former colonial powers (and now with the EU) remained more economically important.

57 (Viljoen and Louw 2007, quote at 2).
58 (Nye 1965; 1967).

African nationalism was probably the greatest impediment to international legal efforts, but economic relationships with colonial powers also created impediments for African actors advocating transnational regional cooperation.[59]

A Lack of International Courts in Asia and the Middle East

Asia and the Middle East remain outliers to this day. Like Europe, Asia experienced mass atrocities in World War II. Unlike Europe, however, the blame for these atrocities could be placed on outsiders—the Japanese. South Asian independence wars succeeded before African independence wars, without giving rise to any pan-Asian integration movement. Asia also experienced Cold War conflict, including the Korean and Vietnam Wars, but China's Communist Party remained domestically and regionally powerful throughout the Cold War and beyond, able to support local leaders and fight battles with the United States. The robust presence of the Communist alternative in the region kept any demand for liberal reform at bay.

Middle Eastern history largely mirrors what occurred in Africa—colonialism gave way to self-rule, and during the heady nationalist days that followed, populations believed that waning colonial influence would bring with it respect for human rights and greater economic justice. Also as in Africa, Cold War tensions protected problematic political leaders. There are three key differences, however. First, a number of Middle Eastern countries have significant oil deposits. The mutually beneficial oil relationship originally kept Arab leaders close to Western powers, and oil wealth meant that Middle Eastern leaders were not dependent on colonial powers or international institutions for financial and economic support. Second, Middle Eastern politics have long been polarized around the issue of the existence of Israel. Third, the 1979 Iranian revolution exacerbated Islamic tensions, creating a crosscutting cleavage that pits secularly oriented against theocratic actors.

A key question among oil producing countries has been how to use oil power in the service of other political objectives, such as promoting Arab unity and challenging the existence of Israel. In 1967, politically conservative oil producing leaders—Saudi Arabia, Libya, and Kuwait—created the

59 For example, as Nigerian leaders worked to create the Economic Community of West African States (ECOWAS), Francophone countries responded by creating the West African Economic and Monetary Union (WAEMU) among Francophone member states. The Francophone community was intended to serve as a counterbalance to Nigerian hegemony within ECOWAS (Bach 1983, 66), and local participants often see WAEMU states voting as a bloc and undermining ECOWAS initiatives (Adebajo and Rashid 2004, 40–41; Kufuor 2006, 27–29).

Organization of Arab Petroleum Exporting Countries, originally intended to be an exclusive club that would shield the economic weapon of oil from street pressures by excluding more radical member states. In the 1970s, nationalist objectives led a number of Arab countries to seize control of their oil industries. Organization of Arab Petroleum Exporting Countries also succumbed to political pressure following the 1973 Yom Kippur War, expanding membership and becoming a coordinating organization for Arab responses to the conflict with Israel. The Organization of Arab Petroleum Exporting Countries actually includes a permanent international court with jurisdiction over interstate disputes and disputes between oil companies and governments. In 1980, Arab League nations signed a Unified Agreement for the Investment of Arab Capital in Arab States. Both initiatives envisioned international courts that investors could invoke, but these bodies remained defunct.[60]

International Courts at the Close of the Cold War: Economics, Human Rights, and Mass Atrocities Regimes

By the mid-1980s there were two global legal systems—the ICJ and the dispute settlement system of the General Agreement on Tariffs and Trade (GATT). The International Court of Justice became a venue for Cold War politics, hearing a number of cases linked to practices associated with proxy battles and decolonization struggles. Most ICJ cases involved European and American governments, with a few cases that involved African and Middle Eastern countries. Assessments as to the ICJ's good functioning and influence varied.[61] In 1984 the ICJ agreed to rule on American intervention on behalf of "freedom fighters" challenging Nicaragua's socialist political leader. Nicaragua's filing of this case led President Reagan to withdraw from the ICJ's optional compulsory jurisdiction provisions, and the ICJ's invocation of its compulsory jurisdiction in the case and subsequent condemnation of US policy generated a maelstrom of critiques in the US legal academy, hardening American conservative opposition against international law and the ICJ.[62] Robert Bork was most vehement in his critiques, essentially accusing the ICJ of rendering international law immoral by suggesting that politically and morally valid fights against Communism might be illegal.[63]

60 See the online appendix for more. On the Arab Investment regime, see Ben Hamida (2006).

61 For studies of the ICJ during the Cold War and beyond, see Boyle (1985); Franck (1986); Schulte (2004); Singh (1989).

62 ICJ judgment of November 26, 1984—Jurisdiction of the Court and Admissibility of the Application. In 1987, the American *Journal of International Law* published a number of analyses of the ICJ's ruling by American legal academics (volume 81).

63 (Bork 1989/90; 2003).

Economics: The advent of the Cold War had ended international efforts to build a global trade system, leaving the GATT as a default trade institution for Western countries. In the 1950s and 1960s trade diplomats constructed an informal system to resolve trade disagreements in the GATT. This system allowed state parties to initiate mediation and then compose a panel of experts to render a ruling. Defendant states had to consent for a panel to be formed and for the panel's ruling to be accepted. When developing countries sought to make the GATT system more useful for themselves, by creating financial remedies and by allowing for remedies even if a country had not participated in the original case, Europe and the United States stopped using the GATT dispute settlement system. From 1965 to 1979, only nine disputes reached the stage of a panel's formal decision being accepted.[64]

Frustration with the dysfunctional GATT dispute settlement system combined with growing American trade deficits in the 1970s to provoke the passage of the United States Trade Act of 1974. Under Section 301 of this act, the United States Trade Representative was to investigate complaints of American exporters and sanction unfair trade practices of other states. The Section 301 system (relaunched in the 1990s under the name Super 301) was better at engendering resentment among trading partners than it was at resolving intractable trade disagreements.[65] The United States complained, however, that the GATT system had no other effective means to address "unfair trade" by its trading partners.

Mass Atrocities: Once the Nuremberg trials ended, there were no other international criminal tribunals. The consequences of having no international judicial bodies to deal with war crimes were increasingly apparent. Few of the war crimes committed during the wars of liberation were prosecuted, and the United States' response to American war crimes during the Vietnam War, and especially the My Lai massacre, appeared insufficient. Meanwhile, the instigators of Cambodia's killing fields have to this day largely escaped accountability. It became abundantly clear that without an international impetus, war crimes would not be punished. But so long as the permanent members of the UN Security Council would tolerate crimes by allies, no international efforts to address this problem were possible.

Human Rights: As democracy returned to Latin America, US President Carter made enforcement of human rights a priority, facilitating the ratification of treaties needed for the creation of IACtHR. Although Ronald Reagan eschewed this priority and renewed the fight against Communism, Carter's legacy included congressional legislation linking the provision of

64 (Hudec 1993, 31–34).
65 (Noland 1997).

military aid to improvements in a government's human rights record. This legislation created a source of political leverage human rights advocates could draw on.

As of 1989 neither Europe's nor Latin America's human rights courts were used very often. Insiders saw the human rights commissions as fairly effective in promoting respect for human rights among signatory states. In Europe, advocates claim that Commission recommendations were often enacted.[66] Kathryn Sikkink credits the Inter-American Commission's 1980 report on human rights violations in Argentina for being "the first source in print" to request domestic prosecution of responsible parties. According to Sikkink, the report helped to spur demands in Argentina for prosecution (but so did the delegitimization of the military because of the disastrous Falklands War). Together these events made Argentineans distrust their government.[67]

In the 1980s, the European Commission began to forward more cases to the ECtHR because, as Schermers explained, the threat of member state exit was no longer politically viable. Also in the 1980s, Inter-American Commission reports grew increasingly courageous and critical. In 1986, the Commission forwarded the first cases to the Inter-American Court of Human Rights, which involved the Honduran government's practice of "disappearing" political opponents. Other Latin American governments had worse records for making political opponents disappear, but Honduras was the Latin American government that had used this practice *and* submitted to the IACtHR's compulsory jurisdiction. The IACtHR's rulings in the Velásquez Rodríguez cases broke legal ground in that the Court rejected the government's arguments that Velásquez Rodríguez had probably run away from his family, since no body could be found. In a first for Latin America, the Court required the Honduran government to punish responsible parties.[68]

Figure 4.2 shows the relatively low level of litigation in existing international legal systems before the end of the Cold War. The ECJ, with its compulsory jurisdiction and legal revolution, is a clear outlier in terms of level of activity. Litigation rates in systems lacking compulsory jurisdiction—the ICJ, GATT, ECtHR, and IACtHR—barely register. Although the BENELUX and Andean systems largely copied the new-style ECJ model, both systems were yet to become active, let alone effective.

66 Moravcsik cites Mower's claim that member states display a "high degree" of cooperation with the Commission 75 percent of the time, and a moderate degree of cooperation 25 percent of the time (Moravcsik 1995, 171).

67 (Sikkink 2011, 67–69).

68 "Velásquez Rodríguez" case. The political importance of this case is discussed in Sikkink (2011, at 105–6).

FIGURE 4.2: Binding rulings issued by ICJ, GATT, ECJ, ECtHR, ATJ, and IACtHR (founding to the end of the Cold War)

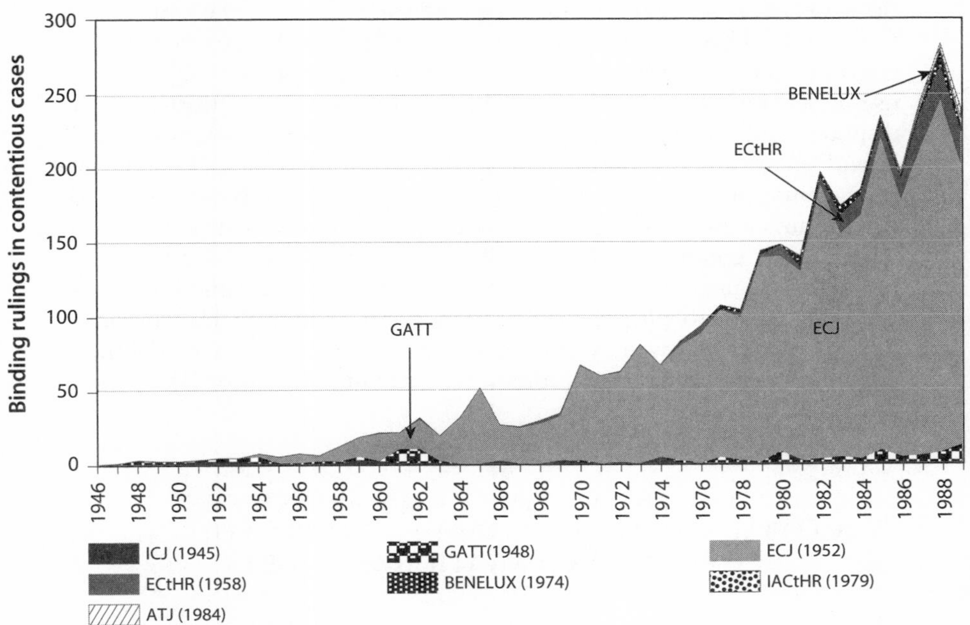

Figure 4.2 helps us understand why, at the close of the Cold War, scholars were beginning to associate the ECJ with effective supranational adjudication. Although activity is not the same thing as effectiveness, scholarly accounts suggest that the ECJ was an international legal system where the desire for law enforcement met with an IC willing to demand respect for European rules despite the wishes of recalcitrant governments.[69] Europe's supranational courts appeared exceptional, but they were for this reason models for the world. The ECtHR influenced the formation of the IACtHR, and the ECJ provided a model emulated by the BENELUX and Andean systems. And scholars looked to Europe to better understand how international legal review becomes politically effective.[70]

The focus in this chapter on the international judiciary obscures other important changes occurring in legal practice at the national level—namely, an increase in the extraterritorial law enforcement by American actors. The discussion of the GATT system mentioned one such change.

69 (Cichowski 2007; Conant 2002; Stone Sweet 2004).

70 (Helfer and Slaughter 1997).

The United States Trade Act of 1974 required the United States Trade Representative to investigate "unfair" trade, and section 301 allowed for the imposition of trade sanctions against states found to be engaged in unfair trade. The Section 301 system revealed how public-private partners generated a pool of legal claims governments might pursue,[71] but the US use of Section 301 spurred renewed interest in working with the GATT dispute resolutions system, if only to stave off and redirect American unilateralism. The US Second Circuit's 1980 decision in Filártiga v. Peña-Irala, reinterpreting a defunct part of the 1789 Judiciary Act, asserted federal jurisdiction for courts to hear torts claims for violations of international law committed abroad. This ruling opened the door for additional torts claims to be raised in US courts, giving NGOs and litigants a venue in which to pursue their human rights agenda. Each American move was later followed by European moves to expand the reach of their law and to prosecute crimes committed abroad in violation of international law.[72]

III. THE END OF THE COLD WAR AND THE GLOBAL SPREAD OF EMBEDDED INTERNATIONAL LAW AND INTERNATIONAL COURTS

The previous section explained the emergence through legal practice of an "embedded law approach," where implementing international law requires authorizing domestic courts to enforce international legal rules at home and sometimes extraterritorially. International legal bodies interpret international statutes, but since domestic law has been linked to international law, international and domestic legal actors end up applying a common set of legal rules. This section explains the global spread of this embedded approach. The end of the Cold War, and with it the discrediting of Marxism and Socialism, led to the end of Soviet economic subsidies and the ascendance of neoliberal economic thought in international institutions and the American and European foreign policy elite.[73] Henceforth, any state that wanted help from foreign investors, the International Monetary Fund, and the World Bank needed to show that they were undertaking economic and political reform. The dismantling of the Soviet empire also unfroze the political dynamic whereby the Soviet Union and its satellites blocked multilateral efforts and membership in Western institutions. Countries escaping from the Soviet orbit rushed to bind themselves to the

71 (Shaffer 2003).
72 (Putnam 2014).
73 (Dezalay and Garth 2002a).

international institutions of the West. In anticipation of expanding membership and legal rules, states moved quickly to address problems in existing international judicial systems.

My focus is on world history and changing legal practice rather than explaining the creation of every IC. I begin with key political events and legal changes that had systemic effects with respect to the three issue areas where international courts are most prevalent: economics, mass atrocities, and human rights. I then discuss international judicial changes in European, Latin American, and African international judiciaries.

Three Global Legal Changes Coinciding with the End of the Cold War

(1) International economics systemic change: Creating the World Trade Organization (WTO)

GATT members were already engaged in broad multilateral trade talks when the Berlin Wall fell. It soon became clear that the collapse of the Soviet trading system would lead to an increased membership of the GATT. The Uruguay Round trade talks (1986–94) became the moment to address known problems, in part because structural reform would only become harder once membership expanded, but also because new members could then be forced to accept a package deal. The Uruguay Round's "single undertaking" made every item of negotiation part of a package. The United States and Europe forced the single undertaking package on other signatories by planning to exit from the old GATT while embracing the new WTO.[74] The final agreement included an expansion of GATT trade rules, an end to the "multiple geometry" approach that allowed countries to selectively adopt GATT agreements, and a major structural change in the GATT's dispute adjudication system.[75]

The impetus for changing the GATT dispute settlement system was the growing dissatisfaction with the US unilateral enforcement strategies combined with a desire to simplify and universalize the GATT system before membership expanded. The US Trade Representative became particularly aggressive in its pursuit of Section 301 violations whenever the president sought trade negotiation authority from Congress, appeasing Congress but creating much disgruntlement among trading partners. The lead up to and beginning of the Uruguay Round led to enhanced US monitoring of "unfair trade" of trade partners, making the 1980s an especially contentious period.[76] US negotiators sought a more effective trade remedy, and other states sought a reprieve from US unilateralism.

74 (Steinberg 2002, 359–60).

75 (Barton et al. 2006, 67–73, 160–78).

76 (Dunoff 2009, 342–45).

The Uruguay Round changes meant that all current and aspiring WTO members faced the prospect of compulsory judicial enforcement in the transformed WTO dispute settlement system. This reality, along with the perceived superiority of economic liberalism, helped to reinvigorate regional trade agreements.

(2) Mass atrocities systemic change: The United Nations creates an international court to adjudicate war crimes

Chapter VII of the United Nations Charter allows the United Nations Security Council to "determine the existence of any threat to the peace, breach of the peace, or act of aggression" and to take military and nonmilitary action to "restore international peace and security." During the Cold War, the threat of a veto by one of the five permanent members of the Security Council blocked many Chapter VII initiatives. The end of the Cold War generated optimism that the United Nations Security Council might finally become a body that could address major threats to peace and security. The Yugoslav crisis led to the first United Nations decision to create an international war crimes court.

When the Cold War ended, a number of Yugoslav territories sought independence. European governments fumbled in their early efforts to deal with the situation, contributing to the outbreak of war by recognizing the legitimacy of the Slovenian, Croatian, and Bosnian independence claims. The United Nation's failed intervention in Somalia (1992) had sapped enthusiasm for UN intervention. Meanwhile, the United States wanted regional organizations to become security providers so that it could capture a peace dividend from the end of the costly Cold War. The United States and the United Nations hoped that the European Community, with its new foreign policy apparatus, might deal with the regional crisis. While Western political leaders tried to avoid involvement in any humanitarian intervention, human rights groups published accounts of concentration camps, bringing images to America and Europe that greatly resembled the concentration camps of World War II. Political inaction became increasingly embarrassing for American and European leaders.

Eventually the West responded through the United Nations, establishing a "commission of experts" to gather evidence of war crimes. According to Gary Bass, this commission was set up to go slowly. UN officials obstructed its efforts, and a paltry budget starved the commission of the resources needed to carry forth its task. But commission member Cherif Bassiouni raised funds from private foundations and relied on students and nongovernmental organizations, amassing strong evidence of war crimes. Embarrassed by UN inaction, especially in light of the mounting evidence of mass atrocities, yet still unwilling to use military force to counter Serbian atrocities, the United Nations Security Council agreed in

1993 to create an international tribunal to prosecute war crimes committed in Yugoslav wars.[77]

The International Criminal Tribunal for the Former Yugoslavia (ICTY) broke the mold of past war crimes systems, leading to a new form of international war crimes court. Already different was that the Nuremberg trials and the Genocide Convention had created legal precedents so that the ICTY did not face the legitimacy problem of enforcing legal rules that did not exist at the time of the crime. More significant were the ICTY's political and institutional innovations. The Nuremberg tribunal had been established by victorious powers. The Yugoslav tribunal was created by the United Nations using its Chapter VII powers to adopt measures that promote peace and security. The ICTY's international prosecutor focused on individual accountability for mass atrocities, investigating crimes by multiple parties so that war crimes prosecution would not be victor's justice. Also, the tribunal was created while the war (and thus war crimes) was ongoing.

The very limited nature of the ICTY's authority in itself raised questions. On what logic could one prosecute crimes in Yugoslavia but not crimes elsewhere? And on what logic could "crimes" of NATO forces be exempted from investigation?[78] The 1994 Rwandan genocide provided an early test of international resolve. Especially after the debacle in the UN's Somalia intervention, Western powers did not want to commit troops to stop the genocide, nor did they want to suggest that African lives were of less value than European lives. The international community responded by again using the United Nations' Chapter VII powers to create another International Criminal Tribunal for Rwanda (ICTR). Participants understood that although the tribunal's jurisdiction might be temporary, the doctrines and practices developed to prosecute mass atrocities would be enduring. The ICTY's and ICTR's charismatic prosecutors, Richard Goldstone, Louise Arbour, and Carla Del Ponte developed legal arguments applicable to any military context, using their prosecutorial prerogatives to shape what these tribunals and subsequent international war crimes tribunals would become.[79]

Inspired by these political advances, human rights activists advocated for a global model. Surely a global war crimes court made more sense than multiple ad hoc war crimes tribunals. The political impetus for a permanent criminal court came from the United Nations General Assembly. Working groups gave way to an ad hoc committee, which became a

77 (Bass 2000, 210–14).

78 Slobodan Milošević tried to create a focus on the crimes of NATO, and the prosecutor did investigate complaints that NATO had bombed a prison. See Hagan (2003, 217–19).

79 (Hagan 2003; Hagan, Levi, and Feralles 2006).

preparatory committee for multilateral negotiations. By the time formal negotiations for the International Criminal Court began, more than sixty states had united into a "like-minded caucus" committed to a number of key propositions that were at odds with the preferences of permanent members of the Security Council. The "like-minded caucus" pushed for inclusion of core crimes (genocide, crimes against humanity, war crimes, and, in the future, aggression); for the elimination of any Security Council veto on prosecution; for an independent prosecutor with the power to initiate investigations and issue indictments; and for a rule that would prohibit reservations to the statute.[80] These provisions ultimately prevailed, leading the United States to oppose the Rome Statute. The result was the new International Criminal Court, created in 2002, and a host of ad hoc hybrid systems to deal with crimes that were committed before and outside of the framework of the new International Criminal Court (ICC) (for example, abuses in Sierra Leone, East Timor, Kosovo, and Cambodia).

The old approach to punishing war criminals had the military victors prosecuting the crimes of the losing force, an other-binding form of victor's justice. The ICTY and ICTR were not much different in that they were created by the United Nations and imposed on Rwanda and Yugoslavia. By contrast, the ICC represents the first-ever self-binding commitment to ongoing international oversight of how states conduct war, at least for 121 state parties to the Rome Statute.[81] For other countries, the Rome Statute reflects other-binding in that the Security Council can use its Chapter VII powers to refer cases to the Office of the Prosecutor, and permanent Security Council members can still veto such references.

The ICC also reflects an embedded European approach to international law enforcement. Part of ratifying the Rome Statute entails creating domestic laws and processes to deal with war crimes in the national system. The ICC's complementarity principle creates an incentive for domestic officials to deal with war crimes, so as to stave off the assertion of ICC jurisdiction. Decisions about prosecuting political leaders who instigate or abet mass atrocities now take place in the shadow of potential ICC prosecution.

(3) Human Rights: The rise of extraterritorial human rights adjudication

American willingness to adjudicate the international legal violations of foreign actors evolved during the Cold War. In the 1960s Congress ordered federal courts to adjudicate disputes involving Cuba's nationaliza-

80 (Schabas 2001, 14–16).

81 This distinction between other-binding and self-binding delegation to courts is developed in chapter 2, section I.

tion of certain industries. Extraterritorial law enforcement accelerated with the United States Trade Act (1974), the revision of the Foreign Sovereign Immunities Act (1976), and the Filártiga v. Peña Irala ruling (1981) that woke up the long dormant Alien Tort Statute, allowing for federal jurisdiction for violations of international law abroad.[82] The Convention against Torture and Other Cruel, Inhuman or Degrading Treatment or Punishment (signed in 1984) universalized this trend because it required state parties to take effective measures to prevent and punish any act of torture, including prosecuting or extraditing for prosecution individuals who violate the treaty. Ratification of this convention reinvigorated the idea of personal accountability for violations of international human rights laws, and it led to the creation of domestic legislation empowering judges to prosecute torture and other cruel and inhuman systems of punishment that occur abroad.

In the 1990s national courts in Belgium, the United Kingdom, and the United States became more willing to adjudicate human rights abuses in Latin America and Africa and to limit claims of foreign sovereignty immunity. A key turning point was the serious treatment given to the Spanish indictment of Chilean Senator for Life Augusto Pinochet. Although the United Kingdom decided to return Pinochet to Chile for humanitarian reasons, the 1998 House of Lords ruling suggested that mutual ratification of the Convention against Torture by Chile, Spain, and the United Kingdom created an international legal prohibition against torture and a duty to prosecute torture violations regardless of who committed the crime or where the crime occurred.[83]

The greater willingness to hold domestic trials for violations of international human rights law committed abroad meant that individuals not prosecuted at home for gross atrocities or torture faced prosecution in Europe and the United States. This experience, as well as indictments of leaders involved in Argentina's dirty war, led national judges to rescind amnesty promises granted to other Latin American leaders (and the IACtHR to later echo this demand). As of this writing, both Belgium and Spain have significantly curtailed their legislation authorizing universal jurisdiction,[84] but domestic laws associated with ratification of the Convention against Torture and the Rome Statute still allow countries to prosecute war crimes committed abroad. Indeed, few people bother noting

82 On changing notions of extraterritoriality in the United States, see Putnam (2014).

83 The House of Lords made this ruling even though Pinochet's "crimes" occurred when he was the sovereign leader of Chile, and he still enjoyed diplomatic immunity from prosecution because he was a "senator for life" in Chile seeking medical attention in the United Kingdom. See Pinochet ruling and Roht-Arriaza (2005); Sikkink (2011, 123).

84 On Belgium's foray into universal jurisdiction, see Roozbeh (2009). On the declining use of such provisions, see Arajärvi (2011).

as exceptional decisions like the 2008 ruling by an American court giving Charles McArthur Emmanuel (a.k.a. "Chuckie" Taylor Jr.) a ninety-seven-year prison sentence for acts of torture in Liberia between 1999 and 2003 or the 2009 Canadian decision finding Désiré Munyaneza guilty of war crimes in Rwanda. In the first ruling, the American judge applied a 1994 US law adopted during ratification of the Convention against Torture. The second ruling was a bit more noteworthy in that it was the first time Canadian judges applied Canada's Crimes against Humanity and War Crimes Act, passed as part of the ratification of the International Criminal Court's Rome Statute.

The Uruguay Round, developments concerning universal jurisdiction, and the Yugoslav and Rwandan genocides spurred legal mobilization, contributing to the proliferation of ICs. Legal developments in Europe, the United States, the United Nations, and the WTO altered the default condition most governments faced. No longer did governments face the choice of international legal systems or no enforcement of international law. Instead, the new global reality is that absent any domestic or regional enforcement systems, the United States, Europe, or the United Nations could use domestic and global systems to enforce international economic, human rights, and mass atrocities laws. These changes combined with forces unleashed by the end of the Cold War to propel the global spread of new-style ICs and the embedded approach to international law enforcement.

Europe: More Deeply and Widely Embedding European Law

The end of the Cold War led both the Council of Europe and the European Union to greatly expand their membership. West European governments decided to improve the European Community and the Council of Europe systems before enlargement, while negotiation of such changes would be relatively easier. For the European Community, the impetus to reform its system was a sense that compliance with EC law and ECJ decisions was uneven.[85] In the late 1980s and early 1990s member states streamlined the Commission-initiated noncompliance procedure for enforcing European law, created a Tribunal of First Instance (now named the General Court) to relieve the growing caseload pressure on the ECJ, and added to the European legal system financial sanctions for those states that persistently ignore ECJ decisions.[86] This new system, as well as the common law *acquis communautaire*, applied to all new member states.

85 According to Tanja Börzel, the perceived "compliance crisis" was a result of Commission action, and it was rather overstated, designed to build support for a more resourced and muscular European legal system (Börzel 2001; Tallberg 2003, 48–53).

86 (Tallberg 2003, 54–91).

For the European human rights system, the impetus to reform was a growing backlog of unresolved cases. In the 1960s and 1970s, few European governments had accepted the ECtHR's jurisdiction, and the Commission dealt with most cases on its own. The part-time ECtHR judges could handle the caseload during their regular meetings. But when more states accepted the ECtHR's jurisdiction, and when the European Commission on Human Rights began to refer more cases in the 1980s, the existing apparatus became overburdened and slow. After years of studying problems in the system, a majority of existing member states finally agreed to accept Protocol 11, which abolished the European Commission on Human Rights, required that all member states accept the ECtHR's compulsory jurisdiction and the right to individual petition, and converted the ECtHR into a full-time body.[87] New Council of Europe members thus joined a fundamentally different system from that of the original member states.[88] Formally speaking, the ECtHR's power is much the same. But with private actors able to pursue cases on their own, the ECtHR became a de facto review body for national court decisions involving human rights violations.[89] In the 1950s, European governments would have soundly rejected these developments, but by the 1990s European leaders sought to extend to others the constraints they already experienced.

The newly liberated post-Communist regimes rushed to bind themselves to Western Europe's institutions, embracing the Council of Europe as an external guarantee against political backsliding.[90] Russia even joined the Council of Europe's human rights system. Expansion of the European Community proceeded more slowly because West European leaders required significant economic and political change before new members could accede. The membership conditions the European Community set helped to lock in human rights promises and economic reforms.

Europe also added two post–Cold War ICs. The Economic Court of the Commonwealth of Independent States was created to facilitate the resolution of disagreements among what were now formally independent yet structurally dependent post-Soviet states.[91] Many states that had been part of the European Free Trade Association decided to join the EU, but those that remained outside negotiated a European Free Trade Association that comes with its own IC.

87 (Bates 2011, chapter 11).

88 Moravcsik argues that formerly Communist systems embraced these changes to demonstrate their deep commitments to democracy and the rule of law (Moravcsik 2000).

89 According to Laurence Helfer (2008), these changes are best understood as an acknowledgment that Europe's human rights obligations and the ECtHR's authority have become deeply embedded into Europe's national legal orders .

90 (Moravcsik 2000).

91 (Danilenko 1999).

Latin America: Sleeping Bears Awake

Latin America's two ICs were largely moribund in the 1980s. The Cold War thawed legal initiatives earlier in Latin America, beginning in the inter-American system. By the 1990s, proxy wars and military regimes were over in Latin America, domestic courts in Argentina were prosecuting violations of the military government, and Spanish prosecutors were also pursuing prosecutions of Latin American human rights violations. Membership in the Organization of American States human rights system grew from eleven countries in 1979 to twenty-two countries today. In this context, the Inter-American Commission became increasingly willing to refer cases to the IACtHR.[92] These new cases, in turn, allowed the IACtHR to establish legal precedents, including expanding access to nongovernmental organizations, invalidating amnesty agreements granted at the end of civil conflicts, and raising the bar for countries that might want to withdraw from the IACtHR's compulsory jurisdiction.[93] The IACtHR's rulings have generated some controversy and at times noncompliance,[94] but undeniably the influence of the IACtHR in Latin America has grown since the end of the Cold War.[95]

The promarket Washington Consensus pulsed through Latin America in the 1990s. Domestic lawyers and economists transformed the legal institutions creating new administrations and legal institutions to promote economic liberalism and human rights protection.[96] The rise of liberal economic thought in the region contributed to the end of the Andean Pact's controversial rules regulating foreign direct investment and the re-

92 We don't really know why the Inter-American Commission, which had begun operating long before the creation of a court, initially hesitated to refer cases to the Court. Perhaps the commission needed time to learn how to best use the Court. Perhaps the Commission was concerned that legal references and rulings might be used to criticize the Commission's work, member states might use a legal case to challenge Commission findings, or that a focus on private cases might detract from a focus on a broader range of violations within a state. See Cosgrove (2000, 52–53).

93 The IACtHR ruled that countries must withdraw from the entire Inter-American Human Rights system, not just the jurisdiction of the court. This means that countries can decide whether or not to accept the authority of the IACtHR when they opt in to the Inter-American Human Rights system, but once they are in the system they must withdraw from the entire human rights system if they want to escape IACtHR oversight. For more, see Romano (2007, 821–24).

94 (Hawkins and Jacoby 2010; Huneeus 2011, 2013).

95 (Cavallaro and Brewer 2008).

96 Dezalay and Garth discuss changing economic and human rights policy brought by the diffusion of the Washington Consensus (Dezalay and Garth 2002b). An edited volume discusses a growing willingness of what are in some cases newly created supreme courts to confront governments, and with this a shifting legal culture (Huneeus, Couso, and Sieder 2011).

launching of Andean integration efforts.[97] The prospect of WTO membership, and with it the binding Trade Related Aspects of Intellectual Property Rights contributed to changes in Andean intellectual property legislation, national intellectual property management, and the activation of the Andean legal system's preliminary ruling mechanism. And a desire to make the Andean legal system work better contributed to the 1996 Cochabamba Protocol expanding private litigant access to the ATJ's noncompliance procedure. The ATJ has become the third most active international court, but its docket is skewed. Andean intellectual property rules are regularly enforced, while loopholes written into Andean law continue to allow national derogations to the free movement of goods, capital, and people.[98]

The spread of liberal economics, and the United States' commitment to the North American Free Trade Agreement in 1994 led to the strengthening of the Southern Common Market system. Brazilian leaders supported improvements in the dispute settlement process as a sign of their commitment to free trade in the Americas. This common market system, and the Andean system, can hear complaints about member states violating free trade rules. But trade in the region continues to be regulated mostly through bilateral and multilateral agreements with the United States, the WTO remains a key venue for regional trade disputes, and Latin America's two other ICs (the Central American Court of Justice and the Caribbean Court of Justice) have struggled.

Africa: The Creation and Activation of Regional Courts

The largest and least investigated changes in the international judiciary have occurred in Africa.[99] We lack histories regarding changes within Africa's regional integration systems, but it is clear that the end of the Cold War led African leaders to look for new sources of financial support, and American and European donors to increasingly require human rights and economic reform. This confluence of incentives provided an excellent opportunity for African lawyers trained in Europe and the United States to advocate for international judicial changes. African leaders embraced the creation of many international courts, perhaps to demonstrate their commitment to economic reform.

Most of Africa's ICs emulate the ECJ model, but they tend to add political hobbles to protect national sovereignty. This fact may explain why violations to free trade rules abound in Africa, with adjudication of such

97 (O'Keefe 1996).

98 (Helfer, Alter, and Guerzovich 2009, 36–39).

99 An exception is Gathii (2011).

violations practically nonexistent.[100] There are, however, African courts that are becoming increasingly active. Chapter 5 discusses the impetus to create the Organization for the Harmonization of Business Law in Africa (OHADA), and to add an IC to oversee national application of its Uniform Acts. The OHADA court has issued over five hundred rulings to date.

As in Europe and Latin America, the African human rights systems have been slow to evolve. Although the Banjul Charter became legally binding in 1986, it took the end of the Cold War for movement toward creating oversight mechanisms. As of this writing, key African states still do not accept the African court's jurisdiction, which makes both the Commission and the Court hesitant to use their formal powers. But a recent turning point seems to be the conflicts in Libya and the Ivory Coast. In 2011, leaders of these two countries decided to employ violence to hold on to power. The African Union took the side of the people, demanding that African leaders stop targeting noncombatants. This intervention seems to have unfrozen the concern about referring cases to the African Court of Human and Peoples' Rights. In 2011, the ACtHPR received fifteen cases from the Commission, a trend that is continuing in 2012. But abuses in the Congo, Zimbabwe, and the Sudan remain unaddressed.

Only in a few countries do private litigants have direct access to the ACtHPR, and the Court recently ruled that state ratification is the only way for private litigants to gain access to the Court.[101] Frustrated by the slow growth of the African human rights system, regional integration systems have expanded their human rights actions. The largest change has occurred in the Economic Community of West African States (ECOWAS), which in 2005 gave its Court of Justice the authority to hear private appeals of human rights violations. The difficulties human rights activists face in the African Union system was a key catalyst behind the decision to give the ECOWAS a human rights jurisdiction, with direct access for litigants.[102] The ECOWAS court has been willing to make bold demands of member states with respect to human rights—as discussed in the modern-day slavery case study (chapter 7).

African countries did not embrace the Washington Consensus to the same degree as in Latin America. Instead, the awakening of African

100 Elsewhere we investigate why the ECOWAS court has not been more involved in adjudicating economic cases (Alter, Helfer, and McAllister 2013). Richard Oppong undertakes a systematic review of the legal aspects of Africa's economic integration agreements, finding that institutional overlap and a failure to address certain legal deficiencies undermines regional economic integration efforts (Oppong 2011).

101 ACtHPR "Femi Falana ruling." As of Aug. 2013, Burkino Faso, Ghana, Ivory Coast, Malawi, Mali, Rwanda, and Tanzania had agreed to allow private litigants to bring cases directly to the ACtHPRs.

102 (Alter, Helfer, and McAllister 2013; Nwogu 2007).

regional systems has been triggered in part by the United Nations Millennium Development Goals. In May 2000, a hundred governments committed to the seven specified Millennium Development Goals, which brought with them a promise of international aid (a.k.a. global partnerships) to help signatory governments. Millennium Development Goals are not about economic liberalism or human rights per se, but they include promises to eradicate extreme poverty, expand access to education and health, and promote gender equality. Starting in 2000, regional integration movements and national governments infused national and regional legislation with promises aimed at helping achieve the Millennium Development Goals. Good governance, gender equality, and the right to free basic education were thereby added to the agenda of regional institutions and were embedded within national legal orders. African ICs have been also been involved in adjudicating cases involving these provisions, at times generating some political backlash.[103]

Asia and the Middle East Remain Outliers

Asia continues to eschew international courts. The Association of Southeast Asian Nations (ASEAN) agreed in 2004 to add a compulsory dispute settlement system, modeled on the WTO, and there are constant studies of the benefits that could come from further legalizing ASEAN. Judges are yet to be appointed, and states are yet to ask for the formation of an adjudicatory panel. As recently as October 2012, ASEAN leaders reaffirmed their "strong commitment" to establishing a legalized regional dispute settlement system.[104] I have no good explanation for the absence of the international judicialization of Asian politics, which others have also observed.[105] Certainly China remains adverse to legal checks on government power, and the economic productivity in Asia perhaps helps legitimize Asian governments, keeping citizens content enough to continue to trust central governments. ASEAN leaders also clearly worry about inciting ethnic tensions, preferring consensual over adversarial forms of dispute adjudication.

Populations in the Middle East have, by now, had time to sour on the early nationalist euphoria and to become deeply disenchanted with their governments. In the post–Cold War era, the Arab League actually constituted the Arab Investment Court to adjudicate a Saudi investment dispute with Tunisia.[106] As I finish this book, the Middle East is convulsing through

103 On the prospects for Africa's regional economic courts, see Gathii (2010). On the political challenges to the SADC and EACJ, see Ebobrah (2011); Ebobrah (2010).

104 http://www.asean.org/news/asean-secretariat-news/item/great-reaffirmation-put-in-place-for-enhanced-dispute-settlement-mechanism-in-asean, last visited January 11, 2013.

105 (Kahler 2000).

106 (Ben Hamida 2006, 712).

the aftermath of the Arab Spring. Arab populations are becoming increasingly frustrated with their own transitions, and with the reality that Syria's leadership may well escape international prosecution for its crimes (because Syria has not accepted the ICC's jurisdiction and Russia has blocked Security Council efforts to crack down on Syrian leaders). Perhaps in the Middle East the conditions are more ready to embrace international judicial oversight. Indeed, the government of Bahrain recently asked the Arab League to consider establishing an Arab Human Rights court. But the Israeli-Palestinian problem is as vexing as ever, and theocratic rule may well be at odds with the liberal values associated with international judicial oversight. These regions are likely to remain outliers for the time being.

IV. POLITICAL FORCES GENERATING A PROLIFERATION OF INTERNATIONAL COURTS

This chapter has focused on how global historical events and legal practice have shaped the development of the international judiciary. This section extracts from this history five general political factors that make governments more willing to consent to international judicial oversight.

First, a distrust of governments is the key impetus behind the political support of international judicial oversight, with major disappointments creating the permissive conditions to move ahead. John Locke long ago argued that "it is unreasonable for Men to be Judges in their own Cases, that Self-love will make Men partial to themselves and their Friends. And on the other side, that Ill Nature, Passion and Revenge will carry them too far in punishing others. And hence nothing but Confusion and Disorder will follow."[107] Major political unrest and human rights violations have led populations to extend this logic to governments, creating the permissive conditions that facilitate delegation to ICs. Governments only sign on, however, once their legitimating suggestions of other options ring too hollow to be convincing. Europeans' experience of World War II and Communist rule, Latin Americans' experience with brutal military dictatorship, and Africans' experience with corrupt nationalist governments that become increasingly violent once they overstay their welcome have led populations to favor self-binding to international judicial oversight. These events occurred at different times in different places, and populations first had to give up on the notion that a different government, chosen by the people or overseen by domestic structures, would respect the rule of law and citizen rights. The varied time it took for disenchantment

107 (Locke 1957, §13).

with domestic checks and balances to grow helps to explain the variation in the timing of embracing ICs across regions.[108]

Each permissive moment creates the possibility for international judicial evolution because advocates stand ready to push for international judicial models that address limitations and problems faced by past international legal and judicial initiatives. The first iteration of IC creation draws on successful European models, but adds political hobbles to protect national sovereignty. When and if governments later desire more effective international legal systems, some of these hobbles might be removed, as occurred with respect to the WTO and the Andean Tribunal of Justice and in the European and ECOWAS human rights systems.[109]

Second, global initiatives have aided the implantation of international law in domestic legal systems, and thus facilitated the spread of the embedded approach to international law enforcement. This chapter discussed how international initiatives increasingly generate domestic law and domestic legal enforcement mechanisms. The Washington Consensus, the Convention against Torture, the ICC's Rome Statute, and the Millennium Development Goals all included demands that domestic legal economic and political institutions change in fundamental ways. The World Bank has also promoted structural changes to enhance the domestic rule of law. When international judicial oversight combines with embedded international law, the possibility for delegation to ICs to generate altered politics increases.

Third, the overlapping nature of national, regional, and international jurisdiction propels advancements at each level. Institutional histories tend to downplay how developments in parallel regimes create a permissive environment for change. But dissatisfaction with United Nations human rights efforts led Europe and Latin America to pursue their own human rights system. Dissatisfaction with the African Union human rights system propelled ECOWAS to add a human rights jurisdiction to its court.

Later, global and extraterritorial law enforcement changed the default choice of individual governments. Where international litigation advances take hold, liberal democracies find themselves already constrained by international legal rules. These countries then advocate for the spread of binding rules and for improvements in the international legal mechanisms to address noncompliance by others, so that other states will be equally bound by international legal commitments. Regionally based activists simultaneously learn from developments in the United States and Europe,

108 This argument is consistent with Reus-Smit's (2011) discussion of the expansion of individual rights in the international system.

109 (Barton et al. 2006; Alter, Helfer, and McAllister 2013; Alter, Helfer, and Saldias 2012).

adapting foreign models to the specific needs of the region. Meanwhile, the least attractive enforcement system for international rules has courts in one country sitting in judgment over the behavior of actors in another country, which occurred when the United States passed its 1974 Trade Act, when American and European courts started to assert jurisdiction over crimes committed in Latin America and Africa, and when the UN Security Council started creating ad hoc war crimes bodies. American unilateralism and Euro-American extraterritorial legal assertions made multilateral legal systems newly attractive. And where multilateral systems exist, governments still prefer to resolve disagreements close to home rather than experience international adjudication, and thus multilateral enforcement gives rise to regional enforcement mechanisms and to domestic enforcement of international rules so as to stave off external assertions of jurisdiction. Today's discussion of adding criminal chambers to African legal systems is the latest example of this cross-institutional reverberation.

Fourth, legal and political dynamics interact to produce institutional change between conjunctural moments. This discussion offered a number of examples of how legal practice contributed to changing existing international legal institutions. The starkest example is surely the ECJ's *coup de la loi*. When the ECJ declared direct effects and the supremacy of European law in national legal orders, it created legal rights that European citizens could invoke in domestic courts and fundamentally changed how the European legal system operated. Another example of legal evolution concerned the IACtHR's very first ruling where the Court created an obligation for Honduras's government to punish people involved in disappearing political opponents. A third example involves changes in national legal practices including extraterritorial assertions of legal jurisdiction over economic and human rights violations committed abroad, as occurred in the revisions of the Foreign Sovereign Immunities Act and Filártiga v. Peña-Irala ruling that reinvigorated the American Alien Tort Statute and the British Pinochet rulings.

There are many reasons why these legal developments occurred.[110] But it is also true that legal dynamics sometimes evolve because political change is blocked. In the European case, legal advocates were frustrated by the success of French efforts to block European integration from proceeding. It is rare for international judges to be as legally innovative as the

110 The IACtHR and national courts were arguably responding to legislation that governments had adopted. The Inter-American Convention gives the IACtHR the authority to demand restorative remedies; the Foreign Sovereign Immunities Act explicitly limits the sovereign immunity of foreign leaders; the British House of Lords responded to commitments made in ratifying the Convention against Torture.

ECJ and ECtHR have been. These courts arguably faced permissive conditions that facilitated greater judicial activism.[111]

Legal practice also evolves because litigants detect a greater political willingness by governments to accept adjudication and adverse legal rulings. As governments become habituated to defending their policy in court, and to sometimes losing, litigants become more willing to raise bold cases and judges more willing to apply existing legal rules. This evolution in legal practice need not take the form of judicial activism. Indeed, the baby steps of change involve judges conservatively applying clear legal rules to compelling cases. Advocates may then draw on the acculturation of governments and later permissive opportunities to garner decisions that ratify or extend the jurisdiction of international courts.[112]

Fifth, the United States (and Europe) facilitate the spread of international law and international adjudication when leaders articulate, accept, and respond to legalist arguments. Europe's support for international law and international legal institutions is well known, thus I focus here on the less intuitive case. The United States' record vis-à-vis international law and international courts is schizophrenic. The United States helped to found the United Nations, enabled and supported European integration to create a strong counter to the Soviet Union, promoted human rights in Latin America, developed the WTO system, promoted robust domestic rules of law, and early on American administrations supported the creation of an ICC. During the Cold War, Congress essentially ordered American courts to adjudicate legal violations of Fidel Castro's Communist regime and the United States Trade Representative to adjudicate violations of GATT trade rules.

But American conservatives have also been a constant force challenging the authority and legitimacy of international institutions. In the 1940s, Republicans ran against President Franklin Delano Roosevelt on a platform that opposed many initiatives in the United Nations that Roosevelt had supported. Conservatives lost the election, but the Republican vice presidential candidate from 1944, John Bricker, became a senator in 1946. In 1949 Bricker proposed to the Republican dominated Congress a constitutional amendment, the so-called Bricker Amendment, which would have significantly restricted the ability of the United States to negotiate and ratify international treaties. The Senate rejected Bricker's amendment in 1954, but the amendment failed by just one vote. To win

111 Judicial power in general was growing in Europe in the 1960s and 1970s, which made national judges sympathetic to the argument that judicial checks must also exist at the international level. For more on how context shapes international judicial lawmaking, see Alter and Helfer (2010).

112 (Goodman and Jinks 2004).

the fight against the Bricker Amendment, the secretary of state (John Foster Dulles) testified that the administration did not intend to submit the Genocide Convention or the Covenant on Civil and Political Rights to the Senate for approval.[113] The Brickerite coalition and sentiment has remained an enduring force in American politics.

One possible explanation for the United States' apparent schizophrenia is the willingness of powerful countries to bind others, and unwillingness to bind themselves to international law. But this answer is insufficient. Powerful countries do not systematically avoid legal checks, and the United States is not consistently opposed to international courts and tribunals.[114] A better explanation of the US position is that the United States is a divided nation that includes deep wells of support and highly mobilized opposition to international law and international courts. America acts schizophrenically because Congress is only sometimes able to shape US positions on international legal issues. When it comes to ratifying treaties,[115] and to political positions taken by Republican administrations,[116] the political power of the Brickerite coalition reveals itself. The conservative movement has been able to limit the American embrace of international legal instruments, including the Law of the Sea Convention and Inter-American initiatives, with the one exception of the United States' support of a more robust legal system for the World Trade Organization. But the United States often demonstrates its commitment to international law, especially when congressional support is not needed.

The US (and European) commitment to legalism ends up contributing to the spread of international adjudication. There remains a strong base of support for multilateralism, the rule of law, and for international courts in both the United States and Europe.[117] This support leads Western governments to search for useful legal and political strategies to promote their objectives. Since legal arguments *do* shape US and European policy positions, using international law to challenge these positions is an effective political tool. This reality means that international law provides a useful means for governments around the world to resist or push back against Western pressure.[118] As long as Americans use and respond to legal arguments, American (and one might add European) support for the rule of law remains a powerful force for the legalization of international relations.

113 (Borgwardt 2005, 267–69).
114 (Romano 2009).
115 (Moravcsik 2005).
116 (Nzelibe 2011).
117 (Kull and Ramsay 2009).
118 (Hurd 2005).

CONCLUSION: EMBEDDED INTERNATIONAL LAW AND THE EVOLVING INTERNATIONAL JUDICIARY

This whirlwind world historical account of the changes contributing to the spread of ICs helps us see how the same global forces—the Cold War, disenchantment with governments, and the end of the Cold War—shaped developments in economic, human rights, and war crimes legal regimes. Local conditions generate varying permissive environments for advocates to pressure governments to accept international judicial oversight.

This chapter stressed how many of the global changes were facilitated by incremental changes in legal practice at the national and international level. These changes occurred in part because governments and legislatures embedded international law into national legal orders, changing constitutions and passing laws that either made international law part of domestic legal orders or encouraged national adjudicators to help enforce international law.

Embedding international law into domestic legal orders makes international litigation locally effective because it increases the prospect that domestic compliance partners will respond to international legal pressure. National actors tend to be more concerned with domestic law and domestic legal perceptions than they are with international law or foreign perceptions. But the more domestic law mirrors international law, the harder it is for domestic actors to defend behavior that has been condemned by international or foreign judges.

The embedded approach to international law enforcement has developed furthest in Europe. Section II of this chapter explained that Europe did not set out to create a model of international law; indeed, European governments in the 1950s and 1960s displayed the same aversion to international oversight as one finds today in Africa and parts of Latin America. Nor have European leaders worked hard to export their legal model. European governments generally support the strengthening and spread of international judicial oversight, if only so that other countries might be as constrained by law and international courts as European governments already are. But Europe cannot force its model on others, nor is there evidence that European actors systematically use economic or political leverage to promote the spread of their international legal model. Instead, the European model draws its own adherents. Advocates for international legalization wait until the moment presents itself, and then they draw inspiration from Europe's experience with international law.

A focus on world history suggests that the spread of ICs in the post–Cold War period reflects the dominance of American and European hard and soft power. Even when the United States and Europe do not directly pressure regions around the world to create or enhance their international legal systems, belief in the benefits of liberal economics, democracy, and the rule of law drives US and European actors to support political parties and interest groups that pressure their governments to submit to judicial accountability. Moreover, the willingness of the United States and Europe to respond to well-developed legal arguments and judicial rulings makes emulating legalism an attractive strategy.

A fuller account of the proliferation of international courts will need to take local histories into account and explain the choices leaders make as they embrace and adapt European legal models. A fuller account will also need to explain how legal practice shapes what international judicial institutions become.

As I write this, democratization movements seem to be faltering. Venezuela, Russia, and Hungary have been moving in increasingly authoritarian directions, with the democratic support of the people. Arab Spring movements are also giving rise to the democratic election of Islamic parties that do not necessarily support democracy or Western conceptions of human rights and the rule of law. And people are questioning whether liberal economic orthodoxy actually delivers its promised goods. International legalization may depend on the permissive condition of liberal values and Euro-American power. But to the extent that democracy, the rule of law, and the binding nature of international law are associated with progress and modernity, domestic and international forces may continue to push toward realizing the goals inscribed in international law. This chapter has shown that international judicial systems evolve slowly over time, propelled by conjunctural events and shifting legal practice. What may look like near collapse may actually contribute to an awakening if supporters mobilize to maintain support for the rule of law. Development of international legal systems will depend to some extent on the opportunities for litigation, but also on the actions and decisions of participants in the legal process to prioritize legality and judicial independence over other objectives.

Part II: International Courts in Action

CHAPTER 5

International Dispute Settlement

Hedley Bull once argued that international society, like all societies, organizes to achieve the elemental, primary, and universal goals of peace, property protection, and the keeping of covenants.[1] International systems of order have changed over time, from empires to religious orders, to the rule of kings and colonial powers, to the current international state system, but all of these systems have included mechanisms to facilitate the peaceful settlement of disputes. In more recent history, kings, queens, and colonial officers dealt with transborder disputes within their spheres of influence. Often proceedings were more diplomatic than legal in nature, with adjudicators using their power and authority to make decisions stick. International courts (ICs) are twentieth-century additions, created to provide an alternative and perhaps more modern mechanism for states and transnational actors to resolve their disputes. ICs have largely replaced the role of colonial powers in adjudicating international disputes, but many other means for dispute settlement also exist.

International law does not require governments or private litigants to resolve their disagreements; the only requirement is that disputes be peacefully resolved. Alternative dispute resolution mechanisms, including diplomacy, mediation, and arbitration, remain common approaches to international dispute settlement. In mediation, a third party works with the disputants to help craft an agreement that both parties can live with. In arbitration, litigants select a third party to adjudicate the dispute and issue a binding decision. The benefit of these methods is that the parties can choose who adjudicates their disagreement and influence the process, and the entire proceedings may take place behind closed doors and thus

1 The three "elementary, primary, and universal" goals of any society, according to Bull, are to create norms to ensure security and avoid bodily harm, to establish a system of property governance, and to create mechanisms to ensure that covenants are kept (Bull 1977, chapter 1).

away from public scrutiny. Legalized dispute settlement differs from these alternatives in a number of respects. Disputants do not get to pick their judges or define the universe of legal rules that will be applied, and arguments will generally be written down, generating a more public government position. The fact that judges will issue a binding ruling also creates a legalized backdrop for negotiations that differs from mediation and even arbitration.[2] Scholars have shown that where legalized dispute settlement exists as a compulsory option (that is, one that defendants cannot block), out of court negotiation is more likely to occur in the shadow of the law because parties know they can bring their disagreement to a judge to garner a legal resolution.[3]

This chapter focuses on international courts in their dispute settlement role. Section I documents the variation in how states have delegated dispute settlement jurisdiction to different international courts. Section II focuses on state-initiated dispute settlement, discussing the International Court of Justice's (ICJ) contribution to the Qatar v. Bahrain territorial dispute, and the International Tribunal for the Law of the Sea resolving a dispute involving Russia's seizure of Japanese vessels illegally fishing in contested waters. Section III focuses on private litigant-initiated dispute settlement, including the United States–Iranian mass claims tribunal and Organization for the Harmonization of Business Law in Africa (OHADA). These are least likely cases involving issues that touch on long and deep antagonisms and/or countries that generally avoid international adjudication. Section IV considers the extent to which ICs alter politics in their dispute settlement role, bringing additional ICJ cases into the discussion. The key compliance partners for ICs in the dispute settlement role are the litigants themselves, which is to say that disputes end because the parties decide to let the legal decision govern their disagreement.

Those familiar with the workings of international law will find this chapter's case studies rather normal. This is the point. This chapter resides in the familiar old terrain of international law. The cases show how international courts offer a modern way to address issues that have long vexed international relations. Pretty much everyone agrees that sometimes ICs helpfully resolve disputes, and that the existence of ICs with dispute settlement jurisdiction is neither surprising nor problematical. The only question is whether ICs should only be a mechanism for governments to selectively use, should they desire legalized dispute settlement. The conclusion considers the stakes of keeping ICs within the old terrain of international dispute settlement.

2 (Shapiro 1981, 8–17).

3 (Edelman, Uggen, and Howard 2000; Mnookin and Kornhauser 1979).

I. DELEGATING DISPUTE SETTLEMENT ROLES TO INTERNATIONAL COURTS

One might see all ICs as having an implicit dispute settlement jurisdiction since all cases that appear in front of an IC involve two parties and a disagreement about the meaning of the law. In my coding of Court Treaties, however, I looked for explicit jurisdiction to adjudicate disputes in cases raised by state and nonstate litigants. This grant of dispute settlement jurisdiction was surely the most vague of all of the roles.[4] ICs in an enforcement role have a clear jurisdiction to assess state compliance with a specified international legal agreement; ICs with administrative and constitutional review jurisdictions can assess the validity of state and international institutional acts. ICs with dispute settlement roles have jurisdiction to adjudicate any matter that parties raise. The devil is, of course, in the details. The first questions the court will consider are whether the IC has jurisdiction, the case is admissible, the parties have legal standing, and the law in dispute is binding law. In my coding of Court Treaties, dispute settlement was the second most common role delegated to ICs, after law enforcement.

Figure 5.1 identifies the universe of permanent operating ICs explicitly authorized to adjudicate disputes between states, and sometimes between international actors and private litigants, seventeen in all. Fourteen ICs have jurisdiction to adjudicate interstate disputes; eleven have jurisdiction to resolve disputes involving private actors and international organizations (IOs); four have jurisdiction over disputes between states and international institutions;[5] four allow private litigants direct access to litigate a dispute with another member state; and three can hear disputes involving two private parties. Nine ICs also have preliminary ruling mechanisms that allow domestic courts to channel cases involving community

4 The jurisdictional assignment tends to be vague for a few reasons. Sometimes negotiators expect subsequent agreements to define the terms of dispute settlement, and sometimes state parties might want the IC available to adjudicate a broad range of disputes, in which case the less said about the jurisdiction the better. Sometimes dispute settlement clauses are lowest-common-denominator clauses, intended to allow states to list their caveats in reservations to the treaty. For example, Article IX of the Genocide Convention stipulates that disputes "relating to the interpretation, application or fulfilment" of the convention can be brought to the ICJ, but a number of countries then objected to this clause by filing reservations as they ratified the treaty. The Law of the Sea Convention also allows states to specify limitations to their consent to dispute adjudication for certain maritime and territorial issues.

5 I am not including jurisdiction regarding staff cases. The chapter appendix notes whether courts can also adjudicate employment disputes involving staff of the international institution.

FIGURE 5.1: International courts' dispute settlement jurisdiction (N = 17)

<table>
<tr><th colspan="2">State initiated dispute settlement</th><th colspan="3">Private dispute settlement</th></tr>
<tr><th>State v. state
(Interstate dispute settlement)
N = 14</th><th>State v. IO
N = 4</th><th>Private
litigant v. IO
N = 10</th><th>Private
litigant
v. state</th><th>Private litigant v.
private litigant</th></tr>
<tr><td rowspan="2">Andean Tribunal of Justice (ATJ)
Caribbean Court of Justice (CCJ)
Central American Court of Justice (CACJ)
Central African Monetary Community (CEMAC)
Court of Justice for the Common Market of Eastern and Southern Africa (COMESA)
East African Court of Justice (EACJ)
Economic Court of the Commonwealth of Independent States (ECCIS)
Economic Community of West African States Court (ECOWAS CJ)
European Court of Justice (ECJ)
International Court of Justice (ICJ)
International Tribunal for the Law of the Sea (ITLOS)
Southern Common Market Dispute Settlement Permanent Review Tribunal (MERCOSUR)
Southern African Development Community (SADC)
World Trade Organization Permanent Appellate Body (WTO)</td><td rowspan="2">ECJ
CACJ
ECOWAS CJ
SADC</td><td rowspan="2">ATJ
CACJ
COMESA
CEMAC
EACJ
ECJ
ECOWAS CJ
European Free Trade Area Court (EFTAC)
West African Economic and Monetary Union (WAEMU)
ITLOS (Seabed Authority & staff disputes)
SADC</td><td>*Direct access:*
ATJ
CCJ
SADC</td><td>*Direct access:*
ATJ
ITLOS (Seabed Authority)
Common Court of Justice and Arbitration for the Organization for the Harmonization of Corporate Law in Africa (OHADA)</td></tr>
<tr><td colspan="2">*Preliminary ruling mechanisms allow cases in national courts to be referred to the IC*:
ATJ
ECJ
BENELUX
CACJ
CEMAC
COMESA
EACJ
SADC
WAEMU</td></tr>
</table>

The first listing on the table identifies the court's full name. Repeated listings use the acronym.

rules to the IC for resolution (see chapter 6 for more about preliminary ruling mechanisms). The full name of the court is used for the first listing, with an acronym for each additional listing. The chapter appendix paraphrases each IC's dispute settlement jurisdiction as defined in Court Treaties. The dispute settlement role often overlaps with other roles. For example, the Andean Tribunal's noncompliance procedure defines the rights of states to initiate disputes involving other states, essentially ensuring that the disputes will involve compliance with Andean rules. Although one could surely add ICs and quasi-legal bodies to this table (the chapter appendix also includes the African Court of Justice, ASEAN, OAPEC, and Arab Investment Dispute settlements systems), the most relevant insight is the variety of ways that ICs can be invoked in their dispute settlement role. We are far from the world of kings and queens adjudicating the complaints of local leaders or their subjects.

It is interesting to note that from this list, the Economic Court of the Commonwealth of Independent States (ECCIS) and ICJ are the only ICs that have not also been delegated other judicial roles. Observing what is omitted starts to reveal the limits of this old terrain of international law. Excluded from figure 5.1 are human rights courts and criminal courts, which instead have a clear mandate to oversee compliance with human rights or criminal law. The rest of this section provides more detail about ICs' state-initiated and private litigant-initiated dispute settlement jurisdiction.

State-Initiated Dispute Settlement

Nothing is lost, and much can be gained, by allowing ICs to be available should state parties desire a legalized resolution of disputes. As scholars have noted, there are many reasons for governments to turn to ICs for dispute settlement. The Qatar and Bahrain case study shows how turning adjudication over to a legal process can help political leaders by removing the need for diplomatic agreement regarding each step. The Japan/Russia case study shows how governments use international adjudication to address important concerns of domestic actors. Research by Paul Huth, Todd Allee, Christina Davis, and Beth Simmons extends these insights via quantitative analyses, affirming the many economic and political benefits of a clear legal resolution for certain types of international disputes.[6]

6 Todd Allee and Paul Huth see the desire to deflect blame as the chief motive for states choosing legalized dispute resolution. Simmons focuses on the economic benefits that accrue when territorial disputes are resolved. Christina Davis shows the United States initiating WTO litigation for domestic reasons and WTO litigation bringing economic benefits. (Allee and Huth 2006; Davis 2012; Huth and Allee 2006; Simmons 2002; Simmons 2006).

The only real question is whether ICs should have exclusive and compulsory dispute settlement jurisdiction. Figure 5.2 provides more detail on the fifteen ICs with a jurisdiction to adjudicate interstate disputes.[7] Of the twenty-four operational ICs today, seven ICs have dispute settlement jurisdiction for specified international agreements; an additional seven allow member states to adjudicate a broad range of disagreements. Unless clearly indicated in a treaty, a court's jurisdiction is presumed to be optional, something both parties must agree to before a case can proceed. Compulsory (jurisdiction) means that defendant states are obligated to participate. Some courts have "optional declarations" that countries can sign in advance, committing to compulsory adjudication of disagreements. If the countries involved in the dispute have each signed optional declarations, the court's jurisdiction will be compulsory. This table reflects what is written in Court Treaties; specific agreements can confer compulsory jurisdiction on an IC with respect to the agreement. The table also identifies the ICs that have additional enforcement roles, meaning jurisdiction to adjudicate state compliance with the agreement.

Optional jurisdiction ensures that ICs will mostly act as interstate arbiters adjudicating disputes only where both parties so desire. Although the commitment to interstate dispute settlement is in principle self-binding, where ICs lack compulsory jurisdiction governments can block inconvenient cases from proceeding.

Compulsory dispute settlement jurisdiction arguably transforms dispute settlement into law enforcement. The state with law on its side becomes advantaged in negotiations because of its power to initiate litigation. Figure 5.2 notes that most ICs with compulsory jurisdiction in their dispute settlement role also have enforcement jurisdiction. If ICs also have compulsory enforcement jurisdiction, there is no reason to deny an IC compulsory jurisdiction for their dispute settlement role; indeed, this dispute settlement role becomes largely redundant. ICs without an additional enforcement role include the Central American Court of Justice, the Central African Monetary Community's court, and the Economic Court of the Commonwealth of Independent States, which adjudicate disputes among members with respect to a range of issues and agreements.

ICs with compulsory dispute settlement provisions can turn into enforcement courts, making international legal agreements binding. But the objective of dispute settlement is somewhat different from that of law

7 Figure 5.1 also included a second category of state-initiated dispute settlement for disputes between states and international actors. My intuition is that this particular IC dispute settlement role is rarely activated. International institutions are more like member organizations, designed to serve the needs of the member states. Important decisions are usually undertaken by consensus, and international officials are unlikely to let a dispute escalate to the point of litigation.

FIGURE 5.2: ICs with interstate dispute settlement jurisdiction

ICs N = 14	Subject matter jurisdiction	Voluntary or compulsory jurisdiction	Additional enforcement jurisdiction
Andean Tribunal of Justice (ATJ)	Any issue states bring	Compulsory	X
Caribbean Court of Justice (CCJ)	Any issue states bring	Compulsory	
Central American Court of Justice (CACJ)	Any issue states bring	Mostly optional[A]	X
Central African Monetary Community (CEMAC)	Any issue states bring	Compulsory	
Court of Justice for the Common Market of Eastern and Southern Africa (COMESA)	Any issue states bring	Compulsory	X
East African Court of Justice (EACJ)	Any issue states bring	Voluntary, unless a special agreement includes compulsory jurisdiction	X
Economic Court of the Commonwealth of Independent States (ECCIS)	Most CIS agreements	Compulsory[B]	
Economic Community of West African States Court (ECOWAS CJ)	ECOWAS agreements	Compulsory	X
European Court of Justice (ECJ)	Consolidated European Treaties & Investment Bank	Compulsory	X
International Court of Justice (ICJ)	Any issue states bring	Optional Declarations	
International Tribunal for the Law of the Sea (ITLOS)	Law of Sea, related side agreements, and most maritime issues	Optional Declarations; Compulsory for Seabed Authority and prompt release of vessels	
Southern Common Market Dispute Settlement Permanent Review Tribunal (MERCOSUR)	MERCOSUR agreements	Compulsory	X
Southern African Development Community (SADC)	Community rules and subsidiary agreements	Compulsory	X
World Trade Organization Permanent Appellate Body (WTO)	WTO agreements	Compulsory	X

[A] CACJ—Technically the Court's jurisdiction is compulsory, but the dispute resolution jurisdiction applies "when the parties have requested" the Court to rule. Moreover the Court's jurisdiction is explicitly not compulsory for frontier, territory, and maritime disputes.

[B] Treaty is ambiguous, but according to Danilenko the Court has declared its jurisdiction compulsory (Danilenko 1999, 899–901).

enforcement. Interstate dispute settlement is a nonexclusive means to facilitate the peaceful resolution of disagreements, useful mainly where legal clarity helps and a failure to resolve the dispute might harm international relations. By contrast, enforcement aims at inducing respect for international law both for specific cases and more generally. State-initiated compulsory dispute settlement can help enforce legal rules governments care about, but we would not expect a government to instigate adjudication where the issue mostly concerns citizens of another state, and many governments will avoid adjudication even when the issue concerns their citizens. For this reason, many violations of international law—including human rights and war crimes violations, and violations that affect external more than internal actors—cannot or will not appear in ICs as dispute settlement cases.

Private Litigant-Initiated International Dispute Settlement

It may seem somewhat surprising that private litigants are authorized to initiate international litigation against foreign governments, but this situation has long existed. Guilds have long adjudicated trader disputes, and firms have sought the right to pursue contract breaches by foreign governments.[8] Today, firms tend to prefer arbitration over litigation because it is cheaper and faster, and disputants can influence the selection of adjudicators and the legal terms applied. Indeed, firms often mandate arbitration rather than litigation in contracts. The International Chambers of Commerce, the Permanent Court of Arbitration, and the International Centre for the Resolution of Investment Disputes (discussed in the next chapter) as well as numerous ad hoc systems and lawyers provide such services.[9] Repeals of sovereign immunity for commercial disputes also allow firms to bring cases in domestic courts, and for foreign governments to raise suits within domestic systems where courts can order remedies and assets can be seized as payment. These plentiful alternatives diminish the attractiveness of invoking ICs.

Governments also at times have intervened to facilitate adjudication of transborder private litigant disputes. The most common example involves mass claims, situations where the number of parties affected is too large to ignore or resolve through informal or diplomatic means. During the nineteenth century, approximately eighty claims commissions adjudicated private litigant cases arising out of war and civil unrest. In the twentieth

8 A famous example is the law-merchant, discussed by Milgrom, North, and Weingast (1990). Historians, however, dispute the stylized narrative in this account.

9 For an interesting analysis of international commercial arbitration trends, see Dezalay and Garth (1996).

century, the Hague Peace Conferences led to the creation of the Permanent Court of Arbitration, which provides arbitration for cases involving private litigants suing governments. Between World War I and World War II nearly thirty commissions and arbitral bodies adjudicated private litigant disputes.[10] The case study of the US-Iran Claims Tribunal shows how states can circumscribe the mandate of these bodies for the purpose at hand.

Only following World War II were private litigants given access to permanent international courts with broad jurisdictions. Often, these grants of private access remain other-binding extensions of IC jurisdiction. For example, private litigants have been authorized to raise cases against international organizations. Usually such cases involve employment issues or disputes between vendors and international agencies.[11] Section III will discuss one system for private litigant cases, the Organization for the Harmonization of Business Law in Africa, in more detail. The ITLOS's jurisdiction also includes private contract disputes related to the mining of the deep seabed. The SADC, Andean, and OHADA systems have arbitration mechanisms for private litigant disputes (although to my knowledge these mechanisms are not used). The Organization of Arab Petroleum Exporting Countries (OAPEC) authorizes oil companies to bring disputes with governments to a special OAPEC court, and the Arab Investment Court can adjudicate contract disputes between firms and states.[12] ICs with preliminary ruling mechanisms can rule on private disputes raised in national courts. For example, an Ecuadorian court asked the Andean Tribunal to rule on one litigant's claim that World Trade Organization rules trumped Andean rules for the case at hand.[13] IC jurisdiction for such cases is compulsory but not exclusive; the defendant cannot block the case from proceeding but litigants can opt for alternative dispute settlement approaches.

The next two sections consider international legalized dispute resolution initiated by states and by private parties. These case studies are focused on how and why legalized dispute settlement proved attractive and helpful for resolving these particular disputes. The next chapter includes

10 (Crook 2006, 41–42).

11 Because I am most interested in ICs enforcing the law vis-à-vis states, I do not include these disputes in my litigation data or offer any examples in this book, but even the least active ICs seem to hear such cases.

12 See the book's online appendix for more. The OAPEC court appears to be moribund, but the Arab Investment Court has appointed judges, and it has issued some rulings.

13 Andean ruling 158-IP-2006 (see the legal decision appendix for more on where to find Andean rulings). The case arose from a contract dispute involving the transfer of ownership in a dispute with a foreign investor. The defendant suggested that the General Agreement on Trade in Services, rather than Andean rules, had precedent.

private-actor-initiated dispute settlement under the auspices of NAFTA and ICSID (International Centre for the Settlement of Investment Disputes), where private actors are drawing on compulsory enforcement provisions to adjudicate disputes with foreign governments. Chapter 6's case studies are more controversial, and they generate less compliance, perhaps because they are self-binding, constraining rather than extending the power of the central state.

II. INTERSTATE DISPUTE SETTLEMENT IN ACTION

Chapter 3 showed that the Middle East and Asia tend to avoid committing to compulsory IC jurisdiction. Russia is a member of regional ICs and in 2013 it joined the WTO, meanwhile Bahrain and Qatar only accept the jurisdiction of the World Trade Organization. Concern about IC's compulsory jurisdiction does not mean, however, that countries are entirely adverse to international adjudication. This section discusses two long-standing interstate disputes where IC involvement led to meaningful changes in state behavior and a settlement of the conflict at hand. In the "Qatar v. Bahrain territorial dispute," the government of Bahrain initially contested the ICJ's assertion of jurisdiction so that Qatar's decision to approach the ICJ appeared to escalate the conflict. The "Japan v. Russia seizing of vessels" case study shows that ICs can create tailored solutions within their limited grants of jurisdiction. The changes induced by IC involvement clearly left both governments better off, and thus the immediate compliance with the IC rulings is neither unexpected nor surprising. These cases are strong illustrations of the interstate arbiter conception of how ICs influence political outcomes. Section III will briefly discuss two more ICJ cases involving the United States and Iran which did not garner compliance.

5.1. "Qatar v. Bahrain territorial dispute"—International Court of Justice resolves a territorial dispute, which facilitates regional economic development

The Hawar Islands are located 1.4 kilometers from the Qatar coast, and almost 20 kilometres from Bahrain. Geography notwithstanding, Bahrain asserted ownership over these islands and over Janan, which is so close to Qatar that at low tide one can walk to the islands. Bahrain also claimed ownership over Zubarah, which is actually on Qatar's land mass. With the Hawar Islands part of Bahrain, the government could claim gas and oil located in the territorial waters of both countries. Supporting Bahrain's claim was the fact that its leaders had been able to extract British promises regarding the disputed islands. The ICJ's solution split the difference, awarding each side some of the disputed lands, generating an outcome that was not all that different from the decision created by colonial Britian. The passage of time, the carefully crafted compromise, and the sense that the ICJ was the most neutral arbiter for the case allowed the ICJ to create a resolution that had eluded both the British and Saudi Arabia. There are many excellent legal analyses of the ruling;[14] this case study focuses instead on how the ICJ was able to resolve a long-standing dispute that had eluded resolution by others.

The first question to address is how Bahrain came to have a legally legitimate claim over land that was much closer to Qatar? Britain became involved in the Persian Gulf region in the 1800s because pirates based in Qatar and Bahrain were plundering British ships. What is today known as Bahrain attracted colonial attention because of its strategic location along important trade routes in the Persian Gulf. Bahrain's reserves of fresh water also attracted interest from powerful families in the region. Bahraini tribal leaders saw agreements with the British as a way to secure their claims over the territory. The Preliminary Treaty for Maritime Peace of 1820 was the first agreement between Britain and Bahraini tribal leaders. Continuing wars led Bahrain to bind itself even closer to the British, essentially ceding sovereignty to British rule. The 1892 Exclusive Protection Agreement between the Chief of Bahrain and the British Political Resident in the Gulf stipulated that neither the Bahraini chief nor his heirs were to enter into agreement or communication "with any other power other than the British Government." This agreement also stipulated that agents from other countries could not enter Bahraini terrain without British approval.[15] These agreements are how Britain came to generate documents justifying Bahraini land claims.

Qatar had a less attractive geography, and thus it generated less interest from the British or from Qatar's neighbors. Under duress, the tribes governing Qatar had also entered into agreements with British powers in the 1800s. Qatar's agreements promised to maintain maritime peace and pay tribute to Bahrain. The more Bahrain turned to the United Kingdom for support, the more Qatar's Al Thani family turned to the Ottoman Empire for backing, to the point that tribal leaders allowed a Turkish garrison in Doha. Meanwhile, to escape taxes the Na'im tribe living near Zubarah in the north of what is today Qatar appealed to Bahrain's leaders for help. Responding to their pleas, Bahrain claimed control over Zubarah, and the Na'im tribe then immigrated to Bahrain, leaving the territory unoccupied. When Ottoman influence declined in the early

14 See, for example, Tanaka (2003). There is an entire book about this case (Al-Arayed 2003).

15 (Burgis 2005, 561).

1900s, Qatar's tribal leaders signed more agreements with the British (in 1913 and 1916) guaranteeing Qatar's independence and banning Bahraini influence in its territory. Although none of these agreements addressed specific land claims, because of these various agreements Britain became the first arbiter for the Bahrain-Qatar dispute.

In the 1800s, political loyalties were more important than land. The territorial disagreements could thus persist without provoking violence. But in May 1932, the Bahraini Petroleum Company discovered oil, at which point the unoccupied land became valuable. Qatar's leader claimed the Hawar Islands, signing an oil concession in 1934. This agreement led Bahrain to establish a military outpost on the largest Hawar island and to reassert its authority over the deserted town of Zubarah. Qatar fought back, ejecting Bahrain from Zubarah. The skirmish led to British intervention to adjudicate their territorial dispute. In a 1939 decision, Britain found that Bahrain had rights over the Hawar Islands but not over Zubarah. Qatar had agreed in advance to abide by the decision, but it remained unhappy with the outcome. Britain then sent clarifying letters to the leaders of both countries, which left open the question of whether the Janan Islands could be seen as part of the Hawar Islands as well as questions about certain reefs located to the north of Qatar.

In the 1950s and 1960s, leaders in both Qatar and Bahrain sought to develop their regions. British rule over the Persian Gulf kept the peace, but Qatar continued to complain about Bahrain's claims to the disputed lands. In 1971 Britain withdrew its protectorate and new nation-states were created. At this point, the contested land claims once again flared. Over the next twenty years, Saudi Arabia tried to keep the peace. Leaders of Bahrain and Qatar continued to claim interference in each other's affairs, and Qatar continued to question the validity of Britain's 1939 settlement of the territorial dispute. Saudi Arabia succeeded in quelling the periodic violent escalations that occurred as each country sought to assert its authority over contested islands, but it too was unable to resolve the underlying territorial disagreement. Meanwhile, in 1981 the United Arab Emirates, Bahrain, Saudi Arabia, Oman, Qatar, and Kuwait established the Gulf Cooperation Council to promote mutual interests in the region.

After another skirmish in 1986, Qatar, Bahrain, and Saudi Arabia agreed to let the Gulf Cooperation Council try to resolve the dispute. Qatar by then wanted to bring its territorial claim to the ICJ, but Bahrain continued to insist that the Gulf Cooperation Council handle the issue. Saudi Arabia crafted a compromise; if no "brotherly solution" could be reached by May 1991, the case would go to the ICJ. The compromise defined which aspects of the disagreement would be referred to the ICJ, an arrangement known as the "Bahraini formula," to which Qatar at first balked but later reluctantly assented.[16] When the stated deadline to resolve the disagreement passed, Qatar decided to unilaterally pursue the case at the ICJ. Qatar's application raised only the issues that the Qatari leadership wanted the ICJ to resolve. Bahrain accused Qatar of violating the Bahraini formula. Bahrain's leaders wanted the Gulf Cooperation Council to continue to mediate the issue, and they insisted that Qatar withdraw its ICJ complaint as a precondition to working with the Gulf Cooperation Council. Qatar refused to withdraw the suit, insisting that it would only work with the Council if an agreement could be promised. Given the stalemate, at first it looked like Qatar's filing the dispute in front of the ICJ made the conflict even more difficult to resolve.[17]

The case arrived at the ICJ in July 1991. Bahrain immediately filed two letters contesting the ICJ's jurisdiction in the case since it had not agreed to have the dispute adjudicated. After much back and forth, in July 1994 the ICJ ruled that the minutes of the Gulf Cooperation Council meetings constituted an international agreement to bring the controversy to the ICJ if no solution could be reached by the specified date.[18] The ICJ agreed with Bahrain that Qatar's list of contested issues was incomplete, essentially insisting on the Bahraini formula that allowed it to issue a ruling on the whole of the contested claims.

In 1995, the son of Qatar's then leader initiated a bloodless coup and seized control from his father. In this way, one of the leaders entrenched in the controversy ended up removed from negotiations. In 1996, Bahrain accepted the ICJ's jurisdiction in the case although the Bahraini leadership continued to insist that the issue would be best resolved through the Gulf Cooperation Council, and at times Bahraini leaders threatened to boycott ICJ proceedings. Eventually, however, both parties prepared to bring the entire case to the ICJ.

The merits phase of the proceedings took another five years. The specific promises regarding the contested Hawar and Janan Islands, and Bahrain's claims over Zubarah, were hard to sort out, especially because each side assembled a jumble of historical documents and put on the table every possible claim they could use, invoking at times conflicting legal arguments.[19] Also complicating the litigation were submission of forged documents by Qatari officials. During these five years, the governments of the two countries continued to provoke each other in ways that

16 (Burgis 2005, 563; Evans 1995, 691–92).

17 (Fry 2010, 53).

18 ICJ, "Qatar v. Bahrain territorial dispute."

19 (Burgis 2005, 572–84).

undermined regional development and greater political cooperation.[20] The Gulf Cooperation Council convinced Qatar to withdraw the forged documents, but leaders in both countries repeatedly rejected solutions to the dispute suggested by the Council. As the political mediation process continued without any real progress, the legal suit wound its way through the ICJ.

In 1999, the leader of Bahrain died and his son assumed office. The two regional leaders most entrenched in the dispute were now gone from office. Crown Prince Harnad immediately instituted political reforms, and in December 1999 the new leaders of Qatar and Bahrain established a Joint Higher Committee for Cooperation. The territorial disagreements, however, continued and partisans committed to the conflicting ownership claims still held sway in each country. In mid-May of 2000, only days before the ICJ's oral proceedings were set to convene, negotiations mediated by the United Arab Emirates and Saudi Arabia once again collapsed. Following this failure, the Qatari and Bahraini governments decided to wait for the ICJ ruling before proceeding with greater cooperation.

Public hearings before the ICJ began in May 2000, nearly ten years after Qatar first filed its case. At this point, adjudication proceeded with fewer accusations or efforts to undermine the process. It helped that the legal process has its own rhythm. Where mediators sought compromises that both sides could endorse, judges simply proceeded through each step of the litigation process. The ICJ issued its ruling ten months after oral proceedings. The ruling included a number of split decisions speaking to different aspects of the territorial disagreement. The complicated ruling essentially gave each side part of what it wanted, without deeply upsetting the status quo the British had created in 1939.

Both parties immediately embraced the ruling, declaring the day following the judgment a national holiday to celebrate the end of the dispute and the beginning of better relations between the countries. Bahrain quickly invited foreign companies to begin oil exploration in the Hawar Islands, without the sort of protest from Qatar that would have been expected a few weeks earlier.[21] The Hawar Islands now has Bahraini tourist resorts, Zubarah's historic fort is now a Qatari tourist site, and Bah-

20 For example, in 1995 the Bahraini government announced its provocative decision to establish a tourist resort on the Hawar Islands, while continuing to criticize Qatar for taking the disagreement outside of the region instead of relying on "brotherly" arbitration. Qatar accused Bahrain of interfering in its internal affairs by encouraging a coup. As the vitriol escalated, Saudi Arabia, the United Arab Emirates, Oman, and Kuwait repeatedly tried to craft compromises via the Gulf Cooperation Council.

21 (Paulson 2004, 454). *The Bahrain-Qatar Border Dispute: The World Court Decision: Part 2, The Estimate*, April 6, 2011. http://www.theestimate.com/public/032301.html, last visited December 15, 2011.

rain and Qatar have planned to build the world's largest bridge to connect the two countries. All is not perfect in this relationship. The bridge project is perennially delayed (which may be because of the bridge's high costs). And more recently Qatar has started to use force against Bahraini fishermen in its waters, acting in ways some see as signaling deeper disagreements over policy in the region.[22] But the basic territorial dispute appears to be resolved.

Why was the ICJ able to create a resolution of territorial dispute that neither Britain nor regional leaders could resolve? The change in Bahraini and Qatari leadership certainly helped, but the ICJ also was advantaged in that it did not need to rely on political mediation. Britain had been able to impose compromises in the past, but British solutions were always suspect because of historic biases toward the leaders of Bahrain and because of Britain's clear self-interest in regional oil reserves. Because Qatar's leadership never accepted as legitimate the British solution of 1939, the dispute continued. Meanwhile, according to Michelle Burgis, the Gulf Cooperation Council contained leaders with too many historic grievances and crosscutting relationships for any solution offered to be seen as neutral.[23] The first Gulf War, triggered by the Iraqi invasion of Kuwait, only made it harder for the Gulf Cooperation Council to be a helpful mediator. Compromises the Council suggested became tainted by other disagreements, and since both sides needed to agree to any compromise, the Gulf Cooperation Council process could be easily blocked. By contrast, ICJ judges could issue a binding compromise under the guise of a legal solution. And it was likely easier for the new leaders to have a solution imposed.

Some have questioned whether the ICJ could have resolved the dispute if the Court had found that the Hawar Islands belonged to Qatar. The Bahraini government is on record insisting that it would not accept any ruling against its claims to the Hawar Islands.[24] But it is also true that there was no clearer competing "legal" solution to choose. The disputed lands lay within both countries' exclusive economic zones, and the British government had the best records of promises made, which made it hard for the ICJ to reach any law-based conclusion that did not heavily favor

22 In May 2010, Qatari coast guards injured a Bahraini fisherman. There have been more arrests, although incidents are sporadic, suggesting that actions are meant to send a signal to Bahrain and other members of the Gulf Cooperation Council. See David B. Roberts, "Rhetoric and Fishermen Belay the Myth of GCC Unity," June 25, 2010, http://www.thedailynewsegypt.com/global-views/rhetoric-and-fishermen-belay-the-myth-of-gcc-unity-dp3.html, last visited March 14, 2012.

23 (Burgis 2005, 584).

24 Bahraini dissident Sa'id al-Shihabi argued, "Had the judgment gone the other way, it would have had disastrous consequences" because the islands constitute a third of Bahrain's total land claim, and they justify Bahrain's claim to be an archipelago that includes the islands (Paulson 2004, 545).

the written record Bahrain had built through cooperation with its colonial patron. Thus it is possible that the politically convenient outcome was also the most plausible legal outcome.

5.2. "Japan v. Russia seizing of vessels"—International Tribunal for the Law of the Sea assures fair treatment of Japanese vessels seized for illegal actions in Russian waters (Tomimaru and Hoshinmaru cases)

Governments generally support the United Nations Third Law of the Sea Convention (UNCLOS III) as a way to secure access to the sea and end the practice of individual states extending territorial claims. Although UNCLOS III sets clear limits to future territorial claims in the oceans, the agreement leaves many overlapping territorial claims unresolved.[25] Countries with extensive coasts were concerned about the International Tribunal for the Law of the Sea (ITLOS) being invoked to challenge territorial claims involving overlapping and historic ocean rights. To overcome disagreement, governments were allowed to designate among four possible means to resolve disputes involving the key provisions of the convention, with arbitration being the default choice when parties have not both selected the same dispute adjudication mechanism.[26] This compromise leaves ITLOS, the legal body overseeing the Law of the Sea Convention, with a Swiss cheese jurisdiction. ITLOS has exclusive and mandatory jurisdiction regarding disputes involving the International Seabed Authority, and mandatory jurisdiction with respect to disputes involving the seizing of vessels.[27] But governments were able to file objections to the ITLOS jurisdiction for certain disputes, and they can refuse to adjudicate territorial claims.[28]

This case study concerns two disputes where Japanese fishing vessels were impounded for violating Russian licensing rules. The interaction

25 (Oxman 2001, 285–86).

26 Article 287 of the UNCLOS III Law of the Sea Convention.

27 There is no clear statement indicating state consent to the ITLOS compulsory jurisdiction for such cases, but legal scholars tend to see ITLOS jurisdiction as compulsory (Oxman 2001, 280, n. 14; Seymore 2006, 15–18; Tuerk 2007, 304).

28 Countries may file special "Article 298" statements that explicitly reject adjudication of specified issues. Russia explicitly accepted ITLOS jurisdiction for disputes involving the seizing of vessels, but its Article 298 declaration asserts limits on ITLOS jurisdiction: "The Russian Federation declares that, in accordance with article 298 of the United Nations Convention on the Law of the Sea, it does not accept the procedures, provided for in section 2 of Part XV of the Convention, entailing binding decisions with respect to disputes concerning the interpretation or application of articles 15, 74 and 83 of the Convention, relating to sea boundary delimitations, or those involving historic bays or titles; disputes concerning military activities, including military activities by government vessels and aircraft, and disputes concerning law-enforcement activities in regard to the exercise of sovereign rights or jurisdiction; and disputes in respect of which the Security Council of the United Nations is exercising the functions assigned to it by the Charter of the United Nations."

between Japan, Russia, and ITLOS in these cases is very normal, and that is the point. Japan and Russia continue to dispute ownership of the Kuril Islands, and disagreements over fishing rights in the disputed territories repeatedly escalate to violence. This case study suggests that a contribution of ITLOS is that it allows disputes involving fishing vessels to be handled in a regularized way, so that they do not aggravate an already fragile political standoff.

For at least three centuries Russia and Japan have been disputing ownership of parts of the Kuril Islands, an archipelago of over fifty large and small islands that stretch 1,250 kilometers from the southern tip of Russia to the northern tip of Japan's Hokkaido Island. Japan has historically claimed ownership over the southernmost Kuril Islands, where its peoples have long resided. Ownership of the contested islands has passed back and forth, through various treaties and peace settlements. Japan gained a clear ownership of some of the contested islands following the Russian-Japanese war of 1904–5, but the Soviet Union reasserted its ownership following Japan's defeat in World War II, expelling 17,000 Japanese people from the southern islands of Shikotan, Iturup, the Habomais, and Kunashir, which are just 21 kilometers from Japan's Hokkaido Island.[29] The two parties never resolved the territorial disagreement.[30] But the countries have been able to reestablish diplomatic relations and arrange for people in both countries to make personal visits to the disputed areas. Under the auspices of the Law of the Sea Convention, Japan and Russia have also reached agreements about preserving fisheries in the region.

Amid this cooperation, however, are constant conflicts involving fishermen that stray into Russian waters and violate fishing licensing rules. Russia has routinely seized Japanese fishing vessels traveling in Russia's Exclusive Economic Zone (EEZ), including three vessels in 2004, two in 2005, and four in 2006. In a 2006 seizing, a Russian patrol boat fired a warning shot at a Japanese crab-fishing vessel near the Kuril Islands, killing a Japanese crew member.[31] There is no suggestion that Russia is singling out Japanese fishermen for harsh treatment. Instead, there is a sense that Russia has a right to protect its territory and oversee fishing, especially because of the precarious ecobalance of fish in the region. But the Law of the Sea Convention requires that governments set a reasonable bond for the retrieval of the vessel, and that adjudication of any dispute

29 Soviet leader Joseph Stalin claimed that his country gained ownership over the entire chain of islands in a secret agreement at Yalta, and the Soviets occupied Japanese-owned islands as part of the international occupation of Japanese lands at the end of World War II (Hara 2001, 264–66).

30 The United States arguably worked to block an agreement reached between Japan and Russia in 1956 (Hara 2001, 376–80).

31 (Song 2007, 2).

be prompt. These rules try to strike a balance between the right of a country to police its territory and the harsh reality that impounding a vessel can destroy valuable cargo and severely impact the livelihood of fishermen.

A majority of the cases adjudicated by the ITLOS involve the seizing of vessels. Through these cases, the ITLOS has established some basic ground rules for countries, and for itself.[32] The ITLOS's jurisdiction is circumscribed to ensure that a bond for a vessel's release is promptly set, and that the bond is reasonable. The tribunal does not involve itself in disputes about the merits of the case. In both the *Tomimaru* and the *Hoshinmaru* disputes, the boats were seized for misreporting fish they had caught, in violation of their Russian fishing licenses. The *Tomimaru* had a Russian license to fish a specified amount of walleye and herring. The Russian Coast Guard found walleye that was not reported on the ship's registrar, and once the ship arrived in port officials found nearly twice as much walleye as was authorized, plus 19 illegal tons of frozen halibut, 3.2 tons of ray, 4.9 tons of cod, and 3 tons of other bottom fish.[33] The *Hoshinmaru* had a license for a specified amount of sockeye and chum salmon.[34] While the fishermen were far from exceeding their quotas, they had hidden the more expensive sockeye salmon under a layer of chum salmon and misreported this fish on their registry.

In both cases, the Russian legal process proved slower than legally required. Article 292 of the Law of the Sea Convention allows the flag state to raise a case involving the prompt release of vessels ten days after the boat has been seized, if no reasonable bond has been set. The *Tomimaru* case occurred in 2006, and the alleged offenses were the most serious. Russian officials charged the ship's captain with illegal fishing, and they seized the boat as evidence in criminal proceedings. The ship's owner then sought to get his boat back. The prosecutor in the case promptly set a bond, but an administrative court rejected the bond. The Japanese government made several requests on behalf of the ship's owner, but the case was the subject of ongoing legal proceedings that Russian officials did not want to interrupt. The Russian administrative judge then found that the ship's owner had violated his licensing agreement, imposing a fine and ordering the vessel to be confiscated. Meanwhile, a criminal court imposed a fine on the ship's captain and added a penalty for damages that was eighteen times the amount of the fine. The captain paid the fine, but not the damages, and he was released while the damages fee was being appealed.

The case reached the Law of the Sea Tribunal while the administrative and criminal rulings were awaiting appellate review. The main legal issue

32 (Treves 2010).

33 (Blut 2007, n. 25, at 55).

34 ITLOS "The Hoshimaru case" ¶¶27–28.

before the ITLOS was whether the tribunal had the authority to set a bond for a ship after the domestic court had issued its ruling and confiscated the vessel. Russian officials argued that the confiscated vessel no longer belonged to Japanese owners, and thus the tribunal lacked jurisdiction. ITLOS judges rejected this argument, noting that if confiscation terminated legal rights then ITLOS rules for the prompt release of vessels would lose all meaning.[35] But, the judges emphasized, the tribunal's role is to ensure the prompt release of vessels while domestic cases are still proceeding. Since domestic proceedings had ended, the tribunal held that Japan's application was without object. To avoid the situation of rushed proceedings leading to confiscated vessels, the judges noted that their ruling might be different had the domestic court issued a confiscation judgment with "unjustified haste" or if the domestic confiscation proceeding violated international standards of due process.[36] Individual judges noted in separate opinions that the flag state must petition the ITLOS in a timely manner in order to ensure a reasonable bond.[37] In short, Russia's confiscation of the ship was reasonable given the offense, and Japan had waited too long before invoking ITLOS.

Three months after the tribunal issued its decisions, Russian border guards seized four more Japanese fishing boats in the disputed waters near the South Kuril Islands.[38] Then in June 2007 Russian officials seized the *Hoshinmaru*. Japan wrote the Russian Ministry of Foreign Affairs within days of the *Hoshinmaru* seizing. Although Russia began administrative proceedings promptly, a month later the bond still had not been set and Japan filed its legal suit. Russian judges then set a bond price based on the cost of the vessel plus the maximum possible fines. Given that the boat had not exceeded its quota, and thus was at most guilty of having unrecorded sockeye salmon, Japanese officials viewed the bond as excessive. In this case, the ITLOS court agreed with Japan, finding the imposition of maximum penalties for the purpose of the bond to be excessive. In response to the ruling, Russian officials set a new bond price that was 40 percent of the original sum, which the boat's owner paid ten days following the ITLOS ruling.

The ITLOS system seems to have largely worked as is expected in both of these suits. But Japan and Russia continue to find themselves embroiled in cases where Japanese boats are caught illegally fishing in Russian waters. In 2009 Russia and Japan negotiated an agreement to facilitate

35 ITLOS "The Tomimaru case" at ¶65.

36 Ibid., at ¶74–76.

37 (Gautier 2008, ¶41 at 387).

38 (Song 2007), and Mari Yamaguchi, "Russia Seizes 4 Japanese Fishing Boats," *Seattle Post-Intelligencer*, December 13, 2007, available at http://www.redorbit.com/news/international/1180653/russia_seizes_4_japanese_fishing_ boats/index.html.

cooperation in criminal matters.[39] Then, after Japanese fishing vessels were found to be bribing Russian border guards, Japan's and Russia's fisheries agencies began cooperation to try to address the problem of illegal fishing in Russian waters. In the meantime, there is still no armistice agreement between Japan and Russia and no postwar settlement of territorial disputes in the region.[40] Japanese officials continue to call for a comprehensive peace agreement, while Russian officials deflect the issue, stressing the two countries shared economic interests.[41] The ITLOS system thus appears able to deal with a small range of maritime disputes, while fundamental disagreements on sea-related territorial and fishing persist.

The Kuril Islands dispute, like a number of territorial disagreements involving overlapping claims in exclusive economic zones, persists mostly because neither the ICJ nor the ITLOS have compulsory jurisdiction for such cases. The old saying "possession is nine-tenths of the law" applies; those exercising possession have little incentive to adjudicate the dispute. Mediation, when it occurs in such cases, is a way for the country with ownership to demonstrate a willingness to find a solution so as to stave off intervention or litigation. The Qatar-Bahrain dispute was in mediation for years, a situation that was fine for the Bahraini government until the point that developers demanded legal certainty before making investments. By contrast, Russia does not need greater legal certainty because it mainly wants to maintain military control over strategically important land. Russia and Japan can, however, use the ITLOS system to deal with domestic outcry that occurs every time Japanese fishermen get caught cheating in Russian waters. The system allows Japan's government to demonstrate its concern for fishermen. At the same time, both countries know that strong enforcement of fishing rules is needed if the fishing stock in the region is to survive.

III. PRIVATE LITIGANT-INITIATED DISPUTE SETTLEMENT

This section focuses on international dispute settlement initiated by private actors. Both are examples of other-binding delegation to ICs and

39 Treaty between Japan and the Russian Federation on Mutual Legal Assistance in Criminal Matters signed May 12, 2009, and mutually ratified November 13, 2010. The treaty became effective in February 2011. Treaty No. 12 and Ministry of Foreign Affairs Notification No.483, available at http://www.mofa.go.jp/policy/treaty/submit/session174/agree-1.html, last visited December 21, 2011.

40 (Hara 2001).

41 A recent example of this was the joint press conference between Japan's and Russia's prime ministers, January 2009, available at http://www.kantei.go.jp/foreign/asospeech/2009/05/12kaiken_e.html, last visited December 21, 2011.

both case studies have delegation to international legal bodies extending rather than compromising the power of central states. These case studies analyze the overall dispute settlement systems rather than the resolution of specific disputes. The systems themselves represent changes in the behavior of governments and national judicial systems. My question is, to what extent does the existence of an international dispute settlement system help resolve important disagreements that span two or more countries? The assessment is mixed.

5.3. "Iran-US Claims Tribunal"—Adjudicating disputes arising from the Iranian revolution

The Iran–United States Claims Tribunal is perhaps most remarkable for having been able to deal with a large number of complicated legal cases despite very poor relations between the governments of the United States and Iran. During the nearly forty-year reign of Mohammad Rezā Shāh Pahlavī, the shah of Iran, Americans and Iranians had friendly relations. Close government ties facilitated economic relationships where American firms sold products and invested in Iran, and Iranian assets were held in American and Western banks. Economic difficulties at the end of the shah's reign led to the flight of foreign investment and a near collapse of the Iranian banking system, creating additional debts owed to Western banks. The Iranian revolution then disrupted many of the contractual relationships in place. For a while American firms waited to see how the political situation would unfold, but when US-Iranian relations deteriorated, American firms filed claims in US courts for property lost due to the Iranian revolution. American officials refused to block such claims, creating the prospect of American judges repeatedly ruling against Iran and ordering the seizing of assets held in US banks or in foreign banks with US subsidiaries.

Iranian revolutionaries blamed the United States for keeping the shah in power and for tolerating brutal and corrupt practices. Condemnation of the revolution in the United States Senate further angered Iranian revolutionaries. When the United States then allowed the shah to seek medical treatment in the United States, hundreds of thousands Iranians demonstrated in the streets, calling for the shah's extradition so that he could be prosecuted for his crimes. Demonstrations ended with students sacking the United States Embassy, taking at least sixty-two people hostage including many American diplomats. Under international law, an embassy belongs to the foreign country and diplomats enjoy immunity, thus invading an embassy and holding diplomats hostage is legally akin to a direct invasion of the United States. Iran's Ayatollah Khomeini endorsed the hostage seizure, and Iran's Constitutional Council refused to intervene to stop the "students" unless the shah was extradited to Iran. President

Jimmy Carter responded by ending all US oil purchases from Iran, after which Iran threatened to withdraw all deposits from US banks. Carter then issued an Executive Act blocking all dealings in Iranian property within the possession or control of people who fall under US jurisdiction. This meant that anyone who returned Iranian assets could be legally liable in the American legal system. Carter's action led to the freezing of $12 billion of Iranian assets held around the globe, and the filing of many lawsuits in American courts. The US Department of Justice and Iran called for a Judicial Panel on Multidistrict Litigation to hear the cases, and asked that cases be consolidated and dealt with collectively. The Judicial Panel, however, refused to consolidate cases with such disparate fact patterns, which made it impossible to reach any quick settlement to the many pending claims. These events gave rise to the 1981 Algiers Accord, which facilitated an end to the hostage standoff and created the Iran-US Claims Tribunal. Under the Algiers Accord, Iran promised to release the hostages and the United States promised to terminate or block litigation against Iran by US persons or institutions. The United States also agreed to release Iranian assets but to first transfer $1 billion of frozen assets, plus interest, into an escrow account. Iran promised to replenish the escrow account every time it fell below $500 million, an agreement that held until 1995.[42]

Despite its name, lawyers consider the Iran–United States Claims Tribunal to be an arbitral body rather than a court because it was set up after the fact by the United States and Iran with the sole purpose of resolving claims that arose because of their dispute.[43] The tribunal has ended up as a functional equivalent to the formally constituted and more permanent courts that are the focus of this book. Governments and private parties submitted 3,861 cases, ranging from individuals who "had to leave their cars and refrigerators behind" to the seizing of drilling rigs, the nationalization of companies, and the cancellation of military contracts. All claims were adjudicated by a three-judge panel that applied a preexisting system of rules created by the Algiers Accord, supplemented by model rules that have been created by the United Nations Commission on International Trade Law (UNCITRAL), and further developed through the practice and case law of the tribunal.[44] Adjudicating these cases has been challenging, and the environment within the tribunal has often been politicized and

42 The fund fell below $500 million at that point, but most disputes had already been resolved so arguably the need for the full reserve no longer existed (Seymore 2006, 1–13).

43 In theory, the fact that it is an arbitral body means that the state parties setting up the body create an "internal world," where judges are supposed to focus on the objectives of the state parties (Caron 1990, 109).

44 (Seymore 2006, section 1.4). See also http://www.iusct.org/background-english.html.

tense.[45] But observers see the tribunal as making a number of broader legal contributions. The tribunal has created many procedural and jurisdictional precedents and helped to clarify the law of state obligation. And it has issued rulings on a number of complicated political-legal issues including the application of friendship agreements, how to assess damages, the application of agreements of the International Monetary Fund, and how to deal with dual nationals, expropriation, exchange controls, and wrongful expulsions.[46]

The Iran–United States Claims Tribunal is arguably an island of legal success in the US-Iran relationship. American invocation of the ICJ failed to help resolve the hostage crisis.[47] And when the United States attacked Iranian oil platforms in the Persian Gulf, Iran's invocation of the ICJ resulted in a split decision that did not noticeably tarnish the legality of the United States' retaliatory attacks.[48] In neither of these cases did IC intervention appreciably affect government decision making.

The fact that the Iran–United States Claims Tribunal was helpful, while the ICJ could not meaningfully contribute to dispute settlement in other areas, seemingly provides credence for Posner and Yoo's claim that state consent is the key to ICs being able to shape political outcomes. But the difference between government positions vis-à-vis the Iran–United States Claims Tribunal and ICJ's intervention may turn on the default condition of having no international judicial intervention. With respect to disputes adjudicated by the tribunal, the default outcome permitted by the US government was national court adjudication of legally legitimate claims. By creating an ad hoc tribunal, the US and Iranian governments could set the terms for dispute settlement and control which judges adjudicated legal claims. This solution proved acceptable to litigants and domestic judges, who relinquished domestic litigation rights. By contrast, the default outcome for the ICJ cases was the status quo of stalemate. Iran

45 Iranian appointees often protested proceedings and asserted that there was a Western bias. While American lawyers saw the tribunal as unbiased, this may be because Americans are used to the type of legalized dispute settlement the tribunal practiced. Meanwhile, the third-party judges were seen by American participants as bending over backward to try to satisfy what were at times unreasonable Iranian demands. (Hara 2001, 177; Seymore 2006, 18–22, 29–36).

46 (Crook 2006, 43–46).

47 The United States brought Iran to the ICJ demanding an interim order for Iran to end the hostage crisis, and then later requested a ruling against Iran because of the hostage crisis. Iran refused to participate in ICJ proceedings, issuing instead a statement listing what it saw as many crimes of the United States against Iran. The ICJ proceedings continued anyway, and the ICJ ordered Iran to end the hostage crisis (ICJ Consular Staff case.) The United States withdrew any pursuit of these actions as part of the Algiers Accord. This case is discussed further in Section IV.

48 ICJ Oil Platforms ruling. This case is discussed in Section IV.

preferred to allow the hostage crises to persist, and the United States preferred to threaten Iran's oil outputs to pressure the Iranian government.

Rather than say that Iran's revolution created a force majeure that abrogated extant legal rights, Iranian and US governments responded to litigant assertions of legal rights through a financially costly system. The initial idea of the Iran–United States Claims Tribunal may have been to create an arbitration system, but advocates suggest that in practice the tribunal became increasingly legalized and judges increasingly independent:

> The Tribunal's power is based on its raison d'être: there was a demand for third-party intervention in order to offer compromise and to encourage cooperation. No one wanted the disintegration of the Tribunal once it was established. Accordingly, the will to cooperate prevailed over the forces of discord . . . As the Tribunal grew older and more experienced, it laid down more rigorous rules and precedents. By invoking past practice, the regime has been able, in latter years, to protect itself from pressure exerted by the United States, Iran and non-state actors. With the lapse of time, the regime has relied more on its rulings and precedents than on other sources of law. Similarly, with the passage of time control by the United States and Iran over the Tribunal has decreased.[49]

This was a costly solution. In addition to the costs of staffing the tribunal, Iranian litigants received $2.1 billion from US escrow accounts, and US litigants received $2.2 billion in reparations from Iran.[50] Martin Shapiro would surely smile at the symmetry of the final balance, but nonetheless this outcome shows the costs governments paid to settle property claims in the shadow of the law.

5.4. "OHADA Business Law"—The Organization for the Harmonization of Business Law in Africa as an appellate body for cases involving OHADA "Uniform Acts"

The Organization for the Harmonization of Business Law in Africa (OHADA), formed in 1993, creates unified business codes.[51] Its members are predominately Francophone African countries, all of which had anachronistic business rules left over from French colonialism and adapted in a hodgepodge fashion so that few lawyers or judges even knew what governing law applied. The result, everyone seemed to agree, was

49 (Hara 2001, 150).

50 "Senior presidential official says only 17 cases remain in Iran, US claims," British Broadcasting Corp., August 4, 2005. http://www.accessmylibrary.com/article-1G1-134852128/senior-presidential-official-says.html.

51 Thanks to Jean-Allain Penda, Claire Dickerson, Gustav Kalm, and Paul Bayzelon for their help in understanding OHADA.

legal uncertainty that was worrisome to potential investors.[52] Lawyers and judges were unsure of what law applied, so firms that wanted to follow the law had a hard time knowing what rules to follow. Adjudication was uncertain, because one never knew which set of rules judges would apply. In such a context, legally opening and securing new businesses became difficult. This in turn made it hard for local businesses to secure loans, and banks were generally hesitant to lend money because it was not clear whether legal redress existed for loans not repaid.[53]

The impetus to create OHADA came both internally and externally. Foreign investment in the region fell in the 1980s due to political instability and the reorientation of financial supports in the post–Cold War era. Political leaders wanted more foreign investment, and they became convinced that legal and juridical insecurity made investing in their markets less desirable. Adopting common commercial codes offered many advantages. OHADA created a single set of rules to guide business practices, and it created a business registration system that could help private and public actors keep track of local businesses. By having the same set of rules across countries, foreign investors could save on the legal expertise needed for each national system. OHADA Uniform Acts were also adapted specifically for the needs of developing countries, so that they became more attractive than competing rules—existing French, American, or European Union business law.[54] Member states may not amend the Uniform Acts, and the acts are widely available on the Internet and in source books, providing legal stability and certainty.

The supranational legal system was also one of OHADA's chief attractions. Foreign lawyers have little faith in Africa's national legal systems, where judges are perceived to be ill informed and often corrupt. International dispute resolution through, for example, the Paris-based International Chamber of Commerce or the Swedish Arbitration System offer an alternative, but African-based firms find it expensive to litigate outside of the region. OHADA created its own legal system, managed by the Common Court of Justice and Arbitration (CCJA), which offers appellate review of national judicial rulings and arbitration services.

Externally the OHADA system was strongly supported by the French government, with the encouragement of the French Council of Investors in Africa (Conseil Français des Investisseurs en Afrique, CIAN). The French government was interested in any solution that might help to stabilize the franc zone, because regional instability could generate currency

52 (Mouloul 2009, 10–11).

53 Interview with officers of the Conseil Français des Investisseurs en Afrique (CIAN), Paris, April 12, 2010.

54 (Dickerson 2005, 25–30; Mouloul 2009).

pressures felt in France. A 1991 meeting of African finance ministers from African franc countries, held in France, led to the commissioning of a study on the feasibility of creating regional business law.[55] The French Foreign Ministry reached out to Kéba Mbaye, a former Senegalese Supreme Court judge and president of the International Court of Justice, who in the 1960s had advocated legal harmonization among newly independent states. The French Foreign Ministry underwrote and provided technical support for Mbaye's efforts, which led to the founding of OHADA.[56] France, other EU and non-EU countries, and other international institutions provided financial support to pay for OHADA.[57] While member states now also provide support for the system, it is safe to say that foreign support has been instrumental to the functioning of OHADA. The French Foreign Ministry to this day supports at least one attaché at the OHADA secretariat, and the next paragraph explains how a French-based NGO provides outreach on behalf of OHADA.

Part of the OHADA system included the creation of the Regional Institute for the Judiciary (Ecole Régionale Supérieure de la Magistrature, ERASUMA) to train local judges. This school, located in Porto-Novo, Benin, seeks to educate judges and interested practitioners about OHADA law. The school, however, is remote, which makes travel and lodging too expensive for most local professionals.[58] When it appeared that the soon-to-be-implemented OHADA Uniform Acts had been largely forgotten, French patrons, with the support of funding from various international institutions, created a nongovernmental organization to promote awareness of OHADA and its laws. The Association for the Unification of African Law (l'Association pour l'Unification du Droit en Afrique, UNIDA) helps with training sessions and maintains a website—OHADA.com—that makes available OHADA Uniform Acts and CCJA and national court rulings applying OHADA law. The French journal *Juriscope*, with the support of Coopération Français, publishes commentary and compendiums of Uniform Acts and community case law, which UNIDA helps to distribute throughout the region. This is important because journals publishing laws and legal rulings tend to be irregularly maintained and hard to access in OHADA countries. Members of UNIDA's network regularly visit national courts to collect rulings that pertain to OHADA. The rulings are transcribed and published online. While the collection of national legal rulings on OHADA.com is surely incomplete, UNIDA's website supplies what may be the only publicly available searchable source for case

55 (Tiger 2001, 23–24).
56 (Katendi and Placca [an undated web-based documentation]).
57 (Mouloul 2009).
58 For more on ERASUMA, see Dickerson (2005, 58–59, 69).

law in OHADA member states. Ohada.com also maintains an e-mail listserv that distributes information about OHADA events and new publications.[59]

The promulgation of ten detailed multilaterally crafted Uniform Acts and the extensive networking of UNIDA has activated the OHADA system. The OHADA system offers the prospect of private litigant dispute resolution at the supranational level. There has to date been no systematic study of the OHADA system's legal output or effects, thus it is hard to tell the extent to which this prospect is being realized. If litigation is a sign of legal demand, then there appears to be a significant demand for international adjudication of business disputes in Francophone Africa. The OHADA court is the fourth busiest international court, after Europe's Court of Justice and Court of Human Rights and the Andean Tribunal of Justice. There is also a significant amount of legal mobilization in the OHADA system. Most African international courts operate in obscurity. The OHADA system, by contrast, seems to mobilize grassroots adherents. UNIDA did not organize any OHADA clubs, but it helps to coordinate their activities by listing the club coordinators and publicizing events via its e-mail listserv. As of June 2012, there were forty-eight OHADA clubs in the region and abroad.[60] These clubs, usually founded by law students, legal scholars, or practicing lawyers, host discussions, conferences, and meetings about legal issues. OHADA clubs also offer a way to network and build expertise that can hopefully attract clients.

The practice of the OHADA system has generated mixed reviews, which is not surprising given that the legal systems in most OHADA countries face a multitude of challenges. Lawyers and government officials seem to agree that OHADA is better than what existed before, if only because what constitutes the applicable law is now very clear.[61] The establishment of an OHADA rule of law, however, remains a work in progress. There is no question that OHADA law is the supreme business law of the land.[62] According to one lawyer I interviewed, "Since 2000, OHADA law is taught in the law schools. This is their law—there isn't anything else. So now new lawyers and judges are learning the OHADA Uniform Acts—and these people are the future leadership of the area."[63] There is a question, however, whether OHADA law regulates business relations in the

59 Based on interviews with UNIDA staff and founders, Paris, March 22, 2010.

60 Ibid. For a list of OHADA clubs, see http://www.ohada.com/clubs-ohada.html, last visited December 19, 2012.

61 Based on interviews conducted by the author in Paris, March 2010, and research by Gustav Kalm in Cameroon, where the OHADA secretariat is located, in March 2011.

62 (Dickerson 2005).

63 Interview with a French lawyer involved in the drafting of OHADA rules, March 24, 2010, Paris.

region. The OHADA arbitration system has been slow to take off. Contracts need to be written with arbitration clauses specifying the OHADA system, and there is still great uncertainty about how OHADA's arbitration mechanisms will operate.[64] There is also much judicial corruption in the region. The transparency of OHADA sometimes serves as a helpful antidote. One lawyer explained: "I can't say that business investment has changed a lot. I can't say that more business came—it wasn't a sea change. But our clients were happy to know that there were common rules that they knew. Also the transparency of OHADA rules obliges the magistrates to have a certain rigor and transparency. Lawyers could bring in OHADA rules and decisions to try to influence judges. Lawyers really kept track of what was going on, and they would bring the OHADA decisions in. And [local] judges are generally receptive to these arguments."[65] Another lawyer I interviewed relayed the following example, which I paraphrase:

> African judges are under a lot of political pressure—from government officials who don't hesitate to pick up the phone and call judges, from ethnic groups of which the judge is a member, and from corruption. In this domain of the national judiciary, things haven't really changed. One has tried to change this. I was just pleading a case in Chad—all of my information suggested that the judges were corrupted—bought off by the other side. I went to see the appellate judge. There wasn't any jurisprudence on this topic—OHADA was new and the case involved a provision that had yet to be applied, but the law was clear. I explained that his would be an important decision, that it would set a precedent. I asked him to apply the law—however he would—but just make clear how he was applying the law because the decision would be published and written about [by the lawyer himself]. I leave the material we [meaning UNIDA] produce with courts, I give them my articles, I give materials to the court's library. One year later, I got a ruling that was well reasoned, which applied the law.[66]

To some extent, these changes are independent of the existence of the OHADA court. Most disputes are still resolved out of court or in local courts, in large part because litigation fees are prohibitive for most small businesses. Compared to the number of cases adjudicated, relatively few are appealed to the CCJA (the OHADA.com website includes 3,100

64 Interview with officers of the Conseil Français des Investisseurs en Afrique (CIAN), Paris, April 12, 2010.

65 Interview with a lawyer with years of experience living in and practicing law in OHADA countries. This lawyer has since moved to France. Interview March 30, 2010, Paris.

66 Interview with a French lawyer involved in the drafting of OHADA rules, March 24, 2010, Paris.

rulings involving OHADA law, of which 567 are CCJA rulings).[67] But the existence of this supranational appellate venue is nonetheless important. The CCJA can decisively resolve disagreements about the meaning of OHADA law, filling in legal lacunae and facilitating a more uniform interpretation of the law.

OHADA is generating stakeholders. But at the end of the day, the value of a clear law depends on whether domestic actors want to follow the law. If national judges are corrupt, ignorant of OHADA law, or otherwise unwilling to follow OHADA law, legal clarity will count for little. Researchers on the ground report that most businesses—large and small—are registered in the OHADA system, but the registration does not as of yet mean very much. Mineral and other resource contracts are still negotiated diplomatically, with political pressure counting more than legal pressure in ensuring that agreements are kept. Most local businesses are still too small to claim bank loans, and the OHADA system is not integrated into microlending regimes, which tend to rely more on social than legal pressure to ensure that money lent is spent for its intended purposes and later repaid. These contracts likely do not violate OHADA law, but nor do they depend on OHADA rules or dispute adjudication for their smooth functioning.

IV. THE ALTERED POLITICS OF INTERNATIONAL DISPUTE SETTLEMENT

The altered politics framework works by connecting ICs with actors within states that want to see the law followed. ICs and compliance constituencies work together to encourage those actors with the power to choose compliance—usually key state officials—to make choices that cohere with what the law requires. Dispute settlement is rather different in that it is designed to encourage the litigants to voluntarily accept a legal outcome, and thereby stop disagreeing. Delegation of dispute settlement jurisdiction is primarily an other-binding judicial role, one where courts and governments generally share an interest in seeing disputes peacefully resolved in the shadow of the law. The dispute settlement function works better where legal certainty is helpful, and where governments also prefer that the law be applied and followed. These are the conditions presumed by the interstate arbiter model, which sees ICs as able to construct focal point definitions of the law that individuals and governments can use

67 This sample of national court rulings is surely incomplete. See http://www.ohada.com/jurisprudence.html, last visited June 5, 2012.

going forward. The four case studies in this chapter fit with the interstate arbiter model.

I chose four fairly unlikely cases where international adjudication could be seen as compromising national sovereignty, relations between litigating governments were poor in general, or specific disputes were linked to larger controversies that governments were unwilling to resolve. In all of these cases, domestic adjudication strategies were insufficient to assure foreign actors, or they were likely to aggravate fragile international political balances. International adjudication offered a solution that governments, national judges, and the litigants themselves could embrace.

Figure 5.3 maps these four disputes onto the altered politics framework from chapter 2. The shaded boxes indicate changes in government behavior. The Qatar v. Bahrain territorial dispute and OHADA business law case studies did not involve initial violations of the law, whereas the Japan v. Russia seizing of vessels and Iran-US Claims Tribunal cases did adjudicate alleged violations of contracts or laws. In all cases, bargaining in the shadow of the law during T1 reached a political impasse—litigants needed a binding ruling for the dispute to be resolved, and ICs could provide neutral, authoritative, and final decisions where domestic legal institutions could not. Litigation politics in T2 provide legal certainty that helped disputants move forward. Since governments preferred to see law followed, there was no need for leverage strategies in T3 to induce compliance. Information and publicity, and perhaps a special request by a governmental actor, might be needed to encourage substate actors to embrace the international solution, but since governments wanted to follow the law, this minimum of support could be easily obtained. For this reason, politics focused on bargaining and litigation phases more than the leverage politics stage. Arrows indicate pressure for change in state behavior.

In at least three of the four case studies, governments had a significant say over the laws and processes used in adjudication, or governments were largely indifferent to the range of solutions the court might adopt. ITLOS review only concerned promptness and reasonableness of fines levied, and Russia's and Japan's governments were happy to channel Japanese complaints into the ITLOS legal proceedings and then absolve themselves from further responsibility. The United States and Iran could channel the adjudication of property claims into a specialized legal body that could provide a remedy without further aggravating US-Iranian relations. And Francophone African governments could address investor complaints about judicial corruption by allowing for a supranational review of national court rulings applying OHADA law. These cases thus show ICs extending rather than meaningfully constraining the power of national governments in international and domestic affairs.

The possible exceptions were the cases involving the International Court of Justice. In the Qatar v. Bahrain territorial dispute, the ICJ claimed jurisdiction despite Bahraini protests. But the ICJ remained dependent on the parties filing their briefs and resolving the dispute over the forged documents the Qatari government submitted. Litigating this dispute took over ten years, with the ICJ decision finally emerging once the parties were ready to submit their papers and thereby exchange conflict for legal certainty.

The US-Iran Claims Tribunal discussion involved two additional ICJ rulings in disputes between the United States and Iran. The ICJ case involving United States diplomatic and consular staff in Tehran proceeded despite Iran's opposition to adjudication. The United States won a ruling in its favor, which Iran ignored. Iran's government did eventually insist that the United States withdraw this ICJ suit as a condition for submitting to the Algiers Accord, but the ICJ's ruling was not key to ending the conflict over the hostages or the frozen assets. Iran later brought a suit against the United States over its attack on Iranian oil platforms. The ICJ's "Oil Platforms" ruling has been much critiqued. Some suggest that the ICJ's claim of jurisdiction was tenuous at best. Others criticize the convoluted ruling with many separate opinions and dissents. The need to speak to the use of force through the lens of a commerce treaty, and the apparent disagreement among ICJ judges, led to a ruling replete with "creative avoidances" and "tortured analysis."[68] Harvey Rischikof observes that if the ICJ could have spoken with one voice, and if this voice had found support among member states, such "unanimity of voice would have placed the United States on notice that as a hegemon it was losing legitimacy and becoming an imperial power—establishing and enforcing bilateral treaties based on force and not international norms."[69] There are a lot of "ifs" in this sentence, but surely it would have been better if the ICJ's jurisdiction were undisputed and if ICJ judges were able to agree on the proper legal solution for the case. It is hard to know, however, if such clarity would have allowed the ICJ to alter politics regarding the use of force. The US-Iran controversy is so entrenched, and Iran ignored the ICJ in a case where the violations of international law was very clear, thus it is hard to imagine any international legal body making much of a difference for this particular relationship.

The dispute settlement role resides in the old terrain of international law. The Iran-US Claims Tribunal and OHADA Business Law case studies

68 The *Yale Journal of International Law* published a symposium on the ICJ "Oil Platforms" decision in 2004, with contributions from participants and observers in the case. Quote from Rischikof (2004, 331–32).

69 Ibid., at 341.

FIGURE 5.3 Political dynamics of international dispute settlement

	National system		**International system**			
	Domestic enforcement strategy	Compliance partner required change	International legal strategy	IC ruling (no remedy)	Post-ruling political strategy	Policy change by compliance partner
ICJ Bahrain-Qatar territorial dispute	No domestic resolution would be acceptable to the other country.	Executive branch needed to stop contesting land ownership.	Qatar pursued ICJ adjudication.	ICJ defined border (split the difference).	None needed.	Leaders of Qatar & Bahrain embrace declaratory ruling.
ITLOS Russian seizing Japanese vessels	Delays and excessive fines upset Japanese boat owners. There was no Japanese remedy for this problem.	Japan needed to drop case, or Russian judge needed to act in a timely fashion, setting appropriate bonds.	Japan pursued ITLOS adjudication.	ITLOS rejected Tomimaru case, ordered reduction in of bond for Hoshinmaru.	None needed.	Japan dropped Tomimaru case. Russian judge reconsidered bond in light of ITLOS ruling.

US-Iran Claims Tribunal	US court rulings would upset Iranians, and vice versa, undermining diplomacy regarding other issues.	US & Iranian judges needed to reject claims raised in domestic courts. ←	A political deal: Iran consented to claims tribunal, US transferred some frozen assets to compensation fund and released the rest.	3,861 cases adjudicated, with varying awards.	None needed (existence of compensation fund ensured payment of awards).	National judges refuse domestic adjudication. Other than Iran replenishing compensation fund, no domestic action needed.
OHADA Business law disputes	Uncertainty about the applicable law and judicial outcomes hindered business formation and foreign investment.	National judges need to accept OHADA law as governing law.	Governments cannot change OHADA Uniform Acts. National court rulings can be appealed to CCJA.	CCJA defines law in cases appealed from domestic system.	Publicity to → discourage corruption (with limited effectiveness).	Lawyers persuade (where possible) domestic judges to follow OHADA law
	T1: Bargaining in the shadow of an IC			T2: Litigation politics	T3: Leverage strategies (not salient in dispute settlement role)	

involved other-binding new-style ICs, international legal bodies with compulsory jurisdiction and access for nonstate actors to initiate litigation (the Iran-US Claims Tribunal has exclusive, and the OHADA CCJ has exclusive appellate jurisdiction). But the dispute settlement role depends on litigants and governments preferring a legal resolution for the dispute. The contributions of the ICJ, ITLOS, Iran–United States Claims Tribunal, and OHADA systems are undeniable. The legal rulings are the reason Qatar gave up its claim over the Hawar Islands, Japan dropped the Tomimaru case, Russian judges decreased the bond for releasing the *Hoshinmaru*, American judges refused jurisdiction with respect to US claims involving the Iranian revolution, and Iranians no longer fight for the release of assets frozen by Jimmy Carter. I have yet to find a clear example of OHADA adjudication changing the behavior of a public actor within an OHADA state, but I do not think that lawyers would bother to have raised over five hundred legal appeals at the CCJA if doing so were pointless.

CONCLUSION: BEYOND IC DISPUTE SETTLEMENT

This chapter focused on how ICs facilitate dispute settlement, when they are seized. ICs can helpfully settle complex legal and political disagreements, but the dispute settlement role especially depends on litigants and governments wanting to use law to resolve a disagreement. In each case study, litigation settled legal controversies. But one can question whether the IC intervention resolved the dispute. For the Qatar-Bahrain territorial dispute, international adjudication helpfully generated legal certainty while absolving state leaders of responsibility for disappointing partisans. In other cases, the larger underlying conflict continued. For these issues, ICs contributed "dispute management." Case studies explained how the ITLOS helps manage conflicts regarding vessels seized, the Iran–United States Claims Tribunal dealt with complex claims arising from the revolution in Iran and the United States' decision to freeze Iranian assets, and the OHADA system provides legal certainty and the prospect of legal oversight, which can be a partial antidote for widespread judicial corruption. Addressing these types of contentious cases helps to keep private litigant complaints off the bilateral diplomatic agenda.

Any analysis of the role of international courts today would be incomplete without discussing ICs in their dispute settlement role. The converse, however, is not true. No one is claiming that permanent courts are generally better at settling disputes than ad hoc or less formal systems of dispute settlement. Where parties retain the right to seek a legal remedy, ICs arguably increase the shadow of international law in legal negotiations.

But international law does not require that states resolve disputes or that governments use ICs when they seek a resolution, legal or otherwise.

Since my goal was to understand how ICs facilitate dispute settlement, I focused on cases that were litigated. Because ICs usually have neither exclusive nor mandatory dispute settlement jurisdiction, such cases are likely more the exception than the rule. One can find no more than a handful of government-to-government cases in legal systems that emulate the ECJ. When one considers how many countries are members of the WTO and the prevalence of violations of WTO and MERCOSUR rules, WTO and MERCOSUR litigation seems to be fairly rare. The ICJ has existed for more than sixty-five years, and its geographic and jurisdictional reach is arguably the broadest of any IC in this study, but as of June 2012 only 152 cases had been filed in the ICJ's general list. This is especially surprising given that for many issues and treaties, the ICJ is the only legal body, domestic or international, with jurisdiction to adjudicate disputes.[70]

Given that international dispute settlement appears to be relatively rare, it is somewhat surprising that dispute settlement remains such a prevalent analytical lens for assessing international courts. The structure of international litigation—with two legal adversaries approaching the court for a ruling—lends itself to the dispute settlement framing. But there are also normative reasons why some people cling to the dispute settlement lens. International treaties, by definition, are negotiated and signed by governments. If treaties are nothing more than a contract between governments, then international legal duties remain bilateral. Contractual promises arguably cease to exist when one government abrogates the contract, and the contractual perspective suggests that treaties generate no duties to nonsignatories, and no rights for substate actors or governments that are not directly involved in a dispute. Limiting the role of ICs to dispute settlement tends to keep ICs as the handmaiden of powerful governments. ICs can either bind weaker parties and nonstate actors—in which case powerful states may happily extend compulsory jurisdiction and private access to the court—or IC jurisdiction can be optional. Either

70 The old-style nature of the ICJ, and especially its lack of compulsory jurisdiction, surely limits the ICJ's usage. Its very broad jurisdiction may also lead litigants to shy away from the Court. The diversity of ICJ judges, the paucity of cases adjudicated, and the politicization of the ICJ lead the Court to speak with multiple voices. A more specialized mandate might lead to more cases being raised, although as long as states are the only actors able to initiate binding litigation, appeals are likely to remain relatively rare. There are calls, however, to extend to the ICJ jurisdiction to review decisions and actions of United Nations agencies, and to allow for preliminary references from nonstate actors. Either of these changes would increase usage of the ICJ, but arguably not facilitate the ICJ's dispute settlement role.

situation circumscribes the influence of ICs to the interstate arbiter model discussed in chapter 2, where international adjudication was not really about what law required but rather about what the litigating parties would accept.

The OHADA system is possibly a bridge to the new terrain of international law. The OHADA system creates legal stability by making it impossible for any single government to unilaterally change governing business law. If OHADA bodies manage to build political support within national judiciaries, business relations in the region will be transformed. The next three chapters move more fully into the new terrain of international law. The administrative review role still has ICs serving a narrow legal role defined by governments, but IC jurisdiction is compulsory, nonstate actors can initiate litigation, and ICs can connect with substate administrative actors. The enforcement and constitutional review roles move further into the new terrain of international law, where international adjudication becomes constraining of government decision making. These chapters also move further in creating actionable human and economic rights.

CHAPTER 6

International Administrative Review

The administrative review role of ICs is often underappreciated because the implementation of international law garners less attention and most regulatory issues (for example, environmental regulation, regulation of manufacturing, employer-employee relations) remain primarily national. Lawyers who deal with intellectual property issues, foreign contracts, and mergers and acquisitions involving multinational corporations are surely aware of the importance of international law regulating these issues, but unless administrators are grossly misapplying international rules, there will be no reason to seek recourse in international adjudicatory bodies. That said, the body of global regulatory law has grown significantly since the end of World War II, and one might even say that global governance is increasingly regulatory in nature.

The rising prevalence of international regulatory rules has led to the creation of a new academic subfield, known as global administrative law (GAL). Benedict Kingsbury, Nico Krisch, and Richard Stewart argue for considering global governance as administrative action even when such governance focuses on issues that are not per se regulatory in nature (for example, security, human rights, and humanitarian intervention), because they believe the quality and legitimacy of global governance would be improved by adhering to the well-known practices of administrative law—transparency, participation, reason giving, and accountability.[1] Even if one does not embrace this normative objective, GAL scholars are clearly correct in pointing out that global regulatory rules take many forms, and can have informal, judicial, and loosely coordinated origins.[2]

This chapter seeks to understand what ICs contribute to administrative review of international law. Administrative review checks that administrative decisions adhere to correct procedure, are not arbitrary, and

1 (Krisch and Kingbury 2006).

2 (Kingsbury et al. 2005, 17).

faithfully apply the law. Although administrative review examines the decisions of public administrators, both the dispute settlement and administrative review roles contribute to the regulative role of law, using law to shape expectations and guide the decisions and actions of civil servants, firms, and private citizens.

The broader reach of global regulatory rules has expanded the legal domains ICs now influence. Chapter 5 noted that some ICs have jurisdiction to adjudicate cases involving staff members and contract disputes with vendors. Large international institutions that lack an associated court sometimes create internal administrative tribunals to adjudicate staff and employment disputes.[3] These bodies are not my focus. Rather, my discussion of international administrative review is consistent with what GAL scholars mean—mechanisms to review the application of global regulatory rules. GAL scholars define the field of global administrative law to include hard and soft regulatory rules made by groups of states, transnationally coordinated national actors, networks of public and private actors, and international institutions. These rules can be interpreted, reviewed, and applied by a broad range of legal and quasi-legal actors at both the national and international levels. Compared to GAL's far-reaching conception of administrative law, my focus is narrow. ICs conducting administrative review adjudicate the application of binding international regulations, which means a focus on ICs inherently narrows the aperture to the application of hard law by public bodies.

Eyal Benvenisti argues that international administrative review is a problem-solving device of states, a way to address the reality that law is inherently general and thus unable to speak to every contingency. Judges, in conjunction with national and global administrators, adapt global regulatory rules to new situations, filling in the content of the rules as they apply them to specific cases. Administrative review also provides a fire-alarm system of oversight, a way for private actors to contest problematic administrative decisions and to identify where administrators are captured by powerful governments or otherwise corrupted.[4] Daniel Kelemen adds that global governance through administrative review provides a way for underresourced international institutions to harness private litigants to monitor firms' and national governments' adherence to supranational rules.[5]

Peter Lindseth, by contrast, stresses the legitimacy contributions of international administrative review. Lindseth observes that as international

3 For example, the United Nations, International Labor Organization, International Monetary Fund, World Bank, Inter-American Development Bank, Organization of American States, Asian Development Bank, African Development Bank all have administrative tribunals. For more on administrative tribunals, see Amerasinghe (2014).

4 (Benvenisti 2005).

5 (Kelemen 2011).

administrative actors became more politically powerful, nationally based firms and politicians started to question the legal and legitimacy basis of supranational actors' authority. The standard answer—that states delegated authority to supranational administrators—started to seem insufficient.[6] Administrative review helps legitimize international administrative policy making. As GAL scholars suggest, the legal requirements judges engaged in administrative review demand—transparency, participation, reason giving—help to bolster the legitimacy of global administration. Martin Shapiro explains that the "giving reasons" requirement judges impose is "a form of internal improvement for administrators. A decision-maker required to give reasons will be more likely to weigh pros and cons carefully before reaching a decision than will a decision-maker able to proceed by simple fiat. In another aspect, giving reasons is a device for enhancing democratic influence on administration by making government more transparent."[7] Administrative review also increases accountability by giving the subjects of administrative decision making a chance to have their concerns adjudicated. This sort of check is exactly what the Court of Justice of the European Union and others were demanding in the seizing private assets (Kadi) case discussed in the chapter 8. More often than not judges affirm the validity of the administrative action, thus international administrative review can enhance legitimacy without compromising national sovereignty or the pursuit of valid public policy objectives.

Section I explores where and how states have delegated administrative review jurisdiction to ICs and where states are avoiding creating private litigant rights to seek an annulment of administrative actions that violate international law. Section II considers four case studies of international administrative review in action, comparing permanent and ad hoc courts and review of national and international administrative decisions. American academics encouraged me to include an investor dispute case study. For investor disputes, legal review does not involve assessing the legal propriety of administrative decision making per se, and investor adjudicatory bodies have no authority to annul or remand decisions of national administrative actors. Rather, adjudicatory systems can award compensation for public policy decisions that undermine the value of an investment. Lawyers consider investor treaties to be an example of global administrative law,[8] and ICSID fits in this chapter because the investor dispute system

6 (Lindseth 2005; Lindseth 2010). Bignami and Lindseth link European administrative law to European legal traditions (Bignami 2005; Lindseth 2003). Martin Shapiro and Francesca Bignami, and many others, show how judges have been key architects developing administrative law in ways that help legitimize the administrative state (Shapiro and Stone Sweet 2002, 228–57).

7 (Shapiro and Stone Sweet 2002, 228–57, quote at 229).

8 (Van Harten and Loughlin 2006).

can give rise to costly litigation and awards, to the point that litigation threats by investors can have a chilling effect on the local regulatory politics. But as the case study shows, the investor dispute system is a rather unique transnational hybrid that upsets the careful balance between private rights and public goals that judges generally seek.

Section III considers ICs altering politics in these case studies, bringing into the discussion case studies from other chapters that involve review of administrative actions. Administrative agencies are the key compliance partners for ICs in their administrative review role. The case studies together suggest that ICs are more likely to have their rulings respected when they are aiding rather than constraining administrators.

American lawyers expect administrative review to invariably morph into constitutional review, since judges are reviewing the actions of public actors. Civil law lawyers, by contrast, expect robust administrative review to be able to coexist with parliamentary supremacy and even authoritarian rule.[9] The conclusion considers the extent to which international administrative review avoids crossing into constitutional review, and thus into questioning decisions and actions of the sovereign itself.

I. DELEGATING ADMINISTRATIVE REVIEW JURISDICTION TO INTERNATIONAL COURTS

ICs with administrative review roles have jurisdiction to assess the validity of administrative decisions and a corresponding authority to annul illegal administrative actions. All ICs with administrative review jurisdiction are new-style ICs. The subjects of administrative decisions, invariably private actors, will initiate review with the defendant being a public actor, either a supranational or national administrator. IC jurisdiction is also compulsory. Although ICs with administrative review jurisdiction are new-style courts, IC administrative review is not necessarily sovereignty compromising. As the introduction to this chapter explained, administrative review provides a way for legislative bodies to harness private actors to monitor administrative actors, which themselves rely on delegated authority. So long as administrative review is limited to questions of procedure and law, rather than questions of fact, and whenever administrative review ratifies administrative decision making, international administra-

9 Civil law systems still separate administrative review from constitutional review. Administrative judges are expected to stay entirely within their administrative role, leaving any constitutional question for specialized constitutional courts. For more, see Merryman and Pérez-Perdomo (2007); Stone (1995).

tive review mainly reinforces the objectives and goals of the central state, which helped to write the rules judges are applying.

The key interlocutors of ICs in the administrative review role are the administrators themselves. Administrators generally do not have a personal stake in how the rules are applied (it would be a conflict of interest if they did), and professional administrators value a reputation for being evenhanded and technically skilled. Noncorrupt administrators generally avoid nullification and the issuing of awards by following the interpretations of judges. These interpretations clarify vague rules and specify the proper procedure to follow so as to avoid legal reversal. There should be a natural life cycle for administrative review. Once legal rules are clear, litigation should decrease because the more administrators follow legal rules, the less likely it becomes that firms will prevail in their legal challenge. But it is also true that firms may choose to play the lottery, appealing a ruling in the hopes that a judge will reverse an administrator. In the Andean context, administrative review increased over time not because questionable administrative actions increased but rather because the number of applications for patents and trademarks increased, thereby generating more appealable decisions.

International administrative review systems tend to emulate the European Community's system. Thus I begin by explaining the origins and design of the European Community administrative model so that we can better understand its specialized design features. Figure 6.1 will list the universe of operational ICs with explicit administrative review roles, documenting the copying of Europe's supranational administrative review model.

The European Supranational Administrative Review Model

Chapters 4 and 8 discuss the European Court of Justice's legal revolution, which reoriented scholarly focus toward the Court's constitutional and enforcement roles. For this chapter, however, I want to stay within the ECJ's administrative review role, which is a mostly unproblematic template that has been readily emulated.

France's Robert Schumann proposed the European Coal and Steel Community as a way to subject German firms to supranational oversight and thereby ensure that German dominance in a sector crucial for industrial manufacturing (and war making) did not undermine reconstruction efforts in the rest of Europe.[10] Smaller European countries worried that French and German governments would unduly influence the Coal and

10 For more on the origins of the European Coal and Steel Community, see Gillingham (1991); Milward (1984, chapter 12).

Steel Community's main regulatory body, the High Authority. They created the European Court of Justice (ECJ) in 1952 as a check against the High Authority's abuse of power, providing a means for states and firms to challenge and invalidate illegal High Authority actions, and to demand that the Authority act when legally obliged.

The European Community's regulatory role expanded with the creation of the European Economic Community. The Treaty of Rome envisioned that supranational legislative bodies would enact "regulations," directly applicable regulatory rules that do not require the traditional step of national incorporation. In other words, for regulations European administrative law *is* domestic law. Indeed, one might say that the "regulations" are the legal embodiment of European Community supranationalism. There are also European "directives," rules crafted by the Council of Ministers that must be domestically implemented. The legal obligations for directives are somewhat different, but governments must incorporate directives by a specified date and adhere to the overall objective of the directive.

The ECJ's administrative review role was the Court's initial raison d'être, and it is the reason why member states gave the ECJ what was—at the time—an unusual design.[11] The EC legal system includes two complementary administrative review mechanisms. Firms and private litigants can raise "direct-action" challenges to European Commission decisions, actions, and nonactions. Initially, direct action cases went to the ECJ, but when the ECJ's docket became overburdened, member states created the Tribunal of First Instance (now called the General Court), and the ECJ became an appellate body for these cases. National administrators also apply European regulations and directives, and they help implement decisions of the Commission. For this reason, member states added a preliminary ruling mechanism to the EC's legal system. Private litigants bring suits in national courts challenging High Authority/Commission actions or the implementation of European regulations and directives by national administrative actors. National judges suspend national legal proceedings and refer questions about European law to the ECJ. After the ECJ has ruled on their questions, the case returns to national judges, who apply the clarified law to the facts of the case. In the European system any national court can refer a legal question to the ECJ, and courts of last instance are required to refer such questions. The ECJ remains a first and last instance body for preliminary ruling references.

The European Community's new international administrative tools—directives, regulations, and the preliminary ruling procedure—needed to

11 The ECJ was actually modeled on the Conseil d'État, France's highest administrative court. On the origins of the ECJ, see Boerger-De Smedt (2008; 2012); Pescatore (1981).

be assimilated into domestic legal practice. Given that European regulations were directly applicable within national legal orders, European judges had to update dualist conceptions that only allowed international law to be domestically binding once formally incorporated by domestic legislative actors. National legal change took time. Some European judges questioned whether the ECJ should adjudicate issues that in their view should remain national rather European in nature. But national governing bodies clearly wanted to regulate certain domains at the supranational level. Supreme courts did not want to suggest that European integration was legally impossible, and supranational legal review was obviously a good idea. National judges lack jurisdiction to review Commission decisions, and they are not experts on complex European regulatory rules (for example, rules regulating labor benefits for migrant workers, agricultural subsidies for farmers, and such). Rather than introduce errors of law, apply European regulations in ways that disadvantage national producers, or generate conflict among member states, national judges could refer legally and politically complex cases to the ECJ. The preliminary ruling mechanisms allowed, for example, German judges to let the ECJ decide how they should to treat letters from Italian doctors that by all appearances were designed to extend vacations rather than address medical emergencies. As long as a small fraction of national regulatory rules were supranational in origin, domestic judges were quite open to referring questions involving community rules to the ECJ.

Much of the ECJ's law making in its administrative review role has also not been contested. Francesca Bignami documented how the ECJ, Commission, and member states responded to concerns about supranational policy-making power by constructing new administrative law legal rights: the right to a hearing for proposed European regulations, the right to transparency in Commission decision making, and the right for parliamentary and civil-society participation in European regulatory rule making.[12] As the first case study in this chapter will show, European administrative law has become a high-stakes enterprise. Furthermore, as more aspects of regulatory governance transferred from the domestic to the European level, and as the ECJ increasingly delved into questions involving the compatibility of national law with European law, national judges *have* started to worry about the ECJ's ever-expanding jurisdiction.[13] But there is no disagreement that the Commission's actions must

12 EU administrative law today is part common law constructed by the ECJ and part legislation codifying practices developed by the Commission in response to ECJ rulings. See Bignami (2005).

13 Firms and government officials question whether certain policy issues should be regulated at the European level. They question whether the Council of Ministers and the ECJ have overstepped the regulatory form of a directive, which should leave national and

be subject to judicial review. There is also widespread agreement that national judicial review of Commission decisions is neither practicable nor desirable since national judges are less informed about European law, already overloaded, and national review would likely give rise to varied legal interpretations and forum shopping by litigants.

The Global Spread of the ECJ Administrative Review Model

International administrative review jurisdiction has spread with the ECJ template, because emulation is a powerful factor in the multiplication of ICs and because delegating administrative review jurisdiction vis-à-vis the interpretation and application of supranational rules makes compelling sense. International administrative review has two forms. Type 1 review involves the review of decisions of supranational administrators. ICs engaged in this type of international administrative review provide a legal check of supranational administrators that would otherwise not exist. This type of review is exclusive and mandatory, meaning that ICs are the only venues where international administrative acts are subject to be challenged and annulled. Type 2 review involves review of state regulatory decisions. Type 2 review aims to facilitate a coordinated and correct interpretation of supranational regulatory rules across borders. This second form usually indicates that international administrative law is embedded within domestic legal orders, meaning that international law *is* domestic law, or domestic law is intentionally linked to international law. IC review of the national application of international administrative rules is generally mandatory, but national judges are yet to fully understand their legal obligations within supranational legal systems so that in practice ICs are often not approached unless litigants insist on a reference.

Figure 6.1 identifies thirteen ICs with jurisdiction to review the validity of acts or decisions made by supranational administrative actors and/or national implementation of supranational regulatory rules. With the exception of the International Tribunal for the Law of the Sea's Seabed Chamber and the EFTAC, ICs with administrative review jurisdiction can also review the validity of administrative rules themselves, which may lead administrative review to morph into constitutional review in practice.[14] Thirteen ICs (plus the MERCOSUR system) have copied the ECJ's preliminary ruling mechanism, authorizing ICs to receive from national

---

local governments meaningful discretion regarding how they achieve directive goals. There is also concern that the tendency to make European law enforceable by private actor suits has introduced an American style adversarial legalism into Europe.

14 The Seabed Chamber can hear charges that the Seabed Authority misused its power. EFTAC administrative review concerns penalties imposed by the Surveillance Authority. See the chapter's appendix for more.

judges questions about either supranational administrative decision making or the national application of supranational regulatory rules. Sometimes the copying of the ECJ administrative review structure is identical, and sometimes it is adapted.[15] The appendix to this chapter provides more information about each IC's administrative review jurisdiction, and information about three additional international administrative review systems: the MERCOSUR dispute settlement system, which contains a preliminary ruling mechanism and allows a supranational political body to review private complaints about abusive national administrative practices, and the NAFTA and ICSID mechanisms that are the focus of section III.

Many ICs in figure 6.1 are not very active. In general we can say that the presence of supranational rules that are applied in practice is a necessary condition for IC administrative review to occur. Where international regulatory rules are actively applied, ICs tend to be regularly and fairly frequently invoked. Indeed, the vast majority of what some of the most active ICs do involves ruling on private litigant complaints regarding the application of supranational regulatory rules. A rough estimate of ECJ caseload suggests that 75 percent if not more of what the ECJ does involves straightforward administrative review of the application of European regulatory rules.[16] A perusal of BENELUX's 139 rulings suggests that most legal rulings of the BENELUX court involve administrative review.[17] Having coded all Andean preliminary rulings, I can more definitively say that at least 90 percent of ATJ rulings involve review of the application of community regulatory rules by national and international administrative actors.[18] My sense is that the overwhelming majority of the

15 Some common market systems still require community regulations to be incorporated into national law. Some preliminary ruling mechanisms require last instance national judges to refer cases to the supranational courts, and others authorize but do not require national judges to refer questions about community law to the IC. For more, see Alter (2012, 141–43).

16 Stone Sweet and Brunell's coding of the ECJ caseload reveals that the ECJ heard 4,003 annulment actions (e.g., challenges to EU regulatory rules or Commission decisions applying these rules) and 5,216 preliminary ruling references from its founding through 2005. Preliminary ruling cases can also involve state compliance with European law, but the vast majority of preliminary ruling cases are about the straight-up application of European regulatory law. By comparison, the ECJ heard 2,645 suits involving state infringement of European rules during this time. http://www.eu-newgov.org/datalists/deliverables_detail.asp?Project_ID=26, last visited August 8, 2012.

17 BENELUX cases list the two parties, which are often private parties fighting over intellectual property rights. But the stated objective for the BENELUX court is to facilitate a uniform interpretation of common regulatory rules, thus presumably most cases involve reviewing the application of these rules by national actors. See the book's online appendix for more.

18 Larry Helfer, Maria Florencia Guerzovich, and I coded 1,338 of the ATJ's preliminary rulings from its founding through 2007; all but thirty-two of the preliminary ruling

FIGURE 6.1: ICs with delegated administrative review jurisdiction **(by year created)**

	Type of International Administrative Review				
ICs with role	1) Review international administrative actions	2) Review state administrative actions	Compulsory jurisdiction	Direct private access	Preliminary ruling mechanism
European Court of Justice (ECJ) (1952)	X	X	X	X	X
BENELUX (1974)		X	X	Via national courts only	X
Andean Tribunal of Justice (ATJ) (1984)	X	X	X	X	X
European Free Trade Area Court (EFTAC) (1992)	X		X	X	Advisory opinions only
Central American Court of Justice (CACJ) (1992)		X	Partial	X	X
International Tribunal for the Law of the Sea—Seabed Chamber (1996)	X		X	X	
West African Economic and Monetary Union (WAEMU) (1995)	X		X	Via national courts only	X

Court of Justice for the Common Market of Eastern and Southern Africa (COMESA) (1998)	X	X	X	X	X
Central African Monetary Community (CEMAC) (2000)	X	X	X	X	X
Caribbean Court of Justice (CCJ) (2001)	X		X	X	X
East African Court of Justice (EACJ) (2001)	X	X	X	X	X
Economic Community of West African States Court of Justice (ECOWAS CJ) (2001)	X	X	X	X	X
Southern African Development Community (SADC) (2005)	X		X	X	X
Total N = 13	11	8 (plus NAFTA + Investor disputes)	13 (plus NAFTA + Investor disputes)	11 (plus NAFTA + Investor disputes)	12 (plus MERCOSUR)

ECJ's, BENELUX court's, and ATJ's administrative rulings are not controversial because administrative review is extending and legitimizing rather than curtailing state legal and regulatory power.

What about Other Instances of IC Conducting Administrative Review?

All ICs listed in figure 6.1 are part of international institutions that include (or at least envision) the creation of international regulatory rules by supranational bodies, and the implementation of such rules by supranational and/or national administrative actors. If NAFTA's Chapter 19 system included a permanent court, it would also be listed in figure 6.1. And if the Southern Common Market relied on a legal rather than a political mechanism—the Common Market Group—to adjudicate complaints about national administrative practices, MERCUSOR would also be listed.[19] But there are other unlisted ICs that end up reviewing administrative decision making without explicit administrative review jurisdiction. For example, GAL scholars would surely consider ITLOS's review of the prompt release of vessels (case study 5.2) as a review of the administrative handling of decisions to impound vessels. The many decisions involving safeguards and countervailing duties undertaken by WTO panels can be seen as de facto administrative review raised in the form of an enforcement action.[20] GAL's broad definition of administrative review would likely include human rights cases reviewing decisions to deny benefits to gay partners, or significant adjudicatory delays in national legal systems as involving administrative review. Given that a far broader range of bodies may be called upon to practice administrative review, why not explicitly delegate administrative review jurisdiction to these bodies?

A potential answer emerges by considering the nature of ICs' explicit administrative review jurisdiction. Credible review of administrative action

references involved the application of Andean intellectual property rules and the rest included questions of administrative practice (Helfer and Alter 2009, 893–900). The ATJ also heard six omissions cases, which clearly involve administrative review. I did not code the 105 noncompliance cases or the forty-six nullification cases. Most of these cases probably are administrative review cases, but if one assumes that none of them are administrative review cases, we are still left with the finding that administrative review accounts for 90 percent of the ATJ's total output through 2007. This coding will be updated in Alter and Helfer (2014).

19 These disputes will only be adjudicated if a state pursues the issue or a national supreme court refers a case to the Permanent Review Body. See the chapter's appendix for more.

20 A coding of WTO litigation finds that 13.8 percent of all cases initiated involve antidumping, countervailing duties, or challenges to safeguard decisions, thus challenges to national administrative decision making (Horn, Johannesson, and Mavroides 2011, 1119).

only exists where the subjects of administrative decision making can initiate review. This is why all ICs with delegated administrative review powers have compulsory jurisdiction, all allow the private subjects of administrative decision making to instigate administrative review, and all can nullify illegal actions. Where states do not want to subject their national decision makers to international judicial oversight, administrative review may still take place via dispute settlement and enforcement mechanisms. But such review tends to be different.

The subjects of administrative decisions often lack standing to instigate international dispute settlement or enforcement review. For example, the WTO and ITLOS systems require states to initiate litigation on behalf of private litigants. A second difference concerns remedies; IC decisions in enforcement or dispute settlement cases create costs for noncompliance but they do not nullify contested domestic regulatory actions. Case study 6.3 shows how this difference matters: WTO decisions finding "illegal" dumping apply prospectively, creating a legal right for state retaliation if the defendant state does not cease to collect illegal duties. This retaliation is of little practical benefit to a firm harmed by illegal countervailing duties. By contrast, NAFTA rulings involving "illegal" dumping apply retrospectively, so that private litigants may be refunded illegal fines and duties.

A third more subtle difference concerns legal understandings. International law enforcement can occur entirely at the international level. The ruling is binding on governments, but it does not necessarily penetrate the realm of domestic legality, which is to say that domestic judges may not be legally obligated to follow international legal rulings. International administrative review of national regulatory actions suggests that international law is embedded into the domestic legal order, and that national actors *are* legally obliged to respect international regulatory rules.

From these differences we can surmise that states may not want to extend international administrative review jurisdiction to ICs because they do not want to allow private actors to initiate review, they do not want to be liable to pay compensation to private actors, and they do not want to suggest that international law is somehow part of domestic law. The hybrid review system of NAFTA and quasi-legal MERCOSUR systems offer compromise solutions. ICSID, by contrast, involves a morphed and perhaps unintended administrative review role.

II. INTERNATIONAL ADMINISTRATIVE REVIEW IN ACTION

This section reviews four examples of international administrative review. The first two case studies involve the two ICs most actively involved in international administrative review adjudicating cases involving powerful

American firms. The European case study involves type 1 administrative review. I intentionally sought a non-European example of type 2 judicial review to show that the European Community's administrative review model also works in non-European regulatory contexts. The Andean case is especially challenging because governments took conflicting positions in the controversy. The second set of case studies examine type 2 administrative review by ad hoc bodies. The NAFTA rulings contributed to changes in government behavior in the direction of relatively greater respect for the law, whereas the Metalclad ruling generated compensation but also a reinterpretation by signatory states to narrow the legal basis for future claims.

It is tempting to argue that the first two case studies are not very contentious because ICs upheld administrative decisions, while the NAFTA and ICSID case studies are controversial because international legal bodies rejected administrative decisions. But other chapters involve case studies where ICs rejects administrative acts. In the Japan v. Russia—Seizing private vessels case study in chapter 5, ITLOS rejected a Russian decision setting a bond; in the second use patent case study in chapter 7 the ATJ invalidated both a national law and a national administrative decision. In the seizing private assets (Kadi) case study in chapter 8 the ECJ invalidated both a community regulation and a Commission administrative decision. I bring these case studies into the discussion of how administrative review alters politics. Overall, my sense is that cases become "controversial" when a ruling is problematic or because some political factions would prefer policies that cannot pass legal muster.

6.1. "Microsoft" and "GE/Honeywell Merger"—The Court of Justice of the European Union reviews Commission decisions involving violations of community competition laws

Henry Kissinger famously said, "Who do I call if I want to call Europe?" With respect to competition policy, there is no question. Competition law is one of the legal arenas that European governments definitively transferred to the European Community very early on. The Commission can issue fines against firms that abuse their dominant position in the market and reject company mergers that might undermine market competition. The only legal bodies empowered to review these decisions are Europe's General Court and its renamed Court of Justice of the European Union (which at the time of this case still carried the name of the ECJ). As long as the Commission follows specified procedures and provides plausible reasons to support its decision, the ECJ tends to defer to the Commission's expert assessments.[21] In the seizing private assets (Kadi) case (8.2),

21 This is of course a generalization. European administrative law is extensive, and there are literally thousands of ECJ and General Court rulings. Surely the level of deference varies across domains of administrative practice.

the Commission did not meet this standard, and its decision was thus rejected, but for the Microsoft and Honeywell/General Electric cases the Commission had arguably fulfilled the criteria the ECJ defined.

Before mobile phones replaced computers and Google supplanted Microsoft in software dominance, Microsoft was the behemoth of the computer world. Microsoft has been accused of a number of anticompetitive practices. As a condition for using its Windows operating system, Microsoft required computer companies to include and make its Internet Explorer product the default browser. Microsoft could thereby increase usage of Explorer's search engine so as to garner more advertising revenue. The company also bundled products, writing its software in an integrated way that meant that consumers opting for competitors' products would not be able to achieve full functionality with Internet websites. These practices were investigated in both the United States and Europe. Often Microsoft negotiated settlements, with deal making occurring in the shadow of judicial review. For example, in a July 1994 settlement Microsoft promised the US Department of Justice not to tie other Microsoft products to the sale of Windows.[22] After arguably violating this agreement, the Department of Justice sued Microsoft for forcing computer makers to include Internet Explorer as a part of the installation of Windows. The district court sided with the Department of Justice, finding that Microsoft had threatened to retaliate against other companies if they supported Microsoft's competitors, forced computer makers to preinstall Internet Explorer while prohibiting users from removing the program, and withheld necessary software information from developers unless they promoted Microsoft products. In November 2001, Microsoft reached a settlement that a district court then approved.[23]

Regulatory oversight in Europe proceeded in a similar fashion, the only difference being that decision making and judicial review took place at the supranational level. The European Commission considered two Microsoft practices largely overlooked by American regulators: (1) requiring Microsoft Access (a database program) to be used in conjunction with Microsoft server software to achieve full functionality, and (2) tying Windows Media Player to the Windows PC operating system.[24] In 2004, the Commission held that these practices abused Microsoft's dominant position in the PC operating system market. The Commission imposed a fine of €497 million and ordered Microsoft to disclose proprietary data so that non-Microsoft manufacturers could make their products fully in-

22 Sandra Sugawara, "Justice to Launch Probe of Microsoft," *Washington Post*, August 21, 1993; Keegan (1993, 167–74).

23 These cases are discussed in Cohen (2004, 335–43).

24 Ibid., 355–57.

teroperable with Windows PCs and servers. The Commission also required that Microsoft release a version of Windows that did not contain Media Player.[25]

Microsoft paid the fine in full and released the required European version of its Windows operating system.[26] But the company was, in the Commission's view, too slow in releasing proprietary data. In July 2006, the Commission levied a fine of €1.5 million per day, backdating the fine to December 16, 2005, and threatening to increase the fine to €3 million per day if Microsoft did not comply.[27] Microsoft appealed this decision. The then named Court of First Instance took the side of the Commission, finding that Microsoft had not demonstrated that the Commission's analysis was in "manifest error."[28] Microsoft appealed this ruling to the ECJ. The company then reached a settlement in October 2007, after which it dropped its appeal and agreed to pay an additional €280.5 million fine.[29] The pattern then continued with the Commission issuing new fines whenever Microsoft failed to do as the Commission required, with the company appealing the fines to the Tribunal of First Instance and then the ECJ. As in the United States, Microsoft can often negotiate a decrease in sanctions, but it cannot avoid Commission investigations or complying with Commission requirements. This deal making takes place in the shadow of legal review, which is costly and usually favors the Commission. Allowing the Commission to negotiate on behalf of member states helps to leverage European countries' power. Microsoft may well have been willing to remove its products from the French or Italian market rather than comply with a national demand to release proprietary data. But Europe's collective market is too valuable.

A second competition policy case, which was never litigated, shows how ECJ jurisprudence shapes European administrative procedure, which then protects the European Community in controversial cases. Americans sometimes criticize the European Commission for making decisions based on politics rather than hard economic analysis. This is especially so when the Commission reaches a conclusion that differs from that of American regulators. One such example includes the Commission's decision to block

25 (Potter and Constantine 2009).

26 Matt Hines, "Microsoft Pays E.U. in Full," CNET, July 2, 2004, http://news.cnet.com/2100-1014_3-5255715.html.

27 "Brussels Poised to Fine Microsoft," BBC, June 27, 2006, http://news.bbc.co.uk/2/hi/business/5120536.stm; Dawn Kawamoto, "'No Alternative' to Microsoft Fine," CNET, July 12, 2006, http://news.cnet.com/No-alternative-to-Microsoft-fine/2008-1014_3-6093104.html.

28 Case COMP/C-3/37.792-Microsoft Corporation v. Commission Decision, 2007 O.J. (L 32) 23, discussed in Ahlborn and Evans (2009).

29 *Antitrust Law Updates*, 156 Antitrust Counselor Article II (December 2007).

a proposed merger between two American firms—Honeywell and General Electric. US regulators had endorsed the merger, but then the Commission demanded that each company first divest itself of ownership of highly attractive and profitable units. In addition to a concern about dominance in the airline engine market, the Commission argued that the merged firm could offer one-stop shopping, bundled products, and capital financing for the purchase of a variety of products, including navigational systems, environmental control systems, wheels, breaks, landing gear, auxiliary power units, aircraft lighting, and engine starters.[30] The Commission's eighty-four-page justification adhered to the sort of procedure administrative judges tend to require. By all appearances, the Commission listened to concerns of a broad range of European manufactures and gave reasoned substantive opinions to support its decision. Perhaps this is why Honeywell and General Electric decided to abandon the merger rather than raise a legal challenge, and no member state raised a challenge to the decision.[31]

Since the Microsoft decision upheld the Commission's finding, the ruling required no change in Commission policy. The ECJ is known for hewing closely to the decisions and actions of the European Commission.[32] With respect to administrative review, critics fault the Tribunal of First Instance and the ECJ for allowing "too much discretion to the Commission."[33] The ECJ and the General Court do sometimes question Commission actions, as the discussion of the Kadi litigation (in chapter 8) documents. The Microsoft and General Electric/Honeywell decisions, however, concerned a highly complex review of companies with unusually dominant positions and a record of using their market power to the detriment of European competitors. The Commission may be given a wide swath in such contexts, but the same is arguably true of national administrators in other contexts.[34] In any event, there is little reason for European governments to want to curb either the Commission's power or the ECJ's review of Commission actions. Allowing the Commission much discretion enhances the leverage of member states vis-à-vis foreign firms. Meanwhile,

30 Commission Decision of July 3, 2001, declaring a concentration to be incompatible with the Common Market and the EEA Agreement (Case No. COMP/ M.2220 General Electric/Honeywell), discussed in Holland (2003, 81–86).

31 The reasons for the decision are discussed in Holland (2003). For a discussion of the political basis of Commission merger decisions, see Bagchi (2005).

32 Eric Stein first pointed out the tendency of the ECJ to follow the Commission (Stein 1981). Stein's intuition is empirically borne out over time. See Stone Sweet and Brunell (2012).

33 (Ahlborn and Evans 2009, 928).

34 Scholars of comparative administrative law find meaningful national variation in the extent to which judges review administrative fact finding and other elements of administrative procedure. See Bignami (2011).

ECJ review provides a legal redress that creates an extra incentive for the Commission to listen to the concerns of European firms and governments, and an actor to blame when powerful interests disagree with a contested outcome.

6.2. *"Belmont Trademark Case"—The Andean Tribunal fills lacunae and coordinates transnational administrative decision making*

Chapter 7 will discuss the second use patent case where the Andean Tribunal of Justice invalidated a Peruvian executive act. National administrators embraced the ATJ ruling because they saw the contested decree as corruptly enacted and agreed that it violated Andean law. In this case, however, it really was not clear what Andean rules required. Trademarks are designed to protect the value of firm investment in developing brand recognition and protect consumers who associate quality and value with established brands. This case involves contestation over well-known cigarette brand names. The companies involved were foreign, but the stakeholders—smokers and cigarette vendors—were local. Although rather convoluted, I chose this case because the Belmont litigation is perhaps the most politically salient Andean litigation to date. ATJ review filled in Andean law, reversed the effects of a problematic national precedent the ATJ had previously endorsed, resolved questions about ownership of the disputed Belmont trademark, and facilitated the uniform application of Andean community rules.

In 1963, British American Tobacco through a subsidiary (Cigarrera Bigott) claimed ownership of the trademarked name "Belmont" for marketing tobacco products in Venezuela. The company also filed for the "Belmont" trademark in Ecuador, but its competitor, Philip Morris, secured the twenty-year trademark. This was not an isolated occurrence; around the world Philip Morris claimed trademark ownership of British American Tobacco brands.[35] Bigott had tried many times to challenge Philip Morris's claim to the trademark; notwithstanding the fact that Philip Morris was not using the Belmont trademark in Ecuador, Philip Morris succeeded in influencing Ecuadorian officials to validate their ownership of the mark.[36]

Renewed conflict over the Belmont trademark started in 1989 because of changes in the global context. The American market for cigarettes had become increasingly limited by health regulation, leading American firms to seek growth in international markets. The reinvigoration of common

35 I found BENELUX litigation between Philip Morris concerning ownership of the Kim trademark. See case A 87/2 by the BENELUX court, available at http://www.courbeneluxhof.be/fr/arresten.asp?RID=45, last visited April 24, 2012.

36 These various challenges are described in "Andean Belmont Noncompliance Case against Ecuador."

market strategies around the world offered a new prospect of using regional free trade rules to penetrate markets that had been previously closed. British American Tobacco decided to use the Andean market to develop a new regional legal and marketing strategy, because it saw the Andean community as "being in the vanguard" of regional integration processes.[37] British American Tobacco undertook to influence the development of Andean intellectual property rules, which member states redrafted five times in the next eleven years.[38]

When renewed conflict over the Belmont trademark began, British American Tobacco had registered rights to the Belmont name in Venezuela and Peru, and Philip Morris had registered rights over the name in Ecuador and Colombia.[39] Colombia and Peru granted these trademarks, but national regulations effectively closed local cigarette markets to foreign tobacco products, so as to favor local brands. But Belmont and Marlboro products were regularly smuggled in to these closed markets, stoking brand loyalty. Although Philip Morris owned rights to the Belmont name in both Ecuador and Colombia, it did not actually use the Belmont trademark in the region until 1989, when a Philip Morris subsidiary started to export Belmont products from Ecuador.[40] These exports were designed to meet an emerging use requirement in Andean law, which allowed for exports to serve as evidence of a trademark's use. The sudden decision to export small amounts of Belmont cigarettes, while still not using the trademark within Ecuador, suggested that Philip Morris was still primarily interested in blocking access for rival products.

In 1992 British American Tobacco filed papers to register the Belmont trademark in Colombia, Bolivia, and Peru and undertook an extensive lobbying campaign in Venezuela and Colombia to influence Andean

37 (Holden et al. 2010, 2).

38 Andean intellectual property law dated from 1974. The ATJ started to issue decisions interpreting existing intellectual property law in 1987. When the Cold War ended, Andean governments became converts to liberal economic ideas and mobilized to join the World Trade Organization. New intellectual property rules included Andean Decision 311 (adopted in December 1991), Decision 313 (approved in February 1992), Decision 344 (January 1994), and Decision 486 (December 2000). For more on evolving Andean intellectual property rules, see Helfer, Alter, and Guerzovich (2009, 9–13).

39 Earlier Andean legislation left it entirely up to national bodies to determine when marks could be registered and what constituted use. Each subsequent articulation of Andean law specified provisions. These clarifications allowed exports to serve as evidence of "use" of a trademark. Article 100 from Decision 311, repeated in Decision 314 (Article 99) and Decision 344 (Article 111) stated, "A mark shall otherwise be deemed to be used when it distinguishes products exclusively intended to be exported from any of the Member Countries."

40 This fact is noted in ATJ ruling "Andean Belmont Noncompliance Case against Ecuador," 4, no. 12.

legislation under negotiation and bolster support for legal interpretations of Andean law that would favor its trademark claims.[41] In 1993, a fourth iteration of Andean intellectual property legislation (Decision 344) entered force. Parts of Andean law remained unchanged. Andean law continued to allow trademarks to be canceled for nonuse, leaving it to national bodies to determine what constituted use.[42] The newest version of Andean law still allowed exports to serve as evidence of use of a trademark.[43] But a new provision incorporated into Decision 344 stated that imports from other Andean countries were allowable so long as no other goods bearing the same name were present in the local market.[44] This provision provided a way around Philip Morris blocking rival products via ownership of the Belmont trademark. Bigott immediately invoked the new Andean law to secure a certificate from the Ecuadorian Patent and Trademark office recognizing its right to import products using the name Belmont. Bigott then began legally exporting its Venezuelan Belmont product into Ecuador.

Philip Morris responded immediately. Although the company had not used the Belmont trademark for products sold in Ecuador for over thirty years, acting via local subsidiaries Philip Morris demanded that the Ecuadorian Duties Office, Ministry of Industries, Intellectual Property Office, and Central Bank ban imports of Bigott products. British American Tobacco responded by appealing to similar Ecuadorian agencies, and to a first instance judge, asking the judge to find that under Andean law Philip Morris no longer had rights to the Belmont name because of disuse of the mark. Philip Morris preempted British American Tobacco, however. Ten days after Venezuelan Belmont cigarettes entered the Ecuadorian market, Philip Morris started marketing products in Ecuador using the name of Belmont. It also got Ecuador's government to undertake an aggressive campaign advising the public that "illegal" Venezuelan Belmont cigarettes would be confiscated, and that people involved in trade or marketing of Belmont contraband would be prosecuted.[45] Philip Morris thus simultaneously substantiated a claim to domestic use while discouraging consumption of any Belmont cigarettes.

41 The strategy is described and documented in Holden et al. (2010, 20–22).

42 The 1974 Andean intellectual property law left national actors in charge of registering trademarks. Over time, use requirements for trademarks were shortened from five to three years, and what constituted use was specified in greater detail. But national bodies were still in charge of determining whether or not a mark was being used (Article 108 of Decision 344).

43 See note 38.

44 Article 107 of Decision 344.

45 These facts are summarized in "Andean Belmont Noncompliance Case against Ecuador," 4–5, points 12–23.

Venezuelan officials took up Bigott's case, turning to the Andean legal system to stop Ecuador's government from restricting importation of Venezuelan Belmont products. At the time, the General Secretariat avoided bringing cases to the ATJ, instead arguing that its own resolutions were legally binding. The Secretariat found that Ecuador had violated Andean law by restricting British American Tobacco imports, but that once Philip Morris began to use the trademark for locally manufactured products, Bigott lost the right to market Belmont goods in Ecuador.[46] Venezuelan officials believed that free trade claims should win over a hastily constructed use argument. Venezuelan officials decided to pursue a noncompliance suit against Ecuador in front of the Andean Tribunal.[47]

In its noncompliance suit, Bigott argued that Ecuador's intellectual property office had no right to ban imports of its Belmont product. Bigott argued that it had made the larger investment in developing the Belmont name, that Andean intellectual property rules were intended to help resolve conflicts regarding the same mark being used in multiple countries, and that Andean free trade principles should lead the ATJ to prioritize Venezuelan imports over Philip Morris's claim to a trademark it never actually used in the region.[48] These arguments did not, however, win the day. Venezuelan officials were trying to get the ATJ to rule that Bigott had a better claim to the mark, but such decisions clearly reside at the national level. Instead, the ATJ's decision affirmed the compromise position of the General Secretariat. The judges found that four Ecuadorian administrative decisions violated Andean law, because the local administrators had failed to consider whether or not Philip Morris was using the trademark in the national market as required by Andean law. The ATJ also clarified that export use may be good enough to avoid cancellation of a mark, but Andean law still allows for the importation of goods where trademarks are not being used in the national market.[49] The tribunal dismissed, however, the last alleged violation because Philip Morris was by then using its trademark in Ecuador.[50] Thus on the key issue of trademark rights, Philip Morris came out the winner, but only because Ecuadorian actors accepted Philip Morris's use claims.

46 This decision was discussed in Mancero-Bucheli (1998, 128).

47 This step was highly unusual in that it violated a gentlemen's agreement to resolve disputes bilaterally or through compromises worked out with Andean officials. This dispute remains a relatively rare example of one Andean government circumventing the Secretariat by initiating a noncompliance procedure against another government.

48 These arguments are discussed in the "Andean Belmont Noncompliance Case against Ecuador," 1.b, "La Demanda."

49 (Mancero-Bucheli 1998, 134).

50 See "Andean Belmont Noncompliance Case against Ecuador."

Legal suits over Philip Morris's claim to the Belmont trademark, to whether the right was exclusive or concurrent, and to the use of various associated names (for example, Extra Suave) continued in Ecuador, but the real prize was Colombia's market, where Philip Morris also held an unused trademark for Belmont. The ATJ's ruling created a problematic precedent. The decision rewarded what many saw as a bad faith effort by Philip Morris to hinder Bigott's valid use of the Belmont trademark. More problematic was that the ATJ ruling suggested that firms could follow Philip Morris's strategy of claiming rights to competitors' brands so as to block their entrance into new markets, sustaining this claim by hastily starting to use a mark locally.[51] The root problem, however, lay in Andean intellectual property rules, which did not specify what constituted "use" of a trademark. Colombian officials participated as a third party in the Venezuelan/Ecuadorian Belmont litigation, arguing that the ATJ should bring in secondary principles to interpret legal lacunae, by which it meant Colombian laws on what constitutes "use" of a trademark.[52] But national administrators clearly retain the final say in any determination of product use, which is why the ATJ required national administrators to check for use but accepted without question Ecuador's fact-finding regarding Philip Morris's use of the Belmont trademark.

Colombian officials responded by enacting a law designed to close the loophole Philip Morris had helped create. According to the ATJ's own legal doctrine, member states may legislate about issues not regulated by regional law so long as national regulatory rules complement and do not violate Andean rules. The Colombian president used his "constitutional and legal powers to create domestic legislation that complements Andean rules," to pass a legal act that protected an importer's legal right to use a trademark not previously in use.[53] The Colombian rule did not contradict Andean law, but it only applied to Colombian administrative actors.

The litigation battle then turned to the Colombian market. In a preemptive move, Bigott filed suit in the Colombian Trademark Office to cancel Belmont's trademark on the grounds of nonuse.[54] Philip Morris argued that Colombian import restrictions, rather than a decision to

51 (Mancero-Bucheli 1998, 135).

52 Interview with a former trade negotiator for Colombia (1998–2005), September 14, 2007, Bogotá, Colombia.

53 Decree Number 698 of March 14, 1997, on file with the author. Article 1 of the decree states: "The right established in article 107 of decision 344 of the Committee of the Cartagena Agreement to import products or services will *not* cease if, after an import, the right holder of the trademark in Colombia started to use the trademark in national territory" (emphasis added). For a discussion of the Andean Tribunal's doctrine allowing complementary national legislation, see Alter and Helfer (2011, 711–12).

54 Based on an interview with a lawyer involved in the dispute, September 11, 2007, Bogotá, Colombia. Both Venezuela and Colombia had local rules regulating "use," which

focus on its Marlboro brand, explained its disuse of the trademark. When the trademark office sided with Philip Morris, Bigott brought suit in the Colombian Consejo de Estado, which used the Andean preliminary ruling mechanism to refer the case to the Andean Tribunal.

The ATJ seized upon the opportunity of a new ruling, this time focused on the legal question of canceling a trademark, to address its critics. The tribunal argued that use of the mark had to be real and effective from before the date of filing in order to cancel the grant of a trademark. Intentions to use the mark, or mere symbolic use of the mark, were not sufficient.[55] The ATJ's ruling built a common law basis for canceling a trademark.[56] As required under Andean law, the tribunal left it for the Consejo de Estado to make a factual assessment regarding reasons for the trademark's disuse by Philip Morris. The Consejo determined that Philip Morris's disuse of the trademark preceded the import restriction so that the trade restriction did not itself explain the disuse of the mark. Based on this finding of fact, the Consejo canceled Philip Morris's right to the Belmont trademark.[57]

One question to ask is why Ecuadorian and Colombian administrators were so easily swayed by Philip Morris's claims to own the Belmont trademark, when clearly the company was not using this mark in the region? I cannot answer this question except to observe that vague rules offer administrators latitude and rich firms are able to incentivize administrative decision making. In the 1970s questions regarding intellectual property rights were resolved at the national level because there was no supranational route of appeal. Starting in 1984, firms could ask national courts to refer contested intellectual property decisions to the ATJ. Clarifying rules, as the ATJ has done many times, makes it harder for firms to gain by influencing administrative decision making.[58]

---

provided a basis for Bigott's claim that Philip Morris forfeited its right to the Belmont trademark through nonuse.

55 "Belmont litigation, Colombian preliminary ruling," based on a reference from the Colombian Consejo de Estado, Andean Decision 486, the governing Andean law as of 2000, adds clarity to what constitutes "use" (see Article 166), but ATJ doctrine is still more specific regarding the issue of how agencies should determine use.

56 How this precedent would affect Ecuadorian litigation is unclear, because consistent with Andean law Ecuadorian administrators continued to affirm Philip Morris's right to the trademark based on export use.

57 World Trademark Law and Practice, § 6.05, n. 5 (2011). German Cavelier Associates, *The Belmont Trademark Case*, Managing Intellectual Property, November 1, 2000. There were a number of different cases involving other issues related to the Belmont trademark, such as whether similar names and pictures infringed on trademarks, and whether the Philip Morris trademark was properly canceled. Belmont cases include: TJCA 11-IP-96, TJCA 2-AI- 96. TJCA 15-IP-99, TJCA IP-17-2004, TJCA 47-IP-2004, TJCA 04-IP-2006 (see legal ruling index for more on how to find these rulings).

58 The ATJ also clarified a number of additional questions of Andean intellectual property law concerning coexistence, oppositions to registration of marks, and the rights for

A footnote is that Venezuela ended up withdrawing from the Andean Community. An Internet website listing popular cigarette brands in different countries notes that Belmont cigarettes still dominate the market in Chile and Venezuela, but not in any of the other Andean countries.[59] A recent British American Tobacco company report notes that the company acquired Protabaco, the second-largest cigarette company in Colombia, on October 11, 2011. While Belmont may not be an important brand in Colombia, as of January 2012 Protabaco and British American Tobacco Colombia are operating as one entity with a market share of almost 50 percent.[60] Meanwhile, Philip Morris continues to dominate the Ecuadorian market through its subsidiary Tabacalera Andina.

6.3. "Softwood Lumber" case study—NAFTA binational review and WTO review of national determinations of dumping and countervailing duties

This case study involves a unique system of supranational administrative review. NAFTA Chapter 19 panels cannot be considered international courts. Not only are panels ad hoc, composed on a case-by-case basis, they also do not apply international law. Rather, NAFTA's binational panels review the decisions of national administrators applying *national* law. A concern about national administrative decision making has arisen because free trade agreements make it increasingly difficult for governments to legally block foreign goods from entering national markets. Quotas are not allowed under WTO law. Most Favored Nations provisions prohibit raising tariffs on goods from specific WTO members or countries where free trade agreements exist. WTO rulings regulating the use of safeguards make it increasingly difficult to legally enact safeguard protections, and in any event safeguard protections can only be used to address temporary and unforeseen market disruptions. Given these constraints, one of the few remaining protectionist tools involves administrators invoking health or environmental reasons to limit market access, or finding that a good is being "dumped" into a national market.[61]

Dumping is a predatory practice used to drive competitors from the market, so that dominant firms can then extract monopolistic rents. At the domestic level, firms can be fined for anticompetitive practices (as occurred in the Microsoft case discussed earlier). The remedy for international dumping is to levy a countervailing duty that raises the cost of the

---

holders of "notorious" (meaning famous) trademarks. See Helfer, Alter, and Guerzovich (2009, 21–25).

59 http://www.tobacco-facts.net/trends-in-tobacco-use/best-selling-cigarette-brand-in-each-country, last visited March 30, 2012.

60 http://www.bat.com/ar/2011/business-review/regional-review/americas/index.html, last visited March 30, 2012.

61 (Napoles 1993, 469–72; Powell 2010, 236).

good in local markets. Countervailing duties are legal under WTO law, so long as these duties are used only to offset the benefits obtained by illegal dumping. In practice, dumping claims are easier to make than they are to disabuse. A clear case of dumping would involve selling a product for less than the cost of production so as to drive a competitor from the market. But cost claims are subject to dispute, and it can be impossible to know how to compare costs across different economic systems. The softwood lumber dispute, discussed in a moment, exemplifies the challenge. Lumber firms in both the United States and Canada harvest wood grown on public lands. But Canada charges a stumpage fee while the United States leases harvesting rights. Even if one agrees that the stumpage fee system is less costly than leasing harvesting rights, in neither system are firms paying the full costs of production. Since true costs cannot be ascertained, administrators have relied on proxies to assess when international dumping is occurring. American and European administrators have defined dumping as occurring when manufacturers export a product to another country at a price either below the price charged in its home market or in quantities that cannot be explained through normal market competition. National administrators adjudicate dumping claims, and their decisions are subject to administrative review by national courts. Foreign firms see national review as favoring the claims of domestic producers.

Complaints about questionable national administrative dumping determinations have been plentiful enough for firms and countries to demand international review mechanisms. The WTO dispute settlement system offers one route of appeal, but it is not a very attractive one. States can no longer block panel formation or the adoption of panel reports, thus as of 1994 national administrators' questionable dumping findings can be internationally adjudicated.[62] But strategically speaking, dumping cases are often unattractive litigation prospects. Every individual finding and calculation of a countervailing duty must be legally contested. WTO rulings apply only prospectively, which allows a defendant country to levy illegal duties up until the day a WTO ruling becomes binding. The country can then modify the dumping assessment, restarting the litigation clock. Amounts involved tend to be small, and international litigation costs high. Because WTO rulings do not nullify the contested administrative decision, the WTO system also does not create a remedy that helps firms. The defendant country can accept the ruling but maintain its practice in the hopes that any retaliation will be economically and politically insignificant. And even if, for example, India levies retaliatory duties on American products, the Indian textile producer that has been falsely

62 See note 20.

punished for "dumping" may still face countervailing duties in the United States.[63]

NAFTA offers an alternative and some might say improved mechanism to deal with complaints about suspect dumping determinations. The United States and Canada created the precursor to NAFTA's Chapter 19 in 1989, as part of the US-Canada Free Trade Agreement.[64] The hope was that binational review could "act as a discipline on enforcement of the anti-dumping and countervailing duty laws in both [Canada and the United States], but especially aimed at the United States."[65] This hope has been borne out in practice. Scholars find that binational panels are more likely to decide in favor of Canadian firms, that compared to non-NAFTA countries there are fewer administrative findings of dumping, and as a result fewer dumping investigations are initiated by firms.[66]

Whereas the WTO system only lets states initiate review, the Chapter 19 system provides the subjects of administrative decision making a chance to instigate a legal review by a body that is less likely to defer to national administrators, and that can provide a useful remedy. Binational review panels may not be able to nullify illegal decisions, but they can repeatedly remand the case back to national administrators for a new assessment. NAFTA review also offers the prospect of refunding illegally collected duties. The NAFTA system generates praise from lawyers who are familiar with the inner workings of the system. But there is one very well known case of failure—the softwood lumber dispute. This dispute arguably contributed to the creation of the NAFTA Chapter 19 system,[67] and its problematic resolution keeps lawyers cautious in their endorsement of NAFTA review.

The softwood lumber dispute has existed for many years, but when GATT panels could be blocked and before the advent of the binational review system, there was nothing Canada could do to challenge US

63 Cunningham notes, however, that the WTO system has some advantages. Binational review is sometimes even slower than WTO review, the WTO system has an appellate mechanism, and governments rather than firms bear the costs of WTO litigation (Cunningham 2000, 88).

64 (Cunningham 2000, 80). See also Napoles (1993, 504).

65 (Cunningham 2000, 80). The Canadian government was frustrated that the United States refused to let GATT panels review US countervailing duties on Canadian softwood lumber. Canada tried to have the Free Trade Agreement disallow countervailing duties, but the United States refused. Binational review panels were a compromise solution that facilitated adoption of the Free Trade Agreement (Napoles 1993, 491–504).

66 On the greater likelihood of binational panels to decide in favor of Canadian firms, see Colares (2008). On how binational review decreases dumping findings of administrative actors, see Goldstein (1996). For more recent data suggesting relatively fewer antidumping charges and findings against NAFTA member states, see Powell (2010, 223).

67 See note 65.

countervailing duties. The unchanging facts are that American producers cannot meet US demand for softwood lumber, and Canadian lumber is cheaper, high quality, and very abundant. American firms insist that Canada subsidizes its softwood lumber industry through low stumpage fees "so as to dump softwood lumber in the American market."[68] American dumping rules are written in a way that makes it fairly easy for firms to show material injury and to use this finding to support a dumping claim.[69] American administrative agencies and judges have thus repeatedly sided with American firms. At least five NAFTA Chapter 19 panels have found US softwood lumber duties to be illegal, and firms have also used other NAFTA legal mechanisms to argue that policies designed to inhibit sales of Canadian lumber represent illegal "takings."[70]

The United States participates in the panel process, but administrators have at times refused to comply with some panel rulings.[71] Frustrated by repeated remands, one NAFTA panel arguably overstepped its jurisdiction by instructing the United States International Trade Commission to find that the evidence on record does not support a finding that Canadian practices create material injury to US firms. Such a finding would require the United States to return $5 billion worth of collected countervailing duties.[72] The United States responded by bringing countersuits in the WTO, most of which it lost. But the United States did win one finding of material injury, which seemed to directly contradict the NAFTA panel's insistence that there was no material injury.[73]

The softwood lumber dispute was only resolved through a political deal that allowed the United States to keep $1 billion of the $5 billion of "illegally collected" duties, Chapter 19 to remain in place, but softwood lumber disputes to be adjudicated by a special arbitral body that may not interpret or apply domestic law but instead is instructed to adjudicate disputes under the guidance of a special softwood lumber agreement. Jeffrey Dunoff sees litigation as mostly successful: "One result was a gradual, albeit partial, reduction in the composite antidumping and

68 (Adams 2008, 218).

69 (Potter 2000, 96).

70 The many decisions are cited and discussed in Dunoff (2007); Pauwelyn (2006).

71 Stephen Powell notes, "I have not [before] . . . witnessed the degree of defiance seen with some Chapter 19 remands. In one case [involving softwood lumber], the agency publicly announced that, although it would obey the direction given in the Panel's fifth remand, it had no intention of revoking the order, even though the results of the remand would be a de minimis countervailing duty margin." (Powell 2010, 230–31).

72 Opinion and Order of the Extraordinary Challenge Committee, in the matter of certain softwood lumber products from Canada, Secretariat File No. ECC-2004-1904-01USA, August 10, 2005, discussed in Pauwelyn (2006, 204).

73 The United States was partially successful in the "WTO softwood lumber dispute." See Dunoff (2007, 333); Pauwelyn (2006, 198).

countervailing duty rate paid upon the importation of softwood lumber from Canada. In addition, the litigation helped produce a negotiated settlement."[74] Others see both the NAFTA and WTO systems as having failed because Canada won numerous legal cases but nonetheless had to accept a political bargain that involves taxing and restricting exports to maintain a price floor for lumber.[75] In other words, the United States may no longer levy illegal duties, but it has exchanged illegal duties for what are arguably illegal quotas in the guise of voluntary export restrictions.

Politics clearly overtook law in the resolution of this dispute, but does that mean that international legal systems were ineffective? Indeed, one might argue that pressure from the NAFTA system is the reason why the United States worked out a political arrangement that is far more favorable to Canadian interests. Before the advent of the WTO and binational review, Canada had to accept US countervailing duties. Now Canada has achieved a political compromise that allows the Canadian government and firms to harvest the rents extracted via the price control policy. This bargain is short term. Every time the agreement nears expiration, Canada's legal leverage is renewed.

This may be a resolution in the shadow of the law, but it is hardly a happy status quo. Firms and governments engage in forum shopping that results in conflicting legal findings.[76] Being a review panelist has become so unpleasant that it is increasingly hard to find lawyers willing to accept small compensation in exchange for thankless service.[77] Meanwhile, neither the WTO nor alternative systems of panel review seem able to address the larger issue of governments using countervailing duties, and other measures, to protect national markets. At least five WTO panels have condemned the US practice of "zeroing," which leads to inflated calculations of countervailing duties.[78] Still, the United States continues its practice.

Since both the NAFTA and WTO systems seem equally limited, we cannot lay the blame on the ad hoc nature of NAFTA's binational panel system. The crux of the issue is that both NAFTA and WTO seem to lack supportive US compliance constituencies, groups of legal and political actors who want to see global administrative rules regarding dumping neutrally applied. Of course US trade officials are professionals who value the rule of law, but American antidumping rules are written to facilitate

74 (Dunoff 2007, 332).

75 Adams sees compromising instead of complying as exposing fundamental flaws of the Chapter 19 system (Adams 2008, 231).

76 (Adams 2008; Lopez 1997, 200–208; Pauwelyn 2006).

77 (Potter 2000, 94–95).

78 (Nye 2009; Vermulst and Ikenson 2007; Voon 2007).

dumping findings.[79] Defenders of the American position suggest that it is wrong to legally handicap American firms when remedies do not exist for other countries' "unfair" trade policies. Stephen Powell, chief counsel for import administration at the US Department of Commerce from 1982 to 1999, noted that

> we have all witnessed such blatant politicization of dumping that some of us may be permanently cynical of those who claim to be following the WTO rules. I have seen a WTO Member A openly threaten to impose an [antidumping] duty on an imported product from Member B if B did not open its market further to a product from Member A. I have seen dumping margins that coincidentally matched the level of an offered price settlement agreement that was not accepted. I have seen affirmative injury determinations that read more like a summary of foregone conclusions than an analysis of injury indicators and trends.[80]

This argument essentially suggests that reciprocity is the basis of the free trade system. Since one wrong with no remedy is unfair, two wrongs actually can make a right.

Dumping is clearly a misused protectionist tool, but it is also true that the economic playing field probably cannot be made level. Production costs will vary because some countries offer public health care, while some require firms to pay for workers' health benefits. Some countries have low wages and no social safety nets, and others have high costs of living and extensive social safety nets that increase labor costs. Meanwhile, currency fluctuations can create price advantages even where costs are similar. The WTO system cannot address these underlying causes of production price differentials, and it is undesirable and politically unfeasible to unleash a race to the bottom that rewards countries with the lowest regulatory standards and smallest social safety nets. Defending protectionism is unpopular, and the United States is loath to be seen as ignoring international law. Thus critiques of adverse rulings are usually framed in terms of defending national autonomy and the integrity of the US legal system.[81] Some see less than full compliance as a sign of legal

79 Potter mentions how US rules create "unbelievably soft" criteria for establishing injury (Potter 2000, 207–8).

80 (Powell 2010, 236).

81 One hears that NAFTA and WTO adjudicators are biased, that international adjudicators are less qualified especially with respect to interpreting American law, that the lack of any appellate process to correct bad legal decisions violates the American Constitution, and that unequal applications of US rules threaten the good functioning of the US legal system. These charges have been repeatedly investigated, with scholars finding NAFTA legal rulings to be mostly solid, generally conservative, and untainted by national biases. See

failure, while others see extralegal arrangements as safety valves that are necessary to ensure the political stability of the entire system.

6.4. "Metalclad"—ICSID investor dispute settlement systems to compensate for administrative "takings"

The investment dispute settlement system is not like the other systems discussed in this chapter, and it requires some explaining. Investment treaties are intended to ensure fair compensation for foreign investors when investments are directly or indirectly expropriated. The rationale for such a system is that legal security is important in encouraging foreign investment, and many domestic systems do not supply sufficient and fair legal protection for foreign investors. The legal rights of investors are established in Bilateral Investment Treaties (BITs), with the rights and obligations extending only to signatory states.[82] In theory, these treaties are easily revised by mutual agreement, but often there are significant power differentials between investor states and states that very much need foreign investment, with the result that BITs get offered on a take-it-or-leave-it basis. BITs generally specify the form of dispute adjudication, and increasingly BITs include provisions whereby signatories preconsent to arbitration of investor disputes.[83]

The International Centre for the Settlement of Investment Disputes (ICSID), an autonomous international institution within the World Bank, has adjudicated many of the contested investor-government disputes. ICSID has existed since 1966, but only recently has it become active.[84] The investment dispute settlement system allows firms to initiate arbitration by a three-person panel, with members chosen by the investor and state defendant. The Convention on the Settlement of Investment Disputes between States and Nationals of Other States, signed by over 140 states, defines procedures for adjudicating disagreements. The specific legal terms guiding adjudication, however, are defined in BITs.

There are few features of the investment dispute system that set it apart from most international adjudicatory systems. First, the framework convention for investment disputes, which serves as boilerplate for most BITs, does not include a general provision that allows exemptions for state

---

Colares (2008); Gastle and Castel (1995); Jacobs (2007, 192); Pan (1999, 389–94). According to a US General Accounting Office study, practitioners report that the NAFTA system is faster than traditional judicial review, that panelists demonstrate expertise in analyzing disputes, and that the decisions are thorough and carefully reasoned.

82 This section discusses a case governed by NAFTA, a multilateral treaty involving three countries. But most investor treaties are bilateral.

83 (Supnik 2009, especially 346–54). See also Ratner (2008).

84 Some three hundred investment cases either have been arbitrated or await arbitration in the ICSID system (Supnik 2009, 354).

regulatory autonomy for important public policy concerns such as public health and the environment. Such exemptions could be specified in BITs, but only powerful countries are able to insist on such provisions. Second, since BITs include arbitration provisions, there is no requirement that firms first seek compensation through domestic legal mechanisms. Third, ICSID awards can be claimed in any domestic legal system by an enforcement action that garners state assets held anywhere in the world. Even if domestic systems provided legal protections and remedies for forfeited investments, the distinct features of the bilateral investment treaty system would still make ICSID arbitration more attractive to investors than adjudicating disputes in domestic legal systems.[85]

Where both governments and firms want a clear determination of "fair compensation" for an investment gone wrong, ICSID litigation is mostly helpful. Controversy emerges when the question is whether government actions amount to indirect expropriation. Normally administrative review checks that proper procedure has been followed, and that administrators provide sufficient reasons for their action, at which point judges tend to defer to administrators. For investment disputes, however, the legality of the administrative act is not pertinent. All that matters is that expropriated investments are fairly compensated. Litigation tends to center on the question of whether governments are responsible for lost investments, and if certain government actions amount to de facto expropriation of the investment. Many BITs lack clear legal guidelines about how to balance investor rights and valid public policy objectives, and there is little consensus regarding how rights should be balanced.[86] Thus even good faith and generally competent adjudicators can be entering a legal and political minefield. The upshot of the investor dispute system is that where bilateral investment treaties so allow, foreign firms can demand the formation of an ICSID panel, influence the selection of the panelists, win a "just compensation" award judgment, and then call upon a US or European national judge to effectuate the award by ordering the seizing of assets held abroad as just compensation for their losses. This entire process can occur via conversations among a handful of lawyers and perhaps an appellate judge, who will determine that significant sums of public monies can be garnered.

85 Gus Van Harten argues that the investment dispute system should be seen as public law rather than private law (2007, 131).

86 Schneiderman argues that "one can search far and wide in vain for a clear and workable distinction between regulations exempt from and expropriations caught by the [takings] rule" (Schneiderman 2008, 75). Ratner summarizes the areas of agreement and notes how doctrinally thin consensus perspectives are, leaving much area of disagreement (Ratner 2008, 482–84).

This case study focuses on the Metalclad litigation because much is written about this case, and the case exemplifies the concerns of critics and the challenges of adjudicating investor disputes. Steven Ratner points out that Metalclad is an outlier. Its definition of "indirect expropriation" has not been picked up by other adjudicators, no other legal claims invoking the same NAFTA legal provision have prevailed, and in fact most investor disputes litigated under NAFTA investor rules do not lead to findings of expropriation.[87] We will see that upon appeal, a Canadian judge rejected key parts of the ICSID panel's decision in the Metalclad litigation, which is why subsequent expropriation claims have failed. NAFTA is an unusual three-party investment treaty. Canadian opposition to the Metalclad ruling allowed for a legal readjustment in the terms guiding adjudication of investor disputes. Bilateral treaties among very unequal parties are harder to adjust. The fact that a controversial ICSID ruling still resulted in a financial settlement compensating the investor suggests the legal and political strength of the investor dispute regime.

In 1993 the American firm Metalclad obtained a construction permit from Mexico's federal government, after which it decided to purchase an industrial waste processing plant owned by the Mexican company Coterin, located in the municipality of Guadalcazar in the state of San Luis Potosí. Metalclad executives knew that federal authorities had closed Coterin for environmental violations, and that the plant's poor environmental record had generated major state and local opposition.[88] Mexican officials at the federal level led Metalclad executives to believe, however, that approval at the federal level would allow renewed operations at the Coterin facility. The federal government shared Metalclad's desire to have a well-run hazardous waste processing plant inside of Mexico, and converting the Coterin site would seemingly address existing environmental problems and allow Mexico to meet global environmental standards. Although Mexico is a federal system, in the past assurances of the central state were enough because the Partido Revolucionario Institucional (PRI) controlled policy making throughout the country. But in the 1990s Mexico's hegemonic party was losing its political dominance. Metalclad became a business casualty of decreased central power over the provinces.

After satisfying federal officials and obtaining a permit from the state government, Metalclad began to transform the Coterin facility into a "state of the art" hazardous waste processing plant.[89] Soon after, municipal officials demanded that construction cease until Metalclad obtained a construction permit. Local officials still had outstanding complaints and

87 (Ratner 2008, 511 and 512).

88 (Tamayo 2001, 74–76).

89 These facts are discussed in the decision "Metalclad arbitration ruling."

distrust left over from their experience with Coterin, a company the federal government had also backed and provided with ample permits. Because local officials distrusted federal inspections, they insisted on a comprehensive construction plan including new and independent environmental assessments. As a matter of law, municipal construction permits are required. But according to Metalclad lawyers, federal officials assured Metalclad executives that federal and state approval were all that really mattered, and that federal approval would lead to the issuing of local permits, since there was no valid reason to deny such permits. Mexican officials framed their advice differently and denied that federal officials ever suggested that a local construction permit might be unnecessary.[90] All parties agree that Mexico's federal government recommended that the company work closely with local officials to facilitate good relations.

Metalclad tried to convince local officials that it would run an environmentally clean facility,[91] and in November of 1994 Metalclad applied for a local construction permit after which it continued its construction. State and local advisors suggested that Metalclad find another site for its plant in the state of San Luis Potosí, but the firm rejected this advice because it had already purchased Coterin's facility.[92] Metalclad built its new facility without proper local permits, but with numerous required federal approvals and permits. It opened the waste processing plant ten months later, in March 1995. Shortly thereafter, the municipal government denied the construction permit, citing similar decisions with respect to Coterin's permit requests.[93] Local officials were concerned about the extent to which Metalclad would remedy the environmental problems Coterin introduced at the site, and they distrusted lobbying and close relations between Metalclad executives and state and federal officials.[94]

Metalclad challenged the denial of its construction permit through national legal and political channels. Local authorities waged their own legal campaign, securing an injunction against the federal operation permits in large part because Coterin had left a messy trail of environmental violations committed despite federal permits and oversight.[95] The Metalclad plant then became a subject of contestation in state elections in 1995.

90 Ibid., paragraph 41.

91 (Tamayo 2001, 76).

92 Ibid., 74.

93 (Schneiderman 2008, 82–83).

94 (Tamayo 2001, 76).

95 Although Metalclad had obtained a federal permit for its waste processing plant, a federal injunction on Coterin dating from 1991 was never revoked. Local officials used the Mexican legal system to obtain an injunction against federal permits, barring Metalclad from operating its new plant (Dodge 2001, 911).

State officials, who were also members of the Partido Revolucionario Institucional, clearly supported building a waste processing plant in San Luis Potosí, and they may have even offered to go along with federal authorities with respect to the Guadalcazar location. But in the course of the elections the state governor reversed his support. In December 1995, state officials issued a statement in which they rejected the agreement between Metalclad and the federal government over the Guadalcazar location, because neither state nor local officials were included in negotiations. The governor backed the municipality's position: only municipal governments could issue construction permits. This changing state position meant that unless Metalclad secured a local construction permit, it would lack the state permits needed to operate.[96]

In 1995, after $22 million of investment and with the facility having already begun operations, municipal authorities definitively rejected Metalclad's permit request. By this time, two environmental studies had raised serious concerns about geohydrological and ecological risks for storing hazardous waste in Guadalcazar. These reports recommended that the area be declared an "ecological reserve." The departing state governor followed this advice, declaring a site for the protection of a rare cactus that included the area of land Metalclad intended to use to store its processed hazardous waste.[97] By mid-1996, Metalclad's stock had lost 80 percent of its value.[98] Metalclad brought a suit in ICSID requesting $90 million in compensation to cover its lost investment and loss in company value.

The Metalclad dispute was the first case adjudicated under NAFTA's new investment provisions. The ICSID panel composed by Metalclad and the Mexican government included a former US attorney general, a Mexican legal practitioner, and a British law professor. Many Metalclad critics suggested that the company should have realized that the investment was risky given Coterin's difficult past, and given the history of political opposition to the central state in the region. But the panel held federal officials responsible for the decisions and actions of state and local officials. The Metalclad panel ruling had many problems. Even if federal officials could generally lean on local party members to follow their will, as a matter of law local officials have autonomy to issue permits and to challenge federal actions that might be corrupt or represent a dereliction of duty. In the end, Metalclad had assurances but it lacked the required legal permits to build and operate its plant.[99] The panel invoked the preamble to NAFTA's investment agreement, which stated an objective was to "ensure a predictable commercial framework for business planning and investment"

96 (Tamayo 2001, 79).

97 (Schneiderman 2008, 83).

98 (Tamayo 2001, 69).

99 "Metalclad arbitration ruling," ¶71 and 99. The many problems in the ruling are discussed by Schneiderman (2008, 83–86).

and argued that "there should be no room for doubt and uncertainty" regarding which permits are required.[100] Expropriation was the result of the federal government's failure to resolve the disagreement over the issuing of a municipal construction permit and the decision to establish an environmental conservation zone that included the landfill site.

The Metalclad arbitration decision was itself problematic because the ICSID panel never fully addressed a key point of legal contention regarding environmental permits, in light of Coterin's past problems. The panel demanded greater transparency in whether and under what conditions local permits would be issued. But the issuing of permits was complicated because of Coterin's past. Local permits had been denied to Coterin, and they were denied to Metalclad for similar reasons. Federal permits were subject to appeal, and given the history of poor federal oversight of the Coterin facility it is unsurprising that Mexican judges scrutinized the federal government's decision making strictly. The fact that permits were subject to contestation and repeal was not something that transparency could resolve, and it was not clear that Metalclad had been treated less fairly than a domestic firm would have been treated in similar circumstances. These problematic features of the Metalclad arbitration decision led to a reversal of key elements of the decision.

Most BITs do not allow for legal appeals, but since the NAFTA investment system is governed by UNCITRAL rules, limited appeals are possible.[101] The ICSID panel had convened in British Colombia, thus a Canadian appellate judge reviewed the ICSID settlement. After a review of the base NAFTA legal text, the judge rejected all panel findings of breach based on a lack of transparency in decision making. According to Judge Tysoe, NAFTA leaves decisions regarding transparency or the lack thereof to local officials and diplomatic resolution.[102] But the Canadian judge upheld the basic finding that creating the environmental preserve amounted to a taking. After this appeal, Mexico was left owing over $16 million, an amount similar to the finding of the ICSID arbitral panel.

Soon after the appellate ruling, US, Canadian, and Mexican officials exercised their authority to issue an "interpretation" of Chapter 11, which supported the narrower legal reading of the appellate judge. The statement affirmed the legal requirement of "fair and equitable" treatment as generally understood under customary international law and rejected bringing in other provisions of NAFTA (such as the preamble) to supplement this minimalist requirement.[103]

100 (Del Duca 2003–4, 40).

101 (Aguilar, Alvarez, and Park 2003, 375).

102 "Appeal of Metalclad arbitration ruling," discussed in Del Duca (2003–4, 91–93). On NAFTA rules allowing the issuing of binding reinterpretations, see Ginsburg (2005, 662–63).

103 The agreement is summarized in Del Duca (2003–4, n. 321 at 93).

NAFTA has contributed to important changes in Mexico, but so have domestic politics. Democratic authoritarianism via one-party rule has given way to multiparty democracy and with it serious legal reforms. The judiciary is becoming more independent, and it is becoming more open to international law. A 1999 ruling by the Mexican Supreme Court supported the supremacy of international treaties within Mexico, and the long-standing Calvo doctrine, which prohibited foreigners' recourse to their home governments particularly with regard to property disputes, is no longer operative. Said differently, NAFTA's chapter 11 investment system has firmly established the right of investors to seek third-party arbitration of investor disputes. This is a major change in Mexican law, since the Calvo doctrine had been enshrined into Mexico's constitution.[104]

Administrative review exists to ensure that proper administrative procedure is followed during policy and decision making, that decisions are supported with transparent and adequate reasons, and that administrators respect the law as written. ICs tend to combine administrative review with deference to national administrators. ICSID is different by design, since it is meant to circumvent local adjudicatory mechanisms and consider only whether administrative actions amount to expropriation. Assuming the appellate judge was right that the governor's final act constitutes a taking, then the ICSID process would seem to have largely worked despite the controversial arbitral ruling. Still, the notion that four individuals—a US district attorney, a Mexican practitioner, and a British law scholar selected by the parties, and a Canadian judge who happened to hear the appeal—can adjudicate the behavior of Mexican, American, and Canadian administrators and issue an award that must be paid with public funds remains politically controversial.

III. THE ALTERED POLITICS OF INTERNATIONAL ADMINISTRATIVE REVIEW

Administrative review is also a mostly other-binding role, where governments, judges, and administrators largely share an interest in seeing regulatory rules correctly applied. Administrative review should exert its

104 The Calvo doctrine asserted that "foreigners are to be treated on a plane of absolute equality with the nationals of a given country. Foreigners should not lay any claim to diplomatic protection or intervention by their home countries since this would only provide a pretext for frequent violations of the territorial sovereignty and judicial independence of the less powerful nations." The Mexican Constitution Article 27 limits acquisition of "lands and waters" to Mexican companies and citizens, with an exception for foreigners who accept a Calvo clause and agree that its breach means forfeiture of the property at issue (Del Duca 2003–4, 51, nn. 64 and 65).

greatest influence through prophylactic improvements in administrative process and decision making, and by decreasing litigation once ICs have filled legal lacunae, addressed conflicts, and facilitated a uniform application of existing rules. Scholars have credited the ECJ and the ATJ with such contributions,[105] and even the NAFTA system is seen as leading to better factual records and improved transparency in administrative decision making.[106]

This book is concerned with how ICs induce greater respect for international law by influencing state decision making and international relations. Figure 6.2 maps IC influence over those actors with the power to choose compliance, applying the altered politics framework. Arrows indicate pressure to influence the key compliance partner.

During the bargaining phase (T1), the administrators made their decision. For the ECJ, Andean, and NAFTA systems, it was clear that controversial administrative decisions would be subject to administrative review. The European Commission made sure that it faithfully adhered to the ECJ's legal requirements. It solicited input from European competitors and justified its decisions in detail. Since the Commission's actions were likely to be upheld, the prospect of review generated very little leverage for Microsoft, General Electric, or Honeywell. Microsoft complied with the Commission's decision, but did challenge a Commission fine added because of a delay in releasing programing information. Microsoft lost, however, and ultimately it acceded to the Commission's demands.

Firms had more leverage in the Andean case study, but primarily because the legal rules and their interpretation were in flux. In T1 Bigott worked with Venezuelan officials to influence both the creation of Andean rules and Colombian interpretations of existing Andean law. Once Andean rules were in place, litigation politics in T2 aimed at influencing ATJ's interpretation of these rules. Bigott got Colombia to intervene in Venezuela's noncompliance suit against Ecuador, but the Venezuelan efforts failed to reverse Ecuador's decision to award the Belmont trademark to Bigott's rival. One can presume that firm pressure led the Columbian executive to issue its decree clarifying how Andean rules should be understood in Colombia. This clarification then influenced the ATJ as it responded to the preliminary ruling reference by the Consejo de Estado. Political maneuvering in both the European and Andean cases ended after the relevant legal rulings because the key administrators complied in full with supranational legal requirements.

105 Regarding European administrative law, see note 6. On the Andean Community, see Helfer, Alter, and Guerzovich 2009, 21–25).

106 (Potter 2000, 94–95; Powell 2010, 233).

FIGURE 6.2 Political dynamics of international administrative review

	National system		International system				
	Domestic enforcement strategy	Compliance partner required change	International legal strategy	IC ruling	Legal remedy	Post-ruling political strategy	Policy change by compliance partner
ECJ Microsoft case	None—case involves an issue delegated to the European Commission.	Commission must ensure legality of decision.	Out of court bargaining to influence Commission decision making.	Commission decision upheld.	None	Microsoft negotiates reduction of fines. →	Commission reduces fines but sticks to its decisions.
ATJ Belmont litigation	Efforts to invoke Andean rules to influence national decision-making. →	National trademark agencies & national judges must make proper determinations.	Venezuela noncompliance case + domestic lobbying.	ATJ specifies requirements to demonstrate trademark use.	National bodies determine trademark ownership.	Political lobbying of Colombian officials. →	Colombian government promulgates "use" rule; Colombian court annuls Phillip Morris' Belmont trademark.

NAFTA Softwood lumber	Political pressure & Canadian appeals within US administrative system. →	US administrators should limit dumping determinations.	← Canadian firms demand binational panel review, US seeks WTO review.	NAFTA panels find no dumping; WTO finds material injury.	Most illegally collected countervailing duties refunded.	US officials negotiate extralegal deal; Canada agrees to limit exports. →	Fewer firm dumping complaints and fewer softwood lumber dumping determinations
ICSID Metalclad	Domestic law was not on Metalclad's side. Firm lobbied for federal support. →	Local officials should issue valid permits, or sue federal government.	← Metalclad lobbies federal level and later convenes ICSID panel.	Uncertainty created by regulatory environment illegal. Creating environmental zone amounted to taking.	Compensation for Metalclad.	Canada, US & Mexico issue "interpretation" that more narrowly construes investor rights. →	Compensation paid. Change in Calvo doctrine; acceptance of investor dispute adjudication.
	T1: Bargaining in the shadow of an IC			T2: Litigation politics		T3: Leverage strategies	

For the NAFTA case, bargaining in the shadow of the law (T1) included forum shopping with Canadian softwood lumber producers drawing on NAFTA legal institutions, and American producers encouraging the United States Trade Representative to challenge Canadian policy in the WTO system. During the litigation politics (T2) the United States lost a number of NAFTA binational appeals, generating a legal obligation to refund illegal countervailing duties. The likelihood of future losses in the NAFTA system served as leverage for Canadian officials. Americans were clearly unwilling to sustain the job losses that would ensue if they let cheaper Canadian imports flow into the US market, and thus Canada faced the prospect of continued litigation battles. Seeking to diffuse a political controversy that could further undermine support for NAFTA in the United States, Canadian officials used their legal leverage to negotiate the softwood lumber agreement in T3. Because law was on their side, Canadian actors could negotiate a settlement that allowed Canadian actors to capture the rents collected as a result of decreased supply and price floors. The deal protects US jobs by creating higher prices for lumber, allowing Canadians firms to capture the profits. The temporary nature of the softwood lumber agreement allows Canadian officials to maintain their legal leverage.

The ICSID system, by contrast, cast less of a shadow over administrative decision making in T1. The federal government *did* lobby local and state officials on behalf of Metalclad, but not because they feared litigation. Rather, the federal government had many reasons to hope that Metalclad would take over the flawed Coterin waste processing facility. Local actors neither knew nor cared about possible ICSID arbitration. As long as federal actors pay ICSID awards, the prospect of litigation is unlikely to increase firm bargaining leverage in T1, and in any event local officials were committed to stopping the operation of the waste processing site. ICSID arbitration did create a legal ruling in Metalclad's favor (T2). Mexican officials accepted the loss in this case and paid the demanded compensation. To do otherwise in the first ruling implementing the new NAFTA investment agreement would have sent a poor signal to future investors. But along with Canadian and US officials, Mexican leaders elicited a clarification that stripped away the legal extension the arbitration panel created. To the extent that the ICSID adjudication has influenced bargaining in the shadow of the law it has been to encourage firms to obtain all the required permits *before* purchasing a local enterprise or undertaking construction. The NAFTA investment regime has, however, led to a major change in Mexico—namely, the elimination of the Calvo doctrine, which barred foreign intervention in national property disputes.[107]

107 See note 104.

Other chapters provide more evidence of ICs facilitating compliance with the law by co-opting the support of administrative decision makers and/or national judges. The ITLOS ruling in the seizing private vessels case (chapter 5) led Russian judges to decrease the bond for the *Hoshinmaru*. The ATJ's ruling in the second use patent case led the Peruvian intellectual property agency to repeal Pfizer's patent (chapter 7). Chapter 8's case study involving Britain seizing private assets of blacklisted supporters of terrorism (the Kadi case) led to a redrafting of the contested regulation and a change in Commission practices. Some of these cases led to larger changes too. The United States stopped pressuring Andean countries to agree to second use patents, and ECJ review contributed to changes in UN procedures.

The first two case studies in this chapter were not controversial. In these cases, administrative review mostly bolstered the legal credibility of administrative decisions. The second set of case studies and the seizing private assets (Kadi) ruling were more politically controversial because governments disagreed with IC decisions. In the Metalclad case, the arbitral decision was itself problematic, but in the softwood lumber case the American officials wanted to address the concerns of American lumber companies regarding abundant and cheap Canadian lumber.

Administrative review is not intended to address problems that are inherent to rules themselves. The ATJ could not, or would not, rectify a fundamental tension in Andean law between the free trade aspirations of Andean law and the deference toward national determinations of trademark usage. The NAFTA system also hit an impasse because American antidumping rules make it easy for firms to show material injury.

I included an ICSID because lawyers see the investment dispute system as part of the new terrain of international law and global administrative law.[108] Investment treaties increasingly require compulsory arbitration that can be instigated by private litigants. Arbitration results in binding rulings that usually generate compliance in the form of compensation. The prospect of ICSID review provides insurance (and in the Metalclad case generates moral hazard) for investors, but since the actor who must pay an award (the central government) is generally not the actor whose decisions compromised the value of an investment, it is hard to see how the ICSID system casts a legal shadow. It really is not the job of local officials to avoid actions that may later be seen as a "takings," nor are most local officials in any position to intuit how an ICSID panel might decide the case. This is especially so since ICSID arbitral panels tend to be more favorable to investor rights than are local judges.

108 (Van Harten and Loughlin 2006).

Perhaps the critical key test of all administrative systems is whether the subjects of administrative decisions gain more faith in the quality and fairness of administrative decisions. Although firms might prefer less European regulation, ECJ review has generated legal predictability for firms facing European regulation. Andean intellectual property administrators regularly reference ATJ rulings, and our interview with intellectual property lawyers revealed that at least in Colombia and Peru, Andean intellectual property law is professionally applied and faithful to what the law requires (although corruption is still sometimes a problem). Simon Potter evaluated the NAFTA Chapter 19 system on the following terms:

> Canadians saw American judicial review as inspired by protectionism and political influence, and the deference . . . in the United States [as] protectionism. Americans saw Canadian courts as . . . too timid to do anything about [bad administrative decision making]. That is the reason that Chapter 19 came in. It was to rekindle a business person's faith in the system, looking at both sides of the border. I think it has done it. I think we have done it. I think there is a much greater confidence in the system. There is a confidence that in the end, one way or the other, we will get to some better result than [existed] without Chapter 19.[109]

ICSID and other investment dispute settlement systems, by contrast, are not faring well. Business clearly likes ICSID arbitration because it offers the prospect of a remedy for government regulatory decisions that compromise the value of their investments. Governments are less enthusiastic about the ICSID system, in part because firms can win through ICSID awards that would not be possible within domestic systems. Critics see the ICSID system as generating conflicting findings, subordinating valid public policy objectives to private property rights, undermining democratic choice by creating hidden costs for regulatory decisions, and creating problematic incentives for adjudicators who as free agents for hire might want to satisfy clients so as to be hired again.[110] Quantitative studies repeatedly show that the balance of decision making is not as bad as the critics suggest.[111] Lawyers continue to rack up hefty litigation fees. Meanwhile, the notion that firms can pick adjudication venues, that investment awards can be claimed in domestic courts around the world, that panel decisions are often not subject to appeal, and that foreign investors have more legal rights than domestic investors, strikes many as

109 (Potter 2000, 93).

110 See discussions about problems with the system in Ratner (2008, 477–80); Schneiderman (2008, chapter 3).

111 (Franck 2007; Schneiderman 2008; Van Harten and Loughlin 2006).

problematic even if ICSID arbiters are legally evenhanded. Latin American countries especially but also Americans and Europeans continue to be unhappy with the ICSID system. Increasingly Latin American governments are refusing to pay awards, and they have found a host of ways to unbind themselves from BIT and ICSID arbitration requirements.[112]

CONCLUSION: ROLE MORPHING IN ADMINISTRATIVE REVIEW

International administrative review is part of the new terrain of international law. International regulatory rules penetrate the surface of the state, addressing issues that used to fall under the exclusive domain of national governments. New-style ICs allow private litigants to initiate review of contested national and supranational administrative decisions, and international review improves state adherence to international regulatory rules while promoting accountability for national and international administrative actors. The case studies in this chapter provide a window into the intersection of national regulation and global markets as they became subjected to global market forces and internationally coordinated legal review. The case studies are perhaps most revealing for how normal the politics are, which is to say that these international regulatory politics are similar to the rough and tumble of domestic regulatory politics.

Many American lawyers are convinced that administrative review will inevitably slip into constitutional review. On the one hand, this concern is difficult to assess given that eleven of the ICs with administrative review jurisdiction also have explicit constitutional review jurisdiction, meaning jurisdiction to assess the validity of community rules with respect to higher order legal principles.[113] The ECJ clearly did exercise constitutional powers in the seizing private assets (Kadi) case, but then again the ECJ clearly has jurisdiction to do so. On the other hand, there are a number of critics of WTO, NAFTA, and ICSID review, even when this review does not trespass beyond the boundaries delegated to adjudicatory bodies.[114]

Scholars are justly concerned about international judges overstepping the jurisdiction that governments have delegated to them. When binational NAFTA panels order American administrators to make a different factual assessment, they arguably overstep their jurisdiction. When

112 (Fach Gómez 2011; Harout 2007).

113 The two exceptions are the ITLOS court, which can only examine errors in the decisions of the Seabed Authority, and the EFTAC court, which can only review competition decisions of the Surveillance Authority.

114 See Jacobs (2007); McGinnis and Movsesian (2004).

investment arbitration panels find legally enacted and defensible public policy decisions to be akin to expropriation, the investor dispute regime seems to be morphing into a tort-based foreign assessment of state practices. But my sense is that such oversteps are rare. In their administrative review roles, international judges invariably generate procedural requirements for national and supranational administrative decision making and fill in details of law that has been left unspecified, but generally without much controversy. Indeed, such legal clarifications are expected and are even seen as a functional reason for governments to create robust administrative review procedures.[115] If the Microsoft and Belmont case studies are any guide, ICs conducting administrative review seem to show great deference to administrative actors, perhaps because they are so dependent on national administrators embracing their rulings. Although the NAFTA and ICSID examples continue to generate controversy, my sense is that the problem is not courts exceeding their mandates. Rather, sometimes governments want to maintain policies that do not pass legal muster.

The complaints about the investment review system fall into a different category. The investment arbitration system by design creates contractual legal rights for foreign investors that can be internationally enforced, while domestic actors lack similar rights. Perhaps having a permanent court would help remedy complaints about the structural problems in investment and the binational NAFTA system. Ad hoc bodies will inevitably generate rulings of varied quality. Once the ruling is issued, governments can complain about "the system" but there is no actor that can remedy the problem. A permanent appellate review body could specify decision-making criteria, put pressure on panel bodies in the form of a threatened reversal, and provide clearer guidance for governments as they try to diplomatically resolve investor and countervailing duty disputes. Moreover, negotiations regarding the new body's Court Treaty could provide an opportunity for governments to specify the extent to which judges are allowed to question national fact finding, and governments could use the appointments process to influence judicial decision making and thereby address concerns about adjudicators for hire. Governments could also have a target to pressure if they remain unhappy with the overall adjudication system.

Global administrative law by design constrains state administrative decision making. International administrative review brings IC interpretations of global administrative rules into national legal orders via alliances with national administrators and judges, strengthening the ability of domestic and international administrative actors to push back against powerful private interests. Where the objective is to reassure private

115 (Benvenisti 2005).

actors that regulatory rules are being evenly applied, cooperation between international and domestic legal interpreters seems to be unproblematic. Where firms and states want to discriminate against foreign actors, tensions will arise because domestic rules will be purposefully ambiguous or favorable to domestic actors, and national administrators may find themselves being asked to choose between competing interpretations of administrative rules that have powerful political backing. These problems seem to exist regardless of the presence or absence of international administrative review, but on balance lawyers seem to prefer having legal checks to no legal checks, and to believe that administrative decision making improves when subject to robust judicial oversight.

CHAPTER 7

International Law Enforcement

Many people assume that courts exist to enforce the law. As this book makes clear, courts play a number of roles besides law enforcement. Indeed, international law enforcement is a relatively new role for international courts (ICs). The first ICs were created to provide a peaceful means to resolve disputes should state parties so choose. The Permanent Court of Arbitration (1899–present), the Central American Court of Justice (1908–18), the Permanent Court of Justice (1920–40), the International Court of Justice (1945–present), and even the original dispute resolution system of General Agreement on Tariffs and Trade (1945–94) all required state consent before a case proceeded. Governments might agree to let an IC decide a case where they were open to a range of possible outcomes. But governments would not consent to let an IC rule against them where significant national or governmental interests were at stake.

Scholars have come up with many plausible reasons for why governments may want to self-bind to compulsory international judicial oversight. Governments might want to lock in policies that promote market openness, human rights, and the prosecution of war crimes, making it harder for future governments to deviate from such agreements. Agreeing to international oversight can send a helpful signal, reassuring foreign investors that their rights will not be compromised by national bias, political pressure on national judges, or judicial corruption. Delegation to ICs can also help assure domestic populations that their government is seriously committed to keeping markets open, respecting human rights, or prosecuting mass atrocities.[1] Although benefits of delegating compulsory enforcement authority to ICs surely exist, one must wonder why these arguments became so much more persuasive in the last twenty years, especially since there are also compelling reasons *not* to self-bind

1 (Cooley and Spruyt 2009; Elster 2000; Ikenberry 2001; Moravcsik, 1995).

to international judicial review. Letting ICs rule on state compliance with international law compromises national sovereignty. One hears concerns that international review might call into question the authority of domestic judges, encroach on the authority of states and localities within a federal system, violate national constitutional requirements, and inflame those domestic interests that dislike the substance of international law, making it more rather than less politically difficult to address international legal breaches. Given that every country has policies that clash with international legal obligations, we might expect governments to err on the side of caution. Optional procedures provide the greatest flexibility, letting states choose where and when IC review is convenient.

If it were not for the reality that states have in fact created ICs with an enforcement jurisdiction that is not easily controlled or blocked, and they do so increasingly often, we might be left wondering if benefits of submitting to compulsory international judicial review could ever outweigh the compromise of national sovereignty that occurs every time ICs review state actions. Perhaps because international judicial review is now compulsory, more common, and increasingly tolerated by governments around the world, the remedies that ICs authorize have also become more intrusive. In any event, the attributes of the IC enforcement role—a formal mandate to oversee state compliance, compulsory jurisdiction, and a growing willingness of domestic actors to embrace IC interpretations—allow domestic and international actors to leverage the threat of international litigation and to create political costs for continued noncompliance. These features also make delegating enforcement authority to ICs among the most sovereignty compromising of all international judicial roles.

ICs are participants in international law enforcement; they do not themselves enforce the law. The role of judges is to name a state practice as legal or illegal, and sometimes to specify remedies. ICs are not unique in primarily flagging noncompliance. As chapter 1 explained, no court actually enforces its rulings or the remedies judges create. Rather, judges rely on their own authority to encourage compliance, and if that fails, on the power of others to pressure reluctant actors. At the domestic level, one can assume that governments will provide support for the enforcement of domestic judicial rulings because courts are helping to enforce state law, and because coercive power, when used, is employed against individual subjects of the law and not the government itself. With the expectation that states *will* enforce legal rulings, there is perhaps an assumption of coercion behind a national legal ruling. Clearly this assumption does not hold internationally since the international system lacks a centralized enforcer, and state actors are usually the subjects of noncompliance suits. It is worth reiterating that ICs share this limitation with all courts involved in public law roles (for example, constitutional courts, administrative review bodies, and even domestic criminal courts when the law violation involves high-level government officials).[2] The scarlet letter of illegality, the specification of the actions requiring change, and the formal or social sanctions that courts order or that ensue by virtue of the IC ruling, are the court's contribution to law enforcement.

Chapter 4 sought to explain the trend of states consenting to compulsory international judicial oversight. This chapter is concerned with the politics that follow from this decision. Section I identifies which ICs have been delegated enforcement jurisdiction and variation in the design of international courts' enforcement systems. Section II investigates four hard cases where ICs with enforcement jurisdiction ended up changing state policy. The cases span economic, human rights, and mass atrocities issue areas. Section III compares how ICs altered politics in the case studies. Together this chapter's case studies identify a number of different ways that ICs alter the political balance in favor of law compliance. The conclusion recaps how new-style design features contribute to different enforcement politics.

I. DELEGATING ENFORCEMENT JURISDICTION TO INTERNATIONAL COURTS

The European Court of Justice was arguably the first IC with an enforcement role. The Court had explicit jurisdiction to assess state compliance with European law, and this jurisdiction was compulsory. Nineteen ICs today have a formal mandate to oversee state compliance with an international treaty; fifteen have compulsory jurisdiction for this role. Whereas the defendants in international administrative and constitutional review cases may be international institutions, the defendants in enforcement cases will primarily be state actors.

Figure 7.1 identifies the universe of operational ICs with jurisdiction to review state compliance with international law, dividing ICs by the subject matter the court adjudicates and organizing within each category by the year litigants were first able to raise enforcement actions. The ECOWAS court is listed twice (signified by the acronym for the second listing), as it has both an economic and human rights subject matter jurisdiction, and its design varies depending on if it is enforcing economic or human rights law. The table also identifies salient design features of ICs with enforcement jurisdiction, as they existed in 2012 (see figure 3.3. in chapter 3 for more on these changes). The WTO, Andean, and ECOWAS

2 (Goldsmith and Levinson 2009; Staton and Moore 2011).

case studies demonstrate the importance of these design changes, as none of these cases would have proceeded if the original IC designs had been retained. Figure 7.1 also lists the different remedies specified in Court Treaties. The chapter appendix elaborates on the court's formal jurisdiction and further specifies formal political checks on ICs with enforcement jurisdiction. All ICs listed can issue binding rulings declaring state noncompliance, and some ICs have fashioned their own rules about remedies for legal violations.[3] This chapter's case studies suggest, however, that only sometimes are the treaty-defined remedies a key factor in changing state behavior.

Compulsory jurisdiction is a necessary feature for an IC to play an enforcement role; otherwise, defendant states would block inconvenient cases from proceeding. Most ICs listed have compulsory jurisdiction for their enforcement role. The exceptions are the IACtHR and ACtHPR, which deal with sovereignty concerns by allowing countries to opt in to the IC's compulsory jurisdiction. (Chapter 3's diagrams of regional judicial complexes [figures 3.8–3.10] identify which countries have signed up for the court's compulsory jurisdiction.) Opt in may be optional, but the ability of a country to later opt out will depend on the domestic and international political costs associated with such a choice. The IACtHR has raised the political bar for countries that want to withdraw, but countries can still opt out if their domestic populations will tolerate such a choice.[4] The ACtHPR recently upheld the opt-in requirement, ruling against a private litigant that encouraged the Court to assert jurisdiction or otherwise require his government to opt in to the Court's jurisdiction so that he could pursue legal suits.[5]

While compulsory jurisdiction is crucial, rules of access end up being key determinants of whether or not a court is invoked. WTO-style ICs allow only states to initiate litigation. Although in theory member states can pursue any noncompliance suit, in practice there is an expectation that governments will only litigate cases where a significant national interest is at stake. Thirteen international enforcement systems allow supranational prosecutorial type actors to field and investigate noncompliance complaints from states and/or individuals. Where international actors can

3 See, for example, Shelton (2005). The ECJ has also created state liabilities through its "Francovitch ruling."

4 Trinidad and Tobago opted out of the IACtHR's jurisdiction (Helfer 2002), Peru tried to opt out, and recently Venezuela decided to opt out. Cesare Romano explains the difference between the Trinidad and Tobago case and Peru's effort to opt out, which the IACtHR rebuffed (Romano 2007, 820–24). It is unclear what Venezuela's opt out will mean. The pending cases can still be adjudicated, and as in Peru leadership change can lead to a change in the opt-out decision.

5 ACtHPR "Femi Falana ruling."

FIGURE 7.1: International courts with enforcement jurisdiction (by issue area and year created) (N = 19)

		Actors authorized to initiate litigation			
International Courts with Enforcement Jurisdiction	Compulsory Jurisdiction	State Party	Supranational Prosecutor	Private Actors	Treaty-Defined Remedies
Economic Law Jurisdiction	(N = 11)				
European Court of Justice (ECJ) (1952)	X	X	European Commission	Via national courts	Declaratory rulings plus the potential for hefty fines for continued noncompliance.
Andean Tribunal of Justice (ATJ) (1984)	X	X	General Secretariat	Direct access & via national courts	Declaratory rulings and retaliatory sanctions for ongoing noncompliance (tit-for-tat enforcement).
World Trade Organization Permanent Appellate Body (WTO) (1994)	X (Since 1994)	X			Declaratory rulings and retaliatory sanctions for ongoing noncompliance (tit-for-tat enforcement).
European Free Trade Area Court (EFTAC) (1994)	X		Surveillance Authority		Penalties imposed by Surveillance Authority.
West African Economic and Monetary Union (WAEMU) (1995)	X	X	Commission	Via national courts	Declaratory rulings. Political bodies may agree to additional unspecified sanctions for ongoing noncompliance.
Court of Justice for the Common Market of Eastern and Southern Africa (COMESA) (1998)	X	X	General Secretary	Direct access	Declaratory rulings. The court may also prescribe unspecified penalties.

Central African Monetary Community (CEMAC)(2000)	X	X	Executive Secretary	Direct access & via national courts	Declaratory rulings. A council of the heads of states can be convened to authorize additional unspecified sanctions for ongoing noncompliance.
East African Court of Justice (EACJ) (2001)	X	X	Secretary General	Direct access & via national courts	Declaratory rulings.
Economic Community of West African States Court of Justice (ECOWAS CJ) (economic system) (2001)	X	X	Executive Secretary	Via national courts	Declaratory rulings and possible suspension of Community loans, assistance, appointment to posts, and voting rights.
Southern Common Market Dispute Settlement Permanent Review Tribunal (MERCOSUR) (2002)	X	X		**	Arbitral awards collectable by retaliatory sanctions.
Southern African Development Community (SADC) (2005)	X	X		Direct access & via national courts	Declaratory rulings plus a Council can agree to unspecified sanctions for persistent noncompliance. A WTO style ad hoc arbitration system can authorize retaliatory sanctions.

FIGURE 7.1: (*Continued*)

		Actors authorized to initiate litigation			
International Courts with Enforcement Jurisdiction	Compulsory Jurisdiction	State Party	Supranational Prosecutor	Private Actors	Treaty-Defined Remedies
Human Rights Jurisdiction (N = 5, including ECOWAS, which is also listed above)*					
European Court of Human Rights (ECtHR), as changed in 1998	X Since 1998	X	(Eliminated 1998)	Direct access as of 1998	ECtHR can require "just satisfaction" going beyond national provisions for compensation.
Inter-American Court of Human Rights (IACtHR) (1979)	Optional protocol but hard to rescind acceptance	X	Inter-American Commission on Human Rights	Private litigants can bring cases to the Commission for review	The IACtHR can specify remedies, including public apologies, changes in rules and statutes, and fair compensation to the injured parties.
Caribbean Court of Justice (CCJ) (2001)	States must consent to the CCJ replacing the role of Privy Council			Appellate review of national court decisions	For appellate review, CCJ has recourse to the remedies available in the domestic system.
ECOWAS CJ (Human rights jurisdiction added in 2005)	X			Direct access for human rights case as of 2005	ECOWAS CJ can order compensation.

African Court on Human and Peoples' Rights (ACtHPR) (2006)	Optional Protocol	X	African Commission on Human and Peoples' Rights	Optional protocol for private litigant access to the court	None stated, but Court will be changed as it merges with the African Court of Justice (the African Court of Justice can order reparations).
Mass Atrocities Jurisdiction (N = 3)					
International Criminal Tribunal for the Former Yugoslavia (ICTY) (1993)	X		Office of the Prosecutor		Incarceration and return of illicit proceeds (no death penalty).
International Criminal Tribunal for Rwanda (ICTR) (1994)	X		Office of the Prosecutor		Incarceration and return of illicit proceeds (no death penalty).
International Criminal Court (ICC) (2001)	X		Office of the Prosecutor		Incarceration, fines and property forfeiture (no death penalty).
General Jurisdiction (N = 1)					
Central American Court of Justice (CACJ) (1992)	X	X		Direct Access	None specified.
Totals ICs for each category	17	14	13	11 (excluding SADC)	

Relevant treaty articles listed in the appendix.

*I have not listed the ECJ's human rights jurisdiction, as it pertains only to review of Community acts. This role is discussed in Chapter 8; **The MERCOSUR system allows national supreme courts to refer legal questions to the Permanent Review Tribunal, but this has not yet become a means of law enforcement.

pursue noncompliance cases, governments tend to rely on supranational bodies instead of raising their own cases. Eleven international enforcement systems allow private litigants to bring cases directly to the IC (direct access), or individuals can raise enforcement actions in national courts. If the legal system has a preliminary ruling mechanism, the national court may refer the case to the IC. If the legal system lacks a preliminary ruling mechanism, national courts will rule on their own with their decisions subject to review by the IC.[6] The wider the access to the IC, the more likely the IC is to be invoked and the more difficult it will be for a government to use political pressure to avoid unwanted litigation.[7]

Since 80 percent of ICs today (nineteen of twenty-four) have been delegated an enforcement role, it is worth asking why certain ICs lack jurisdiction to assess state compliance with the treaty. The International Court of Justice (ICJ) and the International Tribunal for the Law of the Sea (ITLOS) are dispute settlement bodies. Additional treaties can confer enforcement jurisdiction on these courts, but the Court Treaties do not themselves establish such jurisdiction. The common market systems for the Commonwealth of Independent States and the Caribbean Community are still works in progress.[8] These ICs do not yet have jurisdiction to enforce common market agreements, but they are likely to be given such jurisdiction in the future. The BENELUX system creates common regulatory rules for the Netherlands, Belgium, and Luxembourg in areas not covered by European Community rules and allows for administrative review of national application of these rules. The BENELUX system is likely to remain as is, since most enforcement issues are handled by the European Union. The Organization for the Harmonization of Business Law in Africa, discussed further as a case study in chapter 5, does not have explicit enforcement jurisdiction, but private actors' dispute settlement cases will provide a means to enforce OHADA rules. From this list of exceptions we can conclude that most, but certainly not all, ICs are intended to help enforce international law.

6 Human rights courts are reluctant to be seen as appellate bodies. International courts are usually not reviewing national legal rulings, nor do their decisions reverse national decisions. But since most human rights mechanisms first require the exhaustion of domestic remedies, recourse to an international human rights body is akin to an appeal of national adjudication of the issue.

7 See chapter 1 section I for more.

8 The Caribbean Court of Justice (CCJ) appellate jurisdiction is listed, but as of yet the CCJ lacks an enforcement role for the Caribbean Community's common market and economic agreement.

II. INTERNATIONAL LAW ENFORCEMENT IN ACTION

The case studies in this chapter compare ICs involved in economic, human rights, and mass atrocities law enforcement in diverse countries so as to underscore the altered politics dimensions across issues and contexts. For each case, what compliance required varied, so that the actor with the power to choose compliance differed. Variation in the "problem structure" of compliance affected the strategies of litigants and IC compliance partners. Remember that my goal is not to explain compliance per se, but rather to understand how pressure on governments gets raised and diffused by the actions of IC interlocutors so as to ascertain how an IC's existence and actions contribute to changes in state behavior in the direction of greater respect for international law.

7.1. "Foreign Sales Corporation"—WTO review of the United States special tax treatment for goods exported abroad

This conflict over US tax policy began in 1971 when Congress decided that it needed to create a remedy to address American businessmen's complaints about the US system of taxing profits. The nature of the United States' legal violation did not change over the thirty-three years of this dispute, nor did the global trade regime's formal sanctioning system.

What became the Foreign Sales Corporation (FSC) case began in 1971 when the United States introduced the Domestic International Sales Corporation (DISC), which allowed US companies to create a subsidiary where export earnings could escape taxation. Congress hoped that the DISC legislation would reduce the US trade deficit. From the US perspective, providing a way for multinational corporations to escape American taxes only served to moderate the disadvantages the US approach to taxation inadvertently created.[9] The crux of the issue was that Europe levels value-added tax on goods sold in its market, and thus its system of taxation does not apply to goods exported abroad. Meanwhile, the United States taxes profits. American firms have to pay both US profit taxes and European value added taxes. Even if one accepts that the European system implicitly subsidizes exports, the intent behind the European system is not to provide a subsidy for exports so much as to tax consumption. By contrast, the intent behind the American DISC system was to provide tax relief for exporters. Thus arguably the American system was more illegal than European tax rules.

9 Gary Hufbauer explains the US position: GATT rules have a territorial notion of taxation that many see as making little sense in the modern system (Hufbauer 2002, 1–4).

As soon as the United States introduced its DISC system, Europe asked for a GATT panel arguing that DISC provided American firms with an unfair trade advantage. In response, the United States brought countersuits against European taxes that it claimed provided analogous export subsidies. Under pressure from Europe, the United States allowed the DISC case to proceed to the point that US practice was declared illegal. The United States was able to win its countersuits against the European practices, though according to Robert Hudec, the legal reasoning supporting the US victories was questionable.[10] All panel rulings were released at the same time. The United States offered to have the four panel rulings accepted, which would lead to mutual nullifications and impairments and thus no authorized retaliation. Europeans refused to accept the rulings against them, and thus all the panel rulings were blocked under GATT era rules that required unanimous consent for panel reports to be adopted.

Throughout the 1970s and 1980s the United States maintained its claim that the European system was also illegal. But in the politics that followed, the United States ended up isolated, with most countries believing that the DISC policy clearly violated GATT law, while the European systems were probably legal. In 1981 GATT bodies created a compromise collective position that arguably exonerated the European taxation systems while implicitly leaving the DISC policy discredited and illegal. In this compromise, the three European panel reports were separated from the DISC report, and the United States supposedly agreed that the European tax system was acceptable. The United States later claimed that the compromise position also exonerated DISC.[11] A basic détente set in. While the United States continued to violate GATT rules, the fact that its argument was not legally tenable undermined the US Trade Representative's ability to use reforming the DISC as a bargaining chip against other countries.

From a domestic perspective, the US tax system was entirely legal. The United States Trade Representative's office surely saw the DISC law as a strategic liability, but it had no power to address the issue. Only Congress

10 Hudec surmises that either political concern about the US position or inadequacies in legal reasoning allowed for the four panel decisions. According to Hudec: "Finding the right answer to the nasty interpretative problem presented by Article XVI:4 would have required legal work of the highest order. The level of legal practice would have had to provide the panel with a broad and sophisticated exploration of the issues, the data, the possible solutions, and the ramifications of those solutions. In 1976, however, GATT litigation procedure was just beginning to scrape off the rust that had accumulated during the antilegalist period of the 1960s. It was simply not ready to operate at this level." (Hudec 1988, 1486).

11 Ibid., 1493–96.

could change the contested policy. Congress had contradictory preferences. Its members supported the GATT and the enforcement of GATT fair trade rules, and it saw the United States as largely complying with GATT rules and with the rule of law in general. But members also supported US policies that violated GATT rules.

The compulsory WTO dispute resolution system came into effect in 1994. Now it would take unanimity to reject a panel ruling. Changes in the WTO enforcement system transformed a losing international legal argument into a ticking-bomb legal violation, which Europe could unleash whenever it chose. By then the United States had replaced its DISC system with tax rebates for exports and foreign production (goods sold through a Foreign Sales Corporation) so that goods sold in Europe could escape the double taxation of the US profit tax system. But creating a discount for the part of a corporation's products that were exported still looked like an illegal export subsidy. Europe knew that the FSC policy violated WTO law. Although the new WTO system made the FSC legislation a greater political liability, the US could avoid making any changes until Europe acted. The lurking possibility that this case might be filed was not enough to stop the United States Trade Representative from bringing suits to satisfy those American exporters who disliked European Union policies involving bananas, beef with hormones, and genetically modified foods. Only after losing these cases did the European Union raise the FSC suit.[12]

When the new FSC suit appeared in the WTO system, the substantive issue remained largely the same. US firms may believe that Europe's value added tax system provides benefits for exporters, but this does not change the reality that Europe's system of consumption taxes is WTO compliant. According to Gary Hufbauer, when the WTO ruling condemned the FSC system, it "gutted the understandings that the United States had relied on for nearly two decades." A first WTO ruling left open a door for the United States to maintain the heart of its FSC system. The United States adopted modest legal reforms, which were then challenged, leading to a second WTO ruling where it became clear that if the United States did not eliminate the entire system, Europe could levy $4.03 billion a year in retaliatory sanctions.[13]

The WTO system allows the winning country to choose which products it targets for retaliation. The winning country can first create tariffs on, for instance, US automakers right before quarterly reports are due or

12 Hufbauer argues that Europe raised the case to create bargaining chips after it lost the bananas and beef hormones case, and because it anticipated losing cases involving Airbus and agricultural subsidies (Hufbauer 2002, 5).

13 (Hufbauer 2002, 5). WTO United States Tax Treatment for "Foreign Sales Corporation."

when credit agencies are making their calculations, then add tariffs on Hollywood movies, American computer products, and perhaps wine from Napa Valley, and later add tariffs on citrus products shipped from states where there are tight elections. For Europe, this award was a bargaining chip it could use in future conflicts with the United States. Europe won the right to put a 5 percent levy on American goods, rising 1 percent for every month the legal violation persisted up to a 17 percent tariff ceiling. The European Union published a target list for retaliation, making quite clear the costs of defending this subsidy for American exporters.[14] Moreover, American legal leverage vis-à-vis Europe was undermined as long as this fine existed. The United States could continue to bring and win cases against Europe, but doing so merely risked that Europe would find even more products to target as it implemented $4.03 billion worth of annual retaliation.

According to one estimate, European countries collected between $200 and $300 million in 2004 and were poised to collect another $666 million in 2005.[15] The prospect of rising retaliation ultimately changed domestic calculations by mobilizing businesses like Boeing, General Electric, and Caterpillar, which faced retaliation. With these major firms now wanting the FSC system eliminated, the political costs of changing the US tax code diminished. The American Jobs Creation Act of 2004 changed the contested US tax law while providing tax breaks to many.[16] It may be urban folklore, but the press reported that even Starbucks earned a classification as a "manufacturer" that could benefit from the tax reform.

The United States was particularly intransigent regarding the FSC case because so many American firms believe that they are unfairly disadvantaged by double taxation, yet there continues to be deep political opposition in the United States to switching from taxing profit to taxing consumption. The United States has complied more quickly with WTO rulings where far smaller sums were at stake. For example, the US government on its own volition respected the WTO's finding of a violation regarding safeguards levied on Australian and New Zealand lamb, ending the safeguard protections nine months before they were set to expire at a cost of $42.7 million.[17] Compliance was arguably easier in this case because the United States' International Trade Commission could choose to end the safeguard without congressional assent. In other words, the United States is not always reluctant to comply with WTO laws or decisions. Meanwhile, Europe's record of compliance with WTO rulings is

14 (Stancil 2005, 422).

15 Ibid., 434–35.

16 H.R. 4520, 108 Congress 2004.

17 "US ends lamb import quotas." 2001. Agra Europe, November 16, 2001, 7.

also spotty. Instead of immediately complying with the WTO's banana and beef hormones rulings, Europe brought the FSC suit so that it could counterretaliate should the United States target its products. Arguably European firms were disadvantaged by the tax-break subsidy for exports, but the impetus for the suit seems to have been annoyance and a desire to gain bargaining leverage. Thus we might conclude that the WTO system brings both incremental compliance and dueling legal suits.

7.2. "Second Use Patent"—Andean Tribunal's review of Peru's policy granting patents for new medical uses

Andean intellectual property law requires absolute novelty for inventions to garner a patent. It thus bars recognition of so-called second use patents—new patents for when a medication is found to be beneficial for a different purpose. In the 1990s, the American pharmaceutical company Pfizer discovered that its heart medication pyrazolpyrimidinones (renamed Viagra) had the side effect of treating male impotence. Latin America promised to be a lucrative market for Viagra. Notwithstanding clear Andean rules to the contrary, Pfizer filed second use patent applications in all of the Andean countries in an effort to prevent the sale of generic erectile dysfunction medications.

In Peru, the office charged with issuing patents (the National Institute for the Defense of Competition and the Protection of Intellectual Property [INDECOPI]) applied Andean law and rejected three patent applications for Viagra. A few months later, in June 1997, President Fujimori issued a decree that purported "to clarify and interpret various articles of [Andean] Decision 344."[18] Article 4 of the decree recognized that patents could be issued when there were new uses of existing drugs.[19] Immediately thereafter, Pfizer ask INDECOPI to reexamine its application to patent Viagra. Relying on the new law, the agency granted the application in January 1999. Pfizer then threatened to sue Peruvian drug companies that were manufacturing or selling generic copies of Viagra. With domestic litigation looming, the Association of Pharmaceutical Industries of National Origin (ADIFAN) filed a complaint with the Andean General Secretariat alleging that Peru had violated Andean rules requiring absolute novelty for patents. This case would not have occurred under the original Andean system, because the General Secretariat originally could

18 Supreme Decree No. 010-97-ITINCI (June 5, 1997).

19 Article 4 provided that "a distinct use included in the state of the art shall be the subject of a new patent if it complies with" the normal patent requirements of novelty, inventive step, and industrial applicability. Ibid.; see also Pascale Boulet, *Campaign for Access to Essential Medicines—Patents and Medicines in Peru* 4 (November 2001); Ena Matos Jaqui, *Las patentes de segundo uso* (undated), available at http://www.dlh.lahora.com.ec/paginas/judicial/PAGINAS/D.Autor.4.htm.

only pursue noncompliance cases raised by states. The 1996 Cochabamba reforms, however, allowed any affected party to complain about state noncompliance and to bring the case directly to the ATJ if they were not satisfied with the Secretariat's actions. ADIFAN was thus able to approach a former member of the Andean Secretariat to help with the case, someone it knew from conversations regarding Andean intellectual property law.

After failing to convince Peru to abandon its second use patent legislation, the General Secretariat submitted the case to the ATJ. In a judgment issued in September 2001, the ATJ upheld the complaint and the Andean ban on second use patents and directed Peru "to leave without effect the patent conferred to Pfizer."[20] The Andean enforcement system allows for retaliatory sanctions when a trading partner's rights have been nullified or impaired. In this case, however, sanctions were never part of the political calculation because the generic producers raising the suit were Peruvian. The ATJ decision was actually enforced by INDECOPI, which upon the request of ADFIAN revoked Viagra's patent. INDECOPI's decision undermined Pfizer's legal claim that generic companies were violating its patent, and thus INDECOPI's decision also put an end to Pfizer's legal efforts against regional producers marketing generic alternatives to Viagra.

One of the most interesting aspects of this case is that neither the administrative agencies nor national courts were willing to disregard an executive legislative act that was valid within the domestic legal order until the ATJ ordered them to do so. Why did Peruvian patent officials follow the ATJ? According to INDECOPI officials, adhering to the Andean Tribunal's judgment was a straightforward matter: "When the ATJ tells us what the supreme interpretation of the law is, then our own interpretation is void." In interviews INDECOPI officials also expressed frustration at the Peruvian law authorizing second use patents. Not only did this law represent political interference in their decision making, there was also a widespread sense that the Peruvian decree was the result of corruption. Both Andean and national intellectual property (IP) officials try to walk the line between protecting the rights of intellectual property holders while remembering the needs of local stakeholders. The winners of the second use patent rule were foreign pharmaceutical companies that could extend patents; the losers were consumers and local producers of generic medicines. Nevertheless, before the ATJ's ruling, the officials refused to ignore the Peruvian decree. Since the Viagra case, the agency has not granted any second use patents. The Peruvian government never repealed the law, but nor did it pressure INDECOPI to enforce it, suggesting that government officials had been willing to circumvent Andean law, yet

20 ATJ "Second use patent case," at 40.

unwilling to fight their intellectual property officials or repudiate the ATJ on behalf of Pfizer.[21]

Litigation in Venezuela and Ecuador followed a similar pattern. The intellectual property agency in each country registered a second use patent for Viagra prior to the ATJ ruling against Peru, and generic drug manufacturers turned to the Andean legal system to challenge the registrations. The General Secretariat and the ATJ reaffirmed their prior rulings and the administrative agencies reversed their positions and invalidated the patents.[22] The end result of this wave of litigation was that all domestic intellectual property agencies in the Andean Community denied or annulled patents for Viagra.

This case study contrasts with chapter 8's Colombia and Ecuador alcohol-related practices. In that case, Colombian courts refused to see an ATJ ruling as requiring them to create a legal remedy, and Colombia remains in violation of Andean rules notwithstanding an authorization for Ecuador and Venezuela to retaliate. The difference across these cases turns on the support of domestic interlocutors. Andean intellectual property agencies see themselves as bound by Andean rules, which they support in part because they had a say in creating the rules. Andean national courts see themselves as obliged to apply Andean interpretations of Andean rules, and they agree that Andean law is supreme.[23] But as chapter 8 explains, Colombian judges do not see the primacy of Andean law as requiring them to disapply conflicting domestic laws, especially if the domestic legislation in question is considered a higher order law.

Beyond inducing compliance, the ATJ's second use patent ruling affected multilateral politics involving intellectual property issues. The WTO has established a multilateral floor for intellectual property protection, but this floor leaves a number of issues involving intellectual property rights unaddressed. The United States has been trying to fill the holes via bilateral agreements (so called TRIPS plus agreements). The ATJ's ruling against Peru took the issue of second use patents off of the bilateral negotiating agenda, frustrating American pharmaceutical companies. The US pharmaceutical industry's 2008 Special 301 Report to the US Trade Representative places the blame squarely on the ATJ:

> The Andean [Tribunal] of Justice [has] issued several legal opinions . . . forcing Andean Community members to refuse recognition of patents for second uses. . . . Such decisions constitute law in Bolivia, Colombia, Ecuador, and

21 Interviews with officials in INDECOPI's National Institute for the Defense of Competition and the Protection of Intellectual Property, Lima, Peru, June 21, 2007.

22 See "Related Second Use Patent Cases" judgment against Venezuela and Ecuador.

23 For more on why intellectual property agencies supports the ATJ, see Helfer, Alter, and Guerzovich (2009, 21–25).

> Peru. Andean member countries have either been compelled by the [ATJ] not to grant second use patents or chosen to honor Andean Community obligations. . . . The failure to provide patents for second uses particularly affects the pharmaceutical industry, which has dedicated substantial research dollars to evaluating additional therapeutic benefits of known molecules (second uses) in order to provide effective solutions for unsatisfied medical needs. The [ATJ] position is dispositive on the issue and no further domestic appeals/remedies are possible.[24]

Without the ATJ's interventions, Andean countries would likely have succumbed to external pressures to grant second use patents. Indeed, the legal landscape looks quite different elsewhere in Latin America. El Salvador, Guatemala, Honduras, Mexico, and Paraguay recognize second use patents; Chile, Panama, and Uruguay do so in certain instances; and the status of such patents in Brazil is uncertain. Only Argentina, Costa Rica, the Dominican Republic, and Nicaragua share the Andean Community's prohibition of all second use patents.[25] Thus this litigation not only enhanced compliance with Andean rules, it altered US-Andean relations on intellectual property related issues.

7.3. "Modern-Day Slavery"—ECOWAS court finds that Niger's government has not done enough to remedy family law

The Economic Community of West African States (ECOWAS) is, as the name indicates, an economic community with the formal objective of building a common market supporting economic development in the fifteen West African member states. The community's meager accomplishments in creating a common market are eclipsed by ECOWAS's role as a regional security organization and, more recently, as perhaps the boldest and most active international human rights court in Africa. Starting in 2005, the ECOWAS CJ became a rare international legal institution with jurisdiction over economic suits raised by the ECOWAS Commission and member states, and human rights suits raised by both NGOs and individuals.[26] Human rights advocates were key actors creating the change in

24 Pharmaceutical Research and Manufacturers of America (PHRMA), Special 301 Submission 236 (2008), cited in Helfer, Alter, and Guerzovich (2009, n. 144).

25 (Helfer, Alter, and Guerzovich 2009, n. 146).

26 For more on how the ECOWAS CJ gained its human rights jurisdiction, see Alter, Helfer, and McAllister 2013); Nwogu (2007). The ECOWAS CJ remains unusual in that it has become at this point primarily a human rights court, despite the fact that ECOWAS is in theory primarily an economic community. But other economic courts also hear human rights cases. Chapter 8 discusses the ECJ Kadi case, where the ECJ examined the rights protections for a European Union regulation. The Caribbean Court of Justice regularly reviews death penalty appeals. The East African Court of Justice has claimed a human rights jurisdiction for itself, as did the court of the Southern African Development Community. The

the ECOWAS CJ's jurisdiction. These advocates have gone on to find a number of important cases for the ECOWAS CJ to rule on. The Hadijatou Mani case was one of the earliest ECOWAS CJ human rights rulings, and it has a particular resonance because a savvy media campaign led to broad international recognition, and because the ECOWAS CJ could portray itself as taking the side of slave girl.[27]

The Hadijatou Mani case arose because Timidria, a local antislavery association, and Anti-Slavery International, a British based NGO, undertook a law-based strategy to address the problem of slavery in Niger. While slavery was banned in Niger's 1999 constitution, what constituted slavery was not defined and slavery itself was not a crime. Timidria first worked with Anti-Slavery International to document indigenous forms of slavery in Niger. The two organizations then lobbied for national laws criminalizing slavery, leading in 2003 to a statute that created potentially severe repercussions for anyone found to be holding slaves.[28] The organizations then worked to have the laws enforced.[29] The advocates' efforts bore mixed results because of local customs. Even when formally liberated, former slaves found many barriers to beginning a new life. When former slaves turned to local judges, these judges often refused to recognize the condition of slavery or the relevance of constitutional protections against slavery, favorable legal rulings were often reversed on appeal, or penalties applied were so small that litigation became meaningless for the plaintiff and defendant. By the time of the ECOWAS judgment, there had been only one prosecution for slavery, which ended in a one-year prison sentence.[30] Anti-Slavery International concluded that it needed a big win, one that would attract international attention, shaming the Niger government and national judges into recognizing that slavery is a crime.[31]

SADC court's human rights jurisdiction has been compromised by a member state decision in August 2012 to remove the right of individual appeal.

27 "Former Slave Wins Historic Case against Niger Government," *The Telegraph*, October 28, 2008; "Free at Last: Female Slave Who Dared to Take Niger to Court," *The Times*, October 28, 2008; "Court Rules Niger Failed by Allowing Girl's Slavery," *New York Times*, October 27, 2008; "Une-Cour-Regionale-Africaine-Condamne-le-Niger-pour-Esclavage," *Le Monde*, October 27, 2008, cited in Duffy (2011).

28 Penal Code of Niger as amended by Law No. 2003-025 of June 13, 2003, in its Article 270 (1) to (5).

29 Anti-Slavery International helped organize events like the 2005 ceremony in the western Niger town of Tillaberi, where government officials explained that the new laws meant that people who had spent their whole lives as the property of their masters were now free. See "Niger Begins Enforcement of Ban against Slavery," *The Guardian*, March 5, 2005. At http://www.guardian.co.uk/world/2005/mar/05/sarahleft, last visited August 15, 2011.

30 (Duffy 2011, 4).

31 Interview with the African Program Coordinator for Anti-Slavery International, April 5, 2011, via Skype.

Part of Timidria's enforcement strategy involved hiring a judge to speak in marketplaces around the country, to explain how enslavement is a crime. After one speech, an individual came to Timidria's office to complain about a man who treated his slaves very badly. Timidria investigated, learning that El Hadj Souleymane Naroua had seven slaves. Local advocates threatened criminal prosecution, which could bring up to a thirty-year sentence, and the master issued a formal "liberation certificate," signed by the "chef du village" the "master" and the "beneficiary," who was the brother of Hadijatou Mani. The certificate stating that "I El Hadj Souleymane Naroua have liberated Mme Hadijatou Koroua on this day 18 August and she is now free and is no-one's slave" lent an aura of legality and official support to the master's declaration, making it harder to deny that Hadijatou Mani was now free. When Hadijatou Mani learned of the certificate, she ran away and then tried to have her right to freedom recognized.

Hadijatou Mani's situation presented as straightforward a case of modern slavery as one can find. Her master had paid about $400 to buy Hadijatou Mani when she was just twelve years old. Hadijatou had provided unpaid labor for ten years and bore children as a result of forced sexual relations. There was a liberation certificate, and Hadijatou was asserting her right to freedom. Problems began, however, when Hadijatou Mani tried to remarry. Her former master argued that under local tradition she was married to him. The first instance judge found that she was free to leave her former master because there had been no marriage ceremony and no dowry. This decision was reversed on appeal, with the Tribunal de Grand Instance finding that under Niger's customary law, a slave girl is de facto married to her master once she is released. The appeal court ordered Hadijatou Mani to return to her former master. This ruling was appealed to the Supreme Court, which acknowledged that Hadijatou Mani was initially a slave, although it did not make this fact determinative of the outcome. Instead, it ruled that advisors unduly influenced the Tribunal de Grand Instance, and thus it sent the matter back for another determination.[32] When Hadijatou Mani became pregnant by the man she had tried to marry, her former master sued for bigamy. Hadijatou Mani, her new husband, and her brother (who had consented to the marriage) were detained, convicted, ordered to pay a fine equivalent to $120, and sentenced to six months imprisonment. Hadijatou Mani appealed this case to the Court of Appeal in Niamey, which deferred judgment pending divorce proceedings for the nonmarriage with her former master but

32 These cases are referenced and discussed in Duffy (2009, 155), and in the ECCJ ruling itself.

allowed her to be temporarily released from jail after two months.[33] Meanwhile, El Hadj Souleymane Naroua claimed custody of the children he had fathered with Hadijatou Mani, and he tried to gain custody of the child Hadijatou Mani bore with her new husband.[34] Based on these cases, Anti-Slavery International decided that Mani was not going to get any justice in the Niger legal system. Hadijatou Mani's case was such blatant evidence of the failure of the Niger legal system that it provided a perfect test case. The question then became where the case should be brought.

Anti-Slavery International teamed up with Interights, and both organizations provided critical aid to Timidria's local lawyer Abdourahaman Chaibou. Lawyers chose the ECOWAS Court because it could provide a quicker remedy than the African Commission on Human Rights, and it could create a binding ruling that would be immediately useful for Hadijatou Mani, who was serving a jail sentence for bigamy when the ECOWAS CJ case began.[35] For Anti-Slavery International, the possibility for ECOWAS CJ to change the venue of hearing provided an additional attraction. Timidria's lawyer argued that Hadijatou Mani lacked the means to pursue the case in Abuja, the seat of the ECOWAS CJ. ECOWAS judges agreed to move the legal proceedings to Niamey, the capital of Niger. This move to Niamey proved key. The government took the proceedings seriously. On the first day of the proceedings, the entire Niger Supreme Court, the prime minister, and the speaker of the Parliament were in attendance, as were newspaper reporters.[36] Timidria arranged for there to be local television coverage, and Anti-Slavery International prepared an international media strategy. The court heard the case over four days. ECOWAS judges later returned to Niamey to publicly read their ruling.

The government argued that Hadijatou Mani's case was inadmissible because it was still proceeding in national courts. It refuted that Hadijatou Mani was currently enslaved, arguing that Hadijatou Mani was perhaps in a position of servitude, but that she was El Hadj Souleymane Naroua's wife and they "had more or less lived happily as in the lives of

33 Based on a briefing paper provided by Anti-Slavery International.

34 (Duffy 2011, 6).

35 Choosing such a confrontational and public strategy was risky. There was no budget to cover the legal expenses due if they lost the case. But Anti-Slavery International felt that it had tried to work with the government to no avail. Moreover, as lawyers argued, "Hadijatou Mani's case is as clear a case of slavery as one is likely to encounter." The only risk was that the ECOWAS CJ might "chicken out," which was a very real risk. Based on notes provided by Hadijatou Mani's Interights lawyer, and interviews with the African Program Coordinator for Anti-Slavery International (April 5, 2011, via Skype) and Helen Duffy, the Litigation Director for Interights (February 10, 2011, via Skype).

36 Based on an interview with Ibrahima Kane, AU Advocacy Director at the Open Society Institute, February 3, 2011, via Skype.

all couples."[37] Hadijatou Mani's advocates contested this claim, arguing that the system of *sadaka*, "the act of selling a woman to a man to serve as a concubine for him," and *wahiya*, the customary practice of considering slave/concubines to be supplementary wives (fifth wives) created conditions of enslavement.[38] Identifying the many ordeals Hadijatou Mani had suffered, the lawyers argued that Hadijatou Mani's life conditions met the definition of slavery defined by the International Criminal Tribunal for the Former Yugoslavia. "Slavery and other violations cannot be reduced—as the state agent sought to do yesterday—to a 'private matter,'" they claimed, instead the state becomes responsible when it fails to prevent or to respond appropriately to the violations of individuals.

The ECOWAS Court refused to hold the Niger government accountable for the discrimination Hadijatou Mani faced, including the very questionable bigamy conviction. But it found that Hadijatou Mani was indeed enslaved by *sadaka* and *wahiya* customary practices. The Court's potentially far-reaching argument asserted:

> Even with the provision of square meals, adequate clothing and comfortable shelter, a slave still remains a slave if he is illegally deprived of his freedom through force or constraint. All evidence of ill treatment may be erased, hunger may be forgotten, as well as beatings and other acts of cruelty, but the acknowledged fact about slavery remains, that is to say, forced labor without compensation. There is nothing like goodwill slavery. Even when tempered with humane treatment, involuntary servitude is still slavery.[39]

The Court went on to identify a number of specific failings of different public actors. The Konni High Court should have recognized the condition of slavery and put into place procedures to end it. The judge who heard the case of Hadijatou Mani Koroua v. El Hadj Souleymane Naroua should have prioritized stopping slavery instead of upholding another aspect of the Niger penal code that says that "the marriage of a free man with a slave woman is licit, in as far as he does not have the means of marrying a free woman, and if he fears falling into fornication." The failure to take positive action on Hadijatou Mani's behalf, or to create appropriate measures to end slavery, made the government responsible for the human rights violations she suffered.[40]

The court demanded 10.000.000 CFA francs in compensation for Hadijatou Mani. The minister of justice was present for the reading of the

37 ECOWAS modern-day slavery ruling, paragraph 73.

38 Islamic law permits four wives. Each additional wife or concubine is a *sadaka*.

39 ECOWAS modern-day slavery ruling, paragraph 79.

40 Ibid., paragraphs 82–86.

ruling, and as soon as the court issued the ruling, the minister announced that Niger would implement the Court's decision.[41] Within four months, the government had paid the compensation.

Why did Niger's government comply? Perhaps the government wanted to show that it was, as its representatives had stated at the outset of the legal proceedings, a rule of law country. Perhaps officials in the capital wanted to distance themselves from what they too saw as backward practices in the provinces, especially given the publicity the case was generating. Perhaps the government was concerned about a threat that had been made, that advocates might draw on the finding and invoke International Labor Organization laws to undermine the preferential trading status of Niger in the United States. Or perhaps the public officials who watched the trial felt they had to follow through to save face. Any or all of these forces could have been at play. Given the many obvious benefits of compliance, perhaps it makes more sense to ask why would we expect the government not to comply?

Niger complied with the ruling in full. But it is also true that the ECOWAS court asked fairly little. The court refused to examine national statutes that might conflict with the right to be free, because it said that considering the compatibility of such statutes with the national constitution and international conventions is the responsibility of national judges. Since the ECOWAS court did not examine the validity of national statutes, it did not require that any national rules be changed. The judges also found that the government was not liable for any discrimination that Hadijatou Mani faced because she was a former *sadaka*. It did not even require that Niger enforce its antislavery law by prosecuting Hadijatou Mani's former master (although the master was eventually prosecuted in 2009; his one-year sentence was then reduced to a three-year suspended sentence and the fine reduced).[42] And the court did not require training or deeper change by the judiciary.

One should not overlook the effect this ruling had for Hadijatou Mani. The African Human Rights Commission can investigate violations and issue reports, but these efforts seldom provide something useful for the victim of the abuses. The ECOWAS CJ's ruling literally transformed Hadijatou Mani's life. The bigamy charges against Hadijatou Mani went away as the case proceeded to ECOWAS court, and the compensation has allowed Mani to establish a life for herself. Hadijatou Mani won a "woman of courage 2009 award." In a trip to Washington, DC, Hadijatou Mani

41 Interview with Ibrahima Kane, AU Advocacy Director at the Open Society Institute, February 3, 2011, via Skype.

42 The prosecution is discussed in Duffy (2011, n. 78). Duffy also discusses the many limitations she sees in the Court's ruling.

met with Hillary Clinton and Michelle Obama who formally recognized the courage it took a twenty-two-year-old uneducated former slave to pursue her case. Impediments, however, remain. Hadijatou Mani's former master continues to assert custody of the children he fathered. While Hadijatou Mani can now provide for the children, local law still favors the father, and the custody battle has continued for many years.[43]

The ECOWAS ruling also rewarded the ECOWAS CJ's compliance supporters. The ruling gave the case an international profile. Anti-Slavery International leveraged the ruling by teaming up with the Danish Institute of Human Rights, which had a planned training session for Niger judges. An entire day of this session ended up focused on the antislavery laws in place and national judicial mistakes in handling the Hadijatou Mani case. Timidria also gained because the ruling clearly recognized *sadaka* as slavery. No longer could the government claim that the issue was merely a problem of "forced labor" or customary practice. In a press release for the decision, Ilguilas Weila, Timidria's president, said, "For 17 years we have been working towards bringing slavery to the attention of authorities. Previously there has been a lack of political will to deal with the situation on the ground. The law in 2003 was passed only as part of a charm offensive to please westerners. This verdict means that the state of Niger will now have to resolve this problem once and for all."[44] The media attention has made Timidria's lawyer a national figure, and many more women have come to seek Timidria's help.

The implications of this ruling for Niger are clear: customary practices that create conditions of slavery violate international human rights obligations. In all likelihood, such conditions also violate Niger's constitutional ban against slavery. What the ruling will mean in practice, however, is less clear. According to Anti-Slavery International, one can detect small but meaningful changes in the Niger government's attitude. An official associated with Timidria was appointed to government office in a region with a high incidence of slavery. The government also took the side of a former slave in a contest over who could become a chief. Local residents insisted that former slaves lacked the status to be a chief. Government officials, however, helped alter the balance, so that for the first time a former slave became a local chief.[45] Slower to change are the attitudes of people who continue to condone slavery and make life difficult for any individual who dares to challenge the status quo. It remains difficult to get local prosecutors to enforce the crime of slavery, and punishments for slavery continue to be too unlikely and small to discourage the

43 Interview with the African Program Coordinator for Anti-Slavery International, April 5, 2011, via Skype.

44 On file with the author.

45 Interview with the African Program Coordinator for Anti-Slavery International, April 5, 2011, via Skype.

widespread practice of slavery. In other words, the same types of social factors that limit the generalized enforcement of the "rape as a war crime" ruling (discussed in chapter 8) also limit the prosecution of slavery. This is exactly the problem that Gerald Rosenberg identified in his discussion of the "hollow hope" that courts can bring social change. At the end of the day, people backed with political power, not judges, create social change.[46]

7.4. *"Charles Taylor"—Convicting Charles Taylor, president of Liberia, for crimes committed in a neighboring country*

When the Special Court for Sierra Leone indicted Charles Taylor (March 7, 2003), Taylor was the president of Liberia, where he was embroiled in an ongoing civil war.[47] The prosecutor of the Special Court for Sierra Leone issued the indictment on the first day of multilateral peace negotiations to end the civil war (June 4, 2003). The Ghanaian host of the peace talks refused to honor the indictment, expressing outrage that his government had not been notified in advance. Nigeria later granted asylum to Taylor to facilitate his exit from Liberian politics. Taylor spent over two years in asylum in Nigeria before he was finally turned over to the Special Court on March 23, 2006. This case study explores how the creation of the Special Court for Sierra Leone contributed to politics that led to Charles Taylor's removal from regional politics and his prosecution. I pay special attention to the interaction between international judicial and domestic judicial processes so as to highlight the value added by international criminal courts.

Although Taylor was tried in The Hague, the Special Court for Sierra Leone, not the International Criminal Court (ICC), prosecuted his case. The newly elected president of Sierra Leone, Ahmad Tejan Kabbah, had asked the United Nations to use its Chapter VII power to create a special international legal body because Sierra Leone's judiciary had been decimated during its civil war. Relying on the ICC was not an option because the ICC lacks jurisdiction to prosecute crimes that occurred before it was formally constituted on July 1, 2002. The creation of another ad hoc international criminal body provided a chance to improve upon the 1990s model of the international criminal tribunals for Yugoslavia and Rwanda. Dissatisfied with the slow and expensive process of the Yugoslav court, the United Nations gave the Special Court the mandate to focus on "those who bear the greatest responsibility."[48] Also different, the Special Court

46 (Rosenberg 1993).

47 (Tejan-Cole 2009, 210).

48 Security Council Resolution 1315 (2000) explains the reasons for creating a Special Court. The resolution is available at http://www.un.org/Docs/scres/2000/sc2000.htm, accessed August 19, 2010. The founding of the Special Court is explained in Perriello and Wierda (2006, 10–12).

was crafted as a "hybrid court" including both international and national judges. The hybrid nature has advantages. International criminal tribunals have been criticized as being less effective because they operate outside of the arena of conflict. By contrast, the Special Court undertakes all of its activities, except the Taylor case, inside of Sierra Leone.[49]

When the UN Security Council agreed to create the Special Court for Sierra Leone, it was not clear that Taylor would be a target. At the time, Taylor was president of Liberia. While the conflict in Sierra Leone was over, Liberia was still embroiled in a civil war. Taylor could still slow any progress toward peace, create refugees, and foment trouble in neighboring countries. Perhaps for this reason the patrons of Sierra Leone's request—the United States and the United Kingdom—were not at the time proposing that Taylor be indicted.[50] But the crafters who wrote the UN resolution kept the indictment option open by including that "the official position of any accused persons, whether as Head of State or Government or as a responsible government official, shall not relieve such person of criminal responsibility nor mitigate punishment."[51] Taylor became the second sitting head of state to be indicted by an international criminal tribunal, the first being Slobodan Milošević.

By all accounts the Special Court's prosecutor, David Crane, made the decision to indict Taylor without first consulting with governments involved. Most people saw Taylor as ultimately responsible for crimes in Sierra Leone because of his support of the Revolutionary United Front (RUF), the rebel army blamed for some of the worst atrocities during Sierra Leone's civil war. The indictment originally remained secret because of ongoing peace negotiations regarding the Liberian civil war. But Crane decided to make the indictment public on the first day of peace negotiations for the Liberian conflict. With great publicity, Crane issued an indictment accusing Taylor of eleven specific crimes, including the direct responsibility and command and control authority for unlawful killings, terrorizing the civilian population, rape and sexual violence, forced labor, and the

49 The UN has created hybrid courts in East Timor, Bosnia, Kosovo, and Cambodia, relying on national institutions to contribute to international prosecution (Shabas 2014). The Sierra Leone Court is distinct, however, in being located within the arena of conflict and because it is completely independent from national courts (Nmehielle and Chernor Jalloh 2006, 108).

50 Based on interviews with a key intermediary for President George Bush regarding the Liberian conflict, Chicago, Illinois, September 9, 2010. Sierra Leone's request had the strong backing of the United Kingdom and the United States, the United States and the United Kingdom funded the Special Court, and the main prosecutors were from these countries.

51 Statute Creating the Special Court for Sierra Leone Article 6 (2). Security Council Resolution 1315 (2000) explains the reasons for creating a Special Court. See note 48 for full citation.

recruitment and use of child soldiers.[52] Since David Crane is an American, one might presume that he coordinated his actions with American officials. But this does not seem to have been the case. When Crane made his decision, the US government was supporting ECOWAS efforts to keep the Liberian conflict contained. In order to get Taylor to negotiate peace, African leaders had promised Taylor that he would be secure at the peace talks in Ghana, and that he would be given a graceful exit from the presidency. Crane's actions made these promises hollow. Apparently Crane kept his intentions secret out of a concern that Ghanaian officials might warn Taylor, keeping him from traveling to the peace talks. Crane's lack of diplomacy likely contributed to the open condemnation of the public indictment by countries involved in the peace talks, including Americans present.[53]

More important than the diplomatic slight was the real concern that the indictment might undermine the peace negotiations. ECOWAS, under Nigeria's leadership, had been trying to stop Taylor and end the regional wars since the early 1990s. The underresourced military force created by ECOWAS lacked the power to control the contested territories, and by 2003 regional and domestic support for continued intervention had waned. The Nigerian leader who had begun the regional intervention departed from office in 1999, and Nigeria's internationalist president, Olusegun Obasanjo, wanted to end an intervention that had proved costly in political, economic, and human terms.[54] The Taylor indictment came during an extremely volatile time. Rebels were closing in on the capital of Monrovia, and the United States had sent troops to protect its embassy and stationed 2,300 soldiers offshore, a clear sign of US displeasure with Taylor. Negotiators were focused on a peace agreement for Liberia, not on accountability for crimes in Sierra Leone.

Taylor left the peace talks shortly after Crane publicly issued the indictment, but the Ghana conversations nonetheless ended with an agreement that the parties implemented. Priscilla Hayner saw the surprise indictment as aiding peace negotiations. Hayner stressed that Taylor had broken a number of promises in the past, suggesting that a peace agreement negotiated in the absence of an indictment had an equally likely chance of failing. In her view, the indictment helped in the short run because it undermined Taylor's ability to demand a role in the new Liberian political regime:

> The indictment de-legitimized Taylor, both domestically and internationally. It effectively removed any last support for him from international partners. Once

52 (Tejan-Cole 2009, 208, 214).
53 Ibid., 213–14. See also Hayner (2007, 8).
54 (Bach 2007, 307–12).

> it was evident that [Taylor] could not rely on international support, and especially that the US had publicly turned against him, it became clear that he would have to leave the presidency. Equally important, it affected the morale of his own troops, which was already low because the soldiers had not been paid in months.[55]

Taylor may well have agreed to leave office on his own, as he was under considerable pressure to do so. But if Taylor faced a real threat of prosecution in another country, as opposed to an international court, he may have insisted on retaining a political role in Liberia that could allow him to claim sovereign immunity. Even while Taylor tried to escape arrest, his lawyers invoked the International Court of Justice's (ICJ) ruling in Democratic Republic of the Congo v. Belgium, where the ICJ had prohibited national indictments of high officials of foreign governments. The ICJ ruling had left open that Belgium could indict officials once they leave office, and it allowed international courts to indict sitting government officials. The ICJ ruling meant that if Sierra Leone were dealing with mass atrocities on its own, no country would have been able to indict Taylor so long as he held high office in Liberia. The Special Court dismissed the appeal, however, since it was both an international court and it had been explicitly authorized by the United Nations Security Council to pursue heads of state.[56]

Taylor also tried to make amnesty part of the peace agreement for Liberia, but the parties involved refused. They did, however, agree that Liberia would use the model of a Truth and Reconciliation Commission instead of requesting a mass atrocities tribunal, thereby ensuring that Taylor would not be subjected to prosecution for crimes committed in Liberia. Taylor tried, but failed, to obtain a promise that the Special Court for Sierra Leone would not prosecute him. Since the Special Court operated under a UN mandate, this was not something Nigeria could promise. Instead, Taylor received a promise that Nigeria would not turn him over to the Special Court.[57] Nigeria's asylum agreement, as we shall see, was later rescinded.

The indictment provided ongoing leverage to use against Taylor and his protectors. To facilitate his exit from the president's office, Nigeria granted Taylor a comfortable landing pad: three houses where he and his entourage could entertain visitors in private and where Taylor would be protected from the reach of the Special Court. The terms of the asylum

55 (Hayner 2007, 9). Hayner is cofounder of the International Center for Transitional Justice.

56 ICJ "Arrest Warrant" ruling. For more on Taylor's effort to invoke the ICJ's arrest warrant precedent, see Tejan-Cole (2009, 222–24).

57 (Hayner 2007, 15–18; Tejan-Cole 2009, 215).

agreement, which reportedly had the backing of the United States, United Kingdom, the African Union, the United Nations, and ECOWAS, were never made public. It is rumored that Nigeria promised to rescind the asylum agreement should Liberian leaders request extradition, although given that Taylor could not be prosecuted in Liberia it is not clear why Liberian leaders would seek Taylor's return. Subsequent events suggest that the agreement also involved Taylor promising to refrain from intervening in regional politics.[58] The asylum agreement held for two years. What political pressure led Nigeria to revoke Taylor's asylum promise?

The international indictment provided a basis for governments and nongovernmental organizations around the world to demand that Nigeria rescind its asylum agreement. NGOs, including Human Rights Watch, No Peace without Justice, the Soros Foundation Justice Initiative, and Amnesty International, continued to call for Taylor's arrest and pursued a local legal strategy of raising suits inside of Nigeria. NGO pressure helped to keep the media and politicians focused on the issue of arresting Taylor, and one of the legal cases made it up to the Nigerian Federal Court.[59] Still, there is little reason to believe that the transnational legal strategies or the NGO pressure directly influenced the position of the Nigerian government.

NGOs were more successful in influencing legislative actors in Europe and the United States. In late 2003, the US Congress authorized a $2 million reward for Taylor's capture. In March 2004, the Security Council added to the travel ban on Taylor by freezing the assets of Taylor and his immediate family. In February 2005, the European Parliament called for Nigeria to send Taylor to the Special Court, followed two months later by a similar resolution passed in the United States' Congress. In November 2005 the UN Security Council expanded the mandate of its Liberian peacekeeping initiative to include arresting Taylor, signaling that Taylor would be arrested if he returned to Liberia.[60] These public rebukes—facilitated by the existence of the Special Court's indictment—reminded local actors that Taylor had not been forgotten, and they tightened the net on Taylor, keeping his regional range of action limited. The protection of the Nigerian government, however, held steady.

Taylor seems to bear some responsibility for his reversal of fortunes. Taylor allegedly broke the asylum agreement by continuing to interfere in regional politics. Abdul Tejan-Cole notes that "by mid-2005, persistent

58 (Tejan-Cole 2009, 215).

59 Activists hoped for an important precedent, but the Federal Court eventually declared the case moot once Nigeria had turned Taylor over to the Special Court. See the discussion of Anyaele v. Taylor at http://www.soros.org/initiatives/justice/litigation/taylor, accessed August 13, 2010. See also Tejan-Cole (2009, 216).

60 (Tejan-Cole 2009, 216).

claims were emerging that Taylor was violating the terms of his Nigerian asylum deal to refrain from political interference in West Africa, including that he had been involved in an attempt to assassinate Guinean president Lansana Conteh in January 2005, that he continued to back armed groups, and that he was attempting to influence forthcoming post transition Liberian elections."[61] The accusations led the leaders of Sierra Leone, Liberia, and Guinea to issue a joint statement calling for a review of the asylum arrangement. The leaders also threatened to refer the case to the ECOWAS political system. Nigeria continued to resist pressure by refusing to act without a formal request from the president of Liberia. Taylor's actions undermined the support of African governments, making travel in the region risky, but Taylor remained safe as long as his supporters could keep the pressure on the politically fragile Liberian president.

When Ellen Johnson Sirleaf won the Liberian election in November 2005, Taylor lost his local protectors, and American officials found they had a president they could work with. Once the election outcome was decided, the United States wanted Taylor to be prosecuted. President Sirleaf at first refused to request Taylor's arrest, as it was not yet clear which members of Liberia's military and government still supported Taylor. But there was an understanding that she would consolidate her power and then request Taylor's extradition. The United States then worked to convince Nigeria to renege on the asylum agreement. On March 17, 2006, just three months after taking office, Sirleaf requested that Nigeria turn Taylor over to the Special Court.[62] After some drama when Taylor disappeared inside of Nigeria, on March 29, 2006, Nigerian forces turned Charles Taylor over to the Special Court. The Nigerian president received a White House visit in return for his support. Officials at the Special Court, backed by the governments of Liberia and Sierra Leone, requested a change of venue for the trial out of stability concerns.[63] In 2012, the Special Court for Sierra Leone found Charles Taylor guilty of war crimes and sentenced him to fifty years in jail, which is the equivalent of a life sentence. This ruling was upheld on appeal, after which Taylor was transferred to a British prison.

The Taylor case may prove somewhat unusual in that the crimes were so atrocious that NGOs remained mobilized and Taylor refused to lay low, which made it harder for the United States and regional governments to ignore him. Even if Taylor had not burned his protective bridges, the standing indictment limited his room for maneuver. Once Taylor lost his

61 Ibid.

62 Based on interviews with a key intermediary for President George H. W. Bush who was involved in resolving the Liberian conflict, Chicago, Illinois, September 9, 2010. Tejan-Cole gives an excellent account of all of these developments, including the dramatic endgame where Taylor for a short time went missing in Nigeria (Tejan Cole 2009, 214–18).

63 (Tejan-Cole 2009, 219; Williamson 2012).

protection, his energies were consumed by his trial, and his hidden resources became harder to employ (Taylor had claimed poverty so as to avoid paying his own legal expenses).

Most people are happy to have Taylor held accountable, but the prosecution had many problems. The Special Court's jurisdiction only covered crimes in Sierra Leone, and since Taylor and his troops never went to Sierra Leone it was harder to prove command responsibility. Taylor ended up being convicted for abetting war crimes including terrorism, rape, using child soldiers and murder.

For now, the cycle of violence in the region is held at bay at least in part because of Taylor's forced removal from regional politics and the continued scrutiny of Taylor and his supporters. These are outcomes that follow from the creation of the Special Court for Sierra Leone. Indeed, it is doubtful that either domestic actors (judges or activists) or international NGOs could have on their own created accountability for Taylor and his crimes. Liberia is still unable to deal with the crimes of Taylor's regime, and there is little to suggest that Sierra Leonean courts could have handled the Taylor case on their own. Advocates may have been able to draw on domestic courts willing to exercise universal jurisdiction,[64] or perhaps Taylor would have faced a situation similar to that of Chad's former ruler Hissène Habré.[65]

III. ICS ALTERING THE POLITICS OF INTERNATIONAL LAW ENFORCEMENT

For dispute settlement cases, the IC's compliance partners were the parties to the dispute. For administrative review, IC compliance partners included national and international administrative actors and sometimes also national judges. In enforcement, the pathways of inducing change vary based on which actor has the power to choose compliance and the factors that motivate these compliance partners.

For the WTO case, compliance required new legislation. Only the threat of European sanctions persuaded the US Congress to eliminate the

64 Taylor's son was prosecuted for his crimes, and he is now serving a ninety-seven-year sentence in the United States. http://news.bbc.co.uk/2/hi/americas/7820069.stm.

65 Hissène Habré, president of Chad from 1982 to 1990, had been living in Senegal under political asylum. In 2005, a Belgian court issued an international arrest warrant for Habré with the intention of using universal jurisdiction to prosecute his crimes. Senegalese authorities then arrested Habré, and Habré then used legal channels to block his extradition and prosecution. Most recently, the International Court of Justice ordered Senegal to proceed with prosecution, and the African Union has agreed to create a special tribunal to deal with the case. See ICJ decision "Hissein Habré." See also http://www.bbc.co.uk/news/world-africa-19351938, last visited October 22, 2012.

illegal policy. For the second use patent and Niger slavery cases, the binding nature of ruling itself tipped the balance. For the Charles Taylor case, high-level power politics shaped the ultimate outcome. Figure 7.2 maps how ICs are altering politics. In time 0, the violation occurred—the United States created its DISC law (which changed its name but otherwise persisted over time), President Fujimori's office issued its decree authorizing second use patents, local judges helped El Hadj Souleymane Naroua block Hadijatou Mani's efforts to establish a new life for herself, and Taylor committed his many crimes in Sierra Leone. T1 considers the domestic options available to injured parties. For the FSC case, there were no domestic options. The American law was fully legal, and GATT rules are not self-executing in the American political system. For the second use patent case, litigants could have challenged the grant of a patent to Pfizer. But they would have needed to raise the suit in INDECOPI's own tribunal, asking INDECOPI judges to ignore a legally valid national law. For the ECOWAS slavery case, Hadijatou Mani had already tried many legal appeals. Appellate bodies were slowly rejecting lower court rulings, but Hadijatou Mani found herself in jail for bigamy in the meantime. For the Charles Taylor case, domestic courts in Liberia and Sierra Leone lacked law on the books, and the legal and political capacity to prosecute Taylor. T2 represents international enforcement strategies—the prelitigation and litigation phases. For mass atrocities cases, most of the political energy is focused on the prelitigation stage, which involves decisions to indict individuals and many decisions related to the pursuit of indicted war criminals. T3 involves leverage strategies once the IC has ruled. These strategies target the national actor with the power to comply with the law. Arrows indicate pressure exerted at each stage.

One could see these IC enforcement cases as shifting the cost-benefit calculations of states, but I'm not sure that the cost-benefit metaphor best captures what happened. It certainly became less costly for American senators and congressmen to repeal a popular tax once American firms supported the repeal, but given the inevitable outcome it seemingly would have made more sense to change US policy before incurring over $200 million in retaliatory fines. The cost-benefit calculus in the Peruvian case is also a little odd. The Peruvian government never actually changed its policy, and by failing to act it may have gotten the best of all worlds. Fujimori received the benefit of having cooperated with Pfizer, without paying the cost of damaging its generic producers of Viagra. For Niger, immediate compliance helped the government begin to recover from an embarrassing public rebuke. But no doubt the government would have preferred to have never been publicly shamed. Moreover, the government actually did intercede once the case was raised in the ECOWAS system, but it got no credit for facilitating Mani's release from prison, or for later ensuring that the bigamy suit disappeared. In the Taylor case, the costs and benefits of Nigeria's asylum agreement didn't really change, if only because rescinding the asylum agreement also had associated costs. Rather, the political context changed: Taylor was out of office, Liberia had a Western-oriented president, neighboring governments were tired of Taylor's continuing political antics, and the United States now wanted Taylor turned over to the Special Court. The Nigerian government got the benefit of a White House visit for its troubles, but surely the other changes mattered more.

In all of these cases the international judicial system provided points of political leverage that state and nonstate actors could exploit and defendant governments could not eliminate. In the FSC suit, European officials gained a tool to pressure specific American corporations and to create local electoral vulnerabilities that might harm intransigent politicians. ADIFAN, the Peruvian association of generic medication producers, could leverage the Andean legal system to provide a service to its members while promoting a reversal of a Fujimori policy that was widely seen as corrupt and counterproductive. Timidria could use the Hadijatou Mani case to force Niger's government to respond and to draw attention to its cause. As the Taylor case shows, even actors who are not parties to the suit can build on international legal mechanisms as points of leverage. NGOs and West African governments could use the fact of the Taylor indictment in their legal and political strategies aimed at influencing European, American, and Nigerian officials.

The long-term legacy of these cases varies. The FSC case is resolved, and we are unlikely to see new tax policies designed to benefit exports. For the second use patent case, lawyers for pharmaceutical industries learned that only political deals inscribed in Andean law will give them the type of protections they seek. When pharmaceutical companies sought to prolong the terms of their patents by prohibiting the release of data in patent applications, Colombian lawyers worked to insert into Andean law provisions that allow member states to protect data in patent applications, thereby hindering generic companies from assembling competing products until a patent has expired.[66] Meanwhile, pharmaceutical companies have found other ways to enhance the market power of trademarked pharmaceutical products. The international politics of intellectual property rules have primarily been redirected, not halted, by ATJ rulings. There are some meaningful shifts in government support to end slavery in Niger, and the precedent set by the ECOWAS CJ's Hadijatou Mani v. Niger ruling may well end up helping slaves in Niger and beyond. Taylor's prosecution by the Special Court will leave a longer legacy, both in terms of the

66 See Helfer, Alter, and Guerzovich (2009, 30–34).

FIGURE 7.2 Political dynamics of enforcement cases

	National system		International system				
	Domestic enforcement strategy	Compliance partner required change	International legal strategy	IC ruling	Legal remedy	Post-ruling political strategy	Policy change by compliance partner
WTO FSC	None available (US tax law is legal).	Executive branch + Congress ←	EU/US negotiations.	US FSC policy illegal.	Retaliatory sanctions.	Europe retaliation list. →	Executive branch + Congress change FCS legislation.
ATJ 2nd use patent	Domestic legal challenges would fail given legal validity of Fujimori's decree.	Executive branch could rescind law and/or national judges or INDECOPI could choose to apply Andean law instead. ←	Secretary General tries to negotiate to rescind illegal decree.	Fujimori second use patent decree illegal.	Sanctions not possible since no other state is affected.	ADIFAN asks INDECOPI to rescind 2nd use patent. →	National judges and INDECOPI apply ATJ ruling instead of Fujimori decree.

ECOWAS slavery case	National level litigation resulted in rulings favoring Hadjitou Mani's former master.	Higher courts could have reversed lower court judges, rather than remanding the case.	NGO first supported domestic litigation, then wanted a public international ruling.	Customary practices perpetuate slavery.	Compensation for violation.	Media campaign which put Niger government in bad light, and could potentially trigger trade sanctions.	Government pays fine. Some positive actions to help former slaves. Training for judges.
SCSL Charles Taylor	National prosecution hampered by absence of law and capacity in national system, and concern that arresting and prosecuting Taylor might rally supporters to violence.	Nigerian executive can rescind amnesty and order extradition. Nigeria waiting for a request from Liberia.	International Prosecutor issues indictment. NGOs & later US pressure for extradition.	Taylor guilty of aiding and abetting Sierra Leone rebels.	50 year prison term.	Leverage politics occur during T1.	Once Liberia requested extradition, governments aid prosecution. Since Taylor is already in jail, no follow-up politics are needed.
	T1: Bargaining in the shadow of an IC			T2: Litigation politics		T3: Leverage strategies	

precedent and because the Special Court also has a broader mandate to facilitate reconstruction of the rule of law in Sierra Leone.[67] Taylor's case shows that even though indicted war criminals may find havens, any asylum or amnesty agreement is precarious. A government can at any time choose to help arrest indicted war criminals; thus indicted war criminals need to constantly work to sustain their havens.

All of the courts discussed in this chapter have issued a variety of rulings, which have had mixed influence. The discussion of the WTO case study noted that the United States and Europe do not always comply with WTO rulings; the chapter 6 discussion of the softwood lumber dispute is an example of this. The discussion of the second use patent case noted that Colombia is yet to comply with the court's ruling regarding violations of municipal alcohol policies (see the case study in chapter 8 for more). The ECOWAS court has issued a number of rulings with varying compliance rates. The Gambia has neither produced a body of a disappeared journalist nor has it paid compensation for the journalist it tortured.[68] The court's rulings regarding the right to free compulsory education and the Nigerian government's failure to crack down on oil companies that violate environmental policy are going to be more difficult to enforce.[69]

CONCLUSION: IC DESIGN AND INTERNATIONAL LAW ENFORCEMENT POLITICS

International courts name state actions as violations of international law, create concrete remedies that advocates can demand of governments and international actors, and generate legal precedents that litigants facing like scenarios can invoke. International enforcement bodies cannot actually make states follow the law. But they can provide resources that alter politics in favor of domestic and international actors using national, multilateral, and transnational strategies to encourage greater government respect for international rules.

The new style of ICs has made these enforcement politics possible. One key new-style design ingredient is compulsory jurisdiction for the IC. The Foreign Sales Corporation case study showed how the United States

67 The court actually has a Legacy Working Group that identified specific legacy goals. Legacy projects include an endowment to maintain the buildings the Special Court will leave behind, a radio-based system to independently disseminate information (Radio Justice), a library of resources at the main university, and a public defender system. See Nmehielle and Chernor Jalloh (2006); Perriello and Wierda (2006, 39–40).

68 ECOWAS "Gambian disappearance" and "Gambian torture" cases. For more, see Alter, Helfer, and McAllister (2013).

69 See ECOWAS "Environmental damage in the Niger Delta."

sustained a tax policy designed to favor exporters at the same time as the United States condemned other countries for their unfair trade practices. Giving the WTO compulsory jurisdiction changed the politics, leading American firms to actually prefer elimination of this tax benefit. The United States is now in full compliance with the WTO ruling, but chapter 6 included the softwood lumber case where the advent of compulsory jurisdiction (this time for the Canada-US Free Trade Agreement) did not create compliance. Rather, the prospect of repeated litigation led the United States to negotiate a new arrangement with Canada to protect its softwood lumber industry. Although the terms of the Softwood Lumber Agreement are much more favorable to Canada than what had existed before, the whole arrangement arguably violates WTO rules. The point is that compulsory jurisdiction provides leverage to actors with law on their side. How these actors use such leverage, however, is subject to political influence.

A second key new-style design feature is access for nonstate actors to initiate litigation. This chapter included three case studies where access for nonstate actors proved crucial. Peru's violation of Andean law did not compromise the interests of other member states, and it is safe to assume that no other state would have raised a challenge to Peru's second use patent law. But changes to the ATJ's jurisdiction in 1996 allowed private litigants to appeal to the Secretariat to raise cases on their behalf (and to bring the case themselves if litigants remain unhappy). The Hadijatou Mani case also could not have been raised in the original ECOWAS legal system since private actors lacked access to the Court (and the ECOWAS CJ lacked jurisdiction over human rights cases). For the Charles Taylor case, the fact that the prosecutor, and not states, controlled the indictment process led to the indictment notwithstanding peace negotiations underway for Liberia, and this indictment meant that no political leader could offer Taylor immunity from prosecution.

ICs with enforcement capabilities are among the most active ICs. It is also true, however, that not all enforcement ICs are active, and that the shadow cast by the prospect of IC enforcement is highly uneven. Design limitations account for some of the inactivity of existing enforcement courts. A number of systems that copy the design of the ECJ put limits on the types of cases that international secretariats can pursue.[70] New-style design features may be necessary conditions for international litigation to

70 For example, the original Andean legal system only allowed the Secretariat to investigate noncompliance complaints raised by states. This requirement inhibited the Secretariat from pursuing clear violations of Andean law. The COMESA system requires political assent before the Secretariat refers a case. The ECOWAS system does not limit the types of cases the Secretariat can raise, but nor does it require the Secretariat to pursue noncompliance cases raised by private actors.

proceed, but they will never be sufficient conditions for ICs to alter politics. Many factors hinder international law enforcement. Two ICs with a global reach have a limited capacity to handle claims: the ICC focuses only on the top perpetrators of mass atrocities and WTO litigation can be prohibitively expensive. And Asia and the Middle East have thus far largely escaped the shadow of regional enforcement courts, and Syrian leaders are at the time of writing escaping ICC investigation or indictments because Russia is blocking any effort to refer the matter to the Office of the Prosecutor. Moreover, even where ICs exist, potential litigants may choose not to raise suits, contributing to the sidelining of law and legal institutions.[71]

Barriers to international law enforcement persist, but delegation of enforcement jurisdiction to ICs, and the strengthening of existing international enforcement systems, has undoubtedly introduced a new dynamic in international relations. The Special Court for Sierra Leone's prosecutor was able to pierce the cozy bubble diplomats constructed in order to encourage Charles Taylor to step down. And the prosecutor's actions gave NGOs new tools of political leverage. Once legal suits are initiated, a spotlight is focused on questionable government behavior, and the political environment is thereby fundamentally changed. Publics, NGOs, lower-level government officials, and national judges that see themselves as rule of law actors may choose to comply with an IC ruling even without high-level direction, as occurred in the second use patent case, and perhaps also the modern-day slavery case. Indictments for mass atrocities limit political leaders' ability to travel abroad, make individuals a greater political liability at home, and provide a ready way for opponents to remove indicted leaders once their protectors lose power. Legal suits and indictments also shame actors whose tacit support facilitates illegal behavior.

Shaming and litigation strategies may fail in the short term. But eventually power shifts, as happened in the Taylor case. Political leadership changes, related concerns come to the fore, new actors arise. The indictment and IC precedent, however, endures. New governments may find that outstanding indictments are creating new or unanticipated difficulties, or warrants and legal rulings that seemed unhelpful at one time may come to be seen as a helpful later. It may take a very long time for states to comply with IC rulings, and the power of certain governments may be too strong for ICs to affect, but advocates may nonetheless be able to elicit concessions along the way.

Compared to the other judicial roles of ICs, enforcement politics may well be the most variable. In dispute settlement cases, compliance with an IC ruling often does not require positive government actions for the ruling

71 (Ellickson 1991).

to have a legal impact. A government's endorsement of the ruling will surely help to reassure state and nonstate actors, but usually all that is required is for litigating parties to embrace the decision of the court. Administrative review cases require administrative support for IC rulings, but they generally do not require legislative or executive actions for compliance to occur. By contrast, enforcement cases will vary significantly with respect to what compliance entails. Sometimes governments can reinterpret existing legislation or open their coffers to facilitate compliance with an IC ruling. But sometimes compliance will require a positive action. Even if a government wants to turn over an indicted war criminal, change problematic domestic legislation, or encourage national judges to heed an international judicial ruling, a government may lack the ability to influence key substate actors to follow their will. Since what compliance entails varies, the actor with the power to choose compliance varies. For this reason, litigation and leverage strategies must also vary.

ICs want to have their rulings respected. But as chapter 2 explained, quite often compliance concerns do not even enter the judicial calculus, and even when compliance concerns are relevant usually legal factors will still matter most of all to judges. Said differently, an independent judge with a clear legal mandate that is presented with a clear violation of the law will condemn a legal violation even if such a ruling is likely to be ignored. Indeed, following the clear letter of the law is arguably the safest political strategy for legal actors, and the strategy most likely to build future support for the IC.

Potential litigants consider whether investing in litigation will be worth the expense, and judges worry about making demands that are likely to be ignored. Compliance concerns shape the legal strategies of litigants and judges, influencing whether cases are raised and the types of remedies litigants demand and ICs require for legal breaches. ICs can vary what compliance with its ruling requires, and ICs can reach out to those actors best placed to facilitate respect for international law. As international legal institutions build alliances with compliance partners, as compliance partners become politically stronger, and as public support for following the law grows, ICs become more politically powerful. Growing support for the law has a feedback effect that in itself shapes litigant strategies and the ability of ICs to use their naming power to encourage greater respect for international law.

CHAPTER 8

International Constitutional Review

The previous chapter discussed international courts in their enforcement role of declaring states' noncompliance with international law. An international judicial finding of state noncompliance may make violating international law more costly, but it does not invalidate conflicting domestic laws. Constitutional review differs in that it is designed to check sovereign power. I adopt Alec Stone Sweet's definition of constitutional review as the judicial authority to invalidate laws and government acts on the basis of a conflict with higher order legal obligations.[1] Constitutional review raises the stakes of law enforcement because where the legal conflict concerns a higher order law, the only way to resurrect unconstitutional laws will be to change the conflicting practice or the higher order law. Constitutional review also differs in that legal review challenges the validity of actions of highly legitimated sovereign actors—legislatures and governments.

Giving judges—domestic or international—constitutional review power can be controversial. Those who embrace a Lockean perspective of legitimate authority tend to view judicial review as contributing to democracy by ensuring that individual rights are not trampled by the collective will. But a finding of constitutional invalidity can become a judicial trump card. By specifying what it would take for a policy to be constitutional, judges can become policy makers and veto players. The harder it is to change a constitution, the more difficult it is to reverse a constitutional veto. For these reasons, wherever constitutional review authority exists one hears concerns about a "government of judges," meaning a political system in which unelected judges replace accountable politicians in making

1 (Stone Sweet 2000, 21). The notion of higher order international law does not mean that international law is generally or necessarily natural law. All that matters is that constitutional, treaty-based, or other international law is seen as legally binding and trumping conflicting "lower order" domestic laws.

law. The losers of the legal case usually voice such concerns, but their arguments resonate because citizens cannot vote judges out of office.[2]

The notion of *international constitutional review* raises perhaps even more concerns about the possible deleterious effects of judicial review on democracy.[3] Changing domestic statutes or the national constitution will not suffice where the conflict is with higher order international law. States cannot change international rules on their own, and legal principles that fall under the category of *jus cogens* (a.k.a. preemptory norms) cannot be changed at all. The contentious notion that international courts can be seen as constitutional bodies enforcing higher order international laws against strongly legitimated domestic actors has generated active debate. Critics of the constitutional analogy question whether treaties can or should create higher order legal obligations, whether one can have an international constitution without a corresponding *demos* that supports it, and whether international legal orders contain the types of foundational *grundnorms* one associates with legitimate constitutional orders. Meanwhile, even the most revered domestic constitutional systems exhibit at least some of the problems and limitations critics point to when they challenge international constitutional orders.[4]

Most lawyers engage this fraught issue from the domestic perspective, debating the legal space that domestic constitutions allow for international law and IC rulings.[5] From this vantage point, the constitutional import of international law is not something that international actors can or should have any say over. Moreover, to the extent that domestic lawyers see international law as a hermetically separate legal domain or the national constitution as the only higher order law of the land, the concept of a higher order international law feels like an oxymoron. But the reality is that international laws are legally binding, and judges and policy makers increasingly see international legal commitments as constraining what is permissible at home. As this chapter will demonstrate, ICs also conduct constitutional review of both international and domestic acts. Practice

2 The United States is a strange outlier in that some judges are elected to office. This is not typical, and election rules do not apply to federal and supreme court judges that practice constitutional review.

3 Some examples about these concerns include Barfield (2001); Bork (2003); Rubenfeld (2003).

4 This debate exists mostly with respect to the European Union, the European Convention on Human Rights, and the World Trade Organization. For a good overview of the different positions in this debate, focused on the case of the WTO, see Cass (2005, 3–25). On the benefits and limits of constitutional analogies for international courts, see Helfer (2003); Stone Sweet (2009). Other voices in this debate include Cass (2001); Dunoff (2006); Hartley (1996); Helfer (2003); Maduro (1998); Mancini (1989); Petersmann (2008a, 2008b); Stone Sweet (1998); Stone Sweet and Brunell (1998); Trachtman (2006).

5 See, for example, Monaghan (2007); Rabkin (2005).

thus evokes the question of how we understand the political influence of ICs in their constitutional review role.

From an international perspective, there are two different conversations to have regarding ICs' constitutional review role. The less controversial conversation concerns the role of international courts in assessing the validity of *international* legislative acts. Domestic judges will agree that although they may rule on the legal applicability of international rules in the domestic order, they lack jurisdiction to review the legal validity of international acts. This means that the choice facing policy makers is to either make international rules beyond any judicial check or to empower ICs as the international counterpart to domestic judges, giving them authority to review the legal validity of international acts. Most lawyers and governments see IC review as preferable to having international law and policy beyond any check, and in fact most delegations of international constitutional review authority are designed to address a concern that arises because international legislative actors can create domestically binding international legal rules that may not be subject to legal review.

More controversial is whether international courts should have jurisdiction to assess the validity of state acts vis-à-vis higher order international legal principles. Many ICs have been empowered to rule on state compliance with international law. Where this law is deemed to be higher order law, international judicial rulings can render domestic law inapplicable, thus de facto nullifying the conflicting national practice.

It is important to note that ICs have, in fact, been delegated constitutional review jurisdiction. But the real question is, when do ICs become international constitutional review bodies in practice? For ICs, to inhabit a constitutional review role requires a corresponding culture of constitutional obedience where domestic actors see violations of higher order laws as ipso facto illegitimate. ICs can help define when international law creates a higher order legal obligation, but in the end national supreme courts must support these assertions if international judges are going to draw on their delegated or assumed constitutional review roles, at least with respect to the review of national acts.

Section I identifies the ICs with explicitly delegated constitutional review roles and explains how cultures of constitutional obedience underpin the constitutional review role. Section II examines two cases of ICs nullifying international legislative acts for conflicts with higher order legal requirements. Both are hard cases because ICs rejected legislative acts that enjoyed considerable government support. The Kadi case is an especially hard case because the ECJ asserted the supremacy of community law over United Nations acts.

Section III examines four cases where ICs are reviewing the validity of state acts vis-à-vis higher order international law, covering all of the domains that constitutional review usually operates: state responsibility, minority rights, and criminal law. The cases are also selected to serve as contrasting examples, and they also are hard cases in that the IC required positive actions to rectify constitutional breaches. Section IV considers how ICs alter politics in their constitutional role and identifies the critical role national supreme courts play in international constitutional review politics.

The conclusion considers the extent to which international constitutional review differs from domestic constitutional review. Domestic constitutional courts also build coalitions with compliance constituencies to influence political outcomes, and they also worry about maintaining the support of lower court judges. Where domestic supreme courts are weak, IC backing can bolster their constitutional authority in the domestic order. The stronger the domestic supreme court, however, the more likely that domestic constitutional court judges will construct barriers to the penetration of international law in the domestic domain. This tension between international courts and domestic supreme courts can, however, help to keep international law attuned to domestic legal and political concerns, enhancing the accountability of ICs.

I. INTERNATIONAL CONSTITUTIONAL REVIEW JURISDICTION AND CULTURES OF CONSTITUTIONAL OBEDIENCE

After World War II, constitutional review spread around much of the globe as defeated countries emulated constitutional models developed elsewhere, as democratization displaced authoritarian rule, and as new leaders sought to instantiate their rule of law legitimacy and programmatic objectives.[6] IC constitutional review jurisdiction mirrors the growth of judicial review powers across domestic political systems. Delegating constitutional review jurisdiction to international courts arguably extends to the international level the requirement that public power submit to the rule of law.

As with administrative review, delegation of constitutional review jurisdiction to ICs spread with the European Court of Justice (ECJ) model. The ECJ has always had jurisdiction to rule on the legal validity of the binding legislative acts passed by the Council of Ministers. Access to the ECJ remains widest for the Court's constitutional role. Governments, firms, and private actors can bring suits directly to the ECJ, or private litigants can raise challenges to European acts in national courts, with last

6 (Ginsburg 2008; Hirschl 2004; Stone Sweet 2000).

instance national judges obliged to refer such challenges to the ECJ for a preliminary ruling. European officials then immediately worried that the constitutional review of community acts could lead to political paralysis. In 1962, ECJ Advocate General Lagrange voiced the concern that "extremely grave consequences . . . could follow from even a partial annulment of texts that [have] 'quasi-legislative character' and [have] been adopted with considerable difficulty, and sometimes after a compromise reached in the Council."[7] These concerns influenced the ECJ to limit the contexts in which private actors could claim legal standing to challenge the validity of community acts, so that initially it was extremely difficult for constitutional challenges to succeed.[8] Over time, the ECJ demonstrated that its constitutional review jurisdiction would not undermine the integrationist project of governments.

In my coding, ICs are seen as having an explicitly delegated constitutional review jurisdiction when they have jurisdiction to assess the validity of legislative acts. Unstated is that this review will assess contested laws and acts vis-à-vis higher order legal principles—usually the organization's founding treaty and human rights obligations that are binding on the organization and its members. Figure 8.1 summarizes the universe of operational ICs with constitutional review jurisdiction. As with administrative review, an IC's constitutional review jurisdiction can take two distinct forms. Type 1 review assesses the legality of supranational legislative acts. This jurisdiction tends to be exclusive and mandatory, extending to the international level a constitutional check on supranational legislative actors that would otherwise not exist. Type 2 review, sometimes explicitly delegated but sometimes an assumed role, assesses the legality of domestic legislative or constitutional acts. The columns on the right identify which actors are allowed to initiate a constitutional challenge to international actions (parentheses explain if access extends to challenges of state acts as well). The chapter's appendix provides greater detail on the Court Treaty articles pertaining to the IC's constitutional review jurisdiction.

All of the ICs explicitly delegated constitutional review jurisdiction are located in common markets, and all but one replicate the general design of the ECJ. The Caribbean Court of Justice (CCJ) can exercise constitutional review when it serves as an appellate body for national judicial

7 Conclusion of the Advocate General Legrange in Confédérations nationals des producteures contre Conseil des CEE, Case 16-62.

8 Litigants had to show that the harm applied to them personally and illegally. For more, see Biernat (2003); Hartley (1998, 350–55). Treaty revisions regarding Article 263 of the Treaty on the Functioning of the European Union make it somewhat easier for litigants to challenge community acts today.

rulings.[9] The other ICs have jurisdiction to assess the validity of international acts, state acts, or both. All ICs listed have compulsory jurisdiction for this role, and access to ICs for constitutional challenges tends to be relatively wide, which is to say that all ICs with constitutional review jurisdiction allow state and nonstate actors to initiate international constitutional review of IO statutes and policies.

Five of the ten ICs with constitutional review jurisdiction also have jurisdiction to review the legal validity of state acts. The COMESA court, SADC tribunal,[10] and the CCJ envision that litigants will appeal challenges to state acts once domestic appeals are exhausted; the EACJ allows litigants to challenge the validity of legal acts in member states. The EACJ also can review the extent to which the community and its members adhere to the principles of good governance, rule of law, gender equality, and human rights.[11] The SADC tribunal had an initial jurisdiction to oversee whether the community and its members act in accordance with principles associated with protecting human rights, sustaining democracy, and adhering to the rule of law. Direct access to these courts and to the ECOWAS court can, and has, led to the review of the validity of state actions.[12] The CACJ has jurisdiction for cases involving noncompliance with judicial rulings, and for challenges regarding the "fundamental powers of organs," which in practice has meant disputes within countries involving the separation of powers. The CACJ expressly does not have human rights jurisdiction, which is conferred exclusively on the Inter-American Court of Justice.

Figure 8.1 captures ICs' explicit jurisdiction to conduct constitutional review. A less clear grant of constitutional review jurisdiction concerns ICs enforcing international legal agreements that codify what are arguably higher order laws. In practice, IC review of state compliance with human rights treaties, mass atrocities law, good governance requirements, and sometimes even economic agreements may generate rulings that are seen as implicitly invalidating conflicting state acts. The list of ICs with "morphed" constitutional review roles is thus arguably larger. The case

9 The Caribbean Court of Justice (CCJ) is unusual in that it lacks the formal authority to invalidate community rules, but it allows states to substitute the CCJ for the British Privy Council, which serves as the final court of appeal for a number of Commonwealth countries. See the chapter's appendix for more.

10 In August 2012, governments decided to revise the SADC court's jurisdiction and to remove direct access for private litigants. No new agreement about the court's jurisdiction existed at this book's publication, thus my discussion focuses on the SADC court's original jurisdiction.

11 Treaty for the Establishment of the East African Community Articles 6 and 7.

12 Ibid., 259. See the appendix to this chapter for more detail.

FIGURE 8.1: International courts with constitutional review jurisdiction **(by year created)**

ICs authorized to review the legality of validity of legislative acts (N = 10)	Compulsory Jurisdiction	Type of Constitutional Review		Litigants authorized to initiate review of community acts		
		(1) Review of Community Acts	(2) Review of State Acts	States	Supranational Actors	Private Litigant
European Court of Justice (ECJ) (1952)	X	X		X	Commission	Via national courts
Andean Tribunal of Justice (ATJ) (1984)	X	X		X	Secretary General	X
Central American Court of Justice (CACJ) (1992)	X	X	Limited[A]	X	Any community institution	X
West African Economic and Monetary Union (WAEMU) (1995)	X	X		X	Council or Commission	X
Court of Justice for the Common Market of Eastern and Southern Africa (COMESA) (1998)	X	X	X	X		X (access to challenge state acts too)
Central African Monetary Community (CEMAC) (2000)	X	X	X	X	Any community institution	X (access to challenge state acts too)

East African Court of Justice (EACJ) (2001)	X	X	X	X		X (access to challenge member states acts)
Economic Community of West African States Court (ECOWAS CJ) (2001)	X	X		X	Council of Ministers and Executive Secretary	
Caribbean Court of Justice (CCJ) (2001)	X	This authority is under discussion	For countries where CCJ replaces the Privy Council	Under discussion		Via national courts on case-by-case basis[B]
Southern African Development Community (SADC) (2005)	X	X		X		X
Totals in each category (N = 10)	10	9	3 full + 2 partial	9	6	8

[A] The CACJ can hear cases involving the "fundamental powers" or organs of the member states, and regarding noncompliance with judicial verdicts. In practice, these involve violations of the separation of powers.

[B] The Caribbean Court of Justice (CCJ) can determine that specific laws create *locus standi* for private actors, leaving open the possibility that the CCJ can extend direct effect to Caribbean laws on a case-by-case basis (Article XXIV). See Bastide (2007).

studies in section III offer examples of what might be seen as "morphed" constitutional review roles.

Whether an IC assumes a morphed constitutional review role turns on the remedies required for a breach of international law. In the enforcement role, legal violations by states generally give rise to sanctions or compensatory awards. Administrative review nullifies illegal administrative decisions and perhaps generates compensation for harms done, but since an administrative decision rather than the legislation itself is the subject of review, the law on the books stays the same. Constitutional review, by contrast, renders the "unconstitutional" act politically inapplicable. If a government wants to resurrect the contested policy, some positive action is required: either the law must be changed, or the constitution adjusted. If IC judicial review de facto invalidates conflicting domestic legislation, or builds new constitutional requirements for rule of law public actors, one might say that international law enforcement becomes constitutional review in practice.

For law to be rendered politically inapplicable requires that some set of actors see unconstitutional actions as unacceptable. Thus for ICs to inhabit a constitutional review role, explicitly delegated or otherwise, there must be a corresponding culture of constitutional obedience wherein constitutional violations of the law are seen as ipso facto illegitimate. The rest of this section considers what a culture of constitutional obedience entails, and what we know about how such cultures emerge.

Creating a Culture of Constitutional Obedience

A culture of constitutional obedience, by which I mean a political culture in which any legislative text or government action found to violate higher order law becomes inherently illegitimate, gives constitutional courts the political power to inhabit a constitutional review role. I call this a culture because it is a shared expectation that is socially enforced. A government that demonstrates clear indifference to the law violates a taboo, conveying to the larger public their unwillingness to adhere to the legal and political rules of the game.[13] Where cultures of constitutional obedience exist, constitutional review becomes a tool political actors use to defend the validity of their positions. Influential constitutional courts insert themselves as essential arbiters of disagreements about what is and is not constitutional. Through their constitutional interpretations, judges help define legitimate political action and determine whether specific contested acts are "constitutional."

13 For a discussion of the benefits and liabilities of invoking legal cultures, see Huneeus, Couso, and Sieder (2011).

Scholars have studied how new domestic courts generate constitutional authority. The process begins with governments publicly defending the constitutional validity of their policies. Litigants then challenge government actions in court, and judges respond by invoking higher order bodies of law as they provide rulings that opposition forces can embrace. Since litigants are only likely to seize a court where existing policy does not reflect their political preferences, a necessary condition for constitutional review to occur may be access provisions authorizing those actors who get outvoted in the political process to raise legal suit. According to Stone Sweet, when these conditions exist a virtuous circle can emerge where legislative bodies and governments create rules, litigants invoke judges to interpret existing rules, judges build law through their legal rulings, which leads litigants to keep challenging policies through litigation.[14] Kim Scheppele adds that for new constitutional courts to become both relevant and powerful, they must be seen as expressing a moral authority and siding with issues of concern to the people.[15] Ran Hirschl adds that judicial interests must align with the interests of key hegemonic groups.[16]

It is interesting to note the factors that do not appear as necessary for these accounts. Stone Sweet and Scheppele do not require an official judicial mandate to conduct constitutional review, nor do constitutions have to include basic rights provisions. While constitutional rhetoric generally comes with the territory, constitutional rhetoric is neither necessary nor sufficient for constitutional review to exist in practice. Nor does there need to be a constitution that was drafted in a certain way so as to create a basis for its legitimacy. Indeed, in the United Kingdom judges arguably review the legal validity of public acts despite the fact that the country lacks a constitution. If formal mandates and bills of rights are not required for constitutional review, then treaties can gain a constitutional status through practice, through government assertions of the validity of their actions and legal challenges that lead judges to invoke higher order legal principles. This is precisely what occurred in the European Union where the ECJ transformed the Treaty of Rome into a constitution for the European Community.[17]

14 Others see constitutional review as instantiating the power of political hegemons or as part of separation of powers political bargains, suggesting that there may be additional antecedent conditions that contribute to the emergence of constitutional review authority. These conditions may facilitate the emergence of constitutional review, but access for outvoted actors seems necessary for constitutional review to exist in practice. See Ginsburg (2003); Hirschl (2004); Staton (2010); Stone (1995); Stone Sweet (1999; 2000; 2008; 2009).

15 (Scheppele 2006, 1760). Martin Shapiro reviews a number of hypotheses that one used to think might influence the success of constitutional courts. See Shapiro and Stone Sweet (2002, 149–83).

16 (Hirschl 2004, 215–22).

17 (Mancini 1989; Stein 1981; Weiler 1991).

By all accounts, cultures of constitutional obedience develop over time, and creating such a culture involves litigants, judges, opposition groups, and governments testing and building political support. Governments, lawyers, and judges sometimes gauge the extent of social support by publicly questioning the validity of legal rulings that criticize public acts, and even by impugning judges. Kim Scheppele's account of the growth of constitutional review authority in Hungary and Russia is, in her words, a tale of "the separation of powers as a contact sport." Scheppele invokes Hannah Arendt's famous argument that "successful constitutions do not just constrain power, they create power through the opposition of interest to interest." According to Scheppele, "States (and courts) can fail. What prevents their failure in the early fragile days of a new constitution is the willingness of new institutions to deploy their power and to parry off the power of others in return."[18] In other words, an essential part of building broad-based cultures of constitutional obedience may involve judges making rulings that governments then contest, thereby rousing lawyers and the public to mobilize in support of the rule of law.

A somewhat different process may be needed to generate constitutional obedience to international law. ICs can sometimes skip the step of building grassroots support for international law through alliances with domestic legal actors, and especially national high court judges. Where domestic and international judges are in agreement about the higher order nature of an international legal obligation, governments are more likely to respond to an IC ruling by changing their policy. The support of national high courts is key because otherwise governments are able to argue that they respect the rule of law notwithstanding what may be a blatant disregard for an IC ruling. The Colombia and Ecuador alcohol-related practices case study in this chapter makes this point as it shows how the Colombian Constitutional Court's actions contributed to the persistent noncompliance by Colombia, in direct contrast to Ecuadorian supreme court justices who found that Andean law *required* them to remedy Andean law violations.

This analysis suggests that domestic judges have a choice in how they understand the binding force of international law. Many lawyers will argue that national constitutions, not judges, define when and how international law becomes binding within domestic legal orders. While legal provisions surely matter, interpretations of key constitutional provisions have been known to change over time. For example, both France and the United States have constitutions that clearly declare the supremacy of international law. In France, judges at first interpreted their constitution's supremacy clause as binding on Parliament but as not creating any corresponding

18 (Scheppele 2006, 1760).

role for judges conducting judicial review. Over time French judges came to believe that they had a role in upholding the supremacy of certain international laws, even though the relevant provisions of the French constitution did not change.[19] Doctrinal change in the United States went in the opposite direction. According to David Sloss, the fairly recent understanding that treaties are only binding in the US legal order if they are explicitly "self-executing" does not find its origin in the constitution, but rather in a relatively recent academic reassessment of foreign relations law in the United States.[20] Constitutional review traditions vary considerably, and much more could be said about when, how, and why legal interpretations evolve, but the main point is that the words on the constitutional paper do not in themselves create fundamental barriers to national judges finding that international legal obligations are domestically binding.

Why might national judges embrace or reject the legal authority of international law and international judicial rulings? There are books focused on the question, and no clear conclusion is in sight.[21] But one can speculate. Most judges actually do believe that the general principle of *pacta sunt servanda*, the Latin version of a basic good faith standard, requires governments to adhere to international agreements especially if these agreements have been domestically ratified. Moreover, the rule of law is generally seen as a package deal; national judges may worry that any precedent allowing governments to pick and choose their legal obligations, or to unilaterally repudiate legal obligations embraced by past governments, could have corrosive effects on the rule of law. Also, where international law is embedded into the national legal order, national judges may see compliance with international law as pretty much the same thing as compliance with domestic law. And especially where national supreme courts are relatively weak political actors, national judges might welcome an external corroboration of the illegality of a government's action.

But there are also reasons for national judges to reject the notion that international law and IC rulings generate domestically binding higher order laws. In the United States, opponents of international legal authority regularly argue that the national democratic will should trump international legal obligations, that governments should not be able to use international law to circumvent domestic processes, and that national court rulings should be based purely on analyses of domestic laws and the

19 On the French relationship to international law, see Alter (2001, chapter 4).

20 Restatement (Third) of Foreign Relations Law § 115(3) (1987) discussed in Sloss (2009b). See also Sloss, Ramsey, and Dodge (2011).

21 (Nollkaemper 2011; Nollkaemper and Nijman 2007; Sloss 2009a). See also Benvenisti (2008).

national constitution.[22] The European version of this argument goes by the name of "constitutional patriotism," the belief that the national constitution reflects the country's heritage and as such provides the best protection for citizens compared to other constitutions or international legal texts.[23] The fact that the American and German constitutional systems tend to generate these arguments suggests that systems with powerful domestic constitutional courts may see embracing higher order international law as unnecessary if not undermining of the national constitutional order.

This discussion shows that international constitutional review is not about a simple binary choice of compliance versus noncompliance with the international law. Compliance decisions may occur independently of any sense that international law is higher order law. Moreover, not all international legal obligations will be seen as higher order law. This makes sense. It is the job of judges to engage in proportionality balancing and to resolve conflicts across disparate legal provisions. Thus we should expect judges to create pecking orders among competing international and constitutional provisions.

The key insight is that the tacit endorsement of national high court judges is a necessary condition for international law to draw on the domestic cultures of constitutional obedience as a resource for international law. National judges can decide on a case-by-case basis whether a specific international law trumps a specific domestic law, or they may find domestic legal reasons to justify adhering to international law. Domestic judges can reject an IC's interpretation of this law as legally binding, or they can embrace the broader notion that certain international laws create higher order limits on what is domestically allowed.[24] In other words, even if constitutional obedience to international law may, once given, be difficult to rescind, its terms can be constantly finessed through legal and political contestation.

Critics of international courts suggest that international judges inevitably overstep their authority. For this reason, it is important to note that certain ICs have in fact been delegated jurisdiction to review the validity of state and international acts. It is also important to remember that the

22 See, for example, McGinnis (2007); Rabkin (2005). For a counter to these arguments, see Buchanan (2006).

23 Jan Werner Müller provides one example of the idea of constitutional patriotism as a less nationalistic way to create a sense of belonging to a society, which suggests that social attachments are national rather than global or cosmopolitan (Müller 2007). Of course the German version of this argument is not nearly as skeptical about international law as the American version, suggesting that constitutional patriotism can coexist with higher order international law.

24 An edited volume identifies variation in national judicial willingness to help enforce treaties. See Sloss (2009b).

alternative to ICs conducting constitutional review may be that international actions are beyond any judicial review. But the real question is when and how ICs are able to contribute to or partake of cultures of constitutional obedience. The next two sections discuss ICs as they exercise a constitutional review role. Section II shows ICs reviewing international legal acts, and acting carefully so as not to overreach. Section III shows ICs in morphed constitutional review roles that are limited or bolstered by national judicial positions regarding the supremacy of international law in the national legal order.

II. CONSTITUTIONAL REVIEW OF INTERNATIONAL LEGISLATIVE ACTS

ICs with constitutional review jurisdiction over international acts have an exclusive and mandatory jurisdiction that provides litigants a legal means to challenge and perhaps invalidate supranational acts. The most prevalent arguments made in such challenges are that international acts exceed the competence of the institution, conflict with higher order laws, or were made without allowing the full voice and participation of constituent actors. While there are many examples of ICs reviewing the validity of international acts and making constitutionally important rulings, there are fewer examples of ICs' invalidating international legislative acts. This section considers two cases selected because the IC invalidated an international legislative act that enjoyed strong government support. In both cases the ICs defended their constitutional review prerogatives and developed constitutional principles with a prospective reach, while being careful to make their rulings politically palatable.

8.1. "Peru Exemptions Case"—ATJ invalidates a decision exempting Peru from Free Trade Area

The Andean Tribunal of Justice has a separate nullification procedure for challenges to Andean Secretariat *Resoluciones* (administrative review) and *Decisiones* of the collective Andean Council of Foreign Ministers or the Andean Commission (a supranational legislative body analogous to the European Council of Ministers). By the end of 2011, the ATJ had issued fifty-two nullification rulings. The case discussed here involves the Junta, the General Secretariat's precursor body, challenging a legislative Decisión authorizing Peru to derogate from the Andean Free Trade Area.

A cornerstone of a common market agreement is the commitment to eliminate internal barriers to trade. The Andean Community has struggled with this commitment, in part because member states have faced a series of severe economic disruptions that have limited the political feasibility of opening markets to regional goods. The Andean General Secretariat has tried to navigate economic crises by allowing exceptions to Andean provisions while trying to make sure that these exceptions are limited in nature, sanctioned by supranational agreement, and temporary. Starting in August 1992, Andean member states passed a series of Decisiones allowing Peru to be exempted from the Andean Free Trade Area. At the time Peru's president was pursuing an economic policy referred to as *Fujishock*, which involved eliminating price and exchange rate controls and reducing subsidies. When prices for basic commodities skyrocketed, the government enacted trade restrictions to stop low-cost regional products from displacing demand for what were now more expensive Peruvian products. The International Monetary Fund encouraged these structural adjustments, rewarding Peru's president with loans. Over time, capital investment flowed into Peru, seemingly vindicating the governments' choice for economic shock therapy.

The economic turmoil called for exempting Peru temporarily from Andean free trade rules. Although the Junta did not like the many Decisiones passed by member states to help Peru, it tried to work within the political process to address what was clearly an exceptional situation. After its efforts to encourage member states to address Peru's situation differently had repeatedly failed, the Junta challenged Decisión 387. This Decisión was not more problematic than others, but because of time limits on raising legal challenges the Junta focused on the most recent Decisión allowing Peru to derogate from the Andean Free Trade Area.[25] The ATJ's discussion of the legal issues included a concern that Peru might be resorting to bilateral agreements in lieu of Andean multilateral policy making, that the Decisión did not adequately address that the Tariff Reduction Program promised an irreversible lowering of internal trade barriers, that the Decisión violated the most-favored-nation trade principle, and that it was the job of the Junta to decide on temporary derogations from common rules.[26]

When the case appeared on the ATJ's docket (November 22, 1996), Peru's situation in the Andean Community was under active discussion. The Sucre Protocol, adopted in 1997, relaunched the Andean integration project and set 2005 as an end time for Peru's special status.[27] The Junta

25 Thanks to Osvaldo Saldias for his help understanding this case.

26 "Peru exemptions case" Point 1.1.

27 Sucre Protocol of July 30, 1997, amended a number of provisions of the Cartagena agreement and included a "transitory provisional chapter" that declared that the Free Trade Area would become operational no later than December 31, 2005, and it allowed Peru to work out with the Commission its entry into the common external tariff system. See http://www.comunidadandina.org/INGLES/normativa/ande_trie4.htm, last visited May 1, 2013.

then tried to withdraw its suit, since the legal issue was now moot.[28] Representatives of the member states also argued that it would be invalid for the ATJ to review this Decisión since so many similar Decisiones had been enacted through the same legal means without the legal validity of the process being challenged. It would undermine legal certainty, they argued, to question a decision adopted many years earlier with the support of the member states.[29]

The Andean Tribunal, however, refused to dismiss the suit, arguing that the Decisiones were "public acts" giving rise to a general interest in ensuring the legality of laws on the books. This interest still existed, the ATJ argued, notwithstanding the Junta's change of mind.[30] The larger issue was that the series of Andean Decisiones pertaining to Peru kept revising the terms of Peru's participation in an ad hoc fashion and without setting a clear end to the derogations. Also, some of the Decisiones allowed Peru to continue to participate in discussions of rules that would not bind it.[31] Although the Sucre Protocol ended the legal and political crisis, ATJ sought to review the precedent that had been set. The ATJ declared that the Decisión in question did in fact violate Andean law primarily for the way it was enacted, but that any illegal aspects of the Decisión had been "purged" by the Sucre Protocol. In other words, Decisión 387 did not need to be nullified because valid law had superseded it. The ATJ distinguished between Decisiones, which are acts adopted by member states, and the Sucre Protocol, which was decided during a "reunión de plenipotenciarios," and which was thus more akin to a constitutional convention than a legislative decision.[32]

The politically astute ruling used the judicial tactic associated with the US Supreme Court's Marbury v. Madison decision.[33] The ATJ defended its constitutional jurisdiction and asserted its power to nullify illegally enacted Decisiones while finding that the particular situation did not require the court to exercise this power. The ATJ did not actually address the legal substance of the Junta's initial complaint, since it is clearly within the power of states to revise the Andean Treaty by adopting the Sucre Protocol. The ruling means that governments must meet at the presidential level

28 "Peru exemptions case," Point 1.4.1.

29 Ibid., Point 1.2.

30 Ibid., Point. 2.2.

31 Decisión 353 (April 4, 1994) had modified the situation allowing Peru to once again be involved in harmonization negotiations. This decision was superseded a few months later by Decisión 377.

32 "Peru exemptions case," Points 2.4 and 2.5.

33 US "Marbury v. Madison." This is a common technique, used also by the ECJ in its "Costa v. Enel ruling" establishing the supremacy of European law. Tom Ginsburg (2003) discusses the importance of this technique in developing judicial authority in Asia.

and issue a formal protocol in order to amend the treaty. But it is actually not very hard to amend the Andean Treaty because there are only four states in the Andean Community, and because it is fairly easy for Andean leaders to convince their national legislative bodies to ratify treaty amendments.[34] The constitutional bar in the Andean context is much lower than the European bar, discussed next.

8.2. "Seizing Private Assets—the Kadi Case"—ECJ invalidates a Council regulation implementing an act of the UN Security Council

In the 1970s, after national courts raised serious questions about the lack of basic rights protection in the European legal system, the ECJ asserted jurisdiction to review the validity of community acts vis-à-vis human rights norms. Eventually, the ECJ's doctrine was incorporated into treaty revisions so that the consolidated European treaty now demands that European acts respect human rights and the rule of law.[35] There are thick casebooks and many journal articles dedicated to the constitutional doctrine of the European Court of Justice, yet law scholars I consulted could identify few ECJ rulings that actually invalidate community legislation. Indeed, the ECJ has a reputation for being less critical of European than it is of national legislative acts. The ECJ's 2008 Kadi decision, however, provides a landmark example of the ECJ playing its explicitly delegated constitutional review role. The Kadi rulings are especially controversial because the law in question implemented an act of the United Nations Security Council.

Chapter VII of the United Nations (UN) charter allows the United Nations Security Council to take any action needed to maintain peace and security. The Security Council resolutions are, for all practicable purposes, binding United Nations legislation. All UN members are obligated to implement UN Security Council resolutions.[36] Since the end of the Cold War (and arguably even before then), the United Nations Security Council has generated a number of resolutions to coordinate state actions so as to address transnational threats to international peace and security. Among these efforts is a system to freeze the assets of people who provide

34 It isn't entirely clear what qualifies as a *reunión de plenipotenciarios*. Would a meeting of heads of states suffice? One difficulty in answering this question is that "Decisiones" are the formal label attached to all Andean laws, and it often isn't clear whether a "Decisión" was adopted at a *reunión de plenipotenciarios* or in a Commission meeting.

35 This requirement is inscribed in Article 6 of the Consolidated European Treaty. De Burca (2011) discusses the EU's legal and political evolutions with respect to human rights starting from the origins of the European Coal and Steel Community through the present.

36 Article 25 of the United Nations Charter states: "The Members of the United Nations agree to accept and carry out the decisions of the Security Council in accordance with the present Charter."

financial support to groups involved in terrorist activities. A special Sanctions Committee, comprised of members of the Security Council, oversees this system by maintaining a "consolidated list" of individuals accused of supporting terrorism. Security Council resolutions require member states to act on decisions of the Sanctions Committee by freezing assets and using all other domestic legal means possible to thwart terrorist activity.[37] From the perspective of UN law, "in the event of conflict between the obligations of the Members of the United Nations under the present Charter and their obligations under any other international agreement, their obligations under the present Charter shall prevail."[38] Moreover, the European Commission, the Council of Ministers, Spain, France, the Netherlands, and the United Kingdom supported the contested Security Council policy, which they had helped to incorporate into European Community law.

Yassin Abdullah Kadi and Al Barakaat International Foundation separately challenged the validity of a European regulation that froze assets of actors identified as supporters of terrorism by the Sanctions Committee. Kadi is a Saudi Arabian businessman seen to be a supporter of terrorism based on connections to Blessed Relief, a Muwafaq charity that allegedly channels support to Al-Qaeda. Al Barakaat is a Swedish organization that is part of the Hawala banking system used by the Somali diaspora to transfer funds back home. Both litigants ended up on the United Nations' consolidated list because they appeared on a US list of "specially designated global terrorists." Targeted individuals can ask their government to request that the Sanctions Committee delist them, but it takes unanimous consent within the Committee for this to occur. Thus in reality, a single country can create an internationally binding listing that results in the freezing of assets around the world. While amendments allow for the release of funds for food, medical expenses, and legal fees, an individual's ability to travel and run a business is severely impacted by the freezing of assets. The Swedish government intervened on behalf of Al Barakaat, trying to determine why Al Barakaat had been listed as a supporter of terrorism. A diplomat I spoke with about this case expressed frustration that his request to see the evidence against Al Barakaat was basically ignored. Both Kadi and Al Barakaat were investigated by a number of European governments based on their listing, but all criminal investigations ended with charges being dropped.[39]

37 There are many resolutions to this effect. One example is: S.C. Res. 1363, U.N. Doc. S/RES/1363 (July 30, 2001). Elsewhere De Burca discusses the increasingly legislative nature of UN acts and the challenges Security Council actions create for international law more generally (De Burca 2010, 9).

38 Article 103 of the UN Charter.

39 (Zgonec-Rožej 2009, 306).

The Kadi and Al Barakaat cases were heard in the ECJ's first instance General Court (at the time called the Tribunal of First Instance), which in the past has required meaningful due process protections for European procedures that sanction individuals.[40] On behalf of the member states, the Council argued that for the Tribunal of First Instance to question the validity of UN acts would put member states in a difficult legal position vis-à-vis their UN obligations, and perhaps undermine the entire UN system.[41] The Commission and Council suggested that the appropriate route of appeal was for Saudi Arabia to argue Kadi's case in front of the Sanctions Committee. In the Al Barakaat case, the Tribunal of First Instance suggested such intervention can be effective, noting that Swedish intervention led to two individuals being removed from the consolidated list.[42] Accepting the general thrust of these arguments, the Tribunal of First Instance refused to review the contested EU regulation arguing that UN legal obligations ipso facto trump European law.[43] The two cases were combined in the appeal that was lodged in front of the ECJ. For space reasons, I focus on only a few salient aspects of the ECJ's ruling.

In the appeal, community institutions and member states reiterated their arguments about the lack of community competence and the supremacy of UN rules. The ECJ approached UN law much like a domestic judge approaches the question of the binding nature of international law in the domestic order.[44] The ECJ found that acts of the UN Security Council may have primacy over secondary European legislation but not over primary European law. The ECJ noted that respect for human rights is a condition for the lawfulness of community acts, thus "the obligations imposed by an international agreement cannot have the effect of prejudicing the constitutional principles of the EC Treaty, which include the principle that all Community acts must respect fundamental rights, that respect constituting a condition of their lawfulness."[45] Indeed, the ECJ rejected the Tribunal of First Instance's willingness to defer to the United Nations, arguing that the idea that "the principle of the primacy at the level of international law of obligations under the Charter of the United Nations . . . cannot find a basis in the EC Treaty."[46]

The ECJ identified specific procedural problems with the way the UN Sanctions Committee dealt with applicants who requested their removal

40 (Eckes 2008, 210–20).

41 "Kadi I decision (Tribunal of First Instance)." See especially ¶174.

42 "Al Barakaat decision." ¶318

43 For a discussion of the limitations of a "radical monist" view regarding the supreme authority of UN obligations, see Kumm (2009); Murkens (2009, 274–79).

44 (De Burca 2010, 3).

45 "Kadi I (ECJ decision)."

46 "Kadi I (ECJ decision)." ¶¶299–300.

from the sanctioning list, indicating which elements of the Sanctions Committee process needed reform. In specific it noted that evidence used against individuals must be communicated, and plaintiffs must have a way to contest such evidence. Because no legal body could review the appropriateness of the Sanctions Committee's listing of Kadi and the Al Barakaat International Foundation, the ECJ found that the plaintiffs had not been given their fundamental right to a legal remedy.[47] The ECJ annulled the offending regulation with respect to the plaintiffs and ordered the community to pay half of the applicants' legal fees. But the ECJ allowed the European Council to continue its restrictive measures vis-à-vis Kadi and Al Barakaat for three more months.

The first and more vocal political reaction was to criticize the ruling as trespassing on the authority of the United Nations, while putting member states in a bind since they are obliged to implement decisions of the Security Council. But the ECJ was not alone in its critique of the UN system to list supporters of terrorism. National courts within member states have also raised concerns,[48] and there exists a less vocal basis of support for the ECJ position among governments, judges, and civil society groups, though not per se for the litigants' claim that they had been wrongly listed. Indeed, the ECJ faced the very real prospect that national courts within member states might find the EU regulation to be unconstitutional,[49] as might the European Court of Human Rights, which also insists that European rules implementing Security Council acts are subject to review.[50]

The United Nations Sanctions Committee (a.k.a. the 1267 Committee) had already taken note of growing national legal concerns about the sanctions regime. In its first report, issued in 2004, the monitoring team noted that "a further issue that needs resolution is the procedure by which a name may be removed from the list, whether by a listing state, or as a

47 "Kadi I (ECJ decision)." ¶351.

48 The national cases are noted in "Kadi II (ECJ/General Court) decision." See ¶122. Monitoring team reports for the Sanctions Committee include lists of national litigation. See notes 51, 52, and 62 for citations.

49 Murkens quotes from an interview with the president the German Constitutional Court, issued before the Kadi decision, in which the judge suggested that if a case arose involving a German national, the German Constitutional Court would need to explore a number of legal questions because Security Council resolutions lacked effective judicial protections for affected persons. "Ohne Wenn und Aber," in *Der Spiegel*, March 24, 2008, cited in Murkens (2009, n. 145).

50 The ECtHR has adjudicated cases where the the ECJ had previously issued a preliminary ruling, and thus the ECJ arguably was right to be concerned that both the General Court and its own rulings might be found wanting by the ECtHR. See the discussion of the Bosphorus Hava Yollari Turiizm ve Icaret Antonim Sirketi v. Ireland, 45036/98 Eur. Ct. H.R. 30 (2005) in Kumm (2009, 280–86). In fact, the ECtHR has gone on to confirm the ECJ's Kadi ruling in "ECtHR ruling on UN Sanctions System: Nada v. Switzerland."

result of appeal by the individual or entity concerned."[51] Subsequent reports included a summary of litigation proceeding in a broad range of countries. The ninth Sanctions Committee report, issued in 2009, noted that

> the decision of the Court of Justice of the European Communities in Qadi [Kadi] has changed the terms of this debate. Action by the courts has largely pre-empted any initiative that the Security Council might have taken, however unlikely, to create its own independent review mechanism. The fact that European courts have joined American courts in asserting their jurisdiction over national implementation procedures means that in this context they will in effect offer an independent review of listing decisions by the Committee when these are challenged before them.[52]

Following the ECJ's ruling, France requested the reasons for Kadi's listing by the Sanctions Committee. A newspaper article concerning this dispute suggested that the United States then presented "no direct evidence linking Mr. Kadi to terrorism," but instead "made public a dense labyrinth of associations and business and personal ties that it says establishes Mr. Kadi's relationship with Mr. bin Laden and his allies." Since there were no criminal charges, Kadi never had a chance to challenge the evidence.[53] The Commission incorporated the divulged information in a letter conveyed to Kadi, who then asked to see the evidence against him. The Council changed the contested regulation,[54] after which the Commission noted that it took into account Kadi's letter but determined again that Kadi's assets should be frozen. In its second letter to Kadi, the Commission explained that in changing the regulation, conveying the reasons for his listing and considering his response, the European Community had now fully complied with the ECJ's Kadi ruling.[55]

51 First report of the Monitoring Team: Letter dated August 23, 2004, from the chairman of the Security Council Committee established pursuant to resolution 1267 (1999), ¶41, available at http://www.un.org/sc/committees/1267/monitoringteam.shtml, last visited May 2, 2013.

52 Ninth report of the Monitoring Team: Letter dated May 11, 2009, from the chairman of the Security Council Committee established pursuant to resolution 1267 (1999) concerning Al-Qaida and the Taliban and associated individuals and entities addressed to the president of the Security Council, ¶27, available at http://www.un.org/sc/commit tees/1267/monitoringteam.shtml, last visited May 2, 2013.

53 Landon Thomas, "A Wealthy Saudi Mired in Limbo over an Accusation of Terrorism," *New York Times*, Saturday Profile, December 12, 2008, http://www.nytimes.com /2008/12/13/world/middleeast/13kadi.html?pagewanted=all, last visited March 20, 2012.

54 Commission Regulation (EC) No 1190/2008 of November 28, 2008, amending Council Regulation (EC) No 881/2002 (OJ 2008 L 322, p. 25).

55 France's response is noted in the "Kadi II (ECJ/General Court) decision," ¶49. The reforms and new procedures are discussed in ¶¶60–62.

In 2009, fifteen months after the ECJ's Kadi decision, the Security Council adopted Resolution 1904, which explicitly acknowledged the "legal and otherwise" challenges to the existing regime required greater transparency of information supporting an individual's listing. The resolution also created an ombudsman that private actors could appeal to directly to challenge their listing. The ombudsman gathers information from member states and individuals, and assembles a "comprehensive report."

Supporters of the UN sanctions regime remained adamant that members of the Committee alone determine who gets listed as a supporter of terrorism. Its eleventh report suggested that the Sanctions Committee saw the ombudsperson as siphoning away pressure on national courts. Putting a positive spin on the reality that litigants were still pursuing national and regional litigation, the October 2012 report notes that "the locus of the legal debate around listing and delisting has moved back to the Security Council and the Committee and away from national and regional courts. Petitioners for delisting have benefited accordingly. While national and regional courts and treaty bodies may have had some indirect impact on a very small number of the Committee's decisions on delisting the ombudsperson process has resolved a substantial number of cases relatively quickly."[56] Later, however, the report notes that the Kadi litigation was still proceeding, and with it "the potential to damage the regime or to distract it from looking forward."[57]

Yassin Abdullah Kadi challenged his relisting in front of Europe's first instance General Court. During legal proceedings the Commission noted that its review only concerns "manifest errors of fact or assessment, such as an error to the identity of the person indicated," because it is not for the community to substitute its own assessment of evidence for that of the Sanctions Committee. The General Court noted that the ECJ's Kadi decision had generated significant controversy. Even though the General Court declared that it is "not bound to the points of law" in the ECJ's Kadi ruling, judges found that the appellate principle of legal hierarchy meant that it was also not for the General Court to reverse the ECJ's Kadi ruling. The General Court thus faithfully applied the Kadi decision, rejecting both the revision of the regulation and the Commission's response to Kadi. The ECJ, the General Court's judges argued, clearly intended legal review to include "not only the apparent merits of the contested measure

56 Twelfth report of the Monitoring Team: Letter dated October 1, 2012, from the chair of the Security Council Committee pursuant to resolutions 1267 (1999) and 1989 (2011) concerning Al-Qaida and associated individuals and entities to the president of the Security Council, ¶30, available at http://www.un.org/sc/committees/1267/monitoringteam.shtml, last visited May 2, 2013.

57 Ibid., ¶33.

but also . . . the evidence and information on which the findings . . . are based." The General Court's criticism of European Union and Security Council actions was even more blunt this second time. The ruling noted that the "Security Council has still not deemed it appropriate to establish an independent and impartial body responsible for hearing and determining, as regards matters of law and fact, actions against individual decisions taken by the Sanctions Committee." It found specific European and UN procedures lacked in due process, and it characterized the Commission's correspondence with Kadi as containing "general, unsubstantiated, vague and unparticularised allegations." As to the Commission's claim to have complied with the ECJ's ruling, the Court noted that "the applicant's rights of defense have been 'observed' only in the most formal and superficial sense." The Commission "failed to take due account of the applicant's comments . . . [and] did not grant him even the most minimal access to the evidence against him."[58] This time the General Court annulled the regulation as it concerned Mr. Kadi, because the European Union had violated his right to property and effective judicial review.

This second criticism, after the many Sanctions Committee reforms, stung. By the time of the General Court ruling, the United Nations was publishing individuals and entities listed as supporters of terrorism, and making a narrative of the reasoning for the listing available on the Internet.[59] It had an ombudsman, who had managed to facilitate the delisting of some individuals. But under Resolution 1904 the Sanctions Committee retained absolute and unquestionable control over the listing of individuals.[60] The latest available report of the Sanctions Committee (December 31, 2012) noted that although the reformed sanctions regime seemed to have reached a stable equilibrium, two factors could upset this stability. The first was the General Court's criticism in its second Kadi ruling. The second was a recent ruling by the European Court of Human Rights that confirmed the ECJ's Kadi I ruling and legal analysis.[61]

Its most recent report shows the Sanctions Committee struggling to maintain its relevance as the primary authoritative source for naming supporters of terrorism. Compliance with the regime remains a problem, with governments under pressure not to block assets.[62] Moreover, the list

58 "Kadi II (ECJ/General Court decision)," ¶¶94–96. Quotes from ¶¶96, 115, 121, 135, 128, 157 and 171–73.

59 The website of the Committee has much information. The narratives on individual listings are located at http://www.un.org/sc/committees/1267/narrative.shtml, last visited May 2, 2013.

60 UN Security Council resolution 1904 (S/RES/1904 [2009]), adopted December 17, 2009.

61 "ECtHR ruling on UN Sanctions System: Nada v. Switzerland."

62 Twelfth report of the Monitoring Team: Letter dated December 31, 2012, from the chair of the Security Council Committee pursuant to resolutions 1267 (1999) and 1989

remains fairly stagnant: "The Committee has devoted a great deal of effort to improving its list. It has accepted proposals by the Monitoring Team to make around 400 amendments to the list since March 2004, turning vague references to poorly identified targets into actionable entries with sufficient identifying details to allow States to apply the measures." The ombudsman has dealt with a number of complaints, but it seems to be mostly removing dead individuals and defunct organizations from existing lists so as to make the lists shorter and thus more useful.[63] The report's authors saw the Committee's many efforts as meaning that "Member States have little justification for incomplete compliance with the sanctions measures on the grounds that the regime lacks fairness," so that the committee might then adopt a stricter approach to insisting that member states comply with the regime.[64] Still, "one disappointment for the Security Council and the Committee must be that, despite all these efforts to improve the list and the procedures for listing and delisting, more States have not come forward with the submission of names. It is still generally the same small group of countries that is most active in proposing new entries (or deletions)."[65] The report subtly suggested that the regime be assessed to ascertain whether the costs associated with the regime bring with them meaningful benefits, in the form of effective limitations of the flow of money to terrorist organizations.[66]

Mr. Kadi continued a variety of legal campaigns to gain access to his assets around the world. In response to a General Court decision releasing the assets of other listed supporters of terrorism, the British government noted that, "We accept . . . that the application of targeted measures to individuals and entities must take account of their fundamental rights and respect due process. . . . The UK will work with EU partners to address the reasons identified by the court as to why they found in favour of [the plaintiff]."[67] According to web blogs, the European Commission, Council, and the United Kingdom have appealed the General Court ruling. Meanwhile, the United Nations apparently delisted Kadi as a supporter of terrorists in October 2012. Critics note that the EU only delisted Kadi once the Sanctions Committee decided that he was not a supporter of terror-

---

(2011) concerning Al-Qaida and associated individuals and entities to the president of the Security Council, ¶27–29, available at http://www.un.org/sc/committees/1267/monitoring team.shtml, last visited May 2, 2013.

63 Ibid., ¶37.

64 Ibid., ¶23.

65 Ibid., ¶39.

66 This was one of many recommendations, including improving the outreach of the Sanctions Committee in an effort to build support for the regime. Ibid., ¶¶20–29.

67 Alan Travis, "EU Court Releases Abu Qatada Assets," *The Guardian*, June 11, 2009, http://www.guardian.co.uk/uk/2009/jun/11/abu-qatada-assets-released-binladen, last visited March 20, 2012.

ism.[68] The UN system has greatly changed. There is more transparency, a publication of evidence and a way to challenge listings. It remains unclear, however, whether the new review mechanisms are what the ECJ asked for. Clearly erroneous listings can now be addressed, but there is still no means of obtaining an independent review of ambiguous evidence. The situation remains in flux.

Section IV will review the altered politics of these two cases, in comparison to the next four cases.

III. INTERNATIONAL CONSTITUTIONAL REVIEW OF STATE ACTS

The question remains whether in demanding state compliance with international rules, international legal bodies become de facto constitutional review bodies. Thirty years ago, most domestic lawyers would have answered this question with a resounding "no," explaining that IC rulings leave domestic acts legally intact. Although this is still true formally speaking, increasingly we find that IC rulings undermine political support for existing policies. Knowing that their rulings will be embraced, some ICs have asked for changes in national policies that have engendered the same substantive effect as a national constitutional review. These case studies suggest that the varying ability of ICs to draw on domestic cultures of constitutional obedience shapes how ICs exercise their constitutional law-making authority. Where ICs expect their ruling to be seen as domestically obligatory, they are more willing to create positive obligations for domestic actors. Where ICs cannot draw on domestic cultures of law obedience, they will usually still declare violations of the law and their rulings may help to build compliance constituencies, but ICs may also limit the remedies they order so as to avoid provoking greater noncompliance.

8.3. "Women in Combat Support Roles"—ECJ rejects a German constitutional provision disallowing women in combat support roles

The requirement for gender equity is based in the Treaty of Rome, which stipulated that there must be equal pay for men and women.[69] This treaty provision has been elaborated through secondary legislation into a requirement of equal treatment for men and women. For a long time, gov-

68 "Kadi de-listed—A cause for celebration?" The posting notes that the EU followed the UN in delisting Kadi, still never conducting its own review of Kadi's listing. http://europeanlawblog.eu/?p=1192, last visited May 2, 2013.

69 This provision is currently Article 141 of the Consolidated Treaty.

ernments and European officials presumed that the military was exempt from European gender equality requirements. Article 2(2) of the European Community's 1976 Equal Treatment directive included a provision noting that "this Directive shall be without prejudice to the right of Member States to exclude from its field of application those occupational activities and, where appropriate, the training leading thereto, for which by reason of their nature or the context in which they are carried out, the sex of the worker constitutes a determining factor."[70] The military was seen as falling under this exception.

Angela Maria Sirdar challenged the military's blanket exemption from Europe's equal treatment laws in 1994, raising a suit in a British court against the decision to deny her a job as a cook in the British Royal Marines. British law, which had been created before the European Equal Treatment directive, created a clear exception to gender equality requirements for the military.[71] As required under European law, the British court referred the case to the ECJ. The ECJ's Sirdar v. Army Board ruling rejected the British argument that the military was exempt from European equality law requirements, but the ECJ agreed that the Royal Marines can exclude women even from positions as cooks because the Royal Marines are a "special force" within the British military relying on the military cohesion of its all male membership.[72]

While the Sirdar case was pending, Tanja Kreil applied for a job in the German Bundeswehr in weapon electronics maintenance. The German constitution expressly forbids women from military positions involving armaments.[73] As in the Sirdar case, this challenge appeared in a domestic court, which referred the case to the ECJ. During legal proceedings, the German, Italian, and UK governments once again argued that decisions concerning the organization and combat capacity of the armed forces lay outside the scope of community law.[74] The European Court again rejected this argument, asserting: "Although it is for the Member States . . . to take decisions on the organization of their armed forces, it does not follow that

70 This case discussion is adapted from Alter (2009, 252–56). Council Directive 76/207/EEC of February 9, 1976, on Equal Treatment for Men and Women in Employment. OJ [1976] L 39/40.

71 Article 85 (4) of the United Kingdom's 1975 Sex Discrimination Act states: "nothing in this Act shall render unlawful an act done for the purpose of ensuring the combat effectiveness of the naval, military or air forces."

72 ECJ "Sirdar decision."

73 German Basic Law stated: "If, while a state of defense exists, civilian service requirements in the civilian public health and medical system or in the stationary military hospital organization cannot be met on a voluntary basis, women between eighteen and fifty-five years of age may be assigned to such services by or pursuant to a law. They may on no account render service involving the use of arms." (Article 12 a (4)).

74 ECJ "Kreil decision," Points 12–13.

such decisions must fall entirely outside the scope of Community law." The ECJ found that the exclusion of women from working with armaments violated the European Community's Equal Treatment directive.[75]

The ECJ's ruling suggested that the German constitution needed to change. The government was happy to see itself as bound by the ECJ's ruling. German opinion on the role of women in the military had been evolving. In the 1970s, the peace movement was a chief opponent of a greater role for women, mainly because without an army of sufficient size deployment would not be an option. Staffing shortages in the past led to adjustments in the constitutional ban on women in the military. In the 1970s, notwithstanding the Social Democrats' general desire to promote "The Year of the Woman," opposition to women in the military was such that the German Parliament could only agree to allow women in the military's medical services, thereby relieving a shortage of medical service staff in the Bundeswehr.[76] In 1991 women were granted the right to serve in the band.[77] Then in the 1990s, Germany's Red-Green coalition agreed to deploy the German military as part of NATO operations in the former Yugoslavia, which in itself signified a defeat of the peace movement and a change in German attitudes. This shift also put the military under new resource constraints. German law prohibited the stationing of conscripts outside of Germany. If the German government wanted to participate in more international missions, it needed to grow its volunteer army. While the German military initially opposed a broader role for women, participation in NATO deployments also contributed to attitudinal shifts within the military.

Notwithstanding the growing support for wider female participation in the military, German policy would not have changed without the ECJ decision—at least not when it changed. Writing in *Die Zeit* the week of the ECJ decision, Constanze Stelzenmüller argued that it was not a question of "if" Germany would change its constitution—since it *must* in light of the ECJ ruling—but rather *how* Germany would change its constitution.[78] Gerhard Kümmel concurred: "recent steps to open the Bundeswehr to women do not stem from genuinely political initiatives as one may have thought, but from a court ruling that required the political sphere to take some action."[79] Indeed, most observers credit the ECJ's Kreil ruling with provoking the change in the German constitution. And most observers saw the change as required by the ECJ's ruling.

75 Ibid.
76 (Liebert 2002, 13).
77 (Kümmel 2003, 3).
78 (Stelzenmüller 2000).
79 (Kümmel 2003, 4).

This sense that change was required is a result of the culture of constitutional obedience to both basic rights law and to higher order European Union law. The German Constitutional Court has created a constitutional obligation to ensure that litigants have access to their legal judge, and they have interpreted this obligation to mean that German judges are constitutionally obliged to refer cases involving European law to the ECJ, and to apply ECJ rulings wherever the ECJ is the "legal judge." One can question whether the ECJ was in fact the legal judge in this case, especially given that the German Constitutional Court has also asserted the supremacy of the German constitution over European law.[80] But this issue never arose because the government readily declared itself bound by the ECJ's ruling. Changing the German constitution did not prove difficult. Only one member of the Bundestag spoke against the ECJ decision as "a clear transgression," because in his view the domain of the military does not fall under the jurisdiction of the European Union.[81] Within ten months Germany had changed its constitution and initiated an extensive transformation of the German military, allowing women to assume more roles and working to dismantle remaining social resistance to women in the military.[82]

The ECJ has not been immune to political concerns regarding the issue of women in the military. A few years after the Kreil decision, Alexander Dory invoked European law to challenge the validity of Germany's policy of compulsory military service for men.[83] The German government again argued that the organization of the military remained part of member states' exclusive powers, and thus was entirely outside the scope of community law. The ECJ again rejected this argument, but it found that male-only conscription does not violate European law and suggested that certain aspects of military organization do remain fully within national control.[84] Some commentators interpreted the Dory decision as a response to criticism of the Sirdar and Kreil decisions. For example, Beate Rudolf suggests that the ECJ avoided for political reasons the logical finding that either Germany conscript women or eliminate military conscription altogether.[85] But the ECJ is not alone in limiting equality provisions to allow for gender-biased military drafting laws. In Rostker v. Goldberg, the US

80 This German doctrine is discussed in Alter (2001, 103–8).

81 (Liebert 2002, 16).

82 The number of women in the military went from 4,173 in 1999 to 7,734 in 2002, with 2,752 women serving in armed troops. For more on the larger changes brought by the incorporation of women into a wider variety of military roles, see Kummel (2003); Liebert (2002).

83 ECJ "Dory decision."

84 (Rudolf 2005, 674–75).

85 Ibid., 678.

Supreme Court also found the practice of requiring only men to register for the draft to be constitutional.[86] In any event, Germany decided to end conscription in June 2011 primarily for financial reasons.[87]

8.4. *"Colombia and Ecuador Alcohol-Related Practices"—ATJ finds that municipal practices in Colombia violate Andean free trade rules*

The ATJ has incorporated the ECJ's supremacy doctrine so that as a matter of law[88] Andean countries have the same obligation to prioritize community rules as Germany faced in the Kreil case.[89] But the Andean Community has not been able to create the sort of constitutional obedience one finds in Europe. Chapter 6 discussed the ATJ's ruling regarding second use patents, where national intellectual property agencies embraced the legal obligation to comply with the ATJ ruling. Chapter 7 discussed complex litigation over the Belmont trademark. National judges asked to ratify the legal outcomes proved willing to follow the lead of national intellectual property administrators. This rather complicated case study, however, shows that some Andean supreme courts embrace the supremacy of Andean law while others remain hesitant to grant to Andean law a higher order legal status within the national legal order.

The Colombia and Ecuador alcohol dispute unfolded over many years and in a number of different venues. Ecuador first challenged Colombian alcohol licensing and tax policies in 1991. Ecuador also unilaterally retaliated by creating restrictions that essentially barred Colombian alcohol products from entering the Ecuadorian market. Venezuela later brought a new complaint against Colombia's municipal alcohol practices in February 1996. The Venezuelan complaint led to Resolución 453, a reasoned opinion by the Andean Junta condemning Colombia for violating Andean law. When Colombia's government ignored the Resolución, the Junta raised a noncompliance suit in front of the Andean Tribunal.[90] There was also a parallel case involving Ecuador's retaliation against Colombian practices. The Andean Junta refused to link the two cases, and instead issued a reasoned opinion condemning Ecuador's restriction of Colombian alcohol imports.[91] The upshot of these investigations was that both

86 US *Rostker v. Goldberg* 453 U.S. 57 (1981).

87 Quentin Peel, "Germany's CDU Votes to End Conscription," *Financial Times*, November 17, 2010. http://www.ft.com/intl/cms/s/0/69d7359c-f179-11df-8609-00144feab49a.html#axzz1peOuJXcH, last visited March 19, 2012.

88 Thanks to Larry Helfer, Ryan Mellske, and Osvaldo Saldias for their help untangling this complicated case.

89 (Alter and Helfer 2011, 706–7).

90 For a number of years the Junta insisted that its Resoluciones had the same legal effect as an ATJ decision. The case was raised October 20, 1997. Resolución 453, Gaceta Oficial del Acuerdo del Cartagena, Año XIII—Número 249.

91 Resolución 454, Gaceta Oficial del Acuerdo del Cartagena, Año XIII—Número 249.

Colombia's municipal alcohol practices and Ecuador's retaliation violated Andean law.

While the noncompliance case against Colombia was still pending, a private citizen (Maria Carolina Rodriguez Ruiz) asked the Colombian Constitutional Court to review the constitutionality of the base law that allowed for a state monopoly on alcohol. The law in question is part of the Colombian constitution, and as such it falls under the purview of the Constitutional Court. But the constitution does not define the terms of the national monopoly, and all actors involved seem to agree that having an alcohol monopoly does not per se violate Andean Community rules.[92] Instead, Colombia's noncompliance with Andean rules is a result of municipal practices that set minimum price and licensing requirements, undercutting price advantages from other Andean countries and making it onerous for alcohol produced outside of Colombia to be sold locally. These practices fall within the prerogatives of local governments, and as such they were arguably not part of the Constitutional Court's legal purview. Still, one could imagine that the Colombian Constitutional Court might see itself partially responsible for ensuring that Colombian policy coheres with international legal obligations, or that it might follow the German Constitutional Court's approach of requiring national judges at the appropriate level to ensure respect for Andean law.

Instead, the Constitutional Court seemed to undermine the legal status of Andean rules in the Colombian legal order. The Constitutional Court reasoned that unlike human rights treaties that have quasi-constitutional status in Colombia, Andean laws were equivalent to domestic legislation. Because such laws "and the Constitution do not share the same hierarchy, nor are [they] an intermediate legal source between the Constitution and ordinary domestic laws . . . contradictions between a domestic law and Andean community law will not have as a consequence the non-execution of the [domestic] law." The Court also noted that community law has "primacy" over conflicting national law—a concept that the Constitutional Court interpreted to mean that community law "displaces but does not abrogate or render non-executable" conflicting national legislation.[93]

92 This view was upheld in the Junta's reasoned opinion (Resolución 453) and in the subsequent ATJ ruling. Such a position is compatible with both European and WTO legislation, which permit monopolies so long as state practices do not discriminate against foreign producers.

93 Article 93 of Colombia's 1993 constitution states: "International treaties and agreements ratified by the Congress that recognize human rights and that prohibit their limitation in states of emergency have priority domestically." (Under ATJ "Colombian Constitutional Court Alcohol Ruling" Section 3.1.) The Constitutional Court ruling notes that international human rights agreements ratified by Colombia are part of a "bloque de constitucionalidad," which gives them a status superior to the national law.

Probably unbeknownst to the Colombian court, the Ecuadorian Supreme Court ruled two weeks earlier on a private litigant case that challenged Ecuador's retaliation against Colombia's alcohol policy. Ecuador's Supreme Court also failed to make a preliminary ruling reference as required under Andean law, but in contrast to the Colombian Constitutional Court the Ecuadorian Supreme Court invoked its obligations under Andean law and accepted the "preeminence of community over national law," which it interpreted as "requir[ing] that national regulations not conflict with the higher-level legal norms" of Andean law.[94] There were thus conflicting supreme court precedents regarding the supremacy of Andean law in national legal orders issued in cases that were substantively linked.

The ATJ issued its noncompliance rulings nearly six months later, quoting from the national court rulings. The ATJ refrained from condemning the national supreme courts for failing to refer the cases, but it openly (and separately) condemned both Ecuador and Colombia for their violations. The ATJ made it clear that it concurred with the view of the Colombian Constitutional Court, explicitly noting there was no inherent conflict between the Colombian Constitution's authorization of an alcohol monopoly and Andean law. It was the implementation of this monopoly that was a problem. The Colombian government had tried to introduce a common system of taxation for alcohol products, but municipal licensing and price floor policies persisted. The ATJ found that municipal practices were in violation of Andean law, and declared that Colombia was obliged under Andean law to correct the problem.[95] The respective governments ignored both of these rulings. Ecuador's governments had, however, accepted the ruling of its supreme court. But a different Ecuadorian agency then issued a new barrier to Colombian alcohol imports, reintroducing the Ecuadorian violation in explicit contravention of the ATJ ruling, which had barred the enactment of *any* barrier not authorized by Andean law.[96]

The litigant who had instigated the Colombian Constitutional appeal went on to ask the Colombian Consejo de Estado to nullify a presidential act that clarified details of the alcohol monopoly. As required, the Consejo referred the questions involving Andean law to the ATJ. The legal issue at stake was not straightforward. Rodriguez Ruiz argued that that the

94 Judgment of May 15, 1998, cited in "Internal Judgment of Ecuador, Alcohol dispute," section XIII.

95 ATJ "Colombia alcohol decision." The ATJ acknowledged the "la Ley 223 de 1995 sobre Racionalización Tributaria" attempted to address the problem (see p. 12). See also "ATJ alcohol ruling condemning Ecuador."

96 Resolution No. 004, Ecuador Board of Foreign Trade and Investment (COMEXI), published in *Gaceta Oficial* No. 372 of July 30, 1998.

president lacked the power to issue his decree. Meanwhile, the legislature had subsequently passed legislation on the issue, and the contested decree also did not create the municipal practices that violated Andean law. The plaintiff's claim rested on an assertion that the president's decree had created an encumbrance to the circulation of alcohol products.

The preliminary ruling reference gave the ATJ a chance to speak directly to a Colombian court about a violation of Andean law that it had recognized and condemned. The ATJ had in the past embraced ECJ jurisprudence that requires national judges to set aside national laws that conflict with community law, but it refused to reinforce this position, perhaps out of fear that its edict would be ignored.[97] One might argue that neither the Colombian Constitutional Court nor the Consejo were empowered to nullify the domestic legislation in question, especially because the real culprits—municipal practices—were not part of the cases. In any event, the ATJ avoided confronting the Consejo de Estado. The ATJ did not follow the ECJ in requiring national judges to on their own initiative fill in for what their government had failed to do.[98] Instead, the ATJ declared its own lack of jurisdiction to assess the meaning of domestic legislation and reiterated that the Colombian government is legally bound to change practices that conflict with Andean law.

Meanwhile, a private litigant in Ecuador raised a challenge to the new trade barrier levied on Colombian alcohol products, this time in front of Ecuador's Constitutional Court. Although Ecuador's Constitutional Court, like the Supreme Court before it, eschewed its legal obligation to refer the case to the ATJ, it embraced the supremacy of Andean law and invalidated the illegal administrative action. The Constitutional Court's ruling was the deathblow to Ecuador's retaliation. Ecuador thus complied with the ATJ's noncompliance ruling, but only because its national supreme courts acted to invalidate the illegal regulations.

The Colombian government continued to ignore the ATJ's noncompliance ruling, leading the Secretariat (which replaced the Junta) to initiate a new noncompliance procedure against the government. In March 2000

97 The ECJ sees the Treaty of Rome provision that requires member states to "take all appropriate measures . . . to ensure the fulfillment of obligations arising out of the treaty" as creating an obligation for national courts to do what it takes to apply European law supremacy. (Bebr 1981, 639; De Witte 1984; Pescatore 1983). The Cartagena agreement contains an analogous provision. In its Simmenthal ruling the ECJ argued that "it follows from the forgoing that every national court must, in a case within its jurisdiction, apply Community law in its entirety and protect rights of individuals and must accordingly set aside any provision of national law which may conflict with it, whether prior or subsequent to the Community rule." The ATJ seemingly incorporated this Simmenthal doctrine in its first preliminary rulings (Alter and Helfer 2011, 709–10).

98 ATJ decision 29-IP-98, conclusions 1 and 2 (see legal ruling index for information on how to access ruling).

the ATJ found that Colombia was in noncompliance with its ruling, and in November 2001 the ATJ authorized retaliatory sanctions against Colombia, authorizing the other member states to "impose an additional tax of 5% on up to five products" of Colombian origin, sanctions that were to remain in effect until Colombia provided "clear evidence" that it has "strictly complied" with the noncompliance judgment.[99] There is no evidence that Ecuador, Venezuela, or any other Andean country imposed the penalties authorized by the ATJ, and as of November 2011, Colombia still had not complied with the ATJ's 1998 decision.[100]

Why did the Colombian Constitutional Court seemingly lower the status of Andean law within the Colombian system at the same time that Ecuadorian supreme courts affirmed the supremacy of Andean law? One can only guess at the answer. One plausible explanation is that Andean law only indirectly entered the Colombian cases challenging the alcohol monopoly, meanwhile the contested policy had a long pedigree, and municipal authority over regulating alcohol was well established. Indeed, Colombia's breach of Andean law is not very easy to rectify. The Colombian legislature would need to organize local governments to completely overhaul municipal policy regulating alcohol, all in the service of complying with Andean free trade rules. In other words, what compliance entailed was far more complicated in Colombia than Ecuador. One might also argue that rather than lowering the status of Andean law, the Constitutional Court mainly affirmed the higher-law status of international human rights treaties. Until the 1991 Colombian constitution, international treaties had *no* special standing in Colombian law. The Colombian Constitutional Court's ruling clearly endorsed the notion that human rights treaties have domestic priority. The Constitutional Court has applied these provisions, confronting Colombian leaders regarding human rights abuses, at times invoking the IACtHR's jurisprudence, and repeatedly has suggested that the Inter-American system's human rights obligations are domestically binding.[101] Of course embracing international human rights treaties does not mean that the Colombian court cannot also embrace Andean law.

99 ATJ Alcohol Noncompliance Judgment against Colombia No. paras. 1 and 2.

100 The General Secretariat issued a report listing all cases in which member states had failed to comply with ATJ rulings. Secretaria General Comunidad Andina, *Estado de Dictamenes y Sentencias Pendientes de Cumplimiento y Relación de Acciones de Incumplimiento ante el Tribunal de Justicia de la Comunidad Andina*, Documentos de Trabajo SG/dt 452, E.5, November 29, 2011.

101 (Uprimny 2007). On the Colombian constitution's elevation of human rights treaties, see note 93. The literature I could find on the "bloque de constitutionalidad" suggests that this is a creation of the fairly new Colombia Supreme Court, and that it is not entirely clear what falls inside and outside of this block.

The current legal status of Andean law in Colombia remains a bit puzzling. The Colombian Consejo de Estado assiduously refers all cases involving Andean law to the ATJ, and the Colombian Constitutional Court recognizes that Andean law has primacy over national law, yet it is not clear what this means in practice. Meanwhile, two high courts in Ecuador have endorsed the position that the supremacy of Andean law requires that they invalidate conflicting domestic legislation but eschewed their legal obligation to send a preliminary ruling reference to the ATJ.[102]

The limited willingness of national judges to work with the ATJ to enforce Andean rules presents a challenge for the Andean Tribunal.[103] The ATJ has stuck to its position regarding the supremacy of Andean law in national systems and to its finding of a legal violation regarding Colombia's municipal alcohol policies. In other words, the ATJ has not let concerns about noncompliance shape its rulings on the merits. Although this case study does not bode well for the supremacy of Andean law within national legal orders, we should not forget that the ECJ contended with national high court rulings challenging the supremacy of European law for many years.[104] If one adopts an evolutionary perspective on this issue, it is possible that the alcohol dispute is merely a bump in the road.

8.5. "Indigenous Land Rights Case"—IACtHR creates a positive obligation for Nicaragua to demarcate land rights for the Awas Tingni

The Awas Tingni are a group of roughly 150 families that traditionally hold their land communally. Each family has a small plot of land, which they farm until the soil is depleted. The family then moves, letting the land sit idle for about fifteen years. The community also hunts and maintains ancestral burial grounds. These customary practices mean that the community asserts land rights over territory that it is not at present occupying.[105] The Awas Tingni became concerned about their land rights when in 1993 the Nicaraguan government authorized a Dominican company to inventory tropical forest resources on land the community claimed. Working with the World Wildlife Fund and the University of Iowa College of Law, the community negotiated a lumber contract with the Nicaraguan-Dominican lumber company and the Nicaraguan government.[106] To guarantee this arrangement, the Awas Tingni community began formal proce-

102 Article 33 of the Amended ATJ Court Treaty.

103 We discuss the preliminary ruling practices of national courts in Helfer and Alter (2009).

104 (Alter 2001).

105 (Vuotto 2004, 226–27). Slightly different numbers are given in Anaya and Campbell (2009, 117), but it could be that the population grew or that groups that were considered separate merged.

106 (Grossman 2008, 1276–77).

dures to recognize the full extent of its territorial claims. With the help of a Harvard University center, the community mapped its land claims.[107] During this process, the community discovered that the Nicaraguan government was negotiating a lumber concession on another part of its land with a large South Korean corporation, Solcarsa. The government claimed that the land in question was not marked or in use by the community, and thus that it belonged to the state. The Awas Tingni community then reached out to human rights lawyers.

After futile efforts to negotiate a compromise with government officials regarding the Solcarsa concession, the community filed an injunction to annul the concession. Initial efforts failed because the claim was filed more than thirty days after learning of the concession.[108] The Awas Tingni appealed the court's decision to the Inter-American Commission on Human Rights, which for nearly three years attempted to negotiate a friendly settlement. Meanwhile, in March 1996 the Regional Council of the North Atlantic Coast Autonomous Region tried again, on behalf of the Awas Tingni, to have the Solcarsa concession revoked. This time the Nicaragua Supreme Court found the concession to be illegal, primarily for procedural reasons. The government tried a number of ways to address the procedural concerns while maintaining the Solcarsa concession, but after more legal suits Nicaragua's Supreme Court annulled the concession.[109]

The different international efforts on behalf of the Awas Tingni had created a long paper trail of documented land claims, which made the Awas Tingni a perfect test case for the Indian Law Resource Center.[110] Nicaragua's 1985 constitution affirms indigenous rights to communal land and natural resources. The Nicaraguan National Assembly gave meaning to this right when it granted regional autonomy to Nicaragua's Atlantic Coast region. But stating a right and granting autonomy is not the same as formally recognizing land holdings.

Its efforts at mediation having failed, in 1998 the Inter-American Commission on Human Rights referred the case to the IACtHR.[111] The government argued that the Awas Tingni lacked the legal title and ancestral rights to the land in question, and that the community had never asked Nicaraguan courts to hear their claims about ownership of the disputed land. But there was no clear system in place for indigenous actors to gain

107 The anthropologist was associated with Harvard's Center for International Affairs' Program on Nonviolent Sanctions and Cultural Survival.

108 (Anaya and Campbell 2009, 123).

109 Ibid., at 128–29.

110 (Vuotto 2004, 220). See http://www.indianlaw.org/projects/past_projects/nicaragua, last visited May 1, 2013.

111 The mediation efforts are discussed in Anaya (2009, 271–73).

such rights.[112] Instead, Nicaragua had a slow and cumbersome *amparo* system that could be used to contest infringements of land rights but not to claim land ownership. During the long course of this dispute, the World Bank funded a study to map the land rights in the region. The World Bank report noted that there were unclear, often overlapping local perceptions of land tenure and no system to resolve such disagreements.[113] This report, which largely reiterated the findings of the Inter-American Commission on Human Rights, had been delivered to Nicaragua's government. The government lawyers, however, continued to act as if the national procedures and rules were in fact protecting the land rights of indigenous groups.

The legal proceedings brought together the diverse range of actors supporting the Awas Tingni's legal position. Three Mayagna Indians from the Awas Tingni, the Harvard anthropological researcher who had documented land ownership, and more than a dozen "expert witnesses" from Nicaragua and throughout the Americas testified. Roque de Jesús Roldán Ortega, a witness with over seventeen years of experience working with regional indigenous land claims, argued that if officials had identified a procedure when Nicaragua's constitution and the Law on Autonomy were passed, "the time taken to grant legal title to those lands could have been shortened considerably, to one, two, or three years."[114] The Nicaraguan government's clear record of refusing to acknowledge or remedy an identified problem regarding land titles and its intransigence during the Solcarsa litigation undermined faith in the government's defensive claim that the community had no valid title to the land.

The IACtHR issued its ruling against Nicaragua on August 31, 2001, finding that the Nicaraguan government had failed to provide rights to property guaranteed by its own constitution and the Inter-American Convention on Human Rights, and that available national remedies were insufficient. Whereas the Nicaragua Supreme Court had considered only the validity of the Solcarsa concession, the IACtHR ordered the government to abstain from any acts that "affect the existence, value, use or enjoyment of the property located in the geographic area where the members of the Mayagna (Sumo) Awas Tingni Community live and carry out their activities" and to create a process for all indigenous groups to demarcate

112 IACtHR "Awas Tingni v. Nicaragua." See the discussion of some of the proceedings, in terms of where they stood, at paragraph 103. Noted in Vuotto (2004, 230). For fuller details, see Anaya and Campbell (2009, 128–29).

113 (Hale, Gordon, and Gurdián 1998). There were also other agreements that the government had made, seemingly recognizing the land right, but then not following through (Anaya and Campbell 2009, 122).

114 "k. Expert opinion by Roque de Jesús Roldán Ortega, attorney," reported in "Awas Tingni v. Nicaragua."

their lands. By recognizing the validity of customary land rights claims, and by requiring governments to create a procedure to demarcate and recognize these rights, the IACtHR created a general human right for indigenous groups that was broader than what Nicaragua's constitution required. The IACtHR also ordered the Nicaraguan government to cover the Awas Tingni's legal fees and to provide reparations in the form of investing in works or services to help the Awas Tingni peoples.[115]

The IACtHR is well known for ordering a broad range of remedies for violations of human rights. These remedies are arguably consistent with the Court's explicit authority "to rule that the injured party be ensured the enjoyment of his right or freedom that was violated" and to demand that the "breach of such right or freedom be remedied."[116] The many changes the IACtHR requires, however, contribute to the reality that most IACtHR rulings generate only partial compliance.[117]

At first the Nicaraguan government seemed to ignore the Inter-American Court's ruling. The Solcarsa concession had by then been canceled, so no ongoing violation of the land rights existed. The Indian Law Center continued to push the issue, filing more domestic legal suits to demand that the government respect the ruling. The government covered the Awas Tingni's legal costs in 2002 and worked out a system to invest funds into the Awas Tingni community as required by the IACtHR.[118] The government eventually agreed to create a joint committee of government and Awas Tingni representatives, which worked with a local consultant to perform a diagnostic land use study of the areas in question. This committee released its final report two years after the IACtHR ruling, in October 2003. The Nicaraguan legislature then adopted a comprehensive law for the demarcation and titling of indigenous lands, and the president of Nicaragua assigned his personal advisor to supervise the implementation of the IACtHR's decision.[119] It took a number of years to resolve the overlapping claims. In December of 2008, the Awas Tingni were granted a formal title to their land.[120] In light of the IACtHR ruling, indigenous groups in Surinam, Belize, and Paraguay have raised claims demanding formal recognition of their land rights.[121]

115 IACtHR, "Awas Tingni v. Nicaragua," conclusion 4.

116 Article 63 of the Inter-American Convention on Human Rights (see Court Treaty Bibliography for full citation).

117 (Hawkins and Jacoby 2010).

118 (Anaya and Campbell 2009, 143).

119 Law 445 discussed in Anaya and Campbell (2009, 144–45). See also http://www.indianlaw.org/projects/past_projects/nicaragua, last visited March 20, 2012.

120 See UN expert praises Nicaragua for formally confirming land ownership for indigenous group, at http://www.ohchr.org/en/NewsEvents/Pages/DisplayNews.aspx?NewsID=8443&LangID=E, last visited March 20, 2012.

121 IACtHR, "Other indigenous land right cases Suriname and Paraguay."

An interesting footnote to this case involves the challenge that the Central American Court of Justice has had in asserting its authority in both Nicaragua and Guatemala. Courts in both countries show a willingness to respect the binding nature of judicial decisions of the Inter-American Court of Human Rights, while at the same time they have explicitly rejected aspects of the Central American court's jurisdiction and law.[122] It is possible that a number of countries see regional human rights law as higher order law, while as in Colombia, regional integration law may have more difficulty finding a domestic legal purchase.

8.6. "Rape as a War Crime"—ICTR creates command responsibility to stop sexual violence

Rape has long been a staple of war, a side benefit given to male troops. Only recently has sexual assault been considered a war crime.[123] Prosecutions following World War II included rape as part of a the list of crimes, establishing the international illegality of rape during war but arguably suggesting that rape is a lesser crime.[124] The international mobilization of women's groups during the founding of the international criminal tribunals of Yugoslavia (ICTY) and Rwanda (ICTR) assured that crimes against women would gain more attention.[125] In Yugoslavia, sexual violence was used to demoralize Muslim forces, shame individuals, encourage people to move, and to shift the demographic profile of the country by impregnating Muslim and Croat women with Serb children.[126] In Rwanda, women and children were often raped and sodomized as a prelude to murder. A report by the special rapporteur of the Commission on Human Rights estimates that 250,000 to 500,000 rapes occurred during

122 Very little is written about the Central American Court of Justice (CACJ), but a local scholar pointed out to me resolution 81-03-05-12-2007 and resolution 09-040-08-1996. The Guatemalan case involved challenges to the immunity granted to members of the Central American Parliament, which according to complainants was being used as a shield of impunity domestically. The Guatemalan court declared the provision void, and the CACJ declared the court's ruling void, creating a stalemate.

123 Kelly Askin describes evolving understandings of rape in war, from a time when women were considered property and rape was merely violation of property, to rape being considered an affront to a women's dignity but not per se a crime (Askin 1997, 24–28).

124 The Nuremberg Charter did not list sexual violence as a war crime (ibid., 48–98).

125 Women's groups were increasingly present during multilateral conversations, appearing at the 1993 Vienna Conference on Human Rights, the 1994 Cairo Conference on Population, and the 1995 Beijing World Conference on Women. United as various NGOs (e.g., Women's Project of Human Rights Watch, the Women's Caucus for Gender Justice, and the Women's Initiative for Gender Justice), women's groups participated in conversations leading to the founding of the Yugoslavian and Rwandan criminal tribunals.

126 Final Report of the Commission of Experts Established Pursuant to Security Council Resolution 780 (1992) S/1994/674—27 May 1994 Section IV Substantive findings, available at http://www.his.com/~twarrick/commxyu1.htm, last visited March 21, 2012.

the period of the Rwanda genocide.[127] These reports suggested that rape was itself a tool of genocide. As evidence of gender violence mounted, women's groups demanded that rape be explicitly listed as one of the prosecutable crimes in the statutes of the criminal tribunals. UN negotiators were reluctant to include mass rape as part of the ICTY jurisdiction, but a number of the provisions of the ICTY charter were written to facilitate prosecuting sexual violence as a war crime, and rape was enumerated on the list of crimes that when systematically employed against civilian populations constituted crimes against humanity.[128]

The legal tools now existed for international criminal courts to focus on the issue of rape as a mass atrocity, but most international prosecutors were neither trained nor interested in doing so. The prosecution of Jean Paul Akayesu provided a breakthrough case establishing rape as a genocidal act. Although women's groups had brought to the attention of the prosecutorial team the prevalence of rape at the communal bureau under Akayesu's command, neither systematic nor genocidal rape had been part of the original indictment against Akayesu. Rather, the topic of rape entered the room during a witness's testimony. Witness J mentioned in passing that her six-year-old daughter had been gang raped by three Interahamwe soldiers. In the civil law tradition, judges can ask their own questions during legal proceedings. The president of the ICTR chamber picked up on Witness J's comment and asked more questions. Witness J testified that she had never been questioned about rape by the tribunal's investigators, and that she had heard that women had been raped at Akayesu's bureau. The witness could not provide direct evidence that implicated Akayesu. But ICTR judges then asked subsequent witnesses about sexual violence at the bureau, exploring whether Akayesu had been in charge when the rapes took place.[129]

Observers of the public trial reported the testimony to women's groups. The timing of the testimony was propitious. A number of human rights groups were studying the issue of gender violence during the Rwanda

127 See special rapporteur of the Commission on Human Rights under paragraph 20 of S.C. Res. S-3/1, Report on the Situation of Human Rights in Rwanda, paragraph 16, E/CN.4/1996/68 (January 29, 1996), available at http://www1.umn.edu/humanrts/commission/country52/68-rwa.htm ("rape was the rule and its absence the exception"), cited in Van Schaack (2009, n. 53).

128 Article 5 of the ICTY Court Treaty and Article 3 of the ICTR Court Treaty include rape among the list of crimes against humanity that the courts have jurisdiction to pursue, with the proviso that the act must be widespread or systematic and targeted at civilians who are singled out on race, ethnicity, political, national, or religious grounds. Rule 96 of the Rules of Procedure and Evidence protects women who are providing testimony and prohibitions against enslavement, torture, persecution, inhuman acts, "willfully causing greater suffering," etc., provide bases to prosecute rape as a war crime.

129 (Van Schaack 2009, 200–201).

genocide. These groups issued reports calling upon the ICTR to fully investigate and prosecute sexual violence as war crimes, crimes against humanity, and genocide.[130] The Coalition for Women's Human Rights in Conflict Situations then filed an amicus brief suggesting that the prosecutor charge Akayesu for using rape as part of a genocidal campaign to "destroy a woman from a physical, mental or social perspective and [to destroy] her capacity to participate in the reproduction and production of the community."[131]

On June 17, 1997, six months into the trial, the prosecution asked to amend the indictment in light of the witness testimony. The prosecutor's office claimed that they had been aware of rape but had been unable to link it to Akayesu before the witness's testimony in court. The prosecutor denied having been influenced by the amicus brief, arguing that the new witness statements made it "duty bound" to request an amendment of the indictment. But the prosecutor did cite the brief as "a factor because . . . it does remind us of the importance of the issue of sexual violence."[132] The chamber allowed the amendment, adjourning the court to give the defense additional time to address the new charge. The continuation of the case brought in new evidence and testimony about the prevalence of rape at Akayesu's bureau, but no evidence of Akayesu's direct involvement.

The ruling in the Akayesu case created a new level of accountability for rape in war. Akayesu was not convicted for having personally committed rape. Rather, among the various crimes committed, the court found that Akayesu "ordered, instigated, aided and abetted" a series of incidents of sexual violence, and was "criminally responsible" for this violence and for a number of specified rapes. The ruling created an extensive definition of criminal sexual violence, one that did not require physical contact and thus which could include forced disrobing and naked gymnastics.[133] Kelly Askin credits the ruling for providing "the first ever conviction of either genocide or crimes against humanity for sexual violence," and for creating "the seminal definitions of rape and sexual violence under international law."[134] Most importantly, the ruling made leaders legally liable for failing to stop and punish sexual violence by troops under their command.

130 See, for example, Human Rights Watch's report: "Shattered Lives: Sexual Violence during the Rwandan Genocide and Its Aftermath," 1996, available at http://www.hrw.org/reports/1996/Rwanda.htm, cited and discussed in Van Schaack (2009, 201).

131 Amicus Brief Respecting Amendment of the Indictment and Supplementation of the Evidence to Ensure the Prosecution of Rape and Other Sexual Violence within the Competence of the Tribunal, Coalition for Women's Human Rights in Conflict Situations, available at http://www.womensrightscoalition.org/site/advocacyDossiers/rwanda/Akayesu/amicusbrief_en.php, at paragraph 19, quoted in Van Schaack (2009, 203).

132 (Van Schaack 2009, 204).

133 ICTR, "Akayesu rape as war crime ruling."

134 (Askin 2003, 318).

Subsequent ICTR and ICTY rulings have built further precedent. Prosecutors have shown how even a single rape can be seen as a serious violation of international law and how sexual violence can be prosecuted without victim testimony. Rulings have recognized coerced nudity as a form of sexual violence and sexual violence as a form of torture. The ICTY case Prosecutor v. Kunarac, Kovoc and Vokovic was the first international legal case to focus exclusively on sex crimes, convicting the defendants of numerous crimes including sexual slavery.[135] These precedents and prosecutorial techniques apply beyond the context of war crimes prosecution. The definition of rape as a form of torture, for example, opened the possibility that rapes in certain contexts might be prosecutable under the Convention against Torture and Other Cruel, Inhuman or Degrading Treatment or Punishment, which can be enforced in national courts in signatory countries even if the violation took place elsewhere.

The prevalence of rape in the Rwandan genocide and Yugoslavia wars was certainly horrific, but so was rape by the Japanese during World War II. The difference was that women were now politically mobilized and pressing the United Nations to address issues of concern to women. Whereas the Yugoslav and Rwandan statutes included rape on the list of possible crimes against humanity, the International Criminal Court's Rome Statute goes further, clearly specifying that "crimes against humanity" include not only rape but also "sexual slavery, enforced prostitution, forced pregnancy, enforced sterilization or any other form of sexual violence of comparable gravity" when committed as part of a widespread or systematic attack directed against any civilian population.[136] This language suggests that although never prosecuted, the forced imprisonment of "comfort women" by the Japanese would today be seen as a crime against humanity.[137] The Akayesu case shows how delegation to ICs creates new opportunities for mobilized actors, in this case women's groups who were able to leverage opportunities created in court into actionable strategies, influencing legal outcomes in real time and building legal precedents that can be invoked in the future.

In the long run, the prevalence of sexual violence in war will change only when social attitudes toward sexual violence change. There are many reasons why rape in war remains underprosecuted. Rape victims often want to keep their experiences secret, and prosecutors often prefer to focus on the crimes where conviction will be easiest and prison terms

135 ICTY, Prosecutor v. Kunarac, Judgment, IT-96-23-T and IT-96-23/1-T, February 22, 2001. Askin discusses legal developments in detail (Askin 2003, Kunaric et al. judgment at 333–41).

136 Article 7 (g) of the Rome Statute of the International Criminal Court.

137 On the legal challenges of classifying Japanese comfort women practices, see Argibay (2003).

longest. Prosecutors may also be concerned that failed efforts to prosecute rape will be worse than no effort. The prohibition against trying a defendant for the same crime twice means that a botched prosecution can effectively indemnify a person. Indeed, a number of international rape prosecutions have failed due to inadequate evidence and unreliable witnesses.[138] The appointment of Fatou Bensouda, a former Gambian justice minister, as the chief prosecutor for the International Criminal Court may signal a turning point, as Ms. Bensouda has made prosecuting gender crimes a top priority. A tentative and admittedly somewhat optimistic study suggests that ratification of the Rome Statute has contributed to changing domestic legislation to facilitate domestic criminal prosecution of sexual violence.[139]

Criminalization and prosecution can help stigmatize acts of sexual violence. But as Sally Merry aptly shows, the behaviors of police and prosecutors will also be critically important in sending signals to offenders that gender and sexual violence are in fact criminal acts.[140] Thus while the Akayesu decision creates an obligation for commanders to control the sexual behavior of their subordinates, such an obligation is but one small step down a path to creating a culture of constitutional obedience to the prohibition of sexual violence in war.

IV. THE ALTERED POLITICS OF INTERNATIONAL CONSTITUTIONAL REVIEW

These case studies present variation in ICs playing their constitutional role. The variation occurred for a number of reasons. To some extent the politics turned on the issue of whether or not legal violations were easily rectified. The exemptions for Peru were already being phased out at the time the ATJ ruled, and Akayesu was already in custody, which made compliance with ATJ and ICTR rulings a nonissue. The German government was open to changing the constitution to allow women in combat support roles, as was the legislature, thus amending the German constitution proved fairly easy. Ecuadorian courts had already condemned the trade barriers enacted in retaliation for Colombia's legal violations. It was thus politically easier for the ICs to make bold constitutional rulings in these cases. The cases where compliance with the ruling was the slowest—the indigenous land rights case where it took years to resolve overlapping land claims, and the Colombia and Ecuador alcohol practices case where Colombia is yet to change its contested policy—were slow in

138 Cases where rape has been poorly prosecuted are discussed in Van Schaack (2009).
139 (Ni Aoláin 2013).
140 (Merry 2003a; 2003b).

part because changing the illegal policy is complicated. Still the ICs did not shy away from demanding full compliance in these cases as well.

Figure 8.2 examines how ICs altered politics in these cases (the Peru exemptions case does not appear because the breach had already been rectified by the time the ATJ ruled). Arrows indicate pressure exerted on compliance partners at each stage. During T1, litigants tried to encourage those actors with the power to choose compliance to change their behavior. For some cases the relevant actors were domestically based, and for other cases they were internationally based. The domestic-level challenges engendered mixed results. The litigation politics (T2) were clearly affected by the larger political context. On the one hand, the ICs in all of these cases acted like typical constitutional courts. They built law, defended their prerogatives, and rebuffed government efforts to shield national and executive prerogatives from judicial review. Nor did political concerns keep IC judges from considering what higher order law required or from condemning illegal actions. One cannot help but observe, however, that the ECJ's jurisprudence regarding women in the military seems to vary based on sentiments within member states.[141] At a minimum, the ECJ seems sensitive to public opinion on these issues. The ATJ was clearly bold with respect to condemning Ecuadorian and Colombian practices that violated Andean rules, but at the same time hesitant to criticize national judges' handling of the cases. Meanwhile, the ICTR judges appeared to be more concerned about the rape occurring in Akayesu's bureau than the prosecutors for the case.

Since the ICs clearly did condemn practices that violated higher order legal obligations, it appears that IC ambivalence is most prevalent with respect to remedies the judges order. In all cases the ICs provided tools of leverage that those actors who preferred changing the policy could use to orchestrate policy change.

How, if at all, did cultures of constitutional obedience or the lack thereof shape the politics in these cases? In the Peru exceptions case, the ATJ used the Marbury v. Madison technique of asserting the supremacy of Andean constitutional requirements without mandating any change in existing policy. In the Colombia and Ecuador alcohol-related practices case, the ATJ remained a legal formalist, circumscribing the extent of its review so as to avoid the question the supremacy of Andean law in domestic systems. By contrast, in the seizing private assets (Kadi) and women in combat support roles cases, the ECJ drew on the culture of constitutional obedience that already existed in Germany and much of Europe.

141 The ECJ condemned Germany's blanket exclusion of women from most military jobs associated however indirectly with combat, but allowed Britain to bar a cook from the Royal Marines, and the ECJ refused to require Germany to integrate its draft.

Many people still question whether it is wise or legal for the ECJ to call into question the legal validity of UN acts or the factual decisions of the Sanctions Committee. But few European political leaders would seriously consider amending the European Treaties so as to undermine human rights protections for individuals. And even if they tried, such an action would not stop the ECtHR or national supreme courts from invalidating the contested practices. Indeed, the ECtHR has gone on to condemn the UN sanctions regime.[142] This political reality gives the ECJ a strong constitutional trump hand, at least as long as many national actors believe the UN delisting procedure is inadequate. As the case study discussion showed, this trumping hand contributed to significant reforms of the UN Sanctions Committee system for adjudicating the correct listing of individuals and organizations.

In the women in combat support roles and indigenous land rights cases, advocates portrayed compliance with the full implications of the IC rulings as somehow required, even though in both cases national law on its own seemingly did *not* require governments to change national laws. Meanwhile, in the alcohol dispute, Colombia's government has not been forced by domestic judges to change practices that the ATJ has found illegal, while Ecuador complied with ATJ rulings because its national courts forced it to do so.[143] These cases suggest that not all international law will be seen as "higher order" law, and that national judges are key actors in determining whether and which international law has a higher order status within the domestic system. Their tacit support is necessary for constitutional obedience to international law, but especially where national cultures of constitutional obedience do not exist, national judicial support may not be enough. In both the indigenous land rights and rape as a war crime cases advocates had to maintain their pressure on domestic and international actors to ensure legal remedies.

The conclusion will argue that national constitutional courts face the same sorts of limitations as the IC judges. Judges seem to be at least partially swayed by public opinion, the extent of social mobilization, and government preferences. But the cases discussed in this chapter suggest that ICs face a political constraint that domestic judges do not. National supreme courts can become de facto arbiters of how international law applies in the domestic legal order.[144] International judges must avoid

142 "ECtHR ruling on UN Sanctions System: Nada v. Switzerland."

143 The ATJ had condemned Ecuador's regulations in September 1998 and reiterated its position in April 1999. Yet only in March 2000, "at the request of an interested party and not at the initiative of the Government," did Ecuador cease its illegal retaliation. "Considering." Resolution No. 004, Ecuador Board of Foreign Trade and Investment (COMEXI), second, third, and fourth paragraphs published in *Gaceta Oficial* No. 372 of July 30, 1998.

144 (Benvenisti 2008).

FIGURE 8.2 Political dynamics of constitutional cases

	National system		International system				
	Domestic enforcement strategy	Compliance partner required change	International legal strategy	IC ruling	Legal remedy	Post-ruling political strategy	Policy change by compliance partner
ECJ Kadi	EU level regulation was the target, but there were also national cases in many courts	The Commission can delist Kadi. National authorities can unfreeze assets.	Challenge validity of regulation & listing in Tribunal of First Instance & ECJ.	EU regulation invalid with respect to Kadi.	Evidence must be shared, Kadi must have right to challenge evidence.	Many legal rulings criticizing UN system. →	Release assets. Reform UN system. Change EU regulation. Eventually delist Kadi.
ECJ Kreil	Kreil raised her suit in a German court and invoked European law.	National judges can refer case to ECJ. Bundestag can change constitution.	Challenge to German constitution referred to ECJ.	German ban on women in combat support roles violates European law.	Kreil must be allowed to compete for jobs involving armaments.	None needed (Culture of constitutional obedience).	Constitution changed. Political and social reforms to incorporate women in military.

ATJ alcohol-related cases	National judicial challenges in Colombia and Ecuador.	Colombia: Legislature must regulate municipal practices. Ecuador: Agency must eliminate trade restriction.	Noncompliance suits + national court reference to ATJ (Colombia).	Colombian monopoly is legal but municipal practices are illegal. Ecuador policy illegal.	Colombia & Ecuador must end violations.	Retaliatory sanctions authorized but never applied. Ecuador-more legal challenges. →	Colombia: noncompliance persists. Ecuador: national barriers eliminated following national court rulings.
IACtHR Indigenous land tights case	Awas Tingni raised domestic challenges to the Solcarsa concession, facing many procedural hurdles. →	Nicaraguan Supreme Court annuls concession. Legislature must pass legislation to recognize land rights. ←	Inter-American Commission mediates and then refers case to IACtHR.	Nicaragua violated the Inter-American Convention.	Nicaragua must provide compensation, and demarcate land ownership.	Domestic legal suits to ensure ruling is implemented in full. →	Compensation paid. Land claims resolved.
ICTR Rape as a war crime	International prosecution seems to have been a goal.	Not applicable	Women's groups pressure prosecutors to pursue rape crimes. →	Criminal liability for rapes under Akayesu's command	Life sentence, imprisonment.	Women's groups push to criminalize and prosecute sexual violence. →	None needed for Akeyesu. Continued pressure to prosecute sexual violence
	T1: Bargaining in the shadow of an IC			T2: Litigation politics		T3: Leverage strategies	

antagonizing national judges by overstepping their formal grant of authority or pushing too far beyond national legal sentiments. This does not mean that ICs have to ignore clear legal violations. The ATJ did rule against Colombia in the alcohol case discussed above, even though it knew that its ruling was likely to be ignored, and the IACtHR ruled against Nicaragua. The constraints are most manifest when it comes to the remedies IC judges order. The IACtHR was quite bold in demanding that the Nicaraguan government create a process to guarantee indigenous peoples' land rights. The ECOWAS court was not as bold in its modern-day slavery case where it required compensation for Hadijatou Mani, but it didn't demand that the government or judges do anything specific to stop the customary practices that created her situation in the first place. This comparison suggests that judges respond to political constraints by adjusting remedies so as to limit the material impact of their rulings.

CONCLUSION: CONSTITUTIONAL REVIEW POLITICS IN THE SHADOW OF INTERNATIONAL COURTS

This chapter has shown that international constitutional review exists as a category. A number of ICs have jurisdiction to review the validity of international and state acts; and ICs have used their constitutional powers to invalidate international and national legislative acts that enjoy state support. International legal systems are seized either because the IC has exclusive jurisdiction for the issue or because domestic litigation strategies have failed (for example, either domestic judges are unwilling to rule against the government in the case, or domestic judges lack the power to compel government compliance).

The cases discussed in this chapter differ from those of the enforcement chapter in that the ICs were invoking higher order legal principles to create positive obligations for governments. For the cases involving constitutional review of international acts, there never was a question of whether or not the ruling would be followed. Indeed, I know of no cases where an international institution has ignored a ruling of an international court, but I can well imagine what would happen if the institution did. Countries that wanted to follow the international policy would do so as a matter of domestic policy, while countries that were ambivalent about the international policy would use the IC ruling to justify a decision to ignore international policy. This seems to be what is occurring vis-à-vis the UN Sanctions Committee system.[145]

145 See the discussion of the latest UN report in the Kadi case study.

The cases involving constitutional review of state acts are more complicated because governments can violate international law while claiming adherence to the domestic rule of law. For the IC to gain a constitutional review authority vis-à-vis domestic acts, morphed or otherwise, ICs need domestic actors to agree that the international law in question constitutes a higher order legal obligation. Such a step may require that international law be embedded into the national system itself. But it mostly requires that domestic actors—judges, governments, and social actors—show constitutional obedience to higher order international law.

Building a culture of constitutional obedience takes time. Because national judges worry about international actions escaping judicial review, it may be easier for ICs to invoke the culture of constitutional obedience for its review of international acts than it is for review of state acts. Governments are highly legitimated actors, and many domestic courts struggle to elicit respect for the national constitution and their rulings. The discussion of the women in combat support roles and the Colombia and Ecuador alcohol-related practices shows that even within a single international legal system, domestic support for the supremacy of community rules can vary.

The unsatisfying part of this argument is its circularity—courts garner constitutional obedience because there is a culture of constitutional obedience. My argument is less circular in that my main claim is that ICs build constitutional obedience through alliances with national actors, and that the tacit support of national high court judges is a necessary condition for constitutional obedience to international law.

ICs are constrained by their need to build support within the national judiciary, but it is an open question whether ICs are more constrained compared to their domestic constitutional counterparts.[146] Gerald Rosenberg questioned the capacity of the US Supreme Court to produce significant change without the support of the government and the larger population.[147] Michael McCann and Charles Epps argue that courts can contribute to political change, but they need to work with societal actors to promote mobilization and change.[148] Georg Vanberg and Jeff Staton argue that supreme court decision making will be affected by the extent of public support for the court, the extent to which constitutional violations are transparent, and thus whether violations are something the public might know and care about, and by public opinion on specific issues

146 Conventional wisdom expects ICs to be more constrained, but no scholar has really examined whether or not this is true. For discussions on the constraints of ICs, see Alter and Helfer (2010); Ginsburg (2005); Steinberg (2004).

147 (Rosenberg 1993).

148 (Epps 1998; McCann 1994).

in question.[149] Gretchen Helmke traces the willingness of Argentine judges to rule against the government over time, finding that judges respond to the changing political winds around them.[150] In other words, scholars of domestic constitutional courts recognize that even powerful courts are constrained and enabled by the support of domestic actors. We lack any real way to assess if international judges are more constrained by their political environment.[151] Indeed, the US Supreme Court has been even more reticent to question executive action in the fight against terrorism than the ECJ.

I suggested that where domestic legal orders are weak, ICs' constitutional authority can serve as a bolster to the domestic system, creating an international-level obligation that adds pressure on national governments. For this reason, national supreme courts may welcome international judicial support for higher order law. But where domestic supreme courts are strong, they may dislike the notion that international judges should have a say within their constitutional order. In other words, the more established the national constitutional courts, the more domestic judges and lawyers may fear that international constitutional law threatens the domestic constitutional system. This argument presents an irony. Section I suggested that the support of powerful domestic courts is necessary and sufficient for governments to give constitutional obedience to IC rulings. Yet the very strength of domestic courts may lead them to deny ICs a constitutional authority. This reality does not, however, preclude the possibility that governments may choose to see an IC ruling in constitutional terms, as occurred in the women in combat support roles case.

The push back created by domestic high court judges is sometimes worrisome to lawyers who fear that international legal systems may fragment or be inconsistently respected if domestic high courts question the validity of international law.[152] But if one can live with a little inconsistency and overcome concerns about a lack of clear judicial hierarchy, then the dependence of ICs on national courts can be seen as a strength. That IC constitutional review authority depends on domestic constitutional obedience means that domestic actors ultimately define the boundaries of IC authority, inserting themselves as mediators between international and domestic law by anchoring international law in the domestic system to the extent that doing so promotes and protects the national constitutional order.[153] ICs may strengthen the domestic constitutional order by

149 (Staton 2010; Vanberg 2005).

150 (Helmke 2005, especially chapter 6).

151 (Staton and Moore 2011). Joerges and Zürn actually find that the ECJ was more effective in curbing subsidies compared to the German Constitutional Court (Zürn and Joerges 2005).

152 (Broude 2008; Kingsbury 1999).

153 (Benvenisti 2008; Nollkaemper 2011).

providing external support for positions that domestic actors may lack the power or courage to demand, as was the case in the indigenous land rights case study. Or national constitutional concerns may serve as political checks on the multilateral order, inspiring ICs to be bolder, as was the case in the Kadi decision discussed in this chapter.

My goal in this chapter was to understand international constitutional review in relation to the other judicial roles of international courts. My constitutional focus has been admittedly thin, and my claim rather modest. I am not claiming that where there is international constitutional review one finds an ethos of global constitutionalism. Nor am I developing a theory of international constitutionalism. Constitutional review and cultures of constitutional obedience are arguably essential ingredients for constitutional legal orders, but clearly they are but one aspect of what is a deeper ontology of constitutionalism.[154]

This debate about the influence of international constitutional review tends to have a missing actor. That government's preferences are not at the center of constitutional review politics makes sense. The whole point of constitutional review is to create a constitutional check on the actions of governments and legislative bodies. Missing, however, is what "the people" might want. In this respect, the starring role of judges—national and international—underplays the importance of public support for the rules judges apply. Where there are gross violations of human rights, one can reasonably presume that most people would support government accountability. And where the option is to have no meaningful legal checks on international actors, "the people" may also prefer that ICs create legal checks. But there are many areas of constitutional law where discerning democratic preferences regarding international law will be difficult. Cultures of constitutional obedience provide a resource that international constitutional courts can sometimes draw on to evoke compliance with their rulings. But what constitutional obedience requires will be a politically contested notion. The altered politics argument mainly suggests that delegation to international courts allows a broad range of actors to participate in debates over the constitutional limitations of legitimate governance. The case studies suggest that national judges, governments, and litigants retain important tools to influence IC decision making but that IC review leads to both domestic and international policy change.

154 A number of legal scholars take up this task, see for example Buchanan and Powell (2008); Nollkaemper (2011). There is a new journal, *Global Constitutionalism*, focused on this topic.

Part III: Courts, Politics, Rights

CHAPTER 9

International Courts and Democratic Politics

The new terrain of international law is an artifact of a number of indirectly connected decisions: the decision to expand the substantive reach of international law, to embed international legal rules into national legal orders, to expand extraterritorial enforcement capacity of domestic judges, and to create more international courts with a compulsory jurisdiction and access for nonstate actors to initiate litigation. The result of these trends is the globalization of judicial politics and the judicialization of international politics. Judicialization occurs where citizens, organizations, and firms see law as conferring upon them rights, and where politicians conceive of their policy and legislative options as bounded by what is legally allowed. Where judges have jurisdiction and litigation becomes a useful way to reopen political agreements, negotiations among actors become debates about what is legally permissible, and politics takes place in the shadow of courts with the lurking possibility of litigation shaping actor demands and political outcomes. This book has documented the substantive and geographical expansion of IC jurisdiction and demonstrated how international law and the prospect of IC legal review is creating a global judicialization of politics regarding a growing range of issues. International law now speaks to how governments respect human rights, how wars can be fought, the terms under which goods can enter national markets and governments can sanction and limit individual and firm choices, and many other issues. As the many case studies in this book demonstrated, international courts are now adjudicating issues that used to be entirely subjects of national determination. And their decisions are affecting both domestic and international politics.

The reality that ICs are increasingly invoked to adjudicate a broad range of issues raises new challenges for the implementers of international law. My goal in this conclusion is to identify theoretical and political implications that emerge from the book's analysis. I do this through the lens of the normative question of how to reconcile national democracy and binding enforceable international law.

I should, however, warn that it is not my intention to develop a normative theory of democratic politics or the legitimacy of international law or courts. The question I address is as follows: given that international law can supplant decisions and laws enacted through the national democratic process, how can one reconcile respect for international law with the priority of allowing a national democratic political choice? I call this dilemma—the reality that democratic choice is legitimate and international law constraining—the "democratic politics conundrum." This chapter suggests that what "democracy" entails is rather ambiguous so that there are a number of ways to reconcile international law and democracy. I put various reconciliations side by side and show that alone, each one of them falls short. But if we throw various reconciliations into the brew we call democracy, the amalgamated outcome is arguably more legitimate and accountability enhancing than relying on any single democratic theory of legitimation.

Section I begins by summarizing the book's theoretical takeaway for international relations theory and identifying ways to build on this study via middle range theorizing that investigates variation in IC activation and influence. Section II returns to the different models of IC influence described in chapter 2 to explore the various ways international relations theorists imperfectly reconcile democracy and international law compliance. I then add the altered politics reconciliation to the brew. Section III concludes by framing a policy question for further debate. Even if we think that international law enforcement enhances rather than usurps democracy, we may still wonder if delegation to international courts promotes certain goals and objectives. I end by asking: Where does associating judicial enforcement with international legal agreements enhance respect for international law? Where is legalized enforcement likely to instead be counterproductive?

I. THEORETICAL IMPLICATIONS OF ICS INSTANTIATING RIGHTS AND ALTERING POLITICS

When international law was unenforceable, governments could write, implement, and interpret the law, thereby determining how domestic and international legal agreements were understood at home. But delegation to independent adjudicatory bodies—in this case international judicial bodies—breaks the government's and the national judiciary's monopoly power to say what international law means at home and abroad. Where national actors insist that their government respect the rule of law and where ICs are able to influence how law is understood, governments will find their political options constrained. Certain choices may even be foreclosed. This compromise of state choice via delegation to international courts is itself a choice of governments, a decision to self-bind. But to state this point does little to address the reality that policy makers today are increasingly finding their options limited by international legal commitments of the past.

The argument in this book challenges international relations' state-centric ontology. Of course it remains true that international organizations are member organizations dominated by states and that only governments can negotiate and sign treaties. But this reality is increasingly less significant because politics—both domestic and international—is becoming increasingly globalized, legalized, and judicialized. Many international relations scholars resurrect their state-centric ontology by invoking what I call the "executive control thesis." This thesis presumes that the international political mechanisms that executive branches can most easily and perhaps even unilaterally control—nominations and the appointment of international judges, international law-making processes, treaty making, the possibility of exit and noncompliance—can be used, and therefore must surely be used, to influence international legal bodies.[1] Some advocates of this thesis suggest that IC rulings are endogenous to and reflective of government control and thus not able to exert any independent influence on state or international politics. Most proponents of the executive control thesis accept at face value the right of executive actors to control the judiciary. Executive control is perhaps even considered a good thing, a way to make compliance with the law seem rational and a way to reconcile democracy and delegation to ICs.

The executive control thesis is borrowed from the American politics debates where the tools of political control are better able to explain judicial behavior. American political parties work hard to shape the composition of the federal and state judiciary with the result that there is a strong correlation between the political party that appointed the judge and judicial behavior.[2] The theory may work in the US context, and in any context where the political parties have successfully made the tight control of the judiciary a high priority. But as a general theory of judicial behavior, the executive control thesis does not travel well.

Theoretically speaking, one might be skeptical of a thesis that makes judicial self-interest and the tools governments wield of paramount

1 For example, Garrett and Weingast (1993); Stephan (2002); Vaubel (2006). Other scholars investigate government control by considering a broad range of tools government can use to influence although not necessarily control IC decision making (see Helfer 2006; Steinberg 2004).

2 (Epstein and Knight 1998; Epstein, Landes, and Posner 2013).

importance in legal decision making. To do so gives short shrift to legal, normative, and social factors that may also be very important, especially in situations of trusteeship, where judicial independence is valued as a means to enhance the credibility and legitimacy of policy making, where judges are appointed based on professional criteria, and where professional criteria are internally valued.[3] Empirically speaking, there is a particular problem in applying this thesis to international courts. Elsewhere I have discussed how the appointments process for international judges is intentionally designed to limit the ability of powerful states to stack international courts.[4] This is not to say that appointment politics are irrelevant, or that the background of judges does not shape judicial behavior. Rather, my point is that as long as governments care about the legality of their behavior, and as long as individual and groups of like-minded governments are limited in their ability to stack ICs, punish international judges, rewrite the law, or convince everyone who matters to ignore IC rulings, governments will find themselves constrained by international law and IC interpretations.

In truth, social science is unlikely to ever validate or falsify the executive control thesis since the theory survives because of assumption and analogy more than evidence. The real issue is that we can never really know why governments or judges make the decisions they do. The best we can do is to rely on theories of causation tested via proxy evidence. Statistical correlations based on deduced state preferences, the strategic arguments state lawyers make in court, or on preferences "revealed" by the fact of state compliance—all of which are questionable indicators of "the government's interest" or "the national interest"—are likely to always generate findings of degrees of affirmation (for example, a statistically significant correlation), which will be enough to keep the executive control thesis alive. Meanwhile, falsifying this executive control thesis would require a shocking correlation in which judges systematically and generally ignore government opinions. This would be surprising indeed. One would hope that judges mostly apply the law as written and intended, in which case courts will inevitably be following the will of governments and legislatures much of the time. Moreover, as chapter 2 noted, governments have a huge stake in the rule of law, and courts and governments are usually partners in the overall enterprise of law enforcement. Indeed, it would be counterintuitive and arguably revolutionary if judges held preferences that were vastly different from those of the political

3 This is a criterion of my definition of trusteeship (Alter 2008a), and it corresponds to Daniel Carpenter's theory of bureaucratic autonomy (Carpenter 2001; 2010). Alec Stone Sweet stresses other factors in his definition of trusteeship (Stone Sweet and Brunell 2013).

4 (Alter 2006a).

leadership since both profess a desire for the rule of law, both have trained in the same elite education systems, and judges are the brothers, sisters, wives, and husbands of government officials. Said differently, a correlation between "government preferences" and judicial rulings may well be as normal as finding fire brigades where there are fires and thus not in itself a confirmation that a fear of executive sanction forced the judge's hand.

Of course we must consider how government preferences and appointment politics influence international judicial decision making. Of course we must recognize that international courts can become politically captive and investigate which ICs are more likely to be controlled by governments or other political fractions. But we must do more than search for political control; we must explore the many factors that influence international judicial decision making and respect for international law. As Beth Simmons persuasively argues in a somewhat different context, these are separate social phenomena, which is to say that the answer to "why do governments commit to international judicial oversight" may be different than the answer to the question of "what shapes international judicial decision making?" and "what shapes state respect for IC rulings?"[5]

To get to better theorizing about the factors shaping IC decision making and influence we need to first dislodge the strong bias in international law and international relations theory that privileges the preferences of governments, thereby updating our fundamental presumptions. At least four standard international relations assumptions are called into question by the evidence and analysis in this book.

First, we should not assume that national sovereignty is the highest order concern even if governments still say that it is. This book shows that the application of law by courts often extends rather than compromises state power. But as judicial power rises, so does the ability of judges to constrain governments. Everyone—and especially my children—would like to be able to do whatever they want at all times. So it is surely true that ceteris paribus, governments will prioritize national sovereignty. The problem with this logic is that all things are not equal. Our preferences do not always win because we share the world with others and absolute selfishness brings with it costs to ourselves and others.

The devaluation of sovereignty as an absolute political priority may simply reflect the reality that international autarky is not a viable political option. But chapter 4 discussed how disappointment and disenchantment with national rule has led people around the world to distrust their

5 Simmons persuasively made the case that the answer to the question "why sign international human rights conventions" may be unrelated to how international human rights conventions shape government behavior (Simmons 2009, chapters 3 and 4).

governments. There is a deep thirst for the rule of law among people. This thirst extends to governments because central powers also lose when populations become convinced that local officials and leaders are corrupt or incompetent, and because as chapter 2 explained, the rule of law is how central authorities extend their power over individuals, firms, and throughout the territory. Especially where domestic checks appear unable to rein in governmental and economic actors, citizens, businessmen, and even politicians may be more likely to trust international judicial assessments and to believe that invocations of sovereignty are designed primarily to deflect criticism and escape accountability. Where the authority of law ascends, and where legal interpretation gains a natural semiautonomy, sovereign rights will inevitably be diminished. Diminishing the absolute power of governments is, of course, the objective of the rule of law. An implication of this book is that the more the rule of law becomes a legitimating discourse, the more governments value their reputation as rule of law actors, the more sovereignty will descend as an absolute or higher order priority of governments.

Second, the rising invocation and influence of international law and international adjudicatory bodies suggests that we live in a postrealist world, one where perceptions of legality shape both foreign and domestic policy. If law has autonomy and perceptions of legality matter, then it is not enough for states to follow narrowly conceived national interest. Only actions that are legally justifiable under international law will be seen as legitimate domestically and internationally. Of course the importance of international legal norms is everywhere apparent. Governments do not cross borders and seize commodities they want, nor do they annex valuable lands. Chemical and biological weapons are considered politically off limits, even though they may be militarily effective. And tariffs are seldom the protectionist tool of choice, even though they bring revenue and provide clear evidence of a political commitment to protecting jobs at home.

This book's addition to the bounty of evidence is to focus on how delegation to courts undermines a government's monopoly power to determine for itself what international law requires and allows international legal norms to become politically salient in places and in ways that may not be directly servicing national interests defined by governments. Given that international power politics and material interests are not the only factors that matter in international relations, it is time to conclude that we live in postrealist world. Power remains a key element of international politics, and power may be the only thing that can deter the "Hitlers of the world."[6] But for the rest of us, international legal concerns

6 Louis Henkin once wrote: "much law is observed because it is law and because its violation would have undesirable consequences. . . . In international society, too, law is not

matter, even when countries face existential threats to cherished national objectives.

Third, if international law serves the interests of people in addition to states, then it is time to move beyond seeing international society, in Hedley Bull's terms, as a society of states. International agreements do still sometimes generate club goods that service the interests of member governments. But increasingly international agreements are aimed at generating international public goods with corresponding obligations and rights, where the beneficiaries are people (and perhaps thereby their governments). It is worth noting that one can believe that international society is a society of states and people without jumping to the conclusion that there must be an international demos or an emerging cosmopolitan ethos. Most people would agree that replacing local governance with a world government would be undesirable, that smaller units of governance, with leaders and decision making taking place closer to where people live and therefore more reflective of local priorities are preferable to global rule.

This book's more modest claim is that the international rule of law signals an intent to define and protect international public goods—goods that serve the rights and interests of people—and not just the rights and interests of governments. International bargaining may well reflect power politics, with governments championing policies that most serve their own or the nation's interests. But a key objective of constitutional politics is to protect the rights of minorities and groups against the priorities of the powerful and the majority. International legal politics take place within a legitimized discourse of the "rule of law," which by design operates according to a different set of logics and rules than the political realm. This "rule of law" discourse allows for law-backed "out group" preferences to trump the law-violating "in group" preferences of those who wield power. Enhancing the rule of law arguably expands the possibility of achieving international public goods, defined in practice as most public goods are defined, by having laws that subordinate individually self-interested behavior to achieve some publicly defined collective benefit.[7]

If international public goods and fundamental rights are perceived to exist, and if access to these rights and goods are defined in humanistic rather than national terms, then it must be the case that international

---

effective against the Hitlers and it is not needed for that nation which is content with its lot and has few temptations. International law aims at nations which are in principal law abiding but which might be tempted to commit a violation if there were not threat of undesirable consequences." (Henkin 1979, 93–94).

7 This is a somewhat different definition from what economists use. I am not concerned with whether consumption by one person in fact harms another but rather with whether private action is regulated/limited in order to promote public goals.

politics and society is merging into a society of states *and* people with both national and international politics increasingly mediated by institutions and politics at multiple levels.

A fourth fundamental implication is that globalization has now extended to the rule of law. We tend to think of globalization in economic terms, and it is of course true that much of the phenomenon we call globalization is driven by market forces. But the rule of law has also become a force for globalization for a number of reasons. Law is a force for globalization because the rule of law is seen as a key ingredient for economic progress and political stability. Law is a force for globalization because judges and lawyers around the world are asserting greater political power. Law is also a force for globalization because people around the world share many of the goals inscribed in international law and agree that powerful governments must respect international law and the rule of law. For all of these reasons law is rising in political salience. The fact that much international law is domestically embedded means that increasingly international and domestic debates about the rule of law are intertwined. In other words, not only is demand for the rule of law a force for globalization, the increasingly global nature of law is a force for internationalizing national law.

Ceding international relations' state-centric ontology inevitably brings one to the democratic politics conundrum. When we presumed that governments were faithful representatives who pursued the national interest, there was no reason to question whether international political developments might in some way be undermining democracy. But we international relations scholars took this assumption too far. This assumption survived even when it became abundantly clear that totalitarian rulers slaughtered hundreds, thousands, and even millions of citizens, and kleptocrats plundered national resources for personal gain. The reason to overlook the issue of democratic support, or rather the justification for doing so, was that international relations was seen as the realm of power politics. There is no space for ideals like democracy and the rule of law in a Hobbesian world of mass insecurity.[8]

One benefit of relinquishing the state-centric ontology is that we stop willfully blind amoral theorizing. Recognizing the power of legal and moral discourse should be a social science objective if, as Christian Reus-Smit argues, every political order is dependent on a moral conception of the state.[9] But the cost is that we then also admit that states *are not*

8 Of course scholars of ethics have long noted that while governments may lose power, states do not really face the existential threat of a Hobbesian world (Beitz and Alexander 1985; Hoffmann 1981).

9 (Reus-Smit 1999).

inherently legitimate so that normatively speaking, sovereignty should not be a trumping value. There are risks to admitting that foreign actors can and perhaps should constrain what other governments do at home. Realists cling to amoral theorizing not because the scholars are themselves amoral, but because realists see outsiders as fundamentally unable to help. Section III of this chapter will open up the possibility that making international law enforceable may *not* help, in which case international legal approaches to deal with fundamentally political or national problems may be ill advised. But for now, I will assume that states lending support to enforce international law vis-à-vis other states *can* help.

This book showed ICs inducing governments to change laws, practices, and even constitutions. If democracy is about elected governments pursuing voter preferences, then the fact that ICs can induce governments to abandon national policies made through democratic means perhaps raises concerns about conflicting political loyalties. If democracy is about adhering to the laws and constitution of the nation, then the fact that ICs can supplant domestic legislation and constitutions with international legal requirements perhaps raises normative concerns about protecting the national constitutional order. If ICs circumvent governments through alliances with substate and transnational actors, then the rising influence of actors based outside of states perhaps raises concerns about protecting the voice of traditional and nationally based stakeholders.

These concerns only "perhaps" exist. In most cases, the application of international law raises *no* democratic concerns. When ICs are resolving legal ambiguities and enforcing rules that governments, judges, and supporters alike want to see neutrally and uniformly applied, IC review should raise no democratic concerns. When ICs are demanding that governments adhere to rules and norms that are also part of the domestic legal order, IC review should raise no democratic concerns. When IC enforcement primarily raises the costs of walking away from international commitments, ICs are not undermining democratic choice as much as they are reminding governments of the international trade-offs associated with their actions. Perhaps more controversially, when ICs are holding delegitimized political leaders accountable for mass atrocities, IC enforcement arguably raises no democratic concerns. In all of these situations—which frankly encompass what ICs do in most cases—IC oversight provides an additional external watchdog that enhances legal accountability rather than fundamentally undermining democratic choice or the democratic process.

Of course the challenge is how do we know if ICs are reinforcing or undermining democracy? In a constitutional system, delegation to courts is meant to be a check on the exercise of political power. ICs cannot make governments do anything. The central argument of this book—the altered politics framework—is that the need for ICs to co-opt the support of domestic interlocutors creates a national check on the exercise of international legal and judicial power. This is an empirical observation, but since I am bringing normativity in, I will add that in my view this is a good thing for democracy because like all actors, governments and ICs can make decisions that are bad, wrong, poorly reasoned, and worth ignoring. ICs' outside and legal voice provides a different perspective in political debates, one that privileges law and helps shore up the position of those domestic actors who want to see predetermined and principle-based goals and objectives realized. International judges' external nature helps to remediate the problem John Locke identified, that domestic actors tend to be partial to themselves and their friends. Meanwhile, their dependence on domestic interlocutors ensures that international judges stay attuned to the priorities and preferences of state and societal actors. I return to this argument in the next section, but first I want to suggest how we might build beyond the executive control thesis.

Next Steps: Building Middle Range Theories of ICs' Differential Influence and Authority

ICs *can* alter politics, but we also need to recognize that not all international courts are up to the task of helping to enhance respect for international law. This book is intended to be a theory-generating enterprise. Social scientists talk about "lumping" versus "splitting" exercises. I first lumped international judicial bodies into similar categories—legal bodies with dispute settlement, enforcement, administrative and constitutional review jurisdiction. I also clustered ICs involved in economic, human rights, and international criminal law issues. I then identified variations within these broad categories, documenting variation in the design of ICs delegated a different role, significant variation in activation rates for ICs (which I see as a sign of whether lawyers consider litigation to be a useful tool to promote their objectives). Finally, I picked case studies designed to elucidate variation in how ICs play a given role and suggested hypotheses that could explain varied IC influence across cases and time. The next step is to explore variation and more systematically test hypotheses, and to also engage in the splitting exercise of exploring important differences within and across international legal systems, issue areas, and cases.

The altered politics framework provides a structure for proceeding, and the role chapters generate hypotheses that one might investigate further. The starting point for applying the framework is the realization that what compliance with international law entails differs depending on the case at hand. Borrowing from theories of international cooperation, we might call this difference the "law compliance problem structure."

Sometimes a single fairly sympathetic substate actor will be in the position to choose compliance by reinterpreting existing domestic laws that they already have the power to apply. Other times, the only way to generate compliance will be to mobilize groups of legislative actors to change agendas and institutions, which is inevitably harder to do and may even be politically impossible. Because structural factors related to the law and the case affect legal and political outcomes, whether ICs are able to induce greater respect for the law is often shaped by the "law compliance problem structure," and thus exogenous to anything that the IC does or might have done.

Holding constant the "law compliance problem structure" (for example, by comparing like situations), the temporal breakdown defined in chapter 2 provides a basis for proceeding. Recall that I broke down the litigation process into three steps, arguing that different actors became salient at different stages of the litigation process. At the *bargaining in the shadow of the law stage*, the actions of potential litigants are decisive. At the *litigation politics stage*, the actions of international adjudicators are decisive. And at the *leverage politics stage*, the mobilization of actors who will follow through on a legal ruling and these actors' tools of leverage gain salience. Since litigation can fail and defendants can choose to settle or comply at any step, we cannot say that factors that shape leverage politics are more decisive or important than factors that matter when actors are bargaining in the shadow of the law or litigating their case. In what follows, I hold constant what compliance with the law might require and draw from the case-study discussions factors that arguably contribute to varied IC influence at each stage of the litigation process.

Time 1: Bargaining in the shadow of the court and litigant mobilization. Law is binding regardless of its enforceability. But the ability of ICs to generate legal remedies enhances the shadow of the law in out of court bargaining by increasing the credibility and value of legal threats. Chapter 2 identified two necessary conditions for ICs to enhance the shadow of the law in out of court negotiations: clear legal rules without loopholes and access for affected litigants. The case studies then offered a number of examples about how the design of ICs enhanced or undermined litigants' ability to influence political outcomes. The Foreign Sales Corporation and softwood lumber case studies showed the importance of compulsory jurisdiction in increasing the credibility of legal threats. The modern-day slavery, Charles Taylor, and second use patent case studies showed the importance of access for nonstate actors in creating credible legal threats.

This is a start. But of course there must also be litigants who *want* to see the law respected, and who have the resources and expertise to invoke IC authority to promote their objectives. I focused in this book on cases litigated, explaining why plaintiffs turned to litigation and how litigation did and did not promote their objectives. But many other legal violations never get litigated. The rape as a war crime and modern-day slavery case studies identified the challenges that stakeholders have in getting international prosecutors to pursue the crimes of rape and slavery, a reality that blunts the credibility of legal threats and the current value of the legal rights ICs helped to generate.

The takeaway insight from this analysis is that the design of ICs is critical in determining whether legal threats are credible. But even if IC design and jurisdiction are necessary conditions for legal threats to be credible, they will never be a sufficient condition. IC design must combine with the existence of applicable and fairly precise law and litigant mobilization to generate the conditions needed for ICs to enhance the shadow of the law in out of court bargaining. Variation may thus come from the nature of international law, the extent and detail of secondary legislation, and the political preferences and mobilization strategies of advocates.

Key next steps will involve researching how the quality and attributes of legal rules and the way interests organize and conceptualize their concerns affect mobilization and political outcomes. Scholars have started to systematically research why states and groups litigate,[10] why certain groups frame their demands in international legal terms, and why nongovernmental human rights organizations promote some human rights objectives but not others.[11] This work is only sometimes connected to international litigation. In any event, we need more work that focuses on when litigants mobilize to claim their international legal rights, and since the likelihood of success is a key motivator (and deflator) of mobilization, we need to study cross-issue and cross-national variation in the success of legal mobilization efforts.

Time 2: Litigation politics and IC decision making. There has actually been very little work that delves into the black box of international judicial decision making. We know, or at least intuit, that compliance with legal rulings is somehow endogenous to legal decision making, which is to say that judges incorporate political factors as they decide cases so as to increase the likelihood of voluntary compliance. This study, however, included cases where ICs applied the law in cases where they could clearly anticipate noncompliance (for example, the softwood lumber and Colombia and Ecuador alcohol cases and the ICJ cases discussed in the context of the US-Iran dispute). Thus to say that ICs tailor their decisions to facilitate compliance is far from sufficient.

10 See, for example, Alter (2009, chapter 8); Conant (2006); Davis (2012); Epps (1998).

11 (Bob 2005, 2009; Carpenter 2007a, 2007b; Cichowski 2007). Some contributions to the 2000 special issue of *International Organization* on Legalization in World Politics investigated these questions (see, for example, Lutz and Sikkink [2000]).

The altered politics argument suggests that scholars and practitioners need to pay more attention to the interaction of ICs and compliance constituencies, which may or many not include national judges and governments. Chapters 2 and 8 argued that national legal structures (civil law versus common law, monist versus dualist) are not key factors shaping reception of international law. But other elements related to national legal culture might be important. I argued that lawyers, legal scholars, and judges are the gatekeepers of domestic legality, passing judgment on the legal quality and the domestic legal validity of international legal rulings. Since ICs' key interlocutors must actually support the notion that being a rule of law actor entails respecting international law and IC rulings, and that IC rulings reflect what the law requires, we surely need to better understand how ICs convince others of the validity of their rulings.

Legal factors surely matter. One part of promoting the validity of IC rulings is likely the sense that IC rulings apply accepted legal techniques that adhere closely to the text of the law and their jurisdictional mandate. But this is not enough. ICs sticking closely to their mandate and applying well-regarded legal techniques can still issue rulings that domestic actors find illegitimate.[12] Other factors that shape national legal understandings—public opinion, systems of training, mechanisms of judicial recruitment, the overall structure of the national judiciary—will also likely shape how law is understood and how IC legal rulings are crafted and received.

Political-legal factors also surely matter. The administrative review chapter juxtaposed two cases where ICs were helping national and supranational administrators with two cases where ICs were challenging national administrators. Whether or not ICs were helping administrators was not determined by IC agreement with national administrators; indeed, the Belmont case study showed the ATJ issuing rulings that led to the reversal of national administrative decisions. But respect for IC rulings was easier to garner in the first set of case studies because judges were generally supportive of desire for legal clarity that can guide and help defend the validity of administrative decisions. ICs were also deferential to the fact-finding authority of administrative decision makers. In the second set of cases, ICs were questioning the fact finding of administrators and making decisions that policy makers rejected, which put the ICs' compliance partners—national administrators—in a damned if you do, damned if you don't situation.

The constitutional review chapter showed how ICs can draw on nationally built cultures of constitutional obedience. In the seizing private assets (Kadi) case, the ECJ drew on national judicial preferences to

12 Indeed, it really is not clear that sticking closely to a judicial mandate makes ICs more legitimate. Some ICs gain legitimacy by building law that stakeholders value (see Helfer and Alter 2013).

push back against the collective decisions of the United Nations Security Council and powerful member states. In the women in combat support roles case study, the ECJ could draw on a German culture of constitutional obedience (and evolving national preferences regarding gender equity in the military). But in the Colombia and Ecuador alcohol-related practices case the Andean tribunal was unable to use the supremacy of Andean law to harness Colombian judges as coenforcers of Andean law. These cases turned in part on whether IC interlocutors accepted the legal validity of the arguments the IC made but also on whether national judges embraced the domestic legal authority of international legal rules. I hypothesized that weaker national constitutional courts might be more likely to embrace the supremacy of international law and IC review compared to more powerful national constitutional courts, and that national judges may be more willing to embrace the supremacy of international human rights law compared to the international economic law because human rights law may resonate more with the objectives and priorities of national supreme court judges.

Many more factors may be shaping international judicial decision making. Indeed, we are yet to systematically explore the importance of factors that students of domestic judicial behavior have identified as being important—attributes associated with the litigating parties, of the legal issues at stake, and the judicial bench, of the way certain rules are written, and such.[13] Incorporating these many different influences may well lead to conjectures that point in opposite directions, so that we may not be able to generate hypotheses that hold across courts or cases. The larger point is that we need to better understand how IC decision making responds to the broader legal and political context of international judging, by which I mean a context where governments alongside other actors are able to influence legal and political outcomes.

Time 3: Leverage politics and variations in leverage resources. If ICs are not able to induce voluntary compliance by governments, administrators, or judges, then ICs will need to connect with compliance constituencies to promote respect for international law. ICs are sometimes able to help build transnational compliance constituencies by connecting domestic and foreign actors who agree with the IC's legal ruling, nongovernmental organizations that share the substantive priority of addressing the identified legal violation, and potential litigants who are themselves affected by governments ignoring legal rules.

The indigenous land rights case shows how the IACtHR was able to bring together the various advocacy strategies employed by different groups,

13 (Staton and Moore 2011; Voeten 2014). Joost Pauwelyn and Manfried Elsig explore how legal methods shape IC decision making. See Pauwelyn and Elsig (2012). For a discussion of legalized and nonlegalized persuasive techniques used in argumentation, see Ratner (2012).

creating a focal goal for these actors to work toward. The IACtHR drew on testimony by US academic anthropologists, the failure of Nicaragua's government to respond to a World Bank–funded study, the testimony of an indigenous rights activist, and the cause lawyering of the Indian Law Center. The evidence presented by these actors allowed the IACtHR to reject the legal arguments of the government. The fact that nonstate actors participated in the litigation helped the IC to directly connect with its compliance constituency. Follow-up litigation by the Indian Law Center and oversight mechanisms of the Organization of American States kept the issue on the government's agenda, facilitating compliance with the IACtHR's ruling.

International criminal law operates somewhat differently from human rights and economics law. Perhaps the most challenging part of international criminal law is indicting and arresting accused war criminals. Leverage politics may thus in practice operate during T1, before the case reaches the court. In the Charles Taylor case, disparate actors collected evidence of war crimes and then drew on the fact of Taylor's indictment to maintain political pressure and to limit Taylor's options. Because of the indictment, Nigeria's president could only offer Taylor a safe haven; no diplomat had the power to offer amnesty or immunity from prosecution. Legal activists could then maintain legal and political pressure to limit Taylor's freedom of movement. Activists got the US Congress to offer a reward for Taylor's arrest and the Security Council to authorize UN peacekeepers to arrest Taylor should he return to Liberia. The combined external pressure arguably helped the new Liberian president by making it impossible for Taylor to return to Liberia. The indictment also meant that Taylor could not freely travel; it kept the issue of Taylor's prosecution on the American, European, and United Nations agendas; later, the use of Taylor's hidden financial assets was constrained by Taylor's claim to penury so as to elicit public support for his legal defense.

There are obviously many questions to ask about how and when ICs are able to successfully connect with compliance constituents. As mentioned earlier, we need to know more about who IC compliance supporters are and how litigation fits into the strategy of domestic and transnational members of the ICs' compliance constituency. We also need to know more about when transnational legal pressure succeeds, and how different sorts of leverage resources shape the strategy and success of compliance constituencies.

The theoretical implications highlighted in this discussion are illustrative; one could draw out many more policy and theoretical implications to explore from the altered politics framework and the book's eighteen case studies. My goal was to raise the floor for theorizing about IC influence by presenting the diversity of IC influence across a wide variety of political and structural contexts, issues, and cases. The next step is to frame hypotheses that are then examined systematically across a like set of cases. Each role-based chapter provided a set of like institutions to compare, in the hope that scholars will expand beyond the "usual suspects" to generate and test theories.

The Policy Implications of ICs Altering Politics

This theoretical discussion generates clear policy implications for those who want enhance the effectiveness of international law. The need for credible legal threats suggests that advocates for the values and goals inscribed in international law should work to close legal loopholes and extend access to ICs for stakeholders either via direct access or by allowing supranational actors to receive individual appeals and pursue valid cases. The mobilization and bargaining leverage of potential litigants increases when litigants can easily predict how legal cases will be decided. Since immediate compliance is clearly preferable to protracted litigation, legal scholars can help ICs to develop, articulate, and publicize legal doctrines that may be helpful to litigants. If ICs do worry about compliance with their ruling, then advocates can help ICs fill in unclear aspects of the law by raising cases that present clear fact patterns and allow for incremental low-stakes doctrinal and legal development that can educate and build support within legal communities. Since international judges also need help understanding perspectives of different governments and compliance partners, advocates can help by submitting amicus briefs (especially when significant points of disagreement exist) and by being constructive critics of problematic IC rulings. International judges also need scholars to synthesize and communicate how legal doctrine cumulates across cases.

The need for ICs to connect with compliance constituents also has a number of policy implications. ICs, and international institutions more generally, need to develop working relationships with their interlocutors. Students of international cooperation have long known that inducing respect for international regulatory rules is easier when the domestic actors charged with applying the rules are involved in their creation.[14] Translating this insight to the international legal realm suggests that international legal actors should regularly engage their compliance partners. Sometimes it will be the Secretariat that will need to reach out to local administrators about community rules they will be applying. But international courts

14 On factors that enhance the effectiveness of international agreements, see Haas (1992); Haas, Keohane, and Levy (1993); Jacobson and Weiss (1995).

also need to actively engage their compliance partners. International judges may be busy, and their main job description may be to issue quality rulings in the cases litigants present, but it is not enough for international judges to respond to cases that are presented. International judges need to engage in diplomacy, to be known by national lawyers and judges, to participate in developing the legal field of expertise, and to reach out to the current and next generation of litigants, advocates, and compliance partners. The only difference of ICs and domestic judges in this respect is there are already many informal ways for domestic judges to dialogue with their compliance partners, and domestic judiciaries are better able to outsource the public relations aspects of their job to law schools. International judges will need to create these opportunities via outreach—internships, changing the venues in which courts sit so as to reach out to local communities, and facilitating visits to international courts.

These straightforward policy implications are aimed at increasing the effectiveness of international judicial institutions. But as noted, delegation to ICs also raises fundamental questions about how to reconcile international law enforcement and democratic choice. The rest of this conclusion shifts to the philosophical and metapolicy extensions of this book.

II. DEMOCRATIC CHOICE IN INTERNATIONAL POLITICS: MOVING BEYOND EXISTING PERSPECTIVES

In assenting to an international court with compulsory jurisdiction, states self-bind to international judicial oversight of their actions. Given that ICs cannot *make* governments follow their legal edicts, the question then becomes how can ICs influence governments to follow their rulings? Chapter 2 identified three different pathways through which ICs can influence political outcomes, each of which corresponds to a dominant theoretical approach in international relations and international law scholarship. Whereas the old terrain of international law circumscribed IC influence to the interstate arbiter pathway, the new terrain of international law allows ICs to influence politics through all three pathways. I return to chapter 2's models but this time focus on how each approach implicitly reconciles IC review and democracy. One can see these as three different answers to the democratic politics conundrum. We will see that each answer leaves much to be desired, so that another limitation of a single model of theorizing is that it stunts our thinking about how to make international law democratically accountable.

The *interstate arbiter pathway* is predicated on the notion that compliance with international law and IC rulings is purely voluntary. ICs that want to encourage voluntary compliance cater to the interests of governments by validating the policy choices of governments, providing a convenient outside institution to blame as they follow international law, or providing information that contributes to greater legal certainty and helps two or more governments coordinate with each other. This international relations and law and economics perspective reconciles IC review and democracy by presuming that ICs are nonconstraining agents of states and that government preferences best represent and reflect the will of the people. The problem with this approach has already been mentioned. What do you do if the government is breaking the law and ignoring the democratic will? To limit international law to serving as a coordination device for governments is to accept the "anything goes" approach to promoting national interests abroad; to refuse other-regarding international responsibility; to reject as relevant values such as the rule of law and its twin sibling, legal obligation; and to limit our expectations about what international cooperation might achieve.

The Law of Nations, which was the name used for international law a long time ago, may have primarily coordinated state policies while letting governments worry about how to legitimate their rule. This old form of political and international organization has been supplanted by the shared understanding that legitimate government serves the interests of the people rather than the whims of leaders or colonial patrons. The shift to the terminology of "international law" reflects a shift in the nature of international law and in acceptable moral discourse, away from a contractual conception of international law toward a non-Austinian rule of law conception where law exists beyond the confines of the nation-state and where law generates legal obligations for nation-states. Changing understandings of international law are also reflected in the substance of law, which recognizes government responsibility and individual rights, and now includes economic regulation, security law, good governance, and respect for human rights. Adherence to international law has also increasingly becomes part of legitimating the nation-state, replacing the older forms of international legitimation—empire, colonialism, spheres of influence, and hegemony—with the notion that legitimate governments respect the rule of law.[15] International law can, of course, still serve as a coordination device for governments. And certain international legal obligations are contractual in nature, applying only to the signatories and self-dissolving when one contractual partner abrogates the agreement.

15 (Reus-Smit 2011).

But the new terrain of international law also includes higher expectations for international law and a domestically perceived normative obligation to comply with international law.

Because one can only achieve collective benefits via self-regulation by states, international law is increasingly multinational in nature yet domestic in its legal effect.[16] The *multilateral politics pathway* has ICs furthering goals endorsed by a multiplicity of states. ICs contribute to multilateral politics by increasing the international costs of governments violating multilateral agreements, filling in legal lacunae, and by building law where minorities of states are blocking advances preferred by a majority of governments. The multilateral politics perspective explains that international judges are able to rule against the preferences of powerful governments and thereby change state behavior so far as there is multilateral power backing the legal ruling. In this view, autonomy from the vice grip of executive retaliation allows ICs to focus on the goals and objectives inscribed in the legal rules rather than preferences of litigating governments, but only so long as ICs promote the objectives endorsed by a critical mass of states. This multilateral politics pathway is consistent with the view of ICs as legal trustees insofar as international law is a trust agreement among a society of states. The power-politics version of multilateral perspectives has ICs respecting hegemonic power so that powerful governments will back IC rulings via responses that discourage internationally destabilizing behavior and severe and destabilizing predation on national resources and peoples.[17]

The multilateral politics perspective resolves the democratic politics conundrum by replacing national democratic choice with multilateral political choice, while allowing national exit as an option. Governments and legislatures consent to the treaties and rules is seen as providing democratic legitimacy, regardless of whether the substance of the legal commitment has changed significantly since the initial ratification. Domestic social contract theories also rely on loose and somewhat implausible markers for consent, and for this reason Allen Buchanan argues that neither the fact of consent nor the backing of multilateral support legitimizes international law. Many states sign on to international agreements

16 Multilateralism involves three or more states coming together to develop general rules to be applied across a body of like cases (Ruggie 1993). Even customary international law, developed through practice rather than multilateral political processes, can be seen as multilateral in the sense that the practice must be widespread and broadly shared for it to be seen as "customary" law. Bilateral treaty law and natural law arguments in support of *jus cogens*, however, arguably do not depend on multilateral state support.

17 (Stone Sweet and Brunell 2013). This argument is a corollary to Ran Hirschl's claim about the constraints on constitutional courts (Hirschl 2004).

as package deals that come with terms they could neither influence nor afford to reject.[18] Time and elections may also shift government preferences. Buchanan argues that consent theory weakly justifies governance even at the domestic level, and that such consent could not in any event create a moral obligation to follow the law governments, courts, or multilateral institutions create.[19]

Allowing exit does not really resurrect the option of domestic choice insofar as the costs associated with exiting an international institution and ignoring international law can be prohibitively high if doing so will mean that foreign infusions of capital dry up, trading states create embargos, or the United Nations authorizes a coercive response. On the one hand it has always been true that there are external costs to internal choices. We cannot will such costs away, just as we cannot demand that external actors respect national choices, democratic or otherwise. On the other hand, does allowing exit render international law democratically accountable? Ultimately weak governments are left with a Hobbesian consent based "choice." Hobbes's Leviathan had been delegated the right to promote the goals of the collective by demanding an individual to lay down his life for the state. Since the Leviathan's power is based on a social contract, Hobbes recognized that individuals retain the free right to refuse to sacrifice themselves and thus to run away. But the social contract also allows the Leviathan to shoot in the back those who flee, all in the name of the greater good.[20] Of course violating international law is rarely such a costly Hobbesian choice. That said, the multilateral reconciliation to the democratic deficit of international law only works for those with enough power to shape the law or go it alone. For policy takers—citizens of countries and governments that had no meaningful say during the formation of international legal rules—and for those who cannot go it alone, this multilateral politics reconciliation of the democratic politics conundrum may well feel like a Hobbesian choice.

Both the interstate arbiter and multilateral politics perspectives maintain the centrality of states in international politics. The transnational politics pathway breaks from this state-centric ontology by assuming that

18 (Gruber 2000).

19 (Buchanan 2004, 243–49, 312–14). Buchanan suggests that we thus need a different basis to legitimate both domestic and international political authority. We may choose to make international law compatible with constitutional democracy, although this is not per se required. But if we do decide to prioritize democratic legitimation, then according to Buchanan and Powell there is still no philosophical justification for debating the abstract compatibility between constitutional democracy and robust international law. Rather, they advocate focusing on specific conflicts between international law and a country's constitution, finding ways to remediate the conflicts through democratic and international political processes (Buchanan and Powell 2008).

20 (Hobbes 1962, chapter 21, "On the Liberty of Subjects").

states are bundles of actors with differing preferences, that governments do not have monopoly power or authority to identify and articulate the interests of national actors, and that there is no single national interest. Rather, government preferences are mutable, changing in response to shifting priorities and electoral outcomes, economic and political turbulence, and external or transnational forces. Transnational politics approaches focus on how domestic actors bring international forces in as a tool of leverage that influences domestic politics. The transnational politics pathway toward compliance is to construct alliances of internal and external support among actors who prefer that national policy better coheres with international law. Policy change occurs because of pressure exerted on governments by substate actors, acting on their own or in concert with external pressure. Democracy in this view comes from ICs promoting the rule of law vis-à-vis governments.

The transnational politics perspective moves in the direction of creating a broader basis of legitimating support for international law. But it does this by assuming that pressuring governments to comply with international law is inherently legitimate. If we believe that law reflects democratic choice, then this reconciliation makes sense. But if we believe that governments, organized interests, or groups of powerful states can capture international and domestic legislative processes, this conflation between rule of law and democratic choice becomes problematic.

Each of the above answers to the democratic politics conundrum is problematic. The interstate arbiter perspective accepts as legitimate whatever governments want. The multilateral politics view accepts as inherently legitimate international law that represents the majoritarian voice of states while ignoring that much international law was written by a small number of actors or foisted on whole countries as a "take it or leave it" option.[21] The transnational politics view accepts at face value that the rule of international law and democracy are one and the same, since most people would likely choose a rule of law.

We may agree that governments that do bad things that a democratic decision-making process would likely reject—kill civilians or pursue venal interests—deserve legal sanction. If domestic systems are too captured to offer such a sanction, many people may support the notion that an international sanction is better than no sanction. But it is a lot more controversial to suggest that governments doing good things populations want—adopting laws through democratic means to promote valid public policy objectives—should be punished because of prior international legal promises. This is where debates about democracy enter the picture. If legitimated domestic actors are arguably "more democratic" than international

21 (Rajagopal 2003).

law, then one might think that law should bend to the will of a legitimate government.

One can question how seriously we should take these democracy arguments. First, such complaints have domestic corollaries. The constitutional review chapter began by noting that wherever judges can render acts of governments invalid, the losing side often complains about a "government of judges" where the choices of judges replace the decisions of elected officials. Such complaints do not mean that constitutional review is antidemocratic. Because political institutions can become captive to power, many people see judicial review as a crucial check on the democratic process, expecting judges to veto majority decisions that did not follow nationally defined democratic procedures or that impinge on constitutionally protected minority interests. Second, we might argue that democracy is a systems goal. The system is to allow judicial veto of certain choices, in conjunction with a democratic right to circumvent this veto by changing the constitution. Third, we may examine where this complaint arises and wonder if the "democracy" complaint is little more than the expression that the faction controlling domestic systems is upset that their objectives are being questioned. I can't help but observe the irony that international relations realists and nationalists are the people who most adamantly defend the right to ignore international law by raising national democracy concerns.

There is, however, something genuine in the democratic politics conundrum. Problematic international law can be difficult to change since revising international law requires multilateral assent followed by national ratification. As Fritz Scharpf long ago observed, the requirement of two chambers of positive ratifying support can create a "joint decision trap" where policy that the majority of actors find suboptimal can become impervious to change.[22] Policy created by judges is just as likely to lead to traps as policy created by legislatures, and this trap applies both nationally and internationally. But to state these truths is of small comfort. Counterproductive national legislation may be resilient to legislative change, and domestic judicial review may be a countermajoritarian antidote that also generates policy that is hard to reverse. But at least democratic political paralysis and domestic judicial review are not both countermajoritarian *and* foreign. And at least domestic actors *can* on their own escape the joint decision trap through building supermajoritarian domestic political support for change.

The altered politics argument is similar to the transnational politics approach in that it focuses on domestic actors bringing international law into domestic politics. It differs mostly in the focuses on legal politics, but

22 (Scharpf 1988).

this is an important difference when it comes to democratic politics. The altered politics argument inserts the rule of law as an essential part of politically legitimate governance, using the legal nature of ICs in combination with dependence on others to build legitimacy for international law. Where IC rulings are seen as legally valid, international judges may be able to engage, mobilize, and build support within the professional community of lawyers, judges, and law professors. Where international law is embedded into domestic legal order, ICs can also directly connect with compliance partners—national legal implementers—who already have the power to orchestrate a state's compliance. Since compliance partners are using their domestically legitimate powers, this argument provides an internal solution to international law's democratic politics conundrum. The political part of this argument is the insight that their legal nature allows ICs to tap into diffuse domestic and transnational political support for the rule of law. The legal nature of ICs does not solve democracy concerns, but it tethers international law interpreters to rule of law constraints that apply to domestic governments and judges alike.

Meanwhile, the international nature of international law and ICs' allows litigants to circumvent national legal barriers, which is also not per se a problem for democracy. In both the indigenous land rights and modern-day slavery cases ICs enforced legal rules that were also part of national constitutions, providing remedies unavailable in national legal systems yet fully consistent with national constitutions.[23] ICs interpretations can also provide legal cover for domestic actors who actually prefer international law. For example, the second use patent case study mentioned that lawyers and administrators suspected that government decisions to authorize second use patents had been purchased by foreign interests. The Andean Tribunal's ruling gave national administrators a reason to ignore legally valid presidential decrees, diverting any political complaint about national administrative decision making to the Andean level.

The international nature of ICs also allows international judges to ask more of governments compared to their domestic counterparts. The second use patent, softwood lumber, indigenous land rights, and modern-day slavery case studies all showed international judges making demands that many domestic judges supported yet felt unable to make, perhaps because of a fear of personal sanction. The linkage between domestic violations

23 In the indigenous land rights case, the problem was that the Awas Tingni had no papers documenting land ownership, and thus their only legal tool was the *amparo* system that could invalidate the lumber contract on their land but not recognize their land ownership. In the modern-day slavery case, the problem was that national judges kept siding with Hadijatou Mani's former master. Even Niger's higher courts recognized that the lower court rulings were problematic, but they were reluctant to intervene to fix the situation.

and international law then allows litigants to create international costs for governments that ignore domestic or international law and IC rulings. For example, antislavery advocates suggested that failure to follow the ECOWAS court's ruling might lead to the revocation of trade benefits from the United States. Opponents of Charles Taylor were able to generate a United Nations resolution authorizing Taylor's arrest if he returned to Liberia. These tools of leverage were easier to create because they were associated with recognized violations of international law. This leverage helps to focus governments on issues that might have escaped their attention, without necessarily undermining the democratic process.

The goal of the altered politics framework is empirically positivist, to understand the ability of ICs to promote state and international level change in the direction indicated by the law. ICs effect change via compliance constituencies, groups of domestic and transnational actors committed to the objectives inscribed in the law and to the rule of law more generally. Who is part of this constituency, and thus which voices get enhanced, varies. But actors committed to the rule of law are likely to always be a key component of the IC's compliance constituency. Actors that for normative, personal, self-interested, ideational, or strategic reasons also prefer change in the direction indicated by the law will also find their voice enhanced. For administrative review, ICs especially need to be able to co-opt stakeholder national administrators and judges. For constitutional review, ICs especially need to build support among domestic high court judges.

From a normative perspective, the altered politics argument provides an additional reconciliation for the democratic politics conundrum. One could argue that building support among these nationally based compliance constituencies is democratic in nature. It may be an imperfect solution to the democratic politics conundrum, but then so is the way electoral accountability works in practice.

We need to remember a few things at this juncture. First, the whole point of international law is to lock in certain commitments, such as promises to prioritize trade vis-à-vis protectionist impulses, and to respect human rights. Second, delegation to courts is inspired by a mistrust in governments to police their own law compliance, and that of their friends. International law is meant to be a backup to domestic mechanisms, allowing for negotiation in the shadow of the law and domestic adjudication first, but for international review should partiality seep into the domestic adjudicatory process. Third, we need to remember that advocates are turning to ICs not because they offer the best, most legitimate, most democratic solution to a problem at hand. It is always preferable when national political bodies on their own choose to do the right thing—to listen to democratic stakeholders; to respect the rule of law; and to honor covenants between themselves, their citizens, foreigners, and foreign governments. ICs are seized because litigants have reached a domestic political and legal impasse. Fourth, if neither governments, rule of law interlocutors, nor citizens want to follow international law, then choosing domestic over international law will be both likely and a politically legitimate course of action.

All of the above duly noted, it is nonetheless true that delegation to ICs will favor goals written into the DNA of the law—freer trade, human rights, protection of noncombatants, and such—in other words, the goals that those with power have managed to write into international law. Powerful states should like delegation to ICs because it adds to international agreements a slow-release mechanism and a self-help tool for state and nonstate actors to monitor for compliance and pressure governments to respect the rules they helped craft. But delegation to courts is also a self-binding check. Those powerful enough to go it alone, especially if they have not learned to distrust self-governance of the powerful, may prefer not to be bound.

We might find ways to justify prioritizing the international rule of law over democratic choice, but so long as international actors are involved in determining how international law applies at home, the international rule of law will involve foreign pressure constraining of domestic choice. External pressure is an international fact of life, and constraining foreign power to the rule of law may be an improvement to the older ways that power operated internationally (for example, colonialism, empire, or advantage of the stronger). But enhancing the international rule of law is also a means to enhance the leverage of those internationally mobilized actors who get to help write the law, and the power of rule of law actors like judges and lawyers.

III. DO WE WANT MORE INTERNATIONAL LAW ENFORCEMENT?

This book has taken a positive (in the empirical sense) approach to the study of ICs. My focus has mostly been instrumental, examining how actors use litigation threats and leverage international law and IC rulings to promote political change. I have barely considered the legitimacy of such actions, and I just admitted the problem in doing so. International law is created via a political process; there is nothing inherently moral, just, or legitimate about crafting multilateral agreements with the force of law. The empirical and normative project of determining what makes for legitimate international law and the confines of ICs' legitimate authority remains, but to address these important and challenging topics would be a different endeavor, one that I cannot tackle in the conclusion of a volume. Instead I will end on a more modest but nonetheless important policy note.

My starting point is to state what I think is obvious. International law is a resource. It is wonderful and somewhat miraculous that reasoned deliberation can lead to the writing and the development of legal rules and rulings that are mostly words on paper imbued with meaning and authority. When words and ideas are powerful motivators, we do not need to rely on coercion or other types of inducements. We must therefore be sure that delegation to ICs does not induce cynicism or undermine the legitimacy of international law. To protect the policy resource that is international law, we need a broader debate about how and when using international judicial enforcement is likely to be a tool that promotes greater respect for international law. My objective now is to provoke a debate about when and how to constructively use delegation to ICs to promote the policy objective of enhancing respect for international law.

In 1964, Judith Shklar developed a powerful critique of legalism as an ideology. Shklar questioned the fundamental legalist assumption that applying the law equally across cases is inherently good, explaining how equal application of the law is often undesirable and at times even unethical. Shklar's broader claim was that legalism's version of justice—equal application of the law—is only one type of justice, and that justice itself is just one of a number of valid public policy goals. She advocated instead using legalism as a policy approach when it is helpful. Since a complete faith that law leads to the best outcome may well do more harm than good, Shklar suggested that we need different criteria to consider when legal approaches make sense.[24] Shklar did not herself try to develop an argument about when legal solutions are useful except to say that we should use law and legal approaches for good public policy ends.

ICs by design support the policy goals that are inscribed in multilateral law. Multilateralism is a commitment to principled decision making, with two or more governments coming together to precommit to a set of general rules.[25] From a policy perspective, using legalist approaches to facilitate multilateral policy objectives seems like a reasonable starting point, so long as lawmakers' good sense in tandem with judicial enforcement actually helps to reach desired objectives. The previous sections limited policy discussion to questions that are somehow related to enhancing the effectiveness and good functioning of multilateralism and existing ICs. We still need to ask how we should think about applying the policy tool that is international law enforcement.

24 (Shklar 1964).
25 (Ruggie 1993, introduction).

Shklar made a rather controversial claim that prosecuting German war crimes was successful because Germany had a legalist culture, whereas parallel efforts to prosecute Japanese war crimes were "a complete dud."[26] Her argument rested in part on poor choices of prosecutors (and American officials), and in particular the decision not to prosecute Japan's emperor. This part of her argument remains as relevant today as it was in 1964; we are in the very early stages of learning how to constructively use the policy tool of international criminal indictments and prosecutions. The other aspect of her argument, however—that cultural factors in Germany made prosecutions a good strategy, whereas the different Japanese culture made prosecutions likely to flop in any event—is problematic.

Political actors might decide to limit adjudication of certain issues, and in essence Shklar was suggesting that governments should use political trials selectively. The decision to create ICs is different from Shklar's focus on case-by-case political trials. It arguably requires even more careful thought because judges and prosecutors do not have the same luxury of choice as policy makers. We all recognize that sometimes litigating violations *is not* the best means to an end. We all hope that advocates will avoid raising legal suits that will provoke political backlashes, and that governments will address the valid concerns of rights holders even if doing so involves creating an extrajudicial strategy that is not 100 percent faithful to the law.

The problem is that governments get busy and distracted and the political process often fails to address valid concerns of litigants. When there are no political solutions at hand, cases are likely to proceed to court. Once in court, international judges cannot avoid naming human rights and economic law violations in the context of legally valid cases. And now that we have a permanent ICC, we cannot selectively prosecute war crimes based on national cultural or political preferences in the target state. To do so will undermine faith in the rule of law and the political legitimacy of international judicial institutions. Meanwhile, the existence of ICs generates expectations about law enforcement. The gap between expectations and reality can generate cynicism about international law and international courts, just as the robust enforcement of existing rules can generate backlash (as occurred when the South African Development Community's Court of Justice applied existing law to rule in favor of white Zimbabwean farmers, to the dismay of many Africans).[27]

In the past, governments could follow the folkloric ostrich strategy of putting their head in the sand. By avoiding delegating authority to ICs, governments might not be confronted with hard choices about which

26 (Shklar 1964, 181).
27 (de Wet 2013).

cases to litigate or what to do about an adverse legal ruling. But chapter 4 showed that the choice facing most governments today is different. The plurality of adjudicators willing to rule on state compliance with international legal agreements means that persistent litigants can obtain a ruling regarding the legality of a state's policy regardless of if the government has consented to international adjudication. This reality means that today ignoring the law brings costs. It may seem like governments avoid paying the piper more often than not, but extraterritorial law enforcement means that governments increasingly face the choice of empowering IC review or being subject to legal review by foreign courts, ad hoc legal bodies, or foreign donors. Indeed, by failing to address known problems governments actually make it more rather than less likely that litigants will use law and courts as a tool to promote their agendas.

The ostrich days are behind us; today, governments are likely to be confronted by lawsuits and power-backed suggestions to improve the effectiveness and remedies associated with international legal agreements. Given this reality, we need to start a more broad-based debate about where and how we should use legalized or other sorts of approaches to address real concerns about violations of international legal agreements.

This book argued that compulsory jurisdiction and private access provisions undermine state control, thus it may sound controversial to suggest expanding access to and the jurisdictional reach of some international legal mechanisms. But for some issues, we actually do need more judicialization. Chapter 2 explained how delegation to ICs can be both self- and other-binding. Where governments actually want to implement international agreements, allowing private actors to identify legal violations and trigger adjudication can helpfully facilitate the implementation of international law. By allowing private actors to pursue litigation at the international level, governments enhance the perception of neutral adjudication while divesting themselves of the responsibility of monitoring state implementation of international agreements and of the blame for adverse legal rulings. Indeed, private actor-initiated litigation might help clarify the law, create transnational uniformity that discourages forum shopping, and provide a face-saving way for conflict-adverse government officials to put pressure on themselves and on actors within their state to make contested but much needed decisions and to implement international agreements. Thus for some issues it will be a wise policy choice to self-bind to new-style international judicial oversight, especially because creating more ICs with compulsory jurisdiction and private access can channel litigation to international legal bodies staffed by more geographically representative judges that governments get to choose.

The terms of private and international actor-initiated litigation, however, must be set with care. The discussion of the ICSID system (in the

Metalclad case study in chapter 6) flagged a number of problems associated with the investor-dispute system. The discussion explained why Western investors are quite happy with the international investment dispute system: it gives them international legal rights that are vastly superior to rights investors have at home and allows investors to help pick their judges and garner awards that can be claimed around the world. Critics have also identified public policy problems with the investor dispute system. It can introduce moral hazard, indemnifying firms that engage in risky international investments. And the investment dispute system is increasingly being creatively used in ways that were not intended. For example, recently Spanish investors won an award by invoking an investment dispute provision of the Energy Charter Treaty that the Russian Duma had never ratified.[28] While we may be happy that Russia's government has finally paid some price for its manipulation of the rule of law as it seized control of the Yukos oil company,[29] it is unclear that an award for Spanish investors provides a helpful remedy. My discussion of the Metalclad case suggested that a permanent court with a balancing mandate might actually work better than ad hoc arbitration. In any event, the case shows the need to more clearly introduce balancing into international adjudicatory systems. Rules of deference, balancing, and proportionality review are especially important for reconciling international law and democratic choice.

The point is that prudently using delegation to ICs as a policy tool for specific objectives makes more sense than sticking one's head in the sand or adopting a hail-Mary strategy of creating an IC and then hoping that the system works as imagined. Legalized dispute adjudication and international law enforcement are useful resources that litigants can and do draw on. Where international litigation options do not exist, domestic bodies may well step in to fill a legal vacuum. The way to avoid others stepping into the void is to talk with stakeholders and use political or less legalized channels to address persistent concerns so as to avoid the international judicialization of issues that are better decided via political channels. Said differently, the political failure to listen to valid and shared stakeholder concerns triggers and facilitates the success of litigation strategies.

We need to debate the trade-off between legal and political mechanisms. There is an active debate about legalized versus nonlegalized approaches with respect to restorative justice, with participants regularly discussing whether peace and reconciliation commissions or local adjudicatory solutions provide a more useful strategy than international criminal

28 (Laidlaw 2012). The decision on the merits was issued after the publication of this article.

29 (Stephan 2014).

prosecution.[30] But such debates are the exception rather than the rule, and as of yet these are not informed debates since we have little real appreciation of when legal enforcement does and does not help to address political and policy problems. We need more debates, and more social science information that specifies options and trade-offs so as to help policy makers evaluate choices. Debating these and other issues is important for the normative project of building an effective, legitimate, and high-quality international judicial system, one that can be part of the system's goal of accountable international governance.

Democratic Politics and the New Terrain of International Law

This chapter has argued that ICs can contribute to accountability in domestic and international politics, which is part of the project of making international law democratically legitimate. I'm suggesting that international law and delegation to ICs should be conceived of as policy tool, rather than an engine of legalist ideology. As a policy instrument, ICs allow stakeholders to trigger international judicial review while keeping in place the reality that ICs—like all courts—are dependent on social support to implement law and legal rulings. This reconciliation tolerates and perhaps even requires the uneven application of law. Noncompliance with the law is certainly not the goal, but it can be a way to allow for democratic choice to trump international law compliance. If stakeholders are allowed to seize ICs and pressure governments when noncompliance is personally harmful, then delegation to ICs can enhance the accountability of governments while promoting respect for the rule of law.

Delegation to courts is not a silver bullet. Courts are in the business of trying to deliver justice, but it is a messy business that almost always falls short of our impossibly high hopes and aspirations. This self-help altered politics perspective tolerates ambiguities and tensions in the law—for example, a lack of clear legal certainty regarding the supreme authority of international law and some flexibility regarding the boundary lines dividing international and domestic legal authority. Indeed, I suggested that the need for ICs to co-opt the support of others is the best way to keep ICs and international law accountable to the desires of political stakeholders.

To expect this unevenness is to make debates about international law and international courts more realistic. Even in the best functioning national rule of law systems, law gets unevenly applied in practice. Even where there are powerful and independent courts, domains of persistent legal noncompliance remain, the countermajoritarian and power-balancing dimensions of the rule of law need constant adjustment, and there are challenging and at times unresolvable tensions between local,

30 For example, see Osiel (1997).

state, federal, and international levels of governance, which undermine the legitimacy of different domestic political solutions. More realistic expectations are a partial ward for the cynicism that occurs when utopian ideals inevitably fall short.

To normalize our expectations for international law and international courts is not to celebrate or condone shortcomings. On the contrary, the ultimate objective is to push toward a fuller and more even respect for a rule of law in international politics and to create systems where legal rights can be realized in balance with the collective pursuit of valid public policy priorities set by governments and peoples. Toward this end, I advocated a specific path forward. We need to build international law by allowing international law to coexist with the pursuit of valid domestic public policy options. We need to build capacity and support among ICs' critical interlocutors, who are those domestic and international actors that believe in the importance of the rule of law and the political objectives that get inscribed in multilateral legal agreements. Since international rules of law are deeply dependent on the domestic rule of law, building support among ICs' critical interlocutors means in practice building support the rule of law at the domestic level. This support must have a grassroots democratic basis if it is to be legitimate.

The rule of law has become a beneficiary of globalization. The international rule of law is an important backup for shortcomings of the domestic rule of law, but it will never be a substitute. Rather, increasingly the international and domestic rule of law are intertwined and codependent, rising and falling in legitimacy and effectiveness together. We will not be returning to the old terrain of international law, just as we will not be returning to the sovereignty of national law. This means that the only way forward is to find a way to reconcile international law and democracy by making international law responsive to its stakeholders, the society of states and peoples who benefit from a rule of law. I hope that this book makes a modest contribution to this goal by leap-frogging scholarly debate to draw on the rich comparative environment that international judicial institutions are creating. This study has surely raised more questions than it has answered, but hopefully it has also generated ideas about how to answer these many questions so that we can learn when and how international adjudication can helpfully encourage respect for the rule of law.

My argument is that delegation to ICs provides a self-help tool in the form of a legal body that resides outside of the control of states. Advocates turn to international adjudication in the hope that political reality can perhaps catch up to the words on paper that constitute international law. I am under no illusion that law will ever replace power as a key element of politics. But I do believe that the rule of law constrains power, and that the more people believe in and demand the rule of law, the more democratic and meaningful legal checks on power become.

Chapter Appendixes

APPENDIX FOR CHAPTER 3: Coding Delegation of Authority to ICs

Functional Role	Court Treaty Language	Sample Treaty Provision
Dispute Settlement Helping litigating parties resolve disagreements that turn on definitions of the law.	Jurisdiction to "interpret the meaning of the law" or to render binding rulings in cases that are brought.	ICJ Statute of the Court, Article 36 1. The jurisdiction of the Court comprises all cases which the parties refer to it and all matters specially provided for in the Charter of the United Nations or in treaties and conventions in force.
Administrative Review Review the legal validity of contested administrative decisions.	Jurisdiction in cases concerning the legality of any action, regulation, directive, or decision of a public administrator, or the administrator's "failure to act."	EC Treaty, Article 230 The Court of Justice shall review the legality of ... acts of the Council, of the Commission and of the ECB ... It shall for this purpose have jurisdiction in actions brought by a Member State, the European Parliament, the Council or the Commission on grounds of lack of competence, infringement of an essential procedural requirement, infringement of this Treaty or of any rule of law relating to its application, or misuse of powers ... Any natural or legal person may, under the same conditions, institute proceedings against a decision addressed to that person or against a decision which, although in the form of a regulation or a decision addressed to another person, is of direct and individual concern to the former. (Article 231 states that "if the action is well founded, the Court of Justice shall declare the act concerned to be void." Article 232 allows "failure to act" suits on similar terms.)

APPENDIX FOR CHAPTER 3: (*Continued*)

Functional Role	Court Treaty Language	Sample Treaty Provision
Enforcement Naming violations of the law and sometimes defining remedies.	Jurisdiction to adjudicate breach of agreement, nullification or impairment of rights under the agreement, or compliance with the agreement.	ATJ Treaty, Article 23 If the General Secretariat considers that a Member Country has failed to comply with its obligations under the provisions or Conventions comprising the legal system of the Andean Community, it shall submit its observations to that Member Country in writing. The Member Country must respond to those observations within a period set by the General Secretariat in keeping with the urgency of the case, which shall not exceed sixty days. Once the reply has been received or the term has expired, the General Secretariat shall issue an administrative ruling, which must include its reasoning, regarding the state of compliance with those obligations. If the General Secretariat decides that the Member Country has failed to comply with its obligations and it continues with the behavior that was the subject of the observations, the former shall request a decision from the Court as soon as possible. The Member Country affected by that noncompliance can join the General Secretariat in the action.
Constitutional Review Holding international and state actors accountable to higher order norms.	Jurisdiction to review the legality or validity of any legislative act, regulation, directive, of an IO and/or a state.	East African Community Treaty Article 28 (2): A Partner State may refer for determination by the Court, the legality of any act, regulation, directive, decision or action on the ground that it is ultra vires or unlawful or an infringement of the provisions of this Treaty or any rule of law relating to its application or amounts to a misuse or abuse of power. Article 30: Subject to the provisions of Article 27 of this Treaty, any person who is resident in a Partner State may refer for determination by the Court, the legality of any Act, regulation, directive, decision or action of a Partner State or an institution of the Community on the grounds that such act, regulation, directive, decision or action is unlawful or is an infringement of the provisions of this Treaty.

APPENDIX FOR CHAPTER 5: INTERNATIONAL COURTS' DISPUTE SETTLEMENT JURISDICTION (ORGANIZED ALPHABETICALLY)

This appendix examines primarily the terms specified in Court Treaties. First listed are the courts in figure 5.1. At the end are four systems not listed in figure 5.1: the African Union, ASEAN, the Arab Investment Court and OAPEC systems. IC jurisdiction for interstate dispute adjudication is neither exclusive nor mandatory. IC jurisdiction for contracts with international organizations and for labor disputes is usually both mandatory and exclusive. Unless otherwise stated, the articles referenced correspond to the legal instruments indicated in the Court Treaty bibliography.

Andean Tribunal of Justice (ATJ)

New style court features: Compulsory jurisdiction. State access. Private litigant access for labor disputes with Community bodies, and for arbitration (see below).
Jurisdiction: The ATJ is primarily a body for enforcement, constitutional and administrative review. The ATJ envisions that most interstate disputes will be brought under the tribunals' compulsory noncompliance jurisdiction. Complaints must first be raised with the General Secretariat, but member states can pursue the matter themselves if they remain unsatisfied (Article 24). There is also an arbitral system that allows the ATJ (Article 38) or General Secretariat (Article 39) to serve as arbiter for disputes between Andean institutions, and with individuals, regarding contracts, should the parties so agree. Private parties may submit to the tribunals' arbitration any disputes that may arise as a result of the application or interpretation of aspects contained in private contracts that are governed by the Andean Community's legal system. The ATJ can also hear labor disputes that arise in institutions and bodies of the Andean Integration System (Article 40).

Caribbean Court of Justice (CCJ)

New style court features: Compulsory jurisdiction. State access. Ad hoc private litigant access.
Jurisdiction: CCJ has jurisdiction to hear disputes between CCJ member states (Article 12(1)(a)). The court is authorized to decide on a case-by-case basis if the interest of "justice" requires private parties' access to the court (Article 12(1)(d) and Article 24). Member states may also use voluntary modes of dispute resolution (Article 188 (4)) including good of-

fices, mediation, arbitration, a conciliation commission and alternative dispute resolution systems (Articles 191–200, 223).

Central American Court of Justice (CACJ)

New style court features: Compulsory jurisdiction. State access. Private litigant access, and private litigant access for labor disputes.
Jurisdiction: The CACJ has wide jurisdiction for contentious cases, including disputes between states (Article 22a) and disputes raised by private litigants (Article 22 ch & g) or members of community institutions. The court's jurisdiction is compulsory, although the jurisdiction applies "when the parties have requested the court" to intervene. Its jurisdiction is explicitly not compulsory for cases concerning frontier, territorial and maritime disputes, disputes between members and nonmembers, and cases where CACJ sits as an arbitral body (Article 22a). The court can also hear appeals regarding internal decisions in disputes with staff (Article 22j).

Court of Justice for the Common Market of Eastern and Southern Africa (COMESA)

New style court features: Compulsory jurisdiction. State access. Private litigant access for contract and labor disputes involving community institutions.
Jurisdiction: The court has "general jurisdiction" to adjudicate any matter that may be referred to it (Article 23), but the rules regarding the types of claims that can be referred suggest that most cases will be noncompliance claims or challenges to the legality of community acts. The COMESA court has jurisdiction to determine any matter arising from a claim by any person against the common market or its institutions for acts of their servants or employees in performance of their duties (Article 27).

Central African Monetary Community (CEMAC)

New style court features: Compulsory jurisdiction. State access. Private litigant access for contract and labor disputes involving community institutions.
Jurisdiction: The court has jurisdiction involving disputes between states (Article 22). The court is the last resort body for damage claims between community institutions and their agents (Article 20), and the first and last resort body for disputes between the community and its agents (e.g., employees) (Article 21).

East African Court of Justice (EACJ)

New style court features: Compulsory jurisdiction. State access. Private litigant access for labor disputes involving community institutions, and where arbitration clauses in contracts so specify.
Jurisdiction: A special agreement clause allows any dispute among states to be heard by the court (Article 32), but most cases brought by states will challenge another state or a community institution for an infringement of the treaty or a failure to fulfill an obligation (Article 28). The court can also hear disputes between the community and its employees (Article 31). Any question arising in national courts involving the interpretation of the treaty can be referred to the court (Article 34). Arbitration clauses and special agreements can also confer jurisdiction on the EACJ, and Article 32 envisions such clauses in contractual agreement and commercial agreements.

Economic Community of West African States Court of Justice (ECOWAS CJ)

New style court features: Compulsory jurisdiction. State access. Private litigant access for contract and labor disputes involving community institutions.
Jurisdiction: The court has jurisdiction over disputes brought by a party, a member state or the authority regarding the application and interpretation of the treaty or secondary legislation (Supplementary Protocol, Article 9 a and b, Protocol of the Court). A member state may initiate proceedings on behalf of a national (Article 10, Protocol of the Court). The court may also hear disputes involving the community and its officials, and actions for damages or omissions in exercise of official functions (Supplementary Protocol, Article 9 f and g).

Economic Court of the Commonwealth of Independent States (ECCIS)

New style court features: Compulsory jurisdiction. State access.
Jurisdiction: The court has jurisdiction in disputes that arise during the implementation of economic obligations under the Charter of the Commonwealth of Independent States (Article 32). The ECCIS can be given jurisdiction over other agreements among ECCIS states (Article 32). The 1992 Moscow Agreement and Regulations is silent as to whether its jurisdiction is compulsory, but the ECCIS has interpreted Article 3(1) of the

1992 Moscow agreement as providing for compulsory jurisdiction (case c-1/1-97). There still seems to be disagreement regarding the extent to which ECCIS rulings are binding. For more on this see Danilenko (1991, 907–8).

European Court of Justice (ECJ)

New style court features: Compulsory jurisdiction. State access. Private litigant access for contractual disputes.
Jurisdiction: The ECJ is primarily a body for enforcement, constitutional and administrative review. But the court has jurisdiction for any dispute between member states that relates to the subject matter of the treaty. Its dispute settlement jurisdiction is regulated by special agreements between the parties (TFEU Article 273/TEC Article 239). The court has jurisdiction regarding disputes involving contractual liabilities of the community (TFEU Article 268/TEC Article 235) and arbitration clauses (TFEU Article 272/TEU Article 238). States can raise disputes concerning the European Investment Bank (TFEU Article 271/TEU Article 237). The Council of the European Union redelegated the ECJ's jurisdiction over employee disputes to a new Civil Service Tribunal in 2005.

European Free Trade Area Court (EFTAC)

New style court features: Compulsory jurisdiction. State access. Surveillance Authority access. Private litigant access for contractual liabilities.
Jurisdiction: EFTAC is primarily designed to monitor the Surveillance Authority as it oversees compliance with the EFTAC agreement and to hear noncompliance cases raised by the Surveillance Authority. EFTAC can hear private cases regarding contractual liabilities of the EFTA Surveillance Authority (Article 39 and Article 46, para. 2).

International Court of Justice (ICJ)

New style court features: None.
Jurisdiction: The ICJ has jurisdiction regarding disputes between states. The conditions under which cases may be raised are defined in the subsidiary agreements (usually bilateral or multilateral treaties) (Article 35). An optional protocol allows signatories to agree to accept compulsory jurisdiction with respect to other signatories of the protocol (Article 36.2). The ICJ can also be designated the interpreter of treaties, and there can be compulsory jurisdiction for these specific treaties (Article 36.2 and 36.3).

International Tribunal for the Law of the Sea (ITLOS)

New style court features: Partial compulsory jurisdiction, partial private litigant access, including for labor and contract disputes.
Jurisdiction: States are obliged to seek the peaceful resolution of disputes (Article 279) and have a choice of multiple forums for such resolution (Article 289), including the ITLOS court. There is an optional protocol to consent to the ITLOS court's compulsory jurisdiction (Article 287, 288, 291). All dispute settlement procedures are open to state parties (Article 291) and by mutual state agreement any dispute can be brought to the ITLOS court (article 299). But there is a long list of rules specifying limits on claims against the rights of coastal states (Article 197). For the seizing of vessels, if there is no agreement on how to proceed within ten days, the flag state of the vessel may bring the case to the legal body that has been prespecified by the detaining state (Article 292). A separate procedure covers disputes related to the Seabed Authority, and states are obliged to resolve disputes through Seabed Disputes Chamber. This chamber can also adjudicate contract cases between private actors (Article 187c). Article 188 allows such disputes to be heard through binding arbitration too. A 2009 agreement also gives the Tribunal jurisdiction for disputes involving staff members.

Common Court of Justice and Arbitration for the Organization for the Harmonization of Business Law in Africa (OHADA)

New style court features: Compulsory jurisdiction. State access. Private litigant access.
Jurisdiction: The OHADA court primarily is an appeals court for national judicial rulings involving OHADA business laws (Article 15). National court rulings will involve disputes about OHADA law, and might be raised by private litigants seeking to enforce OHADA law. In addition, states, national courts and members of the Council of Ministers can request advisory opinions (Article 14) and national courts can send preliminary ruling requests (Articles 15 and 16). OHADA includes an arbitration system, but its arbitral jurisdiction needs to be inserted into contracts or agreed to by parties. In its arbitral role, the court can create awards (Article 25 of Arbitration Procedures). Enforcement of OHADA rulings is governed by national civil procedure rules (Article 46).

Southern African Development Community Tribunal (SADC)

New style court features: Compulsory jurisdiction. State access. Private litigant access, including for contract and labor disputes involving community institutions.
Jurisdiction: The tribunal's original jurisdiction included disputes between states (article 15:1), between states and the community (Article 17), between individuals and the community (Article 18), and between individuals and states (Article 15:2). The tribunal is also the appellate body for panels that are convened to resolve disputes regarding subsidiary agreements made between member states (Article 20a). A new statute of the SADC had not been negotiated at the time of writing. The private access provisions are likely to change, but not the original jurisdiction between states and individuals and the community.

Southern Common Market Dispute Settlement Permanent Review Tribunal (MERCOSUR)

New style court features: Compulsory jurisdiction. State access.
Jurisdiction: An informal dispute settlement system has existed since 1999, but most disputes were and continue to be handled through diplomatic channels. Under the Olivos protocol, any disputes between the state parties regarding the interpretation, application or breach of the Treaties, protocols, agreements, and the instructions of the MERCOSUR Trade Commission can be submitted directly (Articles 4 and 5) or brought to the Common Market Group (Articles 6 and 7). If there is no resolution, disputes can proceed to an ad hoc arbitration panel (article 9), and any party can directly appeal decisions to the Permanent Review Tribunal (Article 17 and 23). Revisions of the Olivos protocol allow litigants can choose the forum for dispute settlement (including the WTO system), but the MERCOSUR system will not consider a case that has been heard in the WTO forum. Revisions to the Olivos protocol also state that the Permanent Review Tribunal can issue advisory opinions for disputes between states and community institutions, and based on questions submitted by national supreme courts (Articles 1, 3, and 4 of revisions).

World Trade Organization Permanent Appellate Body (WTO)

New style court features: Compulsory jurisdiction. State access.
Jurisdiction: The aim of dispute settlement is to preserve the rights and obligations of members under the covered agreements. Procedures allow any dispute involving WTO agreements to be resolved through mediation,

good offices or consultations (Article 5), and be brought to the dispute resolution system (Article 6). In practice, nearly all disputes will involve the rights and obligations of states, and thus the enforcement role.

West African Economic and Monetary Union (WAEMU)

New style court features: Compulsory jurisdiction. State access. Private litigant access for contract and labor disputes involving community institutions.
Jurisdiction: The court can hear cases between the community and its agents (Court Treaty Protocol 1 Article 16) and between member states (Court Treaty Protocol 1 Article 17). The court is the only body authorized to assess contractual damages caused by the community (court's procedural rules Article 15 (5)). The court oversees charges against individual Commission members for alleged malfeasance (Article 30 of the Treaty establishing the WAEMU).

FOUR ADDITIONAL SYSTEMS NOT INCLUDED IN FIGURE 5.1

African Court of Justice (ACJ) (not yet established)

New style court features: None.
Jurisdiction: State parties, the Assembly of States, Parliament, and other African Union Organs authorized by the Assembly may raise cases (the content of which is not specified) (Article 18). This means that the Commission cannot raise cases. States that are not part of the African Union are specifically precluded from raising cases, and the court has no jurisdiction for disputes involving states that have not ratified the court's protocol (Article 18 (3)). These provisions are likely to change should the ACJ be created as an entity that is merged with the ACtHPR or that has criminal jurisdiction.

Arab Investment Court (operational since 2003)

New style court features: Compulsory jurisdiction. State access. Private litigant access.
Jurisdiction: The draft statute for the Arab Investment Court came into force February 2, 1985, but the court only became operational in 2003 when the Arab League's Economic and Social Council decided to activate it. The investment agreement defines the legal terms governing investment, and it indicates that conciliation and arbitration are the first means

for dispute settlement. The Arab Investment Court can be appealed to when an arbitration agreement is not implemented in three months' time. Firms will be the primary instigators of litigation. The court issued its first ruling in 2004.

ASEAN Dispute Resolution Protocol (formally operational, but not yet invoked)

New style court features: Compulsory jurisdiction. State access.
Jurisdiction: The dispute settlement system is overseen by the "Senior Economic Officials Meeting" (SEOM), which can decide by unanimous consent not to form a panel and not to accept a panel report (Article 5). The panel's stated task is to "make an objective assessment" of the dispute (Article 7). Panel reports can be appealed to an appellate body (Article 12). Most cases are likely to involve noncompliance, and thus the enforcement role.

Judicial Tribunal for Organization of Arab Petroleum-Exporting Countries (OAPEC) (defunct but formally operational)

New style court features: Compulsory jurisdiction. State access. Private litigant access (with state consent to adjudication).
Jurisdiction: The tribunal has implicit compulsory jurisdiction over disputes between member states in the field of petroleum operations, disputes referred to the tribunal by the OAPEC Council, and disputes relating to the agreement (Article 23.1). Member states may consent to the jurisdiction of the tribunal in a case raised by a private company operating in the member's territory or belonging to another member state (Article 23.2).

APPENDIX FOR CHAPTER 6: INTERNATIONAL COURTS' ADMINISTRATIVE REVIEW JURISDICTION (ORGANIZED ALPHABETICALLY)

This appendix examines primarily the terms specified in Court Treaties. Unstated is that the remedy is nullification of illegal acts. First listed are ICs in figure 6.1, all of which have compulsory jurisdiction and allow private actors to initiate litigation. At the end are three additional administrative review systems: NAFTA, ICSID, and MERCOSUR. IC jurisdiction is usually exclusive with respect to invalidating supranational administrative acts. Unless otherwise stated, the articles referenced correspond to the legal instruments indicated in the Court Treaty bibliography.

Andean Tribunal of Justice (ATJ)

New style court features: Compulsory jurisdiction. State access. Direct private litigant access and access via preliminary ruling references from national courts.

Jurisdiction: The ATJ can nullify General Secretariat decisions on the basis of a failure to follow provisions of the Andean legal system or a deviation of powers in cases raised by member states, Andean institutions (Article 17) and private litigants if their direct interest is at issue (Article 19). The ATJ may hear failure to act charges against the General Secretariat, Council of Foreign Ministers, and Commission should these institutions abstain from carrying out an activity. Member states and directly affected private individuals can initiate such suits (Article 37). National courts can refer cases involving Andean law to the ATJ, and courts of last instance are required to refer such cases. In practice, all of these cases involve the application of community regulatory rules by national administrative litigants (Article 33). National judges trying the case must adopt the ATJ's interpretation (Article 36).

BENELUX

New style court features: Compulsory jurisdiction. State access. Direct private litigant access and access via preliminary ruling references from national courts.

Jurisdiction: A 1969 treaty establishes administrative and judicial cooperation. The court treaty defining the BENELUX court's jurisdiction notes: "The court's primary charge is to create a uniform interpretation of legal rules within the community in cases heard in national courts or in the envisioned arbitral body (Article 1)." The BENELUX court can hear preliminary references from national courts raising questions regarding community rules (Article 6). The terms for this review are described in Articles 7–9 and in a separate document. Governments can also ask for advisory opinions about community rules (Article 10). Litigants can challenge decision of the Committee of Ministers and its working groups (Articles 1, 2, and 3). Grounds for appeal are the violation of a written law or of due form, the overstepping or abuse of authority, or the violation of any general legal principle (Article 4).

Caribbean Court of Justice (CCJ)

New style court features: Compulsory jurisdiction. State access. Private litigant access.

Jurisdiction: The CCJ has jurisdiction to review fines levied by the Competition Commission for uncompetitive practices. Private litigants and states can challenge these decisions (Article 175 (12) and Article 176 (6) of the Revised Treaty Establishing the Caribbean Common Market). National courts may refer questions of treaty interpretation or application (Article 14). The court can grant private litigants *locus standi* when the treaty confers individual rights or there is a question of prejudice in the enjoyment of community rights, and where member states fail to make a claim on the individual's behalf or to authorize the individual to make their claim directly (Article 20).

Central African Monetary Community (CEMAC)

New style court features: Compulsory jurisdiction. State access. Direct private litigant access and access via preliminary ruling references from national courts.
Jurisdiction: The court has jurisdiction to review the legality of legal acts of the CEMAC and related acts raised by any state or community organ for irregularity, incompetence, abuse of power or a violation of community rules (Article 15). National courts can also refer cases involving the legality or interpretation of CEMAC acts (Article 17).

Central American Court of Justice (CACJ)

New style court features: Compulsory jurisdiction. State access. Private litigant access.
Jurisdiction: The court's jurisdiction is compulsory for disputes, but voluntary regarding questions of law and fact. The court has general authority to hear suits brought by any actor with standing, including states, private litigants, and community institutions, about decisions of any organ of the system, including nullification charges and failure to act charges (CACJ statute Chapter II Article 22(b), (g)). It also has compulsory jurisdiction regarding any legal, regulatory or administrative provision that affect the conventions, treaties and norms of the laws of Central American integration (Chapter II Article 22 (c)). The court may also adjudicate prejudicial consultations referred by national judges so as to facilitate a uniform interpretation of legal principles (Chapter II Article 22 (5)).

Court of Justice for the Common Market of Eastern and Southern Africa (COMESA)

New style court features: Compulsory jurisdiction. State access. Direct private litigant access and access via preliminary ruling references from national courts.

Jurisdiction: Any resident of a member state may ask the court to rule on the legality of any act, regulation, directive or decision of the council, or of a member state if domestic remedies have been exhausted (Article 26). A national court shall refer questions of treaty interpretation, and questions about the validity of the regulations, directives and decisions of the common market to the COMESA Court for a ruling, if the national court considers a ruling on the question necessary for rendering judgment. A national court shall refer a matter to the COMESA Court if no judicial remedy is available under the member state's national law (Article 30).

East African Court of Justice (EACJ)

New style court features: Compulsory jurisdiction. State access. Direct private litigant access and access via preliminary ruling references from national courts.
Jurisdiction: Any member state (Article 28), private actor (Article 30), or national court (Article 34) can send to the court a question about the validity of regulations, directives, decisions, or actions of the community. Private litigants can challenge any act, regulation, decision or action of a partner state or community institution on the grounds that the act is unlawful or an infringement of the treaty (Article 30).

European Court of Justice (ECJ)

New style court features: Compulsory jurisdiction. State access. Direct private litigant access and access via preliminary ruling references from national courts.
Jurisdiction: The ECJ may rule acts of the Commission void (TFEU Art. 264 and 265/TEU Article 230 and 231). Member states, and institutions of the community can raise charges against any European institution for its failure to act. Private litigants may also raise a complaint for failure to address to that person any act other than a recommendation or an opinion (TFEU Article 265/TEU Article 232). The Court of First Instance (now General Court) has first instance jurisdiction in these cases (TFEU Article 265/TEU Article 225). The Council and Parliament can jointly create special bodies attached to the General Court to hear certain specified class actions (TFEU Article 257/TEU Article 225a) An institution whose action has been declared void or whose failure to act has been declared contrary to the treaty must take necessary measures to comply with the court's ruling (TFEU Article 266/TEU Article 233). National courts can refer questions of interpretation to the ECJ, and courts of last instance are required to refer questions involving European law (TFEU Article 267/TEU Article 234). References often include challenges to national administrative decisions applying community rules.

Economic Community of West African States Court of Justice (ECOWAS CJ)

New style court features: Compulsory jurisdiction. State access. Direct private litigant access and access via preliminary ruling references from national courts.
Jurisdiction: The court has jurisdiction over the interpretation and application of the treaty, conventions and protocols of the community, and the interpretation and application of the regulations, directives, decisions and other subsidiary legal instruments adopted by ECOWAS (Amended Article 9 (1a, b, c)). Individuals and corporate bodies have access for proceedings for the determination of an act or inaction of a community official that violates the rights of the individuals or corporate bodies (Amended Article 10 (c)). National courts may refer questions concerning the interpretation of a treaty provision or any regulation or protocol (Amended Article 10f).

European Free Trade Area Court (EFTAC)

New style court features: Compulsory jurisdiction. State access. Direct private litigant access and access via preliminary ruling references from national courts.
Jurisdiction: EFTA court has unlimited jurisdiction regarding penalties imposed by the Surveillance Authority (Article 36). EFTA states can challenge decisions of the EFTA Surveillance Authority on grounds of lack of competence, infringement of an essential procedural requirement, or infringement of any EFTA agreement, (Article 36), and its failure to act (Article 37). Private litigants can bring an action before the EFTA court under the same conditions, if the decision is addressed to them or is of direct and individual concern (Article 36). Private litigants can bring failure to act suits as well (Article 37). These rulings can effectively quash illegal decisions. EFTA court can give advisory opinions in cases raised by states or referred by national courts. States may limit national court references to last instance courts only (Article 34).

International Tribunal for the Law of the Sea—Seabed Chamber

New style court features: Compulsory jurisdiction. State access. Private litigant access.
Jurisdiction: Seabed Disputes Chamber can hear disputes between states and Authority concerning acts or omissions of the Seabed Authority in violation of the convention, acts of the Authority in excess of its jurisdic-

tion, and any misuse of its power by the Authority (Article 187b). The court is not allowed to review the exercise of the Authority's discretionary power, nor the legality validity of the rules, regulations, and procedures of the Authority. Reviews must be confined to individual claims concerning the application of Seabed Authority rules or procedures that is in conflict with the obligations of the parties to the dispute, and claims concerning excess of jurisdiction or misuse of power, or damages and remedies (Article 189). Given the limited deep seabed mining, these provisions are mostly moribund. But should mining become more pervasive, firms and possibly even environmental groups would be likely litigants.

West African Economic and Monetary Union (WAEMU)

New style court features: Compulsory jurisdiction. State access. Direct private litigant access and access via preliminary ruling references from national courts.
Jurisdiction: The Commission has control for competition policy, subject to the review of the court. Implicitly this means that the court can quash illegal decisions (Article 90 WAEMU Treaty). The court can hear cases that involve damages caused by community organs (Rules of Procedure (15 (3)). Since private litigants lack direct access, except for contractual disputes (Rules of Procedure (Article 16)), the case would need to be raised in a national court. National courts of last resort must refer questions about the legality of regulations, laws, directives, and decisions; other national courts may refer questions (Article 8). Legal interpretations in preliminary rulings are binding on all administrative and legal authorities within member states. A failure to observe these rulings may give rise to an infringement charge (Article 13).

Southern African Development Community Tribunal (SADC)

New style court features: Compulsory jurisdiction. State access. Direct private litigant access and access via preliminary ruling references from national courts.
Jurisdiction: The court was originally given jurisdiction to ascertain the validity of all protocols and subsidiary instruments adopted by the community, and all acts of the community (Article 14). The tribunal's jurisdiction covered disputes between member states, and between individuals and member states once domestic remedies were exhausted (Article 15), between member states and the community (Article 17) and between individuals and the community (Article 18). The treaty did not specify whether specific litigants could bring specific suits, suggesting that all authorized actors could raise suits that fell under the tribunal's jurisdiction, thus all actors could ask the tribunal to assess the validity of com-

munity acts. The tribunal also had jurisdiction to hear preliminary ruling references concerning the interpretation, application or validity of provisions at issue (Article 16). Although certain member states were clearly unhappy with SADC rulings, review panels suggest that the SADC was operating within the confines of its delegated jurisdiction when it issued its contested rulings. See de Wet (2013). A new statute of the SADC had not been negotiated at the time of writing

THREE ADDITIONAL INTERNATIONAL ADMINISTRATIVE REVIEW MECHANISMS NOT INCLUDED IN FIGURE 6.1.

North American Free Trade Area Chapter 19

New style court features: Compulsory jurisdiction. State access. Private litigant access (Chapters 19 and 11).

Jurisdiction: NAFTA Chapter 19 replaces and updates a previous binational procedure defined by the Canada-United States Free Trade Agreement (1987).[1] The Chapter 19 system applies only to goods regulated by the importing party's antidumping or countervailing duty law (Article 1901). Each party replaces final domestic judicial review of antidumping and countervailing duty determinations with binational panel reviews. An affected party may request a binational panel review the administrative record that led to the finding of illegal dumping, and records used to generate antidumping or countervailing duty determinations. The panel assesses whether administrative action is in accordance with the antidumping or countervailing duty law of the defendant state. The procedure for such reviews is then further defined (Article 1904). Should a state party interfere with the functioning or application of the binational panel review process, a state party can request (after consultations) the formation of a "special committee" to investigate the issue. The special committee can stay a panel review process and review panel process and findings (Article 1905). Additional specially formulated binational panels may review amendments to national antidumping or countervailing duty laws to see if changes affect preexisting agreements and understandings (Article 1903). Investment disputes are handled under the ICSID framework, but applying UNCITRAL rules (see the Metalclad case study for more).

1 The base legislative document is Chapter Nineteen: Review and Dispute Settlement in Antidumping and Countervailing Duty Matters included in the North American Free Trade Agreement 32 I.L.M. 289 (1993). Available at http://www.nafta-sec-alena.org/en/view.aspx?conID=590, last visited April 20, 2012.

International Centre for the Settlement of Investment Disputes (ICSID)

New style court features: Compulsory jurisdiction. State access. Private litigant access.
Jurisdiction: The ICSID website states that: ICSID is an autonomous international institution established under the Convention on the Settlement of Investment Disputes between States and Nationals of Other States with over one hundred and forty member states. The Convention sets forth ICSID's mandate, organization and core functions. The primary purpose of ICSID is to provide facilities for conciliation and arbitration of international investment disputes. If signatories of bilateral investment treaties are not signatories of the ICSID convention, disputes may be adjudicated by ICSID bodies following different terms. For example, the Metalclad ruling was adjudicate by an ICSID body according to UNCITRAL arbitration rules.

Southern Common Market Dispute Settlement Permanent Review Tribunal (MERCOSUR)

New style court features: Compulsory jurisdiction. State access. Private access also via national courts (preliminary ruling references).
Jurisdiction: Private parties can file claims with national chapters of the Common Market Group, raising a complaint that the adoption or application of legal or administrative measures by a state party has a restrictive, discriminatory or unfair competition effect in violation of MERCOSUR Treaties (Article 39 and 40). The Common Market Group shall call upon a group of experts (defined in Article 43) to review all valid claims, and private individuals and state parties shall have an opportunity to be heard (Article 42). National supreme courts can also refer questions involving MERCOSUR rules to the Permanent Review Tribunal. While not expressly stated in the Olivos protocol, decisions of MERCOSUR's political organs authorize national supreme courts to request advisory opinions.

APPENDIX FOR CHAPTER 7: INTERNATIONAL COURTS' ENFORCEMENT JURISDICTION (ORGANIZED ALPHABETICALLY)

This appendix examines primarily the terms specified in Court Treaties. First listed are ICs in figure 7.1, which have an explicit enforcement jurisdiction. Included is a summary of remedies and formal political checks in each system (in addition to the default check of the appointment process and legislative revisions). At the end are four additional international adjudicatory mechanisms with jurisdiction that could include assessing state compliance with an international treaty: the yet to be formed African Court of Justice, the Economic Court of the Commonwealth of Independent States, the Caribbean Court of Justice, and the ICSID system for investor disputes. International human rights courts have exclusive jurisdiction, after the exhaustion of domestic remedies (The ECOWAS CJ is a partial exception). Violations of trade law can sometimes be adjudicated at either the regional or WTO level. The ICC has complementary jurisdiction, thus national and regional courts may also exercise criminal jurisdiction. Unless otherwise stated, the articles referenced correspond to the legal instruments indicated in the Court Treaty bibliography.

African Court on Human and Peoples' Rights (ACtHPR)

New style court features: Compulsory jurisdiction for states ratifying optional protocol. State access. Commission access. Private litigant access for states ratifying optional protocol.
Jurisdiction: The Commission is charged with the protection and promotion of human rights, and interpreting the charter. The court is intended to complement the Commission's protective mandate (Article 1). The court has jurisdiction for any dispute or case submitted concerning the Charter (Article 3). Any institution of the African Union and any African organization recognized by the African Union can request an advisory opinion (Article 4). The African Commission and any state parties working with the Commission or that have an affected national can initiate a claim in front of the court (Article 5). States signing optional provisions authorize private litigants or NGOs to bring cases to the Commission (Article 5(3)). Only for states that have ratified an optional protocol is the court's jurisdiction compulsory. A separate ratification of a separate optional protocol allows private litigants to initiate litigation.
Remedies: Where a breach is found, the court may order a remedy including compensation, reparations, and it can require provisional measures in cases of extreme gravity and urgency (Article 27).
Formal political checks: States need to consent to the court's compulsory jurisdiction via an optional protocol. The commission can choose which cases to refer. For countries that have accepted both compulsory jurisdiction and private litigant access, there are no political checks to avert an IC ruling.

Andean Tribunal of Justice (ATJ)

New style court features: Compulsory jurisdiction. State access. General Secretary access. Direct private litigant access and access via preliminary ruling references from national courts.

Jurisdiction: The General Secretariat (Article 23), member countries (Article 24), and private litigants (Article 25) may bring to the ATJ a noncompliance case involving a member states. The Court Treaty allows domestic courts to hear noncompliance cases (Article 30), but this provision is subject to domestic legislation and Andean domestic systems have yet to be empowered to adjudicate such complaints. National courts can refer cases involving Andean law to the ATJ, and courts of last instance are required to refer such cases (Article 33). National judges adjudicating the case must adopt the ATJ's interpretation (Article 36).
Remedies: The General Secretariat can authorize retaliatory sanctions for noncompliance with a community law. So far the community levies small tariffs on a small number of goods (e.g., a 5 percent tariff to be applied on five goods). I have heard that countries are yet to actually retaliate, despite being authorized to do so. The ATJ may authorize the adoption of unspecified "other measures" (Article 27).
Formal political checks: None. General Secretariat determines the level of retaliatory sanction.

Central American Court of Justice (CACJ)

New style court features: Compulsory jurisdiction. State access. Private litigant access.
Jurisdiction: The court has jurisdiction to hear noncompliance cases brought by "any interested party" (Article 22c). States can propose questions to the court related to conflicts between treaties and between treaties and the national law of each member state (Article 23). Human rights cases are excluded because such cases fall under the "exclusive jurisdiction" of the Inter-American Court of Justice (Article 25).
Remedies: Rulings are clearly binding, and the court can review noncompliance with judicial decisions (Article 22f), but no remedies are specified.
Formal political checks: Court's jurisdiction is explicitly not compulsory for cases concerning frontier, territorial and maritime disputes, disputes between members and nonmembers, and cases where CACJ sits as an arbitral body (Article 22a). No specified remedies for noncompliance.

Central African Monetary Community (CEMAC)

New style court features: Compulsory jurisdiction. State access. Executive Secretary access. Direct private litigant access and access via preliminary ruling references from national courts.
Jurisdiction: Any state, organ of the community, or person with a legitimate interest can raise any violation of the treaties or subsequent conventions (article 14). CEMAC rulings are explicitly binding on national ad-

ministrative authorities and national judges (Article 18). The Executive Secretary, any organ of CEMAC, and any person can raise a case alleging that a member state has misinterpreted the treaty or subsequent conventions (Article 19). National courts may and courts of last instance are obliged to send preliminary rulings to the CEMAC court (Article 17).
Remedies: Failure to comply with a CEMAC ruling can be referred to a conference of heads of state (Article 16). The court has authority to order interim measures when it has been validly seized (Article 24).
Formal political checks: A political body determines whether noncompliance generates sanctions (see above).

Court of Justice for the Common Market of Eastern and Southern Africa (COMESA)

New style court features: Compulsory jurisdiction. State access. General Secretariat access. Direct private litigant access and access via preliminary ruling references from national courts.
Jurisdiction: Member states (Article 24) or the Secretary General (Article 25.1) may raise infringement charges against a member state. Member states do not need council assent to raise noncompliance suits. Private litigants can ask the court to rule on any act, regulation, directive, or decision of the council or of a member state (for questions about member state behavior, domestic remedies must first be exhausted) (Article 26). National courts must refer questions of interpretation, and questions about the validity of the regulations, directives and decisions of the common market to the COMESA court for preliminary ruling if such ruling is deemed necessary for the national tribunal to make a judgment (Article 30).
Remedies: The court may prescribe sanctions it considers necessary against a party that does not implement its ruling (Article 34).
Formal political checks: A Council of States must agree before the Secretary General's assertion of a legal violation can be referred to the court (Article 25.3). Once the case reaches the court, it can determine the remedies for breach.

East African Court of Justice (EACJ)

New style court features: Compulsory jurisdiction. State access. General Secretariat access. Direct private litigant access and access via preliminary ruling references from national courts.
Jurisdiction: The court's role is to ensure the adherence to the law and compliance with the treaty (Article 23). The Secretary General can investigate noncompliance and submit observations to member states. If the state concerned does not adequately respond within four months, the

matter can be referred to the Council of States. If the Council does not resolve the matter, it can direct the General Secretary to refer the matter to the court (Article 29). Member states can also raises noncompliance suits, without the step of obtaining the Council's assent (Article 28). Private individuals can challenge any act, regulation, directive, or decision of a state that infringes on a provision of the treaty (Article 30). Any question arising in national courts involving the interpretation of the treaty can be referred to the Court (Article 34).
Remedies: The court can issue interim orders (Article 39) and EACJ monetary judgments executed in accordance with domestic procedures of member states (Article 44).
Formal political checks: The Secretary General must refer matters to a Council, which decides whether the matter should be referred to the Court or resolved by the Council (Article 29). National bodies determine any state liabilities for legal violations.

Economic Community of West African States Court of Justice (ECOWAS CJ)

New style court features: Compulsory jurisdiction. State access. General Secretary access. Direct private litigant access (human rights cases only) and access via preliminary ruling references from national courts.
Jurisdiction: Reforms adopted in 2005 transformed the ECOWAS CJ from an interstate dispute settlement body into an ECJ style IC with an explicit human rights jurisdiction. Today, the Court has jurisdiction over the failure by member states to honor their obligations under the treaty, conventions, and protocols, regulations, directives or decisions of ECOWAS (Revised Article 10 a, Article 4 of the Amended Protocol on the Jurisdiction of the Court). Member states or the Executive Secretary can bring cases against a member state for failure to fulfill its treaty obligations (Article 9d Revised Protocol replacing Article 9 and creating new article 10 (a)). The court has jurisdiction to determine cases of violation of human rights that occur in any member state (Article 9(1) and 9(4) of the Amended Protocol on the Jurisdiction of the Court.) Individuals have access for applications for relief for violation of their human rights (Article 10 (b and d) of the Amended Protocol on the Jurisdiction of the Court.) The Supplementary Protocol (revised Article 10a) mentions that another protocol can specify limits on the Executive Secretary's authority to raise noncompliance suits.
Remedies: For human rights cases, the court is able to create "relief" for violations of human rights, which usually means compensation for past violations but can also mean ordering the cessation of ongoing violations. The authority (not the court) may authorize a number of sanctions for

noncompliance with court rulings including the suspension of loans, suspension of any ECOWAS distributions of resources, suspension of voting rights and the right to present candidates (Article 77 ECOWAS Treaty).
Formal political checks: None for human rights cases. For noncompliance cases, a political body must make a positive decision about any remedies for breach (see above).

European Free Trade Area Court (EFTAC)

New style court features: Compulsory jurisdiction. Surveillance Authority access. Private litigant access via national courts (preliminary ruling reference), advisory only.
Jurisdiction: The Surveillance Authority can bring an action against an EFTA state if it considers that the EFTA state has failed to fulfill an obligation under the EEA Agreement or the ESA/EFTA Court Agreement, and the infringing state fails to comply after being duly notified by the Authority (Article 31). EFTAC can render advisory opinions based on references from national courts. It is unclear if such opinions would cover breach of a community obligation. More likely is that such cases would be raised by the Surveillance Authority.
Remedies: The Surveillance Authority can impose penalties (Article 19), which the EFTA Court can review (Article 35).
Formal political checks: None. The Surveillance Authority determines the penalties.

European Court of Justice (ECJ)

New style court features: Compulsory jurisdiction. State access. Commission access. Private access via national courts (preliminary rulings).
Jurisdiction: Commission can raises infringement suits (TFEU Article 258/TEC Article 226). Member states may also raise infringement suits against each other, but must go through the commission first (TFEU Article 259/TEC Article 227). National courts can refer questions of interpretation to the ECJ, and courts of last instance must refer questions to the ECJ (TFEU Article 267/TEC Article 234).
Remedies: Noncompliance with ECJ infringement decisions may lead to financial penalties (TFEU Article 260-1/TEC Article 228–29). ECJ doctrine also creates state liabilities when states fail to implement European directives (the "Frankovitch doctrine"). ECJ decisions are enforceable in national systems, as governed by national civil procedures (TFEU Article 299/TEC Article 256).
Formal political checks: None. The commission determines the level of sanctions in the event of noncompliance with an ECJ ruling, and the ECJ checks commission decisions.

European Court of Human Rights (ECtHR) as changed in 1998

New style court features: Compulsory jurisdiction. State access. Private litigant access.
Jurisdiction: Any state can refer to the court a breach of a treaty provision or protocol by another state (Article 33). Any person, nongovernmental organization or group claiming to be a victim of a state violation can apply to the court (Article 34). The court decides on the admissibility of all applications based on criteria defined in Article 35, and at any time may strike out a case based on criteria defined in Article 37.
Remedies: In the event of a breach, the court is authorized to "afford just satisfaction" to the injured parties (Article 41). The remedies required by the court have expanded over time.
Formal political checks: None. The court determines the remedies that are required.

Inter-American Court of Human Rights (IACtHR)

New style court features: Mandatory for states ratifying optional protocol. State access. Commission access.
Jurisdiction: The commission can investigate cases (Article 48) and it works with the parties to resolve the issue. Where attempts to resolve the case fail, the commission can issue a report, to which states can add their formal dissents. This report is transmitted to the relevant state, but not published (Article 50). The case is either referred to the court (where the court's jurisdiction has been accepted), or if the case is not referred and the issue not resolved the commission may decide by majority vote to publish its report (Article 51). Only state parties and the commission can submit cases to the court and the procedures stipulated in Article 48 and 50 must be met (Article 61). States may sign an optional protocol accepting the IACtHR's compulsory jurisdiction (Article 62). Any member state may consult the IACtHR regarding violations in the "American States." The commission may consult the court too, subject to its competence stipulated in Chapter X of the Charter (Article 64). In 2001 the commission adopted new procedures; it now refers to the court all cases where it finds a violation (and the court's jurisdiction has been accepted).
Remedies: In the event of a breach, the court is authorized to rule that the injured party shall be "ensured enjoyment of his right or freedom" that was violated, that violations be remedied and fair compensation paid (Article 63). The IACtHR has required a broad range of remedies. See Hawkins and Jacoby (2010).
Formal political checks: Commission can screen cases, choosing which violations to refer to the court. But as of 2001, the commission refers all

cases where there are ongoing violations. The Court determines the remedies that are required (see above).

International Criminal Tribunal for the Former Yugoslavia (ICTY)

New style court features: Compulsory jurisdiction. International Prosecutor initiation. Private litigant defendants.
Jurisdiction: ICTY has jurisdiction over enumerated war crimes committed in the territory of the former Yugoslavia since 1991 (Statute of the ICTY Articles 1–5). The prosecutor issues indictments and selects cases to pursue. The ICTY has primacy over national courts (Article 9).
Remedies: Convicted criminals are sentenced to specified prison terms in accordance with Yugoslavian practices with imprisonment being the only remedy (e.g., the death penalty is not allowed). Illicit proceeds may be ordered to be returned (Article 24).
Formal political checks: The prosecutor must convince a Trial Chamber that there is prima facie evidence to continue (Article 19). Rulings may be appealed to an Appeals Chamber (Articles 25 and 26). Less formally, limiting the prosecutorial budget will hinder investigations and prosecutions. The court determines the remedies that are required.

International Criminal Court (ICC)

New style court features: Compulsory jurisdiction. International Prosecutor initiation. Private litigant defendants.
Jurisdiction: ICC has jurisdiction over enumerated war crimes (Rome Statute Article 5). The court also has jurisdiction over cases referred to the prosecutor by a state party or the Security Council, or cases investigated by the prosecutor on its own initiative where the state is a signatory of the Rome Statute (Rome Statute Article 13, 14, and 15).
Remedies: Convicted criminals are sentenced to specified prison terms and fines and property forfeiture may be authorized (Article 77). The death penalty is implicitly excluded.
Formal political checks: A pretrial chamber evaluates if there is reasonable basis for the prosecutor to proceed (Article 15 (4)). The Security Council can ask the International Prosecutor to suspend investigations and prosecutions for twelve months. The suspension must be renewed every twelve months (Article 16). For the ICTY, the IC had primary jurisdiction for the case. For the ICC, the prosecutor must notify all state parties that would normally exercise jurisdiction over the case. These state parties can decide to prosecute the violation, and the prosecutor "shall defer to the state's investigation" unless the pretrial chamber de-

cides to authorize the prosecutor's investigation (Article 18). The accused, or the state that has jurisdiction, can raise a legal challenge to the court's jurisdiction (Article 19). Rulings can be appealed (Articles 81–85). Less formally, limiting the prosecutorial budget will hinder investigations and prosecutions. The court determines the remedies that are required.

International Criminal Tribunal for Rwanda (ICTR)

New style court features: Compulsory jurisdiction. International prosecutor initiation. Private litigant defendants.
Jurisdiction: ICTR has jurisdiction over enumerated crimes committed in Rwanda between 1/1/1994 and 12/31/1994. (Statute of the ICTR: Articles 1-5). The prosecutor issues indictments and selects cases to pursue. The ICTR has primacy over national courts (Article 8).
Remedies: Convicted criminals are sentenced to specified prison terms in accordance with Rwandan practices with imprisonment being the only remedy (e.g., the death penalty is not allowed). Illicit proceeds may be ordered to be returned (Article 23).
Formal political checks: The prosecutor must convince a trial chamber that there is prima facie evidence to continue (Article 18). Rulings may be appealed to an appeals chamber (Articles 24 and 25). Less formally, limiting the prosecutorial budget will hinder investigations and prosecutions. The court determines the remedies that are required.

Southern African Development Community Tribunal (SADC) (Original jurisdiction)

New style court features: Compulsory jurisdiction. State access. Commission access. Direct private litigant access and access via preliminary rulings from national courts.
Jurisdiction: The original SADC treaty gives the tribunal jurisdiction to ensure adherence to the provisions of the SADC and its subsidiary instruments (Article 16 SADC Treaty). States can raise enforcement actions since the tribunal has authority over all cases raised by states (Article 15 SADC Court Treaty). National courts could refer any question to the SADC tribunal (Article 16 SADC Court Treaty). The SADC tribunal's jurisdiction is compulsory in any case that is referred, but subsidiary agreements may not be binding on all member states. The original court treaty allowed private litigants to raise cases against states after domestic remedies were exhausted (Article 15 SADC Court Treaty), but this provision will be revised.
Remedies: Where states that do not comply with arbitral awards, the injured state can be authorized to interrupt concessions or similar obliga-

tions for one year (Article 31). The tribunal can review measures taken (Article 32).
Formal political checks: None specified, which is how the SADC ended up ruling against Zimbabwe on a sensitive issue. But for noncompliance cases, a political body must make a positive decision about any remedies for breach, and the SADC political body refused to authorize sanctions in the face of Zimbabwe's noncompliance. Litigants then filed claims in South African domestic courts, and won awards (de Wet 2013).

World Trade Organization Permanent Appellate Body (WTO)

New style court features: Compulsory jurisdiction. State access.
Jurisdiction: The aim of dispute settlement is to preserve the rights and obligations of members under the covered agreements. "Where there is an infringement, the action is considered prima facie to constitute a case of nullification or impairment" (DSU Annex 2 Article 3.8). If states fail to reach an agreement amongst themselves (DSU Annex 2 Article 3), they may request the formation of a panel (DSU Annex 2 Article 6). Panel rulings go to the Dispute Settlement Body, which adopts them if not rejected unanimously (DUS Annex 2 Article 16.4). Parties to the dispute may appeal a panel ruling to the permanent Appellate Body (DSU Annex 2 Article 17.4). The Appellate Body makes recommendations to the state (DSU Annex 2 Article 19) and the Dispute Settlement Body oversees compliance with the recommendations (DSU Annex 2 Article 21).
Remedies: Compensation or suspension of obligations may be requested to enforce a decision of the Dispute Settlement Body. The WTO's Appellate Body may authorize a country to levy duties against another country's goods, up to a specified amount. (DSU Annex 2 Article 22). The FSC case discusses the authorization of $4.03 billion dollars per annum of retaliatory sanctions.
Formal political checks: Only rulings accepted by the Dispute Settlement Body are legally binding, but the negative consensus rule means that acceptance of legal rulings is assured. The Appellate Body determines the level of retaliatory sanctions.

West African Economic and Monetary Union (WAEMU)

New style court features: Compulsory jurisdiction. State access. Commission access.
Jurisdiction: The Commission can bring to the court any action against a WAEMU state if it considers that the state has failed to fulfill an obligation. States may also bring cases, but they must first work through the Commission (Court Treaty Protocol 1 Article 5). Court rulings are explic-

itly binding on national judges and administrators (Court Treaty Protocol 1 Article 13). The commission can seize the court if it suspects that a national court has failed to refer a case, and the court can inform the highest national jurisdictions regarding the correct interpretation of community rules (Court Treaty Protocol 1 Article 14).
Remedies: If states do not comply with the ruling, the commission can convene a Conference of a Head of States which can, upon 2/3 vote, agree to unspecified sanctions (WAEMU Treaty Article 74 and Court Treaty Protocol 1 Article 6).
Formal political checks: For noncompliance cases a political body must make a positive decision about any remedies for breach (see above).

FOUR ADDITIONAL ENFORCEMENT JURISDICTIONS NOT LISTED IN FIGURE 7.1

African Court of Justice (ACJ) (not yet established)

New style court features: None. Optional protocol for compulsory jurisdiction. States access. Access for organs of the African Union, but not the commission.
Jurisdiction: The original agreement envisions that the court will have jurisdiction to ascertain the existence of any fact that, if confirmed, would constitute a breach of a State's obligation (Article 19f). State parties, the Assembly of States, Parliament, and other African Union Organs authorized by the Assembly may raise cases (the content of which is not specified) (Article 18). This means that the commission cannot raise cases. States that are not part of the African Union are specifically precluded from raising cases, and the court has no jurisdiction for disputes involving states that have not ratified the court's protocol (Article 18 (3)). These provisions are likely to change should the ACJ be created as an entity that is merged with the ACtHPR or that has criminal jurisdiction.
Remedies: The court will be able to determine any reparations that follow from a breach (Article 19g).
Formal political checks: None, but for noncompliance cases, a political body must make a positive decision about any remedies for breach (see above).

Economic Court of the Commonwealth of Independent States (ECCIS)

Jurisdiction: The court has jurisdiction in disputes arising during the implementation of economic obligations under the Charter of the Commonwealth of Independent States (Article 32). In theory, the ECCIS can find in

these cases that a member state has failed to fulfill its obligations under the treaty (Article 32). There is some question as to whether the court's rulings in contentious cases are binding (Danilenko 1999, 906–7).
Remedies: In theory, member states could ask the Council of Heads of States to sanction noncompliance, but this body makes its decisions based on unanimity (Danilenko 1999, 914). Recent observers suggest that in practice ECCIS rulings are not even binding (Kembeyev 2009, 67–68).
Formal political checks: It is not entirely clear that rulings are binding (see above).

Caribbean Court of Justice (CCJ)

Jurisdiction: The CCJ has dispute settlement rather than enforcement jurisdiction, but national courts can refer cases to the CCJ (Article XIV) and private litigants are allowed to raises cases where the CCJ determines that a right or benefit conferred by community rules enures to private litigants, and where prejudice has contributed to the denial of such right, or where a state declines to espouse a claim, or where the issue of justice is concerned (Article XXIV). In its appellate jurisdiction, the court can review superior court rulings involving constitutional and fundamental rights violations and other areas of superior court jurisdiction (Article XXV (2(d&e))).
Remedies: For its appellate jurisdiction, the court can review decisions involving property and rights exceeding $25,000 EC, and the court has jurisdiction and powers that are parallel to that of national court of appeals (Article XXV (6)).
Formal political checks: The court lacks a clear enforcement jurisdiction, which may be why political checks are not clearly specified.

ICSID adjudication of bilateral investment treaties

Jurisdiction: The terms of adjudication are defined in bilateral investment treaties. These treaties vary with respect to the rights of investors.
Remedies: ICSID arbitral awards can be claimed anywhere that assets are held.
Formal political checks: None.

APPENDIX FOR CHAPTER 8: INTERNATIONAL COURTS' CONSTITUTIONAL REVIEW JURISDICTION (ORGANIZED ALPHABETICALLY)

This appendix examines primarily the terms specified in Court Treaties. First listed are ICs in figure 8.1, which have an explicit constitutional review jurisdiction. Unstated is that the remedy is nullification of illegal acts. There are generally no political checks for this role. At the end are five additional international adjudicatory mechanisms that arguably have morphed constitutional review roles: the yet to be formed African Court of Justice, the African, European, and Inter-American Human Rights courts, and the International Criminal Court. IC jurisdiction is compulsory and exclusive with respect to invalidating community acts. The articles referenced correspond to the legal instruments indicated in the Court Treaty bibliography.

Andean Tribunal of Justice (ATJ)

New style court features: Compulsory jurisdiction. State access. General Secretary access. Private litigant direct access.
Jurisdiction: Review of IO acts. The ATJ can nullify decisions of the commission, and resolutions of the General Secretariat on the basis of a failure to follow provisions of the Andean legal system or a deviation of power. Member states, the Commission, the General Secretary, and private litigants whose interests are affected can bring cases (Articles 17–19).
Review of state acts: The supremacy of Andean law allows for the review of national acts. The case study on the Colombia and Ecuador alcohol dispute shows the importance of national cultures of constitutional obedience to Andean law.

Caribbean Court of Justice (CCJ)

New style court features: Compulsory jurisdiction for states that have accepted the courts compulsory appellate review. Private litigant direct access.
Jurisdiction: Review of IO acts: The CCJ has original jurisdiction for cases involving Caribbean Common Market laws, but it has no explicit authority to review the validity of such laws (Article XII). Given that CARICOM is a common market system, it would not surprise me if the court were given jurisdiction to review the validity secondary legislation of the Caribbean Common Market. But for now this power is yet to be defined.
Review of state acts: The CCJ has appellate jurisdiction over supreme court decisions involving constitutional violations of a litigant's human rights (Article XXV d). This jurisdiction applies only when domestic constitutions allow. In practice, only Guyana and Barbados fall under the CCJ's appellate jurisdiction. Nine Caribbean island states have opted instead to have the East Caribbean Supreme Court serve as the highest appellate body. The book's online appendix includes a brief summary of both the CCJ and the East Caribbean Supreme Court.

Central African Monetary Community (CEMAC)

New style court features: Compulsory jurisdiction. State access. All community institutions. Private litigant direct access.
Jurisdiction: Review of IO acts: The court has jurisdiction to review the legality of acts of the CEMAC and related acts (Article 15.) The relevant provision defines the terms under which an act can be deemed illegal including incompetence, exceeding authority or violating rules of law. States, all community institutions, and any individual with a legitimate interest can challenge any violation of the treaty (Article 14). National courts can also refer cases involving the legality or interpretation of CEMAC acts (Article 17).
Review of state acts: Any state, CEMAC institution or private actor with a valid legal claim can at any time question the legality of a legal act of a member state or a CEMAC organ (Article 14).

Central American Court of Justice (CACJ)

New style court features: Compulsory jurisdiction. State access. All community institutions. Private litigant direct access.
Jurisdiction: Review of IO acts: The court has general jurisdiction to hear suits brought by any actor with standing, including member states, private litigants, and community institutions, about decisions of any organ of the system, including nullification charges and failure to act charges (Article 22b).
Review of state acts: The court may hear questions that arise with respect to the "fundamental powers or organs of the member states, and disputes that may arise when judicial verdicts are not respected" (Article 22f). Any member state can refer a question about conflicts between treaties and national laws of each member state (Article 23).

Court of Justice for the Common Market of Eastern and Southern Africa (COMESA)

New style court features: Compulsory jurisdiction. State access. Commission access. Private litigant direct access and via national courts (preliminary ruling reference).
Jurisdiction: Review of IO acts: Any member state may ask the court to rule on the legality of any act, regulation, directive, or decision of the council (Article 24.2). Any resident of a member state may ask the court to rule on the legality of any act, regulation, directive, or decision of the

council (Article 26). National courts can refer questions of interpretation, and questions about the validity or the regulations, directives and decisions of the common market to the COMESA court for a ruling. Last instance domestic courts are obliged to refer such questions (Article 30).
Review of state acts: Article 26 also authorizes private litigants initiate challenges the legality of any act, regulation, directive or decision of a member state, after domestic remedies are exhausted (Article 26).

East African Court of Justice (EACJ)

New style court features: Compulsory jurisdiction. State access. Private litigant direct access and via national courts (preliminary ruling references).
Jurisdiction: Review of IO acts: Any member state (Article 28), private actor (Article 30), or national court (Article 34) can send to the court a question about the validity of regulations, directives, decisions, or actions of the community. Article 28 clearly allows for claims raised by states, for arguments that acts of member state are ultra vires or unlawful. The treaty also clearly states that EACJ decisions have precedence over national court decisions on similar matters (Articles 33 and 34).
Review of state acts: Private litigants can challenge any act, regulation, decision, or action of a member state on the grounds that the act is unlawful or an infringement of the treaty (Article 30).

Economic Community of West African States Court of Justice (ECOWAS CJ)

New style court features: Compulsory jurisdiction. State access. Council of Ministers and Executive Secretary access. Private litigant direct access.
Jurisdiction: Review of IO acts: Member states, the Council of Ministers, and the Executive Secretary may bring proceedings for the determination of the legality of an action in relation to any community text (Article 4 of the Supplementary Protocol, which revises Article 10 (b)). National courts may send questions of interpretation to the ECOWAS court; the text is silent as to whether such references can include challenges to community acts (Article 4 of the Supplementary Protocol, which revises Article 10 (f)).
Review of state acts: Private litigants have access to seek relief for violations of their human rights; the treaty is silent as to whether such relief includes invalidating illegal acts but the court can order the cessation of ongoing violations (Article 4 of the Supplementary Protocol, which revises Article 10 (c)). A culture of constitutional obedience to human rights law would give this court a de facto constitutional review role vis-à-vis

domestic acts. Recent reforms mean that certain community laws have legal supremacy in the domestic realm, raising the possibility of future review of the compatibility of national and ECOWAS rules.

European Court of Justice (ECJ)

New style court features: Compulsory jurisdiction. State access. All community institutions. Private litigant direct access and via national courts (preliminary ruling reference).

Review of IO acts: Member states, the European Parliament, the European Council or the European Commission can raise challenges to the validity of acts adopted by the European Council, Parliament, Commission, and European Central Bank (TFEU Article 263/TEC Article 230). ECJ may declare the act void (Article 231). An institution whose action has been declared void must take necessary measures to comply with the court's ruling (TFEU Article 266/TEC Article 233). National courts may refer cases raised by private litigants where there are questions as to the validity and interpretation of European laws (TFEU Article 267/TEC Article 234). Numerous human rights provisions found in earlier European treaties have now been incorporated into the EU Charter on Fundamental Rights. The Kadi case study shows the ECJ assessing the validity of an EU regulation in light of EU human rights requirements.

Review of state acts: None specified, but the ECJ's judicial revolution, which asserted the supremacy of European law, implicitly allows the ECJ to adjudicate the compatibility of community law and national law. The women in combat support roles case study shows the ECJ reviewing the validity of national acts.

Southern African Development Community Tribunal (SADC)

New style court features: Compulsory jurisdiction. State access. All community institutions. Private litigant direct access and via national courts (preliminary ruling references).

Review of IO acts: The original court treaty included jurisdiction to assess the validity of all protocols and subsidiary instruments adopted by the community, and all acts of the community (Article 14). The tribunal also had jurisdiction over disputes between member states, and between individuals and member states once domestic remedies are exhausted (Article 15), between member states and the community (Article 17) and between individuals and the community (Article 18). The tribunal's competence for disputes between individuals/member states and the community is exclusive (revisions of Articles 17 and 18). The treaty does not specify whether specific litigants can bring specific suits, suggesting that

all authorized litigants could raise suits that fell under the court's jurisdiction. These provisions might be changed.
Review of state acts: The original court treaty allows private litigants to raise cases against states after domestic remedies are exhausted (Article 15 SADC Court Treaty). This provision will likely be changed. Secondary legislation can still authorize private suits and make community rules supreme.

West African Economic and Monetary Union (WAEMU)

New style court features: Compulsory jurisdiction. State access. Council and Commission access. Private litigant access via national courts (preliminary ruling references).
Review of IO acts: A member state, the council, or the commission can ask the court to assess the legality of any regulation, directive or decision. National courts of last instance are obliged to seize the court in such cases (Article 8). The rules of procedure clarify that any state, the council, the commission, or directly affected individual can raise challenges to the legality of community acts (Rules of Procedure Article 15 (2)).
Review of state acts: None specified, but supreme community law would trump conflicting domestic law.

FIVE ADDITIONAL ICS NOT LISTED ON TABLE 8.1 THAT HAVE EXPLICIT OR MORPHED CONSTITUTIONAL REVIEW ROLES

African Court of Justice (ACJ) (not yet established)

New style court features: Compulsory jurisdiction. State access. All community institutions.
Review of IO acts: The court has jurisdiction regarding the interpretation, application, or validity of Union Treaties and all subsidiary legal instruments adopted within the framework of the African Union (Article 19b) and jurisdiction over all acts, decisions, regulations or directives of the Union (19d). State parties, the Assembly of States, Parliament, and other African Union Organs authorized by the Assembly may raise cases (Article 18).

African Court on Human and Peoples' Rights (ACtHPR) (2006)

New style court features: Compulsory jurisdiction. State access. Commission access.
Review of IO acts: Not applicable.

Review of state acts: A culture of constitutional obedience to human rights law would give this court a de facto constitutional review role vis-à-vis domestic acts.

European Court of Human Rights (ECtHR) as changed in 1998 (1952)

New style court features: Compulsory jurisdiction. State access. All community institutions. Private litigant direct access.
Review of IO acts: The ECtHR has adjudicated the compatibility of European Union and UN actions vis-à-vis the European Convention.
Review of state acts: A culture of constitutional obedience to human rights law gives this court a de facto constitutional review role vis-à-vis domestic acts.

Inter-American Court of Human Rights (IACtHR) (1979)

New style court features: Compulsory jurisdiction. State access. Commission access.
Review of IO acts: Not applicable. Review of state acts: A culture of constitutional obedience to human rights law would give this court a de facto constitutional review role vis-à-vis domestic acts. Indeed some Latin American constitutions specify that international human rights treaties are supreme, and in Colombia the constitutional court has ruled that the Inter-American Convention is part of the "constitutional bloc" and thus has the same legal status as the constitution.

International Criminal Court (ICC) (2001)

Compulsory jurisdiction. International Prosecutor access.
Review of IO acts: The ICC can develop international criminal law, but it has yet to adjudicate issues that touch on the power and competences of United Nations bodies.
Review of state acts: Developments in international criminal law can penetrate into the national level, since ratification of the Rome Statute requires domestic legislation to prosecute war crimes.

Legal Cases Index and Citations

Established ICs publish their rulings in compendiums and online. Under-resourced ICs often lack published compendiums, and more recent rulings may only be available online. The easiest way to find rulings is through an Internet search of the name and number. I have indicated the court's website where harder to find rulings can sometimes be found.

Andean Tribunal of Justice Cases (including national court rulings)

ATJ rulings are most reliably accessed on the Secretariat's website. AI (acciones de incumplimiento) = noncompliance cases, AN (acciones de nulidad) = nullification rulings, PI (interpretaciones prejudiciales) = preliminary ruling references. The last two numbers are the year the case was filed, which is how the rulings are listed. The Andean Secretariat's link to the rulings is in transition. The old page is still partly operable: http://www.comunidadandina.org/canprocinternet/procedimientos.aspx. The new page is only partly operable: http://www.comunidadandina.org/SolControversias.aspx?fr=99#.

"Peru exemptions" case TJCA 1-AN-1996. pp. 296–97
"Second use patent" TJCA 89-AI-2000 (against Peru). p. 258
"Related second use patent rulings" TJCA 01-AI-2001 (against Venezuela); TJCA 34-AI-2001 (against Ecuador.) p. 259

African Court on Human and Peoples' Rights

Decisions are available at the court's website: http://www.african-court.org/en/index.php/judgments/other-decisions.
"Femi Falana ruling" Judgment in the matter of Femi Falana v. The African Union African Court of Human and Peoples' Rights, Application 001/2011. Decision of June 26, 2012. pp. 152, 247

Economic Community of West African States Court of Justice (ECOWAS CJ)

Judgments on the merits are given the letters JUD (judgments). Once finalized in a reported form, the ruling gets the name "APP." Most older cases are available in a hard to find compendium: 2004–2009 Community Court of Justice, ECOWAS Law Report. Select recent rulings are available on the court's website: http://www.courtecowas.org/site2012/index.php?option=com_content&view=article&id=157&Itemid=27. A WorldCourts website also has select older rulings: http://www.worldcourts.com/ecowasccj/eng/index.htm.
"Modern-day slavery" Hadijatou Mani Koroua v. Republic of Niger, Judgment No. ECW/CCJ/JUD/06/08. p. 264
"Free compulsory basic education" The Registered Trustees of the Socio-Economic Rights and Accountability Project (SERAP) v. President of the Federal Republic of Nigeria & Ors, ECW/CCJ/APP/12/07. p. 278
"Environmental damage in the Niger Delta" The Registered Trustees of the Socio-Economic Rights & Accountability Project (SERAP) v. Federal Republic Of Nigeria ECW/CCJ/JUD/18/12. p. 278
"Gambia disappearance case" Chief Ebrima Manneh v. Republic of the Gambia, ECW/CCJ/APP/04/07 reprinted in 2004–2009 Community Court of Justice, ECOWAS Law Report 181 (2011). p. 278
"Gambia torture case" Musa Saidykhan v. Republic of the Gambia, ECW/CCJ/APP/11/07. p. 278

European Court of Human Rights (ECtHR)

Ireland v. United Kingdom, 1976 Y.B. Eur. Conv. on Hum. Rts. 512, 748, 788–94 (Eur. Comm'n of Hum. Rts). p. 50
"ECtHR ruling on UN Sanctions System: Nada v. Switzerland" Judgment of the Grand Chamber of the European Court of Human Rights of September 12, 2012, in case Nada v. Switzerland (No. 10593/08); available at http://hudoc.echr.coe.int/sites/eng/pages/search.aspx?i=001-113118, last visited May 2, 2013. p. 301

European Union Court of Justice (EUCJ) and the first instance General Court (GC) (formerly European Court of Justice [ECJ] and Tribunal of First Instance [TFI])

ECJ rulings are indicated with the letter "C" and TFI rulings with the letter T.

International Court of Justice (ICJ)

All ICJ judgments are available on the court's website, listed by the year of the ruling. The date is usually provided so that one can find the ruling. ICJ rulings are currently located at: http://www.icj-cij.org/docket/index.php?p1=3&p2=3. Before official publication, one must look at the case by its title, under the year the decision was made. The website does not note the official publication listing, but older decisions are reported by lawyers with the formal report listing.

"Consular staff case" United States Diplomatic and Consular Staff in Tehran (United States of America v. Iran) 1980 ICJ Reports 3. ICJ Judgment of May 24, 1980. p. 185

"Oil Platforms" (Islamic Republic of Iran v. United States of America) 2003 ICJ Reports 161. ICJ judgment of November 6, 2003. pp. 185, 193

"Hissène Habré" Questions relating to the Obligation to Prosecute or Extradite (Belgium v. Senegal). ICJ judgment of July 20, 2012. p. 273

Inter-American Court of Human Rights (IACtHR)

Rulings available at http://www.corteidh.or.cr/casos.cfm.

"Awas Tingni v. Nicaragua" The Mayagna (Sumo) Awas Tingni Community v. Nicaragua Inter-American Court of Human Rights Serie C No. 79 Judgment of August 31, 2001.pp. 317–18

"Other indigenous land rights cases—Suriname" Caso de la Comunidad Moiwana v. Suriname. Excepciones Preliminares, Fondo Reparaciones y Costas. Serie C No. 124. Judgment of June 15, 2005. p. 318

"Other indigenous land rights cases—Paraguay" Caso Comunidad Indígena Yakye Axa v. Paraguay, Fondo Reparaciones y Costas. Serie C No. 125. Judgment of June 17, 2005. p. 318

"Other indigenous land rights cases—Paraguay" Caso Comunidad Indígena Sawhovamaya v. Paraguay, Fondo, Reparaciones y Costas. Serie C No. 146. Judgment of March 29, 2006. p. 318

"Velásquez Rodríguez case" Caso Velásquez Rodríguez v. Honduras. Judgments Serie C No. 1, 2, and 4. Judgments of June 26, 1987, and July 29, 1988. p. 140

International Criminal Tribunal for the Former Yugoslavia (ICTY)

Rulings available on the court's website, currently located at: http://www.icty.org/action/cases/4.

Prosecutor v. Kunarac, Judgment, IT-96-23-T and IT-96-23/1-T, ICTY February 22, 2001. p. 322

Prosecutor v. Dragoljub Kunarac, Radomir Kovac, and Zoran Vukovic (Appeal Judgment), IT-96-23 and IT-96-23/1-A, ICTY, June 12, 2002. p. 322

International Criminal Tribunal for Rwanda (ICTR)

Rulings available on the court's website, currently located at: http://www.unictr.org/Cases/tabid/77/Default.aspx?id=4&mnid=4.

"Rape as war crime ruling" Prosecutor v. Akayesu, Judgment, ICTR-96-4-A, June 1 2001. p. 321

International Tribunal for the Law of the Sea (ITLOS)

Rulings available on the court's website, currently located at: http://www.itlos.org/index.php?id=37&L=0%2525255CoOpensinternallinkincurrentwindow.

International Center for the Arbitration of Investor Disputes

North American Free Trade Agreement (NAFTA)

Special Court for Sierra Leone

UK legal rulings

US legal rulings

World Trade Organization Appellate Body (WTO)

Rulings available at http://www.wto.org/english/tratop_e/dispu_e/dispu_e.htm.

Court Treaty Bibliography and Litigation Data Sources

A brief description of the twenty-four ICs in this study, and an additional six ICs, can be found at http://press.princeton.edu/titles/10150.html

THE AFRICAN COURT ON HUMAN AND PEOPLES' RIGHTS (ACtHPR)

Court Treaty: Protocol to the African Charter on Human and Peoples' Rights on the Establishment of an African Court on Human and Peoples' Rights CAB/LEG/665 (http://www.achpr.org/english/_info/court_en.html).

Litigation data: Based on a manual count of reported rulings, found on the court's website, currently located at http://www.african-court.org/en/index.php/2012-03-04-06-06-00/finalised-cases-closed.

ANDEAN TRIBUNAL OF JUSTICE (ATJ)

Court Treaty: Treaty Creating the Court of Justice of the Cartagena Agreement (Amended by the Cochabamba Protocol) available at http://www.comunidadandina.org/INGLES/normativa/ande_trie2.htm.

Litigation data: Posted on the court's website under (Estatisticas de Procesos) http://www.tribunalandino.org.ec/sitetjca/index.php.

COURT OF JUSTICE OF THE BENELUX ECONOMIC UNION (BCJ)

Court Treaty: The Treaty Establishing the BENELUX Economic Union 381 U.N.T.S. 165 (1960). A special treaty was adopted for the court March 31, 1965, and modified via protocols June 10, 1981, and November 23, 1984. The updated treaties are available as the Le Traité du 31 mars 1965. Available at http://www.courbeneluxhof.be/fr/basisdocumenten.asp.

Litigation data: Based on a manual count of reported rulings, found on the court's website, currently located at http://www.courbeneluxhof.be/fr/arresten_lst.asp.

CARIBBEAN COURT OF JUSTICE (CCJ)

Court Treaty: Agreement Establishing the Caribbean Court of Justice http://www.caribbeancourtofjustice.org/court_instruments.html (this agreement repeats provisions found in http://www.caricom.org/jsp/community/revised_treaty-text.pdf).

Litigation data: Based on a manual count of reported rulings, found on the court's website, currently located at http://www.caribbeancourtofjustice.org/judgments.html.

CENTRAL AFRICAN ECONOMIC AND MONETARY COMMUNITY (CEMAC CJ) COURT OF JUSTICE

Court Treaty: Convention Governing the Court of Justice of the CEMAC (July 5, 1996) supplemented by various rules of procedure available at http://www.aict-ctia.org/courts_subreg/cemac/cemac_docs.html.

Litigation data: Not available.

CENTRAL AMERICAN COURT OF JUSTICE (CACJ)

Court Treaty: Statute of the Central American Court of Justice 34 *ILM* 921 (1995).

Litigation data: Based on a manual count of reported rulings, found on the court's website, currently located at http://portal.ccj.org.ni/ccj2/Jurisprudencia/tabid/59/Default.aspx.

COURT OF JUSTICE OF THE COMMON MARKET FOR EASTERN AND SOUTHERN AFRICA (COMESA)

Court Treaty: Treaty Establishing the Common Market of Eastern and Southern Africa. Available in Ebobrah and Tanoh (2010, 3).

Litigation data: Not available, but select rulings are available at http://www.worldcourts.com/comesacj/eng/index.htm.

EAST AFRICAN COMMUNITY (EACJ) COURT OF JUSTICE

Court Treaty: Treaty for the Establishment of the East African Community (chapter 8) available in Ebobrah and Tanoh (2010, 37).

Litigation data: http://www.eacj.org/judgments.php.

ECONOMIC COMMUNITY OF WEST AFRICAN STATES (ECOWAS CJ) COURT OF JUSTICE

Court Treaty: Revised Treaty for the Establishment of the Economic Community of West African States. Protocol on the Community Court of Justice. Supplementary Protocol Amending the Protocol Relating to the Community Court of Justice (1991/1996). Available in Ebobrah and Tanoh (2010, 194–201).

Litigation data: Collected from the court registrar. The court is starting to list and publish select rulings: http://www.courtecowas.org/site2012/index.php?option=com_content&view=article&id=157&Itemid=27.

EUROPEAN FREE TRADE ASSOCIATION COURT (EFTAC)

Court Treaty: Agreement between the EFTA States on the Establishment of a Surveillance Authority and a Court of Justice available at http://www.efta.int/~/media/Documents/legal-texts/the-surveillance-and-court-agreement/agreement-annexes-and-protocols/Surveillance-and-Court-Agreement-consolidated.pdf.

Litigation data: Annual reports summarize the litigation to date, and recent litigation is posted on the court's website. The 2011 report was available on the court's website, currently located at http://www.eftacourt.int/the-court/jurisdiction-organisation/introduction/.

COURT OF JUSTICE OF THE EUROPEAN UNION (ECJ) AND GENERAL COURT

Court Treaty: Numerous changes in European Treaties make it hard to stay on top of the articles defining the court's jurisdiction. The EU publishes annexes that map article changes over time. The EU has started to publish consolidated treaties. The latest is the Treaty establishing the Functioning of the European Union

(TFEU), which updates all other earlier EU treaties. OJ C 326, 26.10.2012. Scholars often start with the EC Treaty as a basis, and then update the articles. The treaty on European Union and of the Treaty Establishing the European Community OJ C 321 E/2 OJ 29.12.2006.

Litigation data: Annual reports summarize the litigation to date, and recent litigation is posted on the court's website. The most recent report was available here: http://curia.europa.eu/jcms/jcms/Jo2_7000/. Previous reports are available under the historical section of the website. Alec Stone Sweet and Thomas Brunell have also published their data sets on the ECJ's decisions through 2006, currently available at http://www.eu-newgov.org/datalists/deliverables_detail.asp?Project_ID=26.

EUROPEAN COURT OF HUMAN RIGHTS (ECtHR)

Court Treaty: European Convention on Human Rights and (ETS 5, 213 U.N.T.S. 222) and Additional Protocols (esp. Protocol 11) (ETS No. 155, Strasbourg, 11.V.1994.) recently available at http://www.echr.coe.int/NR/rdonlyres/D5CC24A7-DC13-4318-B457-5C9014916D7A/0/Convention_ENG.pdf.

Litigation data: Annual reports summarize the litigation to date, but they consolidate early years. My data was based on a manual count of a recent report commemorating forty years of activity, and then a reliance on court reports for more recent years. The court has begun publishing statistics, most recently found at http://www.echr.coe.int/ECHR/EN/Header/Reports+and+Statistics/Statistics/Statistical+data/. Erik Voeten also lists a data page for the ECtHR at: http://www9.georgetown.edu/faculty/ev42/ICdata_files/Page364.htm.

ECONOMIC COURT OF THE COMMONWEALTH OF INDEPENDENT STATES (ECCIS)

Court Treaty: Available only in Russian, thus I had to rely on Danilenko (1999), updated by Kembayev (2009).

Litigation data: The court's website in Russian contains information about litigation. Alexander Panayotov helped me with this data. Google translating the website works fairly well. Recently the court's website was located at http://sudsng.org/database/deed/.

INTER-AMERICAN COURT OF HUMAN RIGHTS (IACtHR)

Court Treaty: American Convention on Human Rights, O.A.S. Treaty Series No. 36, 1144 U.N.T.S. 123, entered into force July 18, 1978, reprinted in Basic Documents Pertaining to Human Rights in the Inter-American System, OEA/Ser.L.V/II.82 doc. 6 rev. 1 at 25 (1992).

Litigation data: Based on a manual count of reported rulings, found on the court's website (under Jurisprudencia), currently located at http://www.corteidh.or.cr/index.cfm?&CFID=666614&CFTOKEN=69520161. Annual reports note the number of submissions. Reports are also posted on the court's website, most recently at the following location: http://www.corteidh.or.cr/informes.cfm.

INTERNATIONAL COURT OF JUSTICE (ICJ)

Court Treaty: The Statute of the International Court of Justice published as part of the basic documents on line, most recently located at http://www.icj-cij.org/documents/index.php?p1=4&p2=2&p3=0.

Litigation data: The ICJ lists cases by when they were filed, or when the parties formally closed the case. But many cases are closed when parties ask for the case to be removed from the Court's docket. One must thus consult each case individually to determine if there is a binding ruling denying jurisdiction, removing the case from the docket, or otherwise determining the merits of the claims. Rulings can be found on the court's website, most recently located at http://www.icj-cij.org/docket/index.php?p1=3&p2=2&sort=2&p3=0. Decisions of the Permanent Court of International Justice are also posted.

INTERNATIONAL TRIBUNAL FOR THE LAW OF THE SEA (ITLOS)

Court Treaty: United Nations Convention on the Law of the Sea 1833 UNTS 3; 21 ILM 1261 (1982) discusses the obligation for dispute resolution. A Statute for the Tribunal for the Law of the Sea defines procedures, jurisdiction and the court's operation. Separate agreements govern rules of procedure and additional agreements can confer jurisdiction on the tribunal. These "Basic Texts" are available at the court's website.

Litigation data: Based on a manual count of reported rulings, found on the court's website (under cases), currently located at http://www.itlos.org/.

INTERNATIONAL CRIMINAL COURT (ICC)

Court Treaty: Rome Statute of the International Criminal Court UN Doc. A/CONF. 183/9; 37 ILM 1002 (1998); 2187 UNTS 90.

Litigation data: There were no rulings for the time period in this study, but the ICC reports its investigations on its website.

INTERNATIONAL CRIMINAL TRIBUNAL FOR THE FORMER YUGOSLAVIA (ICTY)

Court Treaty: Statute of the International Criminal Tribunal for the Former Yugoslavia 32 I.L.M. 1203 (1993).

Litigation data: The Court reports on its investigations, but I relied on data collected by James Meernik, available at http://www.psci.unt.edu/~meernik/International%20Criminal%20Tribunals%20Website.htm.

INTERNATIONAL CRIMINAL TRIBUNAL FOR RWANDA (ICTR)

Court Treaty: Statute of the International Criminal Tribunal for Rwanda 33 *ILM* 1598 (1994).

Litigation data: The Court reports on its investigations, but I relied on data collected by James Meernik, available at http://www.psci.unt.edu/~meernik/International%20Criminal%20Tribunals%20Website.htm.

ORGANIZATION FOR THE HARMONIZATION OF CORPORATE LAW IN AFRICA COMMON COURT OF JUSTICE AND ARBITRATION (OHADA)

Court Treaty: Treaty on the Harmonization of Corporate Law in Africa posted as part of the basic documents on the Ohada.com website.

Litigation data: The official OHADA website is poorly maintained. I relied on yearly searches on the ohada.com website (http://www.ohada.com/jurisprudence/), searching for CCJA rulings. This may not be an accurate reporting of the court's complete docket, so that my data might actually understate the litigation trends. Webmasters for OHADA.com also shared their spreadsheets of data.

SOUTHERN AFRICAN DEVELOPMENT COMMUNITY (SADC) TRIBUNAL

Court Treaty: Declaration and Treaty Establishing the Southern African Development Community, Protocol on Tribunal and Rules of Procedure thereof (2000/2001). Available in Ebobrah and Tanoh (2010, 339 and 383).

Litigation data: At the time of writing this book, all rulings were posted online. Data based on a manual count of reported rulings, found on the court's website most recently located at http://www.sadc-tribunal.org/pages/decisions.htm.

SOUTHERN COMMON MARKET (MERCOSUR)

Court Treaty: Olivos Protocol for the Settlement of Disputes in MERCOSUR 42 *ILM* 2 (2003). Revisions to this protocol, including the provision on national court references, are in Acordada 13/2008 MERCOSUR/CMC/DEC. No. 37/03.

Litigation data: The MERCOSUR website only has data from after the adoption of the Olivos Protocol (http://www.mercosur.int/t_generic.jsp?contentid=375&site=1&channel=secretaria&seccion=6). Earlier litigation was reported at http://www.sice.oas.org/dispute/mercosur/ind_s.asp.

SPECIAL COURT FOR SIERRA LEONE (NOT A PERMANENT COURT, THUS NOT INCLUDED IN CHAPTER 3 OR THE CHAPTER APPENDIXES)

Court Treaty: Statute of the Special Court for Sierra Leone 34 *ILM* (1995) 482.

Litigation data: (Not included in this study, but available at http://www.sc-sl.org/CASES/tabid/71/Default.aspx.)

WEST AFRICAN ECONOMIC AND MONETARY UNION (WAEMU) COURT OF JUSTICE

Court Treaty: Treaty Establishing the West African Economic and Monetary Union and Additional Protocol No. 1 relative to the Organs of Control of WAEMU (UEMOA). Done in Dakar, Senegal, on January 10, 1994.

Litigation data: Obtained from Court Registrar, May 2011.

WORLD TRADE ORGANIZATION DISPUTE SETTLEMENT MECHANISM

Court Treaty: Understanding on Rules and Procedures Governing the Settlement of Disputes 1869 UNTS 401; 33 ILM 1226 (1994).

Bibliography of Cited Works

Abbott, Kenneth, Robert Keohane, Andrew Moravcsik, Anne-Marie Slaughter, and Duncan Snidal. 2000. "The Concept of Legalization." *International Organization* 54 (3): 401–20.

Adams, Daniel. 2008. "Back to Basics: The Predestined Failure of NAFTA Chapter 19 and Its Lessons for the Design of International Trade Regimes." *Emory International Law Review* 22: 205–45.

Adebajo, Adekeye, and Ismail O. D. Rashid. 2004. "West Africa's Security Challenges: Building Peace in a Troubled Region." *A Project of the International Peace Academy* xvi, 449.

Aguilar Alvarez, Guillermo, and William W. Park. 2003. "The New Face of Investment Arbitration: NAFTA Chapter 11." *Yale Journal of International Law* 28: 365–401.

Ahlborn, Christian, and David S. Evans. 2009. "The Microsoft Judgment and Its Implications for Competition Policy towards Dominant Firms in Europe." *Antitrust Law Journal* 75 (3): 887–932.

Al-Arayed, Jawad Salim. 2003. *A Line in the Sea: The Qatar v. Bahrain Border Dispute in the World Court*. Berkeley: North Atlantic Books.

Allain, Jean. 2000. *A Century of International Adjudication: The Rule of Law and Its Limits*. The Hague: T.M.C. Asser Press.

Allee, Todd, and Paul Huth. 2006. "Legitimizing Dispute Settlement: International Legal Rulings as Domestic Political Cover." *American Political Science Review* 100 (2): 219–34.

Alter, Karen J. 1998. "Who Are the Masters of the Treaty? European Governments and the European Court of Justice." *International Organization* 52 (1): 125–52.

———. 2001. *Establishing the Supremacy of European Law: The Making of an International Rule of Law in Europe*. Oxford: Oxford University Press.

———. 2006a. "Delegation to International Courts and the Limits of Recontracting Power." In *Delegation and Agency in International Organizations*, edited by D. Hawkins, D. A. Lake, D. Nielson, and M. J. Tierney. Cambridge: Cambridge University Press.

———. 2006b. "Private Litigants and the New International Courts." *Comparative Political Studies* 39 (1): 22–49.

———. 2008a. "Agent or Trustee: International Courts in Their Political Context." *European Journal of International Relations* 14 (1): 33–63.

———. 2008b. "Delegating to International Courts: Self-Binding vs. Other-Binding Delegation." *Law and Contemporary Problems* 71: 37–76.

———. 2009. *The European Court's Political Power: Selected Essays*. Oxford: Oxford University Press.

———. 2011. "The Evolving International Judiciary." *Annual Review of Law and Social Science* 7: 387–415.

———. 2012a. "The Global Spread of European Style International Courts." *West European Politics* 35 (1): 135–54.

———. 2012b. "The Multiple Roles of International Courts and Tribunals: Enforcement, Dispute Settlement, Constitutional and Administrative Review." In *International Law and International Relations: Synthesizing Insights from Interdisciplinary Scholarship*, edited by J. Dunoff and M. Pollack, 345–70. New York: Cambridge University Press.

Alter, Karen J., and Laurence Helfer. 2010. "Nature or Nurture: Judicial Lawmaking in the European Court of Justice and the Andean Tribunal of Justice." *International Organization* 64 (4): 563–92.

———. 2011. "Legal Integration in the Andes: Lawmaking by the Andean Tribunal of Justice." *European Law Journal* 17 (5): 701–15.

———. 2014. *Supranational Legal Transplants: Law and Politics of the Andean Tribunal of Justice*. Oxford: Oxford University Press. Forthcoming.

Alter, Karen J., Laurence Helfer, Petros Mavroides, Franz Mayer, and Joseph Weiler. 2014. "Comparative Dispute Settlement Systems." In *ASEAN Integration through Law Project*. Forthcoming.

Alter, Karen J., Laurence Helfer, and Jacqueline McAllister. 2013. "A New International Human Rights Court for West Africa: The Court of Justice for the Economic Community of West African States." *American Journal of International Law* 107(4). Forthcoming.

Alter, Karen J., Laurence Helfer, and Osvaldo Saldias. 2012. "Transplanting the European Court of Justice: The Experience of the Andean Tribunal of Justice." *American Journal of Comparative Law* 60 (6): 709–44.

Alter, Karen J., and Sophie Meunier. 2009. "The Politics of International Regime Complexity." *Perspective on Politics* 7 (1): 13–24.

Amerasinghe, Chittharanjan Felix 2014. "International Administrative Tribunals." In *Oxford Handbook on International Adjudication*, edited by C. Romano, K. J. Alter, and Y. Shany. Oxford: Oxford University Press.

Anaya, James S. 2009. *International Human Rights and Indigenous Peoples*. Edited by A. Publishers, Law and Business. Austin: Wolters Kluwer.

Anaya, James S., and Maia Campbell. 2009. "Gaining Legal Recognition of Indigenous Land Rights: The Story of the Awas Tingni Case in Nicaragua." In

Human Rights Advocacy Stories, edited by D. R. Hurwitz, M. L. Satterthwaite, and D. B. Ford, 117–54. New York: Foundation Press.

Arajärvi, Noora Johanna. 2011. "Looking Back from Nowhere: Is There a Future for Universal Jurisdiction over International Crimes?" *Tilburg Law Review* 16: 5–29.

Argibay, Carmen M. 2003. "Sexual Slavery and the Comfort Women of World War II." *Berkeley Journal of International Law* 21: 375–89.

Askin, Kelly Dawn. 1997. *War Crimes against Women: Prosecution in International War Crimes Tribunals*. Cambridge, MA: M. Nijhoff Publishers.

———. 2003. "Prosecuting Wartime Rape and Other Gender-Related Crimes under International Law: Extraordinary Advances, Enduring Obstacles." *Berkeley Journal of International Law* 21: 288–349.

Austin, John. 1832. *Province of Jurisprudence Determined*. London: John Murray.

Bach, Daniel C. 1983. "The Politics of West African Economic Co-Operation: C.E.A.O. and E.C.O.W.A.S." *Journal of Modern African Studies* 21 (4): 605–23.

———. 2007. "Nigeria's 'Manifest Destiny' in West Africa: Dominance without Power." *Africa Spectrum* 42 (2): 301–21.

Bagchi, Aditi. 2005. "The Political Economy of Merger Regulation." *American Journal of Comparative Law* 53 (1): 1–30.

Barfield, Claude. 2001. *Free Trade, Sovereignty, Democracy*. Washington, DC: American Enterprise Institute.

Barton, John H., Judith H. Goldstein, Timothy Edward Josling, and Richard H. Steinberg. 2006. *The Evolution of the Trade Regime*. Princeton, NJ: Princeton University Press.

Bass, Gary Jonathan. 2000. *Stay the Hand of Vengeance: The Politics of War Crimes Tribunals*. Princeton Studies in International History and Politics. Princeton, NJ: Princeton University Press.

Bates, Ed. 2011. *The Evolution of the European Convention on Human Rights*. Oxford: Oxford University Press.

Bebr, Gerard. 1981. *Development of Judicial Control of the European Communities*. The Hague: Martinus Nijhoff Publishers.

Beitz, Charles R., and Larry Alexander. 1985. *International Ethics: A Philosophy and Public Affairs Reader*. Princeton, NJ: Princeton University Press.

Ben Hamida, Walid. 2006. "The First Arab Investment Court Decision." *Journal of World Investment and Trade* 7: 699–722.

Benvenisti, Eyal. 2005. "The Interplay between Actors as a Determinant of the Evolution of Administrative Law in International Institutions." *Law and Contemporary Problems* 68 (3 and 4): 319–40.

———. 2008. "Reclaiming Democracy: The Strategic Uses of Foreign and International Law by National Courts." *American Journal of International Law* 102 (2): 241–76.

Berkowitz, Daniel, Katharina Pistor, and Jean-François Richard. 2003. "The Transplant Effect." *American Journal of Comparative Law* 51: 163–203.

Biernat, Ewa. 2003. "The Locus Standi of Private Applicants under Article 230 (4) EC and the Principle of Judicial Protection in the European Community." Jean Monnet Working Paper 12/03. NYU School of Law, New York.

Bignami, Francesca. 2005. "Creating European Rights: National Values and Supranational Interests." *Columbia Journal of European Law* 11: 241–352.

———. 2011. "From Expert Administration to Accountability Network: A New Paradigm for Comparative Administrative Law." *American Journal of Comparative Law* 59: 859–908.

Blut, John. 2007. "Court Watch: Tracking Current Developments in International Law." *International Law Students Association Quarterly* 16: 52–57.

Bob, Clifford. 2005. *The Marketing of Rebellion: Insurgents, Media, and International Activism*. Cambridge Studies in Contentious Politics. New York: Cambridge University Press.

———. 2009. *The International Struggle for New Human Rights*. Pennsylvania Studies in Human Rights. Philadelphia: University of Pennsylvania Press.

Boerger-De Smedt, Anne. 2008. "La Court de Justice dans les négociationis du traité de Paris instituant la CECA." *Journal of European History* 14 (2): 7–34.

———. 2012. "Negotiating the Foundations of European Law, 1950–1957: The Legal History of the Treaties of Paris and Rome." *Contemporary European History* 21 (3): 339–56.

Borgwardt, Elizabeth. 2005. *A New Deal for the World: America's Vision for Human Rights*. Cambridge, MA: Belknap Press of Harvard University Press.

Bork, Robert. 1989/90. "The Limits of 'International Law.'" *The National Interest* (Winter): 3–10.

———. 2003. *Coercing Virtue: The Worldwide Rule of Judges*. Washington, DC: AEI Press.

Börzel, Tanja. 2001. "Non-Compliance in the European Union: Pathology or Statistical Artifact." *Journal of European Public Policy* 8 (5): 803–24.

Boyle, Francis. 1985. *World Politics and International Law*. Durham, NC: Duke University Press.

Broude, Tomer. 2008. "Principles of Normative Integration and the Allocation of International Authority: The WTO, the Vienna Convention on the Law of Treaties, and the Rio Declaration." *Hebrew University International Law Research Paper No. 07-08*, available at http://papers.ssrn.com/sol3/papers.cfm?abstract_id=1249432.

Buchanan, Allen E. 2004. *Justice, Legitimacy, and Self-Determination: Moral Foundations for International Law*. Oxford Political Theory. New York: Oxford University Press.

———. 2006. "Democracy and the Committment to International Law." *Georgia Journal of International and Comparative Law* 34: 305–32.

Buchanan, Allen, and Russell Powell. 2008. "Constitutional Democracy and the

Rule of International Law: Are They Compatible?" *Journal of Political Philosophy* 16 (3): 326–49.

Bull, Hedley. 1977. *The Anarchical Society: A Study of Order in World Politics*. New York: Columbia University Press.

Burgis, Michelle Leanne. 2005. "(De)Limiting the Past for Future Gain: The Relationship between Sovereignty, Colonialism, and Oil in the Qatar v. Bahrain Territorial Dispute." *Yearbook of Islamic and Middle Eastern Law* 12: 557–86.

Burley, Anne-Marie, and Walter Mattli. 1993. "Europe before the Court." *International Organization* 47 (1): 41–76.

Busch, Marc, and Eric Reinhardt. 2000. "Testing International Trade Law: Empirical Studies of GATT/WTO Dispute Settlement." In *The Political Economy of International Trade Law: Essays in Honor of Robert Hudec*, edited by D.L.M. Kennedy and J. D. Southwick, 457–81. Cambridge: Cambridge University Press.

Cappelletti, Mauro. 1981. "The Law-Making Power of the Judge and Its Limits: Comparative Analysis." *Monash University Law Review* 8: 15–67.

———. 1989. *The Judicial Process in Comparative Perspective*. Oxford: Claredon Press.

Caron, David. 1990. "The Nature of the Iran-US Claims Tribunal." *American Journal of International Law* 84: 104–56.

Carpenter, Daniel. 2001. *The Forging of Bureaucratic Autonomy*. Princeton, NJ: Princeton University Press.

———. 2010. *Reputation and Power: Organizational Image and Pharmaceutical Regulation at the FDA*. Princeton, NJ: Princeton University Press.

Carpenter, R. Charli. 2007a. "Setting the Advocacy Agenda: Theorizing Issue Emergence and Nonemergence in Transnational Advocacy Networks." *International Studies Quarterly* 51 (1): 99–120.

———. 2007b. "Studying Issue (Non)-Adoption in Transnational Advocacy Networks." *International Organization* 61 (3): 643–67.

Carrubba, Clifford J., Matthew Gabel, and Charles Hankla. 2008. "Judicial Behavior under Political Constraints: Evidence from the European Court of Justice." *American Political Science Review* 104 (4): 435–52.

Cass, Deborah Z. 2001. "The Constitutionalization of International Trade Law: Judicial Norm-Generation as the Engine of Constitutional Development in International Trade." *European Journal of International Law* 17 (3): 623–46.

———. 2005. *The Constitutionalization of the World Trade Organization: Legitimacy, Democracy, and Community in the International Trading System*. New York: Oxford University Press.

Cavallaro, James L., and Stephanie Erin Brewer. 2008. "Reevaluating Regional Human Rights Litigation in the Twenty-First Century: The Case of the Inter-American Court." *American Journal of International Law* 102 (4): 768–827.

Chayes, Abram. 1974. *The Cuban Missile Crisis: International Crises and the Role of Law*. New York: Oxford University Press.

Cichowski, Rachel. 2007. *The European Court and Civil Society: Litigation, Mobilization, and Governance*. Cambridge: Cambridge University Press.

Cohen, Amanda. 2004. "Surveying the Microsoft Antitrust Universe." *Berkeley Tech Law Journal* 19: 333–64.

Cohen, Antonin. 2007. "Constitutionalism without Constitution: Transnational Elites between Political Mobilization and Legal Expertise (1940s–1960s)." *Law and Social Inquiry* 23 (1): 109–36.

Cohen, Antonin, and Michael Rask Madsen. 2007. "Cold War Law: Legal Entrepreneurs and the Emergence of a European Legal Field (1946–1965)." In *European Ways of Law*, edited by V. Gessner and D. Nelken, 175–200. Oxford: Hart.

Colares, Juscelino F. 2008. "Alternative Methods of Appellate Review in Trade Remedy Cases: Examining Results of U.S. Judicial and NAFTA Binational Review of U.S. Agency Decisions from 1989 to 2005." *Journal of Empirical Legal Studies* 5: 171–96.

Conant, Lisa J. 2006. "Individuals, Courts, and the Development of European Social Rights." *Comparative Political Studies* 39 (1): 76–100.

———. 2002. *Justice Contained: Law and Politics in the European Union*. Ithaca, NY: Cornell University Press.

Cooley, Alexander, and Hendrik Spruyt. 2009. *Contracting States: Sovereign Transfers in International Relations*. Princeton, NJ: Princeton University Press.

Cosgrove, Michael F. 2000. "Protecting the Protectors: Preventing the Decline of the Inter-American System for the Protection of Human Rights." *Case Western Reserve Journal of International Law* 32: 39–76.

Crook, John. 2006. "Mass Claims Processes: Lessons Learned over Twenty-Five Years." In *Redressing Injustices through Mass Claims Processes*, edited by the International Bureau of the Permanent Court of Abritration, 41–61. Oxford: Oxford University Press.

Cunningham, Richard O. 2000. "NAFTA Chapter 19: How Well Does It Work? How Much Is Needed?" *Canada–United States Law Journal* 26: 79–89.

Dai, Xinyuan. 2007. *International Institutions and National Policies*. Cambridge: Cambridge University Press.

Danilenko, Gennady M. 1999. "The Economic Court of the Commonwealth of Independent States." *New York University Journal of International Law and Politics* 31: 893–918.

Davies, Bill. 2012. *Resisting the European Court of Justice: West Germany's Confrontation with European Law, 1949–1979*. Cambridge: Cambridge University Press.

Davis, Christina L. 2012. *Why Adjudicate? Enforcing Trade Rules in the WTO*. Princeton NJ: Princeton University Press.

De Burca, Grainne. 2010. "The European Court and the International Legal Order after Kadi." *Harvard International Law Journal* 51 (1): 1–49.

———. 2011. "Roads Not Taken: The EU as a Global Human Rights Actor." *American Journal of International Law* 105 (4): 649–93.

de Wet, Erika. 2013. "The Rise and Fall of the Tribunal of the Southern African Development Community: Implications for Dispute Settlement in Southern Africa." *ICSID Review*: 1–19.

De Witte, Bruno. 1984. "Retour à 'Costa': La primauté du droit communautaire à la lumière du droit international." *Revue Trimestrielle du Droit Europóene* 20: 425–54.

Del Duca, Patrick. 2003–4. "The Rule of Law: Mexico's Approach to Expropriation Disputes in the Face of Investment Globalizatoin." *UCLA Law Review* 51: 35–141.

Dezalay, Yves, and Bryant G. Garth. 1996. *Dealing in Virtue: International Commercial Arbitration and the Construction of a Transnational Legal Order*. Chicago: University of Chicago Press.

———. 2002a. *Global Prescriptions: The Production, Exportation, and Importation of a New Legal Orthodoxy*. Ann Arbor: University of Michigan Press.

———. 2002b. *The Internationalization of Palace Wars: Lawyers, Economists, and the Contest to Transform Latin American States*. Chicago: University of Chicago Press.

Dickerson, Claire Moore. 2005. "Harmonizing Business Laws in Africa: OHADA Calls the Tune." *Columbia Journal of Transnational Law* 44 (17): 18–73.

Dodge, William S. 2001. "Metalclad Corporation v. Mexico. ICSID case no. ARB(AF)/97/1.40 ILM 36 (2001)." *American Journal of International Law* 95 (4): 910–19.

Downs, George, David Rocke, and Peter Barsoom. 1996. "Is the Good News about Compliance Good News about Cooperation?" *International Organization* 50 (3): 379–406.

Duffy, Helen. 2009. "Hadijatou Mani Koroua v. Niger: Slavery Unveiled by the ECOWAS Court." *Human Rights Law Review* 9 (1): 151–70.

———. 2011. "Hadijatou Mani Koroua v. Niger. Human Rights Cases in Sub-Regional African Courts: Towards Justice for Vicitims or Just More Fragmentation." Manuscript on file with the author.

Dunoff, Jeffrey L. 2006. "Constitutional Conceits: The WTO's 'Constitution' and the Discipline of International Law." *European Journal of International Law* 17 (3): 647–75.

———. 2007. "The Many Dimensions of Softwood Lumber." *Alberta Law Review* 45: 319–56.

———. 2009. "Does the United States Support International Tribunals? The Case of the Multilateral Trade System." In *The Sword and the Scales: The United*

States and International Courts and Tribunals, edited by C. Romano, 322–94. Cambridge: Cambridge University Press.

Dunoff, Jeffrey, and Joel Tractman. 2009. *Ruling the World? Constitutionalism, International Law, and Global Governance*. Cambridge: Cambridge University Press.

Ebobrah, Solomon T. 2010. "Human Rights Developments in African Sub-Regional Economic Communities during 2009." *African Human Rights Journal* 10: 233–67.

———. 2011. "Human Rights Developments in African Sub-Regional Economic Communities during 2010." *African Human Rights Law Journal* 1: 216–50.

Ebobrah, Solomon, and Armand Tanoh. 2010. *Compendium of African Sub-Regional Human Rights Documents*. Center for Human Rights, University of Pretoria. Pretoria: Pretoria University Law Press.

Eckes, Christina. 2008. "Sanctions against Individuals: Fighting Terrorism within the European Legal Order." *European Constitutional Law Review* 4 (2): 205–24.

Edelman, Lauren B., Christopher Uggen, and Howard S. Erlanger. 1999. "The Endogeneity of Legal Regulation: Grievance Procedures as Rational Myth." *American Journal of Sociology* 105 (2): 406–54.

Ellickson, Robert C. 1991. *Order without Law: How Neighbors Settle Disputes*. Cambridge, MA: Harvard University Press.

Elster, Jon. 2000. *Ulysses Unbound: Studies in Rationality, Precommitment, and Constraints*. New York: Cambridge University Press.

Epps, Charles. 1998. *The Rights Revolution: Lawyers, Activists, and Supreme Courts in Comparative Perspective*. Chicago: University of Chicago Press.

Epstein, Lee, and Jack Knight. 1998. *The Choices Justices Make*. Washington, DC: CQ Press

Epstein, Lee, William M. Landes, and Richard A Posner. 2013. *The Behavior of Federal Judges: A Theoretical and Empirical Study of Rational Choice*. Cambridge, MA: Havard University Press.

Evans, Malcolm D. 1995. "Case concerning Maritime Delimitation and Territorial Questions between Qatar and Bahrain (Qatar v. Bahrain), Jurisdiction and Admissibility." *International and Comparative Law Quarterly* 44: 691–98.

Fach Gómez, Katia. 2011. "Latin America and ICSID: David vs. Goliath?" *Law and Business Review of the Americas* 17: 195–230.

Finnemore, Martha. 1996. *National Interest in International Society*. Ithaca, NY: Cornell University Press.

Franck, Susan D. 2007. "Empirically Evaluating Claims about Investment Treaty Arbitration." *North Carolina Law Review* 86 (1): 1–83.

Franck, Thomas M. 1986. *Judging the World Court*. New York: Priority Press Publications.

Fry, James. 2010. "Non-Participation in the International Court of Justice Revisited: Change or Plus Ça Change?" *Columbia Journal of Transnational Law* 49: 35–73.

Garrett, Geoffrey, Daniel Kelemen, and Heiner Schulz. 1998. "The European Court of Justice, National Governments, and Legal Integration in the European Union." *International Organization* 52 (1): 149–76.

Garrett, Geoffrey, and Barry Weingast. 1993. "Ideas, Interests, and Institutions: Constructing the EC's Internal Market." In *Ideas and Foreign Policy*, edited by J. Goldstein and R. Keohane, 173–206. Ithaca, NY: Cornell University Press.

Gastle, Charles, and Jean-G. Castel. 1995. "Should the North American Free Trade Agreement Dispute Settlement Mechanism in Antidumping and Countervailing Duty Cases Be Reformed in the Light of Softwood Lumber III?" *Law and Policy in International Business* 26.

Gathii, James. 2010. "The Under-Appreciated Jurisprudence of Africa's Regonal Trade Judiciaries." *Oregon Review of International Law* 12 (2): 245–83.

———. 2011. *African Regional Trade Agreements as Legal Regimes*. Cambridge: Cambridge University Press.

Gautier, Philippe. 2008. "The International Tribunal for the Law of the Sea: Activities in 2007," *Chinese Journal of International Law* 7 (2): 371–88.

Gibson, James L., and Gregory A. Caldeira. 1993. "Changes in the Legitimacy of the European Court of Justice: A Post-Maastricht Analysis." *British Journal of Political Science* 28 (1): 63–91.

———. 1995. "The Legitimacy of Transnational Legal Institutions: Compliance, Support, and the European Court of Justice." *American Journal of Political Science* 39 (2): 459–89.

Gibson, James L., Gregory A. Caldeira, and Vanessa A. Baird. 1998. "On the Legitimacy of National High Courts." *American Political Science Review* 92 (2): 16.

Gillingham, John. 1991. *Coal, Steel, and the Rebirth of Europe, 1945–1955: The Germans and French from Ruhr Conflict to Economic Community*. Cambridge: Cambridge University Press.

Ginsburg, Tom. 2003. *Judicial Review in New Democracies: Constitutional Courts in Asian Cases*. New York: Cambridge University Press.

———. 2005. "Bounded Discretion in International Judicial Lawmaking." *Virginia Journal of International Law* 43 (3): 631–73.

———. 2008. "The Global Spread of Constitutional Review." In *The Oxford Handbook on Law and Politics*, edited by K. Whittington, D. Keleman, and G. A. Caldeira, 81–98. Oxford: Oxford University Press.

———. 2012. *Comparative Constitutional Design*. Cambridge: Cambridge University Press.

Ginsburg, Tom, and Tamir Moustafa. 2008. *Rule by Law: The Politics of Courts in Authoritarian Regimes*. Cambridge: Cambridge University Press.

Goldsmith, Jack L., and Daryl Levinson. 2009. "Law for States: International

Law, Constitutional Law, Public Law." *Harvard Law Review* 122 (7): 1792–868.

Goldsmith, Jack L., and Eric A. Posner. 2005. *The Limits of International Law*. New York: Oxford University Press.

Goldstein, Judith. 1996. "International Law and Domestic Institutions." *International Organization* 50 (4): 541–64.

Goodman, Ryan, and Derek Jinks. 2004. "How to Influence States: Socialization and International Human Rights Law." *Duke Law Journal* 54 (3): 621–703.

Greer, Steven. 2006. *The European Convention on Human Rights: Achievements, Problems, and Prospects*. Cambridge: Cambridge University Press.

Grossman, Claudio. 2008. "The Inter-American System of Human Rights: Challenges for the Future." *Indian Law Journal* 83: 1267–81.

Gruber, Lloyd. 2000. *Ruling the World: Power Politics and the Rise of Supranational Institutions*. Princeton, NJ: Princeton University Press.

Guieu, Jean-Michel. 2012. "The Debate about a European Institutional Order among International Legal Scholars in the 1920s and Its Legacy." *Contemporary European History* 21 (3): 319–38.

Guzman, Andrew T. 2008. "International Tribunals: A Rational Choice Analysis." *University of Pennsylvania Law Review*.

Haas, Peter M. 1992. "Introduction: Epistemic Communities and International Policy Coordination." *International Organization* 46 (1): 1–36.

Haas, Peter M., Robert O. Keohane, and Marc A. Levy. 1993. *Institutions for the Earth: Sources of Effective International Environmental Protection*. Global Environmental Accords. Cambridge, MA: MIT Press

Hagan, John. 2003. *Justice in the Balkans: Prosecuting War Crimes in the Hague Tribunal*. Chicago: University of Chicago Press.

Hagan, John, Ron Levi, and Gabrielle Feralles. 2006. "Swaying the Hand of Justice: The Internal and External Dynamics of Regime Change at the International Tribunal for the Former Yugoslavia." *Law and Social Inquiry* 31 (3): 585–616.

Hale, C. R., E. T. Gordon, and G. C. Gurdián. 1998. *Diagnóstico general sobre la tenencia de la tierra en las comunidades indígenas de la Costa Atlántica: Resumen ejecutivo*. CACRC, Central American and Caribbean Research Council.

Hara, Kimie. 2001. "50 Years from San Francisco: Re-Examining the Peace Treaty and Japan's Territorial Problems." *Pacific Affairs* 74 (3): 361–82.

Harlow, Carol, and Richard Rawlings. 1992. *Pressure through Law*. London: Routledge.

Harout, Samra. 2007. "Five Years Later: The CMS Award Placed in the Context of the Argentine Financial Crisis and ICSID Arbitration Boom." *University of Miami Inter-American Law Review* 38 (3): 667–97.

Hartley, Trevor. 1996. "The European Court, Judicial Objectivity and the Constitution of the European Union." *Law Quarterly Review* 112: 95–109.

———. 1998. *The Foundations of European Community Law*. 4th ed. Oxford: Clarendon Press.

Hathaway, Oona, and Scott J. Shapiro. 2011. "Outcasting: Enforcement in Domestic and International Law." *Yale Law Journal*.

Hawkins, Darren, and Wade Jacoby. 2010. "Partial Compliance: A Comparison of the European and Inter-American Court of Human Rights." *Journal of International Law and International Relations* 6: 35–85.

Hayner, Priscilla. 2007. "Negotiating peace in Liberia: Preserving the Possibility for Justice," edited by the Centre for Humanitarian Dialogue, International Center of Transitional Justice, 1–31.

Helfer, Laurence R. 2002. "Overlegalizing Human Rights: International Relations Theory and the Commonwealth Caribbean Backlash against Human Rights Regimes." *Columbia Law Review* 102 (7): 1832–911.

———. 2003. "Constitutional Analogies in the International Legal System." *Loyola of Los Angeles Law Review* 37 (2): 193–237.

———. 2006. "Why States Create International Tribunals: A Theory of Constrained Independence." In *International Conflict Resolution*, edited by S. Voigt, M. Albert, and D. Schmidtchen. Tübigen: Mohr Seibeck.

———. 2008. "Redesigning the European Court of Human Rights: Embeddedness as a Deep Structural Principle of the European Human Rights Regime." *European Journal of International Law* 19 (1): 125–59.

———. 2013. "The Effectiveness of International Adjudicators." In *Oxford Handbook on International Adjudication*, edited by C. Romano, K. J. Alter, and Y. Shany. Oxford: Oxford University Press.

Helfer, Laurence, and Karen Alter. 2009. "The Andean Tribunal of Justice and Its Interlocutors: Understanding the Preliminary Ruling Reference Patterns in the Andean Community." *Journal of International Law and Politics* 42 (4): 871–928.

———. 2013. "Legitimacy and Lawmaking: A Tale of Three International Courts." *Theoretical Inquires in Law* 14: 479–503.

Helfer, Laurence, Karen Alter, and Maria Florencia Guerzovich. 2009. "Islands of Effective International Adjudication: Constructing an Intellectual Property Rule of Law in the Andean Community." *American Journal of International Law* 103: 1–47.

Helfer, Laurence, and Anne-Marie Slaughter. 1997. "Toward a Theory of Effective Supranational Adjudication." *Yale Law Journal* 107 (2): 273–391.

———. 2005. "Why States Create International Tribunals: A Response to Professors Posner and Yoo." *California Law Review* 93 (May): 899–956.

Helfer, Laurence, and Erik Voeten. 2014. "International Courts as Agents of Legal Change: Evidence from LGBT Rights in Europe." *International Organization* 68(1). Forthcoming.

Helmke, Gretchen. 2005. *Courts under Constraints*. Cambridge: Cambridge University Press.

Henkin, Louis. 1979. *How Nations Behave*. New York: Columbia University Press.

Hirschl, Ran. 2004. *Towards Juristocracy: The Origins and Consequences of the New Constitutionalism*. Cambridge, MA: Havard University Press.

Hobbes, Thomas. 1962. *Leviathan; or, The matter, forme and power of a commonwealth, ecclesiasticall and civil*. New York: Collier Books.

Hoffmann, Stanley. 1966. "Obstinate or Obsolete? France, European Integration, and the Fate of the Nation-State." *Daedalus* 95 (3): 862–915.

———. 1981. *Duties beyond Borders*. Syracuse, NY: Syracuse University Press.

Holden, Chris, Kelley Lee, Gary Jonas Fooks, and Nathaniel Wander. 2010. "The Impact of Regional Trade Integration on Firm Organization and Strategy: British American Tobacco in the Andean Pact." *Business and Politics* 12 (4): Article 3.

Holland, Erin E. 2003. "Using Merger Review to Cure Prior Conduct: The European Commission's GE/Honeywell Decision." *Columbia Law Review* 103 (1): 74–110.

Hooghe, Liesbet, Gary Marks,and Arjan Schakel. 2010. *The Rise of Regional Authority: A Comparative Study of 42 Democracies*. London: Routledge.

Horn, Henrik, Louise Johannesson, and Petros Mavroides. 2011. "The WTO Dispute Settlment System 1995–2010: Some Descriptive Statistics." *Journal of World Trade* 45 (6): 1107–38.

Hudec, Robert E. 1988. "Reforming GATT Adjudication Procedures: The Lessons of the DISC Case." *Minnesota Law Review* 72: 1443–509.

———. 1993. *Enforcing International Trade Law: Evolution of the Modern GATT System*. New Hampshire: Butterworths.

Hudson, Manley O. 1944. *International Tribunals: Past and Future*. Washington, DC: Carnegie Endowment for International Peace and Brookings Institution.

Hufbauer, Gary C. 2002. "The Foreign Sales Corporation Drama: Reaching the Last Act?" *International Economic Briefs* PB02-10 (November): 1–13.

Huneeus, Alexandra. 2011. "Courts Resisting Courts: Lessons from the Inter-American Court's Struggle to Enforce Human Rights." *Cornell International Law Journal* 44 (3).

———. 2013. "International Criminal Law by Other Means: The Quasi-Criminal Jurisdiction of Human Rights Courts." *American Journal of International Law* 107 (1): 1–44.

———. 2014. "Compliance with Judgments and Decisions of International Courts." In *Oxford Handbook on International Adjudication*, edited by C. Romano, K. J. Alter, and Y. Shany. Oxford: Oxford University Press.

Huneeus, Alexandra, Javier A. Couso, and Rachel Sieder. 2011. *Cultures of Legality: Judicialization and Political Activism in Latin America*. Cambridge: Cambridge University Press.

Hurd, Ian. 2005. "The Strategic Use of Liberal Internationalism: Libya and the UN Sanctions, 1993–2003." *International Organization* 59 (Spring): 495–526.

Hurwitz, Deena R. 2009. "Universal Jurisdiction and the Dilemmas of International Criminal Justice: The Sabra and Shatila Case in Belgium." In *Human Rights Advocacy Stories*, edited by D. R. Hurwitz, M. L. Satterthwaite, and D. B. Ford, 267–315. New York: Foundation Press.

Huth, Paul, and Todd Allee. 2006. "The Pursuit of Legal Settlements to Territorial Disputes." *Conflict Management and Peace Science* 23 (4): 285–308.

Ikenberry, G. John. 2001. *After Victory: Institutions, Strategic Restraint, and the Rebuilding of Order after Major Wars*. Princeton, NJ: Princeton University Press.

Jacobs, Zachary. 2007. "One of These Things Is Not Like the Other: US Participation in International Tribunals and Why Chapter Nineteen of NAFTA Does Not Fit." *Columbia Journal of Transnational Law* 45: 868–98.

Jacobson, Harold, and Edith Weiss. 1995. "Strengthening Compliance with International Environmental Accords: Preliminary Observations from a Collaborative Project." *Global Governance* 1: 119–48.

Kahler, Miles. 2000. "Legalization as a Strategy: The Asian Pacific Case." *International Organization* 54 (3): 549–71.

Katendi, Francois, and Jean-Baptiste Placca. "Savoir accepter la pauvreté: Interview de Kéba Mbaye." In *L'autre Afrique*, OHADA.com.

Katzenstein, Suzanne. 2014. "In the Shadow of Crisis: The Creation of International Courts in the Twentieth Century." *Harvard Journal of International Law* 55.

Keegan, Laura. "The 1991 U.S./EC Competition Agreement: A Glimpse of the Future through the United States v. Microsoft Corp. Window." *Journal of International Legal Studies* 2: 149–79.

Kelemen, R. Daniel. 2011. *Eurolegalism: The Transformation of Law and Regulation in the European Union*. Cambridge, MA: Harvard University Press.

Keohane, Robert, and Ruth W. Grant. 2005. "Accountability and Abuses of Power in World Politics." *American Political Science Review* 99 (1): 29–43.

Keohane, Robert, Andrew Moravcsik, and Anne-Marie Slaughter. 2000. "Legalized Dispute Resolution: Interstate and Transnational." *International Organization* 54 (3): 457–88.

Keohane, Robert O., and David G. Victor. 2011. "The Regime Complex for Climate Change." *Perspectives on Politics* 9 (1): 7–23.

Kembayev, Zhenis. 2009. *Legal Aspects of the Regional Integration Processes in the Post-Soviet Area*. Berlin: Springer-Verlag.

Kingsbury, Benedict. 1999. "Is the Proliferation of International Courts and Tribunals a Systemic Problem." *New York University Journal of International Law and Politics* 31: 679–96.

Kingsbury, Benedict, Nico Krisch, Richard B. Stewart, and Jonathan Weiner. 2005. "The Emergence of Global Administrative Law." *Law and Contemporary Problems* 68 (3 and 4): 15–62.

Krisch, Nico, and Benedict Kingbury. 2006. "Introduction: Global Governance and Global Adminstrative Law in the International Legal Order." *European Journal of International Law* 17 (1): 1–13.

Kufuor, Kofi Oteng. 2006. *The Institutional Transformation of the Economic Community of West African States*. Hampshire, England: Ashgate.

Kull, Steven, and Clay Ramsay. 2009. "American Public Opinion on International Courts and Tribunals." In *The Sword and the Scales: The United States and International Courts and Tribunals*, edited by C. Romano, 12–29. Cambridge: Cambridge University Press.

Kumm, Mattias. 2009. "The Cosmopolitian Turn in Constitutionalism: On the Relationship between Constitutionalism in and beyond the State." In *Ruling the World? Constitutionalism, International Law, and Global Governance*, edited by J. Dunoff and J. Tractman, 258–325. Cambridge: Cambridge University Press.

Kümmel, Gerhard. 2003. "Changing State Institutions: The German Military and the Integration of Women." In *European Consortium for Political Research*. Marburg.

Lagneau-Devillé, Anne. 1983. "Influences du pouvoir exécutif sur les prérogatives du juge en France, sous la Vème République." In *Fonction de juger et pourvoir judiciaire*, edited by P. Gérard, F. Ost, and M. Van de Kerchare, 469–92. Brussels: Faculté Universitaire Saint-Louis.

Laidlaw, Peter C. 2012. "Provisional Application of the Energy Charter as Seen in the Yukos Dispute." *Santa Clara Law Review* 52: 655–84.

Levi, Werner. 1976. *Law and Politics in the International Society*. Beverly Hills, CA: Sage Publications.

Liebert, Ulrike. 2002. "Europeanizing the Military: The ECJ and the Transformation of the Bundeswehr." Jean Monnet Center for European Studies Working Paper 2002/7. NYU School of Law, New York.

Lindseth, Peter. 2003. "The Contradictions of Supranationalism: Administrative Governance and Constitutionalization in European Integration since the 1950s." *Loyola of Los Angeles Law Review* 37 (2): 363–406.

———. 2005. "Always Embedded Administration: The Historical Evolution of Administrative Justice as an Aspect of Modern Governance in the Economy as Polity." In *The Economy as Polity*, edited by B. S. Christian Joerges and Peter Wagner, 117–36. London: UCL Press (Routledge-Cavendish).

———. 2010. *Power and Legitimacy: Reconciling Europe and the Nation-State*. Oxford: Oxford University Press.

Locke, John. 1957. *The Second Treatise on Government*. Indianapolis: Bobbs-Merrill.

Lopez, David. 1997. "Dispute Resolution under NAFTA: Lessons from the Early Experience." *Texas International Law Journal* 32 (163): 163–208.

Lutz, Ellen, and Kathryn Sikkink. 2000. "International Human Rights Law and Practice in Latin America." *International Organization* 54 (3): 633–59.

Madsen, Mikael Rask. 2010. *La Genese de l'Europe des droits de l'Homme:*

Enjeux juridiques et stratégies d'État. Collection Sociologie politique européene. Strasbourg: Presses Universitaires de Strasbourg.

Maduro, Miguel Poiares. 1998. *We the Court: The European Court of Justice and the European Economic Constitution; a Critical Reading of Article 30 of the EC Treaty*. Oxford: Hart Publishers.

Majone, Giandomenico. 2001. "Two Logics of Delegation: Agency and Fiduciary Relations in EU Governance." *European Union Politics* 2 (1): 103–22.

Mancero-Bucheli, Gabriela. 1998. "Intellectual Property and Rules on Free Movement: A Contradiction in the Andean Community." *NAFTA: Law and Business Review of the Americas* 4: 125–36.

Mancini, Federico. 1989. "The Making of a Constitution for Europe." *Common Market Law Review* 24: 595–614.

Martin, Lisa. 2012. "Against Compliance." In *Interdisciplinary Perspectives on International Law and International Relations: The State of the Art*, edited by J. Dunoff and M. Pollack, 591–612. New York: Cambridge University Press.

McAdams, Richard H. 2004. "Adjudicating in Anarchy: An Expressive Theory of International Dispute Resolution." *William and Mary Law Review* 45 (March): 1229–329.

McCall Smith, James, and Jonas Tallberg. 2012. "Dispute Settlement in World Politics: States, Supranational Prosecutors, and Compliance." *European Journal of International Relations*: 1–27.

McCann, Michael W. 1994. *Rights at Work: Pay Equity Reform and the Politics of Legal Mobilization*. Language and Legal Discourse. Chicago: University of Chicago Press.

McCubbins, Matthew D., Roger G. Noll, and Barry R. Weingast. 1989. "Structure and Process, Politics and Policy: Administrative Arrangements and the Political Control of Agencies." *Virginia Law Review* 75 (March): 431–82.

McGinnis, John. 2007. "Should International Law Be Part of Our Law?" *Stanford Law Review* 59 (5): 1175–246.

McGinnis, John, and Mark Movsesian. 2004. "Against Global Governance in the WTO." *Harvard International Law Journal* 45 (2): 343–65.

Merry, Sally Engle. 2003a. "Constructing a Global Law—Violence against Women and the Human Rights System." *Law and Social Inquiry* 28: 941–74

———. 2003b. "Rights Talk and the Experience of Law: Implementing Women's Human Rights to Protection from Violence." *Human Rights Quarterly* 25 (2): 343–81.

Merryman, John Henry, and Rogelio Pérez-Perdomo. 2007. *The Civil Law Tradition*. Stanford, CA: Stanford University Press.

Milgrom, Paul, Douglass North, and Barry Weingast. 1990. "The Role of Institutions in the Revival of Trade: The Law Merchant, Private Judges, and the Champagne Fairs." *Economics and Politics* 2: 1–23.

Milward, Alan. 1984. *The Reconstruction of Western Europe, 1945–1951*. London: Methuen.

———. 1992. *The European Rescue of the Nation-State*. London: Routledge.

Mnookin, Robert, and Louis Kornhauser. 1979. "Bargaining in the Shadow of the Law: The Case of Divorce." *Yale Law Journal* 88: 950–97.

Monaghan, Henry Paul. 2007. "Article III and Supranational Judicial Review." *Columbia Law Review* 107 (4): 833–82.

Moravcsik, Andrew. 1995. "Explaining International Human Rights Regimes: Liberal Theory and Western Europe." *European Journal of International Relations* 1 (2): 157–89.

———. 2000. "The Origins of Human Rights Regimes: Democratic Delegation in Postwar Europe." *International Organization* 54 (2): 217–52.

———. 2005. "The Paradox of US Human Rights Policy." In *American Exceptionalism and Human Rights*, edited by M. Ignatieff, 19. Princeton, NJ: Princeton University Press.

Mouloul, Alhousseini. 2009. "Understanding the Organization for the Harmonization of Business Laws in Africa (O.H.A.D.A.)." Paris. On file with author.

Müller, Jan-Werner. 2007. *Constitutional Patriotism*. Princeton, NJ: Princeton University Press.

Murkens, Jo Eric Khushal. 2009. "Countering Anti-Constitutional Argument: The Reasons for the European Court of Justice's Decision in Kadi and Al Barakaat." *Cambridge Yearbook of European Legal Studies* 11: 15–52.

Napoles, Robert. 1993. "Dispute Resolution under Chapter 19 of the Nafta: Antidumping and Countervailing Business as Usual." *Arizona Journal of International and Comparative Law* 10: 460–505.

Ni Aoláin, Fionnuala. 2013. "Gendered Harms and Their Interface with International Criminal Law: Norms, Challenges, and Domestication." Minnesota Legal Studies Research Paper No. 13-19, available at http://papers.ssrn.com/sol3/papers.cfm?abstract_id=2247623.

Nmehielle, Vincent O., and Charles Chernor Jalloh. 2006. "The Legacy of the Special Court for Sierra Leone." *Fletcher Forum of World Affairs* 30 (2): 107–24.

Noland, Marcus. 1997. "Chasing Phantoms: The Political Economy of USTR." *International Organization* 51 (3): 365–87.

Nollkaemper, André. 2011. *National Courts and the International Rule of Law*. Oxford: Oxford University Press.

Nollkaemper, André, and Janne Elisabeth Nijman. 2007. *New Perspectives on the Divide between National and International Law*. Oxford: Oxford University Press.

Nwogu, Nneoma. 2007. "Regional Integration as an Instrument of Human Rights: Reconceptualizing ECOWAS." *Journal of Human Rights* 6: 345–60.

Nye, Joseph S. 1965. "Patterns and Catalysts in Regional Integration." *International Organization* 19: 870–84.

———. 1967. *Pan-Africanism and East African Integration*. Cambridge, MA: Harvard University Press.

Nye, William. 2009. "The Implications of 'Zeroing' for Enforcement of US Anti-dumping Laws." *Journal of Economic Policy Reform* 12 (4): 263–71.

Nzelibe, Jide. 2011. "Strategic Globalization: International Law as an Extension of Domestic Political Conflict." *Northwestern University Law Review* 105: 635–88.

O'Connell, Mary Ellen. 2008. *The Power and Purpose of International Law: Insights from the Theory and Practice of Enforcement*. Oxford: Oxford University Press.

O'Connell, Mary Ellen, and Lenore VanderZee. 2014. "The History of International Adjudication." In *Oxford Handbook on International Adjudication*, edited by C. Romano, K. J. Alter, and Y. Shany. Oxford: Oxford University Press.

O'Keefe, Thomas Andrew. 1996. "How the Andean Pact Transformed Itself into a Friend of Foreign Enterprise." *International Lawyer* 30 (4): 811–24.

Oppong, Richard Frimpong. 2011. *Legal Aspects of Economic Integration in Africa*. Cambridge: Cambridge University Press.

Osiel, Mark. 1997. *Mass Atrocities, Collective Memory, and the Law*. New Brunswick, NJ: Transaction Publishers.

Oxman, Bernard. 2001. "Complementary Agreements and Compulsory Jurisdiction." *American Journal of International Law* 95: 277–312.

Padilla, David. 1979. "The Judicial Resolution of Legal Disputes in the Integration Movements of the Hemisphere." *Lawyers of the Americas* 11 (1): 75–95.

Pan, Eric. 1999. "Assessing the NAFTA Chapter 19 Binational Panel System: An Experiment in International Adjudication." *Harvard International Law Journal* 40: 379–447.

Paulson, Colter. 2004. "Compliance with Final Judgments of the International Court of Justice Since 1987." *American Journal of International Law* 98: 434–61.

Pauwelyn, Joost. 2006. "Adding Sweetners to Softwood Lumber: The WTO-NAFTA 'Spaghetti Bowl' is Cooking." *Journal of International Economic Law* 9: 197–206.

Pauwelyn, Joost, and Manfried Elsig. 2012. "The Politics of Treaty Interpretation: Variations and Explanations across International Tribunals." In *Interdisciplinary Perspectives on International Law and International Relations: The State of the Art*, edited by J. Dunoff and M. Pollack, 445–75. New York: Cambridge University Press.

Perriello, Tom, and Marieke Wierda. 2006. "The Special Court for Sierra Leone under Scrutiny." In *Prosecutions Case Studies Series*, edited by International Center for Transitional Justice.

Pescatore, Pierre. 1981. "Les Travaux du 'Groupe Juridique' Dans la négociation des Traités de Rome." *Studia Diplomatica (Chronique de Politique Etrangère)* 34 (1–4): 159–78.

———. 1983. "La clarence du législateur communautaire et le devoir du juge." In

Gedächtnisschrift für L.-J. Constantinesco, 559–80. Cologne: Carl Heymanns Verlag.

Petersmann, Ernst-Ulrich. 2008a. "Human Rights, International Economic Law, and Constitutional Justice." *European Journal of International Law* 19 (4): 769–98.

———. 2008b. "Judging Judges: From Principal-Agent Theory to Constitutional Justice in Multilevel Judicial Governance of Economic Cooperation among Citizens." *Journal of International Economic Law* 11 (4): 827–84.

Pollack, Mark. 2003. *The Engines of Integration: Delegation, Agency, and Agency Setting in the European Union*. Oxford: Oxford University Press.

Posner, Eric A., and Miguel de Figueiredo. 2005. "Is the International Court of Justice Biased?" *Journal of Legal Studies* 32 (2): 599–630.

Posner, Eric, and Alan Sykes. 2011. "Efficient Breach of International Law: Optimal Remedies, 'Legalized Noncompliance,' and Related Issues." *Michigan Law Review* 110: 243–94.

Posner, Eric A., and John C. Yoo. 2005. "A Theory of International Adjudication." *California Law Review* 93 (1): 1–72.

Potter, Alex, and Simon Constantine. 2009. "The EU's Abuse of Dominance Rules and Their Impact on Commercial Policy Setting by U.S. Companies, 24 ANTITRUST ABA 78, (2009)." *Antitrust* 24 (1): 78–84.

Potter, Simon V. 2000. "Chapter 19—Private Party Appeals from Government Rulings: A Dispute Settlement Procedure in Operation, How Effective Is It in the Resolution of Disputes? Are Changes Needed or Possible?" *Canada–United States Law Journal* 26: 91–97.

Powell, Stephen J. 2010. "Expanding the NAFTA Chapter 19 Dispute Settlement System: A Way to Declaw Trade Remedy Laws in a Free Trade Area of the Americas?" *Law and Business Review of the Americas* 16: 217–40.

Putnam, Tonya. 2014. *Courts without Borders: The Politics and Law of U.S. Extraterritoriality*. Forthcoming.

Rabkin, Jeremy A. 2005. *Law without Nations? Why Constitutional Government Requires Sovereign States*. Princeton, NJ: Princeton University Press.

Rajagopal, Balakrishnan. 2003. *International Law from Below: Development, Social Movements, and Third World Resistance*. Cambridge: Cambridge University Press.

Rasmussen, Hjalte. 1986. *On Law and Policy in the European Court of Justice*. Dordrecht: Martinus Nijhoff Publishers.

Rasmussen, Morten. 2010. "From Costa v ENEL to the Treaties of Rome: A Brief History of Legal Revolution." In *The Past and Future of EU Law: The Classics of EU Law Revisited on the 50th Anniversary of the Rome Treaty*, edited by M. P. Maduro and L. Azoulai, 69–85. Portland, OR: Hart Publishing.

———. 2013. "Towards a New History of European Law." *Contemporary European History* 21: 305–476.

Ratner, Steven. 2008. "Regulatory Takings in Institutional Context: Beyond the

Fear of Fragmented International Law." *American Journal of International Law* 102 (3): 475–528.

———. 2012. "Pursuading to Comply: On the Deployment and Avoidence of Legal Argumentation." In *Interdisciplinary Perspectives on International Law and International Relations: The State of the Art*, edited by J. Dunoff and M. Pollack, 568–90. New York: Cambridge University Press.

Raustiala, Kal. 2000. "Compliance and Effectiveness in International Regulatory Cooperation." *Case Western Reserve Journal of International Law* 32: 387–440.

———. 2004. "Police Patrols and Fire Alarms in the NAAEC." *Loyola of Los Angeles International and Comparative Law Review* 3 (Spring): 389–413.

———. 2009. *Does the Constitution Follow the Flag: The Evolution of Territoriality in American Law*. Oxford: Oxford University Press.

Raustiala, Kal, and David Victor. 2004. "The Regime Complex for Plant Genetic Resources." *International Organization* 58 (2): 277–309.

Reidy, Aisling. 2002. "The Prohibition of Torture: A Guide to the Implementation of Article 3 of the European Convention on Human Rights." In *Human Rights Handbook, No. 6*, edited by D. G. o. H. R. C. o. Europe. Strasbourg: Council of Europe.

Reus-Smit, Christain. 1999. *The Moral Purpose of the State: Culture, Social Identity, and Institutional Rationality in International Relations*. Princeton, NJ: Princeton University Press.

———. 2011. "Struggles for Individual Rights and the Expansion of the International System." *International Organization* 65 (2): 207–42.

Rischikof. 2004. "When Naked Came the Doctrine of 'Self-Defense': What Is the Proper Role of the International Court of Justice in Use of Force Cases?" *Yale Journal of International Law* 29: 331–42.

Risse, Thomas, Stephen Ropp, and Kathryn Sikkink. 1999. *The Power of Human Rights: International Norms and Domestic Change*. Cambridge: Cambridge University Press.

Robertson, A. H., and J. G. Merrills. 1994. *Human Rights in Europe*. Manchester: Manchester University Press.

Roht-Arriaza, Naomi. 2005. *The Pinochet Effect: Transnational Justice in the Age of Human Rights*. Pennsylvania Studies in Human Rights. Philadelphia: University of Pennsylvania Press.

Romano, Cesare. 1999. "The Proliferation of International Judicial Bodies: The Pieces of the Puzzle." *New York University Journal of International Law and Politics* 31 (Summer): 709–51.

———. 2007. "The Shift from the Consensual to the Compulsory Paradigm in International Adjudication: Elements for a Theory of Consent." *New York University Journal of International Law and Politics* 39 (4): 791–872.

———. 2009. *The Sword and the Scales: The United States and International Courts and Tribunals*. Cambridge: Cambridge University Press.

———. 2011. "A Taxonomy of International Rule of Law Institutions." *Journal of International Dispute Settlement* 2.

———. 2014. "Trial and Error in International Judicialization." In *Oxford Handbook on International Adjudication*, edited by C. Romano, K. J. Alter, and Y. Shany. Oxford: Oxford University Press.

Romano, Cesare, Karen J. Alter, and Yuval Shany. 2014. "Mapping International Courts and Tribunals, the Issues and Players." In *Oxford Handbook on International Adjudication*, edited by C. Romano, K. J. Alter, and Y. Shany. Oxford: Oxford University Press.

Roozbeh, B. Baker. 2009. "Universal Jurisdiction and the Case of Belgium: A Critical Assessment." *ILSA Journal of International and Comparative Law* 16 (1): 141–67.

Rosenberg, Gerald N. 1993. *The Hollow Hope: Can Courts Bring about Social Change?* American Politics and Political Economy. Chicago: University of Chicago Press.

Rubenfeld, Jed. 2003. "The Two World Orders." *Wilson Quarterly* 27 (4): 22–36.

Rudolf, Beate. 2005. "European Union: Compulsory Military Service." *International Journal of Constitutional Law* 3 (5): 673–79.

Ruggie, John. 1993. "Multilateralism: The Anatomy of an Institution." In *Multilateralism Matters*, edited by J. Ruggie, 3–47. New York: Columbia University Press.

Saldias, Osvaldo. 2010. "Networks, Courts, and Regional Integration: Explaining the Establishment of the Andean Court of Justice." Working Paper of the KFG The Transformative Power of Europe, No. 20, November.

Sassen, Saskia. 2006. *Territory, Authority, Rights: From Medieval to Global Assemblages*. Princeton, NJ: Princeton University Press.

Savelsberg, Joachim J., and Ryan D. King. 2007. "Law and Collective Memory." *Annual Review of Law and Social Science* 3: 189–211.

Schabas, William A. 2001. *An Introduction to the International Criminal Court*. Cambridge: Cambridge University Press.

Scharpf, Fritz. 1988. "The Joint-Decision Trap: Lessons from German Federalism and European Integration." *Public Administration* 66 (Autumn): 239–78.

Scheppele, Kim. 2006. "Guardians of the Constitution: Constitutional Court Presidents and the Struggle for the Rule of Law in Post-Soviet Europe." *University of Pennsylvania Law Review* 154 (6): 1757–851.

Schermers, Henry G. 1999. "Acceptance of International Supervision of Human Rights." *Leiden Journal of International Law* 12: 821–31.

Schneiderman, David. 2008. *Constitutionalizating Economic Globalization: Investment Rules and Democracy's Promise*. Cambridge: Cambridge University Press.

Schulte, Constanze. 2004. *Compliance with Decisions of the International Court of Justice*. Oxford: Oxford University Press.

Seymore, Jillaine. 2006. "International Tribunal for the Law of the Sea: A Great Mistake." *Indiana Journal of Global Legal Studies* 13 (1): 1–36.

Shabas, William. 2014. "International Criminal Courts." In *Oxford Handbook on International Adjudication*, edited by C. Romano, K. J. Alter, and Y. Shany. Oxford: Oxford University Press.

Shaffer, Gregory. 2000. "WTO Blue-Green Blues: The Impact of U.S. Domestic Politics on Trade-Labor, Trade-Environment Linkages for the WTO's Future." *Fordham International Law Journal* 24 (1 and 2): 608–51.

———. 2003. *Defending Interests: Public-Private Partnerships in WTO Litigation*. Washington, DC: Brookings Institution Press.

Shapiro, Martin. 1981. *Courts: A Comparative Political Analysis*. Chicago: University of Chicago Press.

Shapiro, Martin, and Alec Stone Sweet. 2002. *On Law, Politics, and Judicialization*. Oxford: Oxford University Press.

Shelton, Dinah. 2005. *Remedies in International Human Rights Law*. Oxford: Oxford University Press.

Shklar, Judith. 1964. *Legalism: Law, Morals, and Political Trials*. Cambridge, MA: Harvard University Press.

Sikkink, Kathryn. 2004. *Mixed Signals*. Ithaca, NY: Cornell University Press.

———. 2011. *The Justice Cascade: How Human Rights Prosecutions Are Changing World Politics*. New York: Norton.

Simmons, Beth. 2002. "Capacity, Commitment, and Compliance: International Institutions and Territorial Disputes." *Journal of Conflict Resolution* 46 (6): 829–56.

———. 2006. "Trade and Territorial Conflict in Latin America: International Borders as Institutions." In *Territoriality and Conflict in an Era of Globalization*, edited by M. Kahler and B. Walter, 251–87. Cambridge: Cambridge University Press.

———. 2009. *Mobilizing for Human Rights: International Law in Domestic Politics*. Cambridge: Cambridge University Press.

Singh, Nagendra. 1989. *The Role and Record of the International Court of Justice*. Dordrecht: Marinus Nijhoff Publishers.

Sloss, David. 2009a. *The Role of Domestic Courts in Treaty Enforcement: A Comparative Study*. Cambridge: Cambridge University Press.

———. 2009b. "The United States." In *The Role of Domestic Courts in Treaty Enforcement: A Comparative Study*, edited by D. Sloss, 504–55. Cambridge: Cambridge University Press.

Sloss, David L., Michael D. Ramsey, and William S. Dodge. 2011. *International Law in the U.S. Supreme Court: Continuity and Change*. Cambridge: Cambridge University Press.

Song, Yann-huei. 2007. "Prompt Release of Fishing Vessels: The *Hoshinmaru* and *Tomimaru* Cases (Japan v. Russian Federation) and the Implications for Taiwan." *Chinese (Taiwan) Yearbook of International Law and Affairs* 25: 1–28.

Stancil, Jeff. 2005. "Mending Fences: The Real Purpose of the American Job Creation Act of 2004." *Tulane Journal of International and Comparative Law* 13: 421–35.

Staton, Jeffrey K. 2010. *Judicial Power and Strategic Communication*. Cambridge: Cambridge University Press.

Staton, Jeffrey, and William Moore. 2011. "The Last Pillar to Fall? Judicial Power in Domestic and International Politics." *International Organization* 65 (3): 553–88.

Stein, Arthur. 1983. "Coordination and Collaboration: Regimes in an Anarchic World." In *International Regimes*, edited by S. Krasner, 115–40. Ithaca, NY: Cornell University Press.

Stein, Eric. 1981. "Lawyers, Judges, and the Making of a Transnational Constitution." *American Journal of International Law* 75 (1): 1–27.

Steinberg, Richard H. 2002. "In the Shadow of Law or Power? Consensus-Based Bargaining and Outcomes in the GATT/WTO." *International Organization* 56 (2): 339–74.

———. 2004. "Judicial Lawmaking at the WTO: Discursive, Constitutional, and Political Constraints." *American Journal of International Law* 98 (2): 247–75.

Stelzenmüller, Constanze. 2000. "Bürgerin in Uniform." *Die Zeit*, January 5.

Stephan, Paul B. 2002. "Courts, Tribunals, and Legal Unification—The Agency Problem." *Chicago Journal of International Law* 2002 (3): 333–52.

———. 2014. "Taxation and Expropriation: The Destruction of the Yukos Oil Empire." *Houston Journal of International Relations* 35 (1): 102–52.

Stone, Alec. 1995. "Governing with Judges: the New Constitutionalism." In *Governing the New Europe*, edited by J. Hayward and E. Page, 286–314. Durham, NC: Duke University Press.

Stone Sweet, Alec. 1998. "Constitutional Dialogues in the European Union?" In *The European Court of Justice and National Courts—Doctrine and Jurisprudence*, edited by J. Weiler, A. Stone Sweet, and A.-M. Slaughter. Oxford: Hart Publishing.

———. 1999. "Judicialization and the Construction of Governance." *Comparative Political Studies* 32 (2): 147–84.

———. 2000. *Governing with Judges*. Oxford: Oxford University Press.

———. 2004. *The Judicial Construction of Europe*. Oxford: Oxford University Press.

———. 2008. "Proportionality Balancing and Global Constitutionalism." *Columbia Journal of Transnational Law* 47: 74–160.

———. 2009. "Constitutionalism, Legal Pluralism, and International Regimes." *Indiana Journal of Global Legal Studies* 19 (2): 621–45.

———. 2010. "How the European Legal System Works and Does Not Work." Social Science Research Network.

Stone Sweet, Alec, and Thomas Brunell. 1998. "Constructing a Supranational

Constitution: Dispute Resolution and Governance in the European Community." *American Political Science Review* 92 (1): 63–80.

———. 2012. "The European Court of Justice, State Non-Compliance, and the Politics of Override." *American Political Science Review* 106(1): 204–13.

———. 2013. "Trustee Courts and the Judicialization of International Regimes: The Politics of Majoritarian Activism in the ECHR, the EU and the WTO." *Journal of Law and Courts* 1(1): 61–88.

Streeck, Wolfgang, and Kathleen Ann Thelen. 2005. *Beyond Continuity: Institutional Change in Advanced Political Economies*. Oxford: Oxford University Press.

Supnik, Kate M. 2009. "Making Amends: Amending the ICSID Convention to Reconcile Competing Interests in International Investment Law." *Duke Law Journal* 59: 343–76.

Tallberg, Jonas. 2003. *European Governance and Supranational Institutions: Making States Comply*. London: Routledge.

Tamayo, Arturo Boja. 2001. "The New Federalism in Mexico and Foreign Economic Policy: An Alternative Two-Level Game Analysis of the Metalclad Case." *Latin American Politics and Society* 43 (3): 67–90.

Tanaka, Yoshifumi. 2003. "Reflections on Maritime Delimitation in the Qatar/Bahrain Case." *International and Comparative Law Quarterly* 52: 53–80.

Tejan-Cole, Abdul. 2009. "A Big Man in a Small Cell: Charles Taylor and the Special Court for Sierre Leone." In *Prosecuting Heads of State*, edited by E. Lutz and C. Rieiger, 205–32. Cambridge: Cambridge University Press.

Terris, Daniel, Cesare Romano, and Leigh Swigart. 2008. *The International Judge: An Introduction to the Men and Women to Decide the World's Cases*.

Thelen, Kathleen. 2004. *How Institutions Evolve: The Political Economy of Skills in Comparative-Historical Perspective*. New York: Cambridge University Press.

Thomas, Daniel C. 2001. *The Helsinki Effect: International Norms, Human Rights, and the Demise of Communism*. Princeton, NJ: Princeton University Press.

Tiger, Philippe. 2001. *Le droit des affaires en Afrique*. 3rd ed., Que sai-je? Paris: Presses Universitaires de France.

Trachtman, Joel P. 2006. "The Constitutions of the WTO." *European Journal of International Law* 17 (3): 626–46.

Treves, Tullio. 2010. "Human Rights and the Law of the Sea." *Berkeley Journal of International Law* 28: 1–14.

Tuerk, Helmut 2007. "The Contribution of the International Tribunal for the Law of the Sea to International Law." *Penn State International Law Review* (26): 289–316.

Uprimny, Rodrigo 2007. "La Fuerza Vinculante de las decisiones de los organismos internacionales de derechso humanos en Colombia: Un examen de la evolucion de la jurisprudencia constitucional." In *Implementación de las Decisiones de Sistema Interamericano de Derechos Humanos*, edited by C. p. l. J. y. e. D. Internacional.

Van Harten, Gus. 2007. *Investment Treaty Arbitration and Public Law*. Oxford: Oxford University Press.

Van Harten, Gus, and Martin Loughlin. 2006. "Investment Treaty Arbitration as a Species of Global Administrative Law." *European Journal of International Law* 17 (1): 121–50.

Van Schaack, Beth. 2009. "Engendering Genocide: The Akayesu Case before the International Criminal Tribunal for Rwanda." In *Human Rights Advocacy Stories*, edited by D. R. Hurwitz, M. L. Satterthwaite, and D. B. Ford, 196–228: New York: Foundation Press.

Vanberg, Georg. 2005. *The Politics of Constitutional Review in Germany*. Cambridge: Cambridge University Press.

Vaubel, Roland. 2006. "Principal-Agent Problems in International Organizations." *Review of International Organizations* 1: 125–38.

Vauchez, Antoine. 2010. "The Transnational Politics of Judicialization: Van Gend en Loos and the Making of EU Polity." *European Law Journal* 16 (1): 1–28.

Vermulst, Edwin, and Daniel Ikenson. 2007. "Zeroing under the WTO Anti-Dumping Agreement: Where Do We Stand?" *Global Trade and Custom* 2: 231–42.

Viljoen, Frans, and Lirette Louw. 2007. "State Compliance with the Recommendations of the African Commission on Human and Peoples' Rights, 1994–2004." *American Journal of International Law* 101 (1): 1–34.

Voeten, Erik. 2007. "The Politics of International Judicial Appointments: Evidence from the European Court of Human Rights." *International Organization* 61 (4): 669–701.

———. 2008. "The Impartiality of International Judges: Evidence from the European Court of Human Rights." *American Political Science Review* 102 (4): 417–33.

———. 2010. "Regional Judicial Institutions and Economic Cooperation: Lessons for Asia." In ADB Working Paper Series No. 65.

———. 2014. "International Judicial Behavior." In *Handbook on International Adjudication*, edited by C. Romano, K. J. Alter, and Y. Shany. Oxford: Oxford University Press.

Voon, Tania. 2007. "The End of Zeroing? Reflections Following the WTO Appellate Body's Latest Missive." *Legal Issues of Economic Integration* 34 (3): 211–30.

Vuotto, Jonathan. 2004. "Awas Tingni v. Nicaragua: International Precedent for Indigenous Land RIghts?" *Boston University International Law Journal* 22: 219–43.

Watson, Alan. 1993. *Legal Transplants: An Approach to Comparative Law*. Athens: University of Georgia Press.

Weiler, Joseph. 1981. "The Community System: The Dual Character of Supranationalism." *Yearbook of European Law* 1: 257–306.

———. 1991. "The Transformation of Europe." *Yale Law Journal* 100: 2403–83.

Williamson, Richard. 2012. "Charles Taylor and Closing the Gates of Hell." *Journal of the American Enterprise Institute.*

Zgonec-Rožej, Miša. 2009. "Yassin Abdullah Kadi and Al Barakaat International Foundation v. Council and Commission. Joined Cases C-402/05 P & C-415/05 P." *American Journal of International Law* 103 (2): 305–11.

Zürn, Michael, and Christain Joerges. 2005. *Law and Governance in Postnational Europe—Compliance beyond the Nation State.* Cambridge: Cambridge University Press.

Index